Pittsburgh Series in Social and Labor History

Pittsburgh Series in Social and Labor History

Maurine Weiner Greenwald, Editor

The Correspondence of Mother Jones
Edward M. Steel, Editor

Don't Call Me Boss: David L. Lawrence, Pittsburgh's Renaissance Mayor
Michael P. Weber

Women and the Trades
Elizabeth Beardsley Butler

Other titles in the series

The Emergence of a UAW Local, 1936–1939: A Study in Class and Culture
Peter Friedlander

Homestead: The Households of a Mill Town
Margaret F. Byington

The Homestead Strike of 1892
Arthur G. Burgoyne

Immigration and Industrialization: Ethnicity in an American Mill Town, 1870–1940
John Bodnar

Out of This Furnace
Thomas Bell

Steelmasters and Labor Reform, 1886–1923
Gerald G. Eggert

Steve Nelson, American Radical
Steve Nelson, James R. Barrett, & Rob Ruck

Working-Class Life: The "American Standard" in Comparative Perspective, 1899–1913
Peter R. Shergold

Don't call me boss

Michael P. Weber

Don't call me boss
DAVID L. LAWRENCE,

PITTSBURGH'S RENAISSANCE MAYOR

UNIVERSITY OF PITTSBURGH PRESS

Published by the University of Pittsburgh Press, Pittsburgh, Pa., 15260

Feffer and Simons, Inc., London
Manufactured in the United States of America

Library of Congress Cataloging-in-Publication Data

Weber, Michael P.
Don't call me boss.

Includes index.
1. Lawrence, David Leo, 1889–1966.
2. Pennsylvania—Governors—Biography. 3. Mayors—Pennsylvania—Pittsburgh—Biography. 4. Pennsylvania—Politics and government—1865–1950. 5. Pennsylvania—Politics and government—1951– . 6. Pittsburgh (Pa.)—Politics and government. I. Title.
F155.3.L385W42 1988 974.8'043'0924 [B] 87-15166
ISBN 0-8229-3565-1
ISBN 0-8229-5397-8 (pbk.)

*In memory of my parents,
who shared David Lawrence's
love of Pittsburgh*

Contents

Preface

For nearly a century, Americans have been fascinated with the phenomenon of machine politics. Ever since cartoonist Thomas Nast and the editorial staff of the *New York Times* exposed the corruption of the Tweed ring in New York, novelists, journalists, scholars, and political cartoonists have examined, condemned, idealized, and lampooned urban bosses. Early observers criticized them for their greed and corruption, and later, more objective studies pointed out that political machines performed a variety of services needed or desired by their constituents. Jobs for the unemployed, contracts and elimination of governmental red tape for the businessman, and a benevolent law enforcement policy for those providing illegal or illicit "services" to residents were all part of the urban machine. In turn the organization received political loyalty and various kinds of open and clandestine financial support. The boss operated the political organization as a business in which he expected to receive something tangible for himself or the party in return for the goods and services he delivered. Bosses, like the society from which they emanated, were honest or corrupt, benevolent or indifferent, efficient or inefficient. A number brought important reforms to the city that they served.

Historians and political scientists have alternately pointed to the demise and the persistence of machine politics in the mid twentieth century. They generally agree, however, that the style and form of urban politics have undergone a significant transformation during the period from Roosevelt's New Deal to Johnson's Great Society. The old ward-heeling political boss who traded jobs for votes was replaced by a municipal manager who was as comfortable in the corporate boardroom as in the smoke-filled room of party headquarters. Various political reforms, new functions, and a more complex society demanded a more sophisticated mode of operation. David L. Lawrence of Pittsburgh was one of the few political leaders able to make the transition.

Born and raised in one of Pittsburgh's least desirable neighborhoods, Lawrence had an early career typical of that of many upwardly mobile Irishmen who used politics as a stepping-stone to power and respectability. However, when faced with the demands of a statewide office in 1935 and the unwanted mayorship in 1945, he proved to be a man with a broader vision and an innate sense of the operation of government and politics. His understanding of both enabled him to merge them when practicable. Unlike many of his earlier counterparts, he was also able to keep politics out of government, particularly when the mixture threatened the progress of the city's urban renewal.

This study is an account of the career of a single urban leader, whom this author admittedly came to admire during the five years this effort was under way. Fully aware of the difficulty of serving two masters, I hope that it proves instructive to both the professional and the lay leader. Lawrence operated effectively in the local, state, and national political and governmental arenas. His activities shed light on American political behavior, particularly in an urban context. His career between 1945 and 1958 provides important lessons in the implementation of one of America's most successful urban renewal projects. But as a politician, Lawrence also operated on a personal level. Driven by an ambition to raise his two loves, the Democratic party and the city of Pittsburgh, from the doldrums in which he found them, he used his powerful personality to interact with Pittsburghers from every walk of life. From the resident on the street who illustrated a more imagined than real kinship by referring to him as "Davey" as well as the city's wealthiest resident, Lawrence elicited respect, cooperation, and, from some, devotion. Even his political opponents, who dwindled in number as his career progressed, grudgingly admitted that his tenure in office had benefited the city.

An intensely private man operating on a public stage, Lawrence provided no easy access for his biographer. He wrote few letters, kept no revealing diaries, and died before he was able to write his memoirs. The existing correspondence, including the voluminous governor's papers, are primarily short notes in response to queries from constituents or political or governmental officials, which afford little insight into the personality of the man. The paucity of such data presented me with the alternatives of abandoning the project or seeking other sources in an attempt to supplement the material that did exist. The significance of the man's career in terms of longevity, influence at the municipal, state, and national levels, and his success in providing a model for implementing massive urban renewal made the first alternative unacceptable. Fortunately a large amount of data existed and could be supplemented with oral testimony that, in part, overcame the absence of written materials.

Over the course of his career, Lawrence consented to several lengthy and detailed interviews that provide considerable information regarding his motivations in arriving at key decisions or adopting particular positions. An oral history project sponsored by the Buhl Foundation on the Pittsburgh Renaissance produced ninety-five interviews with contemporaries of Lawrence. These works supply important information on the thirteen-year redevelopment project. Sixteen interviews focusing exclusively on the building of Point Park were conducted by Robert C. Alberts for his study of that urban renewal project. In addition, Father Thomas Donaghy generously made available his collection of thirty-seven interviews, all conducted in the early 1970s. The Donaghy interviews, held at La Salle College in Philadelphia, probed deeply into Lawrence's public and private life. Other, more scattered interviews exist at the Columbia University Oral History Collection and the Truman Library. Finally, I conducted an additional eighty interviews with friends, relatives, political contemporaries—both allies and opponents—governmental officials, and urban professionals. The resulting data, often on the same subject, permitted verification as well as offering insight into nuances and often the motivation and personality of David Lawrence. Other important sources included the city's three newspapers—read for the entire period of Lawrence's career—several extensive collections of Lawrence speeches, the minute books of the Allegheny Conference on Community Development, the Pittsburgh Urban Redevelopment Authority, Pittsburgh City Council, several grand jury and court trial proceedings, numerous committee reports, the papers of Senator Joseph Guffey, archival materals in the libraries of four U.S. Presidents, and, of course, a wide variety of published and unpublished works. The materials are not a suitable replacement for a detailed and introspective diary or a lengthy series of letters to and from a loved one or a political acquaintance. Thus not all questions are perused, and the historical record remains incomplete. Many of the intimate details of Lawrence's life remain a mystery. The existing materials, however, do permit one to examine many of the issues surrounding him. The analysis here attempts to deal with a variety of complex issues in a logical and reasonable manner while presenting an accurate portrayal of the fascinating career of David L. Lawrence.

During the five years in which this work was in gestation, I became indebted to a number of people. Colleagues offered encouragement and helpful suggestions; associates of David Lawrence willingly gave their time to respond to lengthy and probing interviews; foundations provided needed funds; and a number of librarians and archivists went out of their way to find a lost document or manuscript. Too many individuals contributed to this work to be thanked individually, but I am indebted to them and appreciate their efforts nonetheless.

Several people, however, made major contributions, and their mention here is my small way of expressing my gratitude. I was assisted along the way by the efforts of a number of Carnegie-Mellon graduate students who conducted and transcribed interviews and secured needed research materials. Tim Kelly, Wendy Rush, Judy Botch, and Mark Knapp gave excellent service. I sincerely appreciate their contributions.

Every librarian and archivist whom I encountered demonstrated the professionalism we have come to expect from those who labor in this important but often unheralded field. Several in particular deserve special mention. Carol Stephan and Marie Zini, reference librarians at the Carnegie Libraries of Pittsburgh, tolerated my often unusual requests for information and refused to rest until they had supplied the desired data. Marilyn Albright of the Carnegie-Mellon University Hunt Library and Frank Zabrosky of the Archives of the Industrial Society were personally interested in the work and often provided unsolicited information or leads on valuable sources. Archivist Roland Bauman made my frequent trips to the Pennsylvania History and Museum Commission pleasant and worthwhile. A former colleague and head archivist at the Lyndon Baines Johnson Library, David Humphrey, first informed me of the valuable Lawrence data in the Johnson collection. He assisted in securing a travel grant, guided me through the intricacies of the library, and opened his home to me on my visit to Austin. He introduced me to new and important information on Lawrence and to Texas ribs. For both I am indebted.

I thank, too, the American Association for State and Local History and the National Endowment for the Humanities, and the Moody Foundation of the Lyndon Baines Johnson Library for important financial support at opportune moments. Their generosity greatly aided the completion of this project.

Colleagues with whom I discussed this work offered intellectual stimulation and important ideas. In particular, John Bodnar, Howard

Chudacoff, Joel Tarr, and William Trimble provided input or support at important times. Bruce Stave generously turned over his entire set of research materials compiled for his study of the rise of the Democratic machine in the 1930s. Father Thomas Donaghy permitted me to see an early version of his own work on Lawrence. I am grateful for their willingness to share their time, research data, and perceptive ideas. Lu Schaefer and Fred Hetzel shared my sense of the importance of Lawrence's career. They offered encouragement in the initial stages of the project and provided assistance in securing funds. Their enthusiasm was contagious, and I thank them. Lu Schaefer also read every word of an early version of this work. His gentle but constructive criticism greatly improved the manuscript. His efforts give true meaning to the terms *colleague* and *friend.*

A special thank-you is offered to Kaye Dudas, who transcribed the hundreds of hours of often barely audible interviews. Without her efforts the work truly could not have been completed.

Individuals with whom I requested an interview cheerfully submitted to my intrusion in their lives. People from every walk of life, whether friend or foe of Lawrence's, appeared anxious to discuss their association with him. Corporate heads, ward chairmen, friends, and relatives provided invaluable details that would have been lost without their cooperation. They supplied the lifebood of the work. I am particularly indebted to Jack Robin and Walter Giesey, Lawrence's executive secretaries, and to Genevieve Blatt and Natalie Saxe, his political associates, who went out of their way to provide information and additional important contacts. Lawrence's daughter, Anna Mae Donahoe, was gracious from beginning to end of the project. She tolerated several interviews and many phone calls and provided access to her personal collection of Lawrence materials. My sincere thanks to everyone who granted interviews. This work is in large part yours.

A special debt of gratitude is owed the copyeditor, Irma Garlick. Her probing questions, gentle prodding, and editorial skills greatly improved the readability of this work. Her ability to cut passages from an overly long manuscript without excessive trauma to the author is much appreciated.

Finally, I am indebted to my wife, Patricia. She gave the encouragement and assistance one comes to expect and too often take for granted from one's spouse. However, her willingness to spend an entire beach vacation clarifying passages, eliminating grammatical errors, and spotting punctuation faults was well beyond the call of duty. Thanks Pat.

Biographical Sketches of Key People in Lawrence's Life

ANNE X. ALPERN. Pittsburgh city solicitor during the Lawrence administration.

FRANK "BANGY" AMBROSE. Lawrence's long-time, always available friend. Held a number of minor political appointments.

GUY K. BARD. Replaced Charles Margiotti as state attorney general during the last months of the Earle administration.

JOSEPH BARR. Lawrence's handpicked successor as mayor of Pittsburgh. Barr played a key role in the Democratic organization during his long term as Pennsylvania state senator.

MICHAEL BENEDUM. Wealthy oil operator. Became the chief financial angel of the Democratic party in 1933. Provided continuous support throughout the Lawrence years.

GENEVIEVE BLATT. One of the earliest active female members of the Democratic party in Pennsylvania. Served as secretary of commonwealth affairs and judge of the Commonwealth Court of Pennsylvania. She defeated Michael Musmanno for the party nomination for the U.S. Senate in 1964.

SPURGEON BOWSER. President, Pioneer Materials Company of Kittanning. Supplied road materials to the state. Allegedly paid kickbacks. Claimed that Lawrence extorted $5000 from him.

WILLIAM J. BRENNEN. Attorney and Democratic County Chairman, 1901–19. Lawrence's political mentor.

AL CONWAY. Democratic chairman of Pittsburgh's Nineteenth Ward for nearly twenty years.

JAMES COYNE. Republican party leader, 1915–33, and a state senator. Business and personal associate of Lawrence's, 1924–66.

HARMAR DENNY. Republican candidate for mayor of Pittsburgh 1941, 1945. Descendant of Pittsburgh's first mayor, Ebenezer Denny.

RICHARDSON DILWORTH. Philadelphia district attorney, city treasurer, two-term mayor.

GEORGE EARLE. Scion of an old Philadelphia family. Ambassador to Austria, 1933–34. Elected governor of Pennsylvania in 1934.

ANDREW "HUCK" FENRICH. Lawrence friend and North Side ward official. He was the unofficial patronage chief in Pittsburgh under Lawrence.

WALTER GIESEY. Mayor's executive secretary, 1949-56. Lawrence's closest aide during his term as governor and as chairman of the President's Committee on Equal Opportunity in Housing.

JOSEPHY GUFFEY. Democratic party benefactor from western Pennsylvania. Served as county and state party chairman. Considered to be the head of the state party during the early 1930s. U.S. senator, 1934–46. Federal patronage chief for Pennsylvania, 1933–36.

FRANK A. HARRIS. Partner in the Lawrence-Harris insurance firm. Served as county chairman of the Allegheny County Republican organization. Was a state senator and key committee chairman during the entire Earle administration.

JOHN HENRY. Pittsburgh attorney. Early Democratic opponent of the Lawrence organization.

THOMAS HESTER. Democratic jury commissioner, 1925–29. Strong opponent of Lawrence and the Democratic organization, 1931–35.

LORENA HICKOK. Appointed by Harry Hopkins to investigate the operation of the WPA in Pennsylvania.

JOHN HUSTON. A Republican who joined the Democratic landslide in 1934. Subsequently rewarded by party support for office of registrar of wills. Huston became strong intraparty opponent of Lawrence's. He was eventually purged from the organization.

K. LEROY IRVIS. Public relations secretary to the Pittsburgh Urban League; supported by Lawrence for assistant district attorney in 1956; elected to state House of Representatives in 1950.

EDDIE JONES. Public safety director in the Republican administration of Mayor Charles Kline; *Pittsburgh Sun-Telegraph* reporter. Became Democratic campaign writer in 1931. Served as secretary of labor and industry during the first half of the Earle administration.

JOHN KANE. President of the pressmen's union in Pittsburgh. Elected to city council in 1933; served five terms as Allegheny county commissioner. Considered to be Lawrence's counterpart at the county level and labor's spokesman in high Democratic circles.

JACK KELLY. Philadelphia millionaire, father of Grace Kelly. Kelly became an important force in eastern and statewide Democratic politics. Served as Philadelphia city chairman, 1934–40.

THOMAS KENNEDY. Lieutenant-governor during the Earle administration. Secretary-treasurer of the United Mine Workers and John L. Lewis's spokesman in Pennsylvania politics. Rejected by Lawrence as the candidate for governor in 1938.

JIMMY KIRK. Lawrence friend and business associate, 1925–46. City treasurer in the McNair administration; first city treasurer under Lawrence.

CHARLES KLINE. Republican mayor of Pittsburgh, 1924–33, convicted of malfeasance in office and forced to resign.

JAMES KNOX. Longtime loyal Lawrence associate. Held numerous public and party offices during Lawrence's career.

GEORGE LEADER. York County chairman, 1948; state senator, 1950; governor of Pennsylvania, 1955–59.

EDDIE LEONARD. President of plasterer's local 31; secretary of the Building Trades Council. Member of the Pittsburgh City Council, 1943–59. Opposed Lawrence in the 1949 Democratic mayoralty primary. Named president of the International Plasterers' Union in 1951.

JOSEPH P. MCARDLE. Son of P. J. McArdle. Democratic city councilman. Staunch opponent of Lawrence and eventually purged from the party organization.

P. J. MCARDLE. Republican city councilman, 1932–34. Became Democratic candidate for council, 1934, after unsuccessful bid to win Republican nomination for mayor. Welcomed into the party by Lawrence.

MATTHEW MCCLOSKEY. Millionaire Philadelphia contractor. Became active in Democratic affairs in 1934. A confidant and supporter of Lawrence's throughout his public career.

WILLIAM MCCLELLAND. Democratic coroner of Allegheny County. Former Pennsylvania boxing commissioner. Long time ally of Prothonotary David Roberts in the anti-Lawrence wing of the party.

CHARLES "BUCK" MCGOVERN. Allegheny County sheriff; Republican voter registration commissioner, 1921–25; county commissioner, 1931. One of the first to defect from the Republican party. McGovern and Caldwalder Barr joined to oppose the regular Republican organization in 1931. Both won.

WILLIAM MCNAIR. Perennial Democratic office seeker; elected mayor of Pittsburgh in 1933. Involved in a constant battle with Lawrence for the next two years. Resigned in 1936.

LAWRENCE MALONEY. A police lieutenant appointed by Lawrence to lead raids against Pittsburgh's gambling establishments. Head of

"Maloney's marauders." Indicted for extorting bribes from the gambling bosses, but never convicted.

CHARLES J. MARGIOTTI. Considered by many to be Pennsylvania's greatest trial lawyer. Named attorney general by Governor Earle in 1934. His uncontrolled ambition led to bitter battles with politicians on both sides of the political aisle. Fired as attorney general during the last months of the Earle administration. Lawrence became his greatest enemy.

PARK MARTIN. Civil engineer, director of the Allegheny County Planning Commission; executive director of the Allegheny Conference on Community Development, 1945–58.

WILLIAM L. MELLON. Nephew of Andrew Mellon, cousin to Richard King Mellon. Co-founder of Gulf Oil. Republican financial supporter, generally conceded to be Allegheny County Republican boss, 1915–35.

EMMA GUFFEY MILLER. Sister of Senator Joseph Guffey. Long-time Democratic National Committeewoman from Pennsylvania. Considered the ranking female Democrat in Pennsylvania for nearly thirty years. Affectionately known as "The Old Gray Mare."

MICHAEL MUSMANNO. Egocentric attorney and later judge. A defense attorney in the Sacco-Vanzetti trial; a judge at Nuremberg. Well-known Communist foe during the early 1950s. Musmanno sought numerous political offices during his long career.

DANIEL PARISH. Co-owner of the Allegheny Asphalt Company. Long-time friend of Lawrence's. Frequently alleged to pay kickbacks to Lawrence in return for city paving contracts.

WILLIAM RAHAUSER. Democratic district attorney of Allegheny County, 1947–51. Battled Charles J. Margiotti in the Marjorie Matson Communist influence case.

DAVID RANDALL. Executive secretary to Governor George Leader, 1955–59.

CHARLES OWEN RICE. Pittsburgh parish priest. Known as the Labor Priest for his support of the causes of organized labor. Often an advocate of liberal social and welfare programs.

WALLACE RICHARDS. Director of the Pittsburgh Regional Planning Association, 1937. Often considered the visionary of the Pittsburgh Renaissance.

DAVID B. ROBERTS. Democratic prothonotary of Pittsburgh. Frequently at odds with the Lawrence administration. Lawrence considered Roberts and his ally William McClelland to be political opportunists who were only interested in their own welfare.

JOHN P. ROBIN. Secretary under Mayor Scully, 1935–43; executive secretary under Lawrence, 1946–48; executive secretary of URA, 1948–54; secretary of the Commonwealth, 1954–55. A trusted Lawrence advisor throughout his public career.

ART ROONEY. Owner of the Pittsburgh Steelers. Life-long friend of Lawrence's.

NATALIE SAXE. Executive secretary to Richardson Dilworth, mayor of Philadelphia.

ADOLPH SCHMIDT. Vice-president of T. Mellon and Sons. Schmidt and Arthur Van Buskirk were Richard King Mellon's closest personal advisers. Later U.S. ambassador to Canada.

CORNELIUS SCULLY. City solicitor of Pittsburgh during the McNair administration. Fired by McNair in 1934. Elected to city council; served briefly as council president. Became mayor upon resignation of McNair in 1936. Reelected 1937, 1941.

CARL SHELLEY. Republican district attorney for Dauphin (Harrisburg) County. Prosecuted Lawrence in both his trials during the early 1940s.

R. TEMPLETON SMITH, MRS. Conservative chairwoman of the League of Women Voters of Allegheny County. A constant and bitter foe of Lawrence.

RAY SPRIGLE. Investigative and sometimes muckraking reporter for the *Pittsburgh Post-Gazette.* Critical of Lawrence's inability to control the police and rackets in Pittsburgh.

STEVE TOOLE. Democratic alderman, First Ward, 1898–1906. As a youth, Lawrence ran errands for Toole.

AL TRONZO. Early Democratic opponent of Lawrence's; elected to state House of Representatives in 1934; later became strong Lawrence supporter. Held several Allegheny County and City of Pittsburgh offices.

ARTHUR VAN BUSKIRK. Executive secretary of T. Mellon and Sons. Aide and confidant to Richard King Mellon. Often spoke for Mellon on the board of the Allegheny Conference on Community Development.

WARREN VAN DYKE. Highly respected Democratic state chairman, 1926–34. Generally considered to be the heir to Governor Earle in 1938. A critical illness prevented his running.

ROBERT VANN. Black attorney, editor of the *Pittsburgh Courier.* Vann led the city's black population into the Democratic party, 1933–34.

JOHN VERONA. Long-time political boss of Pittsburgh's Third Ward. Shifted from Republican to Democratic party in 1934. Implicated in the state gravel scandal but died before he could testify.

FRED T. WEIR. Early Protestant recruit into the Democratic party (1933). Became city councilman and later judge.

JAKE WILLIAMS. Democratic party worker, held numerous patronage positions in the Pittsburgh Democratic administrations. Brother of ward boss Pappy Williams.

Don't call me boss

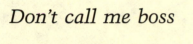

1889–1919

Growing Up: An Education in Politics

Powerful economic and social divisions gripped Pittsburgh during the last decade of the nineteenth century. Industrialization and the development of modern capitalism, technological change and the depersonalization of the worker contributed to growing labor-management conflicts. Social class separation and ethnic rivalries further divided the population, while Catholic-Protestant hostilities were never far from the surface. Anti-Catholic, antilabor, and nativist sentiments dominated the nation that preached freedom for all. Caught in the midst of these struggles, David Leo Lawrence, an Irish-Catholic son of an unskilled laborer, received lasting lessons in American social organization. Religion, ethnicity, the labor movement, and a sharp awareness of social class all became a pervasive part of his youth and later political career.

Between 1885 and 1914, Pittsburgh's industrial production led the American transition into a modern society. Andrew Carnegie, George Westinghouse, B. F. Jones, and a score of others, harnessing new industrial technology, made the city America's center of capital goods manufacturing. Railroad cars, air brakes, river barges, glass products, and iron and steel goods of all kinds poured from their factories. By 1900 the area produced more than half of the nation's coking coal, open-hearth ingots and castings, crucible and structural steel as well as substantial amounts of window glass and steel rails.[1]

Waste materials from these factories, at the same time, polluted the air, poisoned the streams, and destroyed much of the land. "Pittsburgh is not a beautiful city," one foreign visitor observed.

> She is substantially and compactly built, and contains some handsome edifices; but she lacks the architectural magnificence

> of some of her sister cities; while her suburbs present all that is unsightly and forbidding in appearance, the original beauties in nature having been ruthlessly sacrificed to utility. . . .
>
> The hills . . . have been leveled down, cut into, sliced off and ruthlessly marred and mutilated. . . . Great black coal cars crawl up and down their sides, and plunge into unsuspected and mysterious openings. . . . Railroad tracks gridiron the ground everywhere, debris of all sorts lies in heaps, and is scattered over the earth, and huts and hovels are perched here and there, in every available spot. There is no verdure—nothing but mud and coal, the one yellow, the other black. And on the edge of the city are the unpicturesque outlines of factories and foundries, their tall chimneys belching forth columns of inky blackness, which roll and whirl in fantastic shapes, and finally lose themselves in the general murkiness above.[2]

The prosperity of the factories and the dynamic quality of the city prompted thousands of laborers to ignore the horrible environmental conditions. They flocked to the mill towns along the rivers and into the central city, where below-subsistence wages, long hours, and appallingly dangerous working conditions prevailed. Cost-cutting manufacturers replaced highly skilled workers with unskilled labor as quickly as technological advances permitted, and wages fell still further. To counteract the growing power of the corporations and the loss of their status, skilled craftsmen formed labor unions, which promised to defend and assert workers' rights. Labor and management joined in an intense struggle for control of the mills. Between 1877 and 1894, Pittsburgh ranked behind only New York and Chicago in the number of labor disturbances. Companies retaliated by locking workers out, giving the city the dubious distinction of leading the nation in the number of lockouts and in wage losses due to lockouts and strikes.[3] The labor movement failed to end the exploitation of workers, and its near collapse after the 1892 Homestead steel strike gave a clear indication of the subservient position of labor in the Steel City. Sharp class divisions continued to be an important factor for the next forty years.

The development of class-segregated neighborhoods widened the gulf between rich and poor and between labor and management. The masters of industry amassed great fortunes and formed a powerful new social class. They built magnificent homes in the city's suburbs or, like Andrew Carnegie and Henry Clay Frick, abandoned the region altogether. Middle- and upper-class communities such as Shadyside, Oakland, Squirrel Hill, Fox Chapel, and Sewickley developed along the periphery of the city, while formerly heterogeneous neighborhoods were rapidly changing into mixed industrial, warehouse, and blue-collar residential areas.

The Point district, located at the juncture of the Allegheny, Monongahela, and Ohio rivers, was just such an area. "Good honest people . . . live there, but they are, generally speaking, not of the most cultured class. Balls and receptions are seldom held in First Ward residences. The houses themselves are plain, but in many cases substantial, although it must be admitted quite a few are of the ancient time-stained character. . . . Some are half a century or more in age and are unsightly, rickety tenements."[4]

Once a middle-income neighborhood, the Point became a settling ground for Irish immigrants fleeing the Potato Famine of 1845–50. Unlike the other Irish neighborhoods in Pittsburgh, which attracted immigrants from a wide variety of regions, the "Point Irish," as they came to be known, came from the barren moors and rugged mountain villages of Galway. Possessing neither skills nor education, the vast majority became common laborers in the small factories located near the Point. The remainder tended bar in the district grogshops, drove teams hauling goods throughout the business district, or loaded and unloaded barges along the Monongahela wharf. Subject to an unstable Pittsburgh economy, harsh working conditions, and low wages, many engaged in a continuous struggle for survival. A contemporary source described the settlement at the Point as "the filthiest and most disagreeable locality within the city . . . almost entirely composed of the poorer classes, living in many cases in extreme poverty, and occupying the merest apologies for houses."[5]

Separated by class, culture, and language, residents of the Point, not surprisingly, remained isolated from the rest of Pittsburgh through much of the latter half of the nineteenth century. Even into the 1880s, "nearly all spoke Irish [Gaelic] so much that men who had worked more than twelve years could hardly make themselves understood in English."[6] Parents continued to teach their children the ancient language, and most retained close contact with their kin in Ireland.

▽

The families of Isaac Lawrence and Charles Conwell, unlike most of their compatriots at the Point, emigrated from Belfast sometime after 1847. They settled within three blocks of each other. Both families were apparently somewhat better off than their less fortunate neighbors. Lawrence, a stonemason in Ireland, began work as a laborer at the Duquesne Freight House of the Pennsylvania Railroad. Eventually he managed to save enough money to open a small shoe repair shop on Penn Avenue. The Lawrence home occupied the second floor of the shop. Charles Conwell, a stonecutter in Ireland, held a similar job in Pittsburgh until his involvement in politics enabled him to secure a job as a ward assessor in 1866.

Charles B. Lawrence, the second son of Isaac, married Catherine Conwell, the third of nine girls, at St. Mary of Mercy Catholic Church in 1880. The union produced four children: Isaac, Charles, Mary, and David, who was born on 18 June 1889.[7] The young couple rented a home in the Irish neighborhood, two blocks from their parents. Located on the corner of Greentree Alley and Penn Avenue, they coexisted with warehouses, railroad yards, small factories, and several houses of gambling and occasional prostitution.

David lived the first ten years of his life in this area rich with opportunities to satisfy a young boy's curiosity. The Lawrence home, a modest two-story frame structure, was bounded on the north by the Haugh and Keenan storage warehouse and on the west by a planing mill and the Chautauqua Eureka Ice Company. The presence of a boiler works just across the street, two additional planing mills, an iron works, and several machine shops in the immediate vicinity must have produced a constant din in the Lawrence household. The St. Mary of Mercy Convent and Elementary School were directly across Penn Avenue, and the historic Fort Pitt Blockhouse, the only remaining remnant of the eighteenth-century British occupation of the city, lay just two blocks to the east. Railroad tracks carrying Jay Gould's Wabash Line cars intersected the area, bringing additional smoke and dirt to Greentree Alley.

The city's rivers, an easy two-minute walk to the west, were centers of constant activity. Exposition, Mechanics, and Symphony halls, located on the banks of the Allegheny, hosted frequent exhibitions, musicals, and even an occasional circus. A twenty-five-cent fee provided admission to displays depicting the Johnstown flood, the San Francisco earthquake, and the Battle of the Monitor and the Merrimac. Exposition Hall's permanent outdoor balcony for strollers and a roller skating rink made the area a favorite recreation spot. Young boys such as David Lawrence and his friends were no doubt captivated by the Ferris wheel, roller coaster, merry-go-round, and other amusement rides located there. The Monongahela River bank, more commercial than the Allegheny, was usually filled to capacity with barges and stern-wheeler boats loading and unloading goods. Horse-pulled wagons jammed the streets to and from the river banks, carrying products to the warehouses that lined Front Street. Horse auctions were held twice weekly during the summer on Front Street.[8]

Charles Lawrence, a small, mild-mannered man, worked at a number of mostly unskilled jobs including hauler and warehouseman. Known as a hard worker, Charles, like many other blue-collar first- and second-generation immigrants, looked to the saloon for relaxation and social interaction. He spent many evenings at a local pub discussing politics, the labor movement, and working conditions in America. His ability to speak clear English and his somewhat better social class origin as the son of a shopkeeper gave him a slightly elevated status in the neighborhood and recognition as a spokesman for Irish causes in the First Ward. He eventually became involved in both the labor movement and Democratic politics and was named ward committeeman in 1897. His activities, however, were minor, as neither organization exercised any power in late nineteenth-century Pittsburgh.

Undaunted by the apparent futility of his causes, he loved to discuss both, and he could become almost eloquent on the evils perpetrated by the corporate giants of Pittsburgh. His monologues carried into the home, educating the Lawrence boys on the virtues of organized labor and Democratic politics. It was the only vivid memory of his father that David Lawrence would carry into later life. "As just a bit of a kid in my home they would always discuss politics. My father was in it in a minor way in the ward . . . and my grandfather on my mother's side was in it in a minor way . . . he was the ward assessor and did things of that kind. So as long as I can remember hearing anything, it would be about politics."[9]

Charles Lawrence spent little time at home with his young sons, but the passion with which he argued his causes left a lasting impression on his offspring. The eldest son, Isaac, after initially pursuing a career as a professional baseball player, turned to carpentering and occasionally held office in his union's local. He later received a patronage position as superintendent of maintenance for Allegheny County. His appointment, of course, required active, though minor involvement in political affairs. The second son, Charles, became a lifelong champion of organized labor, eventually holding the position of president of the Pittsburgh plumbers' union local. David turned his effort toward politics, and the seeds of much of his later political philosophy were his father's attitudes toward the prevailing turn-of-the-century social conditions. In particular, his views regarding the responsibility of government and big business to correct persisting social ills and to help adjust social class differences became hallmarks of his political career.

It is Catherine Lawrence, however, who emerges as the dominant parent in David's life. A devout Catholic, she ran the Lawrence household with a strong hand. Daily Mass was a regular part of her routine throughout her life, and she expected her young children to participate in this normal way of beginning one's day.[10] A member of the altar society of St. Mary's Church, she washed and ironed the altar garments and spent time almost daily and always on Saturday mornings attending to the routine maintenance of the altar. David frequently accompanied her. Later, when the family moved to the Hill district, Mrs. Lawrence worked as a volunteer for the Catholic Rosalia Foundling Home and Maternity Hospital. Perhaps because he was the youngest and as a result of their constant association, he grew exceptionally close to his mother and remained so until her death in 1939. Stubborn and outspoken, Catherine maintained discipline with an iron hand. "Fighting among the boys was never permitted. We were always expected to reach a compromise on the disputed issue."[11] Compromise was always preferable to confrontation throughout Lawrence's political career.

Mrs. Lawrence's outspokenness, in contrast to her husband's discourses on political and labor causes, was almost always confined to private and family matters. Even in later years she never attempted to offer political advice to her famous son, but she never hesitated to remind him that one had a duty to help the less fortunate. For Lawrence she was the model mother, interested in affairs of the family and the Church. She wished her children well but never drove them to succeed, for her own goals in life remained modest. In common with the Irish community in which she lived, she emphasized employment for her children over education and expected them to lead hard-working, moral, blue-collar lives. The drive to be first, present in so many twentieth-century political leaders, was never a part of the Lawrence upbringing.

Lawrence's parents, like many blue-collar adults in industrial Pittsburgh, struggled to support their offspring, but the children were seldom aware of any serious financial difficulties. David wore hand-me-downs, but they were always kept in excellent repair. Catherine even managed to save enough money to purchase a second-hand piano, and she taught each child in turn. David, like most young boys of his age, preferred to play ball rather than practice the piano. He became what he later described as a "piano thumper." As young boys the Lawrence children worked sporadically but were not required to turn their meager earnings over to their parents.

David, despite poor eyesight, which bothered him for life, played sandlot baseball, fished, and swam in the waters at the Point. He and his companions particularly enjoyed swimming out to meet passing stern-wheelers to "ride the wake" back in toward shore. Unlike his older brother Isaac, he never excelled at sports, but he was remembered as a fierce competitor. He developed an intense love for sports of all kinds and later, during the 1920s, sponsored and managed semi-professional football, baseball, and basketball teams and a stable of professional boxers, including three who gained some local renown: Kid Dugan, Patsy Scanlon, and Pete Connors, who once earned a purse of $350 fighting in Pittsburgh's Duquesne Gardens.[12] As a youth Lawrence especially enjoyed exploring the industrial sites and railroad yards near his home, and the historic blockhouse was a favorite place for him and his friends. "We kids used to play in there and around there. I remember one time an old lady named Powers moved in there and squatted, opened up a candy store and lived there."[13] Lawrence in later years frequently recalled with fondness his early days at the Point, and its redevelopment became a particular source of pride.

David's formal education consisted of primary schooling at Duquesne Public Elementary School and a two-year commercial course at St. Mary's. He later cited insufficient funds as the reason for terminating his education at this point, but this appears to have been only one factor. Few children in working-class Pittsburgh attended school beyond the tenth grade. Young David was different from most in that his education enabled him to secure a white-collar job upon graduation.

His limited education, however, was a source of concern, even embarrassment, throughout his life. "I was no boy wonder in education," he recalled half a century later. "It was always a struggle for me."[14] In his early years he remained attached to one of his former teachers, Sister Casimir, who possessed many of the qualities he admired in his mother—a strong will, outspokenness, and a belief in rigid discipline. She frequently sent him material to read in later years and never hesitated to write him expressing her opinions of his political actions.[15] Later in his career, Lawrence would attribute strong, almost unnatural powers to formal education, driving himself continuously as if to overcome this self-determined deficiency. His political appointments were nearly always highly educated men and women, and he particularly preferred candidates with Ivy League backgrounds.

At the age of nine, Lawrence began his education in the art of practical politics when his father secured a part-time job for him as a helper for Steve Toole, First Ward alderman. For five years David ran errands, set up chairs for political rallies, passed out leaflets at election time, and drove Toole's wagon to help get out the vote. On a number of occasions he was permitted to sit in on party caucuses or other political meetings. Nothing is known of Lawrence's reaction to his association with Toole, but he must have received mixed messages. Toole, an Irish-Catholic Democrat, maintained his strength in the ward by working in collaboration with the Republican Flinn-Magee machine. "He is a Democrat as far as national or state elections are concerned but is for his friends always in local affairs and many of these happen to be ring Republicans. . . . It is a cardinal point of his politics to support a friend. This, he believes, is a debt all politicians owe and favors should be repaid by gratitude at least.[16] In cooperating with the ruling machine, Toole was simply following the common Pittsburgh practice of operating the Democratic party as a branch of the Republican organization. Democrats willing to go along with the ruling duo of Flinn and Magee could expect appropriate rewards. At the height of their power, nearly one-fourth of all city and county jobs were reserved for cooperative Democrats.[17] Toole received a city job and support for his periodic aldermanic elections. In Pittsburgh, one either joined the dominant party, followed their bidding, or withdrew from politics. Lawrence learned this basic fact of political survival well.

Young Lawrence, ironically, also worked inadvertently for the Republican Flinn-Magee machine when he took a part-time job as water boy for the Booth-Flinn Construction Company, which, by virtue of a city-granted franchise, was installing trolley tracks on the city's North Side.

David's association with politics, casual though it was, had already begun. He had seen his maternal grandfather and his father benefit from their political activities, and Steve Toole was clearly the first or second most important person in the First Ward. In addition, David had observed old-fashioned ward politics in operation. The victorious elections attributable to the smoothly operating Republican machine had taught a great deal, but it was the occasional defeat that produced lasting memories. Nearly fifty years later, shortly after his election as governor of Pennsylvania, he vividly recalled: "I've never forgotten watching the men who'd been beaten in elections. Just a few days before, everybody had been rushing up to shake their hand. But when it was over and they'd been defeated, nobody bothered much to speak to them. And that they didn't know how to take. I was just a kid, but it taught me a lot."[18]

The specter of defeat was to remain with Lawrence. More than once he declined to run for office when he concluded that defeat was likely. Moreover, as nearly every associate interviewed for this work revealed, in every election, regardless of the size of his majority, he "ran scared." Associates were counseled to run for office as if defeat were imminent. Finally, perhaps as a guard against the possibility of defeat that would remove him from politics, Lawrence retained his insurance business all his life.

Lawrence's association with his most influential mentor, William J. Brennen, began immediately upon completion of the two-year course at St. Mary's. Brennen, an Irish-Catholic son of an unskilled ironworker, gave Lawrence the male role model his own father could never provide. Born in midcentury, Brennen went to work for the American Iron Works (later Jones and Laughlin) at age eleven. He eventually became a skilled machinist while continuing his education through night school, and he later studied law under James K. Duff. He began his own law practice in 1883, quickly becoming known for his espousal of liberal causes and his support of organized labor, and in 1893 was counsel to the steelworkers in the infamous Homestead steel strike. He later played a major role in the state legislature's enactment of the Commonwealth's first workingmen's compensation law.

Brennen began to dabble in Democratic politics during his ironworker years and served in a number of official capacities including alderman, ward chairman, and Allegheny County Democratic treasurer. In 1876, at age twenty, he became the nation's youngest delegate to the Democratic National Convention. In 1901 he became the chairman of the Democratic party in Allegheny County, a post he retained for seventeen years.

In 1903, fourteen-year-old David Lawrence applied for a job as clerk-stenographer in the Brennen law office in the Hill District. Brennen, acquainted with both Charles Lawrence and his son through their political activities, was attracted by the younger Lawrence's enthusiasm and his devotion to the Democratic cause. He hired David, beginning a political association that was to last until Brennen's death.

Wealthy, educated, and urbane, Brennen nevertheless had much in common with his young protégé. Religion, ethnic and class origin, and training by the strong-willed Sisters of Mercy all drew the two men together. They also shared strong sympathies with the labor movement and, of course, Democratic politics. They even shared a physical ailment, a lifelong vision disability. Brennen worked Lawrence hard—ten hours per day, six days per week—in his law office, and according to Lawrence, "he never broke his bank book by paying us good salaries." As a bonus, however, Brennen began to teach Lawrence the art of politics as he knew it, and the two held long discussions that often lasted until late at night.[19] Unfortunately, little is known about these discussions, although Lawrence later acknowledged their importance in his political development. What does seem clear is that from this relationship, combined with his earlier experiences, Lawrence formed a number of important views.

Both held ambivalent attitudes toward working-class, blue-collar life. It was a life from which they had escaped, and they were always slightly uncomfortable in blue-collar surroundings in later life. Brennen, for example, although known as Pittsburgh's labor lawyer, enjoyed his affluence. He was known to dress in the height of fashion, loved fast cars, and lived in a fashionable home at 2327 Fifth Avenue.[20] He migrated further east into Oakland when the Fifth Avenue district became less desirable because of the influx of Southern and Eastern European immigrants. While he retained his interest in sporting activities, he also cultivated an interest in the theater—a taste Lawrence later acquired—and in other arts. Most important, nearly all of his friends, many of whom visited the Brennen office regularly, were wealthy Republicans. His unusual ability to deal successfully with affluent, Protestant, Republicans while at the same time acting as the spokesman for organized labor was a skill Lawrence also later perfected.

Brennen, perhaps to cover up his blue-collar background, developed a formal style and manner in his relationships with others. Lawrence adopted a similar style. Individuals were addressed by their formal titles. Except in the most private of moments or with a few close friends, a coat and tie were the expected form of dress in Brennen's and later Lawrence's offices. One longtime aide recalled, "You couldn't come into his [Lawrence's] office, or the Democratic headquarters, with short sleeves or no white shirt or tie. 'God damn it, you're a gentleman. This is an office.' he would say. And he really would get mad. . . . Even at political picnics with free beer, sandwiches and games Lawrence would have on his white shirt and tie. He might take off the coat but never the tie." Later his formality extended to his co-workers in the Democratic party. During one campaign he happened to run into two Democratic candidates—one running for county treasurer, the other for a local judgeship. The two, dressed in open-collared, short-sleeved shirts and slacks reported that they were going to a United Mine Workers picnic in Indiana Township. Lawrence exploded. "Listen," he commanded, "when you speak to the miners or visit with them, look like a public official, not like one of them. They expect you to look like a public official."[21]

His formality even extended into his home life, according to his daughter. "I never saw him sit in my house without a shirt and tie and coat on. Once in a while on a hot summer day, he might sit on the front porch or in the back yard without his coat on but he had his tie on. As far as sports shirts were concerned, he might have owned two."[22] In later life Lawrence retained a close relationship with several blue-collar political cronies and continued to enjoy the activities of his youth—baseball, football, and boxing—but the style was strictly formal.

Both teacher and pupil strove to transcend their blue-collar backgrounds, but each struggled in different ways to improve working-class conditions. Legal counsel and legislative action were Brennen's vehicles for redressing the ills of the industrial system. Politics for him was an enjoyable pastime, but, perhaps because of the Republican domination of western Pennsylvania, he never viewed it as an effective method of reform. Lawrence, who "grew up in a law office but never had the chance to study law . . . came up on the political side instead of the legal side."[23] Thus, while he held deep sympathies for the labor movement throughout his life, he could and frequently did oppose organized labor or labor leaders if it seemed politically wise. He viewed political action as the best means to improve working-class lives.

Lawrence's propensity for hard work, no doubt instilled in him by his mother, was certainly reinforced by Brennen. "The hours were terrible. That's where I learned to work. We never left the office."[24] A bachelor with no family responsibilities, Brennen would work alongside his associates from 7:00 A.M. to 6:30 P.M., then remain in the office to greet political workers in an attempt to breathe life into an all but dead Democratic organization. "Lawrence aped Brennan's Beau Brummell style, and until he was thirty-two heeded Brennen's admonition that a man could not 'wive and thrive' in the same year."[25] It may be coincidental, but Lawrence married only after Brennen's death.

The Brennen-Lawrence association lasted for nearly two decades, developing into a father-son type of relationship. Contemporaries of Lawrence often referred to him as Dave "Brennen" Lawrence.[26] He later named his first son Brennen and kept a portrait of his old mentor in his office throughout his career. Lawrence frequently acknowledged his debt to his predecessor, but their long relationship did not result in a strengthened Democratic party.

Brennen treated his own involvement in politics in an almost ad hoc, gentleman-statesman manner. It was a pragmatic, cooperative approach to politics that Lawrence learned to emulate. From the time he became Democratic county chairman in 1901, Brennen, realizing that he stood no chance of upsetting the Republican machine, followed a policy of cooperation with its leaders. He seldom challenged the Republican majority, apparently content with the minority positions legally available to his party. One member of the inner circle, who later became a U.S. senator, explained: "our organization was strictly a bi-partisan affair. All the Democratic factions, and a large number of the Republican leaders . . . wanted to be in on the Federal patronage. In those days, and in fact as long as the Democratic party was in the minority, there were always Democratic leaders more interested in picking up patronage crumbs from the Republican table than they were in winning elections."[27] The Democrats, for example, ran no candidate for mayor in 1902, 1913, or 1917. Only when they could mount a "fusion ticket" such as reformer George Guthrie in 1905 did Brennen's party conduct an aggressive political campaign. To the dismay of some, particularly during the 1920s, Lawrence adopted Brennen's pragmatic brand of politics, with similar results.

It is difficult to overestimate the Brennen's influence on Lawrence's political career. He provided important training, instilled elements of a political philosophy, and taught his protégé a practical approach to the political world. Other factors during Lawrence's formative years, however, also provided important lessons that were apparent in his later actions. The first three decades of the twentieth century were particularly volatile in Pittsburgh politics. Republican boss Christopher Magee's death in 1901 initiated a period of intraparty fighting that raged from Pittsburgh to Harrisburg and continued for nearly a third of a century. Mayors were "ripped" from office by a rival machine headed by state boss Matthew Quay. A local reform administration, supported by the Citizens' League and other independent groups, won election in 1906, and a series of sweeping municipal reforms pushed through both houses of the Pennsylvania General Assembly by a coalition of upper-class businessmen and professionals was initiated in 1911.[28] Meanwhile Republican bosses, including Edward Bigelow, William Magee, and later James Coyne, William L. Mellon, and Charles Kline, all vied for control of the city until the collapse of the Republican machine in 1933.

It is unclear exactly how these dynamic events influenced David Lawrence, but in a young man developing an intense interest in politics they must have generated great excitement. Both the power of a well-organized machine and the disaster of intraparty fighting, regularly reported in the city's press, no doubt, became obvious to him. The Republican organization, in spite of numerous well-publicized charges of corruption and feuds within the party, remained, with the exception of the 1906-9 period, entrenched in power. Regardless of scandals—such as those of 1911, which saw nearly 150 indictments for graft brought against the entire Republican city council, and Mayor William Magee charged with embezzling funds from the city treasury—the well-honed Republican organization brought home winner after winner in both the city and the county.

It became obvious to the young Lawrence that the lack of a well-structured organization in his own party was a major factor in its defeat at the polls. Almost immediately upon assuming the county Democratic chairmanship in 1920, he experimented with the party structure, reorganizing it to create a more responsive ward-level operation. He initiated other reforms following election defeats in 1925 and 1929. Workers were recruited to fill every possible position, and by 1933 clear lines of command existed from ward committeemen through ward chairmen to party chairman.[29]

Less obvious, although certainly apparent, were the long-term debilitating effects of continuous internecine warfare on the Republican machine. The Republicans, whether it was Magee and Flinn battling Quay and Edward Bigelow in the first decade of the century or Edward Kline challenging William Mellon and Coyne in the 1920s, fought their battles in public. They continued to win elections, but the lack of harmony and the rampant corruption became well known. Defections from the party occurred as early as 1909. At first disgruntled Republicans looked to reform groups such as the Civic Club and the Voters' League to correct the abuses within the system.[30] Later they turned to the Democratic party as the best hope for reform.

The lessons Lawrence learned from the Republican intraparty warfare and from several battles within his own party early in his career burned an indelible mark on his approach to party politics. For nearly fifty years at the local, state, and national levels, he struggled to avoid confrontations within the Democratic organization. He always viewed compromise and occasionally even capitulation as preferable to conflict.

Attempts at political reform during the young Lawrence's formative years probably also shaped his development. In 1906, Democrat

George W. Guthrie broke the Republican lock on city hall, defeating his Republican candidate by almost 3,000 votes. Guthrie, whose father and grandfather had held the same office before the years of the Magee-Flinn domination of the city, ran on a reform ticket supported by several independent groups as well as by the Democratic party. Reform strength, however, proved insufficient to gain control of any seats on the city council or of any of the bureaucratic row offices (elected administrative offices such as city treasurer, controller, etc.) held by the Republican organization. Not surprisingly, Guthrie's administration was generally ineffective, for the entrenched machine blocked most of his efforts at reform. Republican William Magee, nephew of the former boss, Christopher Magee, replaced Guthrie in 1909, and all hopes of reform through the existing political apparatus were dead. It is not clear how these event influenced the thinking of David Lawrence, but local newspaper editorials at the time made clear the futility of Guthrie's single-handed attempts at reform. Lawrence, always an avid newspaper reader, could hardly fail to understand the message. In any event, it was a mistake he always avoided. He never undertook political or legislative action without a prior assessment of support, and he often deferred action if he perceived support to be weak or absent. Lawrence seldom ventured out on a limb.

The influence of the success of the 1911 Pittsburgh municipal reform movement on Lawrence, however, is much more difficult to discern, and the analysis that follows is admittedly more speculative. Nevertheless, his reliance on the upper class to carry out the redevelopment of the city in the 1940s and 1950s may have its roots in his observation of the success of that same class in decentralizing the city's political and educational systems. Led by Leo Weil of the Voters' League, nearly 750 members of the city's business, industrial, and professional elites pushed a bill through the state legislature requiring the at-large election of the city council and judicial appointment of the city school board. The bill, ostensibly designed to reduce the power of the political ward system, was supported by, among others, "the presidents of fourteen large banks and officials of Westinghouse, Pittsburgh Plate Glass, U.S. Steel and its component parts, . . . Jones and Laughlin . . . the H. J. Heinz Company and the Pittsburgh Coal Company, as well as officials of the Pennsylvania Railroad and the Pittsburgh and Lake Erie."[31] Lawrence, no doubt, failed to appreciate the significance of their role in this political reform, for its extent has only recently been documented. Several of the presidents, however, were mentioned prominently in the newspapers, and interested readers such as Lawrence could not fail to know that they were involved. Their success, particularly following so closely on the heels of the disappointment of the Guthrie administration and in the face of strong opposition from the entrenched regime, must have impressed him. Thus, when viewed in the light of his early experiences, Lawrence's willingness to embrace Pittsburgh's Republican, Protestant elite to bring about the redevelopment of the city seems much less surprising. It is certainly more than coincidence that the same corporate offices that effected the 1911 reform were also prominent in the post-World War II redevelopment of the city. What changed was that in the latter period they worked closely with the administration in power.

Finally, the Progressive era, during which Lawrence grew up, clearly shaped his later urban liberalism. American historians disagree over which social class provided the impetus for the reforms of the Progressive era, but they generally agree that it established precedents for the later reforms of the New Deal and New Frontier. Lawrence, who straddled two social classes, exhibited some of the traits generally attributed to each, but his blue-collar background proved to be the driving force.

During his early years he was attracted to the Social Gospelers and social scientists who appealed to so many middle-class reformers. At one point he joined the Henry George Club but soon became disillusioned with the single tax as a solution to urban problems. He retained, however, the view that, given economic incentives to do so, private enterprise would develop rather than exploit the resources of the city. He also developed a reliance on experts to examine and provide solutions to the problems plaguing the city. The urban redevelopment known as the Pittsburgh Renaissance owes much of its success to professionals, employed by both public and private agencies, upon whom Lawrence relied.

But he really did not require experts to help him identify the ills of society. Lawrence, to be sure, never experienced the poverty of many of Pittsburgh's working-class families, but he certainly viewed its effects from close range. He knew firsthand the problems of urban life: inadequate housing and health services, unemployment, and a generally unhealthy environment.[32] As a result, he seldom viewed issues on a grand or comprehensive scale but attacked them singly, as they appeared. He offered the comment, "We are practical people, not ideologists," again and again not as an apology but as a sign of strength—a pragmatic politics for a practical people. He viewed government as the vehicle through which one could examine the problem and find a way to solve it. One did not restructure society; one corrected it where necessary. It is possible to see his support of the social reforms from the New Deal through the Great Society, his role in Pennsylvania's Little New Deal, and much of the legislation enacted during his administrative terms as the result of a broad and well-formulated liberal philosophy. However, such does not appear to be the case. His early experience taught him that ills existed in American society, and, as he gained power, he attempted to correct those that became most pressing. The issues he chose to champion—workingmen's compensation, health care, labor legislation, and others—found their origin in his working-class background. He even saw the Pittsburgh Renaissance as a means of providing workers of all classes with a decent living and working environment.

Admittedly, Lawrence did not exhibit many of these beliefs as a young, would-be politician. Like his father and Billy Brennen, he supported the causes of labor and those issues currently popular with the Democratic party. His most intense interest, however, was in seeing a Democrat in office—almost any office or any Democrat would do. Brennen, aware of the competitive nature of his protégé, a competitiveness he did not share, encouraged Lawrence to expand his involvement. In 1912, twenty-three-year-old David accompanied Brennen to the Democratic National Convention as a page. It was, up to that moment, the crowning achievement in the young politician's career. "The proceedings were completely fascinating to a lad of my age and I became devoted to politics even though my favorite candidate, Champ Clark, lost to Governor [Woodrow] Wilson. I later became a major advocate of Wilson."[33]

While at the convention, Lawrence met another rising young politician from south of Pittsburgh, Joseph Guffey, a wealthy Pennsylvania delegate from Westmoreland County. Guffey, a young man of striking appearance, had attended Princeton during the years of Wilson's presidency there and campaigned for his election as governor of New Jersey in 1910. One of the few members of the Pennsylvania delegation who actually knew Wilson, Guffey argued vociferously in his support. When that proved futile, he broke from the delegation to give Wilson his vote for the nomination. Guffey's support of Wilson on each of the forty-six ballots necessary to nominate him, together with his generous financial contributions, earned Wilson's lasting gratitude.[34] More importantly for Guffey, it made him one of the leading Democrats in Pennsylvania.

Lawrence approached Guffey during his convention fight, and the two had several dinners together. They struck up a friendship that, although stormy at times, was mutually beneficial. They met frequently in Pittsburgh during the years immediately following the convention, and Guffey even invited Lawrence to join him for a weekend of deer hunting on the family property. Lawrence decided that he hated hunting, but the experience proved useful, strengthening their relationship.[35]

Lawrence was the first to benefit directly from the Guffey-Lawrence liaison. Wilson rewarded Guffey for his support at the 1912 convention by naming him patronage chief for all of western Pennsylvania, and in 1914 Guffey named his friend to his first official political position: minority commissioner on the Voter Registration Commission for the city of Pittsburgh. The appointment provided Lawrence with his first salaried position, at $4,000 per year, freeing him for the first time from serious financial concern.[36] The position also enabled both men to observe firsthand the lack of organization in the Democratic party as well as the seedier side of Pittsburgh politics. Voters in Pittsburgh were required to register for each election by showing a tax receipt for current paid-up taxes. Those not owning property paid a fifty-cent poll tax. Joseph Guffey was surprised when he discovered the abuses to which such a system could be put.

> I learned early in my first campaign in Pittsburgh, that politics was not entirely a debate over the great issues, as we had so earnestly viewed in our undergraduate discussions at Princeton. I came down to earth with a bump, at half past nine one morning just before a Pittsburgh mayoralty election.
>
> I reached the office quite early. The [Democratic] headquarters rarely opened before noon, but I was eager, and I had things to do. As I approached I saw shadows through the headquarters window. They were dancing up and down in a most peculiar manner. I watched from the outside and finally identified the dancing figures as Dennis Fox and Joe Kraus, both officers of the Allegheny County Democratic Committee. Mustering my courage, I opened the door. My sudden appearance startled them until they recognized me.
>
> "Oh, it's you, is it?" one of them said, with real relief. "Yes," I said, still puzzled, "What are you doing?"
>
> They looked at each other. "Aging tax receipts."
>
> And that in fact was what they were doing. In those days it was necessary, in case your right to vote was challenged, to have a tax receipt either for normal taxes or for payment of the poll tax. Many potential voters had neither and it was ex-

> pensive as well as illegal for political committees to pay a voter's tax.
>
> To meet this situation both sides had obtained a quantity of tax receipt blanks. . . . State Senator William Flinn, a Republican leader, had eight unnumbered books. The Democrats had somehow obtained two unnumbered books from a nearby county. These receipts were given out to ward leaders and political committeemen for distribution to voters. But they couldn't be too clear or too new. That would have aroused suspicion when they were presented to the election board. So Dennis Fox and Joe Kraus were aging them.[37]

In spite of many attempts at reform, the system lent itself to various methods of vote fraud. Voter registration was normally controlled within the wards by paid registrars selected by the ward chairmen. The machine, usually through the registrar, provided tax receipts and/or poll tax fees to individuals who voted under their own and often several other names. Deceased voters, phantom voters, and repeaters were a common occurrence in Pittsburgh during the first third of the twentieth century.[38] The Voter Registration Commission, created in one attempt to deal with such fraud, was charged with investigating and ruling on the validity of all voter registrations. However, its members who were appointed precisely because of their loyalty to their party, were reluctant to disturb the system. An analysis of the commission minutes during the ten years Lawrence served indicates that he was a cooperative member. He seldom spoke, and when he did, his comments, like those of other members, were nearly always in agreement with those of the commission chairman, Republican Charles "Buck" McGovern. Fewer than 10 percent of the voter registration questions that came before the board during Lawrence's membership were rejected as fraudulent.[39] Lawrence, it appears, used his position to hone his skills at working with the Republican majority and to supplement his income. (By the time of his resignation in 1924, he was earning $6,000 per year as commission secretary.) He also secured an appointment for his own political protégé and aide James P. Kirk as clerk and later full commission member.

It is not clear whether the practice of accepting bogus tax receipts as documentation of voter registration bothered Lawrence. If so, he never attempted to act on the concerns of his conscience. But his work on the commission made him aware of the weakness of his own party, and he took steps to strengthen it. Democrats, for example, failed to register at all in four wards in 1915 and 1916 because they could not find people willing to serve as ward registrar. Shortly thereafter, Lawrence supported a commission ruling permitting ward chairmen to serve simultaneously as registrars in their own wards. The funds they received for assisting in voter registration would presumably proved financial incentive to reluctant Democratic party workers. His strongest influence in the commission during the following years was in preventing repeal of the ward chairman ruling.[40] He also waged a mild fight against annual registration, which he correctly viewed as benefiting the large, well-organized Republican operation. Later, as secretary of the Commonwealth, he was instrumental in the enactment of permanent registration.

By 1917 Lawrence was ready to launch his own political career. At Brennen's suggestion, he formed the David Leo Lawrence Political Club and by the summer of that year had nearly fifty followers. The group met monthly to discuss political issues and candidates, and it campaigned in the fall election for Billy Brennen for city council. As usual the mayoralty—for which the Democrats did not run a candidate—and all five available council seats were won by Republicans. Brennen ran a "respectable" seventh.

Lawrence's fledgling organization had barely a chance to get its political feet wet when its activities were interrupted by World War I. Initially turned down for active duty because of his eyes, he enlisted on 17 September 1918 and served in the adjutant general's office for just over a year. Military service in Washington, D.C., in spite of a promotion to second lieutenant, did not prove satisfying, and years later he refused to wear his American Legion pin, reasoning that his efforts did not aid in ending the war.[41] At war's end Lawrence, aged twenty-nine, returned to Pittsburgh to begin the adult phase of his career in politics.

1919–1929

Friends, Family, and Work

There was much to distinguish Second Lieutenant David Lawrence from the thousands of veterans who returned to Pittsburgh in the spring of 1919. He was approximately five feet, nine inches in height, with athletic chest and shoulders, a thick neck, and a large head. His dark brown hair was combed straight back, and his eyes were framed by thick, rimless glasses. A square-set jaw, which could become fierce when he was angered, was made less severe by the roundness of his head and by the second chin that he acquired later in life. A broad smile accented by deep lines and the wrinkles from the corners of his eyes gave his publicity photos the almost stereotyped look of the jovial, happy Irishman. The deep-set eyes and the glasses, however, led to an erroneous characterization of him by some as "cold and steely-eyed." But it was the very big head and shoulders that gave him a strong appearance—"He was such an easily recognizable man."[1]

In addition to his commanding physical presence, Lawrence possessed unusual stamina. During his early years he routinely worked eight hours at his insurance business, met with political associates during the early evening, and ended the night at a sporting event or a dance. Campaigns were even more demanding. Evening whirlwind tours of the city, during which he would speak at five or six sites, usually concluded with strategy sessions at Democratic headquarters lasting until one or two in the morning. Lawrence was always the last to leave. Nearly all of his associates complained that he overworked them, expecting them to maintain his hectic pace. A number noted that his penchant for working weekends, particularly Sundays, nearly ruined their marriages. Several commented on his excellent physical condition, which he worked to maintain. "He went to the 'Y' on a more or less daily basis. He never drank, he didn't smoke, and he generally didn't overeat. He didn't have any physical weaknesses. After Prohibition, according to his daughter Anna Mae, he started to drink beer because he had fought so hard for the twenty-first amendment that he thought he ought to try it. But that didn't last long, for he started to put on weight, and then he quit. "In his later years I never saw him drink a thing. He was very much against drinking." His intolerance for what he considered to be vices extended to excessive gambling and smoking. Anna Mae smoked for years but never dared to do so in her father's presence.[2]

Upon his return to Pittsburgh, Lawrence resumed a position with the insurance agency he and Frank Harris, a state senator and later Allegheny County Republican chairman, formed in 1916. A short time later he encouraged his old friend Jimmy Kirk to join the rapidly growing firm. Adding second mortgage loans to the business, the company experienced moderate success, and Lawrence eventually bought out Harris and became the company president. The firm gave him a modest income throughout his life and became an important source of security at intervals when his political career turned sour. From the time he left state government in 1938, for example, through 1944, it provided the major income for the Lawrence family. During his years as mayor of Pittsburgh, the company provided an annual salary of fifteen to twenty thousand dollars. In spite of occasional attempts by political opponents to embarrass Lawrence, claiming that his firm's sale of surety bonds to the city constituted a conflict of interest, he frequently advised young politicians to develop an outside business as a hedge against sudden unemployment at the hands of the electorate.

Lawrence's early experiences in business resulted in a strong fiscal conservatism that was evident in both his private business dealings and his management of public budgets. In 1920 he and a group of associates, including Jimmy Coyne, the Republican boss of Allegheny County, loaned $80,000 to E. N. Gillespie, a businessman, to purchase stock in the Guffey-Gillespie Oil Company. Lawrence's share was $15,000. No accounting of the fund was ever made, and the group was forced to sue for return of the funds. It was not until 1929 that they were awarded the $80,000 plus $37,919.40 in interest.[3] The award, and other funds, unfortunately would not remain in Lawrence's hands very long. Shortly after, he suffered severe losses in the stock market crash, which nearly caused him to lose the insurance firm. Several costly loans were required to bail out the floundering company. These two occurrences, one following on the heels of the other, relieved Lawrence of whatever speculative urges he may have possessed. He later purchased small amounts of stock in relatively safe utilities and held an interest in a local Pittsburgh beer distributing company, but the investments remained modest. From 1963 through 1965, for example, Lawrence received less than $2,200 per year in stock income.[4] Other funds he invested were always in municipal bonds.

The Harris-Lawrence Insurance Agency and the other investments provided Lawrence with a modest income, but they never sparked his interest. The details of running a business bored him, and he preferred to delegate this authority to others. His friend and political ally Jimmy Kirk ran the day-to-day operations of the firm during the late 1920s, and later, when Kirk assumed administrative positions in the Pittsburgh city government, a full-time manager was hired. Lawrence, except for a four-year interim from 1935 through 1939, when he held the post of secretary of the commonwealth in the administration of Governor Earle, retained the title of president of the company, but he seldom became actively involved. Only in politics did the minutiae hold his interest. The business interests, however uninteresting, provided a financial cushion and a freedom to enjoy sporting events, begin a family, and engage in his true love, politics.

Lawrence had only a few close relationships, all of which were formed during his younger years. He seemed to enjoy most those whose interest in sports matched his own or those who could offer a momentary respite from the rigors of political or governmental life. As teenagers Lawrence and Art Rooney, who would later own the Pittsburgh Steelers, struck up a friendship based upon their mutual interest in football, baseball, and boxing. It was Rooney who introduced Lawrence to another sports passion, horse racing. Beginning in the middle thirties and continuing until he became governor, Lawrence, Rooney, and a number of others would travel to events such as the Kentucky Derby, the prizefights in New York, and Steeler football games. Rooney, also a Republican, later recalled that they would occasionally discuss politics and personal concerns, but mostly it was sporting events or card playing that occupied them. "He relaxed more at sporting events than at any other place I have ever seen him." In 1938, when Rooney ran for the position of register of wills on the Republican ticket, it was Democratic chairman Lawrence who frequently accompanied him to political rallies. Even on those trips, other than advising him not to run because he was sure to lose, Lawrence's discussion with Rooney focused mainly on athletics.[5]

It is not surprising that most of Lawrence's early friends were Republican since nearly everyone in Pittsburgh claimed allegiance to the Grand Old Party. One of his closest friendships, however, later proved to be a source of political embarrassment. Shortly after his return from service in World War I, Lawrence met his Republican counterpart in Allegheny County, Jimmy Coyne.

Coyne, a large red-faced Irishman with an affinity for huge cigars, was a perfect fit for the stereotypical image of the political boss. Aggressive, hungry for power, and generally considered to be corrupt, Coyne was nevertheless easy to like. One of sixteen children, Coyne came to Pittsburgh from Galway in 1900 at the age of sixteen. He worked at several mills in the Lawrenceville section of the city and on construction gangs. His political interest began when he became foreman, then superintendent of Booth-Flinn Construction Company. With financial help from William Flinn, the Republican boss, Coyne opened a saloon on Bates Street in the Oakland area and later entered the wholesale liquor business.

Coyne used his saloon as a center for his political activities, becoming chairman of the Fourth Ward. Following the pattern of the nineteenth-century ward leaders, he could always be counted upon to provide a favor to a "deserving" local resident. The big, fun-loving Oaklander's reputation spread, and he soon developed a following among ward leaders in the Strip District and on the North Side of the city. Following World War I, Coyne joined forces with Joe Grundy and William Larimer Mellon, Republican powers in the state.[6]

The Coyne-Lawrence relationship began around 1924. The two men shared an ethnic and religious heritage, an interest in sports, and, of course, a love of politics. "There was a very close relationship there," Lawrence's daughter recalled. "The first year my parents were married, they bought twenty-one acres of land from Jimmy Coyne out on Babcock Boulevard. They had a house and a barn and we spent our summers there. Jimmy Coyne had a farm down in the back of us so that we spent a lot of time with the Coynes. . . . They became very close associates."[7] Coyne later became a small investor in the Harris-Lawrence Insurance Agency. In 1933, when, for political reasons, Lawrence was forced to dissociate himself from Coyne, their friendship remained intact in spite of Lawrence's blistering attacks. Both men seemed to understand that political expediency demanded the separation.

Lawrence's only other close friendship grew from a teacher-student relationship into one of coequals. Lawrence first met Jimmy Kirk when, still a teenager himself, he hired Kirk to work as a clerk in the Brennen law offices. Several years younger than Lawrence, Kirk came from an identical Irish Catholic background. Born and raised at the Point, he attended St. Mary's, trained in stenography, and began his career at Brennen's. Later, he replaced Lawrence as stenographer on the registration commission when the latter became minority commissioner. In October 1918, Kirk and Lawrence joined the army together, and later, on 14 June 1924, they simultaneously resigned from the Voter Registration Commission to devote more time to the presidential election.[8]

Kirk, a quiet, soft-spoken man whose personality contrasted dramatically with that of Coyne, became Lawrence's closest friend and aide. Andrew Bradley, Lawrence's liaison with the black community in Pittsburgh, had many dealings with Kirk. "If they [the black leadership] wanted me to accomplish something and I knew that the mayor was busy, I could talk to Jimmy Kirk. . . . I always felt that there was no living person at that time in whom the mayor had greater confidence." In 1945, prior to accepting the candidacy for mayor of Pittsburgh, Lawrence supported his friend and business and political associate, but at a caucus the other Democratic leaders objected. They "said Jimmy was a cold fish," Lawrence recalled, "and you couldn't sell him to anyone and we are going to lose the mayoralty. I would have liked to run Jimmy because he would have been the best [mayor] we ever had but he was that kind of person."[9]

Kirk was probably Lawrence's best source of political advice after both left the tutelage of William Brennen. Some suggested that Kirk was intellectually superior to Lawrence and was the driving force behind Lawrence's success, but there seems to be little substance to the charge. Kirk, of course, willingly ran the insurance office, freeing his friend to engage in political matters, and served as an important political aide. Their relationship, however, appears to have been based on strong friendship and mutual respect. When Kirk died prematurely during the first Lawrence administration, he left an unfillable void in the mayor's life. Each Christmas thereafter, following dinner, the Lawrence family would place wreaths on Kirk's grave, as well as those of David's parents, his grandparents, several children, his brother, and Judge Primo Columbus—another of his friends. The ritual continued until his last Christmas in 1965.

With the exception of Rooney, Coyne, and Kirk, few of Lawrence's nonpolitical associates were his intellectual or social equals. Beginning sometime during the early 1930s, he began to develop a coterie of friends whose main role was to indulge his passion for card playing. Some were given important roles in the party organization; Primo Columbus became a judge, and Charles Dinan sat on the city council. Dan Parish, owner of the Allegheny Asphalt and Paving Company, was a regular party contributor and became the subject of much controversy during Lawrence's four terms as mayor. Most, however, worked in ward-level politics and held city jobs. One was an attendant at the Monongahela Wharf parking lot. Each evening around five or five-thirty, some members of this unlikely group would assemble at Democratic headquarters or at the mayor's office for an hour or so of pinochle or gin rummy. Frank "Bangy" Ambrose was a frequent companion on these occasions. "We became fast friends playing pinochle at a quarter a game. I'll never forget the first time I played him, I beat him the first two games, and I didn't want the half dollar. He said, 'When you play me, when I lose I pay, and when you lose you pay.' So that's the way it was from then on." The game apparently relaxed Lawrence, but it was not played without intensity and an opponent whose mind wandered would be reprimanded. Walter Giesey, one of Lawrence's executive secretaries, usually observed the play as he was preparing papers for Lawrence's signature at the end of the day. "There was almost nothing of substance ever said during these games. He played pinochle with people who were certainly not his intellectual or political peers. But it was important for him to relax in this way." When Lawrence moved to Harrisburg as governor and most of his card-playing friends were left behind in Pittsburgh, he attempted to make up for lost time on weekend trips to the city. Ambrose or one of the others was expected to spend part of Saturday and often Sunday at the pinochle table at Democratic headquarters.[10]

▽

Of course, young Dave Lawrence did not spend all of his leisure time playing cards with political cronies or attending sporting events. Little is known about his early relationships with women except that he occasionally took dates to vaudeville shows on Pittsburgh's North Side, where he sometimes played the piano on amateur night. He later told his son Jerry that he dated a Ziegfeld Girl who "danced in the old Ziegfeld shows back in the twenties."[11] He enjoyed dancing and frequented the several dance halls in the city. It was probably at the North Side Social Hall that he met Alyce Golden in the fall of 1920. Alyce, seven years younger than Lawrence, was the seventh child of Irish immigrants John and Anna Golden.[12] John, a North Side liquor dealer, died in 1901, leaving nine children all under the age of seventeen. Anna maintained the business and cared for her children until her death in 1917. Recollections of young Alyce are vague but it appears that she was bright and hardworking, yet quite shy. Unlike her new beau, who by 1920 was widely recognized throughout the city, she shunned publicity and never became comfortable in large crowds or as the focus of attention. She did, however, enjoy her childhood in a home filled with siblings, and later she sought in her own home the constant companionship normal in a large family. That her public husband could not supply such company was a source of difficulty throughout their married life.

Early photographs of Alyce Golden reveal a tall, striking, dark-haired woman whose facial features were set off by high cheekbones. Her thin, almost boyish figure suited the fashion of the "flapper age," and it is easy to understand Lawrence's attraction to her. Moreover, she was Irish and Catholic, she enjoyed dancing, and her family supported the Democratic party. Their courtship lasted approximately seven months, and on 18 June 1921, Lawrence turned his back on the marital advice of his old mentor, William Brennen.

Following a brief honeymoon, the Lawrences returned to set up housekeeping in a middle-class neighborhood in the city's East End. On 18 June 1922 the couple had their first child, Mary, named after David's older sister, who had died suddenly in 1907. On 15 September 1923 a second daughter, Anna Mae, was born. She was followed by three brothers, William Brennen, David Leo, and Gerald (Jerry). Two children born between David Jr. and Jerry died at birth. The Lawrence family also grew through the addition of several outsiders. Shortly after the birth of the second child, Alyce, with no dissent from her husband, invited her sister Helen to move in to help care for the children. Helen remained part of the Lawrence family for over four decades. From time to time other relatives also lived in the Lawrence household—Alyce's single and widowed sisters and orphaned and abandoned nephews. At one point, Anna Mae was forced to share a twin bed with her aunt because there were not enough beds in the house.[13]

The one individual frequently missing was David. Both Anna Mae and Jerry recall the family as being a close one, but their memories of their father's absences are strikingly vivid. Following a practice established during his years with Billy Brennen, he devoted most of his waking hours to his work and the political party. During the 1930s, when he was the state Democratic chairman and secretary of the Commonwealth, Anna Mae recalled, "I didn't see very much of him because in that period of time . . . he was never home. He'd leave on Monday morning [for Harrisburg] and he would come back on Friday night." Parts of those weekends were spent at the city Democratic headquarters, and at least a few hours were reserved for card playing, rubdowns at the YMCA, and often attending sports events. Later, when he became mayor, his time at home continued to be extremely limited, as Jerry explained. "His normal day—well, at the time he was mayor, in that period he would leave home around 9:30 in the morning and would be gone all day and never really get back until around 7 at night and have dinner. Of course many nights he was out. . . . In fact . . . the old William Penn . . . would keep track of his menu because he would eat there three or four times a week."[14]

Even when he was home, much of his time was spent in private activities. Both children remembered his household routine changing little over three decades. After dinner their father would play someone at checkers or dominoes, games that he loved. Usually at about nine he would go upstairs, and always had a book on his night table. He read a great deal of history, particularly Irish history. He was also an avid radio listener, favoring Jack Benny, Charlie McCarthy, and Fibber Magee and Molly. He would be in bed with his light off by eleven o'clock.[15]

Lawrence was apparently devoted to and solicitous of the needs of his children and his wife. He and Alyce attended dances and sporting events and went out to dinner whenever his schedule permitted. Friday nights were reserved for family gatherings at the South Aiken Avenue house, and on other nights, when he was home, he refused to accept calls, rarely made any, and almost never entertained political associates. Like most women of the era, Alyce was not expected to participate in the political activities of her husband, and her own personality would have prevented it in any case. "She was afraid of a lot of the notoriety and the glory that went with it, which was something that he never brought home. He led two very distinct lives; he had a public life and a private life."[16] Alyce was left behind while her husband carried out the public phase of his life.

But certainly, upon their marriage, she did not expect to live her life alone or bear the full burden of raising five children, and Lawrence, in his own way, understood her dilemma. He not only tolerated but encouraged the inclusion of Alyce's relatives in the family home. It appears that he was well aware of the effect of his absences on his family and often sought to compensate. By filling the home with people whom Alyce loved and assisting them when necessary, he, in his own mind, signaled his devotion to her. The surrogate family would provide company and affection during his absences.

▽

Lawrence's own life, meanwhile, was increasingly filled with his work and his political activities. In 1920 he attended his third Democratic National Convention as an aide to the Allegheny County Democratic chairman, Joe Guffey. As at the two previous conventions, he played no role, but his relationship with Guffey once again proved to be fortunate. Guffey chaired the Pennsylvania delegation and acted as floor manager for A. Mitchell Palmer. Palmer repaid Guffey's loyalty by engineering a position as Democratic national committeeman from Pennsylvania. Guffey, in turn, tapped Lawrence to replace him as Allegheny County Democratic chairman. Lawrence now had a base from which to work. By no stretch of the imagination could it be considered one of power, but it did permit him to handpick the men for positions to which the minority party was legally entitled. His next twelve years would be spent trying to create a party following where none existed.

Pittsburgh politics during the 1920s continued to be dominated by a decaying Republican machine challenged at each election by a group of independent Republicans who tried one coalition after another to unseat the entrenched bosses. The Democrats, hopelessly outnumbered, remained far to the rear of the two main contending groups in each municipal election. Lawrence, for his part, offered no comprehensive plan to build the party but attacked aimlessly in whatever direction suited the moment. In June 1920, for example, in his first public statement, he championed the cause of woman suffrage and challenged the state's attorney general to extend the female vote to all state and municipal offices should the national suffrage amendment be ratified.[17] But he failed to capitalize on his stand by recruiting any substantial number of women into the party once the amendment passed. It was not until the mid 1930s that a female wing of the Democratic party was formed in the county. In 1924, taking advantage of his position on the Registration Commission, he initiated a drive to increase voter registrations. The plan unfortunately backfired, for Republican registrations increased by nearly 6,000 while the Democrats gained only 1,120 voters.[18] In another instance of missed opportunities, two small ethnic Democratic clubs were formed before the 1924 national election, but Lawrence was unable to incorporate them into the regular party organization. Both groups disbanded immediately after the election.

Lawrence and Kirk canvased the city before each municipal election in search of Democratic workers, but with little success. In 1921 and 1925, for example, the party was unable to supply poll watchers at each of the polling locations. Not surprisingly, the campaigns themselves were anemic affairs, with the center of attention being the continued squabbles among the Republicans. In 1921 the *Pittsburgh Press* noted a lack of interest in the mayoral and city council races. "The apathy which has been in evidence, if carried into the voting booth, would not be healthy for the community."[19] The fears proved accurate: nearly 30,000 fewer voters turned out for the general election than had cast ballots in the primary. The Republican candidate, William Magee, defeated William McNair by a margin greater than two to one.

The 1925 election produced a bit more excitement but was clearly overshadowed by Robert Jones's victory in the U.S. Open Golf Championship, held at nearby Oakmont Country Club, the Pittsburgh Pirates' defeat of the Washington Senators in the World Series, and the court-martial of Captain Billy Mitchell. All three events pushed the election off the front pages of Pittsburgh's newspapers. The Republicans, as usual, continued to maul one another, although with less publicity than was customary. The machine, controlled by state senators Max Leslie and James Coyne, and financier William Larimer Mellon, eventually settled on Judge Charles Kline to succeed Mayor William Magee. A so-called fusion group consisting of Republicans and independents challenged the Kline domination, offering William Smith, principal of Allegheny High School, as its candidate in the Republican primary. Lawrence and a Democratic executive committee appointed by him nominated Carmen Johnson, a teacher at Westinghouse High School.

While there were few attractive alternatives available, the selection of Johnson illustrates a weakness that would haunt Lawrence all through his political career: an inability to select strong, capable candidates. The slow-talking science teacher had worked for the party in the East End but was virtually unknown in the rest of the city, and he generated almost no enthusiasm during the campaign. Lawrence, usually in the hope of preventing a primary battle, repeatedly agreed to accept a candidate who was least objectionable to all within the party hierarchy. The result was often the selection of a candidate who had done nothing to create political enemies but who also showed little leadership potential. Although the campaign of 1925 was not among them, several important political opportunities were lost because of Lawrence's inability to select strong candidates.

Operating as usual in the shadow of the Republican furor, the Democrats attracted attention only when the fusion group charged that they were acting in collusion with the Republican majority. The slim chance Johnson had of attracting a following ended early in October. Pittsburgh's first World Series since 1909 brought on a frenzy that pushed all political activity far into the background. The Pirates, down three games to one, won three straight games, the last two played in Pittsburgh, to defeat the Senators. Game seven, featuring

Washington superstar Walter Johnson against Rube Oldham, moreover, was postponed because of rain, increasing the suspense. Press coverage, with articles written by Babe Ruth, Ty Cobb, Walter Johnson, Honus Wagner, and others, not surprisingly completely eliminated any concern about the election. By the time the city's excitement abated, the election for all purposes had been decided. The Republican, Kline, received 76,000 votes to 12,859 for the independent, Smith. Fewer than 5,000 voters supported Carmen Johnson. Democrat Thomas Hester's victory for the minority position on the jury commission was explained by the press as another example of the Democrats' subservience to the Republican machine.[20]

Stung by continual charges of bossism within his own party and of bowing to the wishes of the Republican machine, Lawrence turned to a different tactic in the 1929 elections. Ignoring his own executive committee, he appointed a "citizens' committee" of one hundred to select a candidate for mayor. The committee, chaired by a former U.S. district attorney, demonstrated the persisting ineptness of the Democratic party when it turned to Thomas Dunn, a registered Republican and chairman of the Pittsburgh Chamber of Commerce, for its candidate. Dunn accepted the nomination but, showing his own political wisdom, attempted to disguise his new party affiliation by running as the "Good Government" candidate.[21]

The Republicans unwittingly aided Dunn by continuing their decades-old war. Mayor Kline, by announcing his intention to stand for reelection, rejected an unwritten edict by William L. Mellon that no mayor could succeed himself. The Mellon-Coyne faction of the party then turned to the city council president, James Malone, while the independent Republicans backed Judge E. W. Martin. The three waged a heated battle throughout the summer of 1929, obscuring the efforts of the Democratic candidate, Dunn. Nearly 175,000 Republicans voted in the primary, with the plurality going to Kline. In the Democratic primary Dunn received 3,300 votes. The election for all purposes was over. Dunn's only hope was his dual candidacy, and indeed he did attract a considerable number of votes from disgruntled Republicans, including County Commissioner Charles "Buck" McGovern. Lawrence's old boss on the Voter Registration Commission, expressed the mood most eloquently. "Personally I am a Republican," he announced on radio station KQV. "I will, however, vote for Mr. Dunn on the Good Government Ticket as I want to remain one of the 96,000 voters who protested at the primaries against the election of thieves, racketeers and hangers-on who have dominated Pittsburgh's city government for the last four years."[22]

The support of the independents, however, fell far short, and Kline overwhelmed Dunn in the general election 80,000 votes to 37,000, winning twenty-eight of thirty wards. The Democrats had run another listless campaign whose only high note was the announcement by Lawrence that the party had secured enough volunteers to act as poll watchers at all the county's polling places.

That Lawrence's first decade as Allegheny County Democratic chairman was a dismal failure is evident from the city election returns; results from the county and state races, moreover, were similar. Party registration figures during the period are a further indication of his failure. In 1920, when Lawrence assumed his position, 95,000 voters registered as Republican and 12,568 as Democrats; five years later 11,000 additional persons joined the GOP, while the Democratic enrollment slipped to 6,430; in 1929 the comparable figures were 169,000 and 5,200 respectively.[23]

The impotence of the Democratic party under Lawrence was, of course, not new. Democrats had suffered an identical fate in Allegheny County for more than fifty years. The attacks from within, however, were increasing. Democrats began calling, both privately and publicly, for his resignation. In the midst of the election debacle of 1925, Lawrence was accused of collaborating with Republicans to guarantee control of all legally entitled minority positions. Several years later a group of prominent Democrats publicly demanded the resignation of this entire Democratic leadership. The *Pittsburgh Press*, the major critic of the Republican machine, concluding that Lawrence was unable or unwilling to lead the attack on the entrenched organization, criticized him at every opportunity: "The Democratic leadership . . . has lacked virility and courage, and its onslaughts on the 'recognized political boss' [William L. Mellon] have consisted largely of shadow boxing. It has been content, almost eagerly complacent, to accept whatever crumbs of minority representation could be secured through a policy of passivity."[24] Perhaps worse, the city's other two newspapers ignored him.

Two factors saved Lawrence from expulsion as party chairman. First, and perhaps most important, no one else appeared to want the position. Lawrence genuinely enjoyed the challenge of running the party and competing in elections. He was willing to spend great amounts of time and energy and some of his own money. Whether he actually believed that his party would ever succeed is doubtful. His preelection speeches, of course, brimmed with confidence, but one may dismiss those as campaign rhetoric. He had been involved in a futile pursuit of the Republicans for a quarter of a century and was realistic enough to understand that, barring some unforeseen catalytic event, his chances of prevailing remained almost nil. Others could also see the difficulty of the challenge and, while they might criticize him, were unwilling to volunteer themselves as replacements.

Second, Lawrence's liaison with Joe Guffey, now a Pennsylvania national committeeman, strengthened his position in the state Democratic hierarchy. In 1924 he accompanied Guffey to the Democratic National Convention at Madison Square Garden. Lawrence's first convention as a delegate, the most chaotic in the history of the Democratic party, lasted 17 days and required 103 ballots to select John W. Davis, a New York lawyer, as its candidate. As the convention dragged on, the ranks of the Pennsylvania delegation began to thin as one delegate after another depleted his financial resources and returned home. Lawrence, a strong supporter of the Tammany candidate, Alfred E. Smith, organized a pool of rooms to conserve delegate funds and prevent dissolution of the Pennsylvania support for Smith.[25] His decisive action stopped the exodus, and the majority of the Pennsylvania delegation, including Guffey and Lawrence, remained with Smith through all the ballots.

Lawrence left the 1924 convention convinced the Democrats had little chance of victory. We were in great shape to win. But we were manipulated to get into this terrible religious brawl . . . and we wind up, instead of—either one of the candidates was a good man, Bill MacAdoo was terrific but they got the Ku Klux Klan tied on to him because the South was supporting him, because Smith was Catholic. And of course we wind up—of all things—we nominated Pierpont Morgan's chief lawyer, John W. Davis. It was just ludicrous."[26]

The fall campaign probably reflected Lawrence's lack of support for Davis. The *Pittsburgh Press,* noting the party's lackluster effort, suggested that it was near collapse. Not surprisingly, Davis ran third, behind Coolidge and the Progressive candidate, La Follette, in all but two of sixty-two boroughs and townships in the county and in all of the city's twenty-eight wards. He captured only 8 percent of the total votes cast.[27]

The disastrous election results convinced Lawrence of the wisdom of his support of Smith. Three months before the 1928 Democratic National Convention in Houston, Texas, Lawrence called for his nomination. "He is the only candidate that can defeat the reactionary leadership now controlling the country."[28] Smith won the Pennsylvania Democratic primary, as he had done in 1924, and the Pennsylvania delegation traveled to Houston solidly in support of the four-term New York governor, who won easily on the first ballot.

Lawrence and Smith held similar positions on a number of issues, including support for regulation of utilities, the rights of organized labor, and repeal of Prohibition. Lawrence also expressed admiration for Smith's reform of the government of the state of New York. Equally important was an emotional attachment that temporarily blinded Lawrence to Smith's political liabilities. The "Happy Warrior" was a carbon copy of Lawrence's tutor, Brennen, and of Lawrence himself. A product of New York's Lower East Side Irish ghetto and of the city Democratic machine, he had risen to the height of power in his state. A Catholic, he was living evidence that religion need not be a bar to political success. It is unlikely that Lawrence, at this time, harbored any great political aspirations for himself, but, as he often noted later, he viewed Smith as the embodiment of the American dream.

Lawrence's campaign efforts in behalf of Smith were more evident than in any previous election. He worked vigorously for the Pennsylvania senatorial candidate, William McNair, but was most concerned with the presidential election. He spoke almost nightly from September through 5 November at political rallies all over the county. The rhetoric of his addresses, unfortunately, is lost because the city's papers continued their policy of reporting at length on Republican events but announcing Democratic affairs only after the fact. The *Pittsburgh Post-Gazette* did comment that Democratic rallies had grown larger, suggesting the development of a Smith following as election day drew near. A standing-room-only crowd attended the traditional conclusion of the campaign, held at the Carnegie Music Hall on the North Side. Lawrence announced that, for the first time in recent memory, "enough persons have volunteered to act as watchers to enable the party to have watchers at every one of the more than 1,400 districts in the county." Campaign funds must also have been available, for he also announced that he had hired the Burns Detective Agency for duty at Democratic headquarters to answer calls from the watchers regarding vote tampering by Republicans, and that he had retained a lawyer "ready to go to court when any trouble occurs."[29]

Poll watchers and funds, of course, while perhaps an indication of the growing strength of the party, did not guarantee success, and the November election returns in Allegheny County and Pittsburgh reflected the national results, Hoover winning by 56,000 and 8,000 votes respectively. Upon closer analysis, however, the results must have sent mixed messages to the Democratic county chairman. On the one hand, the Smith vote exceeded that of any Democratic candidate in the century. He won nearly one-third of the county boroughs and townships and fourteen wards in the city of Pittsburgh, including several of those dominated by the ruling Republican bosses. Not surprisingly, Smith's support came overwhelmingly from the wards dominated by the blue-collar, foreign-born, Catholic residents of the city. The First and Second wards, with the highest proportion of foreign-born in the city, gave Smith three-fourths of the votes cast. He also won in the Hill District wards, populated by Southern and Eastern European–born workers, the Polish neighborhoods of the Sixth Ward, the Eastern European South Side, and the German and Irish areas on the North Side.[30] Even in defeat, Lawrence must have felt that, given the right candidate, the Democratic party could pull off an upset victory.

Smith, however, in Lawrence's mind had been the near perfect candidate. Only one factor stood against him, and that in Lawrence's later analysis was the deciding factor: Smith's Catholicism. Lawrence's own defeat in 1931 further reinforced his belief that Roman Catholicism was an insurmountable handicap for a political candidate. His concern over the issue became so strong that it bordered on paranoia. Several times he passed over excellent candidates, including on one occasion himself, because of their affiliation to the Catholic Church. In Smith's case, Lawrence rejected the 1932 candidacy of the man he deeply admired solely on the religious issue.

If the Smith campaign of 1928 gave the Democratic party in Allegheny County any hope, it was quickly dashed by the succeeding elections. As was noted earlier, the 1929 municipal elections produced more of the same for the city's Democracy, and John M. Hemphill was soundly defeated for the governorship in 1930.

Guffey and Lawrence, however, by shifting from the Smith to the Roosevelt bandwagon, not only survived to fight another day but emerged from the twenties in excellent position to lead the battle. Guffey endeared himself to Roosevelt by providing needed information and support in the interim years, and Lawrence earned Guffey's support with his loyalty and the energy he brought to the Roosevelt cause. As early as July 1931, Guffey pledged that "not less than sixty-six of Pennsylvania's seventy-two delegates to the Democratic National Convention will support Roosevelt first, last and all the time. . . . This is based on conversations with not only the leaders but the rank and file of our party throughout the entire state."[31] The Pennsylvania Democratic party, led by Guffey, and its Allegheny County branch, directed by Lawrence, would have to wait another year for their first major success, but their efforts in support of Roosevelt were earning lasting political capital that would pay immense dividends for both.

1929–1934

Crumbs No More

On 31 December 1929, Alyce and David Lawrence, his business partner Jimmy Kirk, and State Senator James Coyne joined other merrymakers at Pittsburgh's Roosevelt Hotel to bid farewell to an old year and to toast the coming of a new decade. They remained at the celebration until after midnight, dancing and greeting old friends and acquaintances. But none of the men had much reason to celebrate. The insurance company in which all three were involved was deeply in debt and on the brink of bankruptcy. Republican political boss Coyne, constantly under attack from the city's newspapers and the liberal wing of his party, was involved in a fierce battle to maintain control of his organization. Lawrence's situation was even more desperate. Unlike Coyne, he depended upon profits from the insurance firm for a living. Furthermore, his decade as party chairman had produced only negative results. Each local election ended in a defeat more devastating than the one before. Party registration was only one-half of what it had been when he assumed command. Even the glimmer of hope produced by the strong local showing of Al Smith was dashed by the smashing loss in the most recent mayoralty election. His party had proved unable to take advantage of the deep divisions among the Republicans. Moreover, a serious split had developed within his own organization. Reform-minded Democrats, no longer able to tolerate the party's half-century-old custom of playing for the favor of the Republicans, had grown increasingly shrill in their criticism of Lawrence. If Lawrence spent any time at the gala New Year's Eve party musing on his situation, he certainly saw little reason for optimism in the coming decade.

The financial situation of the Harris-Lawrence Insurance Agency grew worse during the first year of the decade and demanded much of Lawrence's time. As president and major investor he stood to lose the most. His close friend Art Rooney later recalled that he suspended most of his political activities during the year, working six and seven days a week attempting to sell insurance and occasionally real estate to keep the company afloat.[1] Few Pittsburgh residents, however, were in the market for either in 1930. Many were already out of work and desperately holding onto whatever savings they had. In dire times the insurance policy was often the first to go. The real estate market was even worse, with mortgage foreclosures beginning to outnumber purchases by a substantial margin. Only the sale of surety bonds, purchased mainly by the Republican-controlled city and county governments, and several loans prevented the company from succumbing to the growing tide of business failures sweeping the city. Coyne's investment in the firm and his position at the head of the Republican party undoubtedly contributed to the willingness of city and county officials to purchase its bonds from Harris-Lawrence. Although the amounts were small, they provided important help at a crucial moment, adding substance to the charge of Lawrence's willing cooperation with the opposition during the early stages of his career. The bonds later became a major point of contention in his political life.

The Allegheny County Board of Commissioners election in 1931 strengthened the charges against Lawrence and nearly ruined his political career. Unable to defeat the Republican machine, his critics charged, he once again handed his party over to the opposition, causing irreconcilable divisions within the tiny organization. Following in the footsteps of his tutors, Tommy Toole and William Brennen, Lawrence concluded that his party stood to gain only by acquiescing to the dominant forces.

Twelve Republicans, including an incumbent, Joseph Armstrong, state senators James Coyne and William Mansfield, and Charles McGovern, a political maverick, announced their intention to run for the two county commissioners' seats allotted to the majority party. The list was eventually pared to these four. The county organization supported Coyne and Mansfield, while Mayor Charles Kline's city machine openly supported Coyne but quietly backed Armstrong's bid for a third term. A dozen ward leaders showed their independence by rejecting Armstrong in favor of either Mansfield or McGovern. Neither Coyne nor Armstrong, moreover, was willing to accept the other as a running mate, a situation that led to what one Republican called "a crossword puzzle written in a madhouse." To confuse the muddled Republican scene further, a reform Republican, Caldwalder Barr, announced his candidacy on the Square Deal ticket.[2] Within two days, McGovern announced that he would join Barr as his running mate but would also continue his candidacy for the Republican nomination.

The situation seemed ripe for an all-out Democratic attack. Hoping to avoid the primary election battles facing the Republicans, Lawrence abandoned his 1929 experiment of permitting a citizens' committee to select a slate of candidates. He turned instead to a political caucus consisting of the party's executive committee. The caucus quickly agreed upon the solid, if unspectacular, Thomas Daugherty, a jury commissioner, but it became hopelessly deadlocked over the choice of a running mate. It eventually turned to Lawrence as a compromise choice. He resisted initially, arguing first that he could be of greater benefit to the party acting behind the scenes as its chairman, and second, arguing passionately that the county was not ready for a Catholic candidate.

Nevertheless, the widening Republican split presented a great opportunity for the minority party. Ripped apart by ideological and personal divisions, the Republicans seemed vulnerable in spite of their long domination of local politics. A united Democratic party, Lawrence concluded, might capture two of the commissioner positions and would certainly take the minority slot now held by an independent Republican. Reluctantly he agreed to accept the nomination, as he would again later, in order to maintain party cohesion.

Lawrence's selection could hardly be considered a true draft. As the party's most prominent member for more than a decade, he had been considered in several previous elections Moreover, the honor of winning the party's endorsement was a dubious one at best. Democratic candidates considered themselves sacrificial lambs keeping the democratic process barely alive and retaining control of the positions legally allotted to the minority. Others had fulfilled their duty on the chopping block. One loyal Democrat, William McNair, had run for office in five previous elections. If Lawrence was to keep the leadership of the party, it was now his turn. McNair volunteered to serve as campaign manager.

Lawrence's strategy, however, failed to provide the desired united front when Thomas Hester, a former jury commissioner, challenged the Democratic slate. In announcing his candidacy, Hester raised the old issue of Lawrence's alleged subservience to the Republican majority, and his attack haunted Lawrence for the whole campaign.

Regardless of Hester's accusations, the 1931 primary season brought new hope to the Democratic organization. Lawrence reorganized the party structure, creating committees representing teachers, several labor unions, and at least three ethnic groups in an attempt to attract new supporters. He organized dinners and dances for campaign workers, introducing them to one another and making them feel a part of the Democratic party.[3] Lawrence, McNair, and Kirk appeared at rallies all over the county. Curiously, Daugherty did little campaigning in the primary and so lent credence to Hester's earlier charge. Crowds at Democratic rallies remained small, and the major Pittsburgh newspapers paid scant attention to their activities.

The Republicans, on the other hand, provided front-page news almost daily. They branded one another as "subverters of democracy," "despotic bosses" and "despoilers of the public trust." Other less imaginative terms included, *incompetent, indifferent, grafters, racketeers* and *common criminals.*[4] Political posters of all Republican candidates were periodically destroyed, and McGovern's campaign headquarters was ransacked twice.

The Coyne-Kline alliance suffered the most damaging blows shortly before the primary election set for 15 September when it was announced that Mayor Kline, indicted on forty-six charges of malfeasance in office, would stand trial before the year's end. The announcement naturally added fuel to the reform Republicans' fire. Every speech by McGovern and Barr during the final week of the primary campaign mentioned the indictments. The *Pittsburgh Press* meanwhile continued its attack on Kline, charging abuses and extravagances totaling more than $500,000 in two years.[5]

Charges of voter registration irregularities were also laid at the door of Kline and Coyne. The *Pittsburgh Press* ran a photo campaign showing the locations of allegedly "registered voters"—including a wharf at 39 Water Street, an abandoned post office, a vacant building at 601 Grant Street, a billboard at 2842 Liberty Avenue, and a warehouse where thirty-four "voters" lived. In its own investigation, the Allegheny County Bar Association discovered that thousands of citizens were being disenfranchised because unauthorized persons had already paid individual poll taxes in order to collect the receipts, which were then used by "multiple voters" at polling places throughout the county.[6] On 30 August the *Press* revealed that registrants for the primary exceeded the adult population of the city by 11,000. The greatest abuses came from Coyne's home ward, the Fourth, and fifteen others tightly controlled by Kline and Coyne. The courts eventually removed 50,000 illegal registrants from the voting rolls, but by 15 September "Klineism" or "Coyneism," as it came to be called, was synonymous with corruption and election fraud.

The Republican primary, not surprisingly, recorded the extent of the dissatisfaction with the party machine. On election day, voting riots spread throughout the city in spite of the presence of fifty state troopers sent in by Governor Pinchot to guarantee the legality of the election. Several ballot boxes were stolen and the locks broken on thirty-two others. Two recounts were taken, and not until 8 October were the official vote counts released. While an organization candidate, Mansfield, led the ticket, an independent, McGovern, won the second spot. Armstrong and Coyne, placing third and fourth respectively, were eliminated from contention. Given the huge Republican registration majority, Mansfield and McGovern were thus certain to win seats on the county commission. Barr won first place on the Square Deal ticket and had to be considered a serious contender for the third commissioner's seat. A victory by both antiorganization candidates, McGovern and Barr, seriously threatened the party's control of the county. The organization had to gain a second commissionership. At least 3,500 county patronage positions, providing jobs to the Republican faithful, were at stake.[7] To make matters worse, three of four candidates backed by Kline for city council also lost, and both the city and county machines were thus in jeopardy.

The furor of the Republican battle and the continuing ineptness of the Democrats were, as usual, reflected by the treatment of the two parties in the Pittsburgh newspapers. In spite of the Democrats' intraparty squabbles, an examination of the city's papers prior to the primary would convince one that the party did not exist. Campaign rallies received almost no coverage, and the *Pittsburgh Press* underscored its disdain for the party by failing to list the Democratic candidates on its sample ballot three days prior to the primary election. Hester, running without the benefit of the party's meager support, undoubtedly suffered most from the lack of publicity, for Lawrence and Daugherty won the nomination easily. The entire primary campaign cost the Democratic organization $325. The four Republicans, in contrast, had spent nearly $20,000.[8]

In the week following the primary, Daugherty, who led the ticket, announced that he was stepping aside to permit Lawrence to run alone. Upon hearing this, Kline and Coyne decided to turn to Coyne's old friend to solve their election dilemma. They could tolerate one independent, McGovern, on the board of commissioners, but not two. Lawrence, they decided, could be trusted to work with Mansfield, even though he headed the opposition party. Barr, a reform Republican, had to be defeated. Thus the two, originally without Lawrence's knowledge, decided to support him.

Republican party workers were given orders to provide any assistance requested by the Democratic campaign headquarters. Lawrence-Mansfield posters were printed at the expense of the Republican party, William L. Mellon allegedly provided funds for the Lawrence campaign, and Coyne's press agent, Eddie Jones, was loaned to it. Immediately before the general election, sample ballots marked for Mansfield and Lawrence were distributed throughout the city.[9]

Whether Lawrence welcomed the support of the Republican organization is not clear. Evidence of meetings between Lawrence and the Coyne-Kline forces does not exist, although it was certainly possible for the two sides to meet at the secluded Coyne or Lawrence farms. Lawrence never publicly accepted their endorsement. What is equally clear is that he never publicly repudiated it either. As the only Democrat in the race, he probably believed that he had nothing to lose by covertly accepting the endorsement of the entrenched regime. But 1931 was without a doubt the wrong year to become associated with Kline and Coyne. Lawrence was blasted by the reform elements of Pittsburgh and by members of his own party. The *Pittsburgh Sun-Telegraph* and the *Pittsburgh Press* assailed him almost daily as a "tool of Klineism-Coyneism," as a "false Democrat," and as the "candidate of the Democratic-Republican machine." Three times a week the *Press* ran a front-page, four-column editorial headed "Give one of your votes to Barr!" explaining how, although only entitled to vote for two candidates, voters could ensure the election of independents Barr and McGovern.[10]

Lawrence's silence on the matter of support from the discredited Republican regime eventually resulted in a revolt in his own party. John Henry, an attorney, was the first to attack him. When the Lawrence forces made no response, Henry recruited a number of allies in his attempt to oust the party chairman. Four days before the general election, Henry and eight other prominent Democrats, including Hester, defeated in the primary, released a signed letter to all the Pittsburgh papers repudiating Lawrence for exploiting the party for his own selfish benefit and outlining a history of collusion by Lawrence with the Republican bosses. The attack concluded: "We believe that his election will unquestionably give to a vicious Republican organization a continued foothold in the commissioner's office and will perpetuate the bipartisan machine in which David L. Lawrence has long assumed an important role."[11]

Lawrence's response evaded the charges. Speaking the next night at the Garfield Elementary School, he tried to discredit his accusers by questioning their loyalty to the Democratic party. "The real leaders [of the party], familiar with 'who's who' in local party affairs, are wondering what any one of these nine ever did, beyond holding office, to warrant being listed as 'prominent Democrats.'" Warming to the task, he attacked each one by name and concluded by observing that "it is no secret that a majority of the nine expect to be on the county payroll after Jan. 1. I challenge them to come out and declare that if tendered public office during the next four years that they will refuse it."[12] Lawrence, however, failed to deny the charged collusion with the Republican machine. The missed opportunity was a major tactical error—one he would never make again.

Lawrence's failure to reject the aid being offered by Kline and Coyne resulted from three factors growing out of his background and his understanding of the established political situation. First, Lawrence and Coyne, although political foes, were longtime friends and business associates. They saw each other socially; they met occasionally in the course of their insurance activities; and they frequently exchanged views at weekends on their adjoining farms. Coyne and Kline were also in a position to help Lawrence financially. He did not deny the press charge that "the Harris-Lawrence Insurance Agency collected commissions on more than $700,000 in contractor's performance bonds for city work alone," but simply pointed out that the commission on the alleged $700,000 amounted to only $2,100, hardly a sum over which to commit political conspiracy. Lawrence ignored a charge by the *Press* that he once borrowed $4,000 from Coyne.[13] His attitude, according to several political contemporaries, came from the belief that he could weather the political criticism while retaining his friendship with Coyne. One can only speculate on the cost of this friendship to Lawrence and the Democratic party.

Second, the charge against him—a willingness to accept the crumbs from the Republican table—was at least partly true. Lawrence had learned his politics under two men, Toole and Brennen, both of whom aligned themselves with the Republican party. In return for their cooperation, the ruling party customarily reserved a number of patronage positions for willing Democrats. (In 1929, for example, almost half of the 5,200 registered Democrats worked for the city or county government.) Lawrence himself later admitted that "prior to 1932 . . . Democrats always played for the minority places."[14] His own career, moreover, had benefited from his association with prominent Republicans. He attempted to conduct vigorous campaigns for each election, but his candidates were never as critical of the Republicans as critics within the GOP were of themselves. This gentle approach certainly lent credence to the allegation of collusion. More damaging, however, was the charge made by Mrs. J. O. Miller, state president of the League of Women Voters, that Lawrence acquired possession of the minutes of a meeting at which Republican County Commissioner Armstrong illegally created seventy new government positions. Lawrence might have denounced Armstrong publicly, gaining important public credit for himself and his party. Instead, he ignored the evidence and Mrs. Miller, who later brought legal charges against Armstrong.[15] The case was eventually dismissed by a Republican-controlled court but does show a strong reluctance on the part of Lawrence to attack the Republican bosses.

Finally, one must consider that the pragmatic Lawrence simply felt that the Republicans, in spite of their internal battles, were too strong to take on directly. They still had, after years of infighting, a huge voter registration edge. Republicans could fight Republicans, but the winners would still be Republicans. In addition, although the Democrats had gained a substantial number of workers, they still had almost no funding. Campaign posters and sample ballots supporting Lawrence may have been purchased by Republicans, but the financially strapped Democratic leadership looked upon them as a stroke of great fortune. They now had publicity material to distribute. Finally, only when the local newspapers revealed the so-called Coyne-Lawrence alliance did the Democrats receive any press coverage at all. Lawrence might become tainted as a Coyne lackey, but at least his candidacy would not die of anonymity.

Lawrence, for his part, continued to conduct his campaign and build the party as though the tempest were not swirling about him. From 25 October until election day he spoke at thirty-five campaign meetings. He scheduled and attended three meetings per evening on Mondays, Tuesdays, and Fridays and held large rallies Wednesday and Thursday evenings at Carnegie Hall in Oakland and on the North Side. Supporting reform of Pittsburgh's real estate laws, efficiency in government, and relief to the unemployed, he attracted small but enthusiastic crowds and evidently recruited some new party workers. "Once again," he announced on 1 November, "we have enough party workers to man every one of the county's polling places." He also received his party's first union endorsement from Steamfitters and Helpers Local Number 449.[16]

Election day 1931 brought mixed results and presented complex signals to local political leaders. Mansfield, an organization Republican, led all candidates with 171,000 votes, but the independents, McGovern and Barr, claimed the second and third commissioner positions with 163,000 and 127,000 votes respectively. Democrat Lawrence, backed by the Kline-Coyne machine, polled the fewest votes,

119,000. The *Pittsburgh Press,* in a bit of journalistic excess, called the election of the two independent Republicans the biggest political revolution in more than a quarter of a century. The antimachine editors ironically headlined the defeat of a Democrat by an independent Republican running under a Square Deal party label as the destruction of the Republican machine.[17]

A more objective observation would show that the Republican machine was still capable of producing a majority for its own candidates. Both Mansfield and Lawrence rolled up large pluralities in the seventeen Pittsburgh wards and fifteen county municipalities controlled by the Republican organization.[18] The strong machine nucleus, however, could not deliver a Lawrence victory and showed serious signs of vulnerability. A number of independent wards, mostly in the rapidly growing suburban sectors of Pittsburgh, helped deliver the total city vote to McGovern over Lawrence. Three-fourths of the county municipalities, in addition, gave pluralities to both McGovern and Barr over Mansfield and Lawrence. Even more disturbing to the organization, of course, was the potential loss of control of countywide patronage jobs. McGovern and Barr would join together to control nearly all of the 3,500 jobs available to the majority commissioners. Deprived of its patronage, the Republican machine found it increasingly difficult to maintain party discipline in subsequent elections.

The results of Lawrence's campaign are more difficult to evaluate. He received more votes than any other Democratic candidate for local office in the history of the city. Yet it is impossible to determine what proportion derived from the support of Kline and Coyne. The analysis of voter returns by wards and municipalities certainly suggests that the Republican regulars provided strong backing. Equally perplexing is the question of how many votes Lawrence would have received had he decided to attack rather than join the Republican bosses. Certainly, the Republican split and alleged widespread corruption of 1931 offered a tempting opportunity that Lawrence passed by. It was an opportunity he would not miss again. His postelection comment that the results demonstrated the vulnerability of the Republican organization, while mainly the political bravado of a defeated candidate, suggests that he recognized that it was time to chart an independent course.[19] The Republican machine was now terminally ill, and new opportunities would appear in each of the next two years.

The blow the Republican bosses received in the 1931 election had hardly stopped throbbing when they suffered another. Mayor Kline, despite attempts at postponement, stood trial and was convicted of malfeasance in office. He was ordered to resign and sentenced to a six-month prison term. The prison sentence was eventually suspended, but Kline left office in disgrace on 30 March 1933 and died of a stroke within less than four months. The city council president, John Herron, became mayor pro tempore. It was Herron, the city's last Republican mayor, who presided over the demise of a thoroughly discredited political party.

▽

National events, meanwhile, also conspired against Pittsburgh's Grand Old Party. The Depression of the 1930s hit Pittsburgh particularly hard. Orders for steel and the other heavy industrial products manufactured in western Pennsylvania reached all-time lows in the spring of 1932. Unemployment exceeded 25 percent and topped 40 percent among blacks and certain white ethnic groups. One study estimated that in March 1933 more than 200,000 Allegheny County residents were unemployed, while nearly two-thirds of those who did have work were idle more than 40 percent of the time. In the vital steel industry, less than one-third of the 1929 work force remained on full-time status. Those able to hold onto their jobs were forced to take large pay cuts, wages were cut by 60 percent and salaries by 50 percent. "It was terrible," one individual recalled. "My father was out of work for eighteen months. We survived by my parents' booking illegal numbers. We would have lost our home but the savings and loan company didn't know what to do with it so they let us live there for a small amount. Neither my mother nor my father had ever voted for a Democrat, but no one had to convince them to vote for Roosevelt. Shortly after the election, my dad got a job working at the post office. And you know what, they haven't voted for a Republican since." Another Pittsburgher, Raymond Czachowski, remembered, "My father's business went bankrupt. We lived meagerly, but we lived. To this day I don't eat potatoes because I think that's all we ate. My mother made potatoes in every way, shape, and form—bread and everything else—just to keep us going. We took our showers at the boy's club because we didn't have hot water at home."[20]

Cyrus L. Sulzberger of the *New York Times* used Pittsburgh to produce a graphic series chronicling the tragic conditions of the Depression at its worst. Shantytowns and Hoovervilles appeared in several outlying areas and along the Strip District on Liberty Avenue. Soup kitchens and apple carts began operation in the downtown sections and on the North and South sides. Private relief agencies, which shouldered the greatest burden in the early stages, exhausted their resources, and the problem grew worse with each passing month. State and local poor boards, mired in bureaucracy and special interests, squandered the little amount they appropriated on postage and personnel rather than on food and clothing for the needy.[21]

In desperation, Father James Cox of St. Patrick's, spokesman for the city's jobless, led an "army" of unemployed men to Washington, D.C., in January 1932 seeking federal assistance. The well-behaved group was cheered by onlookers as it marched through Harrisburg, then south to Gettysburg and on to the capital. President Hoover met with Cox, assuring him that he was fighting the "final campaign of the Depression," but promised no immediate relief. Unconvinced, Cox returned to Pittsburgh to announce his candidacy for the presidency under the Jobless party banner. The city's workers, meanwhile, began to abandon their old Republican allegiance.

The Democratic county chairman, hardened by the series of previous defeats, could hardly wait for the campaign to begin. The sports-minded Lawrence viewed each election as another season. His "wait until next year" approach enabled him to ignore previous defeats—to look forward to the next contest as an opportunity for a fresh start. Like a baseball manager during the off-season, he utilized the interim to shuffle his team and acquire new "players" to replace those who could no longer fill a useful role or to strengthen the "team" where needed. Successful against an attempt by twenty-two "independent Democrats" including Henry and Hester, to replace him as chairman in March 1932, he reorganized the party, purging a number of ward chairmen who had performed below his expectations in the 1931 campaign, and eliminating several who had sided with the disgruntled element in the party. He streamlined the executive committee, cutting it in size and establishing new lines of command to the ward level. Ward chairmen were ordered to conduct their own fund-raising campaigns, and each chairman was expected to hold party rallies in his own ward during the campaign. Recalcitrant chairmen were called in and told to comply, or the party would support an opposition candidate in the next ward election.[22]

Lawrence, who had reorganized the party structure three times during the 1920s, was well aware, of course, that much remained to be done. Additional workers, funding, and above all, voters willing to abandon their long tradition of voting the straight Republican ticket had to be recruited. The key to all three was an attractive alternative to Herbert Hoover, who, in Pittsburgh, was rapidly becoming the whipping boy for all the ills of the Depression.

Lawrence went to the Democratic National Convention in June 1932 with ambivalent feelings. He was convinced that Franklin D.

Roosevelt, whom he had met at the 1924 convention and again in 1928 when both supported the candidacy of Al Smith, was such a candidate. Indeed, he and Joseph Guffey had spent a good part of 1931 and early 1932 beating the drum for Roosevelt across Pennsylvania. Lawrence's emotional choice for president, however, was still Al Smith, but the negative effect of Smith's Catholicism overruled any other feelings. He simply could not win, and Roosevelt was the logical alternative.

Roosevelt and James A. Farley had openly courted the urban political bosses but at convention time could count upon the support of only Thomas Pendergast of Kansas City, Edward H. Crump of Memphis, and Edward H. Flynn of the Bronx. Frank Hague of Jersey City, Anton Cermak of Chicago, and New York's Tammany machine, on the other hand, remained solidly in the Smith camp. Mayor Curley of Boston supported Roosevelt but was unable to control his delegation at the convention.[23] Lawrence was not yet in the same league, but, as an ally of Joseph Guffey, a national committeeman and generous financial contributor, he had access to the Roosevelt inner circle. The two men corresponded several times with Roosevelt between 1928 and 1932 and by 1932 were firmly in the Roosevelt camp. In addition to canvassing the state on his behalf, they created the Allegheny County for Roosevelt Club and, probably with Guffey's money, supplied buttons bearing the slogan "America Calls Another Roosevelt." Their early support was soon handsomely rewarded.

Lawrence played a minor role at the national convention, but he and Guffey were able to provide fifty-five votes for Roosevelt on each of four ballots, more than any other state. The two returned to Pittsburgh buoyed by their candidate's chances for success, and the rapidly deteriorating economic conditions gave free rein to their organizational talents.[24]

Guffey remained in close contact with the Roosevelt organization throughout the campaign and played the more significant role. His financial support of Democratic candidates—Cox, Smith, and Roosevelt, and numerous Pennsylvania hopefuls—gave him recognition as the state Democratic leader. Warren Van Dyke, the state party chairman, owed his office to Guffey, and Lawrence himself had benefited several times through Guffey's intercession. Lawrence, although with considerable freedom, operated primarily as Guffey's lieutenant during the campaign. As such he was always careful to accede to Guffey in matters of protocol or principle. Lawrence's opportunity to challenge for broader power would come later. In the Roosevelt election he confined his efforts to winning in Allegheny County.

Correctly surmising that the city's blue-collar wards were the most likely to shift to Roosevelt, he focused his attention on the black and ethnic wards. Black voters, who comprised almost 10 percent of the city's population, had consistently delivered the Third, Fifth, Twelfth, and Twentieth wards to the GOP. In return they had received only minor political positions such as ward committeeman, policeman, and court clerk. Their patronage rewards included only the least desirable jobs, such as garbage collector, janitor, and elevator operator. All four black wards were controlled by white chairmen, and not a single black served on the policy-making board of the party. Republican leaders slighted even the most influential black leaders. Robert Vann, editor of the nationally circulated *Pittsburgh Courier,* who yearned for a major federal appointment, had worked diligently for the previous three Republican presidents. All three sought his support and the votes it could offer but failed to deliver the coveted federal post.[25] To make matters worse, as black unemployment soared, the city and county, desperate for funds, began to cut blacks, as well as other lower-income workers, from the payroll.

In March 1932, at the urging of Guffey and Lawrence, Roosevelt invited Vann to Hyde Park to discuss the possibility of a high-level position in a future Roosevelt administration. Vann returned to Pittsburgh a Roosevelt supporter. Using the *Courier* as its chief organ, he established a "parallel organization." Rather than joining the established Democratic organization, Vann created a Negro division of the Democratic National Committee and formed the Allied Roosevelt Clubs of Pennsylvania with himself as head. Black political workers rallied to Vann's call, swelling the Black Democratic Club in Allegheny County to more than 1,000.[26] For the remainder of the campaign, Vann urged black voters in Pittsburgh and across the country to join the Roosevelt following. He went to Cleveland to deliver his first major address before a Democratic audience. It was the most effective of his life. Speaking at the St. James Literary Forum, he chronicled the long history of Republican abuses of loyal black supporters. Focusing on the past three administrations, he charged that "the Republican party under Harding absolutely deserted us. The Republican party under Mr. Coolidge was a lifeless, voiceless thing. The Republican party under Mr. Hoover has been the saddest failure known to political history." But it was the conclusion of his address that captured the crowd and catapulted him into national prominence. "It is a mistaken idea that the Negro must wait until the party selects him. The only true political philosophy dictates that the Negro must select his party and not wait to be selected. . . . I see millions of Negroes turning the picture of Lincoln to the wall. This year I see Negroes voting a Democratic ticket. . . . I for one shall join the ranks of this new army of fearless courageous, patriotic Negroes."[27]

Vann's address was reprinted in many black newspapers and circulated nationally as a pamphlet. The *Courier*, meanwhile, continued to pound at Hoover for a myriad of sins, and black clergymen echoed its sentiments from their pulpits. Blacks faced with the economic realities of the depression undoubtedly had little difficulty accepting their exhortations.

Lawrence also made special attempts to win over the city's ethnic voters. Counting on the support of his own Irish voters, he turned his attention to those from Eastern and Southern Europe. Lawrence, Kirk, and several others spent many evenings on the South Side in an attempt to persuade the city's Eastern European electorate to throw its support to Roosevelt. Inhabited mainly by steelworkers, the Sixteenth and Seventeenth wards had supported Smith in 1928 and La Follette four years before that. With unemployment running at 31 and 42 percent respectively, they were a solid bet to remain in the Democratic column. Priests at St. Adalbert's and St. Josephat (Kuncewicz) Polish Catholic Church permitted their church halls to be used for campaign rallies and temporary South Side headquarters until a permanent location could be found. Workers from all of the ethnic parishes, one Croatian and two Polish fraternal associations, and several small labor locals provided campaign workers and distributed literature among their membership. While each ward continued to have an American-born chairman, usually Irish, the list of committeepersons was liberally dotted with names such as John Karnoski, Peter Dokmanovich, Louise Yarsky, and Magdelina Norkiewicz.[28]

Special efforts were also made in the Sixth Ward, whose Polish Hill neighborhood contained the largest Polish-American population of any ward. Lawrence and Cox—after he abandoned his own presidential hopes—whose parish abutted Polish Hill and who knew many of the community's laborers by name, spoke six times at the Falcon's Nest Hall. Perhaps more important, the party demonstrated its interest in the Polish vote by assuring that every one of the sixteen Democratic committeepersons from the area was of Polish descent. Slightly under one-half of the Republican committeepersons, in contrast, claimed Polish ancestry—in an area more than 90 percent Polish.[29]

Italian-Americans who made up 8 percent of the population, were also singled out for special efforts. Unemployment in the Italian neighborhoods of Bloomfield and East Liberty exceeded the city norm, and both districts had supported Smith in 1928. The city, furthermore, was the national headquarters of the Italian Sons and Daughters of America, publisher of the influential paper *Unione.* Lawrence and Guffey courted its editor, Muzio Frediani, in Lawrence's terms, "like the only girl at the dance," but they were unable to enlist his support. The newspaper, which had supported Harding, Coolidge, and Hoover, eventually called for the president's reelection.[30] Undaunted, the Democratic organization campaigned hard in the Italian wards. Promising a brighter future for the nation's workers—"the Forgotten Man"—they generated a strong Roosevelt following. An Italian Democratic Committee, with branches in the Eighth and Twelfth wards, organized to lead the anticipated groundswell for Roosevelt. Catholic clergy campaigned from their pulpits, and fraternal associations became meeting places for the spreading Roosevelt movement.

The Republicans, of course, did not abandon western Pennsylvania to the opposition, but years of feuding at the local and state levels had begun to take their toll. Locally the organization stood discredited and stripped of much of its power as a consequence of the 1931 commissioners' race and the conviction of Mayor Kline. Statewide, a decade of fighting among William L. Mellon, William Vare, Governor Gifford Pinchot, and Joseph Grundy, the president of the Pennsylvania Manufacturers' Association, had left the party leaderless and inept. An unusual shortage of funding compounded its problems. Grundy, the party's great fund-raiser in past elections, now in semiretirement, refused to solicit businessmen already in difficult financial condition for campaign funds. In addition, Pinchot, a progressive Republican, had thrown his support to Roosevelt and refused to permit the Republican organization to assess state employees for "voluntary" contributions. They had provided the party with more than $300,000 in 1928.[31]

Desperate for funds, Charles Graham, Pennsylvania chairman of the Hoover-Curtis Committee, devised a plan to extract "contributions" and votes from the state's working population. At a luncheon of 1,600 bankers and corporation officials at Pittsburgh's William Penn Hotel, Graham and U.S. Senator David Reed advised employers to urge their workers to vote for Hoover and to work for his reelection. Graham did caution the audience to avoid coercion, but the message was strikingly clear. Workers all over the city were subsequently deluged with the message that a Roosevelt victory would place their jobs in jeopardy. One company, heeding Graham's caution, invited its workers to a voluntary, free lunch at which "company officials will talk to you about the coming election. . . . In order to inject some fun . . . we will have a drawing of ten large hams."[32]

Party chairman Lawrence, no longer cooperating with the Republican majority, responded to the Graham strategy with unusual bitterness. Speaking two and three times daily, he charged Republicans with attempting to intimidate workers into voting for Hoover. "The promise of a full dinner pail has become the threat of the empty pay envelope. . . . The concern manifested by these Republican industrial overlords for the welfare of their employees and their families brings a smile of cynicism to those men and women who saw their life savings swept away through bank failures. . . . The next congress will be asked to take steps to bring to an end such un-American tactics and if I correctly appraise the present temper of the American people, they will see to it that never again will employers be permitted to engage in a campaign of terror and tyranny in an effort to force the election of a President and Congress pledged to a perpetuation of a policy of prosperity for the few and servitude for the many."[33]

Lawrence also successfully sought and won the financial backing of several traditional Republican supporters. Most important, the announced switch to the Democratic cause of Michael Benedum damaged the Republican party's prestige as well as its financial status. Benedum, an oil wildcatter who made his fortune on the famous Texas Spindletop strike, had long-term political and financial ties with William L. Mellon and James Coyne and had contributed large sums to Hoover's 1928 campaign. Nevertheless, he turned his back on the organization in 1932 by contributing more than $50,000 to the opposition. For the first time in its long history, the western Pennsylvania Democratic party was on solid financial ground. The Republicans, on the other hand, in the unusual position of lacking enough funds to conduct a full-scale campaign, closed several campaign offices in mid October.[34]

Finally, Lawrence publicized Roosevelt's support of the repeal of Prohibition (an important issue in the heavily "wet" city) and concern for the causes of organized labor throughout the 1932 campaign. His alliance with both popular issues no doubt added to the growing Democratic strength in western Pennsylvania.

Encouraged by his success at fund-raising and by the growing crowds at Democratic rallies, Lawrence gambled. "We want you to speak in Pittsburgh," Lawrence wrote to Roosevelt in October. "Our organization and your friends here earnestly request that you include Pittsburgh in one of your itineraries. Ordinarily we would not make this request, but for the first time since 1856 we Pennsylvania Democrats feel that the state can be carried and if we can make your lead 100,000 or better we will elect our state ticket. . . . I am confident that Pennsylvania can be carried for you and am convinced that if you will speak here, that will cinch it."[35]

When Roosevelt agreed to appear, Lawrence gambled again, hiring the thirty-five-thousand-seat Forbes Field for the address. The gamble paid off: more than fifty thousand jammed the stadium on 19 October to hear a major Roosevelt address. It was a red-letter day in the history of the western Pennsylvania Democrats. Roosevelt was greeted by huge enthusiastic crowds as his motor caravan traveled from the Pittsburgh and Lake Erie Railroad Station. Thousands lined Smithfield Street to welcome their would-be savior. Public schools were closed to permit the children to join in the festivities, and several bands provided appropriate music. Roosevelt went directly to Wheeling to deliver a morning address and then returned to Pittsburgh for an afternoon meeting with Lawrence and Guffey.

The evening's arrangements were testimony to Lawrence's organizational skills. Each of the key persons in the local Democratic drive played a role in the "warm-up" prior to Roosevelt's arrival. Father Cox, who the day before had announced the abandonment of his own campaign for president, urged his Jobless party followers to give their backing to Roosevelt, and Vann reiterated his support. Several candidates for statewide office spoke, and Guffey and Lawrence offered brief comments. Four black bands representing the Allied Roosevelt Clubs of Western Pennsylvania and half a dozen others representing various ethnic groups and the American Legion entertained the crowd. Several party workers dressed in donkey costumes acted as cheerleaders, spurring the crowd on to greater ovations as speakers concluded their remarks. Finally, at 10:00 P.M. the Greentree Fife and Drum Corps, in striking green uniforms, led a single automobile carrying a lone passenger through the center field gate. The roar could be heard for blocks around. Pittsburgh and Allegheny County gave notice of their impending shift into Democratic ranks.

Lawrence's final and perhaps most masterful touch on the evening was his selection of the person who would introduce the future president: Michael L. Benedum. He spoke only a single sentence, but his presence symbolized the defection of the wealthy from the Hoover camp and cemented his relations with the local Democratic organization. Benedum could be called upon for financial support for the next thirty years.

In his nationally broadcast address (which sounds remarkably contemporary) Roosevelt accused the Republican administration of not caring about the plight of millions of workers, criticized the mounting federal deficit, and declared that he would raise taxes "by whatever sum necessary to keep [the unemployed] from starving." A foolish promise to balance the federal budget would haunt him for the next several years. His reiteration of the Democratic platform plank promising to repeal Prohibition brought a rousing ovation from the standing-room-only crowd.[36]

The 100,000-vote victory that Lawrence anticipated did not materialize. The city of Philadelphia and the state as a whole remained loyal to the Republican party. In Pittsburgh and Allegheny County, on the other hand, years of inept and often corrupt Republican rule, the almost ceaseless intraparty battles, the disastrous effects of the Depression, the Prohibition issue, and the growing effectiveness of the Democratic organization all combined to produce different results. Roosevelt carried the city and county by 27,000 and 37,000 votes respectively. He won an impressive 26 of 32 wards to become the first Democratic victor since before the Civil War.

Not surprisingly, Roosevelt's greatest support came from the city's working-class wards. The Eastern European South Side wards, which had supported Smith in 1928 and La Follette in 1924, gave Roosevelt nearly three-fourths of its votes. The North Side, a mix of second- and third-generation German and Irish blue-collar workers proved to be the second strongest Roosevelt area, with ward totals ranging between 62 and 71 percent. The work of Lawrence and his committee also paid off in the city's Italian wards. Ignoring *Unione*'s endorsement of Hoover, Italians in Bloomfield, East Liberty, and the Lower Hill District gave a substantial majority to the Democrats. Only the black voters, among all workers, failed to produce the expected victory. To be sure, nearly two-thirds of the vote in the Third Ward went to Roosevelt, but the area contained blacks, Jews, Italians, and small numbers of other ethnic groups. It was, in fact, the most integrated section of the city in 1930. Republican Councilman James Malone's Fifth Ward, in contrast, nearly two-thirds black in 1930, gave a slight majority of its votes to Hoover. Blacks were moving toward the Democratic party, but more work remained to be done.[37]

The extent of the Roosevelt victory in Pittsburgh may be judged by the fact that in only one of the more affluent wards, the Fourteenth, could Hoover claim a substantial victory. In addition, one Democratic candidate for U.S. senator, four for U.S. representative, and six for the state legislature all carried the county. The Republican machine held only three of the wards it normally carried. "The Republican party is dead," a jubilant Lawrence told a group of party followers at the Magee Building headquarters the day after the election. He added prophetically, "All that remains is to put in the last nail in next year's mayor's race."[38] Realizing that all the elements of a Democratic takeover were now present, Lawrence could not wait for the next race to begin.

▽

Lawrence and Guffey moved quickly in 1933 to consolidate their gains and prepare for the fall campaign. They attended Roosevelt's inauguration and met briefly with him. A record of their conversation has not been preserved, but Roosevelt lost no time in rewarding his two Pennsylvania supporters. Guffey, as the top Democrat in the state, assumed control of all federal patronage, while Lawrence, working through the Democratic State Committee, would dispense all federal and state patronage in western Pennsylvania. Party loyalty would now be rewarded with jobs. Lawrence himself was named district collector of internal revenue in recognition of his efforts in the 1932 campaign. His new post provided him with a modest income and freed him from the day-to-day operations of his insurance company, which continued to struggle on the brink of bankruptcy. He could now devote more time to building the Democratic party.

Upon his return from Washington, Lawrence, eager to begin what promised to be an enjoyable campaign, called a meeting of the city Democratic leaders to discuss possible candidates for the upcoming mayoral race. Several names surfaced, including those of his 1931 running mate, Tom Daugherty, a jury commissioner; his longtime friend and political ally Jimmy Kirk; his 1931 campaign manager, William N. McNair, a perennial candidate; and Lawrence himself. Lawrence, who initially supported Kirk, waited to hear the opinions of others before presenting his case. When it became clear that little enthusiasm existed for Kirk, Lawrence accepted the will of the majority. It was an approach that was to become standard for him.

Daugherty, the reluctant, often missing candidate from the 1931 county commissioners' race, declined to run again, leaving the field clear for McNair and Lawrence. Each supported the other. Lawrence attempted to disqualify himself on the grounds that the defeat of Al Smith in 1928 and his own loss in 1931 proved what he had long suspected—that Catholicism continued to be a formidable political liability. McNair was not convinced, however, and continued to seek support for the party chairman, insisting that he himself would not be a candidate again after his five previous unsuccessful attempts at seeking office. Eventually, after calling a number of meetings and enlisting the help of state legislators and delegates to the 1932 Democratic National Convention, Lawrence managed to persuade McNair to change his mind and agree to be a candidate.

It has been suggested that Lawrence and the Democratic leaders never expected McNair to win in November. Indeed, the reaction of McNair himself following his victory appeared to be one of disbelief. The evidence, however, indicates that Lawrence carefully and correctly assessed political conditions in Pittsburgh in 1933 and concluded that McNair was the man to capitalize upon the situation. Past practices had been to select a sacrifice to maintain the pretense of an open race. Obviously any willing body would do. For the first time in recent history, however, party leaders selected a candidate with particular attributes in mind and went out of their way to ensure his cooperation. He was just the man to appeal to independents and unhappy Republicans. In prior campaigns he managed to remain free of the taint of collusion with the Republican bosses by running as a loner. He was a Protestant and, although a lifelong Democrat, a Pennsylvania blue blood. Born in Middletown, Pennsylvania, he attended a private military academy, Gettysburg College, and the University of Michigan Law School. He opened a law office in Pittsburgh in 1914. Debonair, handsome, and never at a loss for a quotable comment, he proved to be an attractive candidate. His business and social acquaintances were Republicans, and he appeared to present no threat to the middle and upper classes. The previous campaigns, even though unsuccessful, gave him instant name recognition, if not credibility. Finally, his unyielding advocacy of Henry George's single tax philosophy added to his reputation as a charming if somewhat eccentric intellectual.

Not content with selecting him, Lawrence, acting as campaign manager, engineered every facet of the McNair campaign. He began by educating him on the issues such as housing conditions and the state of the city's water supply. Lawrence hired Eddie Jones, Coyne's hard-hitting former speech writer, as publicity man, who, over the protests of the candidate, breathed some life into the campaign.[39]

Lawrence's old-time foe John Henry also declared his candidacy for the party nomination. The Democrats, however, were able to avoid their own internal division in spite of his attempt to resurrect the old charge of Lawrence's subservience to Coyne. Lawrence, having evidently learned from the 1931 campaign, acted immediately to put the charge to rest. There could not be an alliance between Democrats and Republicans, he declared, for their interests were poles apart. He promised to oppose Coyne, Mellon, and all their candidates.[40]

McNair, although he preferred to discuss the advantages of the single tax, used the best Jones rhetoric to attack Coyne and Mellon at every opportunity. "For when the underlying characteristics of the two men are considered, they will be found to have much in common. Their circumscribed horizons, their limited social vision, their refusal to regard political power as anything except an instrument for personal material gain, their methods of achieving and retaining power—are all about the same." He then accused Coyne of becoming "a Frankenstein creature, mad with and for power, caring neither for public opinion or public favor. . . . Coyneism must be eliminated once and for all."[41]

The message was clear. If Lawrence had earlier struck a marriage of convenience with Coyne, the divorce was now final. Although the two maintained a warm personal relationship throughout their lives, they established a comfortable distance in all political matters. The Democratic organization would settle for the Republican crumbs no more.

The rout of the disorganized Republican party in the 1933 mayoralty race proved comparatively easy. Mayor Kline's conviction and resignation shocked the party. Acting Mayor John Herron could not fill the vacuum, and the usual Republican factionalism emerged. Once again party leaders could not agree on a candidate, and there were three contenders in the primary: Herron, Coyne's choice; Joseph Mackrell, the register of wills, running as an independent Republican; and P. J. McArdle, a member of the city council.

Coyne became the key issue of the primary campaign, with Mackrell and McArdle attempting to outdo each other, and the Democrats, in their attacks on him. They continuously ripped Coyne, Herron, and each other. Herron, for his part, found himself in the no-win position of defending a machine over which he had little control. An indictment in August of Coyne, his brother, several police officers, and twenty-two other Republican officials on vote fraud charges made a difficult task almost impossible.

The arrogant organization, however, refused to lower its profile and continued its bullying and blundering ways. Two weeks before the primary election, for example, Republican ward chairmen began a drive to raise funds by assessing city employees a fee to be used in the purchase of poll tax receipts. The "contributions" ranged from five dollars for city laborers to fifty dollars for police and fire captains. "Macing," as it was known, although illegal, was an accepted practice in Pittsburgh politics, but it was usually handled more discreetly. Within one week of the "collect" order, two of the city's newspapers had received substantial evidence and revealed the effort to their readers. Employees were told to kick in or lose their jobs. The effort allegedly yielded $1,900 before being reported to the local press.[42]

In spite of Herron's difficult position as the whipping boy for the past transgressions of the party, he defeated his badly divided opposition in the fall primary. The party's superiority in manpower and ample funding, provided mainly by the Mellon family, proved too much to overcome. McNair also won his party's primary, but the similarities ended there.[43] The Republican party in decline and the ascending Democratic party perhaps crossed paths at this point, with the Republican plunge accelerating almost daily.

The first scandal of the election broke in September when it was revealed that nearly 20,000 potential voters in the Coyne-controlled Fifth Ward had been assessed a poll tax. Fewer than 6,500 families resided in the ward. Among those assessed was Colonel James Anderson, a long deceased benefactor of Andrew Carnegie. Within two weeks Leo Riordan, a county assessment investigator, uncovered 268 new "voters" in the Second Ward, including: ten men who gave a Penn Avenue speakeasy as their home; twelve persons listed as residents of a notorious Tunnel Street dive; one man assessed as living at 3300 Penn Ave—the site of a billboard; other assessed "voters" also supposedly residing at warehouses, empty lots, a foundry, or in service stations; a number, not surprisingly, were also registered more than once at several addresses.[44]

The *Pittsburgh Press*, now solidly in the McNair camp, dusted off its 1931 anti-Republican tactics and ran photographs of the alleged places of residence. It also issued its own charges, claiming that the Republican organization maced city employees in both the Ninth and Twelfth wards, and ran a series of editorial cartoons depicting the corruption of the Coyne organization.[45]

Perhaps most indicative of the Republican decline was the reluctance of the GOP city council candidates to acknowledge their affiliation with their own party. Their posters carried all kinds of appeals for support, but nothing to show that they were Republicans.[46]

McNair, meanwhile, proved to be the ideal candidate. He delighted in the attention heaped upon him and responded with a genuine warmth. Jumping aboard the Roosevelt bandwagon, he canvased the city night after night. The campaign strategy devised by Lawrence and a small but growing group of supporters worked brilliantly. Fred Weir, assigned to travel with McNair, explained how the plan worked. "The Republicans would hold one big meeting per night while we held half a dozen. . . . On the night, for example that Herron . . .

held a big meeting at the Duquesne Gardens . . . McNair talked to more people than Herron did. At maybe six places. . . . We would just run in and say a few words and they would roar and we would leave. There was nothing significant said."[47]

When he did speak, McNair's standard themes included attacks on Coyne, Mellon, the utilities, and high trolley fares, praise for FDR and the New Deal, and a portrayal of the local Democratic organization as a wing of the New Deal. A vote for McNair was characterized as a vote for Roosevelt, the NRA, WPA, and other New Deal measures. At a rally honoring Roosevelt at Kennywood Park, Lawrence, in Jones's best purple prose, attacked the opponents of the President's program. "Out of the seemingly bottomless man-made abyss dug by avarice, deepened by gold-mad Morgans and Mellons and protected by statesmen of the type of Penrose and Reed, we are at last emerging, following the leadership of the men upon whom today are focused the eyes of the world." Lawrence would frequently conclude a speech by reading a letter from the president. "'Dear Dave'—I want you to get that, 'Dear Dave,'" he would emphasize—"'It is good to know that you and your friends . . . are co-operating in such a splendid way in this fight.'" It was signed 'Franklin.'"[48] The crowd's reaction was unvaryingly enthusiastic.

Campaign advertisements also made clear the Roosevelt connection. A full-page ad that ran at least six times in the Pittsburgh papers prominently labeled McNair as the "Roosevelt Candidate for Mayor of Pittsburgh." "One might think," the *New York Times* observed just before the election, "that it is Mr. Roosevelt who is running for Mayor of Pittsburgh."[49]

The Democrats, attempting to capitalize on the successes of the Roosevelt campaign, repeated their earlier appeal to black, ethnic, and Protestant voters. Lawrence and McNair both courted Vann. Lawrence and Guffey relied upon their association with Washington to appoint five blacks to the Pittsburgh office of the Home Owners Loan Corporation. Publicizing the appointments in the organization newspaper, the *New Deal News,* they also pointed out that blacks, who constituted 16 percent of the voters in Pittsburgh, received only 3 percent of the patronage under the Republican administrations. Vann began to accompany McNair and Lawrence as they spoke repeatedly in the black wards of the city, and his newspaper broke precedent by endorsing the entire Democratic slate of candidates just before the election.

McNair's appeal to Italian-Americans began when he spoke, in Italian, to a crowd exceeding 1,500 at Carnegie Music Hall on the North

Side. In offering a variation of George's single tax on economic rents to relieve the tax burden on small homeowners, he credited the idea to an Italian, Filangeri, and Ben Franklin. The crowd roared its approval. Shortly afterward, the Italian-language newspaper *Unione*, which had earlier supported Herron, began to shift toward McNair, and it eventually called for his election.[50]

Finally, the Democratic organization, wary of its image as a Catholic party, attempted to win a few Protestants into its hierarchy. Councilman Fred Weir, himself a Protestant, helped in the recruiting. He also felt that one of the reasons for his own prominence was Lawrence's concern with the Protestant vote.[51]

The work of the Democratic organization and the influence of the New Deal, of course, might still have been wasted had it not been for the dissension within the Republican party and the work of Pittsburgh's two evening newspapers, particularly the *Press*. The Democrats had gained more than 32,000 registered voters since the last mayoralty election. The Republicans lost almost 12,000 during the same period, but they still held a 122,000 majority.[52]

Lawrence attempted to capitalize on the Republican dissatisfaction by appealing to would-be defectors. He arranged to kick off the fall campaign at the Frick School in the Fourth Ward, Coyne's political backyard, and personally invited McArlde, Mackrell, and other Republican opponents of Coyne to attend. Before a record-shattering crowd, McNair opened his address by promising to crush the Coyne machine. He ended it by inviting his Republican guests to join in the dismemberment. "If elected, I and the [city council] candidates . . . will go into office as uncontrolled and as unfettered as FDR did when he took the oath of office on March 4th of this year.[53] The strategy succeeded almost immediately, and defectors began to line up within the next two weeks. Lawrence, who sat in the audience in order to gauge its reaction, might have been less pleased had he understood the sincerity of McNair's statement. His independence began to show almost immediately after his inauguration.

The Democrats sweetened their call for Republican defections by making it clear that converts would be given important places in their newly adopted organization. Thomas Gallagher, a lifelong Republican, had actually preceded McNair's call for Republican allies by jumping ship in June 1933. He eventually became a McNair candidate for city council. Prominent Republicans, many of whom had little to gain from the New Deal, sensed the end of a dynasty and rushed to place themselves in strategic positions before the new regime took over. Among them were John Huston, the chairman of the Tenth Ward; Republican primary candidate John Mackrell; and P. J. McArdle. But the end of Republican rule in Pittsburgh was signaled by the switch in allegiance of William Magee, a former mayor and nephew of Christopher Magee, a nineteenth-century Republican boss.[54]

Numerous independent political groups such as the Citizens' League and the Council of Churches, and groups that had always supported Republicans, including the Firemen's and Oilers' unions, joined in the stampede to endorse McNair and the five Democratic council candidates. Mrs. R. Templeton Smith, county chairwoman of the League of Women Voters and a bitter enemy of Lawrence's, announced her support of McNair one day before the election. The *Pittsburgh Press*, the city's most influential newspaper, published accounts of each defection on its front page. On one day, 29 October, it announced thirteen endorsements from former Republicans.[55]

McNair proved to be an indefatigable campaigner. In the week before the election he spoke to nearly a dozen crowds per day, the size of each one, according to local estimates, being somewhat larger than the one before. Lawrence expended equal energy in organizing the campaign but remained in the background. Excepting a few major rallies, he seldom spoke and was usually absent from the speakers' platform. Considering the enjoyment he normally derived from campaigning, his behavior may appear unusual. McNair, however, was perceived as independent of the Coyne-Mellon organization, and Lawrence was wary that his presence might resurrect the old charges of political collusion.

The *Pittsburgh Press*, which had campaigned hard against Lawrence in the 1931 county commissioners' race, now saw no connection between him and the Republican machine. Ignoring a Coyne lawsuit for $250,000 for defamation of character, the *Press* ran an almost daily editorial and cartoon campaign against Coyne and Herron, and letters to the editor decried the lack of progress in the city, "standpatism," "dishonesty," and "Coyneism" and called for a "New Deal for Pittsburgh."[56]

The *Press* got its wish when McNair, all five Democratic candidates for city council, and the Democratic candidate for juvenile court judge all won easily. It was the worst defeat ever to a Republican machine in Pittsburgh. The Republicans carried only seven wards, old strongholds, and even there the margin was embarrassingly small.[57] It was a defeat from which the western Pennsylvania Republicans would not recover.

The mop-up that Lawrence predicted following the Roosevelt victory required a few more years than he anticipated, but by 1936 the Democrats controlled the mayor's office and county board of commissioners, held all nine seats on the Pittsburgh city council, and most of the elected row offices. They also had elected Joseph Guffey to the U.S. Senate and put George Earle in the Governor's Mansion in Harrisburg. Lawrence became Earle's secretary of the Commonwealth and the dominant force in the state government. Nearly all of the successful candidates owed allegiance to Pennsylvania's new political boss. Perhaps most revealing was the cause for the celebration held at Democratic headquarters on 10 October 1936. Shortly after the small band of loyal followers gathered at the Benedum-Trees Building, Lawrence, now state party chairman, announced that the local revolution had been completed. As of that date, he proudly proclaimed, Democratic registrants in the city of Pittsburgh outnumbered their Republican counterparts 172,179 to 136,451. A new era in western Pennsylvania politics had begun.

Thus the election of 1933 may be viewed as the turning point in the building of Democratic power in Pittsburgh. Its rise, however, did not occur on that single day in November. Nor did it result from largess flowing from the New Deal offices in Washington, D.C. The genesis of Democratic control lay rather in a complex pattern of circumstances, events, and decisions.

The economic conditions in Pittsburgh and the promise of a New Deal by the Roosevelt administration certainly contributed to the political reversal in Pennsylvania. The party's real and potential ability to provide jobs and social services proved to be a strong magnet. The control of federal patronage, after the Roosevelt election, enabled the party to provide the important quid pro quo to Democratic workers and Republican defectors. The city and county administrations, in addition, controlled thousands of jobs in the departments of public works, parks, highways, and public safety. As economic conditions deteriorated during the 1930s, more and more blue-collar workers abandoned their old Republican ties. By 1936 a majority of the ethnic and black wards in Pittsburgh were safely in the Democratic camp. They remain solidly Democratic today.

Partly regulars, no doubt, were attracted by the same economic opportunities. An increasing proportion of Democratic committeemen received positions on the public payroll each year after 1932. All but four of a 25 percent sample served with the WPA, most as foremen or supervisors, sometime during the Depression. A similarly high proportion of Democratic ward chairmen earned their livelihoods in the public sector.[58]

Public funds and occupational opportunities were clearly crucial in turning the city's blue-collar population into Democrats. However, a substantial proportion of the upper classes of western Pennsylvania also turned their backs on the Grand Old Party. Other factors contributed. Certainly the corruption, both alleged and real, in the Republican organization contributed to its demise. Eighty years of control had produced contempt for the rights of the electorate and an inability among the Republican leadership to reform. This intransigency certainly led to the election results of 1933. McNair, unlike Al Smith and FDR, derived a substantial margin of support primarily from the city's upper-class native white electorate, who cast their votes against the corrupt machine.[59] Its ineptness at governing the city and county and its failure to maintain control over its own party regulars must also be considered. Most damaging to the Republican cause, however, was the constant feuding among its leadership. The inability of William L. Mellon and James Coyne, and later Charles Kline and Coyne, to prevent primary fights and independent Republican tickets sapped the strength of the party, eventually rendering it impotent after 1937.

On the opposite side of the political aisle, the Democratic leaders appeared to learn and gain strength with each election. Their small group of workers, led by Lawrence, strove diligently to attract a loyal cadre. Frequent rallies, combining both social and political activities, produced party supporters. Lawrence's insistence upon local organizations working at the neighborhood and even block level brought others into the fold. As the party grew, so also did its ability to attract funds. Excluding Republican contributions, the Democratic party raised less than $1,000 to support its 1931 county commissioners' race. By 1933, aided by Michael Benedum's $50,000 contribution, the party raised over $100,000, opened a permanent office, and was able to provide financial assistance to local candidates.[60] The number and total amount of contributions increased with each election, providing an important financial cushion to the party.

Lawrence's growing skill at organizing and guiding the party also played an important part in its rise. During the 1920s he struggled to hold together his tiny group of party regulars. One can only wonder how often he must have despaired. That he avoided the temptation to join the Republican majority testifies to his inner strength. His resolve to avoid intraparty battles, although not always successful, contributed to the growing unity of the party.

Finally, one must note the ability of the Democratic party to exploit the loss of public confidence in the Republican organization.

The Democrats successfully abandoned their ties with the GOP machine after 1931 and led the attack. Together with the *Pittsburgh Press*, the Democratic organization branded the party of Coyne, Kline, and Mellon as the party of corruption, indifference, and incompetence. The indictments of the Republican leaders seemed to confirm these charges, and the labels stuck. The Democratic party, as the *Press* editorialized, presented "a focal point around which can gather those who are sick of the old order, who want government freed from utility domination, corporation control and political scandal."[61] In offering its New Deal for Pittsburgh, the Democratic party was happy to play the role of savior while at the same time building its own dynasty.

Building an Organization

The Roosevelt victory in 1932 and the triumph in the municipal election of 1933 ushered in one of modern America's most durable and efficient urban political machines. David L. Lawrence, as its head, remained in power until his death in 1966, and remnants of his machine continue to influence political life in the City of Steel. The Republicans, in contrast, have failed to win an important election since 1938 and in several major races have not even bothered to provide a candidate. When they do offer a candidate, the opposition is only a token.

Political scientists have offered divergent opinions regarding the phenomenon of boss politics in modern America. Some have argued that, in today's world of federally sponsored social security, unemployment compensation, welfare payments, and Civil Service regulations, bosses have become an anachronism. Indigent immigrants or other needy persons no longer look to the local party for financial or social assistance. Similarly, urban parties, stripped of thousands of patronage positions, can no longer bargain employment security in return for votes and party support.[1]

A number of historians, relying upon longer-range perspectives, have challenged this notion. Indeed, they have argued that, while the modern boss is different from his nineteenth-century counterpart, relying on different instruments and methods to retain his power, he continues to exist. Moreover, rather than destroying machine politics, the Roosevelt administration infused new life into the moribund urban administration by supplying the grass-roots of the party with not only federal patronage, but also long coattails. James Curley, Edward Crump, Edward Kelly, Frank Hague, and Thomas Pendergast all benefited from the institution of the New Deal. And the assistance was not limited to Democrats: Republican Fiorello H. La Guardia of New York, a strong New Deal supporter, perhaps more than any other mayor, owed his success in part to his alliance with Roosevelt. This liaison between the urban bosses and the administration in Washington was nearly inevitable. "In a sense, the New Deal Democrats had little choice about using federal urban programs to build their political base, for a newly mobilized urban electorate forced them to do so. In the following years, their successors used these programs to shape that electorate and continually modernize and adapt the organizational base upon which their national majority rested."[2]

The experience of Lawrence and the Democratic organization in Pittsburgh underscores the point that Roosevelt and the New Deal did not destroy the support system of the urban political machine. However, it also suggests that the argument that the New Deal in fact created new machines is simplistic. Of the fifteen major mayoralty elections held within four years of the 1932 Roosevelt victory, only William McNair's in Pittsburgh and George Zimmerman's in Buffalo can be considered coattail victories. Interestingly, more cities shifted from the Democratic to Republican than the reverse—four to three—while four Republican cities remained loyal to the GOP.[3] The Roosevelt coattails may have been broad enough to aid candidates for the national legislature, but they did not extend to the city administrations.

The development of a successful political organization is a complex process. An analysis of the Democratic triumph in Pittsburgh demonstrate that a number of factors were at issue. Roosevelt's popularity admittedly helped, but other factors—including a moribund, squabbling, and certainly corrupt Republican organization, disastrous economic conditions, a successful Democratic strategy to build a broad base of support, a well-orchestrated campaign, and an attractive candidate—must be considered. It is not suggested here that Pittsburgh is representative of all American cities, but the Pittsburgh case does illustrate that the efficient, successful machine is built upon more than the support of the lower economic classes. As such, its power could not be destroyed when the source of financial assistance shifted from the city to Washington.

The Democratic machine in Pittsburgh did not suddenly emerge out of the Roosevelt victory of 1932 and take wing in the municipal election of 1933. Democratic leadership, particularly embodied in David L. Lawrence, worked aggressively for more than a decade to build an organization. The twin victories of 1932 and 1933 were viewed by Lawrence as a vindication of his leadership and just rewards for a long, hard-fought battle. Much, however remained to be done.

Two months before Roosevelt's inauguration in 1933, Joseph Guffey rented a two-room suite in the Washington, D.C., Southern Office Building. The lettering on the door indicated that the suite served as the "Pennsylvania Headquarters." Presided over by Guffey and run by an aide, Richard Bailey, and several staff persons, the office—the only one of its kind in the city—existed solely to provide patronage to the residents of Pennsylvania. Capitalizing on his recognition by James Farley as the "original Roosevelt man" in Pennsylvania, Guffey assumed command of all federal jobs in the state. By September 1934, he had placed at least 500 Pennsylvanians in Washington jobs of varying federal importance, including a position as special assistant to the attorney general for black leader Robert Vann. He also succeeded in placing an estimated 5,000 Pennsylvanians in federal jobs at the state level. Among the political plums Guffey managed to secure were 2,500 administrative positions in the Home Owners Loan Corporation, numerous positions as U.S. marshals, U.S. attorneys, postmasters, and internal revenue collectors. Nearly all of the offices went to registered Democrats. IRS positions went to the democratic state chairman, Warren Van Dyke, and the Allegheny County chairman, David L. Lawrence.[4] In addition Lawrence was given charge of all federal patronage appointments in western Pennsylvania. He theoretically already controlled the locally fincanced jobs and within a year would gain command of the state patronage as well. Jobs thus became the foundation of his political regime.

Initially, the most important jobs the Democratic party had at its disposal during the Depression were the thousands of blue-collar positions provided by state and federal funds. During the first year of the Roosevelt administration, 319,000 Pennsylvanians, including 27,000 from Pittsburgh, secured temporary jobs through the Civil Works Administration. When that program ended, the Relief Works Division and Local Works Division programs, both state funded, provided more than 20,000 interim jobs until the Works Progress Administration (WPA) could take effect in 1935. By that time Guffey, now a U.S. senator, had turned the administration of all patronage over to his colleague Lawrence, giving him virtually unquestioned control over 150,000 jobs, including 57,000 in western Pennsylvania alone.[5] Lawrence named two Pittsburgh-based Democrats, Edward N. Jones and John Laboon, to hire the massive work force at the state and local levels respectively. Both had been active in recent Democratic politics, although Jones had been a Republican up to 1932.

During the first two years of its existence, the WPA spent nearly $70 million in Allegheny County, 80 percent of which went for workers' wages. Projects in the area included more than 530 miles of highway construction, nearly 100 miles of water line and sewer projects, 81 new or renovated parks and playgrounds, construction of the Highland Park bear pits, and more than six miles of concrete stairways on the city's steep hillsides. Generally, the work in Allegheny County fell under control of John Kane, a newly elected commissioner; Lawrence governed patronage in the city. While the two maintained a friendly rivalry for power throughout their parallel careers, they generally cooperated in matters of patronage. They would often "trade jobs" or provided work in their own territory for a favored son of the other.[6] Whether hired by Kane's forces or Lawrence's, the result was the same: another voter in need of work received a job and owed a debt of gratitude to the Democratic party.

"Lawrence actually never saw workers at the lower levels," former committeeman and ward chairman Al Conway revealed. "It all started with the district committeeman or chairman. He was very positive about that. Anyone who ever wrote him a letter for a job or asked for a job was told to go see the chairman. . . . It was John Duggan and later Andrew 'Huck' Fenrich's job to make sure that the patronage system worked."[7] When Lawrence gained control of statewide patronage two years later, he instituted the same system.

The extent of political influence in the hiring of workers for the WPA program in Pennsylvania during the 1930s is unclear. Charges and countercharges were hurled between Republicans and Democrats throughout the decade. Republicans and independent groups such as the League of Women Voters and the anti–New Deal *Pittsburgh Post-Gazette* criticized Lawrence and Guffey for attempting to set up another Pennsylvania machine. Former Governor Pinchot charged in a letter to Roosevelt that the WPA in Pennsylvania had "been sold into political bondage."[8]

Democrats responded to the charges by pointing out that Republicans had made municipal work a political football for nearly half a century in the state. It was a fact of life in Pennsylvania politics. As one official told Lorena Hickok, special troubleshooter for the WPA chairman, Harry Hopkins, "Oh, it's plenty political here in Pittsburgh. . . . But the Republicans would do the same thing if they had the WPA wouldn't they?" Lawrence, reared on nineteenth-century politics, understood and justified the use of the spoils system in terms that the old-time bosses would have understood. The system, of course, often threatened to get out of hand. In 1935, for example, the

Democratic organization's own state relief director, Robert Johnson, threatened to resign unless Democratic pressure for state jobs was reduced. The publicity surrounding his threat forced administration officials to agree to follow a "hands off" policy regarding the relief bureau. Other agencies were not so fortunate. Hickok suggested the extent of political involvement when she reported to Hopkins, "Our chief trouble in Pennsylvania is due to politics. From township to Harrisburg, the state is honeycombed with politicians fighting for the privilege of distributing patronage." Nearly all of the state's 3,000 WPA administrators from 1935 through 1940 were Democrats, as were 18,019 workers classified as "non-certified personnel"—most of them construction project foremen. Among these political appointees was a nephew who grew up in the Lawrence household, Jack Fitzgerald.[9]

To Lawrence's credit, the available evidence suggests that the majority of jobs, those available to unemployed laborers, did not depend on one's political affiliation. A comparison of WPA employee distribution in three wards reveals that jobs went where they were needed most. In terms of the number of WPA workers residing in the ward, the Third Ward, which was highest in four measurements of poverty in 1940, had most, the Fourteenth, the wealthiest ward in the city, had fewest, and the Twentieth, closest to the city average in the four categories, stood near the center.[10]

Republicans, Democrats, and independents could and did petition committeemen for job recommendations. Many, of course, showed their gratitude by shifting to the party of Roosevelt and Lawrence, and the rapidly growing Democratic registrations reflect these newfound loyalties. Higher-level jobs, however, required the recommendation of one's ward chairman and active affiliation with the Democratic party. "I wish you would contact Mr. [John] Duggan [Democratic party secretary]," Lawrence wrote his ward chairmen in March 1935. "Arrange with him your list of endorsements. . . .you should keep in mind that we may not be able to follow suggestions in order, especially in technical places. To illustrate, your first preference might be a laborer or a clerk and we may have available for your ward a stenographer or engineering position."[11]

The system worked so well that by 1935 nearly eight hundred policemen, one thousand firemen, and three thousand craftsmen, public works foremen, aldermen, inspectors, and supervisors had received their employment through the ward chairmen. Not surprisingly, the job recipients willingly contributed time and occasionally money to the continued success of the party. Many were former Republican ward leaders and committee members who became Democrats, seeking to share in the largess of the new organization. Others, correctly viewing politics as the path to financial security, were new recruits to the Democratic cause. Ward committee members and chairmen, in particular, found openings for themselves and their friends on the public payroll. Positions at the highest level, of course, required the direct intervention of the party chairman. Any promotion or transfer needed Lawrence's approval.[12]

The lone break in Lawrence's now smoothly functioning machine proved to be his hand-picked mayor, William McNair. Attempting to assert his independence from the organization, the mayor refused to become involved with federal aid programs, slowing the rush to municipal jobs among Pittsburgh's Democratic activists. By 1936 only one-fifth of a 25 percent sample of party committeemen had found jobs on the public payroll. In October of that year Cornelius D. Scully, an organization man, replaced McNair as mayor, and the number of patronage jobs increased immediately. By 1940 nearly half of the committeemen and most of the ward chairmen were on the government payroll. The proportion of Democratic regulars on the city, county, and state payrolls increased during the subsequent decades as the party became more entrenched. In 1960, midway through Lawrence's term of office as governor, nearly three-fourths of all committeemen and one third of the committeewomen held public jobs, most with the city of Pittsburgh. On the Republican side, less than 25 percent of the men and 10 percent of the women worked for public agencies. Virtually all of them held state or county jobs.[13]

Democratic ward chairmen were even more likely to secure public employment: Twenty-nine of the thirty-two Democrats as compared with four of the Republicans held government positions in 1960. Chairmen also held the coveted alderman position in their home ward. "At one time," Fifth Ward Magistrate Jake Williams recalled, "every chairman was also the alderman. That was his base; he could do favors for his good friends, and punish the enemy . . . the aldermanship gave you an elevated position."[14]

As county party chairman, Lawrence clearly used his control over patronage to build the party and reward its loyal members. He also used it to prevent the development of any would-be opposition. In 1935, for example, shortly after the Democrats' third consecutive victory, he informed all state legislators from western Pennsylvania that local patronage would by handled by ward chairmen exclusively.[15] Thus the ward chairmen, over whom Lawrence held absolute control, were strengthened, while the state legislators were prevented from building a personal following that one day might challenge Lawrence for party control.

Committeemen and ward chairmen, of course, did not receive their positions solely by virtue of their party philosophies. The political system, as Lawrence understood it, functioned on the basis of well-organized ward-level politics. Following the 1933 election victory, each ward was reorganized according to size and population. Party workers, who were elected at the "neighborhood" primary, were expected to remain active in the community.

> The committeemen knew everybody else, because in those days, when they were campaigning or getting new registrations, they went door-to-door. They didn't get on the telephone. One of the first things they would do is to try to get as many new registrations as they could, and try to get people to change parties. . . . And then we would have a big ward meeting or they'd have some kind of fund-raiser to cover the expense of election day. Lawrence would come to that and speak. It was kind of a pep rally. Then the chairman would have meetings with all the committee people. They would all have street lists, and the committee would give one to each payroller [in the ward] and they would go around and ask the people to vote for the candidate. . . . Then, on election day, they'd be at the polls and make sure that the people who they felt pretty sure were going to vote our way . . . got . . . to the polls. . . . They didn't work their regular jobs on election day.[16]

In addition to registering voters, campaigning, and transporting voters, workers at the ward and district (precinct) level were expected to raise funds. Each ward, depending on its size, population, and number of committee members, was assessed a quota. "In our ward," one chairman related, "it was sixty dollars per district. We had thirty districts, so our quota was $1,800.00." This was taken to headquarters and exchanged for five-dollar certificates to be distributed to poll watchers, who would then cash them in. Workers on the public payroll were also expected to contribute to the party.[17]

During the next thirty years city and county workers in all but a few protected departments remained dependent upon the party. The police bureau, in particular, became a cherished political plum of the ward chairmen, who had the power to nominate replacements to the force. Even with the advent of civil service, loopholes prevented removal of the police bureau from the political arena. Magistrate Jake

Williams explained, "Even when they had the Civil Service, they had a loophole in it. You could pick from the highest three [on the Civil Service test], now, if you eliminated the first three, that gave you the pick of the next three. You could go all the way down to the bottom of the list. . . . If you [the ward chairman] were due to get an appointment of a Lieutenant, there's no civil service could stop it. If your man's in it, he would get the promotion.[18]

Good performance in both party service and the municipal job related to it, moreover, became an avenue of upward mobility for many workers. An Eighth Ward committeeman, for example, had been an unemployed steelworker when he secured his first government job as a WPA foreman. Eventually he became a real estate appraiser for the city board of assessors. Another committeeman from the Fifteenth Ward obtained a general foreman's job in the WPA with Lawrence's personal intervention. In 1936 he went to work for the county as a bridge worker and in 1945 joined the city police force, eventually rising to the rank of captain. Jake Williams, brother of the Fifth Ward chairman, "Pappy" Williams, experienced a similar if more meteoric rise. Beginning as a seventeen-year-old truck driver for the city, he landed a clerk's job in the state inheritance tax department through his brother's influence. Several years later he became a tipstaff to Judge Homer Brown of the Court of Common Pleas and eventually succeeded his brother, upon his death, as ward chairman. John McGrady, who became a county commissioner, began his political career as a clerk in a county office primarily because he was an asset to the departmental baseball team. Nearly every judge in Allegheny County served the party in one capacity or another during the early years of their careers.[19]

Clearly, patronage, the party workers it supplied, and the funds it helped raise became the foundation upon which the Democratic party in Pittsburgh was built. Even after the demise of the WPA and other federal programs, Lawrence controlled thousands of ciy and state jobs and could usually call upon Commissioner John Kane for a county position when needed. The longevity of the party as the dominant power in the region, however, depended upon other factors, which assumed greater importance as the economy recovered during World War II and after.

▽

By mid 1934 finding workers ceased to be a problem for the Democratic party. It was now blessed with an abundance of support, from temporary election workers through high-level executive committee personnel. As he had in the past, Lawrence continued tinkering with the party structure, but now he faced new problems. A permanent structure had to be built that would enable the party to deliver on its promises and capitalize on its newfound numerical strength. Shortly after McNair's inauguration in January 1934, Lawrence called a meeting of the Democratic executive committee and several key ward chairmen to wrestle with the problem of party organization. Working with ward-level maps of the city, the group divided each ward into a number of districts depending upon size, population, and unusual physical barriers such as hills and valleys, and decided on an appropriate number of committeemen for each. In all, nearly sixteen hundred of these became the party's eyes and ears at the local level. In addition, individuals who received employment through their district committee or ward chairman operated as block-level workers in their own neighborhoods.

Committeemen and women carried the responsibility for recruiting voters and party workers, for organizing campaign rallies in their districts, for raising funds, and providing services for voters. During the Depression years these services were those normally linked to nineteenth-century political machines—jobs, economic assistance, and help cutting through government bureaucracy, when needed. One Fifth Ward committeeman, for example, purchased fifteen tons of coal, had it dumped in the street, and invited local residents to help themselves. He also purchased barrels of oil to be used for lighting by those unable to pay their electricity bills. "We had Johnny Elmer in my neighborhood in the Hill," Jake Williams reported. "Elmer Square is named after him. He would give baskets to the poor, and loads of coal." Others provided food and clothing to the needy. An Eighth Ward committeeman solicited local businesses for contributions of food and secured a number of jobs at a nearby baking company for area residents. Two Twelfth Ward committeemen held street fairs, bake sales, and other fund-raisers to provide aid to their neighbors. Soliciting assistance from the district fire captain, they rode through the ward in the department pumper each month collecting food for the local unemployed. Later, as economic conditions improved, municipal services replaced personal goods in the grab bag of the committeeman and ward chairman. "We could help get a ballfield, or a swimming pool or a street paved," said Al Conway, chairman of the Nineteenth Ward. Committee members "were the ones to see if you needed a zoning variance to put an addition on to your house."[20]

Above the committee members were the elected ward chairmen representing the city's thirty-two political wards. Many, during the years of Democratic ascendancy, operated their wards as semi-independent fiefdoms, trading votes for jobs and other political favors from party headquarters. Some, such as James Lavuola of the powerful Third Ward, appointed police, firemen, and other municipal workers. They personally selected and controlled their own committeemen and women and frequently ignored the wishes of the party hierarchy. The difficulties between McNair and the organization that broke out shortly after his inauguration prevented Lawrence from acting to limit their independence. He instead maintained a policy of attempting to minimize difficulties within the party by ignoring their indescretions until such times as they could be quietly replaced.

Most ward chairmen, however, delighted to represent the majority party for the first time in their lives, were only too happy to accept directions from headquarters. They performed their tasks zealously and considered it an honor when Lawrence or one of the other top brass attended their ward functions. Several times a year Lawrence hosted a dinner for the chairmen, inviting them to discuss problems in their district. Writing in the shorthand learned years ago at St. Mary's, he would make notes to be directed to the appropriate department head. Corrective action often occurred within days of the meeting.[21] The chairmen, along with their committees, attended a mass meeting annually to hear the choices of the party's executive committee for various elective offices. Although they had no vote in the matter, they always sustained the endorsements with long, enthusiastic applause and pledged their efforts toward victory at the polls.

The committeemen and the ward chairmen sustained the party at the grass-roots level. They were crucial to its continued existence as the dominant party in western Pennsylvania. Lawrence recognized their importance and worked diligently to maintain touch with the workers in the field. But he reserved the decision-making process for himself and a small group at the top that constituted the city's and the county's executive committees. The city group included Lawrence, Jimmy Kirk, the city treasurer, State Senator Joe Barr, and several influential ward chairmen. The mayor joined the executive committee when Cornelius Scully assumed office in 1935. The somewhat larger county committee consisted of Lawrence, the Democratic county commissioners, the officers of the county committee, seven county government department heads, and the chairwoman of the women's division of the party. Immediately following the November general election, these committees met to discuss all potential candidates for city, county, and state offices for the coming year. The meeting was always fairly harmonious: the leaders made their recommendations; the candidates were discussed; and decisions, nearly always in favor of the recommended candidates, were arrived at by consensus rather than voting. All members of the executive committee had a voice, and occasionally a surprise candidate was suggested. "That happened only about twice in twenty years," recalled James Knox, a former county chairman. "I [once] said, 'We ought to consider Robert Vandervort.' And I recall Mr. Lawrence saying, 'Who the hell is he?' and then we talked about him. . . . We came back at another meeting and somehow Vandervort just rose to the top. He was a Protestant and he was from the north end of the county. Eventually it was unanimous."[22]

The Vandervort experience aside, Lawrence remained the dominant force at the slating caucuses, and the apparent openness of the meetings should not deceive one into perceiving a meeting of coequals. The force of his political presence clearly swayed the weaker members of the group, although he often withheld his opinion until last to determine which possible nominees had the strongest support. By developing a potential list of candidates prior to the executive session, Lawrence, Kane, and a few others managed to retain control of the nominating process. Candidates were chosen for their loyalty to the party and their ability to give the ticket geographic, ethnic, religious, and ideological balance. Fred Weir, for example, became a candidate for county court judge because of his religion. Kirk invited him to headquarters, where he was asked to help Lawrence and Kirk find a Protestant candidate. "Believe it or not, they took out the yellow section of the phone book under attorneys and [were] going through that. . . . We got down to the W's and they said 'You're going to have to run.' . . . I didn't want to run, but I had to and damned near won." Lawrence occasionally became obsessed with the notion of a balanced ticket, as in 1935 when he produced an "all nations" slate of candidates for the countywide elections. The slate he described as a "beautiful all American ticket" consisted of candidates of Italian, Polish, and Irish descent, a Protestant, a Jew, and a representative of organized labor.[23] City council membership was distributed geographically even though members were elected at large. The council always had Jewish, Italian, black, and Protestant "seats." Eventually a female seat was added with the election of Erma De Cenzo. (Several members were usually Irish-American, as were the majority of the ward chairmen.) When a vacancy occurred, special care was taken to fill it with a person of similar ethnic or racial background or representing the same special interest. Thus, for example, Pat Fagan was selected to replace

Joe McArdle in 1949 to fill the labor seat; Dave Olbum replaced Abraham Wolk in the Jewish seat; and David Craig was selected to fill a WASP vacancy. Councilmen called Lawrence's practice the "Balkan succession."

Even more important than party balance was party loyalty. Candidates or party officials might disagree in the privacy of the caucus, but they were expected to support the party wholeheartedly once the decision had been rendered. Those who, like Councilman Joe McArdle, refused to comply with this unwritten rule lost valuable party endorsement and support. With the weight of the party turned against them, they stood virtually no chance for reelection and ultimately disappeared from the political scene. That this expulsion was seldom used testifies to its power in effecting party discipline. The mere threat was usually enough to hold all but the most stubborn members firmly in line.

As this analysis of the party organization under Lawrence suggests, the structure permitted a rapid and effective communication flow from the city's streets to the Benedum-Trees Building and back. It would not have been nearly so effective, however, had it not been for the personal touch and guidance of the man at its head. David Lawrence carefully watched over the party as if it were his most prized possession. Unlike his later practice in governmental life, in which the details of day-to-day operations bored him, he administered every facet of the party. Every phase of political life warranted his time and efforts.

The Lawrence style of operating the majority party began to emerge shortly after McNair's election in 1933. It was to become a very personal machine in which party regulars owed loyalty at least as much to him as to the Democratic party. No doubt because of his experiences during the 1920s, in which he was forced to maintain constant contact with his troops in the field lest they be tempted to join the Republican majority, Lawrence established direct links with nearly all party regulars in the city and county. Each was made to feel vital to the noble cause of electing Democrats.

Ward leaders were given open access to the chairman regardless of his current governmental position. During the early years, when Lawrence's position as secretary of the Commonwealth forced him to reside in Harrisburg, he caught the early train to Pittsburgh each Friday afternoon. On Saturday he arrived at party headquarters shortly after 10 A.M. and usually remained there until after 6 P.M. During the first hour or two, he and his close aides attended to party business requiring immediate action. But after noon, the door to his office was opened to any ward chairman who felt in need of his assistance. Jobs, welfare assistance, help in cutting red tape, or simply reassurance of the ward chairman's worth to the party were dispensed throughout the afternoon. He frequently responded with direct action. For example, when a ward leader sought an assistant district attorney's position for a young lawyer in his district, Lawrence called the district attorney. "I got a nice young man here, he's Irish, good name, good looking, I'm going to send him over to see you."[24] The man got the job. In other instances he requested property reassessment, debris removal, restoration of public assistance, and back pay for a worker injured on a city job. In each case the ward chairman could return to his ward demonstrating his own effectiveness in delivering needed services. His allegiance to and dependence upon the party chairman, in turn, was strengthened by the process. While Lawrence seldom engaged in small talk with his ward chairmen, he took the time to learn the names of their wives and children and frequently asked specific questions about them. He asked the chairmen's opinions on political candidates, fund-raising, or political strategy. As long as they performed to expectations, they were permitted to operate their wards without interference. He seldom praised them, but he made them aware of their importance to the party. The cordial but efficient meetings always ended in the same way, with Lawrence clapping his hands sharply or rapping his large ring on the desk to signal that the business had concluded.

On Sunday mornings Lawrence attended ten o'clock Mass at St. Mary's at the Point. Following the collection, at which he always participated as an usher, he held court in the back of the church, talking briefly with those seeking favors. He returned to party headquarters after Mass and repeated the process of the previous day. On slow days his pinochle cronies would be summoned, if they were not already there. When Lawrence became mayor, weekends continued to be reserved for political business, although ward chairmen had virtually unlimited access to him during the week at city hall as well. In 1959, when he became governor and moved back to Harrisburg, the earlier weekend operations at party headquarters became customary again.

Lawrence also used the formal meeting to maintain contact with his important ward chairmen and to keep them active in party affairs year-round. Several times per year luncheons or dinners were held in honor of prominent Democrats such as Roosevelt or Jefferson. Ward chairmen were always expected to attend, and Lawrence made it a point to speak to each one during the course of the evening. Later, as he became more influential in national and international circles, prominent figures were invited to the city to speak to and meet these crucial cogs in the Democratic machine. Those who spoke to the Allegheny County Democratic group at one time or another included, Senators Lyndon Johnson, Estes Kefauver, and Adlai Stevenson, Mayor Willy Brandt of West Berlin, Prime Minister David Ben Gurion of Israel, and numerous governors and mayors. "The luncheons educated us about the affairs of the day, but more importantly they enabled us to rub shoulders with some of the most important people in the world. It made us all feel good about what we were doing." said Knox.[25]

Lawrence also reached out to party workers by attending as many of the numerous rallies in the city and county as possible, speaking briefly and urging those in attendance to increase their efforts on behalf of the party candidates. If there were three meetings on the same evening, he would try to arrange his appearances so that the meeting with the social came last, and it was here that he was at his best. While free beer and sandwiches were served and an orchestra played, Lawrence would go around and talk to party officials and voters. This personal touch, aided by his excellent memory, did much to keep the party close knit.[26]

Even when he was out of town, Lawrence kept a close watch over the activities of the political wards: Jimmy Kirk, Huck Fenrich, Frank Ambrose, and others reported to him by mail and telephone. Loose ends were seldom left dangling beyond the weekend meetings at headquarters. On serious matters he could always be counted on to return home to resolve the issue. During his European vacations, which became more numerous as he grew older, he remained in touch, and on at least one occasion he rushed home to resolve a brewing political crisis. But the care he lavished on the party was almost never viewed as heavy-handed by party regulars. He generally maintained a light touch, preferring to let the principals in any dispute resolve it themselves. A stern warning was usually issued to "get the matter solved." Lawrence became involved himself only when the problem, in his opinion, threatened the welfare of the party.

In disputes involving himself he learned, following several near critical intraparty skirmishes, to choose his battles carefully. Only when he was certain of victory without irreparable harm to the party would he confront a Democratic opponent. In other instances, his patience in tolerating malcontents seems to have been almost limitless.

Like the Irish politician of the nineteenth century, he also maintained contact with his loyal workers through their families. "Visit the sick, and bury the dead," he frequently advised his aide Fenrich, and he lived up to his motto. Frank "Bangy" Ambrose examined the death notices daily and informed his boss of the death of any Democratic worker, and they attended many wakes and funerals together. Lawrence returned from Harrisburg, for example, for the funeral of Jimmy Bates, a loyal Democrat who controlled a district in the black Third Ward, in the Hill District. "People . . . couldn't get over the fact that the governor was there to pay his respects." At another funeral, that of Viola Turner, a committeewoman in the same ward, the preacher invited Lawrence to say a few words in church. "So he spoke for fifteen or twenty minutes about Viola Turner, . . . and there were hallelujahs, hallelujahs."[27] He was particularly solicitous of ward chairmen, whom he considered the backbone of the party. He went to their homes, both on family occasions and when they had troubles. "That was his religion and politics."[28] By his ability to deliver jobs and favors, Lawrence gained the active participation of thousands of party workers. By visiting the wards, whether to take part in a local rally, attend a wake, or visit a regular's sickbed, he earned their unquestioned loyalty. His ability to scold an errant worker at the proper time also earned their obedience.

Not all meetings at party headquarters were the result of ward chairmen appearing to petition for favors. Chairmen whose performance fell short of the expected level were called in to explain. (He didn't call them in if they did a good job.) It was on these occasions that Lawrence's well-known temper would boil over. When, for example, figures showed 68 Democrats to 23 Republicans newly registered to vote in one ward as compared to 310 to 29 and 240 to 16 in two others, he called in the chairman of the first ward and demanded an explanation. On being told that it had rained all day, Lawrence put the figures in the ward chairman's hand and shouted, "How the hell do you think the weather was on the North Side? Now get the hell out of here and get to work."[29]

On another occasion a district committeeman, who had sent Lawrence a barely legible announcement, was called in. When he explained that the copy machine wasn't working properly, Lawrence replied, nearly shouting, "I didn't ask you if there was anything wrong with the copy machine. . . . Don't you ever send me a thing like this again. First of all, you can't read it. Second, it makes no sense. I'm near blind in one eye and I don't want to lose the other one."[30] He then dismissed the man with the customary hand clap.

The threat of party expulsion, while used infrequently, was always present and usually served to keep would-be mavericks or shirkers in line. Inability to perform to expectations, however, was seldom cause for dismissal. Throughout his career, Lawrence found it difficult to dismiss a worker, whether employed by the city or associated with the party.[31] Thus only in cases of real or perceived disloyalty were individuals actually removed from the party. Only one city councilman, Joseph P. McArdle, John Huston, register of wills, four ward chairmen, and a small number of district committee members were removed during Lawrence's forty-six-year tenure as its head. When a decision was made to remove someone, as in the Joseph McArdle case, it was done efficiently and without fanfare. The party's executive committee quietly announced that it would support another candidate in the primary. Funds and workers formerly at the disposal of the errant worker were transferred to the newly endorsed candidate. The Democratic voters at the primary election completed the surgery.

Lawrence's policy of maintaining an open door to ward chairmen did not extend to the district committeemen or residents. They were expected to operate through their chairmen, and this chain of command was strictly observed at all times. When he became mayor, he maintained the same policy. Unlike Richard Daley, for example, who customarily held court with citizens of Chicago each day in his office, Lawrence seldom met with private individuals or even small groups at city hall.[32]

The formal structure of the organization reflected Lawrence's desire for regularity and tidiness. His somewhat formal nature prevented him from engaging in the charismatic interchanges often associated with urban political bosses such as Boston's colorful James Curley or New York's "Little Flower," Fiorello H. La Guardia. An average speaker in his early years, he attended a public speaking class sometime in the 1930s and gradually became more than accomplished. "You could always tell when Lawrence learned a new word. He'd use it over and over again . . . One word in particular was *sanguine*. . . . Lawrence used it for months. . . . 'I'm not sanguine about this.' 'I'm not sanguine about that.' " "He could read a speech better than anybody I ever knew. . . . If it came to a place where a little table pounding would help, he could do that very effectively." He later became polished at presenting a formal address on radio or television, but he never became comfortable with the glad-handing, back-slapping style of modern politics. His 1958 campaign for governor was particularly distasteful to him because of its informal style of the hurried address delivered from the top of a station wagon or the back of a truck. Heckling from the audience often unnerved him, and he refused to answer back. La Guardia's style of "mixing it up" with the audience—"I can out-demagogue the best of the demagogues"—was not for Lawrence. He dealt with issues and facts and remained a comfortable distance from the crowd even when pressing the flesh.[33]

Lawrence's formal approach, surprisingly, never hampered his ability to develop a strong emotional bond with the city's electorate. His masculine, no-nonsense style seemed to capture the spirit of the city, and he consciously exploited the relationship. A workingman's political leader in a workingman's town, he appeared able to tackle the eight-hour shift at the open hearth, at the glassworks, or at Iron City Brewery. To the old Irish and German residents he was "their boy"—one who was the epitome of the self-made man. When he became mayor, citizens referred to him as Davey, signifying their intimate relationship with him. His aides and close associates, however, and even news reporters, always addressed him by his formal title.[34]

The sport-consciousness of the blue-collar city matched Lawrence's own love for physical contests, and he benefited from the parallel interests. In a city that idolized twice-defeated heavyweight contender Billy Conn, turned out over a million fans to see the hapless Pittsburgh Pirates of the 1950s, and supported the even less successful Pittsburgh Steelers, Lawrence and his friend Art Rooney were the area's greatest fans. He was seen and photographed at many sporting events and frequently in the company of athletic greats such as Conn, boxer Fritzie Zivic, and baseball star Ralph Kiner. He threw out the first ball at nearly every Pirate opener during the 1950s and early 1960s and could frequently be seen sitting in box 209 at Forbes Field. He would often attend Little League, sandlot, or high school games on the North Side, in East Liberty, on Polish Hill, or at the Arsenal Field in Lawrenceville.

His visits to the local games were no doubt calculated to keep him in the public eye, as he seldom did anything for pleasure alone. But it is equally clear that he enjoyed the games, and his natural love of organized sports mirrored the overwhelming interests of a large majority of the city's population. Nearly a thousand guests attended a testimonial dinner in 1957 naming him Pittsburgh's Sportsman of the Year. The honor, greeted with overwhelming enthusiasm by the city's sportswriters, seemed to strengthen the bond between the political leader and the electorate.[35]

To be sure, Lawrence clearly recognized the value of good public relations and took measures to cultivate the image of an active, concerned leader. Beginning with his inauguration as mayor in 1945, he willingly appeared almost daily at ribbon-cutting and other dedication ceremonies, although he generally regarded them as a nuisance.

Local party officials frequently shared in the publicity, but Lawrence understood that the limelight had to shine brightest on the head of the party. An aide to Mayor Joe Barr, Morton Coleman, once violated the principle by announcing to the press the establishment of the city's Community Action Program for neighborhood development. Upon hearing about it later, Lawrence, then governor, sternly admonished Coleman, "Young man, you only announce the bad news. You let the mayor announce the good news."[36]

In addition to being willing to appear at public events, Lawrence, who had experienced firsthand the power of the press in the 1931 and 1933 elections, worked hard to enlist the cooperation of the city's corps of political reporters. John Jones, Gilbert Love, John Townley, Kermit McFarland, and others all enjoyed good relations with Lawrence. His executive secretaries, John Robin and later Walter Giesey, were both former reporters with the *Pittsburgh Post-Gazette.* Beginning early in his first term as mayor, Lawrence hosted, at Robin's suggestion, annual dinners with key newspaper reporters and executives and his own associates at which ideas would be exchanged on urban renewal, industrial development, and other civic problems.

Lawrence's relationships with the press, of course, were not always cordial. John Jones once referred to him as "boss Lawrence" in an article in the *Post-Gazette.* Lawrence, who detested the term perhaps more than any other, refused to see or speak with Jones for nearly six months. Lawrence carried on a lasting feud with the *Post-Gazette*'s crusading reporter Ray Sprigle. Sprigle's continued revelations regarding corruption in the city police force launched a bitter relationship between the two men that lasted nearly twenty years.[37] With most of the press, however, the honeymoon which began when Lawrence inaugurated Pittsburgh's renowned Renaissance lasted for the remainder of his political career.

That Lawrence's friendly relationship with the press paid dividends becomes obvious when one examines the political columns and editorials during his term as mayor. Beginning with his second term, all three of the city's news editors endorsed him for reelection at every election. Reporters, moreover, joining in the spirit of teamwork being hailed as the key to the city's urban renewal efforts, seldom criticized his policies or actions. Blame for problems in his administration was usually laid at the door of the particular department head involved. The chief, as he was sometimes called, usually escaped unscathed.

The positive image of Lawrence as the caring and creative governmental and political administrator, however, took some time to develop. During the early 1930s, even after the McNair and Roosevelt victories, he was viewed by the public and many who later became close allies as the typical urban political boss—trading favors and jobs for votes and political influence, with little regard for the actual operation of government or the welfare of the citizenry. Three key allies and loyal supporters, Genevieve Blatt, John Robin, and Alfred Tronzo, all reported an initial negative reaction to Lawrence. Their assessments were to a large extent correct. Lawrence, until he became secretary of the Commonwealth in the Earle administration, exhibited almost no concern for matters of government. Moreover, it is difficult to detect any philosophical principles that guided his actions. To be sure, he embraced the ideology of the Democratic party and at times exhibited concern for the causes of organized labor, the poor, and the politically weak. But his driving force seemed inextricably linked to the excitement he derived from the electoral process.

Selecting a candidate, organizing and running a campaign, and creating the party structure required for a successful venture stirred the passion within him. In Lawrence's early campaigns, political issues and governmental concerns remained secondary in importance and were seldom debated. Personalities, analyzed in the simplest terms, were highlighted: a candidate was honest or corrupt, capable or foolish, selfish or concerned with the welfare of others. The quality of his ideas or his ideological position mattered only slightly and his ability to embrace former lifelong Republicans during the elections of 1932 and to replace Democratic candidates with Republicans in 1933 testifies to his willingness to ignore party labels and their implied philosophical position. A candidate's potential ability to win elections clearly assumed primary importance: appearance, ethnic origin, religion, social class, and residential location all entered into consideration. Political or social views could be ignored or minimized. McNair's unrelenting adherence to the single tax philosophy, for example, posed no difficulty for Lawrence or other high-level Democrats, although all had rejected it as foolish. The party chairman, instead, viewed it as a potential vote-getting position. Winning elections was his utmost goal, one he retained throughout his political career, and one that contributed to his myopia in selecting political candidates.

Following the two successful elections, Lawrence was faced with the tasks of building a permanent party, administering patronage, and distributing assistance to those in need. That the first two demands worked hand-in-hand, of course, delighted him. Building the party was the initial step toward winning another election and was thus viewed as part of the election process. One built the party, in part, by distributing patronage to able and loyal workers. William McNair's crucial sin, in Lawrence's eyes, as time went on, lay not in his publicity-seeking antics or his almost ludicrous approach to government, but in his deliberate interference in the control of the party spoils—which was essential to establishing a lasting party.

Providing public assistance, similarly, while it gave vital aid to the needy, also helped to solidify grass-roots support. The party was only too happy to provide low-level blue-collar jobs to potential voters, although it never insisted upon a test of party loyalty as a condition of employment or public assistance to the truly needy. Grateful workers, of course, who wished to shift political allegiance or to become politically active on behalf of the Democratic party were given every encouragement to do so.

Nearly all of Lawrence's energy during the 1920s and early 1930s was directed toward winning elections and creating an effective, efficient party. His approach was extremely pragmatic—"Whatever works is acceptable." However, even at this early date several important principles begin to emerge. The corruption in the dominant Republican regime and his own suspicion, inherited from his father, of ineptness in urban government led him to begin to insist that political appointees be at least capable. The spoils system was accepted as standard practice. But workers were also expected to perform the task for which they were hired. Those found incompetent were to be transferred until the proper job was found. Few were ever fired, but Lawrence refused to tolerate a slovenly attitude toward work.[38] Later, when he became mayor, he frequently lectured workers on the virtues of punctuality and an "honest day's work." He clearly expected others to adopt the work ethic that drove him. Nevertheless, the actual operation of the various departments, of course, never ran as cleanly as he expected. Department heads, reluctant to run afoul of ward chairmen, seldom dismissed anyone, and while the degree of job-shirking is impossible to document, various departments within the city no doubt contained as many incompetent workers as other large urban governments. As mayor, Lawrence freed certain departments and the independent authorities involved in the rebuilding of the city from the patronage system to ensure that their directors could carry out their duties without political interference.

Finally, it was at about this time that Lawrence began to use the saying that was to become permanently associated with him, "The best politics is good government." Nearly every aide interviewed commented on the frequency with which he uttered the phrase. Lawrence had viewed firsthand the negative results of incompetent, corrupt government, and his pragmatic attitude to the political realities around him dictated a new approach. Good government—defined by him as efficient, caring, and relatively honest—would result in political success. "He was never a reformer in the nineteenth-century sense. He never worried greatly if anybody in the Police Department or the Democratic organization had made arrangements with anyone who would contribute to their welfare. There was no corruption, however, in anything that was ever done in the city government as a government. . . . There was never any shakedown of contractors or of redevelopers, or others, which is really common in New York, Chicago, or Philadelphia."[39]

The actual operation of good government for the time being, however, would be left in the hands of others. Lawrence, following the election of William McNair as mayor of Pittsburgh, turned to larger political battlefields. The county had not yet been conquered by the Democrats, and the state of Pennsylvania represented the biggest political challenge of all. He planned to leave the day-to-day management of the city in the hands of his new mayor and several close aides, including Jimmy Kirk, whom he left behind to "mind the store." For Dave Lawrence, at this stage in his career, a behind-the-scenes role was enough to satisfy his ambition. Unforeseen events in the next two years would force a dramatic change in his intentions.

1934–1935
Expanding the Network

In late 1933, Dave Lawrence and Joseph Guffey had reason to suspect that the mayor-elect, William McNair, would not be a cooperative member of the new Democratic team, but in the heat of the election they chose to ignore the warnings issued by McNair himself. Shortly after winning the Democratic primary, McNair told a reporter, "You know, I made an agreement with Davey that I'd let the Democratic party handle all the patronage if I was elected. But if I'm elected, who'll be the Democratic party? As mayor of Pittsburgh I'll be the most important Democratic office holder in Pennsylvania and I'll be the Democratic party. How'll Davey like that?" Apparently aware of the risk of this new go-it-alone policy, McNair added prophetically, "If I'm elected mayor, the big interests won't let me serve out my term. They'll rip me out of office; they'll impeach me or throw me in jail."[1]

Lawrence's response, if any, is unknown, and both he and Guffey rejoiced at the victory of their handpicked candidate. Immediately after the election they whisked their protégé off to Washington, D.C., to meet the president. The man who had campaigned as the "Roosevelt candidate for mayor" had the opportunity to meet his champion face-to-face. The meeting was brief but cordial, with McNair giving every indication that he would be a firm Roosevelt ally.

One week later, however, McNair began to signal that he might be less cooperative than Guffey and Lawrence hoped. In response to a complaint about inadequate heating by an office worker, he called for a ladder and began exploring the heating ducts in the city-county building. The press photographers, alerted by the McNair staff, captured the incident of the mayor-elect crawling about the pipes for the front pages of all three newspapers. When questioned by Lawrence about his behavior, McNair refused to back down, and he offered a vigorous defense that appeared on the front page of the *Post-Gazette.* The Democratic leadership was making too much of the incident and claiming that it made him look ridiculous. "I wanted to see how they heated the City-County building lobby and the only way to find out was to get a ladder and get up there. What's wrong with that?" A further comment was aimed directly at Lawrence's "coat and tie policy." "In most of the cases I've observed, public officials try to be dignified to cover up the lack of ability. A man who doesn't know the fundamentals of his job dresses himself all up and assumes what he thinks is a dignified air and tries to fool the public.[2]

More significantly, although he accepted organization men James P. Kirk and Cornelius D. Scully on his administrative staff, he gave an indication that he intended to play an active role in appointments to city jobs. Shortly after his election, he named a Lawrence critic, Mrs. R. Templeton Smith, to the post of budget director. He also refused to appoint Eddie Jones, his speech writer and the organization's choice, as director of public safety, an important position in the distribution of patronage. Deliberately embarrassing the party leaders, he announced that, instead, he would accept the recommendation of a group of local clergy for the post. When they made known their selection, however, he ignored it. The public safety director controversy quickly became a morass of confusion when the mayor rejected party benefactor Michael Benedum's choice, James Malone, a former Republican councilman, in favor of the Republican incumbent, Harmar Denny. Almost immediately he requested Denny's resignation and offered the position to Lawrence's Democratic opponent John M. Henry. When Henry accepted, McNair withdrew the offer and called for the appointment of Malone. When the city council refused to appoint Malone, McNair presented the name of Ralph Smith, whom he admittedly had not consulted. Smith assumed the position, only to be fired a short time later by the unpredictable McNair. The office of public safety director remained the main political football throughout the chaotic administration.[3]

Clearly, if Lawrence expected to play a quiet role in the background of the new administration, brokering power and jobs, McNair had shattered that vision. During the first six months of 1934, Lawrence watched McNair violate one after another of his principles.

The episode of the mayor and the heating system proved to be just the beginning of his publicity-seeking antics. On election day, 2 January, he concluded a five-minute victory speech by inviting job seekers to remain in the corridor of the City-County Building following the festivities, to present their petitions to him personally. The following day he fulfilled an earlier pledge by placing his desk in the lobby of the building to meet with the unemployed. Each day for a week thousands of desperate job seekers jammed the building hoping that the mayor could provide employment. "No matter what you happen to have on your mind, you are at complete liberty to lug it to Mr. McNair's office and unload it," wrote a reporter sent to Pittsburgh to cover the new mayor's bizarre antics. "There is no guarantee that Mr. McNair will do anything about it. To the contrary, it is wholly likely that he will assure you he knows as little about it as you do but that under the single-tax system, it wouldn't have happened."[4] It is unlikely that anyone received a job during these sessions—the mayor retreated to his office within a week—but for the whole of that week, McNair was on the front pages of the city's newspapers.

When the publicity value of the "lobby office" began to die, McNair provided reporters with other stories that kept him on the front pages. He tried to "show the unemployed what could be done with $500," by erecting a small frame cottage on the sidewalk directly adjacent to the county jail. When the building inspector informed him that the city fire code prohibited erecting a structure in a fire zone, McNair replaced him with a more willing inspector. At the mayor's request, his pal, Harrison "Playboy" McCready, moved into the cottage, which the press dubbed "McNair Manor." The building was eventually removed, but not before it added to the mayor's growing reputation as the clown prince of city hall.

The mayor brought the city council into his act when he began traveling about the city offering vacant city-owned lots, and $500 for the erection of his cottage, to the unemployed. When dozens of destitute people arrived at city hall, they were informed that only the city council could issue the deeds. The lots, however, heavily encumbered with deliquent taxes and unpaid mortgages, were unavailable. Nor had the promised building funds been appropriated. When Councilmen John Kane and P. J. McArdle delivered a tongue-lashing to the mayor, accusing him of deceiving the aged and poor, he responded by announcing through the press that he "guaranteed the plan would work if council would enact appropriate measures."[5]

McNair's activities assumed farcical proportions when he purchased a forty by four hundred foot tent to house the poor on the grounds of the state hospital at Mayview. On another occasion he named himself temporary magistrate and presided over the hearings at the night court. The press, informed of his intentions, were not disappointed. The mayor joked and clowned his way through each evening, eventually dismissing charges against nearly all the defendants after extracting a promise that they would raise vegetables on land provided by the city.[6]

In addition to his publicity-seeking stunts, which grew stranger each month, McNair continued to turn his back on the regular Democratic organization in favor of a formerly Republican group labeled the "silk stocking clique" by Kane. He chose as an advisor the sister of R. Templeton Smith, and several members of the elite Citizens' League were appointed to administrative positions. Most damaging, the chairman of the league, Leslie Johnston, was appointed director of public works, a position second only to the public safety directorship in the number of potential patronage jobs. Both important offices were now in the hands of anti-organization men.

Lawrence's attempts to block further appointments and to gain control of his unruly protégé were met with both private and public rebuffs. In a stormy session at party headquarters on 4 May 1934, Lawrence criticized McNair's public actions and charged that Mrs. Smith was turning the mayor against the Democratic organization. McNair responded by accusing the party chairman of trying to establish a dictatorship in Pittsburgh. Lawrence "pounded his ring on the desk and ordered McNair from his office." Relations between the two deteriorated further when McNair used the press to raise the "ripper" issue. Shortly after his battle with Lawrence, he repeated his earlier charge to a group of newsmen at city hall. "David Lawrence will never let me serve out my term. He'll rip me out of office or throw me in jail."[7]

Clearly unable to exercise any control over the man whom he had put into office, Lawrence followed his customary practice. When intraparty battles arose, he did his best to minimize them. McNair's charges notwithstanding, the available evidence suggests that Lawrence would have weathered the storm at least until the next election. He attempted to avoid further confrontation and the risk of splitting the party by divorcing himself from city government. McNair, for the time being, could have his own way. The mayor, unfortunately, was unable to accept the victory or control his own impetuous behavior and eventually forced the issue.

▽

Lawrence's willingness to tolerate McNair's eccentricities was tied to his desire to see the adolescent Democratic party in Allegheny County grow to maturity. Party unity, he reasoned, was essential to a healthy development. His preoccupation in early 1934 with political affairs beyond the county lines, moreover, drew his attention away from purely local matters. The relationship with Guffey had already produced rewards, but many more remained to be collected. After the opening of his patronage office in the nation's capital, Guffey, who already had his eyes on a seat in the U.S. Senate, turned to his loyal ally Lawrence. National office required the defeat of the entrenched state Republican regime and the development of a strong Democratic organization. But Guffey already decided that he enjoyed the heady atmosphere of power in Washington too much to return to the seedy, cutthroat world of Pennsylvania politics. He had several weapons of his own. As state Democratic national committeeman and one of the state's wealthiest Democrats, he was considered by leading party members from Philadelphia, Harrisburg, and Pittsburgh to be the head of the party. In addition, as an early financial and political supporter of Roosevelt, he had the backing and friendly ear of the national administration. Furthermore, as has already been noted, he had virtually unquestioned control of all federal patronage due the state. He also had Lawrence, who had just proved his organizational skills and owed much to Guffey, as an ally. Together, they could unseat the incumbent Republican regime.

The Democratic State Committee, which included Warren Van Dyke, chairman, Lawrence, Guffey, and two rising Philadelphia stars, Jack Kelly and Matthew McCloskey, met several times in January 1934 to map strategy for extending the recent Pittsburgh victories across the state of Pennsylvania. The optimistic group expected to gain control of both chambers of the General Assembly, the governor's office, and a U.S. senatorship, for the first time in the century. Hopeful of avoiding a costly primary battle, it drew up a slate that it felt would bring harmony to the party. To head the party as candidate for the U.S. Senate, the slating committee turned to its brightest star, Guffey. He was by far the most prominent Democrat in the state and was clearly associated with the New Deal, which by now had strong support throughout Pennsylvania. He wanted the position, had virtually uncontested control of the party, and was in a financial position to contribute heavily to his own campaign.

Van Dyke, by virtue of his long service, was the logical choice to carry the party's standard for governor. His candidacy, however, aroused no great enthusiasm among the party leaders. They would have a difficult time presenting him, an old-line regular, to liberal Republicans and independents, both crucial in a state in which Republicans outnumbered Democrats by more than three to one. Van Dyke, meeting with Guffey, Lawrence, Jack Kelly, and a few others, agreed to step aside for the "good of the party." It was generally agreed that the party heads would support him for the same position in 1938.[8]

Guffey then suggested George H. Earle, a multimillionaire Main Line Philadelphian currently serving as Roosevelt's ambassador to Austria. A World War I submarine commander, an accomplished pilot, and one of the nation's top polo players, Earle spent a decade engaging in the pursuits of the idle rich. He held the title of vice president in his family's sugar firm but rarely entered the office or factories. A Republican whose family GOP roots ran back to the founding of the party, he gave no evidence of any political interests until 1931. Shocked by the poverty he saw on a visit to Chicago, he switched parties and came to Roosevelt's attention by contributing $35,000 to the 1932 national campaign and a similar amount to Roosevelt Democrats in Pennsylvania.[9] After Roosevelt's inauguration, Guffey recommended Earle for a diplomatic post, but reports of his excessive drinking nearly led to his rejection. Earle vowed to abstain, and Guffey persuaded Roosevelt to accept Earle's pledge. To his credit, no incidents occurred during his tenure in Austria.

Responding to a letter from Guffey, Earle returned to Pennsylvania in February 1934 to meet with the Democratic State Committee, and he won their endorsement. His willingness to contribute a substantial amount of money to support the state ticket, as well as his ability to attract a following among Republicans and independents in eastern Pennsylvania, were apparently all that was needed to convince the party leaders. Earle made good his promise by donating more than $175,000 to the party war chest before the campaign ended in November.[10]

The slate now appeared to have the ideal balance—an organization regular from the largest city in the western part of the state and a former Republican liberal from the east. Both were well bred, and ardent Roosevelt supporters. Neither, however, could claim to represent the state's several million blue-collar workers. The party had openly courted organized labor since 1928, and Lawrence had succeeded in putting a union representative, John Kane, on the Pittsburgh city council, but the alliance between labor and the Democratic organization was still fragile. The party cemented those relationships when it selected John L. Lewis's man, Thomas Kennedy, secretary-treasurer of the United Mine Workers, as Earle's running mate.

David Lawrence played an important role in choosing the Democratic slate, but it was clear to all that he was still Guffey's man and this was to be Guffey's campaign. He placed Guffey's name in nomination at the slate meeting on 9 February, and he offered support for

Earle even though the two had met only briefly during the 1932 Roosevelt campaign. It is not clear what role, if any, he played in the selection of Kennedy. His activities, however, remained consistent with those in earlier elections. By avoiding a strong stand on any of the named candidates, he was free to offer vigorous support to the choices of the party leadership, whoever they might be. In addition, excepting the Guffey candidacy, with which he was closely associated, his reluctance to offer early identification with any candidate placed him in an ideal position to act as power broker should a deadlock arise. His willingness to accept Earle as the gubernatorial candidate demonstrates both his sense of timing and his readiness to support the party's choice.

Lawrence knew, as did nearly everyone else close to the seat of power, of Earle's reputation for excessive drinking and strongly disapproved. He also disapproved of Earle's life-style before he became ambassador to Austria. Earle had displayed none of the qualities that would suggest that he could lead a state under severe economic pressure. On the contrary, he was the type whom Lawrence would normally hold in contempt. He appeared to be virtually without ideas, totally unprepared, and almost without accomplishment. But he had done nothing to create any political controversy. He was a safe candidate who would not upset the delicate balance among the party factions. In addition, Earle's blue-blood Republican background could be counted upon to win over independents and wavering Republicans. Thus Lawrence overcame his deep misgivings to become an ardent supporter of Earle during the primary and general elections.

The party leaders were mistaken in their belief that the well-balanced ticket would result in an uncontested primary. Roland S. Morris, former ambassador to Japan, opposed the closed slating system and entered the senatorial primary as a protest candidate. The governor's race, meanwhile, attracted four other candidates, including Mayor McNair, who apparently placed his name on the ballot to irritate Lawrence. McNair failed to run an active campaign, but all the other candidates crisscrossed the state promising support for Roosevelt and a New Deal for Pennsylvania. The independents, who offered proposals little different from those of Guffey and Earle, were overwhelmed in the primary by what had become a well-functioning party organization.[11]

In the month following the May primary, Guffey, now without a serious rival, and Lawrence were ready to consolidate their power. Guffey, upon his election, would exercise his influence on the Roosevelt administration in Washington, while Lawrence remained at home minding local affairs including, presumably, keeping an eye on the new governor. Two important events, however, had to be engineered: Guffey had to win the general election, and Lawrence had to be placed at the locus of power in the state. Guffey accomplished the second goal by quietly meeting with key members of the Democratic State Committee to gain support for a plan to elevate Lawrence. The state party chairman, Van Dyke, was to be offered a position from Guffey's patronage bag as collector of the Port of Philadelphia. Lawrence would become state chairman. Guffey and Lawrence met with Van Dyke to present their plan. Van Dyke, who had been in politics too long not to recognize the inevitability of a power shift, accepted the transfer without a fight. Two days later, he announced his resignation as state Democratic chairman under the pretext that the rigors of the campaign required a younger man. Besides, he had been promised the candidacy for governor in 1938 and was reluctant to alienate any potential support from Guffey and Lawrence. In his place, Guffey and the other successful statewide Democratic candidates nominated the logical successor, David L. Lawrence, who was elected to the position on 9 June 1934. There were no other nominees.[21] On 25 July Lawrence resigned his position as Pittsburgh's collector of internal revenue, explaining, "I plan to devote all my time to the campaign as Democratic State Chairman." He had, after nearly three decades in politics, achieved what for him was his ultimate political goal—the full-time professional leadership of the Pennsylvania Democratic party. One hurdle remained. As matters currently stood, he was forced to share his power with Guffey. Within the next six months, Lawrence would challenge him for complete control of the organization.[12]

Lawrence seized the opportunity presented by Guffey's ambition for national office to add to his own power in the state. In return for Lawrence's cooperation in the campaign, Guffey agreed to relinquish formal control over all state-level patronage; accordingly, he informed the state's twenty-three U.S. representatives that they would be required to submit all requests for patronage through Lawrence. The agreement benefited both men.[13] Guffey cleverly distanced himself from the patronage issue, which was threatening to become a statewide scandal, while serving notice on all legislators from Pennsylvania that those who failed to fall into line would be denied the use of the party spoils. Even U.S. representatives would be prevented from building their own independent organizations. Lawrence, at the same time, greatly enhanced his own position. He would shortly exercise his newly won power to depose Guffey as the state's number one Democrat. A victory by Guffey and Earle in November would nearly complete the job by removing Guffey from the local scene and giving Lawrence, as state chairman, control over thousands of state patronage jobs to add to his already substantial total. A Democratic sweep in the upcoming election and some solution to the McNair problem were crucial.

The fall election season in Pennsylvania customarily begins on Labor Day. This gave Lawrence barely seven weeks in which to fashion an effective statewide organization. The 1932 election had demonstrated that many Pennsylvanians were becoming disenchanted with Republican rule, and a victory seemed a definite possibility. However, it was also a fact that, excepting Pittsburgh and Allegheny County, the state had remained loyal to Hoover in spite of Pennsylvania's disastrous economic conditions. The Democratic party in Pennsylvania was no longer an election long shot, but neither was it a solid favorite.

Lawrence utilized the period between his election as state chairman and the beginning of the campaign to canvass the state, meeting with local, city, and organization leaders. His control over patronage enabled him to win new converts to the party and to reward those county and city chairmen who accepted his leadership. Many of these, he quickly discovered, were fiercely independent men who could not be pressured into compliance with the same tactics he had employed on ward chairmen in Pittsburgh. He would have to win them over—convince them that a Democratic victory was not only possible but likely and encourage them to work toward victory as most had never worked before. Democrats throughout the state had grown accustomed to Republican victories and generally followed the old Pittsburgh pattern of acting as a subsidiary of the dominant Republican organization.

The new chairman met with local party leaders throughout the state to discuss election strategy, and these meetings were often followed by a rally of as many workers as possible. The election was a critical matter for Pennsylvania if it was to share in the recovery programs of the New Deal. Party leaders were to organize rallies as often as possible during the campaign and were to be more active than in any previous election. The state organization would help wherever it could, and candidates and party officials, including Lawrence himself, would appear frequently. Each local organization, however, was expected to raise funds to cover its own expenses and would be expected to contribute a specified amount to the statewide campaign. Those who failed to do so could not expect much when the victorious party assumed office in January.[14] Lawrence later explained how his fund-raising system operated. "In my own county of Allegheny, we have a club system. Pretty near every ward, borough and township has an organization. They are asked from time to time to raise funds and contribute them to the county organization; and then the county organization will send in funds to the state committee. . . . A year ago we contributed $10,000 to the state committees. . . . They hold . . . various types of fund raising campaigns, and likewise they asked prominent Democrats to contribute. They asked those who had positions . . . and candidates for office . . . to contribute."[15]

Back in Harrisburg, Lawrence and a small staff developed an election campaign schedule for the major candidates designed to get them into as many municipalities as possible. They scheduled repeat visits in the crucial cities such as Wilkes-Barre, Scranton, Erie, Pittsburgh, and Philadelphia, whose newly elected city chairman, Jack Kelly, was a strong supporter of Guffey and Earle. Particular attention was paid to those regions that narrowly missed returning a Democratic victory in 1932. The Pittsburgh speech writer whom Lawrence employed for the McNair election, Eddie Jones, was brought to Harrisburg to contribute his particular talents to Guffey, Earle, and Kennedy. The slashing attacks on Republican corruption and the obsolescence of its tired leadership clearly carried the mark of his poison pen.

As they had in their two previous defeats in 1932 and 1933, the Republicans again contributed to their own downfall. The bitter battles they waged during the 1934 primary campaign left a number of wounds unhealed, severely hampering any attempt at a united fall campaign. Governor Gifford Pinchot, unable to succeed himself, declared his candidacy for the U.S. Senate seat held by an organization Republican, David A. Reed. He championed the New Deal while not incorrectly attacking Reed as one of its chief roadblocks. Reed countered by attacking the tax policies of the Roosevelt administration and Pinchot as an opportunist who would follow anyone to guarantee himself a seat in the U.S. Senate.

Contention for the office currently held by Pinchot was even more vigorous. No fewer than sixteen Republicans announced themselves candidates for governor, while fourteen entered the race for lieutenant governor. Three serious gubernatorial contenders eventually emerged, pulling the leadership of the party in different directions. Philadelphia boss William Vare and the Pittsburgh followers of Pinchot supported the incumbent lieutenant governor, William Shannon. The Philadelphia organization's rising power, Joseph Grundy, contending with Vare for control of the City of Brotherly Love, rejected Vare's choice. Joining with William L. Mellon, he forced a curious choice,

Attorney General William Schnader, upon the regular Republican organization. Schnader had been a loyal supporter of Governor Pinchot and President Roosevelt for the past four years. Consequently he found it difficult to attack either with enthusiasm and ran a generally listless campaign.[16] The third candidate was Charles J. Margiotti, an independent Republican.

Margiotti experienced no problem in either temperament or viewpoint that would inhibit his attacks on his Republican opponents. A quick-minded trial lawyer from western Pennsylvania, he had already begun to attract a following of cultlike intensity. His representation of celebrated criminal defendants and his ability to win huge financial settlements spread his fame over the entire state. In time, he would defend 150 persons accused of murder: only two received first-degree convictions; most were acquitted. He was equally successful as a prosecutor, sending more than 25 persons to the electric chair. In 1930, he made national headlines "as the eager special prosecutor who sent Irene Schroder, the first female to be executed in Pennsylvania, to the electric chair at Rockview Penitentiary." Always described by his contemporaries as both brilliant and arrogant, the Punxsutawney-born son of Italian immigrants charmed his friends with his acerbic wit and sophisticated manner. He could be cruelly frank and, as David Lawrence would discover, treated his enemies with disdain and vindictive hostility.[17]

In a hurriedly organized campaign financed largely by himself, Margiotti traveled the state by automobile, speaking to large crowds. He proved to be the most liberal of the three Republican candidates, supporting nearly all the efforts of President Roosevelt and promising aid for organized labor and a minimum wage for women and children. Schnader and Shannon could offer only mild opposition. The Republican candidates for governor had all begun to sound like Democrats.

The organization candidates from both sides of the political aisle emerged victorious in the spring primary. Democrats Guffey and Earle easily swept the state as well as both major cities, winning by 333,000 and 250,000 votes respectively. Their opponents hardly figured in the race and, excepting William McNair, who refused to withdraw, agreed to accept the will of the majority. The Guffey-Lawrence forces could enter the fall campaign with a united party.

The Republican forces, however, were less fortunate. Reflecting the division within the party, both Pinchot and Margiotti captured considerable support. Incumbent Senator David Reed, partner in an important Pittsburgh law firm founded by his father, carried the state by less than 100,000 votes. Schnader easily defeated his nearest opponents, Shannon and Margiotti, by 340,000 and 348,000 votes respectively. Five other candidates received more than 50,000 votes each.

The results of the races for the Senate and the governorship, however, suggested serious trouble ahead for the organized Republican forces. First, Governor Pinchot made it clear immediately after the primary that he had no intention of backing Reed, or Schnader for that matter, and gave indications that he might run as an independent. Second, while Schnader won, 53 percent had voted against him. Third, Margiotti, who defeated Schnader in nine western Pennsylvania counties, including Allegheny, and captured a substantial portion of the Italian vote in Pittsburgh and Philadelphia, gave indications that he also was going to be difficult to deal with. On the evening of the primary, when it became clear that he would be defeated, he wired his campaign managers, "Don't make any announcements." His exorbitant demands on the Republican organization in return for his cooperation ultimately led Grundy to instruct Schnader to "tell him to go to hell."[18] Margiotti could take his support elsewhere, and eventually he did.

The general election campaign of 1934 mirrored the Pittsburgh campaign of the previous year: prominent individuals shifted to the Democratic party, and new voting coalitions were formed. Nationally, blue-collar workers, organized labor, ethnic groups, and certain special interest groups had already switched party affiliations. Pennsylvanians, who had held fast in 1932, were now ready to join their counterparts all over the country.

Lawrence began the campaign on the evening of his election as state chairman by attacking the Republican moneyed interests, which, he charged were attempting to buy the election. "There is not enough money in all the Mellon banks or in the treasury of the Pennsylvania Manufacturers' Association to pay for another U.S. Senatorship for the reactionary David A. Reed, . . . nor for a Governorship for Joe Grundy's attorney Bill Schnader; [nor] for a Lieutenant Governorship for the unspeakable Harry Scott, who personifies the vicious system of the Senate of Pennsylvania for the past 50 years. I say there is not enough Mellon money or Grundy Greenbacks in Pennsylvania to buy this election, if we can only get across to all the people of this Commonwealth what they have at stake next November."[19] The wealth of the Republican leadership was a theme to which he and his candidates would return repeatedly. In a state where unemployment continued to hover near 25 percent and welfare recipients approached one million, the charge needed little amplification. Neither Lawrence nor the Democratic candidates, of course, commented upon the wealth of millionaires Guffey and Earle, although Pinchot attempted to raise it as an issue. The attack fell on unsympathetic ears. The Democrats were simply not in the same league. The choice was clear for those who blamed the Depression upon the wealthy or manufacturing interests in America.

But it was the Democratic party platform, presented the same night as Lawrence's attack, that offered promise for the state's working class. The brief statement of twenty sentences advocated numerous social welfare reforms, including a "job for the man who wants to work; the abolition of child labor; regulation of hours and labor for women; a minimum wage; elimination of industrial police; absolute right of collective bargaining for labor; old age pensions and unemployment reserves and the outlawing of sweat shops." Lawrence summed it up by noting that "in our platform we make a solemn covenant with the people of Pennsylvania that if the Democratic Party of Pennsylvania is given the mandate it asks it will bring the New Deal into our state Government."[20] It is unclear whether Lawrence's reference to a New Deal for Pennsylvania was the first use of such a term, but it quickly became popular. The Republican press in Philadelphia first inadvertently publicized the concept, ridiculing it as "a Little New Deal." The term stuck, and it became the popular campaign and rallying slogan of the Democrats for the next four years.

The promises of the Democratic platform and the appeal of the Roosevelt program were perhaps enough to win the election outright, but the newly elected state chairman took no chances. Lawrence would not abandon his practice of "running scared" now. As in previous elections, he left the speaking and public appearances to the candidates and their skilled speech writer, Eddie Jones. Lawrence instead played a low-key role, working behind the scenes to win over important voting blocs and key Republican supporters.

The conversion of the black vote was considerably easier than it had been in the two previous elections. Robert Vann had received the promised federal appointment, and even though it never matched his exectations, he was grateful to his two sponsors, Lawrence and Guffey. He returned to Pennsylvania in the fall to repay his debt. He stumped the state, stressing the willingness of Democrats to provide patronage appointments for blacks and emphasizing the Democratic theme that a vote for Guffey and Earle was a vote for the New Deal. A special issue of the *Pittsburgh Courier* that circulated in both Pittsburgh and Philadelphia provided a lengthy list of state and national jobs provided to blacks by Guffey. Earle strengthened the Democrats' appeal to blacks by emphasizing his family connection to the black struggle for freedom. His great grandfather, Thomas Earle, an antislavery Quaker, had financed an underground railroad station for runaway slaves and had vigorously opposed a Pennsylvania law excluding blacks from voting in state elections. Schnader, on the other hand, had earned the disfavor of blacks by opposing an equal rights bill and a bill establishing two black Pennsylvania National Guard units. "The Negro people of this state are obligated to the Earle family," the *Philadelphia Independent* editorialized. Earle cemented his relationship with the state's black leadership by hosting a lavish dinner for the Negro Citizens' Democratic Committee just before the November election.[21] The Democratic platform's emphasis on social justice, of course, while not specifically mentioning blacks, appealed to a large number and, as contemporary interviews suggest, was the key to winning the black vote.

Another special concern of Lawrence's was the state's large number of Italian-American voters. Those in Pittsburgh had supported both Roosevelt and McNair, but the Italian neighborhoods in South Philadelphia had remained in the Republican camp. In the recent primary, they continued to vote Republican but deserted the organization to follow Margiotti. Throughout the summer Margiotti remained silent on his plans despite many attempts by both parties and the press to sound him out. He controlled nearly 200,000 Republican followers, many of whom were of Italian descent and might conceivably bring them over into the Democratic camp. As an independent candidate he could not win, but his candidacy could throw the election into turmoil. In August 1934, Lawrence requested a meeting—one he no doubt regretted for years after—with the irrepressible Margiotti. The two met in the privacy of the attorney's Pittsburgh office. The tone and direction of the discussion is unfortunately lost, but, as subsequent events made clear, they reached an amicable accord. It now seems reasonable to speculate that Margiotti, highly skilled in negotiating, extracted a steep price for his support of the Democratic ticket. A victory in November would guarantee him a high-level state position, no doubt as attorney general.

The ambitious Margiotti later claimed that Lawrence also agreed to support him for governor in 1938. Lawrence may have intimated as much, but it is doubtful. He desired the potential votes commanded by Margiotti, but the two hardly knew each other. It is unlikely that Lawrence, now fairly confident of victory in 1934 and perhaps 1938, would ransom the future of the party to a virtual stranger. Also, Margiotti knew that Lawrence alone did not control the party. It is improbable that he would have accepted such an agreement, if it had been offered, at face value. Without Guffey's acceptance, it would be worthless. Finally, it is doubtful that Lawrence, who always preferred to keep his options open until the last moment, would agree to such a demand four years before the fact. It was simply not his way of putting together a ticket. Nevertheless, it is clear that the two men did reach an agreement on Margiotti's price for his endorsement of the Democratic ticket—a place in the Earle cabinet.

Margiotti informed Lawrence that he intended to discuss the issue one more time with the Republican leadership before accepting any offer, and in September he attended the Republican State Committee meeting in Pittsburgh. The two sides failed to reach an accord and two days later Margiotti issued his long-awaited announcement. Decrying the "baneful influence" on the Republican party of Grundy and Mellon and their wealth, he proposed "to support the Democratic ticket as the only practical way of securing to the people of Pennsylvania the decent social and economic relief to which they are entitled."[22]

Margiotti carried out his promise to support the Democrats by ignoring his law practice to campaign for the ticket. Concentrating his efforts on the areas where his primary vote had been strong—in the organized labor communities in western Pennsylvania, in the Italian-American neighborhoods in Pittsburgh and Philadelphia, and in his home county, Jefferson—he drew huge crowds to hear his attacks on the "privileged interests of the Republican party." When a five-hundred-car caravan turned out to greet Margiotti and Earle in the attorney's home town of Punxsutawney, Earle was so overwhelmed that he remarked to Margiotti's former campaign manager, "If I am ever elected governor, there isn't any place in my cabinet Charley can't have."[23] Charley would soon get the only job he wanted, that of attorney general.

The efforts of Lawrence to bring Margiotti into the fold paid important dividends, but it was the appeal of Franklin D. Roosevelt and the promise of a New Deal for Pennsylvania that made the greatest impact.[24] Kermit McFarland, a journalist, traveled the state during the campaign interviewing prospective voters. "They are talking about only one man and that man is Franklin D. Roosevelt. . . . It was expressed to me by farmers, soda clerks, waitresses, barbers, hotel desk clerks, laborers, unemployed, hitch-hikers and skilled union workers."[25]

In spite of election eve charges that the Democratic leadership was willing to sacrifice Earle to ensure Guffey's election and that

McNair had endorsed Earle's opponent, the entire Democratic ticket won a narrow but decisive victory. Guffey's margin over Senator Reed was 128,000 votes, and Earle's over Schnader exceeded 66,000, although neither Democrat emerged victorious from the Republican stronghold of Philadelphia. Guffey lost Philadelphia County by 43,000 votes, while Earle was defeated there by nearly 20,000 votes. The Lawrence-Guffey Democratic machine in western Pennsylvania, in contrast, supplied vote margins of 143,000 to Guffey and 122,000 to Earle, more than half of each majority being provided by the Lawrence-controlled Allegheny County. Cambria and Erie counties, each with a large organized labor vote, also provided substantial majorities to the two Democratic candidates. Ironically, they squeezed out the barest of majorities in Charles Margiotti's home county of Jefferson.[26]

In addition to its two major victories, the Democratic party won all other contested statewide offices, 22 of 32 seats in the U.S. House of Representatives, 116 of 206 State House seats, and 16 of 25 State Senate seats. The victory gave the Democrats their first U.S. senatorship in fifty-nine years, the first Democratic majority in the U.S. House in the twentieth century, the first Democratic governor since 1894, and the first Democratic majority in the State House in over half a century. Every Democratic State Senate and House candidate from Allegheny County would be moving to Harrisburg in January. The sweep was nearly total. One crucial missing ingredient, however, as the subsequent years would show, was lack of control of the State Senate. The Republicans, by virtue of their huge previous majority, retained control by 31 to 19.

Lawrence, presiding over his Pittsburgh headquarters, was ecstatic as the results were reported to him. Paying homage to the president and taking a parting stab at the devastated opposition, he declared, "The victory is a sweeping endorsement of the policies and administration of Franklin D. Roosevelt and the New Deal. For the people of Pennsylvania it is a red letter day marking the emancipation of millions from the yoke of the Mellon-Grundy industrial and financial autocracy."[27]

▽

The November victory brought several major changes in Lawrence's life. First, the Pennsylvanian with whom he had shared power for the past twenty-four months, Joe Guffey, would be leaving the state to take up his new duties in Washington, D.C. Thus Lawrence became the top Democrat in charge of state matters. Second, within a week of the election, Earle announced that he was taking the man who engineered his victory to Harrisburg with him as secretary of the Commonwealth. The appointment, while suggested to Earle by Guffey and Lawrence, was not one the governor-elect made with any reluctance. Earle, who had little idea of the workings of government, was now expected to carry out the promise of a Little New Deal for Pennsylvanians. As his chief cabinet official, Lawrence could provide important day-to-day advice and guidance. Within a short time, it became clear to all those working in the inner circles in Harrisburg that Lawrence was managing the policies of the administration while Earle acted as the public spokesman, delivering important speeches and encouraging the press to support the measures designed to bring relief to the state. Third, Lawrence's new position required him to spend a greater amount of time in Harrisburg, away from both his family and the increasing political turmoil in Pittsburgh.

Lawrence returned to the city of his birth nearly every weekend, taking the 3:42 P.M. train out of Harrisburg on Friday and arriving in Pittsburgh approximately five hours later. He usually returned to Harrisburg on Sunday evening. He once remarked that he intended to reserve the weekends for his family, but a diary he kept for a short time in 1935 indicates that most of the time was spent at party headquarters tending to the political and administrative mess that McNair was busily creating. He scarcely had time to see his four children, now aged seven through thirteen, grow into their teens. It was a loss he would later deeply regret.[28]

Several times during the month of November, Earle met with Lawrence and Guffey to discuss and complete his cabinet selections. Their influence can be seen in the number of persons—ten of the top sixteen—from western Pennsylvania chosen for what became known as the "little brain trust." Among those were Eddie Jones, who was rewarded for his efforts as publicity writer by being named secretary of labor and industry. Margiotti, in spite of a lengthy protest to the press, was delighted to cash in on his pre-election deal by accepting the post of state attorney general. "I didn't want the job," he later recalled in a classic self-serving statement, "but I agreed to think it over. It meant a terrific financial sacrifice on my part. . . . I finally came to the conclusion that I had to take it, not for myself, but for the sake of others like myself, men who were Catholics and who had foreign-sounding names. I kept thinking of all the trouble I had had in politics because I was a Catholic and because I was of Italian origin. I kept thinking of my son who has the same name as mine. I kept thinking that it might be another hundred years before people like us would get another chance to rise so high in the government of Pennsylvania."[29]

After the selection of the cabinet, Lawrence called the victorious members of the lower house of the General Assembly together in Harrisburg in December to lay down the procedures to be followed in the upcoming legislative session. With a comfortable majority in the House, the party chairman was determined to establish a united front in carrying out his Little New Deal. "If we are to be successful in enacting this legislative program, you must realize at the outset that it can only be accomplished by concerted team work."[44] He proposed to guarantee such teamwork through a preselected House Steering Committee, which consisted entirely of old-line party regulars who had previously demonstrated that they could be trusted to do the party's bidding. Not a single committee member was nominated from the newly elected representatives, who made up approximately half of the lower body's Democrats. They would have to earn leadership positions. Despite a few mild murmurs of discontent to the press later, freshman members accepted the party nominees without opposition. Lawrence's closing advice to the group established the practice he expected them to follow during the next four years and one that became a hallmark of his government and party work during the next third of a century: keep all disputes within the family. "You name[d] your own leaders whom you can respect and trust," he told them, ignoring his orchestration of the elective process. "Confer with them. Discuss proposed legislation with them. Do not hesitate to voice to them your objections to provisions in measures if you have good grounds for your opposition. If you are out-voted, be good soldiers. Follow your leaders and in doing so, we will stand a better chance of making this coming session the most noteworthy of all the legislative sessions in the entire history of Pennsylvania."[30]

The meeting set the tone for the legislative session that followed and informed the legislators that Lawrence intended to play an active role in pushing through the Democratic program. When the legislature convened in January, the House leadership established a practice of holding regular caucuses at which Lawrence, who acted as chairman, or one of his aides would outline any impending legislation and explain the official party stance. A generally free and open discussion followed, and the caucus chairman fielded questions or responded to criticism or suggestions regarding the proposed legislation. Occasionally, adjustments to the proposal were offered and accepted. Outright opposition, however, was rarely suggested. On the few occasions when the group proved unable to achieve consensus, the proposed bill was withdrawn, to be submitted another day. Party leaders, including Lawrence, employed the interim to persuade recalcitrant members to accept the leadership view. Postponement of legislation, in Lawrence's view, was always preferable to a divided party in the legislature.

This is not to suggest that Lawrence tolerated no opposition within the party. He expected loyalty from party members, but he could accept and respect independence as long as both sides understood the rules. For example, Al Tronzo, a freshman representative, initially refused to accept Lawrence's leadership or the caucus rule and insisted on fighting anything he didn't like on the floor of the House. Lawrence called him in. "Dave wanted to know . . . why I wouldn't attend caucuses. When I gave him the reason, he said, 'Well, if I can fix it up so that you can still walk out and fight on the floor any measure that you don't participate in in the caucus, will you attend?' . . . And by jingo he had the Democratic caucus agree to make an exception . . . and that's how I started attending the Democratic caucus. I really enjoyed it and learned something."[31] Lawrence's tactic had valuable results, for Tronzo eventually became a fierce Lawrence supporter and one of the most loyal Democratic members of the State House of Representatives. Lawrence later demonstrated his appreciation of Tronzo's willingness to cooperate by appointing him director of housing for the city of Pittsburgh.

Occasionally, when the group proved unable to reach agreement on the details of an important piece of legislation, Lawrence removed himself from the deliberative process and ordered the differing member to "work things out." One such incident occurred over a Pennsylvania minimum wage law. Al Tronzo and others were fighting for forty-five or fifty cents an hour. For Jack Kelly, who was the Philadelphia Democratic chairman and was also making bricks there, "it was too damned much, and he kept haggling, arguing. In desperation Dave brought the gavel down and brought the caucus to a halt. . . . Dave was pretty hot at the time and said, 'Well you sit down and work it out with Al, and anything he agrees with will be acceptable with us.'" Kelly did not immediately comply, but they worked it out later.[32]

Normally, however, the group that rode into office on the promise of a social reform program accepted the will of the party leadership. While the caucus vote might not be unanimous, legislators were expected to follow the unit rule on the floor. Not surprisingly, Democratic members of the House nearly always voted en masse for the administration's proposed legislation during the 1935–38 sessions.

Lawrence established the same type of control over the Democratic Senate caucus, but, because Democrats remained a substantial minority during the 1935–36 legislative session, the imposed unity produced few tangible results. It was thus not until the second half of the Earle administration that the Little New Deal began to take effect.

Sports

Lawrence's love of sports in a sports-minded city helped to produce a strong, emotional bond between Pittsburgh voters and "Davey."

The P.F. Toole Athletic Club, around 1910. It was one of the many sports clubs sponsored by prominent ward politicians. Peter Toole was a brother of first ward boss, Tommy Toole. A young David Lawrence, second row center with the handkerchief in his pocket, already appears to be a confident political figure. Carnegie Library, Pittsburgh

Always willing to pose with sports figures, Lawrence joins the starting backfield of the 1949 Pittsburgh Steelers. Left to right: Jerry Nuzum, Charley Seabright, Lawrence, Joe Geri, George Papach. The Steelers' record was 6 wins, 5 losses, and 1 tie that season. Carnegie Library, Pittsburgh

Lawrence, a season ticket holder for many years, displays his exuberance at the Pirates' 1960 World Series victory over the New York Yankees. It was their first championship in 35 years. Courtesy Anna Mae Donahoe

Family

The Lawrence family, although seldom active in David's political life, always shared in his successes and occasional setbacks. Frequently absent from the home, Lawrence nevertheless maintained a strong family loyalty.

David and Alyce attend a Democratic Ball held to raise funds, January 31, 1935. Carnegie Library, Pittsburgh

The Lawrence family share in the joy of David's first primary victory as a candidate for mayor, August 13, 1945. Left to right: David, Mary, Jerry, Anna Mae, Alyce. Carnegie Library, Pittsburgh

Pittsburgh Post-Gazette
WADDELL AND LAWRENCE WIN

Left side of governor's desk in the state capitol in Harrisburg, showing photo of David, Jr., and William Brennen, killed in an automobile accident in 1942. The photo was always on Lawrence's desk, wherever he was located. Carnegie Library, Pittsburgh

Lawrence, accompanied by Alyce and a male nurse, leaves the hospital following one of his frequent eye operations, September 13, 1947. Carnegie Library, Pittsburgh

Lawrence remained impeccably dressed, even when playing ball with his grandsons. The boys are, from left to right: Michael (2), Tommy (12), and David Donahoe (10). Courtesy Anna Mae Donahoe

Politics

Lawrence, although basically a private man, was aware of the value of a good publicity photo and seldom passed up the opportunity to appear in front of the camera.

Looking somewhat uncomfortable in straw hat, coat, and tie, Lawrence appears astride the symbol of his party. The photo was taken in 1931 during the Lawrence campaign for county commissioner. Carnegie Library, Pittsburgh

In a pose reminiscent of those made famous by Calvin Coolidge, Lawrence accepts designation as an honorary Thunderbird by Navajo Silagos Tzo (Big Policeman) in the lobby of the William Penn Hotel. Members of the tribe stayed in Pittsburgh enroute to a show in New York, April 29, 1948. Carnegie Library, Pittsburgh

Mayor Lawrence joins in the birthday celebration of "Baby Penny," one of the elephants appearing in the Police Circus at Forbes Field. The cake-cutting occurred in the rotunda of the City-County Building, August 1, 1953. Carnegie Library, Pittsburgh

Vote tally recorded by Lawrence at party headquarters, November 1957. Lawrence's reported vote total was 137,281; 82,080 was that of his mayoralty opponent, John Drew. Below is Lawrence's shorthand recording of Drew's "near concession" statement as reported by phone to Lawrence by a Democratic aide. The translation of the Lawrence transcription reads "we have not officially conceded. It looks as though it is a landslide victory for Mayor Lawrence. My political advisors have suggested that I hold up sending the Mayor a telegram. As far as I can tell, it is just a matter of time." Lawrence, a one-time stenographer, had obviously not lost his touch. Courtesy James Knox

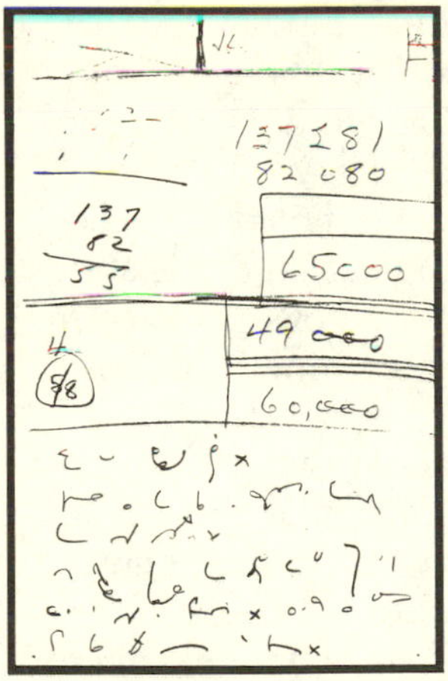

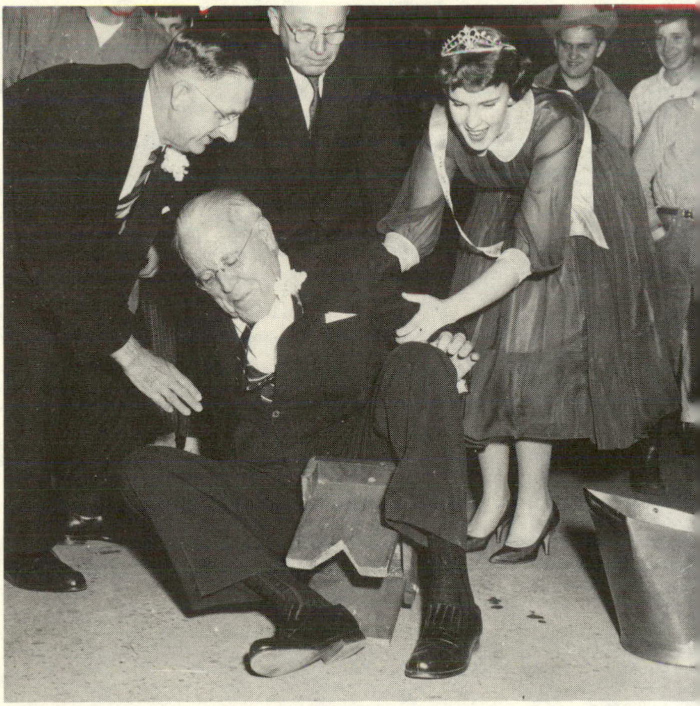

In one of his first official "duties" as governor, Lawrence attempts to demonstrate his milking skills at the Harrisburg Farm Show. Lawrence proved that he had spent little time in rural surroundings. Courtesy Anna Mae Donahoe

1935–1938

Exercising Power: A Little New Deal and a Ripper

It has frequently been suggested that Lawrence underwent the metamorphosis from political boss to urban statesman upon assuming the position of mayor of Pittsburgh in 1945. His political opponents and the press viewed him in the role of the typical boss concerned with winning elections, dispensing patronage and other favors, and building an unassailable power base. He was often accused of showing little regard for the issues of government or the affairs of state. Even close associates confess to an early view of Lawrence as a one-dimensional person concerned only with political affairs. When he was elected mayor in 1945, the *Pittsburgh Press* lectured, "It is a great advantage for a Mayor to be a good politician—provided he does not make politics the be-all and the end-all of his administration. . . . We hope that he will rise above the temptation to be just a political boss and will be a politician in the statesmanlike sense of that word. He has the capacity and the experience."[1]

What the *Press* and even Lawrence's associates failed to recognize, however, was that he had given a strong indication of his ability to separate political and government affairs and of his concern for the welfare of the electorate during his directorship of the Earle program from 1935 through 1939.

When Lawrence moved to Harrisburg in January 1935, Pennsylvania was in as dire an economic and social condition as the city of Pittsburgh had been in 1932–33. Unemployment had fallen slightly since the Roosevelt inauguration two years earlier, but nearly one-fourth of the labor force, 836,359 persons, was still without work when Earle took office. Jobless rates in the major cities and among certain blue-collar groups exceeded the statewide averages. Approximately

 20 percent of the state's farmers were in default and others struggled

to meet mortgage and loan obligations with the sale of food whose prices had fallen 40 percent since 1932. Dairy farmers, a key agricultural group, were hit particularly hard. Their inability to control productivity resulted in wide swings in the availability of milk at certain times of year. Distributors, on the other hand, who controlled storage facilities, could buy at low prices in times of surplus and distribute from their own supplies during short periods. Desperate farmers who thus became victims of exploitation as well as of the Depression looked to Harrisburg for relief. To make matters worse, while the state's Emergency Relief Board had supplied food and other provisions to 1.7 million people during the previous year, its funds were near exhaustion. It could continue operation for less than two months without additional revenues. Unfortunately, the Pinchot administration, reluctant to impose new taxes, had left the state treasury bare. It had, in fact, bequeathed a deficit of $15 million to the incoming administration.[2]

While laborers, farmers, and others hard hit by the Depression were looking to the new administration for relief, organized labor expected deliverance from what it considered half a century of oppression at the hands of capital and industry. Although conditions had improved somewhat from the pre–World War I period, they remained far from acceptable. The twelve-hour day was no longer the rule among Pennsylvania industries, but wages, which had climbed gradually since the war, returned to their prewar rates during the Depression. Many who had jobs could barely maintain their families. Women and children, forced to contribute, labored in sweatshops and unsafe factories.

Attempts by workers to redress their grievances through collective bargaining had been beaten back regularly since the aborted steel strike of 1919. Governor Pichot had attempted to provide some relief by refusing to commission any new "coal and iron" police after June 1930. Companies, however, continued to control police departments in coal and mining towns by paying their salaries. Workers' salaries had fallen, and compensation for job-related injuries and layoffs remained woefully inadequate. Pennsylvania stood thirty-third among all states in workingmen's compensation, fortieth in compensation for widows, and forty-fourth in provisions for medical payments.[3] Organized labor as well as unorganized blue-collar workers in Pennsylvania had given important support to Roosevelt in 1932 and the Guffey-Earle ticket in 1934 and now expected rewards.

Governor Earle and Lawrence, his top cabinet officer, had no grand design based on a set of philosophical principles that would guide them through the murky future. Instead, as Lawrence later admitted, "We had the obvious problems of the residents of Pennsylvania to resolve and we had Roosevelt's New Deal" to serve as a guide. In addition, the lessons of his childhood and the persistent efforts to build a Democratic opposition to what he viewed as the party of privilege and special interests provided a foundation for the difficult times ahead. "He came from a group which had been oppressed. . . . He knew what being poor was all about . . . all his life he always associated himself with the guy who was on the other side of the tracks. . . . That was part of his upbringing."[4]

From the three most influential persons in his life, his parents and Billy Brennen, David Lawrence had acquired a simple but effective outlook. The world was divided into haves and have-nots. The haves possessed the economic power and would use it relentlessly unless checked by an equally powerful opposing force. Lawrence's introduction to the world of the wealthy and powerful through his mentor Brennen also convinced him that those in control were not by nature an evil class to be overthrown, and he came to understand, if not accept, their viewpoint. The mission of the Democratic party when it finally came to power in the midst of the Depression, therefore, would be to check the natural impulses of the economically powerful and to act as the political and economic intermediary for those without power. He retained this view of his party's social obligation throughout his life. In his later years as mayor, for example, he received a long letter from a powerful Sixteenth Ward committeewoman protesting plans to develop a low-income housing project on the South Side. She complained in particular that the project would introduce some undesirable elements into the community and would harm the neighborhood politically. The response characteristically was short and to the point: "Dear Ida: Your letter of February 23rd received. When the Democratic party ceases to be interested in housing for the people, it ceases to be the Democratic party. Very truly yours."[5] His understanding required no lengthy explanation. The party had a clear role to play, aiding the electorate and the less fortunate. The government should be used to assist it in fulfilling that obligation.

The approach, however, was in all cases to be a pragmatic one. Lawrence had examined, admittedly briefly, the popular panaceas of the day and found them wanting. As a short time member of Pittsburgh's Henry George Club, he found the single tax too simple for all the problems of the industrial world. He later privately ridiculed William McNair's adherence to the George philosophy as silly.[6] It is unclear whether Lawrence ever considered socialism or other broad philosophical approaches to restructuring society, but all the available evidence suggests that he remained fiscally too conservative to be attracted by any radical approach. In his relationships with both Democrats and Republicans, he preferred to work through the existing party apparatus rather than restructure the mechanisms of government. Critics during his early life complained that he often avoided or hindered true reform movements through his willingness to work with the ruling Republican interests. The same charge was often leveled against him later, when, as head of Pittsburgh's government, he worked with the corporate heads of Pittsburgh to induce the physical rehabilitation of the city.

Even organized labor, whose merits he had heard extolled since childhood, failed to attract him as an ideology. He did indeed usually support its causes, but he could never be counted upon as a labor politician. Labor, in his view, like any other source of power, acted in its own interests, which usually, but not always, paralleled those of the greater community. When it acted contrary to those interests, the demands of labor should and would be repulsed.

The view of Lawrence during his early years as the consummate politician, bereft of ideological principle, stems from his elevation of party politics to the level of ideology. He had viewed firsthand the debasement of the electoral process through the implementation of one-party rule in Pittsburgh and Pennsylvania and concluded that the two-party system was America's guarantee of a functioning democracy. Only when both parties stood a reasonable chance of gaining power would the diverse elements in society be heard. The competition between the parties, in his view, ensured a voice for all. Rather than apologize for partisan politics, he held that it was the politician's patriotic duty to bring all his powers to bear to win for his party a seat in government. He later chided the Republicans in Pittsburgh when they proved incapable of providing a reasonable challenge to his own party.

The party of Wilson and Franklin Roosevelt represented the great majority of American society and best understood its problems. In nearly all cases the interests of the people, he believed, would be best served by Democratic officeholders. Thus his greatest contribution to society would be made by working toward that goal.

To the occasional consternation of his fellow Democrats, Lawrence's belief in partisan politics clearly did not rule out working with the Republican opposition. His call for bipartisan cooperation was particularly appropriate as he assumed leadership of the Earle government and relegated the slightly talented governor to the role of cheerleader for administration programs. The party controlled the State House of Representatives as well as the chief executive's office. The recent election, unfortunately, left Republicans in control of the State Senate, the state treasurer's and auditor general's offices, and the Pennsylvania Supreme Court. Delivering the promised Little New Deal to hopeful Democratic supporters would require Lawrence's greatest negotiating skills. He had succeeded in cooperating with the Republican party when he represented the emasculated minority. The success of his legislative program depended upon whether he could persuade the GOP to follow his old policy.

The Republican majority in the Senate, however, signaled that it had no intention of cooperating with the new administration. Immediately after assembling in January 1935, the Senate passed a procedure rule requiring the assent of the full majority (twenty-six votes) before a bill could be released from committee. The Democrats, with only nineteen of fifty members, were powerless to act without the cooperation of nearly one-fourth of the Republican side, a defection they could not realistically expect.

Throughout the four years of the Earle administration, Lawrence single-mindedly nurtured the House and Senate Democrats. In addition to presiding over the party caucuses, he met privately with the legislators, nearly all of whom were participating in lawmaking for the first time. On evenings following late caucus sessions, he would hold court with young Democrats at the Elks Club, or at one of several local saloons frequented by House and Senate members. Most often, the group would adjourn from the caucus to Davenport's, an all-night restaurant on Market Street, a few blocks from the capitol. These sessions often lasted well past midnight, at which point Lawrence would collar one or two of the lingering representatives to join him on a walk home along a meandering path, often along the bank of the Susquehanna River. Lawrence would make the last points before dismissing the group for the evening in the lobby of the Penn Harris Hotel.

Not content with coaching the Democratic legislators in caucus and at numerous informal sessions, Lawrence attended nearly every House and Senate session, thus keeping potential strays in line. However, it served another purpose. The Democrats who arrived in Harrisburg in the mid thirties were almost painfully naïve about the legislative and the political processes. Lawrence, although a legislative rookie himself, was almost the only seasoned political executive among the group. Certainly the inexperienced governor, who knew few of his legislators and nothing about the legislative process, was incapable of providing the leadership needed to pass the almost revolutionary legislation promised by the Democratic platform of 1934. The party chairman willingly guided his novice legislators every step of the way, sitting at the side of the chamber, usually with a vacant seat next to him for anyone who needed his advice.[7]

Lawrence's coaching evidently paid off, for every bill proposed in the 1935 session, even the most controversial, sailed through the Democratic-controlled House. The Senate, however, proved unbreachable: the Republican majority, ironically led by Lawrence's associates Jimmy Coyne and Frank J. Harris, beat back nearly every attempt at passing the Democratic program.

▽

Three legislative issues dominated the 1935 session: taxes, a "ripper" bill to remove Mayor William McNair from office, and a labor reform bill consisting of eight distinct pieces of legislation. Lawrence pushed all three through the House, but only on one could he gain even a partial victory in the Senate.

The necessity of tax reform was particularly acute for two reasons. The deficit Governor Pinchot left behind made it impossible for the state to meet its fiscal obligations without additional revenue. In September 1934 the treasury had fallen so low that the state failed to meet its payments to local school systems. A special session of the legislature borrowed $22 million to pay them and meet other outstanding debts, and the Earle administration was obligated to repay the loan. More seriously, the Pennsylvania Chamber of Commerce estimated that the state would need $326 million to meet its 1935–36 budget, while current tax sources would produce only $148 million—a shortfall of $178 million. To compound matters, Harry Hopkins, federal emergency relief administrator, informed the governor that Washington would meet Pennsylvania's relief needs only until 1 April. Thereafter the state would be required to contribute $5 million per month—$120 million over the two-year legislative session—to keep the crucial relief funds flowing from the federal treasury.[8] The amount Hopkins demanded was included in the budget presented to the legislature in 1935, along with a $200 million package of new taxes to support the entire program. The tax package, recommended by a bipartisan blue-ribbon panel appointed by Earle in November, predictably hit hard at utilities, corporate income, capital stock exemptions, and a variety of luxury items.

Lawrence's hand-holding, prodding, and occasionally applying the whip proved successful in the Democratic-controlled House, which passed nearly every piece of requested tax legislation by substantial majorities. In pushing a major portion of the tax program through the House, for example, Lawrence, Eddie Jones, the secretary of labor and industry, and Harry Kalodner, secretary to Governor Earle, stood in a corner of the chamber to observe the deliberations. Twice, when threats of revolt appeared, Lawrence signaled Speaker Herbert Cohen, who gaveled a short recess. The Democratic majority met in caucus to hear Lawrence and the other leaders deliver new pep talks and then rammed four tax bills through on a single day.[9]

In the Senate, however, while the nineteen-member Democratic minority remained firm, neither Lawrence, operating behind the scenes, nor the governor, delivering a series of "little fireside chats" on local radio stations across the state, could sway the Republican majority. Republican State Chairman Harvey Taylor charged that the Democratic tax package would start a "spending spree that, if Republicans would permit, would land Pennsylvania on the brink of bankruptcy." Declaring that $57 million would satisfy Hopkins's demands, Taylor's forces in the Senate whittled away at each part of the package. In April the Democratic leadership arranged to have Hopkins meet with the entrenched state Republicans in Washington. By prearrangement with Earle and Lawrence, Hopkins stood fast on his earlier position. Five million dollars per month must be contributed by the state or it would be cut off from federal relief funds, a fate met by more than a dozen other states since 1933. The Republican leadership departed the capital still convinced that Hopkins was bluffing. They refused to budge from their increasingly untenable position.[10]

Lawrence, meanwhile, put pressure on several Republican senators to abandon their party. His old business partner Frank J. Harris proved to be the key. A long-term, highly respected Republican senator, Harris could be expected to pull a number of colleagues with him if he could be induced to support the administration's program. The two met several times during April. Lawrence, according to one source, never appealed to Harris on the basis of their friendship and long-standing partnership. He argued instead that the residents of Allegheny County and particularly Pittsburgh, unable to count on relief from the erratic McNair administration, were desperate for the state funds. The senator's mail, nearly all supporting the tax package, underscored Lawrence's argument. On 30 April Harris announced to the Pittsburgh newspapers that he was willing to consider a compromise. He was joined two days later by Senator Harry Shapiro of Philadelphia and five other Republicans, who met with Earle to inform him they would support his program for one year only. The shocked Republican leadership denounced the "turncoats." Lawrence called their willingness to support the Democratic package "an act of true courage." But he refused to gloat over the sudden victory and cautioned members of the Democratic caucus to keep a low profile in the days to come.[11]

During the next few weeks Lawrence met with the Republican leadership to work out a compromise. Republicans were adamant that they could support only a limited tax package, while Lawrence insisted that any compromise had to represent some attempts at a fairer distribution of the tax burden. Within a short time they agreed to initiate a 6 percent tax on corporate incomes, a 6 mill increase in the tax paid by utilities, and increases in the taxes on gasoline, cigarettes, and amusements. They also agreed on repeal of the exemption permitted manufacturers on capital stock. The entire package flew through the House, and all but two minor provisions were accepted by the Senate.[12] The victory, although gratifying to Lawrence, was unfortunately only partial. The new package would pay the state's share of relief demanded by Hopkins, but only for one year. Furthermore, it provided only half of the total funds the governor had requested for 1935–36.

It was, however, the only significant victory the governor and the secretary of the Commonwealth were to enjoy that year. Bills to revise the antiquated state constitution, to permit state agencies to participate in various federal relief and public works programs, and an additional revenue program requested by the governor all ran aground in the Senate. In each case the Lawrence-dominated House provided a full majority to the administration.[13]

The difficulties the administration encountered in passing the tax bill presaged events of the 1935 session. Attempting to fulfill the Democratic commitment to organized labor, Earle unveiled an eight-part legislative package to the General Assembly on 28 January. The revolutionary program created by Lawrence, Lieutenant Governor Thomas Kennedy, and the new secretary of labor and industry, Ralph Bashore, called for:

1. a minimum employable age of sixteen (raised from fourteen) and a maximum work week of forty hours for those under eighteen;
2. regulation of industrial homework (sweatshops);
3. penalties for nonpayment of wages;
4. annual registration of industrial establishments;

5. reduction of the maximum hours per week for female laborers from fifty-four to forty;
6. an agency to establish a minimum wage for women and children;
7. abolition of the industrial (coal and iron) police;
8. prohibition of compensation to municipal police or deputy sheriffs by private or corporate interests.[14]

Lawrence hailed his own program as an "emancipation proclamation" for the state's workers, while the Republican leadership, who, the governor noted in his address, had made similar "pledges for a square deal for labor" in its own platform, criticized it as unworkable and unenforceable. Taylor, whose own lengthy career paralleled that of Lawrence, tried to postpone the matter by calling for the creation of a labor study commission.

The four key Democratic supporters of the legislation—Governor Earle, Lieutenant Governor Kennedy, Lawrence, and Bashore—worked hard to get the program through the General Assembly. Earle, acting as the public spokesman, again took to the radio, seeking support from voters across the state. Vehemently attacking the Republican opposition, he urged his listeners to flood the capital with letters supporting the legislative package. He also delivered appeals on behalf of several pieces of legislation on the floor of the State Senate. Lawrence, although he made several trips into key labor areas to encourage workers to demand favorable action from Republican senators, confined most of his activities to working through the Democratic caucuses of both houses. He also met privately with key Republican senators, particularly those from the industrial strongholds of Philadelphia, western Pennsylvania, and the hard coal region in Scranton and Wilkes-Barre. Lieutenant Governor Kennedy and Bashore, both former union officials, worked through the labor organizations to bring pressure to bear on the opposition Republicans. Their efforts produced almost no positive results. The Democratic House, as before, delivered a majority for each piece of legislation. The Republican-controlled Senate, however, effectively killed all but one of the bills. The first four bills listed above never emerged from committee,thanks to the rule requiring a majority of the entire Senate to place a bill on the floor. The proposals to regulate female labor reached the floor, but the committee had so weakened them that the administration rejected both. The wide differences between the House and Senate versions prevented a compromise, and the two bills died in the Senate.

The administration's only success on the entire package, the abolition of the hated coal and iron police, was made moot by the failure to prohibit employers from paying the salaries of local law enforcement officials. Police and deputy sheriffs, supported by company treasuries, could continue to play an aggressive antilabor role in labor-management disputes.

The defeat of virtually the entire labor package was a bitter pill for Lawrence to swallow. While he had never been an uncritical supporter of organized labor, the legislative program represented the culmination of lifelong struggles by both his father and Billy Brennen. It was his gift to them both and he had failed. Friends later attested that they had never before seen him so depressed. Fortunately, he would have a second chance in the 1937 session. The Democrats in the interim, however, had to capture control of the State Senate.

Equally difficult for Lawrence to accept was the defeat, again at the hands of the Republican Senate, of his attempt to remove William McNair from the mayor's office in Pittsburgh. The jousting between McNair and the Democratic organization in the city continued unabated throughout the mayor's first year in office. The immovable single tax advocate blocked all but three of Lawrence's appointments to crucial city positions. He also bypassed the organization's patronage committee in the matter of appointing to city jobs members of minority groups who had supported his candidacy. Black and Italian leaders complained to Lawrence that they failed to receive their share of patronage positions, but the state chairman was powerless to do anything about it. McNair added to the insult when he announced his intention in early 1934 to run against the organization choice for governor. In June, following his defeat in the gubernatorial primary, he twisted the knife when he announced he would support the Republican victor, Ralph Schnader. A few months later, he urged all city workers to do the same. The mayor further galled the organization forces when, before embarking on a one-month European cruise, he named his public works director, Leslie Johnston, as acting mayor, thereby turning the city over to the head of the anti-Lawrence Citizens' League. The Democratic party, except for the offices of city solicitor and city treasurer held by Cornelieus Scully and Jimmy Kirk respectively, was totally shut out of city hall. McNair promptly fired Scully upon his return.[15]

Lawrence effectively shielded his anger from the public, but inside he was seething. In a series of meetings held at Democratic headquarters, it was decided that the situation could no longer be tolerated. Of crucial significance was the method to be chosen for the exorcism. Three avenues appeared available: impeachment; a plan whereby the legislature would strip the mayor of most of his executive powers; or a ripper bill, which would eliminate the office of mayor and replace it with that of a city commissioner. The first two were ruled out because they made the president of city council, Republican Robert Garland, acting mayor until a special election could be held. (Although the Democrats won five council seats in the 1933 election, the GOP retained a majority by virtue of former Republican Mayor William Magee's victory on both tickets. Magee joined the four Republican holdovers in selecting Garland for the president's post.) Thus they would, in effect, return the city to Republican rule, denying the Democrats their hard-earned victory. In early 1935, when the issue came to a full boil, the Senate Republicans made known their support for impeachment, but the Democratic leadership decided to choose another path. They preferred an uncontrollable McNair in office to giving the city back to the opposition they worked so hard to unseat.[16]

The method that McNair himself had predicted, a ripper bill, appeared to have at least a long shot chance of moving through the Republican Senate. Also, it was preferred because the governor selected the interim city commissioner to replace the ripped-out mayor, and Earle was sure to select a Democrat of Lawrence's choosing. The ripper was a tested, if not honored, method in Pittsburgh. In 1902, for example, Mayor William J. Diehl was ripped from office by the Flinn-Magee machine, and two lesser officials were similarly removed by the Coyne regime during the early 1920s. It is not clear that the Democratic leadership actually decided to push for a ripper bill during their discussions of late 1934. Certainly their preoccupation with winning the state elections prevented any action, and it appears uncertain that public reaction to McNair would have supported any attempt to remove him from office. But if they were willing to wait, he would give them a reason. Shortly after the New Year the mayor fulfilled their expectations by precipitating a crisis that generated the needed public support.

On 11 January 1935 McNair initiated a series of sudden firings that, while purging the city payroll of suspected organization supporters, destroyed his own credibility with the public. With no apparent provocation, the fire chief, civil service commissioner, assessor, and zoning board chairman were relieved of their duties. When asked to explain, the mayor responded, "I don't know. It's around the first of the year. Isn't that reason enough? Anyway, I wanted to make some changes." Several weeks later he fired the city court clerk, Evan Thomas. "He's had the job twenty-eight years. Wasn't that long enough? A man oughtn't to mind losing a job he's held that long."[17]

The main event in the mayor's firing spree actually began just before the New Year when he ordered the public safety director, Marshall Bell, on a thirty-day "economy furlough" and appointed himself acting head of the fire and police departments. Three weeks later, again for no apparent reason, he announced the firing of his furloughed director and the appointment of the fourth director in twelve months. This touched off a furor among officials of both parties and in the city's newspapers. The *Pittsburgh Press*, a former McNair supporter, ran a front-page editorial headlined, "It's Time to Get Rid of McNair," in which Edward Leech offered a plea for impeachment but conceded, "The situation . . . is so serious that we believe a 'ripper bill' would be welcomed by a majority of the people of Pittsburgh if it is the only way or the quickest way of ending the cruelties, the clowning and the general mismanagement of the present mayor." After chronicling a long list of abuses, the *Press* concluded, "The time for drastic action—impeachment or ripper—has arrived. The sooner the better."[18]

Lawrence interrupted his work with the General Assembly to return to Pittsburgh. On 5 February, at several hastily arranged meetings with Michael Benedum, Kirk, and the Democratic members of city council, it was decided that the time was ripe for a ripper.

Upon his return to Harrisburg, Lawrence—armed with dozens of letters and petitions from such groups as the "Polish and Slavish Citizens of the Fourth Ward," the "One Thousand Citizens Assembled in the Irene Kaufmann Settlement," and the "Taxpayers of the City of Pittsburgh"—began his campaign to remove his two-year embarrassment from public office. In an initial caucus held in mid February, twenty-four of Allegheny County's twenty-five Democratic legislators supported a ripper bill to be introduced on the following Tuesday. Only Al Tronzo, a former McNair clerk, was opposed. With such solid support from the "home team," gaining backing of the other Democrats in the House appeared relatively easy. When intense pressure from McNair followers and Republican opponents threatened to erode the Democratic support, Lawrence held a second party caucus. He indicated that he felt responsible in part for Mr. McNair's election, regretted it, and therefore felt obligated to correct the situation. The roar of approval from the Democratic group left little doubt of the bill's outcome. On 6 March, with Lawrence pacing the side aisle observing the proceedings, the House voted to replace the mayor of Pittsburgh with a city commissioner to be appointed by the governor. The courageous Tronzo was one of only two Democrats opposing the bill.

"This is a vicious piece of legislation for the express purpose of ripping from office a public official elected by the people and placing instead a rubber stamp appointed by the Governor." While his plea had no effect, it provided ammunition for the bitter Senate battle that lay ahead.[19]

The Republican Senate, since convening in January, had established an unwritten practice of following the wishes of any senator when a bill affected that individual's district alone. In the case of the ripper, the lone Republican from Pittsburgh, Coyne, stood vehemently against the bill. More ominously, he sat on the Senate Municipal Government Committee, which controlled the bill and could prevent it from being reported to the floor. Lawrence's old ally realized that the only way he could regain control of the city was through an impeachment proceeding. Barring that, he naturally preferred the anti-organization McNair to a commissioner handpicked by Lawrence. Lawrence fully understood and anticipated Coyne's position, but he had little choice. He would be forced to rely on his own skills as a negotiator to attempt to swing members of Coyne's committee to the anti-McNair side. The challenge appeared formidable indeed.

For the next three months the committee sat on the ripper issue, apparently unable to decide how to handle the hot potato. A public hearing had indicated strong proripper support from a wide variety of sources, and the Democratic administration announced that it had the votes to pass a ripper if it could pry the measure out of committee. McNair, meanwhile, continued to make a farce of the whole situation. At one point he declared that he would resign if the ripper reached the floor of the Senate; at the same time he moved his bed into his office and said he would eat and sleep there to prevent a newly appointed city commissioner from occupying it.

Neither of McNair's contradictory actions was necessary, for the Senate Committee on Municipal Government, not surprisingly, voted on three separate occasions to keep the bill in committee. Lawrence applied every pressure at his disposal to dislodge it. The governor and five cabinet heads, including Lawrence, lobbied committee members to move it to the floor. "They were in better attendance than some of the Senators," Al Tronzo testified at a Senate hearing investigating charges of illegal activities, primarily by Lawrence, in the attempted ripper.[20] Three Republican senators testified that Lawrence offered jobs and appointments as a quid pro quo. Several House members admitted being pressured by Lawrence, but all stated that he offered them nothing in return for a proripper vote.

Lawrence was not invited to testify but responded to the charges.

"I specifically and emphatically give the lie to the testimony of Senators Graff and Chapman," he told reporters at a news conference. "I never offered favors or patronage for the vote of any Senator or Representative. If these Republican Senators were of the opinion that I offered them such illicit consideration, it was their duty to report the matter immediately . . . instead of many months later."[21] It is impossible to determine the validity of the charges, but one might reasonably infer that they were without substance. The investigating subcommittee, all Republicans, postponed the hearings after two days of testimony. They were never resumed, nor did the committee call for a formal grand jury investigation, the normal procedure when incriminating evidence has been presented.

▽

Lawrence's failure to implement the Democratic program and to rid himself and Pittsburgh of the intolerable McNair left him with one inescapable conclusion. The party had to gain control of the State Senate in the 1936 election, and the prospects seemed good. Twenty-two of the twenty-five contested seats were in Republican hands, while the Democrats retained sixteen holdover seats. Thus the party had to win only ten more to gain a majority. David Lawrence, predicting a close race, expected to win eleven seats and lose ten, and he considered four "up for grabs."[22] The Republicans' opposition to the popular social legislation package made them particularly vulnerable in the large industrial districts, which, excepting Pittsburgh, had remained loyal to the Grand Old Party. Voter registration figures for early 1936, moreover, warned of an impending shift. Nearly 375,000 voters joined the Democratic party in 1936, while the Republicans added only 30,000. In the four years since Roosevelt lost a close race in Pennsylvania, the Republican registration edge had decreased by 1.4 million voters.

The 1936 Democratic National Convention, held in Philadelphia, cast a spotlight on the state's party leaders, Guffey, Earle, and Lawrence. All were given prominent roles, and the relationship between the three and President Roosevelt was emphasized over and over. Newspapers began to speculate that Earle was a likely U.S. Senate candidate in 1938 and a strong presidential possibility two years after. Lawrence was mentioned as the potential gubernatorial candidate.

The entire state Democratic team barnstormed Pennsylvania during the fall of 1936. "We had this Roosevelt Caravan thing going," one campaigner recalled years later. "We would pick up all the local candidates . . . and form this caravan to all places where people wouldn't get to a political rally. . . . We would speak in the public squares of larger cities, a mine entrance, a factory gate, a general store, any place where you could draw a crowd, and we had a built in crowd with us, . . . going from place to place."[23]

Roosevelt underscored the importance of the election outcome in the Keystone State by joining the caravan during the month of October. He also returned to the site of his earlier triumph by making a major address before a standing-room-only crowd at Pittsburgh's Forbes Field on 2 October. In every address he emphasized the importance of voting the party ticket at the state as well as national level.

Roosevelt's broad coattails, the persistent economic difficulties in Pennsylvania, and the Republican Senate's intransigency over relief measures resulted in a statewide landslide of historic proportions. Roosevelt captured the state by an astounding 600,000 votes, while the crucial State Senate changed hands for the first time in two-thirds of a century. Eighteen of the contested Senate seats went to the Democratic party, creating a voting edge of more than two to one. Coyne was defeated by more than three to one, along with Lawrence's business partner, Frank J. Harris, and thus the last vestiges of the Pittsburgh Republican machine were removed from power. The Democratic margin in the House, in addition, was 154 to 54. Roosevelt won in forty-one of the state's counties and captured every major municipality including the cities of Lancaster, Reading, Altoona, Johnstown, Meadville, Scranton, Wilkes-Barre, Erie, Pittsburgh, and Philadelphia. Lawrence's hometown gave the president every ward and a 190,000-vote margin of victory. Even more impressively, the Republican stronghold of Philadelphia provided a 210,000-vote majority, including all the black and Italian wards, to Roosevelt.[24]

Lawrence, Earle, and Guffey, were ecstatic. Lawrence stopped just short of proclaiming a total victory in the coming legislative session. "With Democratic control of the Senate, the people of Pennsylvania can rest assured that legislation in their interest can no longer be blocked by reactionary influences."[25] The pace with which they swung into action after the election gave a clear indication of events to come. Not content to wait until the traditional January date to open the legislative session, Earle called a special session to begin on 1 December. Within four days the House and Senate passed identical bills granting a substantial increase in relief funds to all eligible persons. The governor signed the bill into law on 5 December. Lawrence's special skills in guiding bills through committee and the legislature would be needed from time to time during the 1937 session, but the task was greatly simplified.

When it reassembled in January, the governor reminded the General Assembly of the opportunity at hand. "Our progress in many directions has been retarded by partisan opposition. We have had to wait until this moment for fulfillment of many solemn pledges. . . . We advance to meet the many fundamental problems left untouched by our predecessors." The governor outlined all the programs not passed by the previous legislature and a score more, including such measures as the breakup of the company town and company store, slum clearance and public housing, reform of the Philadelphia court system, recodification of the state's criminal laws, reform of the prison system, and the enactment of a statewide graduated income tax. The mandate of the Pennsylvania electorate demanded nothing less than enactment of the entire progressive program.[26] For the next five months the most liberal legislation ever presented in Pennsylvania sped through the two houses. Only 6 of 371 bills introduced by the administration failed to reach the governor's desk.

Lawrence maintained the same role he had assumed during the previous session, but his duty was now more one of educator and taskmaster than lobbyist. Each evening, Sunday through Thursday, the Democratic House and Senate caucus met to hear an outline of the next day's agenda. Bills were explained and small differences ironed out. Lawrence nearly always presided, but often the principal cabinet members, labor leaders, or other interested persons were present to speak. Matters on which considerable controversy ensued were postponed until additional support could be guaranteed, but this tactic proved hardly necessary. Bills carrying administration backing were submitted to the House or Senate in bright pink covers so that legislators could make no mistake about their origin. To ensure the completion of the entire legislative package, Lawrence, his new Speaker of the House, Roy Furman, and the Senate majority leader, Harvey Huffman, often kept the General Assembly on a twelve- to fourteen-hour work day. Occasionally it would begin early in the morning and deliberations would stretch well beyond midnight.[27]

The Little New Deal, like the national one from which it evolved, had a major impact on life in Pennsylvania. The exhaustive list of legislation, which ranged from funds for public orphanages to cemetery regulations, covered nearly every aspect of life from the cradle to the grave. Organized labor received its long-awaited reward for its conversion to the Democratic party in a comprehensive series of laws including a "Little Wagner Act" protecting the "right of employees to organize and bargain collectively . . . free from the interference, restraint or coercion of their employers." To administer the law, the

Pennsylvania Labor Relations Board of three members was created. Other features of the labor legislation proposed but not passed in 1935, such as a minimum wage law for women and children, the regulation of homework, and the outlawing of company-paid deputy sheriffs, also moved through the legislature with little opposition. A Workingmen's Compensation Act covering workers suffering occupational diseases as well as job related injuries exceeded even the expectations of organized labor in its liberal provisions. Occasionally, the administration became too liberal for its own legislative body, as was the case when it proposed a thirty-five hour work week as the standard throughout the state. Lawmakers arguing that the bill would drive industry out of the state managed to restore the 1935 goal of forty-four hours, then promptly passed the controversial bill. Other important labor legislation requested by the administration and passed into law included a teacher tenure provision and a railroad "full crew" bill, which required that trains of four or fewer cars carry a minimum of four men and that longer trains carry additional crew. Senator Guffey objected to the latter bill, thus giving a hint of the later split that was to occur between him and Lawrence. The House and Senate, however, responding to pressure from Lawrence, passed the bill, which was later declared unconstitutional by the State Supreme Court.[28]

The reform mood of the administration and the legislature did not stop with organized labor. The liberal-minded group hacked away at privilege in all directions. The ability of public utilities, operating as monoplies granted by the state legislature, to gouge the public through excessive rates was severly curtailed by the establishment of the Public Utilities Commission and new regulatory legislation. Cutthroat competition by large commercial enterprises was made more difficult by the Fair Trades Practices Act prohibiting sales at less than cost prices. The administration adopted in total the report by a commission headed by Herbert F. Goodrich, dean of the School of Law of the University of Pennsylvania, which recommended a sweeping revision of the state's system of public assistance. The 374 local poor boards "were havens of corruption and patronage and their practices often degraded the poor." A ripper bill replaced the boards with the state Department of Public Assistance and provided funding for the next several years. Other administration-backed legislation included four slum clearance and public housing bills, revision of banking laws to control loan sharking and other unfair practices, a milk control act, regulations prohibiting stream pollution, and authorization for an industrial home for boys, a new state tuberculosis hospital, and the start of a two-hundred-mile turnpike from Pittsburgh to Harrisburg, the first of its kind in the nation. To support the comprehensive package, the legislature passed a series of tax measures and called for a constitutional amendment permitting the imposition of a graduated personal income tax, a measure rejected by the voters in the subsequent election.[29]

To be sure, not all legislation was altruistic. The Democratic party, in power for the first time in the century, seized the opportunity to enhance its position. An election law making registration permanent for all voters was publicized as a measure to prevent parties from illegally dominating elections by purchasing registration receipts. In reality, however, it helped the Democrats retain their newly won strength by normalizing the status quo. Similarly, the creation of a legislative commission to reorganize the courts and various municipal functions in Philadelphia was a thinly veiled attempt to puncture Republican control in the City of Brotherly Love. Reapportionment of Senate and House districts, while long overdue, created a number of safe Democratic districts and, more important, threw additional power to the now solidly Democratic cities.[30] All three bills, as well as the dramatic social legislation, Lawrence expected, would serve the party well in its reelection bid in 1938. The ambitions of Charles J. Margiotti, unfortunately, upset his well-laid plans.

The 1937 legislative session produced a contagious atmosphere of liberal thought and innovation for the administration as well as for the Democratic legislators. What began as an attempt to emulate the Roosevelt program on a state level proved on a number of occasions to be more far-reaching than its parent. The generous workingmen's compensation provisions and the harsh penalties imposed on violations of the "Little Wagner Act," to cite two examples, reflect the adventurous attitude of the General Assembly. Liberals and potential reformers, attracted by the possibility of a party victory in 1936, became active in Democratic affairs and offered themselves as candidates for legislative office. The freshman legistators arriving in Harrisburg in January 1937 often proved to be more liberal than their counterparts who preceded them two years earlier. In addition to supporting the administration's program, they offered their own bills, including such innovative measures as the abolition of capital punishment and legalization of pari-mutuel betting.[31] While most of these failed, their scope and breadth demonstrate the extraordinary vision of the members of the 1937 General Assembly.

Lawrence, too, was affected by the atmoshere he helped create. Upon his arrival in Harrisburg in January 1935, he espoused the general policies of the New Deal and the cause of organized labor, but he held no clear social or political philosophy. A pragmatic policy—whatever worked to solve the problem at hand—and the desire to win elections appeared to satisfy him. But his battle to push the Democratic program through the intransigent 1935 Republican-controlled Senate and his four-year role as adviser on virtually every piece of legislation broadened his view. In addition, while acting as educator and counselor to the Democratic legislators, whether in party caucus, at Davenport's, on the floor of the House or Senate, or along the Susquehanna River, he educated himself. The long nights, the arguments and discussions, he later admitted, opened his eyes to a number of problems and issues of which he had been previously unaware.[32] Issues relating to health, education, the environment, highway safety, and the penal code all crossed his desk for the first time. In addition, while he had worked politically with blacks and other minority groups, he had never championed their causes, or those of women and children, as enthusiastically as he did during his tenure as secretary of the Commonwealth. Without abandoning his practical approach to politics and government, he adopted these concerns as his own and worked tirelessly during the Earle administration to implement measures related to them—something he would continue to do for the rest of his public life.

Lawrence was understandably pleased with the accomplishments of the 1937 legislative session. The completed package far exceeded the promises of the 1934 Democratic platform, and though additional programs remained to be implemented, he could with much satisfaction call it "the most constructive, liberal and humane [program] in generations."[33] The entire Little New Deal was now law, and he could look forward to the next election, which might elevate him into the chair he had so successfully controlled from behind, that of governor of the Commonwealth.

▽

The only issue left unresolved from the 1935 legislative session, William McNair, had actually resolved itself before the Democrats returned to Harrisburg in control of both houses in 1937. Events spared Lawrence the embarrassment of attempting a second ripper bill and enabled him to gain control of the city of his youth. The behavior of McNair grew more erratic and bizarre with each passing month. On the one hand, many of his capers may be passed off as the frivolous antics of a publicity-seeking buffoon. On the other, he subjected thousands of people to unnecessary physical and economic hardships. His suspicions of the Lawrence organization were clearly well founded, but they led him down a path that proved, in the short run, disastrous for the people of Pittsburgh and for him.

After the unsuccessful attempt to remove him from office, the mayor embarked on a month-long vacation, leaving the city relatively quiet. Upon his return, however, scarcely a week went by without an unusual McNair event. The press, much to his delight, provided full coverage. During the latter part of October 1935, for example, acting as police magistrate, he attempted a series of one-man raids on North Side gambling houses, which resulted in no arrests. Shortly thereafter, for no apparent reason, he wrote to William Randolph Hearst inviting him to "come to Pittsburgh to live." The publisher did not reply, but McNair released the letter to the city's Hearst newspaper, the *Pittsburgh Sun Telegraph,* which displayed it prominently. On 15 November he began a week-long stint as master of ceremonies and sometime performer at the Alvin Theater. He apparently enjoyed himself. His entry into the theatrical world touched off a series of performances on the Rudy Vallee show, the Major Bowes Amateur Hour, and his own amateur show, at which all city employees were expected to perform. He used each occasion to play his fiddle, tell jokes, expound on the benefits of the single tax, and attack the Earle administration. He capped his activities on 11 January 1936 by declaring vacant all but one of the nine city council seats because members failed to attend an organization meeting he called. Nothing came of the declaration, but the mayor, once again, received front-page coverage.

When he couldn't generate press interest in his activities, he contributed directly to newspapers. At one point he drew serial cartoons for the *Pittsburgh Sun Telegraph* poking fun at himself and his political opponents. One prophetic cartoon raised the question, "What is a mayor?" The answer given by the character drawn to resemble McNair was "A mayor is a person who is always firing someone." On another occasion he submitted to the same paper an editorial about himself that, he complained, the paper had neglected to write. The press played into his hands by dutifully printing it.[34]

None of these activities, while unusual for a city mayor, was in itself detrimental to the continuing operation of the city. Certainly New York Mayors Jimmy Walker and Fiorello H. La Guardia, among others, were guilty of eccentric behavior from time to time. Of more serious consequence were McNair's continued tampering with the office of the director of public safety and his refusal to release funds from the WPA and other federal agencies to provide jobs and assistance to the city indigent. McNair did not oppose federal assistance on principle but took his vehement stand "against projects controlled by David Lawrence and Edward Jones," appointed state WPA director in 1936. McNair "despaired in knowing that the hostile Democratic organization would control relief and attempt to use it for political purposes." He publicized his objection to the nation in an article he authored for the *Saturday Evening Post.* Attacking the president, Lawrence, and Eddie Jones, he characterized the WPA as a political octopus. "In the great state of Pennsylvania, in its capital at Harrisburg sits the Works Progress Administrator. His job depends on his political allegiance. This man appoints in every county in the state a local Works Progress administrator whose job depends on his party allegiance. Under this man is an army of staff workers selected and appointed by the party political bosses, whose jobs depend upon their political allegiance."[35] All available evidence indicates that McNair described the operation of the WPA in Pennsylvania accurately. Unfortunately, the poor of Pittsburgh were caught in the political cross fire.

In late 1935, McNair withheld all federal assistance for four months until the governor threatened to cut off all state relief funds to Pittsburgh. The mayor's action delayed twenty-five WPA projects and the allocation of $40,000 appropriated by the city council for shoes and clothing for needy schoolchildren. The governor's threat gave only temporary relief from McNair's obstructionist tactics. On another occasion he rushed off to an Atlantic City vacation to avoid opening bids for notes issued to fund the city's share of the WPA expenditure. The action blocked allocation of $25 million in project funds. On 19 February he refused to sign the appropriate documents to release relief funds for medical care to more than thirty-one thousand individuals in the city. He again eventually relented, but he precipitated one funding crisis after another during the first nine months of 1936.[36]

The fiasco of the McNair administration exploded on 1 October 1936, while Lawrence was introducing President Roosevelt, in the city to deliver a major campaign address, to Democratic candidates and party benefactors. McNair fired the only representative of the Democratic organization in the city administration, the treasurer, Jimmy Kirk.

It is perhaps impossible to explain the firing. Although Kirk was Lawrence's closest political associate, he and McNair had maintained a cordial relationship. Indeed, Kirk was the only row officer to retain his position during the mayor's entire term of office. The publicity surrounding the visit of Roosevelt, of course, may have touched off the incident. The man with whom he had warred constantly in the previous two years was being hailed by the press as a master politician, the "friend of the President." McNair, on the other hand, had not been invited to a reception for the President or to speak at the Forbes Field rally. By firing Lawrence's closest aide on the very day of Lawrence's triumph, the mayor perhaps wished to embarrass the Democratic chairman, to demonstrate his own power to his political enemy.

Of course, McNair's past behavior gave ample evidence that he was an inveterate publicity seeker. Lawrence and the president had dominated the headlines for nearly a week, and it may be that the mayor was simply attempting to reestablish his own position as the premier newsmaker in his own city. Finally, one must at least consider the possibility that McNair merely felt it was time to fire another public official, and Kirk, who had escaped his previous firings, was the logical choice. Whatever the motivation, the action threw the city into crisis. The city council refused to confirm McNair's designated replacement, and, without a treasurer to sign checks, the city government ground to a halt. The matter dragged on for six days until, in a pique, McNair submitted a one-line letter of resignation to the council, which immediately accepted it. When he attempted to withdraw his resignation a few days later, he was informed by council that it was too late; Cornelius Scully, the recently elected council president and an organization man, had already been designated as acting mayor.

The long turmoil had ended, and in Lawrence's mind, the city of Pittsburgh had been returned to its rightful leaders, the Democratic organization. He could hardly contain his jubilation when he wired Roosevelt on the day of McNair's resignation: "Some more Roosevelt luck, Mayor McNair resigned and Cornelius Scully sworn in to fill vacancy by council."[37]

Thus, on the heels of the successful and popular legislative session of 1937, the installation of a statewide patronage system by Eddie Jones, and the return of the city of Pittsburgh to party control, the Democrats reasonably expected to extend their power in 1938. Earle would move to Washington to replace Republican Senator Davis, a step that would place him in an ideal position for the run for the presidency in 1940. In addition, a Democratic candidate would certainly retain control of the governor's mansion; the only unanswered question was the identity of that candidate.

1938–1940
The Empire Crumbles

State chairman Lawrence could look back with much satisfaction as the 1937 legislative session closed. Under his direction the Democratic administration passed a sweeping program of economic and social reform. Abuses of industrial and corporate wealth had been curbed. Organized labor received its long-sought recognition and governmental protection, and an effective attack on the poverty of the Depression had begun. The state, furthermore, assumed greater responsibility in health care, education, citizen protection, and highway safety. The citizens of Pennsylvania would surely reward the party's diligence and foresight in the upcoming elections.

The party organization appeared united and ready to wage a textbook campaign. Lawrence successfully utilized the WPA program and various state public works programs to put thousands of loyal Democrats, and some "deserving Republicans," to work. They could certainly be counted upon to show their gratitude by working in the campaign and turning out the vote for the administration slate in the fall 1938 election. In January, Lawrence predicted a quiet primary and a landslide Democratic victory in the general election.[1] It was probably the worst prediction of his political career.

Several issues emerged during the first four months of 1938 to dampen Lawrence's optimism. First, the party's adoption of organized labor, and its acceptance of Thomas Kennedy, secretary-treasurer of the United Mine Workers, as lieutenant governor in 1934, had produced immediate election results, but it also introduced a critical divisive element. The Democratic party's unexpected entanglement in the political ambitions of John L. Lewis and in the power struggle between the American Federation of Labor (AFL) and the Congress of Industrial Organizations (CIO) were destined to create major election-year difficulties. Second, it quickly became clear that the party's new strength in Pennsylvania made its endorsement and subsequent nomination a desirable commodity. Liberal reformers saw it as a realistic vehicle for a modified social order and rushed to join. The 1937 legislative session merely whetted their appetite for what they considered progressive change. Aspiring, self-serving candidates, on the other hand, viewed the party as an outlet for their ambition and an opportunity to further their own careers. The organization's control of the enormous patronage machinery and the opportunity to benefit from the contracts issued by the newly created General State Authority made governmental service additionally attractive. Both these factors guaranteed a surplus of potential candidates interested in economic entitlements or power brokering. The reform-minded and the opportunists joined the career politicians to form a long line of candidates for virtually every contested office. A struggle for control, while not inevitable, became a definite possibility.

Pennsylvania's constitution prohibited Governor George Earle from succeeding himself, and all factions generally agreed that he deserved the opportunity to run against incumbent Republican James Davis for the U.S. Senate. Earle had received considerable publicity as a potential presidential candidate for 1940 and, with experience as a state leader, might use the senatorship as a springboard to the White House.

With quick agreement on Earle's candidacy, speculation turned to the governorship. Fulfillment of the 1934 pledge by David Lawrence and U.S. Senator Guffey to endorse Warren Van Dyke as Earle's replacement might have produced the desired harmony. Unfortunately, Van Dyke suffered a stroke and lay critically ill in a hospital. He died before the winter ended.

Lieutenant Governor Thomas Kennedy emerged as one substitute. He had carried the labor standard in the 1934 election and had the endorsement of John L. Lewis, president of the CIO, who had made it quite clear that his organization was interested in securing governorships in key industrial states.[2] The results of recent strikes in other states had convinced him that successful labor action required supportive governors.[3] Lewis "nominated" Kennedy nearly a year early, in the summer of 1937, intimating that he supported him for governor of Pennsylvania. The heavy labor support for the Guffey-Earle ticket in 1934 and a $40,000 loan to help the Democrats win control of the State Senate in 1936 entitled him to select the next candidate. But the Democratic State Committee resisted, and Lewis warned that he might walk out on the party organization—either supporting Kennedy as an independent or turning to the Republican candidate, Pinchot—if it did not yield to his demand.[4] But Lewis and the CIO were not the only labor powers that the party had to contend with. William Green, president of the AFL, rejected Kennedy and demanded a voice equal to that of Lewis in the Democratic slate-making.[5] The peaceful primary that Lawrence predicted appeared more remote each day.

A second logical successor to Governor Earle was Lawrence himself. He had proved his ability to administer the state govenment during the past four years and had generated considerable recognition, if not popularity. An Earle-Lawrence ticket gave the east-west balance requisite for political victory in Pennsylvania. In addition, Lawrence already had control of the party apparatus, as well as support from prominent Democrats in Pittsburgh and Philadelphia. An endorsement by the Democratic State Committee was assured should he request it. In addition, a "Lawrence for governor" boom, which developed early in the year, could not have grown so rapidly without his acquiescence. Thus it seems clear that Lawrence was quietly engineering his own nomination.

A third possible gubernatorial candidate was Guffey, though his intentions were not immediately obvious—at first he vacillated in his support between Kennedy and Lawrence. But Guffey had seen what a governorship had done for Franklin Roosevelt, and he made known his willingness to be selected as a compromise candidate. When this did not happen, he made the offer explicitly, but the party leadership showed no interest.[6]

Just one week before the Democratic State Committee meeting to endorse a slate, Lewis played his trump card in the form of an ultimatum to George Earle. The union leader would provide CIO support for Earle's senatorial candidacy "only on the condition that he remain strictly neutral in the gubernatorial campaign."[7] The ultimatum wrecked Lawrence's chances for a united campaign. Without the support of both Earle and Guffey, Lawrence could not expect a unanimous endorsement, and a primary fight between him and Kennedy seemed certain. The party needed a quick solution that would remove both from the scene and produce a new compromise candidate. Lawrence, the master politician, supplied both answers.

Early in the year, Lawrence had conducted a private poll of party leaders throughout the state. Most felt his religion to be detrimental to his chances of winning the election.[8] Lawrence's desire to become governor initially overshadowed his religious fears and he withheld the results of the poll until the day of Lewis's ultimatum. Speaking to the party's executive committee, Lawrence withdrew from contention. The move, while appearing to be prudent, placed a new roadblock in front of the CIO choice. The religious issue affected not only Lawrence, but Thomas Kennedy, who was also Catholic.

At the party's executive committee meeting in Harrisburg on 18 February Lawrence named his new choice, Charles Alvin Jones, Allegheny County solicitor. Actually Jones's name had surfaced several days earlier as a compromise candidate, and he already had the support of Lawrence, McCloskey, and Kelly. He was, however, hardly known, had only limited legal experience, and almost none as an administrator. Yet he carried none of the liabilities of Lawrence or Kennedy. He was sympathetic to both labor and the New Deal, but his activities as solicitor kept him free of the labor or organization stamp. Furthermore, he was a Protestant who had supported Al Smith in two presidential campaigns.

Lawrence's selection of Jones showed a weakness that was obvious throughout his political career: an inability to identify political candidates who could both win an election and lead in a position of authority. McNair, Earle, Jones, and even Lawrence's choice to replace McNair, Cornelius Scully, had almost no experience in government, and none became a strong leader. Critics, of course, charged that Lawrence selected docile puppets who would do his bidding while in office, and in Earle's case the accusation rings true. As a politician, however, he preferred to engineer elections and manage the activities of the organization rather than meddle in the affairs of government. "He became interested in the affairs of state govenment when it became clear that Earle couldn't do the job," a state official close to the Earle administration noted.[9] Lawrence's criteria for a candidate for elective office, unfortunately, often ran counter to those necessary for strong leadership. He sought someone who could create or maintain party harmony and win elections. They were often popular, unassuming, and noncontroversial. They were also usually unknown and exhibited no particular strengths that would qualify them for leadership.

Jones, perhaps the least likely of all the Lawrence choices for public office, nevertheless quickly gained the support of the committee. Guffey, the only member strongly opposed to Jones, startled everyone by jumping from his chair and declaring, "I am a candidate for Governor come hell or high water." After a heated exchange with Lawrence, Guffey stormed out under a shower of boos and catcalls, only to return a short time later, once he realized that he needed the party more than it needed him. "Gentlemen, I have reconsidered," he announced, swallowing a large bite of crow before the assembled group. "I am not going to be a candidate. . . . I shall give my wholehearted support to the slate endorsed at this conference."[10] Lawrence, it appeared, had won total victory, but the triumph would not last.

At the slating meeting on 25 February, the Democratic State Committee endorsed Earle and Jones as its candidates. Guffey repeated his earlier pledge of support and held out the olive branch to Lawrence. "A good deal has been said in the newspapers about a quarrel between Davy Lawrence and myself. . . . If there ever is a separation between us, it will take place only at the grave. . . . You will find Joe Guffey fighting in the front line trenches after the convention and after the primary."[11] Guffey, true to his word, fought on the front line during the primary—but he neglected to tell the committee in which direction his guns would be aimed.

Kennedy informed the press on 9 March that he too was a candidate for the Democratic nomination. Guffey, ignoring his "graveside pledge," announced his support of Kennedy on 11 March. The depth of Guffey's bitterness toward Lawrence, however, did not become clear until 13 April, when, in a speech at the Philadelphia Academy of Music, he hinted that serious corruption existed in the Earle administration. "Here is something for you folks to think about," Guffey told a shocked Democratic audience. "A good many years ago we had the infamous Capitol graft scandal. Five suicides and nine jail sentences resulted from that mess. What the outcome of the present [gravel] contract situation will be I don't know. But don't forget the oldtime Capitol graft scandal."[12] The simple statement that Guffey inserted into his prepared speech that evening, and he later characterized as mere politics, touched off a chain of events that nearly destroyed the career of David Lawrence.

The political world that Lawrence and his estranged colleague, Joseph Guffey, had so carefully built was falling apart, and the party chairman was deeply troubled. The primary battle he had struggled so desperately to avoid promised to be brutal. The long-term remedy, however, seemed obvious. "We need a clear cut victory in the primary," Lawrence told a gathering of party regulars in Harrisburg. "Those who have temporarily left us will return in a wink when the May 17 returns come in. . . . I urge you and the workers in your district to get out and work as if the future of the party depended on it." While Lawrence's statement was similar to those he delivered to party workers throughout his career, in this case the declaration rang true, and his efforts for the remainder of the primary campaign reflected his concern. "He traveled everywhere," Wilkes-Barre Democrat James Law recalled. "He wouldn't neglect anything. . . . In fact I would often wonder how he could do it all and take care of his family." As in nearly every crisis he faced, he considered hard work, doubling or tripling one's efforts, to be the most effective remedy.[13]

▽

Attorney General Charles Margiotti compounded the already difficult situation by initiating a campaign of his own for the Democratic nomination for governor. Calling for "fair play for industry," he stumped the state criticizing the Democratic organization that had welcomed him in 1934. "I am submitting my candidacy directly to the people and not to the political bosses," Margiotti announced in a statewide radio address, ignoring the fact that his own state cabinet position had depended upon the intervention of "boss" Lawrence. "The people of Pennsylvania are through with boss rule regardless of party. . . . Just as surely as night follows day so do corruption and graft follow the concentration of power in the hands of political bosses. Political bosses must keep hands off primaries."[14] Margiotti's reference to bosses was aimed directly at Lawrence, who had earlier vetoed the attorney general's suggestion that he receive the party endorsement for the chief executive's office.

Party officials, with their efforts riveted on the Lawrence-Kennedy battle, initially paid about as much attention to Margiotti's candidacy as they did to another maverick whose hat was also in the race, William N. McNair. Margiotti was, after all, save for the past four years, a lifelong Republican and unlikely to gain much support in the upcoming primary. In mid April, however, the attorney general's interest was piqued by Guffey's Philadelphia Academy of Music speech. "As the chief law officer," Margiotti telegraphed Guffey, "I call upon you to submit whatever information you have to me. If warranted, I will promptly institute criminal prosecution against those involved no matter who they may be."[15] Guffey never responded and later characterized his charge as "merely a political speech." The attorney general, however, grabbed the headlines, as well as the attention of the Democratic hierarchy, with a series of accusations of illegal activities in office, which eventually overshadowed the party-CIO split and hounded Lawrence for the next three years.

Margiotti began his barrage with a series of relatively harmless charges against Matthew McCloskey and John Kelly that induced a collective yawn in the press. Several days later, on 19 April, Margiotti accused the governor of accepting kickbacks, an allegation that Earle quickly disproved.[16] The governor received strong support from most of the state's major newspapers, which correctly accused Margiotti of staging a fishing expedition to gain publicity.

Margiotti's third attempt, however, produced the blockbuster reaction he hoped for. Speaking on 26 April to an audience of approximately a thousand at the Paramount Theater in New Kensington, he attacked Lawrence and McCloskey. "Every time George H. Earle turned his back," he charged in a rather accurate characterization of the operation of the Earle administration,

> David L. Lawrence sat in the governor's chair and ruled Pennsylvania with an iron hand. Much of this time, Satchel Man McCloskey stood at his side. Dictator Lawrence sat in that chair more minutes, more hours, more days, and more months than the Governor himself. . . . He became the chief mogul of the spoils system. . . . He surveyed his domain. He divided it into two parts. He gave the principality of Philadelphia to McCloskey. The balance of the empire, including the province of Allegheny, he retained for himself.
>
> During all legislative sessions, Lawrence and McCloskey dictated the course of legislation. . . . Night and day, at every session, they could be seen hurrying and scurrying about the legislative halls issuing their mandates and forcing their will. . . .
>
> They discovered that the state entered into many contracts for materials and equipment. . . . They discovered the liquor control board, with its vast purchases of liquor . . . was a fertile field, because there is no law requiring that liquor be purchased from the lowest bidder. They discovered that the state was required to rent property. They discovered the rich insurance business and bonding business of the state. . . . These political parasites have their finger in every political pie, their thumb in every political plum. They are a menace to Pennsylvania, a serious threat to Democracy.[17]

Margiotti's shrill accusations might have been dismissed as more charges by a disgruntled office seeker, except that for the first time he cited specific illegal activities. He charged that the two men ordered architects on the General State Authority's $65 million building program to "kickback one third of their six percent commission—one million, two hundred thousand dollars." He also raised a charge similar to the one against Lawrence in 1931. "Lawrence and his insurance associates made $750,000 a year selling insurance and surety bonds to state contractors."[18]

The next evening in a statewide radio address delivered at the Butler County Courthouse, he repeated his charges that Lawrence accepted a $20,000 bribe in return for enactment of a 1935 beer control law favorable to the brewing interests and maced state and WPA employees. Lawrence initially characterized the charges as too ridiculous to talk about, but he soon realized they would occupy a great deal of his time.

Governor Earle called Margiotti to his office the next day to defend his charges before several officials and a number of journalists. The stormy meeting lasted nearly an hour, but Margiotti refused to provide any evidence despite the governor's argument that the supposed offenders could not be arrested without it. Instead, Margiotti insisted that he intended to request a Dauphin County grand jury investigation of all charges. "If you have no confidence in me," he told the governor, "then fire me." Earle, falling into the trap, did just that.[19]

Earle's action constituted the first of several serious blunders he would commit in the next few months. Admittedly, the grand jury investigation Margiotti called for would have undoubtedly lasted beyond the spring primary and placed a cloud of suspicion over the entire administration. But the abrupt dismissal, while not preventing the investigation, prompted immediate charges of a cover-up.

Margiotti wasted no time in carrying out his threat. Twenty-four hours after his firing, he huddled with Carl B. Shelley, Dauphin County district attorney, to present his case. He added two charges. First, he alleged that the prices of highway equipment were increased to permit kickbacks of thousands of dollars by contractors. Second, he charged that Governor Earle had attempted to buy him off by offering him a U.S. Senate seat. Republican Senator Davis had allegedly agreed to accept a bribe in return for his resignation and the governor would then appoint Margiotti to serve the remainder of the term. Both Earle and Davis denied the charge and eventually it was dropped.[20] The Republican Dauphin County Court issued the order to begin the investigation immediately and gave the grand jury broad powers to probe all potentially illegal activities in the Earle era. The order justified the administration's worst fears of a fishing expedition.

A furious Lawrence responded to the charges with a few brief comments directed at the state's voters. "I want to warn you to beware of the smear artists. Don't be misled by these professional mud slingers, don't be led astray by the false hysteria they are creating, and don't be fooled by the false issues they are endeavoring to raise."[21] Otherwise, as was customary with him in times of adversity, he maintained a public silence on the grand jury investigation, which was scheduled to begin one week before the spring primaries. He attempted to conduct a normal campaign, speaking across the state on behalf of his major candidates, Earle and Jones.

Governor Earle, however, unable to maintain the same composure, announced on 3 May that his new attorney general, Guy K. Bard, would conduct the state's own investigation. The press naturally pointed out that the move would place the investigation in the hands of the accused. The governor then aggravated the situation. On 10 May, just eight days before the primary, he attempted to block the grand jury hearings. Bard argued before the State Supreme Court that the judiciary did not have the constitutional right to investigate the governor's office or the affairs of his cabinet members. The court rejected the argument, but not until after the primary. Thus the Democratic organization had to complete the primary campaign under suspicion not only of serious illegal activities but also of an attempted cover-up.

The cloud that now hung over the organization cut into the expected Earle-Jones vote in the May primary but did not produce the "housecleaning" predicted by Margiotti. Governor Earle easily defeated the CIO-Guffey choice for the Senate nomination, Mayor S. Davis Wilson of Philadelphia, but the victory was expected. The real contest centered on the governor's chair. In that race, Lawrence's candidate, Jones, defeated Thomas Kennedy by approximately 100,000 votes, although the Kennedy-Margiotti candidacies captured 55 percent of the votes. The results demonstrated the strength of the organization, now headed by Lawrence alone, but they also indicated the gravity of the division in the party. Unless it could be repaired, the Democratic party, which began the year with such high hopes, faced defeat in November. "It is no exaggeration," a *Nation* correspondent wrote, "to say that the Democratic party in this primary has sowed the seeds of its own destruction in November." Lawrence withstood the attempted coup by Lewis and Guffey, but the victory could prove to be a Pyrrhic one.[22]

First, it was not clear what price Guffey and Lewis would try to extract in return for the 500,000 votes cast for Kennedy or whether the CIO forces would decide to conduct an independent election campaign. Lewis's post primary statement pointed out the narrowness of the Jones victory and gave a hint that he would be difficult to deal with.[23]

Adding to the organization's difficulties, one could not predict how much damage the Margiotti charges had done, but it appeared that the corruption issue, now out in the open, would not disappear before December. The Republicans would exploit it even if the Supreme Court upheld the governor's request to dismiss the grand jury. From Lawrence's perspective no attempt at reconciliation would be made with Margiotti. He would not be welcomed back into the party under any circumstance.

Lawrence, anxious to resolve the other differences which divided the party, began attempts at reconciliation with Kennedy, Lewis, and Guffey immediately after the primary. His efforts eventually succeeded and by September each dissident had announced that he would support the organization ticket.

Ironically, on the same day that Lawrence and Guffey announced the resolution of their differences, Dauphin County District Attorney Carl Shelley presented a new and ultimately more serious one. Responding to a request by the Pennsylvania Supreme Court for more detailed information, the district attorney presented specific charges —macing, demanding kickbacks from individuals and contributions to the party from contractors, and selling legislation—against Earle, Lawrence, four other cabinet members, and several other high ranking officers.[24]

Governor Earle, shaken by the charges and their almost certain detrimental effect on his fall election hopes and White House dreams, reacted by threatening to supersede (replace) the Dauphin County district attorney by having his own state attorney general assume command of the case. Lawrence strongly opposed the idea. The party had already been hurt by charges of attempting a cover-up, and the governor's proposed action would add fuel to the now open fire. He quickly called a meeting of the major figures named in the Shelley presentment to attempt to dissuade Earle and plan further strategy. The governor was eventually persuaded that an aggressive public defense was their best alternative, and he reluctantly gave way, but he retained the right to replace Shelley later if he becamed convinced it was in the group's best interests. Earle, all then agreed, should provide the public response to the charges. The rest, except for denying any wrongdoing when specifically asked, would refrain from any further comment.[25]

Two days later, Governor Earle delivered the official statement via a statewide radio hookup. He began by attacking the proposed grand jury investigation as "a politically inspired inquisition to be conducted by henchmen of the Republican State Committee, before a Republican dominated jury, answerable to a hostile Republican Court, on evidence gathered by a research man for the Republican machine." There was much truth in the charge. Why, Earle asked, had the district attorney and the Republican court ignored a sitting grand jury, which contained seven Democrats, in favor of the nearly all-Republican body to convene in September? Earle then repeated a demand made earlier to Charles Margiotti. "If the District Attorney of Dauphin County has sufficient evidence to warrant any of the charges . . . it is his sworn duty to arrest those whom he accuses. If anyone in my administration is dishonest, he should be promptly arrested, charged, and punished if convicted." He prophesied accurately that "the Republican plotters propose to drag out this Grand Jury inquiry until just before the November election, obtain indictments, and then postpone the trials, . . . until after the election." He closed by repeating his warning that the administration could not permit one branch of government, the judiciary, to act as overlord of another, the executive. The implied safeguard, although he stopped short of naming it, was the executive's right to supersede the district attorney.[26] In spite of the urgings of Lawrence and others, he obviously had not rejected that course of action permanently.

One week later, in fact, the governor, now acting on his own, instructed Attorney General Bard to begin proceedings to supersede District Attorney Shelley in the case. The plea quickly reached the State Supreme Court, which rejected Earle's bid.

The announcement prompted a bizarre reaction on the part of the governor. He contacted Bard and requested legal information on the imposition of martial law. Bard immediately phoned Lawrence, and the two rushed to the governor's office to halt any rash action. When they arrived, they found him huddled with the commander of the state National Guard, General E. A. Shannon. The governor had made up his mind; he would "put a stop to this persecution." Lawrence and Earle, for the first time, exchanged harsh words before Earle finally agreed to forgo imposing martial law, but he would authorize a special session of the state legislature to take over the investigation. Lawrence was opposed to this idea also, and he and Bard suggested that instead all principals cooperate with the grand jury investigation while hitting back at Margiotti with a libel suit. When it became clear, however, that the governor meant to have either martial law or a legislative investigation, Lawrence reluctantly agreed to the latter.[27]

On 25 July, in an evening speech to a specially convened General Assembly and over statewide radio, Earle lashed out at the administration's accusers. The partisan audience frequently interrupted the address with wild cheering and applause. Charging the judiciary with violating the constitutional separation of powers, the governor pledged to resist "the establishment of a judicial dictatorship" and ordered that the legislature investigate the charges against his administration. In addition, he accused Margiotti, Shelley, and the state Republican leadership of slander and libel, "from the safe concealment of Judicial protection," in order to divert public attention from the achievements of the Democratic administration and legislature. The governor concluded his address by calling for the prohibition of the grand jury session scheduled to begin on 8 August.[28]

The leadership of the House, caught up in the supposed urgency of the crisis, introduced a series of measures designed to kill the grand jury investigation and force disclosure of all evidence held by Shelley to a House investigating commission, to be established. The proposals were submitted to the House Committee on State Government within minutes of the conclusion of Earle's address and given a first reading on the floor of the House the next morning. Without benefit of public hearings, five bills designed to accomplish the administration's goal were rushed through the House and Senate and placed on the governor's desk in three days, the minimum amount of time permitted by state law.

The governor immediately signed the bills empowering the Speaker of the House, Roy E. Furman, a Democrat, to name a seven-member board—five Democrats and two Republicans—to investigate the charges originally made by Charles Margiotti. The Democratic floor leader, Herbert Cohen, served as the chairman.[29] The panel convened on 3 August, five days before the scheduled start of the competing grand jury hearings. In its first action it issued a subpoena ordering District Attorney Shelley to present to the House all the evidence in his possession regarding the corruption charges.

The worst fears of Lawrence and Bard were realized when Judge Schaeffer, the presiding judge, announced that the Dauphin County grand jury would convene on 8 August regardless of the recent legislative action. He also said that he had impounded all evidence collected for the grand jury to prevent its disclosure before the House investigating commission. Obeying the judge's orders, Shelley refused to appear. Five days later, Judge Schaeffer issued an additional ruling declaring the hurriedly passed legislation unconstitutional.

The battle continued through the summer and into the fall. The State Supreme Court joined in by issuing temporary injunctions against both investigations until it could rule on the Schaeffer constitutional decisions. On 7 September the high court ruled that the legislature could begin its investigation and ordered Shelley to present his evidence to the panel. The district attorney complied but, in an attempt to sabotage the commission, insisted on presenting every piece of evidence, a full truckload. His six-day testimony reiterated the charges presented earlier and revealed the names of more than sixty persons whom he had interviewed and who had or "might have" evidence to substantiate the charges. However, he failed to produce any evidence implicating any of those named and admitted that he had no firsthand knowledge of administration involvement in criminal activities. Margiotti, who followed Shelley, testified intermittently for nearly a month. He repeated his charges and further cited Lawrence as "principal" in an operation permitting the purchase of eight hundred tons of substandard gravel from the Pioneer Materials Company in return for substantial political contributions.

The investigation dragged on for nearly three months, hearing 119 witnesses and producing 8,165 pages of testimony.[30] The commission, which Earle hoped would exonerate the accused, failed to complete its deliberations until after the fall election, further damaging Democratic hopes for victory. It committed its most serious blunder when it failed to call any of the fourteen accused state officials, all of whom publicly denied any wrongdoing, to testify prior to the election. In any case, unsympathetic newspapers and the Republican leadership and candidates James Davis (U.S. Senate) and Arthur James (governor) denounced the investigation as a whitewash. One minority member of the panel accused the Democrats of "cream puff tactics," while the *Pittsburgh Press,* formerly sympathetic to the Earle administration, attacked the hearings and published each week a list of those state senators and representatives who had supported the investigation legislation. Voters were urged to make known their dissatisfaction at the November general election.

The State Supreme Court added to the Democratic difficulties when, one month before general election, it permitted the Dauphin County grand jury to proceed with its investigation. Judge Schaeffer did nothing to relieve the Democratic anxiety by announcing that he would begin immediately after the election. Thus the Democratic party entered the last month of the campaign under investigation by two boards of inquiry.

The Republican candidates, as one might expect, attacked the legislative record of the administration, charging that the Little New Deal, rife with waste and favor rendering, had actually hurt the average voter by driving industry out of the state. More effectively, they relentlessly attacked the opposition as the party of "corruption, fraud, influence peddlers, and kickbacks." At every opportunity, Republican candidates raised the issue of an administrative whitewash and attacked as a cover-up the Democratic attempts to prevent the Shelley investigation.[31]

In early October, Lawrence who had begun to fear the worst, summoned the Democratic county chairmen from all over the state to Harrisburg to assess the extent of the damage. They reinforced his concern. While Democratic voter registration had increased by substantial proportions since the 1936 presidential election, recruitment of new voters had almost stopped since Margiotti first made his charges. Between 1936 and November 1937, for example, the party reduced the Republican majority in the state by more than 400,000. The comparable figure for the 1937–38 period was less than 25,000. The chairmen also reported substantial unrest and criticism of the administration's handling of the unresolved investigations. Lawrence urged the chairmen to increase their efforts but privately prepared for disaster. For the first time ever, he abandoned the campaign trail three weeks before the election, preferring to remain in Harrisburg to monitor the dissolution of his empire from its center.[32]

On 8 November the expected voter revolt occurred. Braving an early winter storm that affected most of the state, the Pennsylvania electorate produced a near-record turnout—nearly two-thirds of the registered voters. The outpouring rejected Democratic candidates Earle and Jones by 400,000 and 300,000 votes respectively. In addition, the Republican party regained control of the State House and barely missed winning a majority in the State Senate when they gained eighteen of the twenty-six contested seats; Democratic holdovers enabled the party to maintain a majority of one.

The defeat of the two Democratic candidates was statewide; neither man won more than six of the sixty-seven counties. The Lawrence organization managed to deliver both Pittsburgh and Allegheny County to Jones, but the margin of victory in each case was slim. Earle claimed a fifteen-thousand-vote edge in Pittsburgh but lost Allegheny County by one hundred votes. Both candidates lost by narrow margins in Philadelphia County. Small cities, townships, and boroughs that had returned a majority for the Democrats in 1934 fell back into the Republican camp. Rural Pennsylvania, which had remained Republican in 1934 and 1936, continued its traditional pattern.[33]

An analysis of the election returns indicates that while the Republican majorities were not overwhelming, in nearly every district the Republicans received a larger proportion of their total registered vote than did the Democrats. In short, Republicans turned out in record numbers to support their ticket while Democrats, torn by the internal feuding, failed to show up at the polls or supported the

James-Davis ticket. Less than 60 percent of the registered Democrats voted.[34] Centers of organized labor, such as Pittsburgh, Erie, New Castle, Johnstown, Williamsport, Wilkes-Barre, Scranton, and Philadelphia, all produced disappointing Democratic support. The split in the party was healed apparently only on the surface. Many working-class Democrats, denied a labor candidate by the primary, refused to vote.

The graft and corruption charges that hung over the Democratic party throughout the campaign clearly contributed to its defeat. It is difficult to determine what proportion of the voters turned out to register their dissatisfaction against an allegedly corrupt administration, but the number appears to be considerable. James and Davis ran lackluster campaigns, and, while James had a reputation as an excellent orator, neither had the appeal of Governor Earle. They also lacked the organizational or patronage advantages of the Democratic party. Yet record numbers of registered Republicans, in spite of bad weather, went to the polls. Some, of course, may have been disenchanted with the imposition of the Little New Deal and the pro-Roosevelt administration. But the campaign nearly ignored these issues and focused on the difficulties of key members of the administration and the attempts by the governor to obstruct the investigation. The citizens had indeed thrown the rascals out.

A postelection analysis by James A. Farley, an aide to Roosevelt, underscored the impact of the scandal on the voters. Shortly after the election, Farley wrote to each of the state's Democratic county chairmen and the leading figures in the party asking for reasons for the defeat. They gave a variety of answers, but nearly all divided the primary blame between Margiotti and Earle. Margiotti gleefully emphasized the impact of the scandal in the postelection comment, "The people of Pennsylvania have spoken with unmistakable vigor that they will not stand for crime and corruption. The election results are a drastic warning to political leaders that we still live in a Democracy where no individual or group of individuals can rise above the welfare of the people."[35]

Lawrence, as was his custom, joined Pittsburgh Democrats in the city headquarters to await the returns. "As the bad news began to come in," one party worker recalled, "people began to file out one by one. I had never seen Dave so discouraged." Lawrence issued a terse comment to the press. "The Republicans have won a victory. Until I have a chance to analyze the returns, I have nothing further to say."[36] He never issued a follow-up comment.

The debacle of the 1938 election ended all talk of an "Earle for president" move in 1940, terminated the most liberal period in the history of state government after two short years, and seriously tarnished Joseph Guffey's reputation as co-leader of the state Democratic organization. Lawrence did not escape unscathed. His inability to reach a compromise with the Lewis-Kennedy forces and his choice of the ill-prepared and unknown Charles Alvin Jones contributed to the defeat. His dispute with Guffey, furthermore, splintered the party and ensured more strife in the immediate future. In addition, Lawrence had gained a lifelong enemy, Charles Margiotti, who would continue to seek vengeance for the next two decades.

Lawrence barely had time to begin to consider how to resurrect his shattered party when the Earle investigative session resumed its deliberations. The commission, now in lame duck session, moved swiftly to conclude its business by its deadline, 30 November. It called the fourteen officials, one by one, to testify, and each denied all charges and declared his innocence. The testimony proved to be too little, too late.

Lawrence, who was named in nearly all the charges, gave the most extensive testimony. Under sharp cross-examination by the two Republican members, David Perry and Elwood Turner, he denied any knowledge of kickbacks from architects or contractors, of bribes accepted in return for favorable legislation, or of macing of party workers or government officials. On the last of these charges, he explained that each county chairman was assessed a certain amount, based on patronage provided to the county, and local party officials determined how they would raise the funds. It was the method he had used successfully in Pittsburgh and Allegheny County. Furthermore "The specific orders of the Governor and myself, as State Chairman, were that no employees should be coerced or that no employee should be dismissed at any time because they did not contribute to the state fund. That order was given by myself." Of the kickback allegations, he testified that it had indeed been suggested that a syndicate be formed of architects who supported the administration and who would receive General State Authority contracts—by none other than Margiotti. Lawrence had rejected the idea. He concluded his testimony with a blanket denial. "I want to put on the record, a denial of any wrongdoing or that I know of any in the Administration or in connection with me whatsoever. I know that in the time since I came here in 1935, I honestly and conscientiously have served the State of Pennsylvania."[37]

The commission met the following day to hear the governor's testimony and adjourned to prepare its report. Seven days later the

Democratic majority filed its one-hundred-page report finding "no evidence which tends to substantiate the charges it has been appointed to investigate." The report, not surprisingly, was highly critical of Margiotti, accusing him of depending "upon rumor, hearsay and gossip in the proof of many of the charges." The majority further found "gross improprieties" in many of Margiotti's actions while he was attorney general. They also singled Shelley out for criticism, expressing amazement that he could charge public officials with grave offenses without interviewing or taking statements from any of the witnesses he named and without direct evidence of the commission of any offense.[38]

A fifty-four-page minority report responded by pointing out that the Democratic majority on the commission had blocked the subpoena of the books of the Democratic State Committee, refused to interview Matthew McCloskey, holder of $11 million of state contracts, and rejected a Republican demand that state employees be permitted to testify about political payroll assessments. "The legislative session and the committee created during this session have been publicly and widely said to exist for the purpose of whitewashing the accused. We of the minority confirm that opinion." The minority report, calling the "so-called investigation a farce," recommended that the entire case be turned over to the courts where it began four months earlier.[39] Lawrence's ordeal was far from over.

1940–1942
Years of Trauma

Governor Earle's House investigating panel accomplished little more than keep the alleged illegal activities on the front pages of the state's newspapers for the entire fall campaign. It no doubt contributed heavily to the stinging Democratic defeat. The results satisfied no one and failed to prevent the full-scale investigation by the Dauphin County grand jury that District Attorney Carl Shelley began shortly after the 1938 election. He and Margiotti continued to confer during December, and when the newly appointed grand jury convened on 18 December, the prosecution was ready to present its case. The star witness for the district attorney was to be the master barrister, Charles J. Margiotti himself. Judge Paul Schaeffer gave the jury sweeping powers to "inquire into any angle of the state's business," but he specifically directed an examination of five major charges. David Lawrence was allegedly implicated in all. The first was that public officials involved in the insurance business conspired to induce the state to purchase surety bonds from selected firms, identified in the hearings as the Harris-Lawrence and James P. Kirk agencies, both located in Pittsburgh, and two Philadelphia firms. The four companies allegedly supplied 100 percent of all the surety bonds purchased by the state. When evidence was produced to indicate that Lawrence had taken a leave of absence from his agency upon assuming office in 1935, his name was dropped from the presentment. Lawrence's close friend, James Kirk, however, was indicted and eventually convicted of attempting to establish a monoply on the writing of bonds for state highway contracts. Kirk and his business partner, James P. Skok, received small fines. The second charge, that architects were forced to kick back part of their fees as a condition of receiving contracts, was rejected by the grand jury as "being without sufficient evidence to warrant indictment." The third, that Lawrence and other high officials had accepted bribes from the brewing industry in return for favorable legislation, was treated similarly. It was noted that the event allegedly occurred during 1935, at which time the Republicans controlled the State Senate and it was highly unlikely that the Democratic officials could have consummated such a deal. Indictments were returned, however, on charges of extorting political contributions from contractors in return for state contracts and of requiring political contributions from state employees as a condition of employment (macing). Each indictment was to be tried separately.[1]

"Lawrence Indicted in Gravel Scandal," screamed the headlines of the *Pittsburgh Press* on Saturday, 7 January 1939. If convicted, he faced a lengthy prison sentence and a possible twenty-five-thousand-dollar fine. The grand jury case evolved, ironically, not from any of the charges leveled by Margiotti but from a seemingly minor scandal over the sale of road gravel that occurred early in the Earle administration.

In December 1936 an official of the Pioneer Materials Company of Kittanning offered a state highway department inspector a "Christmas present" of eighty-five dollars in cash. The inspector reported the incident to his superiors, touching off the investigation that stalled the Democratic state steamroller directed by Lawrence and changed the lives of dozens of Pennsylvania residents. When other irregularities were uncovered, Governor Earle ordered Superintendent Adams of the state police to conduct a full-scale investigation. Adams's report, delivered to the governor in mid 1937, revealed that two high-level state highway officials ignored specifications for paving gravel to permit them to purchase inferior material from Spurgeon Bowser, the president of Pioneer Materials. The two agreed to overlook the specifications to comply with the wishes of John Verona, political boss of Pittsburgh's Third Ward. Verona, described as a "dapper, well-fed man in his forties," controlled the Hill District long before the Democrats came to power. A longtime Republican, he had followed his friend and attorney, Margiotti, into the Democratic ranks in 1934. The Adams report identified Verona as the go-between for Bowser and the state officials and as the unnamed "Mr. So-and-So" who, according to the chief state engineer, H. H. Temple, "wants this stuff [gravel] moved." Verona, however, died in a bar fight in Pittsburgh on 12 January 1937 and took his version of the story to the grave with him. The governor, noting that Adams found no evidence of any illegal activity on the part of the named officials, dismissed them both for improprieties in office. The report, Earle was quick to point out, "exonerated all other state officials of any knowledge of the scandal."[2] As far as the governor and his aides were concerned, that put a prompt end to a mild indiscretion on the part of two minor officials.

The grand jury presentment of 7 January 1939 tied Lawrence to the so-called minor scandal by charging that he (1) violated election laws by extorting $5000 from Bowser as an election contribution, which he failed to submit or report to the Democratic state treasurer; (2) obtained the payment in cash, by blackmail through a threat to use his power and influence as a state and party official; and (3) along with the deceased Verona and others [including several cabinet members], conspired to cheat and defraud the Commonwealth, to procure unlawful contracts, and to influence officials.[3] The interjection of Lawrence changed the affair in two important respects. First, the scandal now obviously reached to the top of the Democratic party and perhaps into the governor's mansion. (The grand jury asked and received permission to continue its investigation to determine what role, if any, the governor or his other cabinet members played in the conspiracy.) Lawrence, the prize plum, was to be the test case. If he were convicted, other trials would surely follow. Second, Bowser became a victim rather than a perpetrator of the alleged crime. He was supposedly forced to contribute, under threat, substantial campaign funds. In his new role he became a crucial witness for the prosecution.

The first Lawrence trial began on 13 November 1939 in the Dauphin County Court House. In his opening statement to the jury—nine Republicans and three Democrats—the assistant district attorney, Earl V. Compton, painted a vivid picture of corruption, bribery, fraud, and conspiracy in the Democratic administration of George Earle. He told them that Verona was initially promised the job of purchasing agent of the state's $78 million liquor monopoly as a reward for carrying his ward for the Democrats in 1934. When the position was given to someone else, Verona was told he would "be permitted to make some money on gravel."[4] Lawrence, the prosecution suggested, was Verona's sponsor. Bowser, was similarly told that, to sell paving materials to the state highway department, he "would have to have a representative," and it was suggested that he contact Verona. Bowser did so and agreed to pay Verona ten cents per ton on any gravel sold to the state.

Lawrence, Compton told the jury, also intervened at the state level. Whenever Verona arrived in Harrisburg to see state highway officials about gravel purchases, Lawrence's secretary, Mrs. Alice Priddy, with Lawrence's blessing, called the chief highway engineer,

H. H. Temple, to inform him that Verona was on his way. Lawrence also repeatedly phoned E. A. Griffith, the district engineer in the Pioneer Materials Company district, to urge him to use more gravel in order to provide additional business for the Verona-Bowser combination. Griffith allegedly complied.

Compton concluded by explaining various ways in which legal bids were rejected in favor of Pioneer bids and by charging Lawrence with extorting $5000 in cash from Bowser on 2 April 1937 in Lawrence's Pittsburgh office. In addition, Bowser allegedly paid $1000 each to the Democratic committees of Venango and Erie counties.[5]

For the next two weeks, the prosecution introduced an impressive group of witnesses. Most of the thirty-three who testified repeated accounts presented earlier before the Special Legislative Investigative Commission or the grand jury and provided little new evidence. Several gave testimony that appeared to implicate Verona or the chief accuser, Margiotti, but added little to the state's case against Lawrence. For example, one key witness, Arthur Colegrove, former state secretary of property and supplies, testified that he held up the delivery of gravel by the Pioneer Materials Company when informed by an assistant highway superintendent that the "stuff is just awful." In response to questioning, he revealed that Margiotti attempted for the next six months to persuade him to accept the questionable gravel, arguing that Pioneer Materials had submitted a legal low bid. It was Margiotti who called him in and introduced him to Verona. Margiotti arranged meetings with Colegrove in his own office, as well in the offices of Earle, Lawrence, and Colegrove, and added further pressure to force Colegrove to accept the bids by holding up all bid checks of contractors during the five-month period.[6]

Lawrence, Colegrove testified, was present at several of the meetings but took no part in the arguing on behalf of Pioneer Materials. He did, however, support the attorney general. "Mr. Lawrence," Colegrove repeated several times, "maintained the position that if Mr. Margiotti felt it to be a legal bid that I was being somewhat obstinate in not making the award."[7] Governor Earle eventually sustained Colegrove's decision to reject the Pioneer gravel with no objection from Lawrence.

The lone negative note in Colegrove's testimony came when he named Lawrence, not Verona, as the mysterious "Mr. So-and-So." In the course of the negotiations over the Pioneer bids, Colegrove consulted Temple. "He told me he knew these people [Pioneer Materials Company] had a lot of gravel accumulated up there, and that Davey wanted it moved."[8] Temple in later testimony supported Colegrove's statement that Lawrence was indeed "Mr. So-and-So."

The most damaging testimony occurred on the fifth and sixth days, when the president of Pioneer, Spurgeon Bowser, took the stand. Verona, he testified, approached him in the spring of 1935 to make known his ability to assist in securing highway materials contracts. To prove his claim of influence, Verona took Bowser to Conneaut Lake in northern Pennsylvania to visit Lawrence at his summer cottage. Afterward, Verona and Bowser continued to meet until they agreed on a fee, which, on a per-ton basis, would net Verona $30,000 over the next several years.[9]

The testimony of Bowser, Colegrove, Griffith, and others thus far clearly indicated that Verona extorted funds from Bowser. Bowser's evidence showed that he willingly participated in the scheme, while Griffith and Temple probably joined the conspiracy because they believed they were carrying out the wishes of those higher up. In addition, Margiotti had participated. It remained unclear, however, whether Verona ever had the influence with Lawrence and others that he claimed, and the prosecution never attempted to make a case that Lawrence was involved in this first stage.

The involvement of David Lawrence, according to Bowser's testimony, began in February 1937, approximately one month after the death of Verona. Bowser visited Lawrence, at the latter's request, in his Pittsburgh office. "Mr. Lawrence said, 'You know, John owed me $10,000 and he said he was going to get it from you. Now that John is gone, I'm going to look to you for that $10,000.'" Bowser offered a noncommittal reply and agreed to meet Lawrence at a later date to discuss the matter. The later date, he testified, was on 25 March 1937, and the place, Lawrence's Harrisburg office. Lawrence reportedly continued to pressure Bowser for the payoff, telling him at a later meeting, "I know you received a lot of money from the highway department just a few days ago. . . . If you don't get that [$10,000] in here within a few days, you are going to find yourself in a much worse off jam than you already are in." With that, Bowser testified, "I left the office."[10]

Seven days later, on 2 April, Bowser stated, he instructed his company treasurer, Sidney Toy, to draw a check for $5,100. Toy cashed it and gave the money to Bowser. "I went immediately to Mr. Lawrence's [Pittsburgh] office . . . and laid $5000 . . . on his desk. He picked it up and put it in a drawer." Lawrence gave him no receipt and he asked for none. Bowser and Lawrence met several times after that, and Lawrence always inquired how Bowser was going to explain the $5000 should the question arise in an investigation.[11]

District Attorney Shelley's case broke down with the evidence of the five women witnesses. Interest in the courtroom on the eighteenth day focused on three defense witnesses: Lawrence's secretary, Alice Priddy, and two stenographers. All three testified that 25 March 1937—the day on which Bowser said he was threatened by the Democratic state chairman if he did not pay the ten-thousand dollars—was a holiday, and neither Lawrence nor Bowser appeared in the office. While none of the women worked the entire day, they all testified that at least two were present in the office at all times that day. Lawrence's wife, Alyce, later testified that on the second crucial date, 2 April 1937—the date on which Bowser stated that he paid Lawrence the $5000 in his Pittsburgh office—her husband spent the morning in Harrisburg, then caught the afternoon train for Pittsburgh. She met him at the East Liberty train station at 6:00 P.M. Mr. and Mrs. J. Patton of Moon Township in Beaver County also testified that they met with the party chairman in Harrisburg that morning to ask him to attend a political rally.[12]

The defense produced a long list of its own witnesses, including U.S. Senator Joseph Guffey, former Governor Earle, and Jimmy Kirk. Lawrence, testifying in his own behalf, appeared, according to several news reports, "confident but somewhat ill at ease." He systematically denied all the charges against him and maintained that he had not been at either of his offices on the crucial dates. Furthermore, he "had nothing to do with the administrative decisions that made it possible for gravel producers to bid for state work, with the specifications for gravel, the proposals to buy, or with the award of any contract." He was traveling thousands of miles, all over Pennsylvania during the fall of 1936—when proposals to buy gravel were being prepared—in connection with the 1936 campaign. He left for a post-election vacation in Europe 11 November, a day before the opening of bids resulting in the contract award to the Pioneer Company. Lawrence ended his testimony with a brief but fiery attack on his accuser, Charles Margiotti.[13]

Following the summation by the opposing attorneys, Judge Charles Hughes, a Republican, outlined the case for the jury. He discussed forty-one main points and drew attention to the testimony of six persons that Lawrence could not have been at the meetings at which he allegedly demanded and received the payoff from Bowser; the additional charges of blackmail and election law violations could not be upheld if Lawrence was not in his office to demand or receive the money on the dates in question. He concluded by reminding the jury that "a charge of conspiracy is easily made but a mere suspicion or possibility of a guilty connection must be proved beyond a reasonable doubt. . . . There has been offered testimony to raise a reasonable doubt as to the accuracy and credibility of the commonwealth's witnesses, and more particularly that of Mr. Bowser." These instructions seemed almost a directed not guilty verdict.[14]

The mostly Republican jury deliberated six hours before returning a verdict of acquittal on all counts. Lawrence, who had not come to the court to hear the decision, was immediately mobbed by friends and reporters in his hotel room. Feeling obvious relief from the strain that he had endured, he momentarily broke into tears, showing probably his most honest reaction to the crisis. "I knew I would be vindicated," he responded. "It has been a garden of Gethsemane for me." Later, after he had composed himself, he issued a brief statement to the press. "Of course, I am delighted with the verdict. At all times I have had an absolutely clear conscience, since I had done no wrong, and somehow I felt I would be vindicated."[15] He would have much more to say about Margiotti and Guffey, who, he felt, precipitated the entire ordeal, at the conclusion of the second trial, which was to be held early in 1940.

With at least a partial sense of relief, Lawrence returned to Pittsburgh to spend the holidays with his family. Upon his arrival, 5000 cheering supporters, a brass band, and waving banners met him at the Pennsylvania Railroad Station. Harrisburg and the rest of the state might be hostile, but he was loved and respected by the faithful in Pittsburgh. The welcome at the station and at Democratic headquarters the next day reinforced his love affair with the city. Lawrence, looking strained—he had lost about forty or fifty pounds—was obviously touched, but, as always, he had himself under perfect control.[16]

The atmosphere at the Lawrence household was similarly affected. As if seeking solace within the safe confines of his family, Lawrence spent more time at home that holiday season than usual. All the normal family rituals were followed, but "it was different. Christmas was exceptionally quiet that year because he was so quiet. He still had that other trial to go and you could tell it was affecting him."[17] He did not, however, discuss the legal battles with members of his family or other close associates.

He continued to operate at a reduced pace, for him, during the first month of 1940, meeting occasionally with his attorney, Oliver Eaton, and spending his days at his office in the Benedum-Trees Building. For the first time in years, he spent many evenings at home with his family. By 2 February, however, when he arrived in Harrisburg to preside over the Democratic State Committee meeting, he appeared recharged and ready for battle.

Speaking before the 111 members, he made a scathing attack on the Republican party and "those who attempt to crucify the Democratic party. A smoke screen of untruths and half-truths was blown up to obscure the real issues of the [1938] campaign. . . . This caught the party off guard and led to its defeat in 1938. The Democratic party, . . . struck out blindly into tactical errors which prejudiced our case."[18] He made it clear that the party would approach the 1940 presidential and senatorial election with renewed vigor and that he, in spite of the upcoming trial, intended to lead it to victory. The address praised President Roosevelt and the New Deal profusely, and the committee roared its approval of a resolution calling for the renomination of Roosevelt.

Lawrence's address did not mention the Pennsylvania champion of the New Deal, Senator Guffey, an intentional omission that showed the depth of Lawrence's bitterness toward his former benefactor. The executive committee signaled that it shared Lawrence's feelings by refusing to endorse Guffey for a second term. Lawrence's preoccupation with his past and upcoming trials, however, prevented him from rallying the party leadership around a suitable replacement. Jack Kelly received considerable support but expressed little interest in running against such a formidable opponent as Guffey. Auditor General Warren Roberts generated no enthusiasm among the nominating committee. Unable, for the first time in his career, to suggest a suitable candidate, Lawrence supported an unprecedented nonendorsement motion offered by Kelly, which was adopted by the committee by an overwhelming majority. The leadership opted temporarily for an open primary and did eventually agree to support Walter A. Jones, the Pennsylvania Turnpike commissioner, but their inability to act at the state committee meeting turned the nomination over to Guffey.

Following the hectic state committee meeting, Lawrence turned his attention to the upcoming macing trial, remaining largely inactive throughout the primary campaign. The Democrats would have to carry on without a leader.

The trial, which began on 25 March 1940, was potentially more dangerous than the gravel one. Expecting government workers, at all levels, to contribute funds to the political party that provided the job was a common practice in Pennsylvania. The Democratic party willingly admitted that it solicited funds from workers and indeed had established an elaborate system, often known as the "3 percent and

5 percent club," to facilitate the collection and distribution of such funds. Workers earning over $1200 annually were asked to contribute 3 percent of their salaries while those over $1500 were asked to contribute 5 percent. County committees in charge of collection retained two-fifths of the proceeds and were to remit the remainder to the state committee. County leaders, anxious to systemize the collection process, kept ledger books or individual card indexes of all workers, with columns labeled "assessment," "payment," and "balance." Frank Taylor, chief clerk of the Democratic State Committee, kept detailed records of all county and individual payments.[19]

The charges against Lawrence and seven other officials grew out of these practices but rested on allegations of illegal activity in the method of collecting the funds. Payments could not be required, nor could workers be coerced or threatened into making them. Reprisals against those who failed to contribute were similarly illegal. Even unintentional harassment of workers by overzealous party officials might easily be construed as illegal. The potential for conviction appeared strong, and the state had only to prove a single instance of macing to ensure a guilty verdict. To make matters worse, the prosecution succeeded in seating an all-Republican jury. Judge Hughes, a Republican, who had proved to be strictly nonpartisan in the previous Lawrence trial, once again presided.

The prosecution based its case on testimony of employees from Dauphin and Jefferson counties (the latter Margiotti's home county) who claimed that they were "dunned for contributions" by members of their county committee, who informed them that Lawrence or the state committee expected it. Of the seven who testified to such treatment, two were former deputies of Margiotti and four were Republican holdovers from the Pinchot administration. Most damaging was the testimony of J. R. Copenhaver, who stated that he won the backing of the Dauphin County committee for a salary raise by paying a $383 assessment. He also testified that on another occasion he was called to a noon meeting of fifty or sixty state employees, which was conducted by Frank Hean and William Smith, Dauphin County Democratic officials and codefendants. "Mr. Hean spoke of raising money for the campaign and asked us to pay our back assessments." He told them that officials were getting tired of coaxing them and that they expected them to pay up before the election. Smith announced that he "had orders from the State Committee—from Mr. Lawrence—to turn over lists of those back in their payments to Mr. Lawrence and that those who wouldn't pay up would be replaced."[20] Several of the other witnesses gave essentially the same testimony, stating that they had been present at what was evidently a series of attempts by the Dauphin County Democratic leaders to increase payments. However, none of the seven had lost their jobs, even though five failed to meet their payment quotas.

On 4 April, Charles Margiotti appeared on the witness stand for the first time in the two Lawrence trials. He began his testimony by describing a "super-cabinet," dominated by Lawrence, which ruled on all patronage matters. "Immediately upon my appointment as Attorney General he [Governor Earle] gave me and . . . other cabinet members, . . . instructions. It was a condition of the appointment that every cabinet member make only those appointments and dismissals approved by a committee consisting of myself, Mr. Lawrence, Mr. Van Dyke and Harry Kalodner [Earle's secretary]."[21] Contested appointments were to be made by Mr. Lawrence alone and those at the county level by the county Democratic chairmen. Lawrence again served as the final arbitrator in cases of disputes.

Margiotti then gave two specific examples of attempts by Lawrence, which he successfully resisted, at macing his own deputies. Margiotti's allegations crumbled, however, when he revealed that a short time later Lawrence told him that, upon reconsidering, he had decided not to insist that the two Republicans pay their assessment or be fired.[22] Thereafter, Margiotti admitted, he heard nothing more about the matter.

The case for the defense, lasting just over one week, rested on three major points. First, the prosecution failed to produce evidence of a single individual who had been fired or denied a raise for failure to contribute to the Democratic party treasury. Second, an examination of the financial records of all assessed individuals kept by state Democratic treasurer Frank Taylor showed that, in the three and one-half years that the quota system was in operation, the state committee received only $351,000 of the $901,000 quota, slightly over one-third. Lawrence's home county paid only $1943 of its 1935 assessment of $7498 and $5211 of its 1938 assessment of $26,879. The Democratic State Committee, the defense argued, was either embarrassingly inefficient or unwilling to coerce workers to meet their assessments. Third, testimony by several county party chairmen indicated that the quotas were considered targets and the method of fund-raising was left to the individual counties. In Schuylkill County, for example, funds were raised through Democratic clubs and social events. Dauphin County held $100-a-plate dinners, in addition to its luncheon pep rallies at which it urged workers to "pay up." Allegheny

County had an automobile raffle, and Jefferson County held six "victory dinners."[23]

By the time that Lawrence took the stand, the case appeared to be won. In his earlier trial he had exhibited some concern; now, by contrast, he was relaxed and confident. His testimony, which touched on a variety of subjects ranging from party organization to fund-raising to interpersonal relationships, offers one of the best insights into the personality and ability of this largely private man. He began by explaining in great detail the operation of the party from the level of the municipality through that of the state. He indicated differences in operation from county to county and identified those that had difficulty raising funds and those that frequently exceeded their quotas. He told the jury that in his view a functioning democracy required the presence of two political parties and that he believed it his patriotic responsibility to raise funds "to build a strong, virile Democratic party," just as the opposition had a similar obligation.

In explaining the early source of his difficulties with Margiotti, Lawrence showed a sensitivity to the importance of interpersonal relations in the harmonious operation of the organization. At the beginning of the Earle administration all administration-sponsored bills were written in the attorney general's office. "But it became clear that many cabinet members would draw [up] legislation, work out problems . . . and then the . . . Attorney General would give press releases and take away from the department the credit for working it out. It wasn't fair and was causing hard feelings and so the system was changed whereby the bills were prepared and newspaper releases were given out by each of the several departments."[24]

Finally, Lawrence demonstrated flashes of his dry wit and his bitterness toward Margiotti when he responded to questions regarding his relationship with him.

Compton: Mr. Margiotti testified that he held no animosity toward you.

Lawrence: If he had none, then the Lord deliver all of us from friends like that. Machiavelli would have said the same thing.

Compton: But you delivered a birthday cake to him when he was ill in the hospital in April of 1937.

Lawrence: That was my wife's idea.

Compton: As a matter of fact, didn't Mrs. Lawrence bake that cake?

Lawrence: Mrs. Lawrence bakes much better cakes than that.[25]

Lawrence, of course, denied that individuals were coerced into contributing and explained how the 3 and 5 percent assessment developed from a 1935 suggestion that counties be assessed quotas in proportion to the amount of patronage they received. The contributions were to be strictly voluntary, and the quota could be paid through individual offerings or county fund-raising activities or a combination of the two.[26]

Defense and prosecution attorneys, as expected, concluded the trial with ringing denunciations of the two principals, Margiotti and Lawrence, but the case was essentially over. Judge Hughes, in his charge to the jury, once again indicated that the prosecution had not proved its case. Reminding it that the charge against the defendants was "a conspiracy to extort money and not a conspiracy to solicit and collect money for political purposes," he made it clear that this was a "normal and necessary" political activity. He further indicated that none of the fifty-eight prosecution witnesses produced documentary evidence of being coerced to contribute or lost a job because of failure to contribute. "The Commonwealth in offering their case against the defendants," the judge instructed the jury, "have based their proof largely upon circumstantial evidence. The humane presumption of the law is against guilt, and though a conspiracy must ordinarily be proven by circumstantial evidence, you must keep in mind that the charge . . . must be proven beyond a reasonable doubt."[27]

The jury, deliberating less than four hours, returned a verdict of not guilty on all counts against all of the accused. Thus the long nightmare, which ironically began two years to the day earlier with Guffey's Philadelphia Academy of Music address, closed. The trials provided a measure of vindication, but the damage had been done. The events surrounding Margiotti's charges ended a promising Democratic reign in Harrisburg, destroyed several careers, and nearly sent several others to prison. While Margiotti gained some revenge for the party's refusal to endorse him for governor in 1938, none of the principals in the dispute emerged victorious. For all three, the feud would continue.

▽

The conclusion of the trials too, brought an end to the Harrisburg phase of David Lawrence's life. He could return to his beloved Pittsburgh relieved of the heavy burden he had carried for the past two years. Throughout the ordeal Lawrence maintained his composure, seldom revealing its effect on him. In one of the few moments in which he dropped his guard, he told his friend Huck Fenrich, "It's a terrible thing being indicted. It's the first thing you think of when you wake up in the morning and the last thing you think of when you go to bed at night."[28] In later life he almost never commented on this dark period. Yet deep wounds were inflicted that remained partially open for the rest of his life.

Although Lawrence seldom spoke directly of the trials, many associates recall incidents that showed that they were seldom far from his conscious thoughts. His son Jerry, who was born just after the first trial, recalled: "I remember not talking about the trials specifically, but in conversations on other people's trials, his saying how difficult it was and how horrible it was for my sisters and brothers, the abuse they took at school from other kids. I remember my mother talking about it. She was pregnant with me at the time and what a tough experience it was on her. I think that's why he never forgave Margiotti because of all the sadness involved in the thing." The younger Lawrence's reference to the trials of others helps to explain his father's willingness to act as a character reference in many cases involving civil as well as criminal issues. He served in such a capacity at least two dozen times throughout the remainder of his life. "Even if it was someone he didn't like," Walter Giesey explained. "I remember he appeared at Marjorie Matson's trial and he didn't like her. He also in that same week appeared in one for Burgess Ackermann . . . who was a real enemy of Lawrence; but he appeared to testify to his character. . . . I always thought that had some relationship to the trouble he had had and having gone through that he understood."[29]

Lawrence's bitterness toward Margiotti carried with him all his life. He considered Margiotti the most untrustworthy person he had ever met, and he even rebuffed Margiotti's attempt at a deathbed reconciliation.[30] Once, at a political rally, opponents threw gravel on the stage. Lawrence became so livid that he had difficulty completing his talk, a rare break in composure for him.

Most political associates were aware of Lawrence's attitude and were careful never to invite the two men to appear at a function at the same time. But on one occasion during the 1950s, Frank Ambrose accompanied Lawrence to an Italian Day picnic. "We were sitting just getting ready to eat dinner and Margiotti walked in and Lawrence looked at me and said, 'Let's get the hell out of here.' So we left. Even before we ate." At another event, Lawrence found himself with Margiotti at the speakers' table. Monsignor Andres J. Pauley of St. Paul's Cathedral, Margiotti's pastor, was seated between them. The monsignor decided to try to reconcile the two old enemies. He "leaned over to Lawrence and said, 'You know, Charley and I have a contract. He has agreed to keep me out of jail and I have contracted to keep him out of hell.' In a frosty voice, Lawrence replied, 'Margiotti has the easier job.'"[31]

Lawrence was not silent immediately upon learning of his acquittal in 1940. At his first press conference he lashed out at Margiotti and Guffey. "For the second time, a judge and jury have definitely given an answer to the calumny and lies spread . . . by the Margiottis, the Guffeys and their slimy speech writers and press agents. . . . This complete vindication of the Earle administration, my associates and myself makes me feel very happy." Just ten days before the Pennsylvania primary, he told a gathering of seven thousand cheering partisans that the two men "came from the same mold. Their willingness to deceive and destroy for their own selfish ends places them in a class with whom no faction of the Democratic party will now traffic." For the next half hour Lawrence vented his anger. At times his voice broke as he related the ordeal of the past two years, calling the charges against him a "cruel, unfair, indecent, malicious and unscrupulous attack." The mention of Guffey's name drew a chorus of boos. Lawrence brought the house down in a standing, stamping, and tearful ovation when he turned to the members of his family seated in the front row. "I asked Mrs. Lawrence to bring the children here tonight. . . . The children have been subject by innocent playmates to certain references to these false charges against their father. I wanted them to come here tonight to impress on their young minds what the real people think of their father. I've wanted all those weary hours to be . . . back here among my own people, back among the people of Allegheny County, back among the people I'm vain enough to say have some affection for me—to come before you and tell my story." If a dry eye remained among the sympathetic crowd before, none could be found at the conclusion of his talk.[32]

Lawrence's bitterness toward Margiotti certainly appears understandable and justified. The reasons for his vendetta against Guffey, however, remain something of a mystery. Certainly the two men experienced the estrangement that frequently occurs when a student begins to grow and threatens to eclipse the teacher. Lawrence's ascent to the state chairman's post and the top cabinet position in the Earle administration gave him a voice at least equal to that of Guffey, who resented the change. However, they managed to settle their differences on several occasions. To be sure, Guffey's intemperate Philadelphia speech in 1938 had touched off the ensuing scandals, but it was Margiotti who had carried the ball. Lawrence had shown time and again an uncanny ability to patch up differences, but he simply could not accept what he considered Guffey's political disloyalty. He remained blind to the fact that his own activities were counterproductive and actually destructive to him and the party. It was the most obvious lack of political vision in his fifty-year career.

For ten days Lawrence traveled western Pennsylvania in a frantic attempt to upset Guffey's renomination bid. His addresses centered almost wholly on the personality of the senator and were his most vitriolic ever. Guffey, as he saw it, had brought down the party in 1938, had jeopardized Lawrence's freedom during the last two years, and now threatened his leadership across the state. Guffey responded to one of Lawrence's attacks by saying he hoped that it was "a result of momentary hysteria following the strain of his trial," for it came with "ill grace" from a former protégé. He further pointed out that he had appeared as a witness in the trial and contributed $1000 to the Lawrence defense fund. The party chairman countered with a harshness that was becoming common. "Joe Guffey did not contribute one cent to any defense fund for me. Apparently the hysteria is in the Guffey camp. He was not a character witness for me. He was called like a number of others to testify about a fictitious meeting in Philadelphia at the last Democratic National Convention."[33]

Lawrence's preoccupation with the recent trials and the Margiotti-Guffey duo had left him unable to concentrate on election strategy and placed a serious strain on the operation of the party. Contributions declined, and party workers, lacking leadership, divided their efforts between the two competing candidates. Lawrence's brief but harsh attacks on Guffey made it clear to the voters that their primary vote was a choice for one or the other. A reconciliation was out of the question.

The temporary euphoria Lawrence felt upon his acquittal came crashing to the ground on 23 April 1940. Senator Guffey defeated the organization candidate, Walter Jones, by more than 100,000 votes in a light turnout. Guffey carried nearly every municipality in the state and won a surprisingly easy 50,000-vote victory in Philadelphia. Lawrence managed to save face by claiming a solid victory in Allegheny County, but Guffey had won the battle and made it clear that his plans did not include Lawrence. "I shall proceed at once to reorganize our forces for a victorious campaign by eliminating elements of discord and strengthening our organization wherever necessary." His chief press supporter, J. David Stern, publisher of the *Philadelphia Record* made Guffey's intention even clearer with a postelection editorial. "David L. Lawrence the Democratic State Chairman, who opposed Senator Guffey, stands today as an inept politician who let factional hatred and personal ambition override and completely submerge his duty to his party. . . . His resignation is in order forthwith."[34] With the handwriting clearly on the wall, Lawrence announced that he would resign as state chairman effective at the state party reorganization meeting on 20 June.

At the meeting he kept his promise but managed to strike a deal that eventually gave him full control in the state. Guffey wanted Lawrence out and Meridith Meyers, a Lewistown publisher, as his replacement. Lawrence, supported by a small but powerful group including Kelly, McCloskey, and John Kane, Allegheny County commissioner, originally rejected Meyers. After a heated two-hour discussion, the two factions eventually reached an accord: Guffey would back Lawrence for the vacant post of Democratic national committeeman; in return Lawrence agreed to accept Meyers as state chairman and hinted that he would back Guffey in the general election.[35] The agreement severely restricted Lawrence's role in state politics for a time, but gave him a voice at the national level that was to become increasingly important in the next two decades.

At the conclusion of the meeting, Lawrence returned to Pittsburgh to resume active participation in the Harris-Lawrence Insurance Company. He also intended, he informed his old friend Art Rooney, to spend more time with his family. The Lawrence political career appeared to be in eclipse. While he had been named a national committeeman, for the first time in two decades he held no party chairmanship at any level. The battle with Margiotti and Guffey had stripped him of his base of support.

Yet the next two years were happy ones for Lawrence. Shorn of many political obligations, he kept his pledge to spend a greater amount of time with his family. The home at 355 South Aiken Avenue virtually swelled with children and adults. His two daughters, Mary and Anna Mae, had completed schooling at Mt. Mercy Academy and were attending Marywood College in Scranton and Trinity College in Washington, D.C., respectively. Brennen and David Leo, both teenagers, were enrolled in Central Catholic High School and, along with their infant brother, Jerry, lived at home. In addition there were several of the relatives who populated the Lawrence household over the years. Alyce, delighted to have her husband home for the first time in years, presided over the home with charm and serenity.

Tragedy struck on 19 April 1942 and changed the Lawrence household forever. Joe Barr who later became Lawrence's choice to succeed him as mayor of Pittsburgh, was present on the fateful night. "The boys had been playing ball over at the old Shadyside field and that evening they all came over to the Lawrence's home and he fed them. Then we went over to the Athletic Club for dinner, David and Alyce, myself and my wife. After dinner we went out to their house to play some cards. There was this phone call. I answered it. The business manager of [a] hospital wanted to know if the boys were home. I asked Dave. He said the boys were probably upstairs playing pingpong or cards. Pretty soon the phone rang again. The caller said, 'Are you sure the boys are home? There's been an accident.' That's when we found out the car was gone."[36]

It happened in an instant. Seven teen-aged boys returned to the Lawrence home, their informal clubhouse, after losing the opening game of the local sandlot season. In spite of their loss they were pleased with their effort and proud of their new uniforms, their first in several years. The Lawrences fed them sandwiches, milk, and cookies, then left for a dinner engagement. Sometime after 6:00 P.M. the boys decided to take a joy ride in the Lawrence family car. They wandered around, as young boys often do, and eventually found themselves on U.S. Route 19 seven miles north of Zelienople, approximately twenty-five miles from Pittsburgh. Somewhere along the way they changed drivers. Brennen Lawrence moved to the back and John Thomas, nineteen, got behind the wheel. The two Lawrence brothers sat sandwiched in the middle of the back seat between Jack Clinton and Bill Schaub.

As the carefree group began their descent of a long hill, Thomas decided to pass several slower-moving cars on the two-lane highway. Just as he passed the lead auto, an oncoming truck appeared from around the bend. In his haste to move back into his own lane, Thomas apparently lost control of the car. It careened off the road twice, once on the left, once on the right, then it spun around and veered backward, smashing into a huge tree, rear end first. The two boys seated on the outside in the back suffered head and internal injuries and were listed in serious condition by the hospital. The three boys in the front received moderate but not serious injuries. All five recovered. Brennen was killed instantly. His brother David Leo, Jr., died a short time later en route to the Elwood City Hospital.[37]

When they received the news, David and Alyce Lawrence reacted as most parents would at such a time. At first they could not grasp the enormity of the loss. They suffered a blow from which neither would fully recover. It would forever change their lives and the lives of those around them and had its effect on the future of the city of Pittsburgh and of Pennsylvania.

Somehow they managed to struggle through the four days between the accident and the funeral. David refused to attend the public viewing held in the family home but remained upstairs in his room. Jimmy Kirk, Frank Ambrose, and Primo Columbus took turns visiting him late at night to accompany him on long walks. He said little—he just walked.

On the day of the funeral, neither Lawrence nor his wife attended the services at the cemetery. They went home, and a short time later David left the house and went to Democratic headquarters in the city. "When I went in," Frank Ambrose remembered vividly, "Jimmy Kirk pointed to the office and said, 'Why don't you ask him if he wants to play a game of cards. . . . I think it would relax him.' So I opened the door and said, 'How about a game, chief?' And he said, 'Yes, come on in, fine.' And we sat down to play cards. We played four hours that Saturday afternoon, and never a word did he say about the kids, and of course neither did I."[38]

In their search for answers and the strength to continue, David and Alyce naturally drew upon their individual personalities. That their behavior took divergent paths likely made the healing process even more difficult. Unfortunately, they were unable or unwilling to lean on each other for comfort and support. They suffered their grief independently.

Alyce Lawrence surrounded herself with even more people, opening her home to all sorts of relatives down on their luck. Her daughter Anna Mae transferred to the University of Pittsburgh to be near her. Alyce filled her life as much as possible with friends, swimming, horseback riding, and other activities. Her grandson remembers that even when she was older "she would take us to friends of hers who had swimming pools and she would go with us to Schenley Park to ride horses . . . always the accent would be on enjoying yourself and getting the most out of life that you could. My grandmother was sort of a sporty person."[39] She also began to drink more frequently, something that eventually became a serious source of friction between her and her husband, who seldom drank at all.

David Lawrence, needing always to feel in control of his life, responded to the tragedy as one might expect. He threw himself even more vehemently into his work. Just two months after the accident, he actively sought and won reelection to the state chairman's post, which he had relinquished two years earlier. Rita Wilson Kane described him as a workaholic during a three-year period following the accident. A few days after the boys died, "Lawrence went to a political meeting in another county. People said, 'How could he do this?

He must have ice water in his veins.' It was his way of trying to deaden in his mind what the children's death did to him . . . just to keep working, keeping active, and keeping his brain going." Lawrence later advised his own protégé Genevieve Blatt to follow the same procedure when she lost a brother in World War II. "Just keep working Gen. Keep at it."[40]

Lawrence also dealt with his grief as he had reacted to the unpleasant trial experience. He attempted to suppress it, although the tragedy was apparently never far from his consciousness. He almost never spoke of it—not to friends, relatives, or political acquaintances. But on two occasions ten years apart, he happened to be in the Zelienople vicinity and pointed out to companions the exact spot of the accident. He also kept a photograph of the boys, along with that of Billy Brennen, on his desk for the rest of his life, and he never missed the annual ritual of visiting the boys' graves after Christmas dinner. Always afterward, he sent sympathy cards to other parents whose children died suddenly, whether by accident or illness. Finally, many associates attribute his great interest in a strong highway safety program during his gubernatorial years to the 1942 accident.

Although he never expressed it, Lawrence no doubt felt some guilt at not having spent more time with his sons. Immediately after their death, he nearly smothered the surviving son, Jerry, with care. He had a nurse until he started school who watched him like a hawk. Even beginning school did not relieve Jerry of the burden of constant surveillance. For the first five years he attended elementary school on the campus of Mt. Mercy College. None of the neighborhood children went there, and Jerry, finding it hard to relate to them, was very lonely. At the end of fifth grade, he moved to St. Paul's Cathedral School, where his mother's sister was teaching, rather than to St. Lawrence's, where his brothers and sisters had gone. Even later his father continued to watch over him: Jerry attended La Salle College in Philadelphia, where, several associates reported, David Lawrence's political friends could keep an eye on him. It was during that period that Jerry received a highly publicized speeding ticket. His father refused to intervene on his behalf. When the ticket was ruled invalid because of a technicality, Lawrence ordered his son to surrender his license voluntarily to the state police.[41] It was suspended for a brief period.

As Jerry grew older, his father carefully nurtured a close relationship with him and later his grandson David Donahoe. It was as if he were attempting to make up for the time he had missed with his deceased sons. "He made a great point of taking me along with him,"

Jerry noted, "traveling with him as much as possible." "It was great fun," David Donahoe added of his own experience a decade later. "When he was governor, I spent summers with him in Harrisburg. He traveled to various parts of the state and we went to fairs, to funerals, to political gatherings and on tours. I also accompanied him to Pirate games and those sorts of things. We were together a great deal of time."[42]

The four years between April 1938, when Guffey first suggested that illegal activities occurred in "high places" in the Earle administration, and April 1942 were no doubt the most difficult in Lawrence's life. His political career appeared to be on the brink of extinction, and the devastating accident threatened the stability of his family. The three years that followed were indeed the lowest point in his life. He kept busy, but according to numerous associates, his heart did not seem to be in it. The thrill of the political battle had lost its edge. It all, somehow, did not seem as important anymore. Something was needed to provide new direction and motivation to his life. The opportunity struck in March 1945.

Policies, Principles, and Procedures

Numerous models have been proposed to describe mayoral behavior and predict its impact on the city. These include power-brokering mayors, those who build coalitions, public entrepreneurs, policy experts, and those who somehow "muddle through" most decision-making situations. Another model relies on personality as an explanation of the behavior and success or failure of specific urban leaders: Fiorello La Guardia of New York and Anton Cermak of Chicago are two examples of mayors who dominated their city through the force of personality. Each model by itself, however, presents an overly narrow picture of the activities, forces, and behaviors of big-city mayors. Metropolitan leaders often employ a variety of models, for example, acting sometimes as a power broker and sometimes as a public entrepreneur to accomplish a desired goal. Muddling through appears to be the prime mode of action in still other situations. "A good mayor," according to one source, "and an effective one, is a pragmatic guy who. . . . faces the issues which come up and takes small, sure steady steps to deal with them based on the best information he can get and the difficult realities of the situation."[1] The models, rather than being exclusive appear to complement one another. In his actions as mayor Lawrence relied on a combination of these methods, as well as on a broad coalition of public and private groups, to accomplish his goals.

However, the dominant personality of the man was also an important factor. By the time of Lawrence's enforced removal from state politics in 1940, he had been involved in public life for nearly three decades. He had achieved considerable success, although he never held elective office, and had suffered terrible indignities. He thoroughly enjoyed his role as teacher and lobbyist in negotiating passage of the

Little New Deal but was disillusioned that the voters had rejected his party in spite of the impressive legislative package. The treason, in his view, of Charles Margiotti and the feud with Joseph Guffey strengthened a somewhat cynical view of the motivations of his fellow actors in the political world. He was fifty-one years of age, and it appeared that he might be content to spend the rest of his years as a behind-the-scenes power broker. The period from 1942 through 1945 afforded him some opportunity to reflect on his past life and consider future options.

It was an opportunity he almost certainly ignored, for David Lawrence was not introspective. He seldom talked about his problems or his plans or any philosophy of government, and never about his own past career. He was an action man. "Lawrence, of course, had ideas. And he was his own man. Nobody . . . ever controlled him or manipulated him or anything like that. He was definitely . . . going to do what he thought he should do. . . . He was an active politician, he was out in the neighborhood. . . . That didn't mean they [citizens] were always satisfied with him, but they knew . . . it was yes or no; and if it was no, it was no; and if it was yes, it was going to be done. He was that breed of politician." Only near the end of his career did Lawrence feel the need to wax philosophical about politics, and in each case it was in the role of a teacher passing on information to a prized pupil. Rosemary Plessett, who frequently drove Lawrence to political events, and his grandson, who often accompanied him on official trips, spent many hours alone with him. Occasionally, both remarked, Lawrence became expansive about his career, expounding on his ideas about government or society. "I was very interested in politics," Plessett explained. "I would ask a lot of questions. 'What is power? How is it used? Who gets it?' That sort of thing. And, he had a need to be a teacher. . . . He'd go on for half an hour. . . . He was fascinating."[2] For young Donahoe the discussions roamed far and wide, illustrating a broad range of interests in the normally reticent Lawrence.

> In the early years . . . the talk was mostly about athletics, family. Then . . . as I travelled with him and became not so much a grandson . . . but a companion, we talked about politics to some extent; school, what young people were thinking and the attitudes, some of which he couldn't readily understand. But I was interested in national affairs, for which he provided some insight. In the later years we talked about musical theater which we had a mutual interest in. When we were in New

> York we would go and see musicals. . . . Since I was not as interested in athletics as he was, he . . . bent over to find things that I was interested in, including books that we had both read. . . . After he had left the governor's office, we talked about the future—the future of the city and of the nation. . . . He was always thinking ahead and trying to visualize what would come even after he was gone.[3]

It is instructive to note that the only individuals with whom Lawrence felt free to discuss his thoughts on politics, government, and other issues important to him were both much younger than he, held him in deepest awe, and were uninvolved in his day-to-day political life. They were "safe" disciples to whom he could pass on his knowledge and ideas without fear of betrayal. They willingly gave of their time to be in his company, asking little in return. He responded, coincidentally, by giving more of his inner self than at any other time. With his political or governmental associates, however, Lawrence remained guarded, seldom offering a glimpse at his inner thoughts.

To say that Lawrence was reticent with associates does not mean that he was without ideas or a guiding set of philosophical principles. As was noted earlier, his family and the experiences of his youth provided him with a solid base upon which to build a political philosophy. Aid for the less fortunate, support for organized labor, a strong belief in the work ethic, and a suspicion of the wealthy coupled with a fundamental acceptance of the capitalist system, as he understood it, became the bedrock upon which he built his political career. In addition, by the time he returned to Pittsburgh in 1940, he had spent nearly a third of a century in politics. His early career in Pittsburgh and his distasteful but important term in Harrisburg had exposed him to many individuals and ideas. His willingness to compromise, his pragmatic approach to politics and government, an unquestioning acceptance of the two-party system, and an intense dislike for what he termed "political opportunists" all developed during this period. Finally, an association with the Roosevelt administration and in particular the liberal Democrats who gathered around the president crystallized his ideas into the legislative package that became the Little New Deal.

"Dave Lawrence was a marvelous, . . . strong New Dealer and he took compassionate positions, and labor knew that he supported them, and they supported him." The massive public works programs launched by the New Deal, the labor legislation embodied in the

Wagner Act, emergency relief provided to the indigent by the Federal Emergency Relief Act (FERA), and slum clearance and subsidized housing construction were all enthusiastically supported by Lawrence during his period as secretary of the Commonwealth. Each program, as he saw it, provided services or assistance to individuals unable to help themselves. He later added to his reputation as a backer of liberal causes by his early support of the controversial civil rights plank in the 1948 Democratic party platform. Two years later in Michigan he urged the passage of a national fair employment practices act. "In civil rights, the government of this country has an immediate duty, one which will affect not only our material might but our moral might as well. No nation committed to freedom, democracy, and liberty, as we are, can long fight its enemies without first living what it is protecting." Other causes that earned his quick endorsement included women's equality (1944), voting rights for eighteen-year-old citizens (1946), and the establishment of a Jewish homeland (1946). He further showed his interest in international affairs in March 1946 when he criticized Winston Churchill's famous "Iron Curtain" speech as "intemperate and dangerous." "It will take a great deal of patience to undo the harm that Churchill has done. Likewise, it will take great patience to undo the harm that Russian treaty-breaking has done. . . . America must not tie itself to British imperialism nor Russian Communism but must take a strong stand as international mediator and peacemaker."[4]

Lawrence not only endorsed liberal issues but often initiated action to support these causes. During the 1935–39 legislative sessions, he devoted nearly every waking hour to pushing the Little New Deal through the General Assembly. During the same period he was responsible for extending the franchise to uncounted numbers of Pennsylvanians by backing legislation to reform voter registration laws and encouraging minority citizens to register and vote. Democratic platforms, for which Lawrence had major responsibility, always included items to appeal to particular minority groups, which he also included in the distribution of the spoils of victory—jobs. He was directly responsible for the election of the city's first black judge and councilman, and he appointed the first black magistrate when he became mayor. In addition, as mayor he backed the passage of the city's fair housing laws—the second city in the nation to do so.

He attempted to bring women and youth into the political process by encouraging the development of young political organizations and supporting its activists for office. Genevieve Blatt, who became a protégé of Lawrence's, explained that in the early 1930s he was more than a cheerleader. "Although he was practically running the state government, he would spend hours at meetings of Young Democrats, some of whom were not altogether bright, good-humoredly helping them work out their own program in an intelligent way. He didn't seem at all stuffy or pompous, and I couldn't say that for all the cabinet members I ran into in those days." Ambitious women such as Blatt, Anne Alpern, and Grace Sloan could count on his support and encouragement in their bids for elective office. Each of his terms of office in Pittsburgh and Harrisburg was characterized by the presence of bright, aggressive women in both elective and appointive posts. He was the one man of all the political leaders, said Rita Wilson Kane, register of wills, who recognized the value of women in politics and gave them big jobs.[5]

Finally, he demonstrated his support for the Zionist cause by spending a considerable amount of his time raising funds to support Pittsburgh's bonds for Israel program. He once brought the house down at a testimonial dinner honoring him for his efforts by beginning his address with the greeting, "Fellow Jews."

The characterization of Lawrence as a liberal, however, is apt to bring quick disclaimers from friends and opponents alike. Many, of course, point out that all his actions were designed to aid his party. Sponsorship of the New Deal and liberal causes were simply good politics during the second third of the twentieth century, and Lawrence was too skilled a politician not to realize its benefits. "It went beyond simple liberalism and patronage. . . . It was a combination . . . the typical New Deal coalition."[6]

Lawrence's adoption of a liberal view, however, always remained tempered by a strong fiscal conservatism and a pragmatic outlook. While his own modest economic background produced a compassion for those too poor to meet their own needs, it also resulted in what several associates classified as a tight-fisted money policy. Regardless of the value of the program, he always wanted to know where the money was to come from. He was "emotionally opposed" to deficit spending. His daughter observed: "You couldn't classify him as an ADAer. I remember when the ADA [Americans for Democratic Action] was first coming out. There were a lot of things the ADA was doing that he wasn't happy with. He would make comments like, 'Oh, he's an ADAer' or 'that sounds like an ADA philosophy.'" Lawrence's liberalism was much too practical for him to approve of that activist organization. Even when he was receiving an award from the ADA in 1963, he lectured that their views must be tempered by political reality. Politics, he told them "in no way infringes upon my liberal tendencies. On the contrary, politics helped bring into being ideas and proposals . . . converting liberal platforms into law."[7]

While he brought no clearly articulated philosophy of government or ideas about the ideal structure of society to his own activism, Lawrence preferred to be guided by his instincts and a well-integrated set of values. He frequently advised Genevieve Blatt, "Do what seems natural." His oft-repeated phrase, "The best politics is good government," was more than a slogan for him. While he led the way in the implementation of popular legislation and reform measures throughout his career, he also campaigned for unpopular action, such as new taxation and open housing legislation, because he believed it to be necessary. The voters, he firmly believed, would not fail to reward such "right action" at the ballot box. He was astounded in 1962, for example, when voters chose Republican William Scranton over his handpicked successor. The Lawrence administration had produced an impressive package of social welfare legislation, remained relatively free of scandal, and had balanced the budget. The party, in his view, deserved to be returned to office. His surprise when the voters rejected his candidate reflects a simple, almost naïve view of the world of politics. He continued to believe, after fifty years in political life, that "good government" would produce its own rewards.

Clearly the key to Lawrence's beliefs about politics and government lies not in his written statements—he wrote little, and even the voluminous governor's papers carry few useful clues to his thought process. According to his executive secretary Walter Giesey, "he was a telephoner. If you could have taped all his telephone calls you could have gotten some measure of the man." His prepared speeches give some indication of his attitudes, but they cannot be accepted verbatim; they were written by his aides, Robin and Giesey. "What you needed was to get the words after the prepared text was finished. . . . Lawrence was always better after he finished with the text."[8]

Similarly, the best source of information about Lawrence's leadership quality and orientation on issues on the eve of his first election as mayor of Pittsburgh is his own behavior. A number of characteristics stand out.

Perhaps most important among the forces that drove Lawrence was an almost fierce sense of duty. He worked harder and longer than anyone else, only partially because such diligence usually produced victory. Victory to him brought only momentary satisfaction. The lasting reward occurred because office holding enabled one to attain one's goals. Compromises and delays were to be expected, but they should not prevent one from fulfilling one's objectives. In all his administrative offices Lawrence frequently implemented unpopular policies if he believed them to be consistent with what he saw as his duty to his constituency. His policies on smoke control, taxation, and labor negotiations, among others, all generated considerable opposition during his mayoralty. Several were potentially disastrous to his political career, yet he followed the policy he thought correct regardless of political consequences.

Department and cabinet heads were expected to follow suit in carrying out their own duties no matter how difficult or distasteful. When Lawrence assumed office as mayor in 1946, he informed department heads that he would not tolerate interdepartmental disputes and rivalries that jeopardized the city's interests. "We are working for the same employer—the people. . . . We'll work or get off the job." He delivered a similar warning at the start of each administration and in his address to cabinet heads when he assumed the office of governor in 1959. The message, according to many sources, was not idle rhetoric intended for public consumption.[9]

A second trait of Lawrence, often erroneously believed to have developed after 1945, was his ability to separate political interests from governmental responsibilities. He had seen during the Earle years the harmful effects of uncontrolled political ambition. Cabinet leaders such as Margiotti and Edward N. Jones had been selected for their political efforts rather than their ability to contribute to the welfare of the state. Departments became a morass of political infighting and intrigue. In contrast, Lawrence's efforts to push the legislative program through the General Assembly, while certainly partisan, remained relatively free of political maneuvering. Their success was due in part to Lawrence's insistence that legislators subordinate political ambitions to the larger common goal of passing the entire legislative package. In Pittsburgh, while operating as the behind-the-scenes political boss, he admittedly expected that victorious candidates would help build the party by turning the patronage machinery over to the party heads. Beyond that, however, elected officials were free to operate in the manner that they saw fit as long as their actions were judged to be in the best interests of the electorate. Even William McNair was given eighteen months of relative freedom before Lawrence decided to intervene.

When he became mayor of Pittsburgh, Lawrence turned his ability to separate government and politics into policy. To accommodate this principle he adopted a dual hiring policy for the city. Rank and file workers, laborers, non–civil service appointees, clerical help, and police and firemen were selected through the normal patronage process. Candidates for office were selected on the basis of their ability to achieve party harmony. Ability and training were of secondary importance. Most policy-making officials, bureau and department heads, and authority directors, however, were hired on the basis of education and experience. The practice brought an exceptional number of highly qualified people into policy-making positions in city government.

A third quality, Lawrence's willingness to welcome experts into his administration, no doubt grew out of the great respect he had for them, particularly those holding advanced degrees. He always felt a strong sense of inadequacy about his own limited formal education and often appeared slightly ill-at-ease in the company of a number of highly educated people. He welcomed lawyers and educators into the party and the government and supported political figures such as Richardson Dilworth, Joseph Clark, and Adlai Stevenson. "It was brains," Genevieve Blatt pointed out. "He was always on the lookout for someone he thought had the brains to be a good government official."[10] Brains, Blatt correctly noted, were associated in Lawrence's mind with a proper education. Dilworth and Clark, not coincidentally, attended Ivy League colleges, a fact that added to their luster for Lawrence.

Consistent with the high regard in which he held education were the educational reforms he helped initiate throughout his career: teacher tenure and training reforms in 1937, community-supported educational television in Pittsburgh in 1953, and statewide school district reorganization in 1960. Lawrence was aware of his preoccupation. "When I mention education first, you might conclude that I attach the highest priority to that area. And you would be right."[11] Education, he argued, was the foundation of both an enlightened society and a properly functioning community.

The ultimate result for the city of Pittsburgh and the state of Pennsylvania was threefold. First, Lawrence surrounded himself with technical and administrative experts and gave them freedom to perform their jobs without undue interference. Second, his reliance on nonpolitical personnel at many policy-making levels served to insulate much of the municipal and state government from the vagaries of politics. Because many of the bureau heads had numerous outside job opportunities, they could demand that their departments remain isolated from patronage hiring and other well-known political pressures. Lawrence willingly acquiesced. The semi-independent authorities in Pittsburgh, such as the redevelopment and housing authorities in particular, enjoyed a remarkable freedom from politics.

Finally, the talent around Lawrence would have produced few benefits had he been unwilling or unable to learn from them. Such, fortunately was not the case. As mayor, for example, he initially had almost no concept of the complexity of the urban redevelopment task he was about to undertake. Shortly before his election he visited Mayor La Guardia in New York city for advice. "What are you here for?" La Guardia snapped in his well-known abrupt manner. "I'm running for mayor of Pittsburgh," Lawrence replied. "He looked up at me," Lawrence recalled, "and he squatted in his little chair and said, 'you're a god-damned fool.' Well, I said, 'I didn't come here to be lectured. I came here to get some advice.' So he turned me over to Bob Moses." There is no record of the conversation between Lawrence and the irrepressible Moses, but Lawrence later referred to it as the beginning of his education in municipal management. That education never stopped: Lawrence was open to new ideas all his life. Aldo Colautti knew Lawrence only as an older man, in his sixties and seventies. "The thing that struck me about him was that he seemed to be more receptive to changes in federal or state policies in, for example civil rights, than many of the younger people about him."[12]

A fourth element that Lawrence brought to the administration of the city in 1945 may best be described as leadership style, which affected most of his staff. His no-nonsense approach to government and politics stamped both as serious business, with little time for frivolity. There was not a minute of the day when he was not occupied, and his time was compartmentalized into politics, government, family, and leisure. The first two required approximately twelve to fifteen hours per day on the average, and three hours were reserved for the latter two. The four compartments, moreover, were highly organized and almost never overlapped. His work day was organized into fifteen-minute appointments, during which he expected a succinct, precise presentation. For his part, he expected to give an immediate answer. Then he would terminate the meeting with his customary handclap or rapping of the ring on the desk. Many people left the mayor's office with the impression that Lawrence was brusque, even rude, but nearly everyone received the same treatment.[13]

As might be expected in one so highly organized, punctuality was part of his style, and it became almost an obsession with him. Offices were expected to open on time and workers to report promptly. People who kept him waiting felt his swift and certain wrath. In 1958, in perhaps the most extreme example of his insistence on promptness, he had a nearly permanent falling-out with his gubernatorial running mate, John Morgan Davis. Davis, his wife, and three children joined Lawrence on a western campaign swing and managed to appear at every joint speaking engagement a few minutes late. One evening Lawrence arrived at the court house in Kane for an eight o'clock speaking engagement. Davis, true to form, arrived around 8:15 P.M. "You're late," Lawrence roared at him. "I'm only fifteen minutes late," Davis replied. "You're fifteen minutes too *goddam* late," Lawrence responded. With that he walked off the platform and ordered his son to call the state committee. "Get him a staff. I can't travel with him."[14] The two men remained on uneasy terms for the entire Lawrence administration.

The final personal characteristic that contributed to Lawrence's success as mayor came from years of involvement in politics. By 1945 he had developed a sharp ability to remain close to the electorate. Whether through his well-publicized love of sports, a malady common to most Pittsburghers, his down-home speaking style, or the attention he paid to political workers and the voters, a strong bond was beginning to develop. Genevieve Blatt described him as "a true Pittsburgher, of the people." He became a master of the off-the-cuff statement after the formal address: the "now I'm going to give you the real story" type of address. Political crowds, mostly Democrats by 1945, reveled in this seemingly spontaneous informality in a mostly formal man. In addition, the attention he paid to political workers continued to pay handsome dividends. Hospital and home visits to workers or their families, attendance at funerals, weddings, first communion celebrations, bar mitzvahs, and ward-level political rallies—all these signaled Lawrence as a man who cared about one's political effort. Workers usually responded with increased efforts and a strong attachment to "the chief." Finally, Lawrence's background as a self-made man and his lack of pretension enhanced his image in this workers' city. Seemingly insignificant practices strengthened the relationship. For example, although he used a driver during his term as mayor, he almost never rode in the back seat unless accompanied by another rider. It became common knowledge around the Bloomfield-Garfield area that the rear seat in the morning was reserved for cleaning women whom he happened to encounter on his way to work. His mayoral auto was always a simple sedan several years old. When he become governor, he canceled an order for a new limousine placed by the Leader administration, preferring instead a six-year-old auto that had done more than 100,000 miles.[15]

Pittsburgh's perception of "Davey" as "one of us" evolved from more than his commuting habits. A unique ability to interact on a common level with people regardless of their social background was perhaps his most important political asset. Corporate presidents such as Henry Hillman and Edgar Kaufmann, technical specialists such as Wallace Richards and I. Hope Alexander, political associates such as Huck Fenrich and Al Conway, and many individual voters commented on this rare gift of Lawrence's. It became crucial as the administration attempted to carry out the urban redevelopment that became the hallmark of his four terms in office. The public support for the large number of programs spanning nearly two decades was due in large part to Lawrence's ability to remain "close to the people." James Michener commented on Lawrence's gift in 1961: "I suppose the newspapers were right in labeling him 'a typical ward-heeling politician,' but whenever I heard the phrase in connection with Dave Lawrence, I thought, 'I wish my ward were in such hands.' For the thing that impressed me most about . . . Lawrence was that he talked sense. In his speeches that I heard, he hammered away at specific legislation, at specific problems. He seemed to have a delicate radar set tuned in to the minds of the people to whom he was talking, and with each group he discussed the things that they were interested in."[16]

Michener's testimony notwithstanding, Lawrence was not without faults or weaknesses. He was subject to moods of depression or anger, to moments of pettiness, and he could often be accused of insensitivity to the feelings of others. Among fellow workers, for example, Lawrence's temper was well known. He was often short with his office staff, particularly when he was upset by an error or an unexpected interruption in his routine. He was particularly short tempered when he was not feeling well. These periods were rare, but during them Lawrence's cordiality would vanish and "he would really be a bear." Only his closest associates would know why. "Others would say, 'Gee, he is in a hell of a bad mood today. . . .' They didn't know . . . the reason . . . and we certainly weren't about to tell them." But Lawrence gave vent to his anger most frequently when local ward workers did what he perceived to be careless work or failed to carry out an assigned duty. "He let them know he was angry in no uncertain terms. When he began to shout and rap that ring on the desk they got out of there in a hurry." He also became terribly irritated at reporters, particularly when they referred to him as "boss," and at political associates whose ambition, in his opinion, threatened the unity of the party.[17]

Lawrence's temper outbursts, fortunately for his staff and others, were relatively few. Nevertheless, he was not an easy man to work for. He expected his employees to show the same total devotion to the job that he demanded of himself. He was seldom considerate of their need for time outside of work. "He would call you up at night, call you up in the morning. He would expect you to respond," said Jack Robin, who nevertheless called Lawrence a "nice Lyndon Johnson." "He put up with things later on that he wouldn't have tolerated earlier. He just generally mellowed and became a nicer fellow."[18]

Furthermore, he almost never complimented workers on their good efforts. High-quality work was expected and praise was seldom given. Walter Giesey, his highly talented aide, gave absolute loyalty to Lawrence for sixteen years, accompanying him to Harrisburg and Washington, D.C., to remain in his service. "Few people understood the wide range of responsibilities that Walter Giesey exercised," explained Aldo Colautti, his successor in the mayor's office. "He was in effect the budget manager, he was in charge of all the legislative relations with city council, he had all of the city department heads reporting to him, he functioned as, in effect, what other cities would call the city manager." Lawrence was clearly dependent upon him, yet several associates, including Colautti, said that they never heard Lawrence praise Giesey for his important contributions.[19]

Lawrence not only was sparing with his praise but was often gruff or seemingly rude, particularly with those in constant close contact with him. He always answered the phone in a demanding, "What do you want?" tone of voice. He was seldom cordial on the phone and was often unnecessarily sharp with political associates and party workers. Volunteer Rosemary Plessett related, "One time when he was in Harrisburg he asked me to keep him 'up to date on what those ward chairmen are doing.' So I called him . . . and he said, 'Goddam it! I have a whole state to run. I can't worry about two ward chairmen.' Bang! And he hung up. So I had to be very careful about what information I relayed to him." Most of his executive staff and close associates excused his brusqueness as a result of his desire to keep on schedule and his impatience with minor details. Walter Giesey, however, attributed a deeper significance to it. "After being with him for a long time, I came to understand that most of it was a facade. He recognized that that was the kind of image that he had to create to help convey the belief that he was in charge. He would say many times that 'there are only three ways a political leader can run things and that's either out of love, respect or fear. If you don't have one or two, then you simply can't function.' I don't think he ever sought love; he sought respect and in certain instances fear."[20] Giesey's analysis certainly seems on the mark. There was little around him that escaped his attention, and it seems likely that he was indeed aware of his image among his staff and associates. On the other hand, Lawrence often went out of his way to avoid offending political and governmental colleagues, including those whom he could easily have destroyed. Moreover, it was a poorly kept secret around city hall that he could never fire anyone and seldom demoted city workers. On those few occasions when dismissal became necessary, Giesey or a department head was left to carry out the action. In one instance when he did order the dismissal of a worker, he ordered him rehired, in another position, when he learned that he needed only a few more years of work to become eligible for retirement. Thus it appears that his sharp tongue was the result of a carefully orchestrated effort to project a tough-guy, always-in-charge image.

Perhaps more upsetting to those around him was his intolerance of what he considered weaknesses in others. Understandably, he detested Margiotti, who had attempted to put him in prison. However, he was more disdainful of what he saw as the man's dishonesty and uncontrolled ambition. It was a basic character flaw worthy of any ethical person's deepest scorn. Joseph Guffey, Joe McArdle, and David Roberts possessed the same weakness and earned Lawrence's longtime enmity. He worked with all three out of necessity but always avoided any unnecessary contact. Once, while sitting in a car with Art Rooney, owner of the Pittsburgh Steelers, he noticed Roberts approaching along the sidewalk. "I don't want to see this guy," he said, and crouched down on the seat until the prothonotary passed by.[21]

Another longtime opponent, Ray Sprigle, an investigative journalist for the *Post Gazette,* earned his place on Lawrence's enemy list through his crusade against corruption on the city police force. Sprigle, in Lawrence's opinion, was basically dishonest in his reporting—another "sin" that Lawrence could not tolerate—and spoke to the reporter only when absolutely necessary. Sprigle's articles inflicted serious damage on the Lawrence administration, but he never earned the lifelong bitterness that Lawrence directed toward Margiotti. He was doing the job for which his employer hired him, and Lawrence could understand his "indiscretions." When the mayor learned that Sprigle had entered a hospital of questionable reputation for a detached retina operation, he called the owner of the *Post-Gazette,* William Block. His own numerous eye operations had made him something of an expert on eye surgery facilities in the city. "You should get him out of there," he urged. Block complied and later reported that Lawrence's advice had prevented a possible serious medical complication for Sprigle. Sprigle apparently never learned of Lawrence's action, and the two retained their adversarial posture.[22]

Other behavior traits of which Lawrence disapproved, such as drinking, merely aroused the disagreeable side of his personality. "It was a weakness he couldn't understand. He had no tolerance for it," said his son Jerry. Everywhere he turned during his political life it seemed he encountered people who drank more than he thought acceptable. He became most irritated by those close to him. He frequently ridiculed Governor Earle's drinking habits in private, and some felt the sting of his scorn in the company of others, as in the case of one of his aides—it made little difference that the aide always performed to expectations and often contributed well beyond the normal call of duty.[23]

Finally, Lawrence remained somewhat stiff, almost puritanical all his life. On the job he had no time even for occasional levity, and in public he maintained what he considered proper decorum. He enjoyed his pinochle game or an hour at the YMCA, but at both he was businesslike and highly competitive. Even at home he was rather formal and followed a somewhat rigid routine. He greatly enjoyed sporting events, but the enjoyment derived from the competitiveness of the event rather than a lightheartedness on his part. Although Lawrence carried several pages of jokes with him at all times, few associates could recall humorous anecdotes or incidents involving him. John Jones perhaps best captured the serious nature of Lawrence. "He would laugh at others but not at himself. He could tell a joke but the joke was never directed at Lawrence. Most of them were what you might call grocery store humor. But I don't think he had a real sense of humor."[24]

It was perhaps Lawrence's inability to view life in a softer light that prevented him from showing compassion to his wife following the deaths of their sons. He had overcome, or at least controlled, his grief, and he expected the same of Alyce. When she could not and turned to alcohol for solace he treated her as he treated others; in his mind she could refrain from drinking if she so willed it. He retreated further into his work, leaving her alone in a house full of children and relatives to regain control of her life. His absence merely exacerbated her difficulty. That neither could help the other reveals perhaps as much about the state of society in the mid 1940s as it does about either one. One was expected to work out one's problems. The divergent paths taken by David and Alyce Lawrence—one functional, the other destructive—created an unbridgeable gulf between them.

1942–1945
The Interlude

In mid 1942 David Lawrence was struggling to rise from his political and personal disasters. Fortunately for him the method of his ascent existed within his own, now unstable, political career. His running battle with U.S. Senator Joseph Guffey, a new role in national politics, and his efforts to regain control of the state and of western Pennsylvania politics all contributed to his reemergence.

Guffey had momentarily held the upper hand in 1940 when, on the strength of his renomination, he insisted that Lawrence make good on his pledge to resign as Democratic state chairman. By installing his own man, Meridith Meyers, Guffey, at least on the surface, gained new strength in the state organization. He now appeared to be the number one Democrat in the state. It was only Lawrence's standing among the party regulars that prevented Guffey from attempting his total expulsion from the leadership. Rather than risk a dangerous battle that he might conceivably lose, Guffey agreed to back Lawrence for the position of Democratic national committeeman from Pennsylvania. Thus what initially appeared to be a certain Guffey victory, with no quarter given, turned instead into a standoff, with the senator holding a slight edge. Lawrence retained both his prestige and some of his influence. In addition, he gained a degree of national prominence.

During the next two years the two men jockeyed for position, neither able to assert full command. Lawrence, the loyal party regular, had supported, although somewhat less than enthusiastically, Guffey's 1940 reelection campaign. His efforts, by several accounts, won the continued admiration and respect of the organization regulars.[1] Guffey countered by easily winning reelection in November. Lawrence, recognized as the master campaigner, matched him by turning out expected majorities for Roosevelt both in western Pennsylvania and across the state.[2] During the next several years Guffey and Lawrence continued to attack and counterattack each other. To make matters worse for the party, they carried out their war in the media, in full view of the public. Their invective continued without letup for the whole year and promised a battle royal for control of the party in 1942, when two key decisions would be made—selection of a nominee for governor and election of a state chairman.

As was to be expected, the two men differed on both issues. In February 1942, Lawrence, Matthew McCloskey, and Jack Kelly, following a closed-door meeting in Philadelphia, announced that they would support F. Clair Ross—the auditor general and the only Democrat to win statewide office in 1938—for the state committee endorsement for the gubernatorial nomination. A number of Democratic leaders around the state grumbled about the high-handed tactics, and most recognized that they were presented with a fait accompli. Guffey, seeking allies, turned to Allegheny County Commissioner John Kane, who had expressed the most irritation at being left out of the Philadelphia meeting. The two agreed to support an alternative candidate, Judge Ralph Smith, threatening not only to cause another costly statewide primary battle—in terms of both money and party unity—but also to split the Allegheny County party wide open. County Democrats and labor supporters began to line up behind the rising star, Kane, while the city workers and staunch organization members remained loyal to Lawrence. The scenario appeared to be working just the way Guffey hoped. A Smith victory would seriously damage Lawrence's prestige and place Kane in position to claim leadership of western Pennsylvania and perhaps the state chairmanship in June.

For a brief moment during the tragic week of 20 April 1942, it had appeared that Guffey and Lawrence migh reconcile their differences. Guffey visited the Lawrence household several times and attended funeral services. Lawrence met briefly with him on one of these occasions, and the press reported that the two men appeared cordial toward each other. But appearances were deceptive, and the battle continued through the primary and general elections.

Lawrence's first significant triumph occurred in the 1942 primary. In a light turnout, which many attributed to the voters' preoccupation with World War II, Lawrence's candidate, Ross, easily defeated Judge Smith by more than 600,000 votes. Smith lost fifty-seven of Pennsylvania's sixty-seven counties in spite of his endorsement by both the AFL and the CIO leadership and support from important

Democrats from Pittsburgh and Philadelphia. Moreover, he won only one county normally controlled by the Democratic organization. Luther Harr ran a distant third. Senator Guffey brazenly attributed his candidate's defeat to the newly enacted Hatch Act, which prohibited political activity on the part of federal employees. The act, Guffey noted, removed thousands of loyal Guffey supporters, mostly WPA employees, from the political arena. What Guffey failed to note was that by 1942, because of decreased federal funding for Depression relief, the number of federal employees in Pennsylvania had declined drastically.[3]

The exceptionally small voter turnout and the effectiveness of the Lawrence supporters, more likely, produced the easy Ross victory. In organization counties the turnout exceeded that in nonorganization counties. Only in Allegheny County, influenced by the temporary split between the Kane and Lawrence forces and the local residency of Judge Smith, did the organization fail to produce a Ross victory. The election results made it clear that, while Guffey and Meridith Meyers controlled the party offices, Lawrence retained the loyalty of key leaders and, more important, the rank and file workers. The post of state chairman would be Lawrence's for the asking, should he choose to run.

When the time arrived, Lawrence made it clear that he expected to be reinstalled. His unanimous election provided him with the outlet he required to enable him to cope with the loss of his sons. It also eliminated Guffey, once and for all, as an important force in the party. Guffey made one final attempt to place himself in a bargaining position with Lawrence by threatening to back Judge Smith as an independent candidate for governor, but Smith upset those plans by announcing in early June that he would support the party's nominee. Lawrence by the summer of 1942 had no peer within the Democratic party of Pennsylvania.

Once again, however, Lawrence had opted for an unattractive candidate who generated no enthusiasm among the voters in the midwar general election. Ross campaigned on his record as auditor general and the inadequacies of the James administration, and this created no groundswell of support. Pennsylvanians found it difficult to become excited over the activities of the state's number one bookkeeper, no matter how competent. His opponent, the former Republican state chairman Edward Martin, ignoring the not guilty verdicts of the two Lawrence trials, reminded his audiences of the corruption of the last Democratic administration. He also repeatedly, and correctly, charged that Ross was the handpicked candidate of "Boss Lawrence." But Martin's small audiences reacted with the same lack of enthusiasm shown Ross.

The lowest election response in thirty years gave Martin 55 percent of the votes. Pennsylvanians joined in the Republican resurgence occurring across the nation by electing the entire Republican state ticket. This gave the GOP control of the State House and Senate. In Lawrence's home district of western Pennsylvania, Ross defeated Martin in both Pittsburgh and Allegheny County, but by the smallest margins in a decade. The Republican candidate captured seventeen of twenty-four western counties. Republican control in the state had been reestablished for the first time since 1934, and the Democrats were in danger of reverting to their earlier political impotence.[4]

Yet, out of defeat, Lawrence emerged as the sole Democratic power in Pennsylvania. Most Democrats viewed the nationwide Republican victory and the meddling of Guffey as the causes of the Democratic defeat. Lawrence suffered no recriminations, even from those formerly in opposition to him. Kane, Meyers, Leo Mundy, Luzerne County chairman, and James Clark, Philadelphia County chairman, all commented on the national Republican tide and praised Lawrence in their postelection comments. A thoroughly discredited Guffey was no longer a threat to Lawrence or the party. Following an unsuccessful reelection bid in 1946, he retired from politics at age seventy-five.

One unexpected result of the battle his selection as national committeeman, was a recurring source of pleasure for the rest of Lawrence's life. One of his greatest joys as a young politician had been to attend the Democratic National Convention, first as a page and later as a delegate from Pennsylvania. The bartering for votes, the negotiations over candidates and platform, the pageantry, and the frenzied pace thrilled him. Of all his political activities he seemed happiest and most excited when attending a national convention.[5] No evidence exists to suggest that he desired the post of national committeeman, although given his drive for leadership, the thought must have occasionally crossed his mind. He showed no reluctance in suggesting the position in 1940 as consolation for relinquishing the state chairmanship.

As he had done when he assumed the city, county, and state party chairmanships, Lawrence seized the post, which had been largely honorary in the history of the Pennsylvania Democratic party, and turned it into one of major significance. His role at the 1940 Democratic National Convention in Chicago had been marginal, but it would never be so again.

With Roosevelt's nomination for his third term a foregone conclusion, political intrigue and maneuvering at the 1940 convention had rested on the selection of a running mate; "Cactus Jack" Garner had lost FDR's support. Lawrence, who originally favored an old friend, Indiana Governor Paul McNutt, for the second spot on the ballot, visited the Roosevelt headquarters to obtain inside information on the president's choice. He met with Harry Hopkins, who suggested that Lawrence call Roosevelt at the White House. "When I talked with President Roosevelt," said Lawrence, "he stressed very strongly that we were weak in the farm states and that Wallace being on the ticket would be a great help to us." Armed with this information—FDR later issued his "nominate this man or I won't run" edict—Lawrence made his initial speech to the Pennsylvania delegation. "I don't want to see Pennsylvania become a tail on this kite. The word is pretty well around Chicago that Henry Wallace is the leading candidate. We should go to the convention with at least a majority for the candidate who is likely to win. We can play smart politics and lead the vanguard for the Secretary of Agriculture." Pennsylvania gave sixty-eight of its seventy-three votes to Wallace. Ironically, the secretary of agriculture failed to deliver the expected farm vote and predicted as much to Lawrence in the fall of the year. Lawrence agreed to campaign with the vice-presidential candidate "to break down any feeling among the Democrats in Pennsylvania that I was unfriendly to Wallace." They had just completed a swing across the western section of the state when Lawrence remarked, "Well, Henry, I guess we'll do all right in Iowa." "Oh, no," Wallace responded, "we'll lose Iowa. In fact, we'll lose nearly all those states. Nebraska, the Dakotas and so on. . . . They're just not going to vote for the ticket this year." Lawrence later reported that he filed the incident away to use it against Wallace in 1944, but it proved to be unnecessary. The role of the freshman national committeeman from Pennsylvania was not crucial. But he had given a hint of the care with which he intended to operate and clearly signaled that he would not be content to play a passive role in presidential politics. Four years later he got his opportunity to act.[6]

The Pennsylvania delegation to the national convention, under the leadership of Lawrence and national committeewoman Emma Guffey Miller ("The Old Grey Mare") decided as early as February 1944 to support Roosevelt for his fourth term. Once again any dispute would center on the choice for vice president. As he had done four years earlier, Guffey, along with the CIO president, Philip Murray, and Meyers, jumped on the Wallace bandwagon before the convention.

Lawrence, never comfortable with Wallace, leaned toward Senator Alben Barkley of Kentucky but was persuaded by Kane to join the growing list of Truman supporters.

Lawrence and the Missouri senator had met years earlier on an outing arranged by Guffey. They met subsequently over the years, usually for lunch at the Senate dining room and most often with Guffey. Lawrence recalled being neither impressed nor unimpressed with Truman, but Kane was enthusiastic. Then, "in April [1944] Senator Truman came to Pittsburgh to make a speech. . . . The next day I drove [him] . . . to York, . . . to speak to the Young Democratic Society. . . . It gave me my best opportunity to have a real visit over four or five hours of driving across the Pennsylvania Turnpike." Lawrence was impressed that Truman was urging Roosevelt to pardon the senator's old benefactor, Tom Pendergast of Kansas City, then in prison. Lawrence believed Pendergast had suffered at the hands of disloyal associates and admired Truman's loyalty and support.[7]

Shortly afterward Lawrence became a strong and active Truman supporter. He went to Washington, D.C., just before the convention to meet with Mayor Ed Kelly of Chicago, the Democratic national chairman, Robert Hannegan of Missouri, Jacob Arvey of Chicago, and several others to plan strategy for the Truman candidacy. Risking a renewed split with Guffey and, even more important, with organized labor in western Pennsylvania—where Philip Murray and his political action chairman, Sidney Hillman, were campaigning for Wallace—Lawrence returned home to announce his support of the Missouri senator. "It was . . . hard to be on the opposite side from Mr. Murray. . . . And, of course, labor was generally supporting Wallace, and that put me in an awkward position in Pennsylvania, particularly in the Pittsburgh area, which is strongly organized in the labor movement."[8] A split in the Pennsylvania delegation appeared certain.

The convention battle over the vice-presidential choice was waged both within the Pennsylvania delegation and on the floor. A motion to endorse Wallace, introduced by Murray and supported by Guffey, his sister Emma, and Meyers one day before the convention caught Lawrence by surprise. He had called the caucus to discuss voting and other procedures. He immediately ruled the motion out of order but agreed to permit it when reminded that the endorsement did not compel all delegates to support Wallace on the first ballot. The result of the caucus vote was forty-one to twenty-one to endorse Henry Wallace. The Truman backers had considerable work to accomplish in a short period of time.

Angered by the opposition to Wallace, Guffey blasted the Truman candidacy, charging that it was being "bossed by the well known machine leaders Kelly, Hague, and Flynn." He circumspectly omitted Lawrence. His attack might have carried more weight had he added that several of the bosses, as well as Lawrence and Hannegan, had adjoining rooms on the seventh floor of Chicago's Blackstone Hotel. The publication of Guffey's candid but ill-tempered remarks, however, left him with no room to maneuver in the event that the Wallace bandwagon stalled.[9]

Under Lawrence's leadership, Kane, James Clark, and a number of others spent the next several days fruitlessly attempting to sway members of the delegation toward Truman. At one point when it appeared that they might be creating a shift in sentiment, hundreds of telegrams, sponsored by the CIO officials, arrived demanding support for Wallace. Wavering delegates moved back into the vice-president's camp.[10]

Lawrence, unable to control his own delegation, continued to confer with Hannegan, Ed Kelly, Mayor Frank Hague of Jersey City, and the postmaster general, Frank Walker, to plan strategy. Buoyed by FDR's initial cool support for Wallace and a later letter indicating that Truman would be "acceptable to him," this self-appointed executive committee determined that its first task would be to head off a possible Wallace stampede. If that occurred, they decided in private, the convention chairman would recognize Lawrence via a prearranged signal. Lawrence would then call for a twelve-hour recess to stop the nomination and give the pro-Truman forces an opportunity to regroup.[11] The plan worked precisely as arranged.

The CIO-organized Wallace steamroller began to operate on the evening of 20 July, according to schedule. Through the use of counterfeit admission tickets, the union managed to fill the convention floor to overflowing. "I was as afraid as I ever was in my life," Genevieve Blatt recalled. "All kinds of Chicago people . . . were pouring in to try to fill the place up. . . . And I got . . . forced toward the concrete outside wall. I was really afraid I might get crushed into it. I could see the wall coming closer. And some very big men were really shoving and shoving. And when we got to the door . . . they forced us in so hard that I kind of entered the hall in a burst."[12]

When the first ballot was taken, Wallace emerged clearly in the lead but lacking a few votes necessary for nomination. The demonstration planned by the CIO and a few other organizations began slowly because several groups missed their cue. They quickly recovered, however, and "pandemonium broke loose. Wallace was very close to the nomination, and we felt that if it had gone into another ballot, some of the weaker-kneed delegates might run away from Truman to Wallace." The chairman, supposedly spotting Lawrence in the midst of the swelling chaos, gave him the floor. According to Genevieve Blatt, he probably did not even see Lawrence. "He just said, 'I recognize the gentleman from Pennsylvania.' And the gentleman from Pennsylvania had the mike and they turned it on loud for him and he made the motion. . . . [chairman Jackson] stated the motion, put the vote, and it was all over in thirty seconds. All of a sudden there was no more session. The chairman was away from the podium and the people were leaving the stage." The stunned Wallace supporters, in spite of their reinforcements, had been outmaneuvered by a handful of men.[13]

Hannegan, Hague, Ed Kelly, Walker, and Lawrence then met under the stage to assess their situation. "We counted noses. . . . We made plans to check on all the delegations and to have the lines hold. We also contacted all possible wavering Wallace supporters and uncommitted delegates."[14]

By the next day the Wallace balloon had been punctured. Ballot switches in several key delegations gave Truman the nomination on the second ballot. On a somewhat pathetic note, Guffey, in what proved to be his swansong in national politics, grabbed the microphone from the Pennsylvania floor chairman, Judge John Wilson, and tried to move that the nomination be made unanimous. He was ruled out of order, but eight state votes later he again called for a unanimous vote and the motion carried. By this time Truman had 261 votes more than necessary for nomination.

Lawrence, although able to deliver only twenty-four of his state's seventy-two votes for Truman, emerged from the convention as the undisputed leading power in Pennsylvania and an important force in national politics. In an era when city bosses exercised a strong influence in Washington, Lawrence gave notice that he could play in the same league as the most powerful. In succeeding years, as the old guard of Ed Kelly and Hague gave way to younger urban leaders, Lawrence would emerge as the head of the informal delegation of city leaders. It was a role he was to relish during his next two decades in politics. He approached convention politics, as he did all party meetings, as serious business. He discouraged "spontaneous celebrations" on the part of the Pennsylvania delegation and frequently lectured them on proper decorum. He enjoyed the opportunity to meet with old political friends, many representing urban political organizations, and thrilled at the give-and-take of national politics. It was a high-stakes game that reflected his competitive spirit and challenged his ability to win without destroying the party. In the year 1944, when he was still recovering from the death of his sons, it also provided a welcome balm for the pain he carried inside.

Lawrence maintained his frantic pace through the fall election, campaigning in every one of the state's sixty-seven counties. He accompanied both Roosevelt and Truman on their brief visits to Pennsylvania and was particularly active on behalf of the U.S. Senate candidate, Francis J. Myers. He also campaigned for two of his former choices for governor, Charles Alvin Jones and F. Clair Ross, candidates for judge of, respectively, the State Supreme Court and the State Superior Court. The three Pennsylvania candidates were particularly important to Lawrence because all were nominated over the mild objection of Guffey. A sweep would not only revitalize the Democratic party in the state but would probably put a permanent end to the Guffey opposition.

▽

The November election returns did just that, giving Lawrence his greatest statewide victory since 1934. The Roosevelt-Truman margin of victory in Pennsylvania reflected the narrowness of their triumph throughout the nation, but Lawrence's strongholds of Pittsburgh, Allegheny County, and now Philadelphia returned substantial, although not overwhelming majorities.[15] Equally gratifying were the victories of Lawrence's personal candidates for statewide office and the fact that the Democrats regained control of the State House of Representatives. The debacle of 1938 had been partly reversed, and Lawrence's position as the top Democrat in Pennsylvania was secure. He would not have to contend with Joe Guffey again.

In spite of Democratic triumphs at national and state levels, Lawrence remained most comfortable and perhaps most effective in western Pennsylvania. The roots from which he sprang had remained strong during his entire Harrisburg experience. Unlike a legislator, who is required to maintain touch with "the folks back home," Lawrence as state chairman and secretary of the Commonwealth could have abandoned his Pittsburgh ties. His success depended only partly on a Pittsburgh area constituency. However, he did not divorce himself from the Steel City. Making the often uncomfortable, time-consuming train trip from Pittsburgh to Harrisburg and back again, he spent almost as much time in Pittsburgh as in the capital. His family continued to live in the city of his birth and he never entertained the idea that he would not one day return. The tumultuous welcome in April 1940, was, in a way, an inner victory. He could now devote greater attention to the party he had nurtured so carefully during his youth and early adulthood.

It was no longer the organization Lawrence had turned over to William McNair and James Kirk, his successor as Democratic county chairman, when he left for Harrisburg in 1934. Inevitable cracks had begun to form in the coalition that had been created during the early years of the Roosevelt administration. Former Republicans such as P. J. McArdle and rising young Democrats such as John Kane and David Roberts, a prothonotary, had begun to form an opposition. Certain voting blocks, including Italian-Americans, blacks, and, most important, organized labor were pulled in several directions as contending leaders arose within the particular groups. In addition, the Republicans themselves, now leaner and no longer suffering from the complacency resulting from huge registration majorities, had begun to offer stiffer opposition. Lawrence's task was by no means as formidable as the one he had faced a decade earlier, but it still presented a healthy challenge.

Perhaps the greatest problem facing Lawrence in his attempt to strengthen the party was his choice for mayor, Cornelius Scully. Following the McNair resignation in 1936, the mayor's office had been turned over to the steady but unspectacular city council president. Scully was "a gentleman of the old school. Cultured and educated, he was from a long-line family from the uppercrust of Pittsburgh society. . . . He was an Episcopalian, a member of the Duquesne Club, and from Lawrence's point of view he represented a section of Pittsburgh society which was not well represented in the Democratic party. . . . He was wholly inexperienced in politics and was staunchly loyal to Lawrence."[16] Scully, a solid if somewhat bland personality, became the perfect choice to instill confidence in the Democratic party's ability to govern after the chaotic McNair administration. For the same reasons, he proved unable to generate any excitement on the part of the party regulars or the city's electorate. With organization backing in 1937 he had narrowly survived a bid by P. J. McArdle, a former Republican who became a Democratic city councilman in 1933, to deny him the party's nomination and narrowly won a term of his own.

Lawrence returned Scully's loyalty with support for his programs and unwavering political backing. Now, in 1941, amid strong opposition from a group headed by Kane and the county register of wills, John M. Huston, who argued that Scully could not win in the fall, Lawrence again remained faithful. Scully had done a competent job in difficult times and continued to demonstrate his loyalty to Lawrence. The party had an obligation to him and would not abandon him merely to strengthen the ticket. Scully won the primary with relative ease, although the small percentage of eligible Democrats who turned out to vote signaled a potential problem for the general election. Against Scully the Republican organization ran a lawyer who carried a well-known Pittsburgh name. Harmar Denny was a descendant of Pittsburgh's first mayor, Ebenezer Denny, and a member of a well-known upper-class family. He frequently contributed to Republican causes but managed to remain apart from the infighting of Pittsburgh politics. Thus he carried no taint of earlier Republican scandals.

Denny capitalized on his "clean" independent image by making "boss Lawrence, who has returned to Pittsburgh to reclaim the city," the main issue of the campaign. He virtually ignored Scully, consistently referring to the previous five years as the "Lawrence administration." In a typical address at the North Side Carnegie Hall he leveled a brutal attack on Lawrence. "Jersey City has its Boss Hague," he declared.

> Kansas City had its Boss Tom Pendergast—until the law caught up with him, and Pittsburgh has its Boss—Dictator David L. Lawrence. And let me tell you, Davey Lawrence makes Hague and Pendergast, in many ways look like a couple of pikers. . . . There's David L. Lawrence still smelling of the gravel scandal, the insurance scandal, the padded-payroll scandal in the highway department, the iniquitous gag laws with which he attempted to Hitlerize the citizens. With two of his pals convicted by the courts, this Pennsylvania Huey Long boasts that he and his gang are going back to Harrisburg. What's the idea—did they overlook something the last time they were there? . . . Take back your city from the boss ridden crew who have made it a political playground for Davey Lawrence.[17]

As Denny kept up his attack during September and October, the accomplishments of the Scully administration, the local efforts of Roosevelt and the New Deal, and even a whisper campaign regarding a Democratic plan to raise taxes after the election all faded into obscurity. The efforts of Lawrence to reassert his control over Pittsburgh became the sole issue. Lawrence, realizing that he was to be the focus of Denny's entire campaign, tried to remain in the background. That decision, however, gave to Scully the role that he was completely unsuited to play, that of major defender of the party. Denny attacked

Lawrence and the party again and again while Scully recited the accomplishments of his administration and talked of humanizing City Hall.

The results of the election nearly justified the fears of the anti-Scully faction in the party and sounded a clear warning to Lawrence. Mayor Scully won reelection, but by only 3163 out of a total of more than 220,000 votes, in spite of a Democratic registration advantage of more than 81,000. More alarmingly, he lost seventeen of the city's thirty-two wards, including ten that he had carried in the previous election. Scully emerged victorious in all the wards the party normally carried—those composed of heavily blue-collar, ethnic, and black neighborhoods located near the city center, and in the industrial riverbank communities. However, he was unable to carry a single one of the newer and rapidly growing suburbs in the East End, the South Hills, and the West End.[18] Thus, it became clear that the Scully, whose upper-class background should have attracted these "suburban" voters, added little to the party's ticket. The results of the city council races, moreover, confirmed that Scully had become a costly handicap: all six victorious Democratic candidates outpolled the head of the ticket and performed well in the middle-class neighborhoods that supported the Republican mayoralty candidate.

The results of the 1941 municipal elections had showed that the Democratic organization required patchwork and repair in certain places, but not a major overhaul. Immediately following the election, Lawrence met with district committeemen and ward chairmen. He said little to those whose neighborhoods had performed well in the recent election; others were warned to "get their houses in order and increase their efficiency or suffer the consequences. A few who were unwilling or unable to get in line were purged over the next few years."[19] Special efforts were to be made to strengthen the party among the various minority groups and among the city's white-collar middle class.

Fortunately, a decision on the major weakness of the party—Mayor Scully—could be avoided for four years. It is not certain when Lawrence joined the growing opposition to another term for him, but by 1945 he no longer had to be convinced. Scully, who willingly carried out the party philosophy and proved to be a competent mayor, was urged to retire. He could not win reelection, and nine years was as much support as one could expect. The surprise occurred when it came time to select his replacement.

Lawrence filled the difficult period of the early 1940s with power brokering, campaigning for his candidates, and shoring up the local party in areas where it had grown weak. He appeared content, entertaining no thoughts of running for office himself. In Lawrence's pre-1945 view, "you had to make a choice in politics. You either became a candidate-type or a manager-type, and he saw himself as the manager-type, where the job was picking the candidates."[20] It was a role he apparently expected to continue playing for the remainder of his political life.

But "picking the candidate" was for him a consensus activity. With the exception of 1938, when he supported Charles Alvin Jones for governor, he seldom forced his choice upon the party. A good candidate was one who captured the enthusiasm of the majority of the party leaders. A candidate stood no chance of winning if he failed to gain widespread support or if his candidacy split the party. Consensus within the party, he said over and over, was crucial to victory.

▽

The clearest consensus in 1945 was that Scully should be replaced as mayor. Only Scully disagreed, but he was too loyal to Lawrence and too much of a gentleman to make a strong protest. He made no public announcement regarding his candidacy, and it was assumed by all that he was no longer under consideration.

The void was quickly filled by a number of hopefuls who smelled a sure victory if anointed by the party leaders. Huston, who had challenged Scully in 1941, was the first to announce his candidacy. He was quickly followed by Roberts, Edward Frey, the city controller, and Patrick Fagan, former district president of the United Mine Workers. Each brought his own constituency to the potential battle, but none could claim the support of a majority of the party regulars or, more important, of its hierarchy.

Lawrence, Kirk, the county coroner, William McClelland, State Senator Joe Barr, and the other members of the Democratic executive committee at first attempted to persuade Kane to accept the party's endorsement. He was well known in the city, and, as a former labor leader, he could gain the support of the political action committees. In addition, as the second most powerful politician in western Pennsylvania, he could draw strong support from all factions of the party, possibly ensuring an uncontested primary. It was this last factor that caused him to decline the offer. Kane's strength lay in the county, not in the city of Pittsburgh. As a three-term county commissioner, he had carefully built his own organization, which, if he chose, might rival Lawrence's in terms of power and patronage. Indeed, the two had been rivals for a number of years. They frequently disagreed on party matters, and Kane occasionally threatened to challenge Lawrence's leadership. In reality, however, he lacked the competitive nature of Lawrence and was content to remain the number two politician in western Pennsylvania. His political and governmental status was secure as county commissioner, and he had considerable independence. He was naturally reluctant to abandon his constituency to become subservient to Lawrence. When he announced that he would not be a candidate, he stated that he had been elected commissioner by the people and was obligated to fulfill his term.

Searching for a compromise candidate, the party leaders, including Kane, then turned to Judge John J. Kennedy of the Court of Common Pleas. A former Pittsburgh city solicitor, he had been elected to the bench in the same election that gave Scully his first full term as mayor. Isolated from politics for the past seven years, he appeared to be the ideal candidate around whom all factions could rally. He had no known political enemies. Kennedy, flattered by the offer when first approached, gave indications that he might accept the endorsement. A caucus of the executive committee was scheduled for 25 March to hear all the potential candidates and select Kennedy.

The judge, however, sabotaged the planned crowning when he announced on the morning of the caucus that he would not be a candidate. He had been speared by his own sword. He had stated many times in the past seven years that any judge seeking a nonjudicial public office was morally obligated to surrender his commission before beginning a campaign. But financially he could not afford to do so.[21] An embarrassed Democratic executive committee met in caucus as planned that evening but adjourned without endorsing anyone, although Lawrence offered Kirk's name. The proposal generated no enthusiasm, and a second meeting was scheduled for 31 March.

Meanwhile it became imperative for the executive committee to endorse a candidate within the next week. Each of the announced candidates had been busy trying to line up support among the ward chairmen and district committee members. Without a clear indication from the party leaders, a free-for-all primary was likely to break out that could severely damage the party's chances in November. Lawrence was well aware that Scully had barely defeated Denny in 1941, and it appeared that Denny, now a lieutenant colonel in the army, would carry the Republican banner again. To make matters worse, Denny announced that, because of his obligation to his country, he would not campaign for election and would resign from the army only if elected.[22] A factionalized Democratic party might be forced to run its candidate against an absentee candidate, a patriotic image.

The party would most certainly be in serious trouble if it could not agree. The only person left who could unite it was Lawrence himself.

Pittsburgh Democratic folklore has it that the fourteen party leaders turned to Lawrence as the compromise choice at the caucus on 31 March after failing to agree on any other candidate. McClelland suggested that Kane reconsider, and the caucus seemed to be in agreement when Kane took the floor. He again refused to run but named Lawrence in his place. The committee then appealed to Lawrence over his objections. As he liked to recall the story, he excused himself from the meeting to call his wife to ask her opinion. When she agreed, he returned to accept the draft.[23] Other party regulars give essentially the same account. What they fail to mention is the lobbying that occurred in the six days between the two caucuses to persuade Lawrence to accept. His objections were too fundamental to be swept away in the enthusiasm of a party draft.

Shortly after the first meeting, Kane invited Lawrence and Kirk for lunch at the Kane home. When they arrived, Lawrence immediately began to argue for a Kane candidacy, but Kane and Kirk stopped him. They had apparently agreed upon the purpose of their luncheon, and they turned the tables on Lawrence, both maintaining that he should run "for the good of the party." Lawrence countered that he had three strikes against him: his confrontation with Margiotti, his religion, and the public's distrust, as he saw it, of a professional politician. Kane pressed the argument, and Lawrence, perhaps seeking a chance to get away as much as anything else, agreed to consider Kane's argument.[24] While he never voiced any concerns about his personal career, he might also have argued that an unsuccessful bid would have a negative effect on his influence in state and national politics. An affirmative decision involved considerable personal risk.

When Lawrence left, he talked to a few other trusted associates, including Scully's former secretary, Jack Robin, stationed at Camp Livingston in Louisiana. Robin, while working for Scully, had volunteered to write speeches for Lawrence, and the two became close associates. Robin had written to Lawrence early in 1945 urging him to run for the mayoralty, and now Lawrence wanted to discuss the issue further. Robin urged him to seek the nomination. "I told him he had a hell of a lot of people's jobs depending on holding the mayoralty."[25]

It is doubtful that Robin's argument, or even the reasoning of Kane, overcame Lawrence's strong objections. More likely, he realized that the leadership was at an impasse that only his candidacy could resolve. He apparently informed Kane of his decision near the end of the week, and they arranged to orchestrate the Lawrence draft at the party caucus on 31 March. Kane agreed to act as campaign manager. As expected, Frey and Fagan dropped out of the running immediately, and David Roberts joined them in a few weeks. Scully, who had hoped to be a compromise candidate himself, quickly announced his support of Lawrence. One week later, twenty-six of the thirty-two ward chairmen endorsed the executive committee's choice. Four others eventually joined them. Only Huston, a longtime critic of the organization, and a handful of his followers refused to bow to the inevitable. He was, he announced, "in the race to stay."

With nearly the entire city and county organizations lined up behind Lawrence, the primary election produced only a few sporadic sparks, but it indicated the direction the fall election would follow. Huston sprinkled his speeches and published advertisements with the now hackneyed charges against Lawrence. Calling him "Dictator Lawrence," "Boss Lawrence," and "King David," Huston laid all the scandals of the past decade at Lawrence's door. If the public had forgotten the Lawrence trials, Huston quickly refreshed their memories.

The Lawrence campaign, masterminded by George Kelly, director of parks under Kane, worked to create a new image for the candidate. Kelly recognized that the old issues of the New Deal that had brought the Democratic party to power had lost much of their voter appeal. Lawrence needed to overcome his image as the dispenser of the spoils and offer something more. Kelly's experience in highway development and waterfront improvement had fostered a common interest with the business community, which had hitherto been lacking in the Democratic party. Lawrence, he suggested, should use a campaign for public improvements to attract the middle and business classes. Lawrence, whose analysis of the 1941 mayoralty election had pinpointed the same weakness, agreed. To create links with the business community, he would have to win their confidence. George Kelly persuaded him to follow two paths during the campaign: avoid mudslinging and offer an affirmative program of civic improvements.[26] Lawrence accepted the advice, although at times he could not resist responding vehemently to his opponent's intemperate attacks.

On 20 April Lawrence announced the program that in broad form became the guidelines for his administrative efforts. Eventually to become known as the Pittsburgh Renaissance, it proposed the following seven points:

1. public conferences between the mayor and businessmen at which complaints and suggestions would be aired and answered;

2. creation of an "industrial expansion committee" to work for diversified industry in Pittsburgh;
3. public improvements advocated by the Allegheny Conference on Community Development;
4. complete rezoning of the city to "open new home sites within the city limits";
5. new residential construction, especially single dwellings and apartment houses based on federal land purchase and private capital construction;
6. redistribution of the tax load, relief for real estate, and additional state aid for the needy;
7. a program to clean, repair, and beautify the central business district.[27]

Lawrence offered few details about his plan, although he promised additional information during the course of the campaign. The program, however, was a bold approach that sent Lawrence on a mission never attempted before. Only one of the issues—the provision of aid for the poor and the homeless—had been part of his agenda in the past thirty years. His ambitious statement became the guiding concept of his four-term administration.

Lawrence's seven-point plan promised a dramatic departure from the issues that had previously concerned him. But his extemporaneous remarks, offered as always at the end of his address, suggested that his style of execution would remain the same. He preferred action to contemplation, and he remained disdainful of comprehensive utopian programs. To carry out his promise, he told the voters of Pittsburgh, "I am offering two things: leadership and a program. And when I speak of a program, I mean a program in the sense of things scheduled to take place. I do not mean any of the airy plans which are discussed at length and eventually come to nothing. And when I speak of leadership I refer to that quality or knack which I believe I have acquired through years in business and public life. Here is the kind of action Pittsburgh needs and will get from me as your mayor."[28]

Huston offered no competing program but derided his opponent's plan. "Mr. Lawrence's just too wonderful program for the city is just so many more promises." When Lawrence attempted to present a cosmopolitan image by discussing the impact of international issues such as tariff and trade agreements on Pittsburgh industry, Huston urged the voters to "dismiss from your minds the irrelevant clap-trap oratory of my opponent who discusses reciprocal trade agreements, international postwar economics, shipbuilding, Dumbarton Oaks and other world problems." Lawrence's response, delivered over radio station KDKA, enhanced his image as offering more than machine politics as usual. His opponent was a man "whose mental capacities are so limited, so small and taut, that he cannot perceive the relationship of Pittsburgh industries to world trade or do the simple mental gymnastics necessary to fix the part which labor-management policies, industrial reconversion and Federal aid will play in advancing Pittsburgh. The kind of mentality which cannot understand the tariff as a local issue in an industrial city has no part in a political campaign for any leading office. He should rather set himself up in business selling buggy whips, linen dusters and moustache cups."[29]

With the minds of Pittsburghers, along with other Americans, occupied with the conclusion of the war, it is not clear whether anyone was listening to either Lawrence or his opponent. The local newspapers produced several editorials complaining about small crowds at political rallies and apathy on the part of the voters. Election day proved their predictions accurate when less than 40 percent of the voters of either party turned out to vote. With nearly full control of the Democratic organization, Lawrence won the primary election by a more than two to one margin. He captured all thirty-two wards.[30]

The victorious candidate's budding new image was quite unnecessary to win over the already committed party regulars. However, it established a base from which he would launch his election campaign. It also provided him with the key to the office that would vindicate him, in his own mind, from the charges leveled at him during the Harrisburg trials. A victory in November, furthermore, while it would not close the wounds created by the death of his two sons, would create a new outlet for his energies and play a major role in the healing process. Just as the trauma of the war was coming to an end, Lawrence's nomination marked the end of his period of personal tragedy and political eclipse. A new era was beginning.

1940–1945
A City in Trouble

The Pittsburgh of David Lawrence's youth led the nation in the production of iron, steel, and glass and in the mining of bituminous coal. The advantages of location, abundant natural resources, and cheap transportation attracted capital, entrepreneurs, and workers to the city. Men such as Andrew Carnegie, George Westinghouse, and Henry Clay Frick combined creative financing, technological innovation, and organizational talents to build multimillion-dollar national corporations. Their heavy industrial firms dominated the city and spurred the development of the nation. The Pittsburgh central business district became a monument to their genius, sprouting multilevel buildings bearing their names. Their companies, in turn, provided jobs for the thousands of immigrants who arrived in the city in the period between the Civil War and World War I. In the first twenty years of Lawrence's life the city's manufacturing output more than quadrupled, and the population exploded from 343,000 in 1890 to 533,000 in 1910, the greatest period of growth in the city's history.[1] The dramatic expansion of industry and a burgeoning population, not surprisingly, resulted in an unprecedented building boom and the establishment of new neighborhoods and industrial communities all over the Pittsburgh area. Streetcar suburbs and immigrant communities developed within the city, while manufacturing towns such as Braddock, Homestead, and Aliquippa sprang up along the banks of the region's three rivers. The two decades were clearly the most dynamic in the two-hundred-year history of the city.

By 1910, however, the city was already beginning to show signs of economic decline. Growth in industrial production tapered off as the development of by-product coke ovens permitted steel firms to relocate near the source of ore rather than near the coal mines. Investment capital began to flow to new markets, and entrepreneurial talent ceased to find Pittsburgh an attractive field for its creative energies. None of the new industries that have developed in the United States since 1910 had their birth in Pittsburgh. On the contrary, several companies, including Charles Schwab's Bethlehem Steel, abandoned the city altogether.

The "maturation of the Pittsburgh economy" that occurred in the second decade of the century left the city with aging capital goods industries highly dependent upon the condition of the national economy. This dependency "heightened the vulnerability of the district's population to cyclical swings . . . increasing both intensity of fluctuations and vulnerability to depression."[2] The city experienced relatively full employment and economic expansion in times of national growth, such as the periods of the two world wars, but suffered more severely and longer than other areas in times of recession and depression. Its economy in the post–World War II period would be dangerously susceptible to national economic cycles.

If the decline of industry in Pittsburgh left a weakened economic structure in its wake, it also left an indelible mark on the physical and social condition of the city. As many nineteenth- and early-twentieth-century visitors commented in print, the indignities the physical city suffered in the name of profit illustrated all the worst features of the free enterprise system. "In Pittsburgh," one English observer noted in 1913, "man befouled the streams, bedraggled their banks, ripped up the cliffs, hacked down the trees, and dumped refuse in their stead. He sowed the imposing heights with hovels and set beneath them black mills to cover everything far and wide with a film of smoke." The famous *Pittsburgh Survey* of 1907–13 filled several volumes attesting to the uninhabitable conditions in places such as Skunk Hollow in East Liberty; Painter's Row, adjacent to the South Side Carnegie mill; and Tammany Hall, near the neighborhood of Lawrence's youth. The city was legitimately earning its reputation as "Hell with the lid taken off."[3]

During the next thirty years, while some conditions improved, the city continued to stagnate. An overreliance on one basic industry produced violent economic swings of boom and bust. During World War I, the total production of the city rose by nearly one-third, and manufacturing during World War II reached all-time highs. The heights of the boom years were matched by unprecedented lows during the Depression. By 1933 overall production was only one-third of its 1929 level, and one-third of the city's white population and nearly one-half of its black population were without work.

An erratic economy during most of the twentieth century no doubt retarded investment in the city. Few mills opened or expanded except during the war period, and building activity in the central business district remained minimal. The economic malaise contributed to a general blight spreading throughout the city. A survey by the Econometric Institute of New York conducted in early 1945 showed that the city's real estate assessments declined by $206 million during the 1933–44 period, a decline that caused the city to lose approximately $6 million per year in real estate taxes.[4] In the central business district, while several high-rise office buildings had been erected in the 1920s, the last major construction, the Gulf Building, had been completed in 1932. None was planned for the postwar period.

Of equal concern was the condition of the existing structures in the business district. A tour through the central city in 1945 would have confirmed that "when Lawrence first ran for office in 1945, he was seeking the keys to a dying city."[5] Near the Point, where the three rivers join, was a thirty-six-acre area regularly inundated by spring flood waters. This formerly historic section became the site of a major battle between railroad entrepreneurs during the latter part of the nineteenth century that resulted in the city's potentially most valuable land becoming a "dilapidated warren of decayed buildings, warehouses, parking lots, and ugly railroad trestles."[6] Exposition Hall, which young David Lawrence and his companions frequently visited, closed in 1918 and had been recently turned into a city auto pound. The Blockhouse, the only authentic eighteenth-century structure in Pittsburgh, originally part of the British fort, suffered the ignominy of being surrounded by warehouses and abandoned tracks. The grounds and the river banks were littered with debris including tires, automobile parts, and abandoned river barges.

Further back from the river, on somewhat higher ground, stood the former neighborhood of David Lawrence. Most of the single family homes in this once mixed residential, industrial, and commercial area were gone, and it now contained rooming houses, vacant buildings, run-down hotels, and an abandoned railroad station, the Wabash, a marbleized flatiron built by Jay Gould in 1904. Only the Mayfair Hotel exceeded eight floors, and most buildings were under three. The exclusive Pittsburgh Club, a rather pedestrian monument to the area's long-gone importance, gave some relief to the grime of the neighborhood. The entrance to the city was, in short, a commercial slum.[7]

The remainder of the inner city, while not as bad as the apex of the triangle, also contained small pockets of blight. There were vacant buildings and two abandoned movie houes on Liberty and Penn avenues. Only the Jenkins Arcade and Horne's department store on the western end of Liberty Avenue, the historic Moose headquarters on Penn Avenue, and several 1920s-style movie palaces improved the shabby condition of the city's two widest streets. Structures on the Monongahela River side presented a similarly mixed picture. Water Street, separated from the river by an ugly highway built in 1938, offered a continuous string of late nineteenth-century three- and four-story loft buildings, which were structurally sound and, if maintained, aesthetically pleasing, but an estimated 40 percent were in deteriorating condition.[8] Wood and Smithfield streets, two major north-south arteries, contained no structures of significance except the classical style Mellon Building and the Oliver Building erected in 1908. The nineteenth-century financial district, Fourth Avenue contained a number of impressive banking temples built during the height of the industrial era, but these were covered with soot and grime. Two bright spots among the overall decay and neglect could be found: Grant Street, with its historic court house and City-County Building, the striking Gothic Union Trust Building, and several impressive office buildings, and Seventh Avenue, dominated by the Gulf and Koppers buildings erected in the 1930s.

Adjacent to and directly above these sat the Hill District, a large, mixed residential and commercial area that walled Pittsburgh in from the east. Once separated from the city by "Grant's Hill," it became the neighborhood of first settlement for the thousands of new immigrants during the nineteenth century. It was in 1930 the most ethnically and racially integrated and most densly settled area of Pittsburgh. By 1945, although it was becoming increasingly black, it still contained significant Italian, Russian, and Greek pockets. As host to several generations of poor immigrants, the Hill District exhibited all of the characteristics of a slum. Crowded living conditions, inadequate sanitation facilities, dilapidated structures, and a high incidence of disease and crime all pervaded the area.[9]

The Hill District was the city's worst residential slum, but it was by no means the only one. Neighborhoods in East Liberty, Homewood, Hazelwood, and Manchester, on the North Side, and several South Side communities all contained substandard housing.[10] The Pittsburgh Housing Authority erected eight dwelling projects accommodating 18,000 persons by the end of the war, but the effort barely scratched the surface. A new mayor entering office in 1945 could expect housing to occupy a considerable amount of his time.

A deteriorating central business district, inadequate and substandard housing, and an economy dominated by a single industry were not the only problems facing postwar Pittsburgh. Floods, the ever present pall of smoke, health concerns, and the absense of cultural amenities all detracted from the quality of life.

The residents of Pittsburgh expected annual floods. Each spring, as the accumulation of snow in the mountains throughout western Pennsylvania melted, the creeks fed the passing Allegheny River, transforming it into a quickly moving brown ribbon strewn with fallen trees and other debris. By the time the river had traveled its hundred mile course to Pittsburgh, collecting the deposits of numerous streams and creeks along the way, it was well over its shallow banks. Communities along the way such as Franklin and Kittanning, some fifty miles from Pittsburgh, and Sharpsburg and Millvale, nearby streetcar suburbs, were flooded first, and the extent of the damage there usually gave Pittsburgh a hint of its own fate. The city's Strip District, the lower portion of the Point, most of the lower North Side, and parts of the South Side experienced regular flooding. When the waters receded, people performed the familiar tasks. Businesses replaced damaged equipment, and everyone pumped out cellars and attempted to wash away the accumulated muck and sewage. In many cases the smells and dampness did not diminish until midsummer.

Residents who could not afford to move to higher ground and businesses that needed access to railroad or barge transportation learned to live with the problem. Most considered it a serious but unavoidable inconvenience. However, occasionally the flooding became more than a nuisance. A quick spring thaw accompanied by heavy rains could trigger massive destruction along the entire Monongahela and Allegheny river plains. When the two raging torrents reached Pittsburgh, they carried along with them barges, railroad cars, trees, parts of buildings and bridges, and anything else in their paths. The city usually bore the brunt of these major floods.

Five times between 1900 and 1945 the rivers at the Point exceeded flood stage by seven or more feet. The worst of these occurred on St. Patrick's Day 1936, when a combination of a heavy snow accumulation and a sudden thaw in mid March resulted in a forty-six-foot-high wall of water (twenty-one feet over flood stage) that swept into Pittsburgh. It submerged mills, factories, and low-cost housing along the river banks and stores and offices in the central business district, and it halted the city's water and electrical supply. When it crested, eleven feet of water covered nearly half of the main commercial section of the city. The disaster took 47 lives, injured 2800, and left 67,500 homeless. The U.S. Army Corps of Engineers estimated the property loss at $50 million.[11]

The recurrent flooding clearly discouraged any potential entrepreneur from investing in the city. Solving the problem was the single most important factor in the rehabilitation of the city.[12] Federal, state, and local authorities made a start on flood control, but World War II interrupted their efforts. The major reservoirs remained on the drawing boards and Pittsburgh's vulnerability to catastrophic flooding continued.

If floods were the most serious problem Pittsburgh faced, in terms of loss of life and property, smoke was the most pervasive. Pittsburgh deserved its reputation as the "smoky city." The type of industry it sustained, the availability of low-cost bituminous coal, its topography, and increased urbanization all combined to produce a dense pall that hung over Pittsburgh as early as 1845. For a century, city leaders and residents demonstrated a marked ambivalence about it. Industry heads and workers frequently noted that the presence of smoke indicated that the mills were operating, that work was available. Medical personnel were not sure whether smoke was harmful or beneficial. In 1874 Dr. William Denny of the Pittsburgh Board of Health stated: "Strangers with weak lungs for a while find their lungs aggravated by the smoke, but nevertheless asthmatic patients have found relief in breathing it. Coal is . . . undoubtedly the cause of our superior healthfulness."[13]

Attempts were made to control smoke pollution several times during the nineteenth and early twentieth centuries through municipal ordinances. However, officials demonstrated their awareness of the political volatility of the issue by failing to enforce any of them. In fact, in 1939, the city council actually voted to eliminate the Bureau of Smoke Regulation, which had been created during an earlier reform era.[14]

By the beginning of Cornelius Scully's second full term as mayor, it had become obvious that something had to be done about the problem. In 1940, in addition to the numerous factories, which consumed huge amounts of smoke-producing bituminous coal, 141,788 homes, and a number of commercial establishments within the city limits used the same fuel. To make matters worse, the five railroad lines brought more than one hundred smoke-belching locomotives into and out of the city each day. Finally, to heighten the crisis, the winter of 1940–41 proved particularly difficult. Several temperature inversions acted to produce a blanketlike effect that prevented the polluted air from entering the atmosphere. For several days each month—once for as long as a week—the heavy smog hung over Pittsburgh, and lights had to be turned on in the daytime.

Smoke, of course, was not only a nuisance; it was now recognized as unhealthy and expensive. In 1941 Pittsburgh had the highest rate of pneumonia of any city in the nation, with a death rate from it that was 40 percent higher. In addition, the city was among the leaders in other respiratory ailments, the incidence increasing in winter when the coal-burning season was at its peak. During the November through February period, the city received only one-third as much sunshine as did the Allegheny County Airport, only seven miles away.[15]

Smoke also cost money. Industrial and residential smoke dumped more than one hundred tons of pollutants per month on the city during 1940, two-thirds of which fell on the "downtown, the Strip District, Soho, Oakland and the South Side." The cost of additional lighting, building cleaning, and damage to merchandise was estimated at nearly $4 million per year. Estimates of the annual cost of air pollution in Pittsburgh ranged from $2 million to $10 million. Perhaps the only positive aspect of the smoke problem was that Pittsburgh was among the nation's leading cities in the number of laundries per capita. More than 2000 employees earned a living in 128 laundries, which constituted a $4 million industry.[16]

As evidence of the harmful effects of smoke mounted, the opposition to control began to crumble. As a result of urging by newspapers and the public, Mayor Scully created the Commission for the Elimination of Smoke, which, by July 1941 had produced a smoke control ordinance.[17] The city council passed the ordinance with only one member, Edward Leonard, dissenting.

But, as with flood control, World War II hampered implementation, and air quality actually deteriorated during the 1941–45 period. One of the first issues the new mayor would have to address would be smoke control.

The environmental and physical conditions of the city, of course, exercised a powerful force on its residents. Blue-collar workers, forced by economics to remain near the site of their employment, endured the conditions while suffering debilitating health, economic, and psychological effects. Management-level workers, however, began to seek employment elsewhere. Corporate managers complained of the difficulty of retaining or recruiting competent professional workers. "The men were willing," one official testified, "provided salaries were high enough, but their wives objected." (Even Richard King Mellon's wife, Constance, balked at returning to the city from Harrisburg, where Mellon served as director of the state's selective service system.) Corporate heads began contemplating moving out. A number, including Westinghouse, ALCOA, and U.S. Steel "had actually taken options on properties in other cities and were laying plans to . . . move their offices." Of forty businesses that had considered relocating to Pittsburgh during the previous several years, none actually did so. Their major reasons were floods and air and water pollution.[18] Immediate action would be required to prevent the dissolution of the Steel City.

▽

If the environment and the physical plant of the city promised nothing but problems for the two mayoralty hopefuls, the instruments of reform already in place brightened the picture somewhat. Beginning early in the twentieth century, civic-minded organizations became interested in the improvement of the environment. The elite-dominated Civic Club and Voters' League used their influence to reform the organization of the city council, the school board, and to bring about tax reform.[19] The Pittsburgh Chamber of Commerce, similarly, helped to bring about the consolidation of Pittsburgh and neighboring Allegheny into one city and to create the Associated Charities to systematize the administration of charitable agencies. The success of these organizations convinced their members, mostly business and professional leaders, that voluntary private action would succeed where public attempts at municipal reform, through the ballot box, had failed. Their initiative, moreover, permitted them to determine when and where they would intervene. The private voluntary association became the model for municipal reform movements in Pittsburgh for the next three-fourths of a century.

Three significant voluntary organizations existed in the summer of 1945: the Pittsburgh Regional Planning Association, the Pennsylvania Economy League, and the Allegheny Conference on Community Development. Each played a vital role in the redevelopment of the city. Other private sector agencies such as the Golden Triangle Association and later the Regional Industrial Development Corporation also contributed, but to a lesser degree.

The Pittsburgh Regional Planning Association emerged from an earlier organization—the Citizens' Committee on City Plan—formed by men such as William L. Mellon, Richard B. Mellon, and Howard Heinz, which saw as its major task the development of a general physical plan for Pittsburgh. Spearheaded by an architect, Frederick Bigger, it commissioned a comprehensive plan, which the city council adopted but failed to implement.[20] Fifteen years later, the renamed organization, now under the direction of Wallace K. Richards, continued the effort by hiring the famed New York planner Robert Moses to prepare a comprehensive highway program for the city. The design produced by the controversial planner bore a striking resemblance to the earlier one and touched off a furor over who should receive credit, but again no immediate action was taken. The Moses plan, along with ideas from its predecessor, became the basis for the later redevelopment of the central business district. The Pittsburgh Regional Planning Association itself would serve as the technical and planning branch of the renewal.

The Pennsylvania Economy League had been created in 1935. Funded by contributions from business and corporate executives, it conducted research aimed at efficient management of municipalities in Pennsylvania. During the mid 1930s, for example, it recommended to the mayor of Pittsburgh that the government could operate more efficiently if it prepared and followed an annual budget, a suggestion Scully acted upon. The organization originally provided research only for government agencies, but its Western Division soon offered a similar service to the private agencies concerned with urban renewal in Pittsburgh. The Pennsylvania Economy League authored or co-authored a number of pieces of legislation important to the revitalization of the city. League members, because of their dual role in servicing both sectors, soon became an important link between government and private leaders.

The most significant private organization, however, was the Allegheny Conference on Community Development (ACCD). The original idea for the conference (at first named the Allegheny Conference on Postwar Community Planning) is attributed by some to Robert E. Doherty, president of the Carnegie Institute of Technology, alone, and by others to Doherty and Wallace K. Richards, director of the Pittsburgh Regional Planning Association, simultaneously. But all agree that it was after Richard K. Mellon became interested that business and civic leaders were successfully brought together to form the umbrella organization for a "super planning group" to coordinate the postwar redevelopment of Pittsburgh.

During 1944 an organizational structure was created and the conference was incorporated as a nonprofit research and planning organization. A Sponsoring Committee was established consisting of sixty leaders in business, industry, finance, labor, education, and public administration. To ensure cooperation from the public sector, the mayors of Pittsburgh, McKeesport, and Duquesne, the Allegheny County commissioners, and the head of Pittsburgh City Council were invited to become ex-officio members. The heart of the organization, however, was the executive committee, originally ten members from education, business, and planning and research. The group eventually became a who's who of the Pittsburgh business world. By 1950 the committee was made up of the presidents and chief executive officers of the fourteen major commercial, financial, and manufacturing interests in the city. A key feature of the executive committee was the provision that members were elected as individuals, not as representatives of their companies. Composed of what one observer called "action people," the committee could execute any plan it desired without having to clear it with superiors. Thus the members could not send a substitute to represent them. Interestingly, the one exception was Richard K. Mellon, who never belonged to the executive committee but delegated representation of his interests to his aides Adolpf Schmidt and Arthur Van Buskirk. Schmidt explained this exception as a result of Mellon's power. "When Mr. Mellon asked, let's say, the President of the Gulf Oil Corporation or of the Koppers Company or of the Aluminum Company [ALCOA] to participate in this effort, the association through the bank and through the family holdings were such that they were very pleased to assist. . . . The mere fact that he asked them was sufficient."[21] By 1945 the executive committee had established twelve standing committees to investigate such matters as housing and neighborhood development, land use and zoning, health and welfare, cultural development, and public improvements.

Thus, by war's end the city benefited from the presence of three crucial private sector civic service organizations, each with a clearly defined task. The Pittsburgh Regional Planning Association drew up the plans; the Pennsylvania Economy League conducted the research on financing; and the Allegheny Conference on Community Development, in consultation with city and county government agencies, carried out the plans.

However, the presence of such well organized, well financed, private sector organizations, no matter how civic minded, does not guarantee success. The history of urban America is littered with similar reform groups that had little or no lasting impact on their communities. Indeed, the earlier unsucessful attempts by the Pittsburgh Regional Planning Association, the Chamber of Commerce, and other civic organizations illustrate the futility of trying to implement change in the community without the cooperation of both private and public sectors. The inclusion of elected public officials on the Allegheny Conference's sponsoring committee showed that this point had been clearly understood.

A major unanswered question, however, was the degree of cooperation the private organizations could expect from the mayor and city council. To be sure, overtures had been made, and several prominent people serving the private agencies had worked closely with the Scully administration, but public-private cooperation was by no means guaranteed. The Allegheny Conference, the key organization on the private side, was composed of the cream of Pittsburgh's elite. The executive committee was enormously wealthy, Protestant, educated at the best eastern universities, and 100 percent Republican. Several members had contributed generously, and would continue to do so, to the campaigns of local and national Republican candidates. A victory by Republican Robert Waddell in the mayoral election would increase the possibility of private-public cooperation, but the odds were strongly against such an outcome.

A victory by Lawrence and the Democratic candidates for city council, on the other hand, would probably diminish the chances of such cooperation. Lawrence's history as a machine politician, his previous battles with Mellon interests, and his intransigence vis-à-vis state Republicans all suggested he would be difficult to deal with. In addition, as he himself admitted, he had little faith in the initial announced goals. Furthermore Lawrence had little acquaintance with those involved with the early attempts at planning—men who by 1945 were expected to play a major role in the postwar redevelopment. For example, as of the summer of 1945, he had never heard of Richards. It was Fiorello La Guardia's planner Robert Moses who told Lawrence about Richards.[22] Thus Lawrence, who had begun to talk about the redevelopment of Pittsburgh in his primary campaign, relied upon a New Yorker to introduce him to the person many call the idea man behind the city's urban renewal program. Cooperation among the private and public sectors, or among Republicans and Democrats remained an uncertainty in mid 1945.

The problems of postwar Pittsburgh, which would have to be faced by the next mayor, were immense. Urban decay, traffic congestion, floods, air pollution, health problems, and a general lack of amenities robbed residents of the basic elements of a positive quality of life. In addition, serious economic questions and a possible company exodus threatened the very life of the city. Surprisingly, an important number of people in the private sector, maintaining the city's tradition of private intervention, saw value in the city and deemed it worth saving. What was needed was an administration that carried the same perceptions.

1945–1946
From Political Boss to Civic Statesman

David L. Lawrence entered his first mayoralty campaign backed by a united party (even Joseph Guffey and William McNair made appearances on his behalf), an efficient organization, a full campaign treasury, and the outlines of a program designed to provide an image of a candidate deeply concerned with civic problems. His party also held a two-to-one registration advantage. With backing by the rank and file Democrats a virtual certainty, Lawrence's main concern was to broaden the party's traditional New Deal coalition. The business and professional community would be welcomed in a concerted effort to attack the problems plaguing the city. His task during the remainder of the campaign would be to add flesh to the skeleton presented in his seven-point program and to convince voters that the "new Lawrence" was more than a public relations image.

Lawrence's opponent, Robert Waddell, trim and ruggedly handsome at forty-nine years of age, embodied many of the qualities of the ideal political candidate. A lifelong resident of the city, he had financed his own college education through a combination of work and a partial football scholarship. Now he was a successful businessman with his own insurance firm and was listed in the prestigious *Pittsburgh Blue Book*. Waddell became active in Republican circles at age twenty-one and soon gained a reputation as a "man to watch." His timing, however, could hardly have been worse. He ran for city council in 1933, the year of the first Democratic sweep, and finished well down the list of candidates. Undaunted, he ran for mayor in 1937, easily defeating former Mayor William A. Magee, in the Republican primary. Cornelius Scully then defeated Waddell by approximately 30,000 votes in the general election.[1] The two election bids gave him strong support among Republican party leaders, but it was his avocation that brought him widespread popularity. Each fall from 1922 through 1932, he spent his afternoons as head football coach at Carnegie Institute of Technology. During this decade he compiled a record of fifty-six wins and thirty-three losses, including four consecutive victories over the University of Pittsburgh and two each over Notre Dame, Georgia Tech, and Temple University. His teams played consistently before audiences of more than 50,000 at Pitt stadium. Several times his teams shocked the sports-minded with upset victories over those of such coaching giants as Knute Rockne and Jock Sutherland.

Waddell might have had a chance to unseat the Democratic regime had his own party been able to avoid the bloodletting that customarily characterized Republican election behavior. But the splintered and disorganized party followed its usual practice. Five candidates announced their intention to seek endorsement for nomination for mayor. Waddell had the support of the county chairman, James Malone, which gave him a strong advantage; but he was not without opposition. Jimmy Coyne, in the last hurrah of his long career, gave his support to a former city fire chief, Louis Conley. Coyne's now small but loyal following could not be expected to act in the interests of party harmony and, although Conley later withdrew, Coyne continued to oppose Waddell. Harmar Denny, who nearly defeated Scully in 1941, announced his candidacy, assuring the electorate that he would resign his military commission if he won the general election.

Denny's refusal to return to Pittsburgh for the primary forced Waddell to wage an unusal campaign. He wisely refused to attack the absent "war hero" and campaigned instead against the incumbent administration as if he were already his party's nominee. His answer to the city's problems—and to Lawrence's seven-point program—was his own five-point plan. Introduced just before the June primary election, the program raised obfuscation to new heights. Waddell pledged to "give public services that serve," "run the city like a going business," "get Pittsburgh out of the red," "make Pittsburgh a better place to live in," and "never renege on this platform."[2] Perhaps fortunately for him, few voters turned out to hear him, and he defeated Denny by 10,000 votes in a primary in which fewer than 40 percent of the registered Republicans voted. His total of 29,979 votes carried twenty-seven wards, but he lost in all the major Republican districts, an ominous note on which to begin a campaign against the opposition's most able politician.

Neither Lawrence nor Waddell campaigned between the primary and the customary Labor Day starting date, but both were busy. Waddell and his principal supporter, Malone, focused their efforts on bringing the Coyne and Denny followers back into the fold.

Lawrence, his party united behind his campaign, utilized the interim to try to increase the size of his organization. He attended caucuses in the wards, often referring to his "draft" as a call from the party to which "any loyal member would have responded." He emphasized to his followers the distinct possibility that the opponent might win without their efforts and asked for their support. He also spoke with labor leaders and others who usually supported the Democratic party. The normal Roosevelt coalition was to be fully mobilized for the fall campaign.

But, as Lawrence's campaign rhetoric had taken a new thrust, so had his organizational efforts. George Kelly, working for Lawrence's campaign chairman, John Kane, organized "Lawrence for Mayor" committees among attorneys, educators, engineers, and people in business. All were to be welcomed into a new working coalition that would lift the city from its sorry state. Lawrence spoke before each group during the fall campaign, projecting the image of a civic leader concerned about the municipal environment. He naturally concluded by requesting their support in November and in the urban reform programs to come.

The campaign that fall was perhaps Lawrence's best as an organizer and campaigner. He spoke several times in every ward and used the radio as no candidate before him had. He met with groups in churches, school auditoriums, and fraternal and union halls. He delivered major addresses at the Carnegie Music Hall on the North Side, at the Syria Mosque in Oakland, and in the Motor Gardens in East Liberty. On nearly every occasion he built upon his seven-point platform. Speaking before an overflow crowd of more than three thousand at the traditional campaign kickoff at the North Side Carnegie Hall, Lawrence took what was probably the most courageous step of the campaign when he denounced as irresponsible a call by Waddell for a decrease in the city's tax rate. "A lower tax rate for Pittsburgh will come only when we have got at the root of our dropping realty values—especially in the triangle. When acres of idle land are used as parking lots in the heart of our city, only a charlatan would state that a tax cut could be effected by economies in City Hall. You cannot lower taxes when the tax structure has been devaluated. But you can lower taxes when you take intelligent, forthright and determined action to rehabilitate the entire city. That is the only way it is ever going to be done and every intelligent businessman, banker, industrialist, and home owner is going to tell you the same thing."[3]

Lawrence continued to hammer away at the problems of urban deterioration throughout the campaign. Specifically, he promised to support the installation of the proposed flood control system, implementation of smoke control, recruitment of new industry, redevelopment of the triangle area, and overall rehabilitation of the city's infrastructure. In addition, he called for development of a park at the Point, a radically restructured highway system, and construction of a huge public auditorium.

To stress that a Lawrence administration would welcome input and assistance from all concerned citizens, Lawrence proposed the formation of several new groups to work in the coalition he was forging. Early in the campaign he announced that one of the first things he would do if elected would be to establish a Pittsburgh civic unity council, to be comprised of representatives of all religious faiths, youth groups, racial groups, educational, cultural and civic organizations, labor, and management. In mid October he added a second civic affairs coalition: a "business-labor-professional committee to advise on the best future plans for Pittsburgh." While Lawrence did not mention the Allegheny Conference on Community Development by name, he clearly had it or a similar organization in mind. He returned to the theme of a civic unity council and a business-labor-professional committee again and again in his subsequent talks.

Republican Waddell indicated that he too would support flood and smoke control measures, improved housing facilities, and alleviation of inner-city traffic problems. However, he presented no programs, calling only for a "business-like" solution to the problems facing the city. He placed heavy emphasis on the mismanagement and corruption of the current administration. "Lawrence has come out in the open, kicking aside his stooge Scully, to seek election to the office . . . which he has held in fact for the last ten years. . . . Lawrence's organization is a ruthless political machine which has caused untold harm to Pittsburgh." "There is misgiving in the heart of every good citizen of Pittsburgh about Dave Lawrence's political career. Nobody who knows about it trusts him. His own people don't trust him."[4]

When Waddell was not attacking Lawrence, a number of allies were brought out to keep up the invective. Among the most effective was John Huston. A disgruntled Democratic primary candidate for the office now sought by Lawrence, Huston was the main hatchet man for the Republican organization. He had jumped the sinking Republican ship during the Democratic revolution of 1933 and became active in the Democratic party. When his political ambitions were cut short by the 1945 Lawrence "draft," he responded by bitterly attacking the "corrupt machine" and subsequently announced his return to the Republicans. "Today I leave the Democratic party because I not only believe—I know—that it is more corrupt, more reactionary and is dominated by a more ruthless and unprincipled boss than the Republican Party ever was in its darkest days."[5]

Waddell, Huston, and their allies frequently sprinkled their talks with references to Lawrence's two trials, but they all stopped short of declaring him guilty of the charges. In mid October a proposal to bring the Dauphin County district attorney, Carl Shelley, to Pittsburgh to discuss the trials touched off an internal furor when several influential Republicans denounced it as "beneath the dignity of the party." The Shelley speech was eventually cancelled, but Waddell gave a synopsis of the trials in his next major address. The mudslinging campaign reached a new low, however, on 1 November, when the Republican organization placed in the *Pittsburgh Press* a half-page advertisement, which the city's other newspapers refused to run, reprinting newspaper headlines from 1939 and 1940 about the indictment and trials of David Lawrence. It was accompanied by an unusual editorial explaining that, while the advertisement "is questionable . . . we have resolved the question in favor of giving as much freedom of expression as possible."[6]

The *Post-Gazette* and *Sun-Telegraph* both denounced the advertisement, as did several prominent Republicans. Nevertheless, both newspapers endorsed Waddell, while the *Pittsburgh Press* reluctantly endorsed Lawrence. All three papers commented that Lawrence had run a clean campaign, discussed a number of important issues, and offered convincing—one paper called them "tempting"—programs. They also commended Waddell for his programs, although one noted they were "somewhat more sweeping and less definite." All three praised him as a man of character and integrity, although they were critical of the campaign tactics employed by him and his supporters. The crucial point, however, for all three newspapers was Lawrence's career and image as a political boss. Regardless of the effect on the electorate of his attempt to create a new image, he did not convince the city's editors. Even the *Press,* which had supported Democratic candidates since 1933, raised the issue of his indebtedness to his party. "Mr. Lawrence has ability, experience, and an unusual knowledge of municipal affairs and political methods." Those are his assets, and if he put his head and heart into a determined effort to succeed regardless of political considerations, he might do so in an outstanding way. This, however, is a big 'if.' For Mr. Lawrence has been a political boss for a number of years. It is in his blood."[7]

The apathy that characterized the primary election disappeared by November 1945. The war had ended. A few servicemen had returned home, and many more would do so in the next few months. The attention of the city now turned to domestic matters. The campaign highlighted the problems of the city and, for some citizens, identified the potential dangers of turning it over to a political boss. Nearly 80 percent of the electorate turned out to select a mayor and five city councilmen to guide Pittsburgh in its postwar redevelopment. For the fourth consecutive time, the Democratic organization swept all six positions. Lawrence's margin of victory, 14,000 votes, was not overwhelming, but it was the most decisive Democratic triumph since Scully's in 1937. It was also Lawrence's closest mayoral race: each of his subsequent ones brought margins in excess of 50,000 votes. The general election results were never in doubt after 1945. In winning his first elective office in his thirty-year career, Lawrence felt vindicated of the accusations against him earlier in the decade. "I interpret my election as a vote of confidence in me and a vote of approval for my program. My thanks go out to all those who showed their trust in me by voting for me. I assure them I will not betray their trust."[8]

An examination of the returns suggests that Lawrence's interpretation was not far off the mark. He carried eighteen of the thirty-two wards, a not unexpected result considering the party's nearly 100,000 voter registration advantage. A comparison of the results with Scully's in 1941 shows that Lawrence's victory was not due solely to his own organization. The Democratic vote total, for example, suffered surprising deterioration in a number of formerly solid wards, notably in the Hill District, the Twelfth Ward (presided over by Charles A. Papale, one of the strongest of the ward chairmen), the Sixth (Lawrenceville) and Thirteenth (Homewood-Brushton), and the Twenty-second through Twenty-fifth wards (the entire central North Side). Lawrence's support increased in the white-collar, professional, and business wards, a result that suggested that his message of cooperation with those groups had indeed struck a responsive chord. While he failed to win any of those wards outright, he scored impressive gains in upper-middle-class neighborhoods of Shadyside, Squirrel Hill, the South Hills, and Carrick.[9]

Lawrence, who customarily examined vote totals in block-level detail, clearly understood the significance of the returns. None of the so-called powerful ward chairmen could claim that he owed his victory to him. In fact, several would be hard pressed to explain their ward's dismal showing. Although Lawrence was not free of political obligations when he moved into city hall in January, he was not shackled with individuals to whom he owed his career.

Lawrence, no doubt, also realized that if he had not managed substantial gains over Scully's 1941 vote in the independent and Republican wards, he would have been dangerously near defeat. George Kelly's strategy of broadening the party base beyond the traditional New Deal coalition proved an important ingredient in the party's success. Equally important in the long run was the evidence that Lawrence could, in fact, appeal to the business-professional segment of the community. The politician who had always appeared comfortable with ethnic, racial, religious, or labor groups gave every indication that he would be just as adept in the city's boardrooms or at the Duquesne Club. The ability to associate with the elite, which he learned in the law offices of Billy Brennen, was beginning to prove useful.

▽

The mayor-elect wasted no time in moving to implement his program. Within twenty-four hours of his election, he announced his priorities for action. The first was smoke control. The Lawrence administration would immediately implement the ordinances already on the books, including the controversial controls on domestic fuel consumption. He also pressed for the broadening of the statute to include all of Allegheny County. "The winds do not stop at the city line, you know. Nobody has told them where Pittsburgh ends and Wilkinsburg or Bellevue begins." Lawrence had already discussed the issue with County Commissioner Kane, who guaranteed his cooperation.[10] Lawrence also indicated that the proposed Penn-Lincoln Parkway, the Point Park project, the business district restoration, and flood control would all receive immediate attention.

In discussing his plans for his first administration, Lawrence explained two long-held beliefs that would guide his efforts: action would be given preference over planning, and teamwork over individualism. "One of the troubles in this city has been too many planning agencies. . . . I want everybody on one team. We want to get these things done and never mind who gets the credit. We can't be like the Irish band. Every member of the band wanted the parade to go by his house. So there was no parade."[11] The parade, of course, would go by Lawrence's home quite frequently. Most members of the band considered it good politics and good for the project in question to give the band leader the credit. The Republican business community adopted the practice within a short time.

Following a five-day theater-going vacation in New York City with

Alyce, Lawrence returned to Pittsburgh to resume his efforts at bridge building. "You would have thought he was still campaigning for election," one observer recalled.[12]

Lawrence used the month before his inauguration to indicate that his plea for a broad action coalition was not merely campaign rhetoric. He actively sought and accepted as many invitations to business and professional luncheons, dinners, and meetings as he could get. At each gathering the message was always the same: "This administration needs your cooperation and support to solve the problems facing the city. We will work with all groups interested in a better Pittsburgh. In turn we pledge an administration divorced from politics, free of scandal." He accomplished a minor coup five days before his inauguration when he was invited to speak to the city's Chamber of Commerce, a first for a Democratic mayor. The address, Lawrence and his staff realized, would be the first crucial one of his administration and help set the tone for his relationship with the business community. Nearly 500 members of the chamber, many of them skeptical if not hostile to the mayor-elect, attended.

Lawrence began by briefly outlining his dream for Pittsburgh. In language reminiscent of urban visionaries such as Ebenezer Howard and Louis Mumford, he called for "a city of easy access, a center of culture and entertainment, a clean and healthful city of good homes, good public transportation, first rate recreational facilities." The main purpose of the talk quickly became clear. He told the chamber that he accepted the invitation (which his staff had worked to secure) "gratefully because the sooner the government of Pittsburgh and the Chamber of Commerce of Pittsburgh get to working together, the better for all the people of the city. The city administration should not be afraid of the Chamber of Commerce and the Chamber of Commerce should not be afraid of the city administration. The future of Pittsburgh demands teamwork, teamwork between govenment, business and labor . . . we have not always had such teamwork in the past. . . . Government does not operate in a vacuum. . . . To truly succeed, . . . it needs to work in partnership, in tri-partite agreement, with industry and labor, with men and women in every walk of life."[13]

The audience listened attentively but gave no indication that they either believed him or were willing to join in the effort he requested. The applause at the conclusion of his address, the press noted, was "polite." The message, of course, would be heard outside the William Penn Hotel ballroom. Members of the Allegheny Conference on Community Development, among others, apparently found Lawrence's speech encouraging. They were probably not willing to place total trust in the new mayor, but they were certainly intrigued. Lawrence would have to pass additional tests to gain their confidence, but a beginning had been made.

It is likely that no Pittsburgh mayor ever began a term of office facing greater problems. In addition to the persistent major ones, the Scully administration turned over what the *Post-Gazette* called "ten steaming hot potatoes," including $13 million in delinquent tax and water bills (50 percent of the 1946 city budget); outdated building codes threatening to forestall any extensive postwar building program; city streets riddled with potholes; and a desperate need for additional state aid for city projects. The new mayor also faced rampant vandalism of city parks and vacant buildings; traffic problems due to the absence of off-street parking facilities and the inability of the police to enforce parking laws; a shortage of recreation space (the last city park had been dedicated in 1920); and a need to increase taxes to finance general improvement of the city's infrastructure.

In addition, the labor situation in Pittsburgh was volatile. Industrial workers' wages had increased during the war, but the increases were far outstripped by productivity. Workers at first voluntarily restricted pay raise demands to aid in the war effort; the Roosevelt administration later placed mandatory restraints on wage increases. Workers and labor leaders nationally were now anxious to reap the deferred benefits of their labor. A rash of national and local strikes broke out in the fall of 1945 and continued at almost epidemic proportions into early 1946. Nowhere were they more prevalent than in Pittsburgh's industrial valley. Within ten days of Lawrence's inauguration, four major strikes occurred, idling more than 250,000 workers and stopping all three of the city's major industries: steel and aluminum, electrical equipment, and glass. In addition, the administration would shortly face two coal strikes, a cold storage shutdown, a fifty-three-day hotel strike, several bus disputes, a rail strike that threatened food supplies into the city, a brewery strike that resulted in several shootings, and numerous other labor disputes.[14]

If the new mayor worried about the labor situation, he gave no indication of his concern on the morning of 7 January at his inauguration in council chambers. Speaking before a friendly crowd of family, friends, the nine-member Democratic city council, and many of the party faithful, Lawrence did not mention labor problems. He commented briefly on the physical problems of the city, warned the city workers that he expected a full day's work from each one, and spoke of "looking ahead to miracles undreamed of." Most important, he repeated once again the partnership message of the past four months.

"We are all partners in Pittsburgh, everyone of us. Government cannot do the whole job before us. It is a citizen's job; it is industry's job; it is labor's job. I will work to make government in Pittsburgh draw strength and direction from labor and from business, so that working together we can best protect and advance the interests of all the people."[15]

After the inaugural ceremonies and a press photography session, Lawrence spent the remainder of the afternoon closeted in the office with his executive secretary, Jack Robin, County Commissioner Kane, and several of his closest advisers. That evening he used what the *Press* called "the most serious banquet the Democrats have ever held" to inform party workers that he meant everything he said in his inaugural address, particularly the comment that "anybody on the city payroll who doesn't want to work a full day is out." Lawrence left the banquet at ten o'clock to return home for a good night's rest. He intended to begin a full-scale assault on the problems of the city in the morning.[16]

For the next month Lawrence attacked one problem after another. For example, on his second day in office, he resolved an issue that had plagued Scully for nearly five years—garbage collection. Because of political appointees who refused to work, inefficient equipment, and jurisdictional labor disputes, the system frequently ground to a standstill. Residents complained, and garbage collection had been a major issue in the recent election. In a fifteen-minute meeting the mayor issued a blunt edict to his new superintendent of refuse, James Hughes, and three local teamsters' union officials: garbage "must be collected—and collected regularly. I will accept no excuses from anyone." Those who failed to comply would be fired.[17] Lawrence also announced that a new, larger incinerator would be ordered within a few weeks. The issue, which had been a constant source of newspaper editorials and letters to the editor, disappeared from the press almost immediately. It was the first time Lawrence challenged organized labor in the city, and he gave notice that he would not be "labor's boy." He would demonstrate the point over and over again throughout the year.

All of the early efforts of the Lawrence administration were accompanied by extensive publicity and occasional theatrics. For example, in selecting the World War II veterans' housing sites the mayor and a six-car delegation of officials toured the city in fifteen-degree weather. At each potential site the mayor and several officials were photographed climbing small fences, crossing icy fields, and collecting brambles on their clothing, all in the line of duty. Other instances were the garbage problem and the mayor's exchange with the president of the school board, H. B. Kirkpatrick, over what Lawrence considered the underutilization of buildings. But perhaps the most important publicity the mayor could have had at this early date was a newspaper photo of himself and several business leaders, including Alan Scaife, and Leon Falk, announcing the beginning of a fund-raising campaign for a new city nursing school. The formation of that committee demonstrated Lawrence's willingness to work with the corporate heads of Pittsburgh.[18]

The publicity sought by Lawrence in the early stage of his administration may appear uncharacteristic of a man who for more than twenty years was content to wield power from behind the scenes. Even though he was always a public man, Lawrence never went out of his way to seek publicity and often preferred to avoid it. As a politician, of course he always realized the value of a carefully staged photograph or a well-chosen quotation. However, it was the government official, not the politician, whom he expected to stand in the limelight. Citizens should be made aware of the positive activities of their elected officials, whom they would remember and reward with their vote in future elections. Publicity for public officials was simply good politics, and Lawrence acted accordingly.

Lawrence also appeared anxious to convince the citizens of Pittsburgh that he was more than a politician. The actions he initiated—challenging the teamsters' union, announcing a blue-ribbon nursing school committee, government reorganization, and housing—appealed to a broad spectrum of opinion. They provided concrete evidence that the mayor intended to take action on a wide variety of issues, that he was willing to accommodate any group interested in the welfare of the city, and that he would challenge any group, no matter how politically loyal they had been, if he felt their actions were detrimental to the city.

▽

The mayor's best opportunity to demonstrate his ability and intention to lead the city began early in February 1946 and stretched through October. The event, a protracted labor dispute between the Duquesne Light and Power Company and an independent union headed by George L. Mueller, was a crucial point in Lawrence's career. Restrained in his criticism of the company during the war, Mueller began a full-scale attack early in 1945, and his statements gave evidence that the impending contract negotations would be long and arduous.[19] The potential effects of a long power strike on the city eventually involved the mayor. The dispute tested his leadership skills in many ways but ultimately elevated him in the eyes of many residents from city boss to civic statesman.

The dispute began in late 1945 when Mueller presented a 37 percent wage increase demand to the company head, Pressly H. McCance. The company countered by offering a 7.5 percent increase, pointing out that this would place wages "among the highest in the United States including electric utilities in such cities as New York, Newark, Philadelphia, Boston, Cleveland, Baltimore, Cincinnati and others." McCance also reminded Mueller that the existing contract contained a no-strike clause. Negotiations were sporadic and unsuccessful over the next several months. On 9 February Mueller issued a strike notice, effective 4 A.M. on 12 February, that would make Pittsburgh the first city in the nation to experience such a strike and would cut off all but emergency power to both Allegheny and Beaver counties.[20]

Faced with a potential catastrophe, Lawrence swung into action. Proclaiming a state of emergency, he called the secretary of labor in Washington to request that the federal government seize the light company. At the same time he moved to marshal the city's emergency facilities. Police and firemen were ordered on twenty-four-hour duty, and 1000 auxiliary police were to be hired. He also asked the council for a $25,000 appropriation for emergency supplies. During the next twenty-four hours, at the mayor's request, union and management officials and federal and state conciliators met in his office in a last attempt to avert the strike. Lawrence and Robin remained on hand.

When the futility of the effort became clear, Lawrence decided to appeal to the citizens of Pittsburgh to put pressure on the union to continue negotiations. At 9:30 P.M. on 11 February, he delivered an emotional address over radio station KQV "to the people of Pittsburgh and the several thousand men and women who work for the Duquesne Light Company." Using the radio as effectively as an experienced actor, he began by apologizing to the audience for sounding weary. "I have been in almost continuous session for thirty-six hours, seeking to avoid what is rightly called a disaster for Pittsburgh. If my voice is tired, it is because I have worn it out talking." The mayor then explained that the independent union officials, "neither CIO nor A F of L," had refused to negotiate any further. He placed the burden of the strike on the backs of the union workers. "I cannot believe that people whom we know, people who are part of our community, people who are one with us, will plunge our city into darkness—risk the lives of people near death's door in our hospitals, menace the mother going down into the valley of shadows so that life can come into the world. I simply cannot believe it of the good people—the good citizens—the good neighbors whom we know as workers in our public utility system."[21]

He detailed the dire results of such a strike and made a fervent plea to the union. "I ask you even at this late hour, for a reconsideration, for a sober second thought. I have championed the cause of labor all my life, and I am speaking now with that record to support me. I think I have earned a trust. . . . Keep the lights on over Pittsburgh while we work to see that [you] get a fair deal from the community that [you] have treated so squarely." He concluded with a subtle but clear warning to the union. "But my first duty, and my only duty is to all the people of this city. . . . Whatever may take place we will protect the health, the safety, and the welfare of all the people of Pittsburgh."[22]

The appeal brought quick praise in the editorials of the city's newspapers but no action from Mueller. The union struck the power company at 4:00 A.M. as planned. Lawrence resumed his efforts early in the morning. He and Robin met with union and company officials and with state and federal conciliators, CIO and AFL officials, and Commissioner Kane and the Reverend Charles Owen Rice, both considered friends of labor. All pleaded with Mueller to call off the strike, but to no avail. When reminded at one point that "God declared, 'Let there be light'," Mueller responded, "God doesn't run the independent union."[23]

Lawrence's efforts continued all day. He spoke with Governor Martin and with Truman advisers, attempting to pressure the president to act on his seizure request. Truman, involved in his own labor difficulties, reluctantly promised to study the matter and respond within twenty-four hours. The mayor, angered by the postponement, called a midnight press conference at which he assailed the federal government, but not Truman by name, for its failure to act. The president rejected Lawrence's request early on the morning of the thirteenth.[24]

Intervention by the federal government proved unnecessary in any case, for the erratic Mueller, in a surprise announcement over radio station KQV, agreed to suspend the strike and begin negotiations the following Monday.

The strike lasted just nineteen and one-half hours, but that was long enough to create a new role for David Lawrence and enhance the image he had worked to create over the past nine months. He was now viewed as a willing and fair labor mediator who could be called upon to assist in an impasse. His assistance would be requested repeatedly for the rest of his life. Many also began to view Lawrence in a different light. All three newspapers hailed his efforts at resolving the crisis, probably giving him more credit for the temporary solution than he or his aides would have claimed. Praise was heaped upon him, and feature stories and photographs emphasized his stamina and determination and asserted that he had earned a well-deserved rest after "service well beyond the call of duty."[25]

To be sure, not everyone in Pittsburgh joined in the praise. Labor leaders, while not in sympathy with the independent Mueller, began to wonder about Lawrence's loyalties. One even suggested that his actions during the strike were promanagement. Others saw his efforts against an independent union as a political ploy designed to gain the business support he had been courting. One such individual ironically was Walter Giesey, who later became the mayor's executive secretary and closest confidant. "I was working for the *Bulletin Index* then," Giesey recalled, "and my reaction was that of a young liberal—maybe radical—and I recall when he went on the radio and referred to this as 'not an A F of L union . . . not a CIO union, it's an independent union,' I thought you dirty son-of-a-bitch. You wouldn't dare do that if it were one of the others [national unions]."[26] Undoubtedly, Lawrence had inserted himself into a situation where the political risk with regard to labor was real but minimal. The potential for reward, on the other hand, heavily outweighed the danger. In the eyes of most, including the business community, Lawrence's action seemed the right thing to do and demonstrated his independence from organized labor.

Mueller's announcement of his willingness to continue negotiations, unfortunately, did not free the city from the threat of a strike. Union and management had met more than thirty times over the past four months and now had merely agreed to start over. They were no closer to settlement than when negotiations began in September, although the union had demonstrated that its threat to strike was serious. All parties, including the mayor, would rest over the weekend and begin again on Monday.

The following week's discussion in city hall brought no end to the impasse, and Mueller's announcement that he would resume strike action in four days initiated a new round of activity on Lawrence's part. Resorting to public and private channels, the mayor and a team of allies attempted to put pressure on both sides to settle or submit to arbitration. In another radio address, he called for help from five sources: the CIO, the AFL, the Chamber of Commerce, the federal government, and the public. "This is a mighty serious situation. It's time everybody in Pittsburgh arouses himself and uses any influence [he] may have with either the company or the union to prevent the paralyzing of the city." Meanwhile, his office would insist on resumption of around-the-clock talks. Behind the scenes, the mayor's staff contacted any and all organizations that would be affected by the strike to ask them to put pressure on both sides. The response was hundreds of phone calls, telegrams, and letters to the union and company heads. The pastor of one Catholic church even invoked divine intervention by asking his congregation to pray with him for arbitration. The appeals fell on deaf ears—both divine and mortal—and neither side softened its position. Exasperated, Lawrence requested a meeting with the president of Duquesne Light, Pressly McCance, who had steadfastly refused to take part in the negotiations. The two met for more than an hour in a closed-door session on the morning of the twenty-fourth. Reporters huddled outside the door later wrote that "angry voices could be heard . . . and most of the shouting was coming from the mayor." Lawrence later told the press that he told McCance to "do something or the company would be responsible for the strike." That afternoon McCance announced that the company would submit to arbitration. Two hours later Mueller did the same. But both sides still had to agree to arbitration terms. Lawrence called an immediate joint session, but it deteriorated into what he called "filibustering and arguing about where to place semicolons." At 8:00 P.M. the mayor declared, "There will be no adjournments. Meetings will continue all night if necessary."[27]

The meeting continued not only all night but until 11:00 P.M. the next day, when Mueller rushed a negotiated arbitration agreement off to his executive committee for approval. Thirty-five minutes later—twenty-five minutes before the new strike deadline—he phoned the mayor's office: the committee had voted twenty-seven to fourteen to submit the agreement to the membership. Jack Robin shouted to all in the room, "The strike is postponed for one week. The union will vote on arbitration." The membership ratified the agreement, but the settlement satisfied neither side. On 13 April Mueller declared that he expected to negotiate a new contract, beginning in August.[28] Once again the disaster had been averted, but only temporarily.

Lawrence, as earlier, received most of the credit for the settlement. The *Pittsburgh Sun-Telegraph* went as far as to say that he demonstrated the wisdom of Solomon, while the *Press*, which had "reluctantly" endorsed him four months earlier, offered "just another word of praise for our new mayor, and his stamina and energy. Pittsburgh never saw anything like this previously."[29]

Lawrence's growing immersion in labor mediation could hardly help the achievement of his campaign goals during his first year in office. The power crisis, for example, had just been postponed when he became embroiled in the 115-day Westinghouse electrical workers' strike. Once again he emerged as a fair participant, somewhat restoring his standing with organized labor. Lawrence participated in demonstrations urging management to grant the 18.5¢ per hour wage increase demanded by the union. However, when violence broke out, he gently chastised workers for breaking the law, softening his remarks by calling the CIO president, Philip Murray "one of our country's and one of our city's ablest men." When the workers dispersed shouting cheers for Murray and Lawrence, a potentially volatile situation had been defused.[30] Lawrence demonstrated his willingness to meet with both sides when he invited Gwilym Price, president of Westinghouse, to city hall.

A number of other strikes directly affecting the city commanded Lawrence's attention that year. In May he ordered city trucks to cross railroad workers' picket lines and enter warehouses to pick up food destined for city hospitals and other institutions. He also became involved as a part-time mediator in a hotel employees' and a brewery workers' strike.

But it was the power dispute that continued to demand his time. In August, when Mueller set a new strike deadline, Lawrence called McCance and Mueller to his office and lectured them both on the responsibilities of power. "The American people, our own people of Pittsburgh, are long suffering and very patient. But they will not permit the abuse of power they have conferred. . . . The public utilities live by the sufferance of the public. . . . if the terms of that grant are violated, if service is not continuous, the people through their government will act."[31] Lawrence became directly involved in the negotiations early in September, and when the strike was averted by a court-ordered five-day injunction issued one minute before the strike deadline, hundreds of letters and telegrams poured into city hall congratulating the mayor. He and Robin celebrated by taking a rare afternoon off to attend a movie.

But the reprieve was only temporary. Calling the injunction a "scrap of paper," Mueller ordered his workers to strike on 25 September. This time there was no last-minute solution. The city was plunged into darkness. "Night travelers to Pittsburgh had the unnerving experience of coming into a city illuminated largely by candles. And the farther they went into the dimmed-out city, the deeper grew the sense of having strayed into some darker century or into that ice age projected by the gloomier prophets of industrial paralysis. . . . No streetcars and few busses were running. A picket line tie-up of coal trucks knocked out the central steam plant heating most of the big downtown buildings and department stores, restaurants, and other businesses closed down for lack of light and heat. Office workers hitchhiked in and out of town as best they could, climbed long flights of dark stairs to work, huddled in coats and sweaters in stone cold offices. . . . Pittsburgh appeared more than ever a city under siege."[32]

If the situation seemed to have reached its low point, citizens were shocked by the events of the next several days. On 26 September a three-judge panel met to hear the city's request for a permanent injunction. In the process the court demanded that Mueller apologize for his "scrap of paper" statement. He refused. The two Republican judges stunned Mueller and city officials by sentencing him to a one-year prison term for contempt of court. The reaction was almost immediate. National labor leaders attacked the Lawrence-induced injunction, while local union officials called sympathy strikes. The following day, several thousand workers marched on city hall. The Reverend Charles Owen Rice was booed and forced to give up attempts to talk to the group. Chanting "We want Mueller" and "Free Mueller, jail Lawrence," they left no doubt that Lawrence had lost standing among some Pittsburgh workers. "It was horrible," Rice recalled. "I thought I could talk to them, but there were Mueller's friends out there who were like locusts. They were screaming furiously."[33] To make matters worse, Lawrence's own party had adopted a state platform plank condemning the use of injunctions on the very day that the city solicitor, Anne X. Alpern, was in court requesting one. Lawrence's Pittsburgh problems had prevented him from attending the platform meeting.

Lawrence knew he had his back to the wall. He could press the injunction issue; the judges had already indicated that they were willing to find all nine union officials in contempt. Jailing them might persuade the membership to return to work, but the past twenty-four hours suggested just the opposite: the union would have ten martyrs instead of one. A second option seemed even more remote; the city could wait out the strike, hoping that the federal government would step in. Lawrence had been in continuous contact with the secretary of labor, however, and knew Truman was not inclined to act in the face of the growing labor reaction to the injunction. Furthermore, with the growing number of sympathy strikes, delay would cause the city to collapse.

After a meeting of Lawrence, Robin, Alpern, Kane, and several other members of the inner circle, it was decided that only one option was open. Alpern would ask the court to lift the injunction and would request that Mueller be released from jail. The situation had become so desperate that only a complete surrender would get the stalled negotiations moving. The court agreed to Alpern's request the next day.

Mueller's release merely restored the status quo, and Lawrence and his staff spent the next several weeks laboring to maintain negotiations. By mid October Mueller's support began to erode. A committee of rank and file workers called for a vote on arbitration, and sympathetic unions began returning to work. A shooting at one Duquesne Light and Power Company power plant, which damaged a 60,000-volt generator, strengthened the feeling against Mueller. Unable to resist the growing pressure, he agreed to submit the request for binding arbitration to a vote of the union. On 21 October, twenty-seven days after the strike began, the workers voted 1,197 to 797 to accept arbitration. The only strike of its kind against a major city ended in stalemate.

Newsweek pictured Lawrence collapsed at his desk, head in hand, on the cover of its next issue. Letters, telephone calls, and telegrams again deluged city hall congratulating him and thanking him for his resolution. National magazines hailed him as "an outstanding leader" and "a voice of reason." In a local radio poll 92 percent of those asked "thought the mayor did all he could do to avert the strike." In some Democratic circles he was elevated to the level of national hero. More important, he had demonstrated to all but the most immovable of skeptics that he held the interests of the city supreme over the interests of party. His credibility, particularly among Pittsburgh's Republican corporate heads, reached new heights. They would never agree on politics, but Dave Lawrence was a man with whom they could work.

Lawrence's role in the power and other disputes stamped him as a man of courage and integrity, but it was not without its costs. Some members of his own party began to question his loyalty to Democratic causes and to criticize his willingness to deal on a cooperative basis with corporate heads. The charge of his friendliness with management would recur consistently for the remainder of his political career.

His effort in the strike also caused him to lose control temporarily of the state organization. In February 1946, just two days before the first strike deadline, the state Democratic committee, in a split vote, endorsed U.S. Senator Guffey's candidacy for a third term. Lawrence, detained by the strike threat, did not attend the meeting but sent a lukewarm endorsement. The outgoing Republican governor, Edward Martin, easily won GOP support to challenge Guffey. Lawrence also announced his support for the auditor general, Harold Wagner for governor, but Guffey, as usual at odds with Lawrence, supported Judge Guy Bard of Lancaster. The party, without Lawrence's leadership, remained at loggerheads for the next week but eventually settled on a compromise candidate, John S. Rice of Gettysburg. Rice, a former state senator, was virtually unknown outside his home district and stood little chance of upsetting the Republican choice, James Duff, a popular progressive Republican from Carnegie. Lawrence, dissatisfied with his party's leading candidates and preoccupied with the problems of the city, campaigned only sparingly in the primary and general elections for the first time in nearly thirty years. But it is doubtful that active campaigning on his part would have influenced the outcome as Guffey and Rice were overwhelmed by more than 500,000 votes each. What is clear is that the party drifted aimlessly while he attended to one local crisis after another. The adoption of the state party platform condemning injunctions at the very moment when its chairman was seeking one not only embarrassed Lawrence but gave clear indication of his minor role in the election of 1946.

Lawrence also faced personal threats due to his efforts in the power strike. Following the request for an injunction and the ugly scene in front of city hall, he received many threatening letters and phone calls and was placed under armed guard for the only time in his lengthy career.[34] He was also confronted with a potential political problem when, in the midst of the strike, he received a letter from the powerful House Un-American Activities Committee requesting that he appear to explain any Communist participation in the strike. Lawrence risked being branded as a Communist sympathizer when he fired off a telegram in response. "In reply to your letter of October 15, inviting me to testify before your committee, it is my belief that I could serve no useful purpose there. This strike is disastrous in its effects and in my opinion has been unnecessary because arbitration is possible, but I have no reason to believe that any communistic influences are influential in it."[35] Lawrence would later, in the midst of the McCarthy era, risk his reputation by defending those unjustly accused of Communist leanings.

The mayor's role in the Duquesne Light and other strikes during his first year in office distracted him from many of his goals, but it built a basis of trust from which he would operate during the rest of his mayoralty. It was a year in which Lawrence established his credibility with a number of important groups, but it was one that exhausted him. In a year-end interview he summarized his attitude. "I fervently pray the other three years won't be like the first—if I last."[36]

1946–1950

Creating a Renaissance: The Environment

As the Pittsburgh Renaissance unfolded, delegations from nearly 100 cities and reporters from more than a dozen national magazines traveled to Pittsburgh to learn the secret of the city's remarkable redevelopment.[1] What they found, rather than a magic formula for renewal, was a unique blend of people and institutions that managed to overcome fundamental differences to achieve a single goal: the renewal of a dying city. Attempts to emulate the model in other cities frequently failed because of their inability to create the relationships that existed in Pittsburgh during the Lawrence era. When the mayor assumed office in 1946, the private sector forces were already in existence, awaiting a sign from Lawrence that he intended to live up to his campaign rhetoric. What was needed was comparable commitment and purpose in the public sector. Lawrence provided an immediate response.

His long-term passion for orderliness, hard work, and organization soon became the hallmark his administration. He established a set of routines and working relationships that seldom varied during his thirteen years as mayor. Only strikes, election campaigns, an unexpected crisis, or, at times, vacations interrupted his normal procedure. On the typical day his chauffeur, Marion Graves, arrived promptly at 9:00 A.M. at Lawrence's home to drive him to the City-County Building on Grant Street. On the ten-minute ride, Lawrence would glance at the *Pittsburgh Post-Gazette* and often order Graves to pick up commuters along the way. When he arrived at the fifth-floor office, Rita Emmerling, head of a staff of five secretaries and a receptionist, handed the mayor the day's schedule. Copies went to key staff members and to Mrs. Lawrence, in case of an emergency at home. An examination of daily schedules over Lawrence's thirteen-year administration shows that, although details changed from time to time, the routine remained remarkably constant. The following log illustrates a typical day:

9:15 Private meeting with the mayor's executive secretary, Jack Robin, Robin's assistant, Charles McCarthy, and Park Martin, executive secretary of the Allegheny Conference on Community Development to discuss strategy on the Pittsburgh Package, legislation pertaining to the city renewal program, under consideration by the state legislature.

10 Fortieth anniversary convention of ice cream manufacturers in William Penn Hotel.

10:30 Weekly meeting with councilmen to discuss items due before council that week. Representatives from North Side Chamber of Commerce attend to discuss parking problems and a committee from the Fraternal Order of Police offers a presentation on police pension legislation.

12:15 Booster luncheon at downtown YMCA for basketball tournament.

1:15 Meeting with ward chairmen from the South Side to discuss residential relocation plans made necessary by the Jones and Laughlin expansion project.

2 Meeting of Civic Unity Council in mayor's conference room.

2:30 Memorial service for Judge Joseph Richardson in court assignment room.

3 Address to a meeting of the League of Women Voters at the Congress of Clubs on the Pittsburgh Package. Mrs. R. Tempelton Smith raises several objections, to which the mayor responds. (Lawrence is saved from further discussion, which is becoming heated, by a 4:00 P.M. appointment.)

4 Emergency meeting of the Chamber of Commerce to maintain pressure for Federal aid needed in completion of the Conemaugh Dam, a key project in the Pittsburgh district flood control program.

5–7 Signing letters. Brief workout at the YMCA. (Lawrence occasionally used this time to play pinochle with Frank Ambrose, Judge Primo Columbus, or Patsy McGeehan.) Gimbel's reception in William Penn Hotel to meet Edward Millman, one of the artists selected to work on the Gimbel's Collection of Pennsylvania Art.

7 Dinner, Rosalia Foundling and Maternity Hospital.

Meeting with the board of directors, of which Lawrence was a member.

8:30 Opening of the flower show at Phipps Conservatory.

8:30 Tenth anniversary celebration of the Laundry Workers International Union Local 141, Syria Mosque.

9:00 Basketball game between North Catholic High School and St. Joseph's of Philadelphia at Duquesne Gardens. Mayor presents trophy. (The Phipps Conservatory, Syria Mosque and Duquesne Gardens were all within a few blocks of each other.)

10:30 Graves drives Lawrence home.[2]

Thus, in a routine day, the mayor met with his staff and members of city council and several public organizations; mended political fences; and performed a number of ceremonial duties. It is noteworthy that none of his day was devoted to meeting disgruntled citizens to deal personally with their problems, as was the custom of Chicago's Mayor Daley. He felt such problems could best be handled by ward chairmen or committeemen and were a waste of his valuable time. He maintained his relationship with the citizens and with political workers through his evening visits to the neighborhoods. When he was not attending a sporting event, he visited one or more neighborhood functions or made an appearance at a ward-level political meeting. He and his staff usually worked Saturday mornings, and he attended to political matters Sunday afternoons. He reserved Friday evenings for dinner with the family, although he might attend a public function later in the evening. Saturday evenings, which he spent with his wife, were considered off limits for political or government affairs.

Lawrence set a routine upon which his staff and political associates could depend as he led the campaign for the success of the renewal programs; but he seldom dealt with the details of a particular program. He depended heavily upon a small staff led by the executive secretary and his department heads to develop the programs designed to accomplish a particular goal. "He was interested in results," Jack Robin testified, "not in how you achieved them. . . . He was willing to accept the judgment of people he considered had expert knowledge and whom he felt were trustworthy. So he never really worried about the details about who was going to be designer or contractor. Lawrence did not clutter up his head with more than he needed to know." Walter Giesey, who later held the same position as Robin, added, "He would be very upset when things weren't done right. He'd say, 'do it.' But sometimes doing it didn't correct the problem that existed because the system wasn't the correct system. He wasn't concerned with that, he was concerned with the result. . . . He was very pleased to have someone take care of these details which really didn't interest him as long as the end result was some kind of better service."[3]

He initially depended a great deal upon Robin, who wrote his speeches and acted as his adviser, political confidant, and intermediary with the business community. A large man possessed of a quick wit, a brilliant analytical mind, and considerable charm, Robin became associated with Lawrence during the early days of the Scully administration. Educated at the University of Pittsburgh, Robin drifted into newspaper work during the heart of the Depression, then in 1936 became secretary to Mayor Scully. He remained in that position, gradually gaining experience in administration and accumulating political and non-political contacts. Robin's work on the early smoke control laws produced contacts with individuals on the Economy League and the Allegheny Conference staffs that would later prove invaluable to Lawrence. "Lawrence and I became interchangeable in what we wanted to do and how we wanted to do it. I began to be very close to him and after '46 I became, with Jimmy Kirk, the closest person to him politically and to some degree, it was a father-son relationship . . . and that continued for the rest of his life."[4] For the first few years of the administration, until Robin was given other duties, the two men were inseparable. Lawrence placed full trust in Robin, who was sometimes described as the idea man on the administrative side of the Renaissance. It soon became clear to all who came in contact with the administration that, when Robin spoke, he spoke for the mayor.

The department heads, excepting Lawrence's closest friend, James Kirk, never had the authority or confidence that Lawrence granted Robin, but all were given considerable freedom to carry out the duties of their offices as they saw fit. They appear to have been competent, although not highly talented. Several were college trained, and only three of the eight received their positions as a reward for longtime political efforts. They understood their roles in the administration and, with few exceptions, held the goals of the administration above their own self interests. The group became a cohesive unit working toward a singular set of goals.

Mayors can expect loyalty and unity from their own handpicked administration. Legislative bodies, however, can and frequently do change or compromise the efforts of the executive branch. Occasionally they discard administrative policy and attempt to substitute their own. Pittsburgh's city council, elected at large since 1911, had always been proud of its tradition of independence. Councilmen frequently used their positions to initiate their own agenda or launch political careers. One of Cornelius Scully's chief weaknesses as mayor was his inability to control the council. Several times during his administration the council tore his budget to shreds and adopted its own. Lawrence, by virtue of his power and careful planning, had no such difficulties.

Shortly before Lawrence became mayor, council president Thomas Kilgallen, anxious to avoid public criticism over the council's treatment of the Scully budget, instituted the practice of private sessions where differences were aired and compromises hammered out. Actual votes, held at public sessions, became pro forma. When Lawrence became mayor, he continued the practice, meeting each Monday morning in private with the nine council members. The meetings later became controversial when the press and two disgruntled councilmen, Joe McArdle and Eddie Leonard, charged that the mayor was using the sessions to force his will on the council. There was, no doubt, some truth to the charge. Lawrence later proudly announced that he never had to veto an action of the council during his thirteen-year tenure, and most council votes during the period were unanimous. But Lawrence's methods were never as blatant as his critics charged. Following the practice he had established while secretary of the Commonwealth, he held closed-door caucuses to discuss pending issues before they were released for public discussion or a vote. The mayor, his executive secretary, involved department heads or other relevant personnel met with the council for discussion that was usually lively, with considerable give and take. Councilmen felt free to voice opposition, although they were expected to follow the same unwritten rule Lawrence had established with the state Democratic legislators' caucus: a united front would be presented once a decision was reached. If Lawrence felt strongly about an issue, he would argue strenuously for his point of view, but if it was not going to prevail, he would compromise or withdraw the issue temporarily.[5] On legislation of lesser importance, the department head would explain and defend the proposal, and Lawrence accepted the will of the majority.

Of course, the party boss held an unseen but heavy weapon over the heads of council members. Those who consistently opposed his program were almost without exception dropped in a subsequent election. The mayor's willingness to purge rebellious councilmen served as an important reminder of the actual source of power in the administration. Few dared challenge the chief executive. But according to one councilman, while it was true that Lawrence had great power, he seldom had to wield it. "Our political philosophies were so similar. We were all New Dealers."[6] The common philosophy, of course, is quite understandable since Lawrence and the small Democratic executive committee selected council candidates. The system worked so well that, by the end of his first term in office, Lawrence seldom attended the Monday caucuses but turned the discussion over to Robin and, later, Giesey.

Lawrence's hold over council members resulted from a combination of their acceptance of him as the leader whose wisdom they seldom questioned, his power to withold party support in subsequent elections, and a similarity of views—a combination that produced a unity of action seldom seen in Pittsburgh. People from the private sector interested in city redevelopment knew that when Robin or Giesey spoke, they spoke for Lawrence, and that when Lawrence agreed to a program, he spoke for the council. It might offer some resistance, but it would not oppose him.

▽

By mid 1946 a public-private sector relationship began to form among several individuals and organizations. Wallace Richards, the flamboyant, impatient dreamer often known as the visionary of the Renaissance, began his career in Indianapolis as a newspaper reporter, and after several years he became executive secretary of the federal model community of Greenbelt, Maryland. In 1937 he came to Pittsburgh to direct the Pittsburgh Regional Planning Association and soon became associated with Richard King Mellon, probably through Mellon's aide, Arthur Van Buskirk. Richards impressed Mellon with his visions of Pittsburgh, and it was likely he who persuaded Mellon to support the founding of the Allegheny Conference in 1943. Two years later Lawrence and Richards met and quickly developed a mutual admiration. Richards marveled at Lawrence's ability to get things done, while Lawrence stood almost in awe of Richards's visions.

The perfect complement to the dreams of Richards was the extensive technical knowledge of Park Martin, who became director of the Allegheny Conference. Trained as a civil engineer, Martin worked for ten years as chief engineer and director of the Allegheny County Planning Commission. A Republican who once ran for a seat on the county commission, he developed a strong relationship with John Kane and through him met Lawrence. It was Martin who developed the first extensive county improvement plan. He sat on the board of the Allegheny Conference's predecessor and in 1945, at the suggestion of Richards, was appointed executive directore of the conference.

Leslie Reese, head of the western branch of the Pennsylvania Economy League, played a lesser but significant role in the city's urban renewal. A huge man, Reese attracted attention by his very appearance. He was an expert on finances and was respected by nearly everyone who met him. In addition to providing the financial services of the Pennsylvania Economy League, Reese often acted as the go-between when disagreements threatened a project. Like Martin and Richards, he had contacts in both the public and private sectors—in the latter because the league depended upon a number of the city's corporate heads for its funding. Reese met Robin during the early years of the Scully administration when the league helped the city develop its first annual budget. Although Lawrence never liked Reese personally, his work with the city and county governments built a strong reservoir of trust on the part of the public officials. When his organization became a key research group for the Allegheny Conference, Reese began to work for both the government and the conference.

Reese, Martin, Richards, and several other technical experts such as Fred Bigger, head of city planning, Ralph Griswold, a landscape architect, and the conference attorney, Theodore Hazlett, along with Robin, became the principal links between the public and private sectors. Most had had experience on both sides of the fence and knew important people from both worlds. In addition to interacting professionally, they were of a similar age and background, they liked and respected one another, and a number socialized together. "Some nights we would start off by playing pingpong," Ted Hazlett related, "and then end up going into the problems [of the city]; or we'd do a lot of drinking . . . these were nice parties with a lot of fun. We'd go up to Wally's [Richards] house, he always had a lot of cheeses and things like that which is common today but wasn't common then. Then we'd just sit around and talk about what was the immediate problem and what we would do about it, whom we had to see in order to get help. . . . It was just a bunch of guys who got together, who had dedication to the city, who had some imagination."[7]

Hazlett's view of "a bunch of guys" sitting around planning the future of the city is probably overly romantic. Personality conflicts and occasional jealousies had to be overcome. Martin, for example, hinted that not all members of the group were pleased that Richards received most of the credit as the creative genius of the Renaissance. "Don't misunderstand me. I think Wallace had his place and he did his job. He was largely overrated in a lot of respects. He rode on a lot of people's shoulders, and one of them was mine. . . . We put on a great story of Pittsburgh by picture in the museum. Wallace at the time was given credit for that. It wasn't his idea at all; it was mine. . . . That's what I mean. He was the type of man who could take an idea and follow it through, but at times he was off into the wild blue yonder and it was me who had to pull him back to earth. But people believed he was quite a boy and he was in some respects. He was a far better salesman than I could ever hope to be"[8] In spite of his feelings, Martin insisted that he and Richards never "had a cross word with one another." Rebuilding the city, Martin, Hazlett, Richards, and Robin all emphasized, was a such a powerful and exciting goal that it enabled them to surmount personal differences.

Pittsburgh's mid-war crisis prompted a civic consciousness among the business elite. They, in turn, attracted a remarkable group of technical experts and created organizations or used existing ones as the foundation for redevelopment. The city administration, at the same time, followed a parallel course. The technocrats interacted with the administration and in time formed a kind of interlocking directorate that enabled the public and private sectors to work in harmony toward a common set of goals. The formula for success was nearly complete. One crucial ingredient remained absent.

David L. Lawrence and Richard King Mellon were so powerful in their respective fields that resistance on the part of either could destroy the best planning. The business community could not act without the city's power to condemn land, build roads, revise zoning, and so forth. Furthermore, without smoke control, solely the administration's domain, urban redevelopment would be futile. But the city could not act without the support of the business community, which would finance most of the redevelopment and maintain the businesses and corporations vital to the welfare of the city. R. K. Mellon alone, for example, was "largely responsible for getting such companies as Pittsburgh Plate Glass, Westinghouse Electric Corporation, Westinghouse Air Brake, and the other companies to sign twenty year leases [in the redevelopment area] even before the plans were completed."[9] Redevelopment was not possible without the cooperation of Lawrence and Mellon.

Richard King Mellon was to the corporate community what Lawrence was to western Pennsylvania politics. He presided over a vast empire of wealth. Mellon holdings included substantial investment in industrial, transportation, and utility companies and large blocks of valuable real estate throughout the eastern United States. The major Mellon holdings—in excess of $3 billion in assets—were concentrated in western Pennsylvania. They included controlling interest in Gulf Oil, the Koppers Company, Pittsburgh Consolidation Coal Company, ALCOA, and Mellon National Bank and Trust Company. Nearly every other corporation in Pittsburgh had substantial business dealings with the Mellon interests. A liaison between Mellon and Lawrence would almost guarantee the success of any potential renewal plan.

Mellon, however, unlike his uncle Andrew and his cousin William Larimer, originally showed little interest in politics, civic affairs, or even the financial world. When he was seventeen years old his father informed him that he had put fifty thousand dollars in a checking account that the boy might use to engage in whatever business suited his fancy. He left the money untouched. "Dick was universally agreeable. Little seemed worth extending himself for. . . . Blandness required little energy." A poor student, he loved horses, the outdoors, and wild game hunting. His greatest satisfactions during his early adulthood came from fox hunts, the Rolling Rock steeplechase races, and game trips to the Yukon with his wife, Constance, to kill or capture animals. He provided many live specimens to the Pittsburgh Zoo and stuffed animals to the museum. He was at his happiest on horseback or behind the barrel of a large game weapon. "Like most thoroughbreds, he is sensitive, nervous, and high-strung, although he tries to keep such qualities hidden. He also attempts to cover up a large and generous heart, but in this he is not so successful." A shy man, he avoided publicity and had few friends or trusted confidants. When World War II broke out, he quickly volunteered and received a major's commission in the army. In 1943, at Governor Martin's request, he was made director of the Pennsylvania Selective Service System in Harrisburg. "These years of service were perhaps the happiest of R. K.'s life. He had the chance to display his salient abilities—picking men, smoothing over difficulties—without the strain of all but unlimited responsibilities. He loved the crispness, the ritual, the pomp and ceremonial. He made full Colonel—gratifying too, not bad at all for somebody who busted out of Princeton. Nobody finagled that." Mellon eventually attained the rank of general.[10]

It was during Mellon's army tour of duty that Wallace Richards persuaded him to turn his attention toward rebuilding the city his father, Richard Beatty, loved. "Father revered Pittsburgh," Mellon told a reporter at his father's funeral in 1933. "Always he held up Pittsburgh to me as one of the world's greatest cities." Although not evident until the mid 1940s, it was a passion he inherited. "If you ever needed to persuade him to do something [in Pittsburgh], you could point to his father having done the same kind of thing, [and] this always carried the day."[11]

When Mellon returned to Pittsburgh after the war, Richards, Van Buskirk, and Adolph Schmidt decided to get him together with the new mayor, David Lawrence. It was Arthur Van Buskirk who set up the meeting. "The generous offer," Van Buskirk advised Mellon, "would be for you to leave your office and go over to visit the mayor." Mellon initially balked at the suggestion but eventually relented after much persuasion. The pretext his aides used was the offer of a gift of 13.5 acres of family-owned land east of the city to be developed as a public park and recreation center. Mellon went over to city hall to inform Lawrence of the gift and enlist his support in developing the area. "My God!" Schmidt exclaimed even thirty years later. "He didn't even take the car. He walked over with a couple of people and saw Lawrence. It was the first time they ever met. Lawrence was duly embarrassed by this but . . . said there was no problem whatever as far as the park was concerned. . . . Then on another occasion Lawrence did the same thing. . . . It broke the ice."[12]

One can only speculate what went through Lawrence's mind when he saw the head of the family he had fought against for so long walk into his office. Few more incongruous meetings had perhaps ever taken place. The multimillionaire, blue-blood, Presbyterian Republican stood face to face with the Roman Catholic, Democratic son of an unskilled laborer. The two men met in private on both occasions but seldom saw each other under similar circumstances after that. They talked on the phone at infrequent intervals and met at formal gatherings. Nor did they become social acquaintances. But they agreed, perhaps without stating as much, to work together to rebuild the city. Their understanding launched one of the most sucessful urban redevelopment projects ever undertaken.

▽

A formal protocol for action never existed among the groups interested in rebuilding the city. Projects were launched sometimes by the city, often by the Allegheny Conference, and occasionally by individuals. Gradually, however, one unwritten rule came to be observed by all those in the private sector. As work progressed and it became clear that Lawrence was probably an irreplaceable asset, all favorable publicity was carefully shifted in the direction of the mayor. "I'm conscious that I don't have to be elected to anything," Park Martin explained in 1955. "But the man who is to put these policies into effect . . . has to be elected again, and we've been very careful not to do what I call 'front-run' the public official. If we're successful and the public official puts the program through, we're going to get sufficient credit as I think has been proven over these years. As long as the public officials are producing what you want, let them get the credit and you'll get enough for yourself." The Allegheny Conference on Community Development adhered strictly to this policy during the first decade of its existence, and its officials made a point of giving credit to the Democratic city and county organizations and to the Republican state administration. At the same time they refrained from campaigning for any one person by avoiding mentioning names.[13] Lawrence accepted and enjoyed the public credit and kept his part of the bargain. Recognizing the importance of the assistance provided by the conference, he was careful to avoid any suspicion that politics played any role in the redevelopment process. City agencies involved were free to hire employees without adhering to the patronage system. Equally important, the numerous construction projects remained free of kickback and other scandals throughout the redevelopment period.

Lawrence also interceded with the secretary of the treasury, John W. Snyder, when the conference was informed it had lost its tax-exempt status as a result of its lobbying on behalf of the Pittsburgh renewal legislation. Lawrence arranged an appointment with the secretary, and he, Van Buskirk, and Martin went to Washington. At their meeting with Snyder, they "presented him with the work of the conference, what it had already done, what it was planning to do and the lift that the community was getting."[14] Secretary Snyder then called the general counsel of the Bureau of the Internal Revenue and ordered the ruling reversed. The conference received confirmation within a week.

It was agreed that renewal could not take place without flood and smoke control. Enabling legislation had already been passed in both cases, but the war had interrupted execution. Implementing the two programs became the first item of business of the mayor and his fellow proponents of urban renewal.

The economy-minded U.S. Congress threatened the entire flood control program when it omitted the crucial Conemaugh Dam from its 1946 appropriations. Lawrence and the Chamber of Commerce responded immediately. On 10 April—fortunately the first episode of the Duquesne Light strike had been settled by this time—the mayor and a delegation representing the chamber went to Capitol Hill. Dr. James Greene, executive vice-president of the Chamber of Commerce, testified before the House Flood Control Committee. Armed with the report from the New York Econometric Institute that identified floods as one of the main reasons why Pittsburgh had failed to attract new industries, Greene outlined a plan whereby Congress could defer the cost of the entire system by "completing the Conemaugh [Dam] first, then starting work on the other reservoirs in the system." Republican members of the Chamber of Commerce lobbied GOP representatives from Pennsylvania, and Lawrence visited the offices of several important Democratic legislators on the committee. He also met with President Truman, who gave his support. Congress responded to the appeal by appropriating enough funds for the start of preliminary work on the dam, including relocation of railroad tracks, pipelines, and electric lines.[15]

During the next several years, Lawrence continued to work with the chamber to apply pressure to Congress to carry out the flood control program. From 1947 through 1949 he made at least four trips to Washington to use his personal brand of persuasion on Democratic members of Congress, on the members of the Flood Control Committee, and on President Truman. In an attempt to broaden the focus of the issue, he also introduced a resolution at the annual meeting of the U.S. Conference of Mayors urging that Congress continue its appropriations for flood control. The measure passed unanimously. As before, he also accompanied delegations representing the Chamber of Commerce and other prominent Pittsburgh groups in their lobbying efforts and testimony before committees. The effort became a broad bipartisan one with the participation of Republican and Democratic representatives and both senators.[16]

The lengthy campaign succeeded. Congress appropriated funds during the 1948 and 1949 sessions, and work began on the dam in May 1949. There were almost immediate dividends: several months later, the Equitable Life Assurance Society agreed to terms to redevelop the Gateway Center business area adjacent to Point Park. The H. J. Heinz Corporation, located on the Allegheny River, and Jones and Laughlin Steel, on the Monongahela River, also announced multimillion-dollar expansion programs. By September 1953, eight of nine reservoirs approved in 1936 were complete and in operation.[17]

The actual funding and implementation of the Pittsburgh flood control system were beyond the control of Lawrence and the Chamber of Commerce. An unsympathetic Congress had shown its intention to turn its attention elsewhere. The bipartisan efforts of the Democratic mayor and the Republican chamber, however, paid off.

The city has been struck with several small nuisance floods since the catastrophe of 1936, but the flood control system has prevented a recurrence of the St. Patrick's Day disaster.

Also crucial to the redevelopment of the city was passage by the state legislature of a series of bills known collectively as the Pittsburgh Package. Drafted primarily by Ted Hazlett and the city solicitor, Anne X. Alpern, the bills received the strong support of the Pennsylvania Economy League and the Pittsburgh Regional Planning Association. They concerned such diverse matters as county refuse disposal; creation of a city parking authority; creation of a city department of parks and recreation; extension of county smoke control laws to railroads; establishment of a county transit and traffic study commission; completion of the Penn-Lincoln Parkway, a vital link into the city; and broadening of the city's tax base to include sources other than real estate.[18] Hazlett and Alpern presented the completed bills to Lawrence during the first week of 1947. The mayor, who had been kept informed of their general contents by Alpern, endorsed them immediately.

To ensure bipartisan support for the legislation, the conference sponsored three meetings in February and March at the William Penn Hotel to explain the package. Leading city, county, and state officials from both sides of the political aisle attended. The Democrats, as Lawrence had promised, offered enthusiastic support for the package, while Republican legislators dragged their feet. The Republican county chairman, James Malone, and the Senate floor leader, John Walker, both raised objections to various provisions of the bills. One Republican senator, however, probably got to the heart of the matter. "If we support these bills and these things happen, the mayor will get all the credit." He accurately surmised that the Republicans were helpless. Lawrence reached the same conclusion.

> Now, speaking to you fellows as a politician, I'll be perfectly happy if you don't go along with this. But speaking as Mayor of Pittsburgh, I plead with you to support it. Because its going to mean a lot to everybody around here, Democrats and Republicans alike, if we can recapture a lot of the old-time zip that Pittsburgh had. But as a politician, if you fellows oppose it that'd be grist for our mill. . . . We're going to pass these bills anyway, and I have the word of the Governor [Republican James Duff] he's going to sign it. . . . So you put yourself in just the position we want you to be. But as Mayor, I urge and plead

> with you for your own sake and for your family . . . [so] that we can do something for the city.[19]

The mayor's plea, not surprisingly, failed to move the members of the Republican caucus, but pressure applied by Martin, Richards, and Hazlett of the Allegheny Conference, and Leslie Reese of the Pennsylvania Economy League convinced the delegation that united support would bring credit to both parties. There was considerable bickering, but when Malone and Walker agreed to go along, the remaining Republican participants fell into line. A bipartisan Allegheny County delegation presented a united front in the state legislature. It was decided to present eight of the bills together as a package to speed passage. Two that applied to the city only—revising the city's taxing powers and creating a city department of parks and recreation—received support but were to be introduced separately.

The third meeting, a formal dinner, presented a picture of harmony to the invited press. Republican and Democratic leaders pledged their "solid" support and lavished credit on the Allegheny Conference and the other private agencies that developed the legislative package. Lawrence concluded the evening by thanking Malone for his "magnanimous offer of support." While he may have been somewhat effusive in his praise, he demonstrated the basis of his political strategy. "This is a Pittsburgh project, not a Democratic or Republican project. There is no such thing as a Democratic bridge or a Republican highway. It is a civic duty and patriotic duty. We don't want any political advantage, but a full measure of credit to everyone who helps put it through."[20]

The battle to pass the Pittsburgh Package perhaps best illustrates the cooperative spirit of the public and private sectors in the redevelopment process. The bills were introduced in the legislature over both Republican and Democratic signatures on 3 March 1947, amidst considerable opposition. For example, the Allegheny County League of Boroughs, Townships, and Third Class Cities, which perceived threats to local autonomy, objected.[21] Lawrence, State Senator Joe Barr, and County Commissioner Kane met almost weekly with the Democratic House and Senate caucuses to muster support for the program. Governor James Duff, a western Pennsylvanian, and Senator Walker applied equal pressure on the Republican side. Lawrence, in return, agreed to provide enough Democratic votes to ensure passage of a Duff-Republican tax program.

The Allegheny Conference, meanwhile, supplied a delegation to lobby legislators sensitive to business pressure. Several members spent three days per week during the six-month 1947 legislative session in Harrisburg. Attempting to act as individuals to maintain their tax-exempt status, they arranged meetings with Republican and Democratic legislators and wrote to them explaining various parts of the bills and urging support. When problems developed over a countywide smoke control bill, the delegation supplied 48,000 signatures gathered earlier among Allegheny County voters supporting it. Later, when the same bill was introduced by Republican Senator Robert Fleming, Senator Rufus Flynn, assistant general manager of the Pennsylvania Railroad, rose to state that his company opposed the bill. "Wallace Richards and I went directly to the telephone," Park Martin recalled. "Wallace talked directly to Mr. [Richard K.] Mellon in Pittsburgh. . . . Mr. Mellon got hold of the president of the Pennsylvania Railroad, who was in Florida, and told him in no uncertain terms the railroad had to change its position. [Mellon was a director of the Pennsylvania Railroad.] I understand that Mr. Ben Fairless [U.S. Steel president] did the same thing; also several other big shippers. As one man said, 'You know, we can find other railroads. . . .' Almost overnight the opposition evaporated and the bill passed."[22]

The conference delegation intervened directly on another bill, the one to permit the city to establish a parking authority. Strong opposition by parking lot and building owners led to the bill's defeat in the House on the initial vote. "I'll never forget the night of May 5 [1947]," said Ted Hazlett.

> The vote was 71 for and 113 against. That night Wallace Richards and Bob Bassett and I were sharing a room and . . . Bob Bassett got the chills , shaking, and Wally had a fever. I was at least healthy . . . but I was sleeping on a cot and was constantly falling off all night. The bill was resurrected and passed after a great deal of phoning and various pressures were put on. We had begun to learn a little bit about how to operate in Harrisburg by then. . . . You played poker with them [state legislators] and you got to know them by their first names, and maybe there was a little bit of understanding. . . . You also found out that most of the large corporations of this city had very influential lobbyists and there were blocks of votes where their influence was very great. So you would line up these men by making sure their bosses back in Pittsburgh had placed the proper phone call to them to say they ought to be in favor of this Pittsburgh Package. In one case, strangely enough, we got a vote

> because we knew the woman whom one of the members was sleeping with and we were able to get her to sort of talk the bill up while they were enjoying themselves. . . . No stone was left unturned and we finally did get that bill passed on May 14 by a vote of 186 in favor and 4 against.[23]

The combined pressure applied by both parties and by the public and private sectors—and apparently in the bedroom—had the expected effect. It gave the strongest possible signal that a united effort could bring about important change. Eight of the bills were passed during the 1947 legislative session. A separate bill permitting insurance companies to invest in urban renewal areas received the same type of support and also became law.

Besides the flood control program and a partially developed legislative package, Lawrence also inherited a state-sponsored Point Park project when he assumed office in January 1946. Two weeks after Governor Martin's announcement in October 1945 of the project, Richard King Mellon, chairman of the Pittsburgh Regional Planning Association, hosted a dinner meeting at the Duquesne Club at which Wallace Richards presented a design for the park. Lawrence and Kane, both of whom attended the meeting, agreed to sit on the Point Park Steering Committee. Two weeks after his inauguration, Lawrence made good on his promise to cooperate by submitting to the city council a recommendation that a minimum of thirty-six acres be acquired for the park. The recommendation was particularly important in that it committed the city to contribute several acres it owned and the historic Exposition Hall, now a warehouse, to the Point Park Commission. Lawrence ordered an existing Mayor's Point Park Commission to abandon its negotiations with the National Park Service to create a historic monument at the site. He instructed the city planning commission to join with state traffic engineers to create a basic traffic design for the area and to draw up plans to vacate several city streets. Five other city departments and two county departments were later assigned to participate in the planning and development process. Ralph Griswold, chief landscape architect for the project, recalled that Lawrence's action eliminated any further opposition. "Quick to grasp the significance of this new co-operative spirit, all previous conflicting interests rallied to assist the Commonwealth. Point State Park became a popular nonpartisan project."[24] Having successfully launched the plan, the Pittsburgh Regional Planning Association turned its implementation over to the Allegheny Conference in the first of many instances of interaction among the various private redevelopment organizations. A Point Park Committee, chaired by Van Buskirk and Edgar J. Kaufmann, president of the department store, collaborated with the state Department of Forests and Waters to oversee the project.

Planning, design, and land acquisition took nearly four years. Lawrence demanded occasional progress reports and regularly attended the Point Park Steering Committee meetings, but he generally played a minor role in the ongoing development of the project. He participated in the ground breaking ceremony on 18 May 1950. His daughter, son, and grandson represented him at the park's dedication on 30 August 1974, nearly eight years after his death.

Installation of a flood control system and a state park, while time consuming, were relatively easy compared with the efforts to rid the city's sky of noxious fumes and smoke. The city ordinances of 1941 established a three-stage timetable for the elimination of smoke-producing fuel or equipment. Stages one and two, directed primarily against commericial establishments, industries, and railroads, were implemented within sixteen months of the passage of the ordinance, but enforcement remained lax throughout the war. Production of war materials took precedence over pollution control, and the Pittsburgh sky grew darker. All sides agreed that strict enforcement would begin immediately after the war. Implementation of the third stage, aimed at domestic use, was postponed until after the war.

With the fighting in Europe and the Pacific subsiding in 1945, M. Jay Ream, president of the United Smoke Council, sounded out both mayoral candidates, Lawrence and Waddell, about their positions on the issue. Waddell replied that, if elected, he would appoint a "mayor's blue-ribbon" panel to study the question of implementation. Lawrence, on the other hand, indicated that he intended to act immediately to enforce the ordinances already passed. His campaign staff, moreover, unofficially adopted as its own the slogan of the United Smoke Council, "Smoke Must Go!" Lawrence reiterated his commitment in his first inaugural address. "I am convinced that our people want to clean up the air. . . . There is no other single thing which will so dramatically improve the appearance, the health, the pride, the spirit of the city."[25] Several days later, after meeting with members of city council to ensure their support, Lawrence announced the implementation of the ordinances effective October 1946. The date applied to all three groups: commercial establishments and industry, railroads, *and* domestic users.

Lawrence received praise for what members of the Allegheny Conference called a politically courageous step, but letters to the editors of the local newspapers both praised and condemned him. One called him the "savior of Pittsburgh," while another said, "If our mayor thinks so much of St. Louis [he had praised St. Louis's success in controlling air pollution], I sure wish he would move there and see if he could be its mayor." The Western Pennsylvania Conference on Air Pollution, representing the bituminous coal producers, and many residents besieged Lawrence's office with letters and phone calls. He agreed to meet with representatives of the coal producers' organization, who loudly demanded that he postpone implementation for a year because they lacked the necessary equipment and the supply of low-volatility coal was insufficient. They also demanded that the public hearings be canceled. After the intervention of the Allegheny Conference, the United Smoke Council, and the Chamber of Commerce, Lawrence eventually agreed privately to a postponement in return for a guarantee of willing compliance from the producers. But he insisted that the public hearings proceed as planned.[26] He had received considerable favorable publicity for his strong stand against the coal producers' organization and was unwilling to be seen to back down at this late date.

An overflow crowd filled the council hearing room during the hearings. Lawrence, as he had done during his days as secretary of the Commonwealth, sat in a conspicuous spot on the right side of the chamber, but this time he was not attempting to influence legislation. The council president, Thomas Kilgallen, tried to set the tone with his opening remarks. "We are not here today to discuss the merits of our smoke ordinance. This Council is committed to it. For better or worse we are going to enforce this smoke ordinance." When he was interrupted by a mixture of boos and applause, Kilgallen responded, "Now look, ladies and gentleman, here are nine men who have been in council for a long time. We are not affected one whit by applause. It just wastes time."[27]

Representatives of several organizations, including the League of Women Voters and the Civic Club of Allegheny County, spoke in favor of immediate enforcement. The League president, Mrs. J. O. Miller, noted that "if men had to stay home and keep house, the ordinance would go into effect sooner." But it soon became clear that there was overwhelming support for a one-year postponement of the restrictions on domestic users. The coal producers' organization gained public support for the postponement when representatives made clear that they favored enforcement for all consumers except private homes. Its chairman, Walter Schulten, promised support for full enforcement if the council would accept the one-year postponement, after which smokeless stoves should be available at prices ranging from $50 to

$100. Speakers for the United Mine Workers, an important group, also agreed to support the plan in return for the proposed postponement.

Requests for delay by the producers' organization and the mine workers were, of course, expected. Any agreement to postpone implementation as a result of their arguments would be viewed as a sellout by the press and perhaps the public. But the private agreement worked out by Lawrence and the members of the Allegheny Conference provided the needed public support for the postponement. Representatives of the Allegheny Conference, the United Smoke Council, and the Chamber of Commerce all read statements favoring the new date. All three said they accepted the statements of the coal producers and stove makers that neither the low-volatile coal nor the equipment would be ready by the earlier date. Therefore, Martin stated, "the Conference Executive Committee, believing that an effective solution of this problem requires the full cooperation of all interests involved—producers, retailers, consumers, and interested civic groups—agrees to revise its recommendation for an effective date and adopted the date of October 1, 1947." The administration could save face and gain the willing compliance of the coal producers. Kilgallen asked several times, following the testimony, "Is there anybody who will appear before council and tell us that there is coal available now and there are smokeless stoves available now?" When no one came forward, he adjourned the hearing and informed the audience that a decision would be made shortly.[28]

During the next week Lawrence met several times with Park Martin and Councilman A. L. Wolk, chairman of the Health and Sanitation Committee and "father" of the 1941 ordinance, to work out a compromise. On 23 April the council voted to place the commercial users under regulation on 1 October 1946. Residential smoke control would become effective one year later.

Implementation took place on schedule, and the coal producers prediction of shortages, though a gross overestimate, proved correct. Supplies of smokeless fuels were inadequate, and shortages grew worse during January and February 1948, when a cold wave depleted supplies of natural gas. Distributors of smokeless coal raised the price of their precious commodity approximately 25 percent over the cost of bituminous coal. Unscrupulous suppliers peddled inferior grades to consumers. Complaints about the ordinance poured into the mayor's office, city council, and radio stations. City councilmen Joseph McArdle and Edward Leonard tried to have the ordinance suspended, and John Walker attempted to introduce a "smoke control ripper" in the State House of Representatives. Letters of protest to the editors of Pittsburgh newspapers became so numerous that the *Press* took the unusual action of announcing that "space limitations and the repetitiousness of complaints makes it necessary to publish the pertinent extracts of each letter." Letters no longer protested that smoke and prosperity were synonymous. Instead they complained about the quality of smokeless coal, the cost of fuel, and the inability of residents to heat their homes.[29]

The administration sought to muffle criticism by enforcing the law at the sources of supply rather than in the homes of users. Truckers hauling coal were licensed, and those caught hauling illegal bituminous coal were fined. Dealers selling it were likewise subject to fines. The Bureau of Smoke Control's inspectors "deliberately went real easy on the smoke in poor neighborhoods and thought that they would get rid of that by eliminating the trucking of illegal fuel rather than by moving against poor Mrs. Murphy."[30]

In spite of the many problems during the winter of 1947–48, Pittsburgh received 39 percent more sunshine than in the previous year, and the hours of "moderate" and "heavy" smoke decreased by approximately 50 percent. A public opinion poll taken the following summer reflected the improved conditions. A majority of Pittsburghers, regardless of income, found conditions "better than the previous year." Pittsburgh's sky continued to clear each year, particularly after Allegheny County passed its own comprehensive smoke control ordinance. By 1954 "heavy" smoke declined by 98.7 percent and "moderate" smoke by 85.8 percent from the 1946 levels.[31]

Lawrence's efforts in the smoke control battle, following on the heels of the Duquesne Light strike, demonstrated once again that, when he felt he was right, he could be firm on an issue regardless of its political consequences. The ordinance fell hardest on poor families, an important source of Democratic support. Convinced, however, that smoke control held the key to the city's rapidly developing renewal plans, he refused to be deterred. The decision to go ahead was a crucial factor in persuading Equitable Life to proceed with its planned investment in the central business district. In retrospect, Jack Robin noted, "Perhaps if we had waited a year, it could have been done smoothly and with less inconvenience and cost and hardship to some people . . . but again, it cemented the relationship between Lawrence and the civic group [the Allegheny Conference]."[32]

▽

Lawrence's position improved Pittsburgh's air, strengthened his relationship with the business community, and encouraged investment. It also gave rise to a political opponent who presented an immediate and strong threat to his career as mayor.

Edward J. "Eddie" Leonard, an unpolished, tough-talking man of limited ability, grew up in East Liberty. He became active in union politics, was named business representative of Plasterers' Local 31, and in 1930 was elected secretary of the Building Trades Council, an amalgamation of the various construction craft unions. He turned to city politics in 1929, supporting Republican Mayor Charles Kline for reelection. In 1932 he joined the wave of Republican defectors to the Roosevelt cause. Lawrence and Leonard met sometime during the Roosevelt campaign, and Leonard campaigned for Roosevelt and McNair in the blue-collar neighborhoods around East Liberty and among his fellow union members. "I loved politics, but I didn't want to be no political hack. I think Lawrence taught me how not to be a political hack," Leonard observed.[33] He became friendly with another union politician, John Kane, at that time head of the Pressmens' Union, and with Lawrence's protégé Joe Barr. Although he liked to view Lawrence as his mentor, the two were never really close. It is likely that Leonard reminded Lawrence too much of his blue-collar roots.

Leonard continued his political efforts after 1933, working particularly hard for Kane's campaign for county commissioner in 1935. He was rewarded when he was named on Kane's recommendation to fill the vacant "labor" seat on the city council in 1938. He retained his affiliation with the plasterers' union and the Building Trades Council.

Leonard's first seven years on the council were uneventful. He first drew attention to himself three weeks after Lawrence's inauguration by refusing to attend the mayor's Monday morning meetings. Leonard's independent streak was unexpected, and Lawrence treated him much as he had handled State Representative Al Tronzo eleven years earlier—he generally ignored him. Leonard was probably harmless, for he usually joined the majority in open votes in council. As an enemy, however, he might prove troublesome. Leonard clearly had the support of Kane, and Lawrence was not willing to create friction with the commissioner over such a minor issue. It is likely that Kane privately enjoyed the small but constant discomfort Leonard caused Lawrence. Leonard, as the union representative on the council, also enjoyed the support of organized labor. A battle, particularly since Lawrence was increasingly showing his independence from labor, could well prove counterproductive.

Leonard's independence, however, proved to be more than a minor irritation when he opposed the regulations against home use of bituminous fuel even after they had been adopted. At nearly every council meeting as the deadline approached and then during the shortages that occurred that winter, he proposed that the domestic controls be suspended. At one council meeting he spoke for three hours, accusing dealers of price gouging and passing off illegal coal as smokeless fuel.[34]

Leonard was becoming a celebrity and enjoying it. The letters to the editor that deluged the papers during the winter of 1947–48 began to refer to him as the champion of "Little Joe," a term he himself had used at the beginning of his campaign against the domestic regulations.[35] In stating the argument in class terms—the ability of the wealthy to afford smoke control versus the hardships of the poor—the letters raised the issue that would follow Lawrence through the 1949 campaign. His new image as a friend of the wealthy caused serious concern in his political camp.

The smoke control issue died down when the weather turned warm. While he continued to boycott the Monday meetings, Leonard remained silent about them. Lawrence, involved in statewide election battles and still unwilling to risk a split with Kane, agreed to accept Leonard when he petitioned for the party's endorsement for reelection. The councilman's popularity was obvious when he led the ticket in November.

Leonard's silence about the Monday meetings and the smoke control regulations lasted only until the fall of 1948. Even before he won reelection, he began to attack. "He ran more against Lawrence, that campaign," one observer noted, "than against his Republican opponents." In the fall, Leonard demonstrated the inferiority of coal sold by the city's largest company, Consolidation, a Mellon-owned company, by bringing ten bushels of it, along with his fireplace grate, into council chambers. Placing the grate on the table, he showed council members and the previously alerted press that the small lumps of coal could not possibly burn on the grate. "They were trying to rule me out of order. . . . I had two big special lumps. . . . I said, 'Now look.'" He brought them together. "Honest to God they went to dust all over Wolk, who was sweating and all over McArdle who had a new suit on. McArdle says, 'Look what you've done, you'll pay for my new suit.' Oh, the newspapers were full of pictures. . . . I had the shovel in my hand and I waved it and it had a lot of dust on it and [it] went all over McArdle. He said, 'You S.O.B. you.' I said, 'You better smile when you say that or I'll bat you in the puss.' This is in council." Eddie Leonard thoroughly enjoyed the attention he was receiving and continued his taunts against administration policies after the election, but he clearly had no idea where they were leading.[36]

The primary election of 1949 revealed the political costs that Lawrence paid for his cooperation with the city's business community, his independent role in the Duquesne Light and other labor disputes, and his strong stand on smoke control. Leonard's popularity, if one can judge by his council victory and supporting letters to the paper, continued to grow, but no one considered him a serious candidate to challenge the most powerful Democrat the state had known. If Joe Guffey and Charles Margiotti could not succeed, what chance did Eddie Leonard have?

The first shock of the campaign occurred in May when an AFL leader announced that the union had begun efforts to launch a movement to draft Leonard as an alternative to Lawrence in the Democratic primary in September. It began at a meeting of the Central Labor Union (CLU) made up of representatives of the AFL locals. The resolution singled out Leonard's fight against smoke control regulations for family homes and called for enlisting the support of the CIO, Railroad Brotherhood, teamsters, United Mine Workers, and other labor groups. Leonard, flattered, at first appeared uncertain how to respond. In his first public comments he expressed his gratitude but praised Lawrence for his efforts at building the Democratic party. He did not announce his candidacy for the September primary until mid July. In the interim, however, he was pressured by the various local presidents to accept the draft. Leonard denied that John Kane had anything to do with his decision to run but admitted that "he did nothing to dissuade me either." Jack Robin suspected that Kane was not entirely neutral.[37]

By early June, Leonard was apparently over his indecision. He delivered his first personal attack on Lawrence at a Twelfth Ward fund-raiser, focusing on the three issues on which the mayor was most vulnerable. He began by castigating Lawrence for ignoring the problems of the "little Joes" in forcing smoke control down their throats. He then called into question the mayor's loyalty to organized labor and his "sweetheart" arrangement with the financial powers of Pittsburgh.

> Where big city bosses doubled in brass as national committeemen, the people have retired them from local office. Bosses like Hague, Kelly and Crump are ex-bosses. Can Pittsburgh be far behind? When Lawrence set up a labor-management group, he didn't consult me or councilman Tom Gallagher, both labor men or CIO men, or County Commissioner John J. Kane. He chose to ignore all of them and accepted, instead, the labor program of his bungling amateurs.

> He has become a valuable servant of the financial and industrial dynasty that has dominated the economy and political life of the community for three generations.
>
> He is a prisoner of the royal family of high finance. Under the guise of cooperation he helped big business capture both political parties. In secret sessions in their counting houses they determine the policies of his administration.
>
> A coalition of Daveycrats and conservative Republicans [has] detoured the Democratic program from its liberal course.[38]

The attack revived the charges of collusion with the wealthy that John Huston and other Democrats had often made against Lawrence. It also put the Lawrence forces on the defensive. Throughout the primary campaign Lawrence rejected the charge that he was bossed by big business. "Everything that we have done has been part of a single theme—the theme repeated and repeated, that what helps Pittsburgh helps us all. To that end, I have thrown politics out the window, to cooperate in complete harmony with every agency and with every citizen who could contribute to our city." The Lawrence forces were aghast three days later when a telegram from Lawrence congratulating John Dorsey, president of the Central Labor Union, on "63 years in the labor movement" was read at a union dinner. It was greeted largely with boos. "We had a real fight on our hands," Robin admitted. "If we hadn't worked in that election we could very well have lost it. We had to work as if it were the general election—which it was."[39]

Orders were issued from Democratic headquarters to party regulars at all levels to work as if their jobs depended upon their success. They probably did. Lawrence's usual practice of running scared bore a semblance of reality in this primary. The CIO president, Philip Murray, pledged to support the Democratic party "down the line" but extracted a promise from Lawrence that a CIO representative, Pat Fagan, would be named to fill a vacancy on the city council. The continuing CIO-AFL feud probably made the promise unnecessary, for the CIO was unlikely to support Leonard, the AFL choice—but Lawrence willingly gave it to secure the endorsement. The remainder of the primary campaign became a race to see which side could line up the most labor endorsements. Lawrence took the lead early in September, just before the election, when the Railroad Brotherhood, the city teamsters local, and a rump AFL group organized by Charles Lawrence announced its support of the mayor.

The seriousness with which the Lawrence forces considered the Leonard threat was obvious when Lawrence announced that President Truman would appear at the Allegheny County Fair on Labor

Day. It is customary in American politics to ask a national politician to assist in one's campaign, but seldom during the primary election. A holiday crowd estimated at more than 100,000 was on hand to witness the president, Mayor Lawrence, and John Kane riding together in the motorcade to South Park. Lawrence, sitting on the speaker's platform, heard Truman praise him as one of the "greatest Democrats of our day and a great municipal leader."[40]

The election was not as close as Lawrence and his associates had feared, but he would never have a closer one for mayor. Lawrence's final vote exceeded Leonard's by 22,633 (75,838 to 53,205), but he ran behind three of the five organization candidates for the council and lost seven wards. A neighborhood-by-neighborhood analysis of the returns shows a partially unexpected pattern. Lawrence won impressive victories in the city's poorest neighborhoods, where Leonard's "little Joe" campaign was expected to have its greatest impact. Blue-collar workers in the Hill District, Lawrenceville, Bloomfield, Soho, Hazelwood, and the Central North Side all ignored Leonard's appeal and turned in strong majorities for Lawrence. The challenger won his own East Liberty ward, but by only 116 votes. Perhaps most surprising, Leonard's largest victories occurred in four South Side wards—the Sixteenth, Seventeenth, Eighteenth and Thirty-first—in the heart of the CIO-dominated steel district. Both Philip Murray and David McDonald, president of the United Steel Workers, had given Lawrence strong endorsements, and the union officials campaigned in his behalf. Lawrence won the AFL districts he feared losing and lost the CIO districts he expected to win.

The explanation appears to lie in the type of fuel consumed rather than in union affiliation. The four South Side (CIO) wards Leonard won all lagged behind the city average in converting to natural gas. Just over one-half of the households had switched compared with two-thirds in the entire city. The use of natural gas in Leonard's weakest wards (the Second, Third, Fifth, Fourteenth, and Twenty-first), in contrast, exceeded the average by 5 percent or more.[41] For residents still relying upon coal, the enforced use of Disco, or smokeless coal, represented a major portion of the household budget, and many voted their pocketbooks rather than following the advice of Murray and McDonald.

For some, domestic fuel continued to be an issue in the general election in 1949, but Lawrence's victory demonstrated a much broader base of support. He won impressive victories in wards inhabited by the members of the former New Deal coalition—the Third through the Ninth, the Fifteenth, and the Twenty-first through the Twenty-fifth. The combination of loyalty to the Democratic party among the ethnic and black blue-collar workers in these neighborhoods and the effective work of Democratic ward chairmen and workers made them impervious to antiorganization challenges.

Lawrence, however, also showed strength among the white-collar neighborhoods: Shadyside, Squirrel Hill, Stanton Avenue, and parts of Oakland. His vote totals exceeded Leonard's by three and four to one in these districts and signaled his newly won acceptability among the Democratic business and professional community. The effort to cooperate with the city's corporate elite, Leonard's charges of "collusion" and "selling out to Mellon interests" notwithstanding, was beginning to have results.

The mayor probably strengthened his position in the business community when he let it be known that he had rejected a plea by the Central Labor Union to be given seats on the parking and redevelopment authorities as a reward for their support in the general election. Determined to keep the rebuilding process free of politics, he offered it instead a greater voice in the inner circles of the party. The labor organization and Eddie Leonard, who clearly had nowhere else to turn, accepted and publicly endorsed Lawrence for reelection. Leonard showed his appreciation by attending the Monday morning council caucuses. According to both Lawrence associates and Leonard himself, no deal was offered in return for his support. Two years later, however, Lawrence took the unusual course of insisting that Leonard be renominated by the party to retain his council post. The champion of "little Joe" thanked Lawrence for his support but declined to run. Shortly thereafter he became an official, later president, of the International Plasterers' Union.[42]

Lawrence and his aides viewed his victory over Leonard as a signal from the voters to continue to rebuild the city even if the methods were sometimes painful. In Lawrence's words, "the dramatic primary was the final climax for smoke control. . . . Since that time smoke control has had no political challenge. . . . Statistics and the shirt collar both proved that Pittsburgh had become as clean as the average American city. The victory . . . had been the signal for a concentrated attack on the entire range of community problems. It was Pittsburgh's breakthrough."[43]

Clearly, Lawrence viewed the primary victory as a mandate by the party to continue the redevelopment program. It was the last time he would be seriously challenged within his own party, and subsequent general election victories reinforced the commitment to proceed with urban renewal. Lawrence easily defeated subsequent Republican challengers: Tice V. Ryan (1949) by a record-setting 56,000 votes; State legislator Leonard Kane (1953) by 55,000 votes; and former Judge John Drew (1957) by 59,500 votes. He received the support of all three Pittsburgh newspapers in each election. In Lawrence's view the voters provided a consistently strong endorsement of the contract of cooperation that had been written between the public and private sectors. Regardless of occasional criticism from members of his own party, the pattern he set during his first administration would continue unremittingly.

1946–1959

Creating a Renaissance: Bricks and Mortar

On the evening of 22 March 1946, Mayor Lawrence received a call from Fire Chief William Davis informing him of a spectacular fire raging out of control in the railroad warehouse district at the Point. Lawrence, his executive secretary, Jack Robin, and State Senator Joe Barr, who was in the mayor's office, went immediately to the area and watched the inferno from the roof of the *Pittsburgh Press* building. For the next five hours they watched the Wabash Terminal complex, with its rambling sheds and network of overpasses separating the historic Point area from the rest of the city, turn into piles of twisted metal, melted glass, and assorted rubble. They were unable to contain their glee. The fire was a godsend. "We enjoyed the fire," Jack Robin confessed later. "What the hell, we knew the fire was helping us." The state's commitment to build a park at the Point had presented both an opportunity and a dilemma. The park could spur development of the area immediately adjacent to it, yet most of these twenty-three acres were privately owned. Unless they could be redeveloped, the park would become an isolated area, "a haven for the drifters who habitually loitered about the maze of alleys around the railroad operations." Court battles over property rights could delay redevelopment for years. The Wabash fire would make negotiations with the Pittsburgh and West Virginia Railroad, which controlled much of the area, easier. If it agreed to vacate, other, smaller owners would likely fall into line.[1]

Discussions about the condition of the lower triangle had begun sometime in late 1945 among staff members of the Allegheny Conference on Community Development. Wallace Richards and Arthur Van Buskirk approached Charles J. Graham, president of the Pittsburgh and West Virginia Railroad, to enlist his help. During the discussion, Graham mentioned the extensive blight removal work being financed by life insurance capital in New York City. Since the conference staff had originally considered erecting a number of high-rise residential buildings in the area, they decided to contact the Metropolitan Life Insurance Company, which had substantial investments in New York, including two new housing developments. A meeting was arranged for early June. The Wabash fire, meanwhile, heightened the need for a complete redevelopment of the area.

Graham and conference representatives met with the president of Metropolitan Life who told them that, because of the company's large commitment in New York City, it was not interested in their plan. The dejected group was about to return to Pittsburgh when Graham suggested they try another source, Thomas Parkinson of the Equitable Life Assurance Society, a friend of his and a fellow member of the Pennsylvania Society. Parkinson agreed to see them without an appointment, and they outlined their plan for the apartment complex in the lower triangle. Assured that both smoke and flood control were under way, Parkinson agreed to have his staff look into the project. The meeting initiated a series of discussions that resulted in the agreement by Equitable to fund what became known as the Gateway Center project.[2]

At about the same time that they began talks with Parkinson, the group also realized that private action would not be enough. Without intervention and cooperation from the city, the project would fail. They were proposing that hundreds of parcels of privately owned land be acquired for use by other private individuals for a profit-making venture. Refusal to sell by one or two owners in strategic locations could kill the entire project. In addition, price speculation would certainly increase the cost. In July, Richards, Van Buskirk, and Park Martin asked Lawrence to create a redevelopment authority for the city of Pittsburgh. A recent state redevelopment act gave municipalities the right to condemn and acquire land if the area was certified as blighted, and to approve any new development before construction began. Provided the law withstood the inevitable court tests, it gave the city enormous power to bring about urban renewal.[3]

Creation of such an authority was crucial to the success of the redevelopment process. First, it provided the city with an action organization that could interact with the private agencies. Second, an authority could secure private funding for redevelopment projects, thus isolating them from the vagaries of the voting public, which must approve bond issues, and from the state legislature's annual appropriation battles. Finally, an authority would hold the power of eminent domain. It could acquire large numbers of individually held properties, combine them into a site suitable for development, and sell the site to a private developer. Lawrence immediately agreed to the concept and promised to steer the enabling legislation through the council, thereby virtually assuring creation of the state's first redevelopment authority.

The establishment of the Urban Redevelopment Authority of Pittsburgh (URA) gave Lawrence a final opportunity to demonstrate that he intended the renewal process to be above politics. To cement relations with the Allegheny Conference, Lawrence planned to name the conference chairman, Van Buskirk, as chairman of the authority. Van Buskirk, however, presented a counter idea: the executive committee of the conference wanted the mayor to chair the authority. "Arthur, that's ridiculous!" exclaimed a surprised Lawrence. "You're going to put me in a very ludicrous position. I don't think there's a case in all the history of this country where any man ever appointed himself to the job. I just can't do that."[4] Lawrence eventually agreed, on two conditions: first, if Van Buskirk served as vice-chairman, and second, if the conference executive committee, the Chamber of Commerce, and the newspapers all asked him to be chairman. Van Buskirk agreed to arrange the "requests," which came in the fall of 1946. In December the mayor sent a letter to the city council requesting the creation of a five-member redevelopment authority.

By prearrangement the council suspended the rules to allow an immediate second and third reading of the bill. One of the most significant pieces of legislation to be passed by that body sailed through without debate. It received unanimous support. Within twenty-four hours Lawrence announced his five appointees: himself, Councilman William Stewart, Arthur Van Buskirk, Edgar Kaufmann, owner of the department store, and J. Lester Perry, head of Carnegie Illinois Steel. Van Buskirk, Kaufmann, and Perry, all Republicans, also sat on the board of the Allegheny Conference. "It was the first time in my public career I knowingly put myself in the minority with three Republicans and two Democrats on the board," Lawrence later exclaimed. At its first meeting on 18 November 1946, Lawrence was elected chairman and Van Buskirk vice-chairman, and Robin was named acting director. Fifteen months later Robin became the full-time director, and Ted Hazlett, counsel for the Allegheny Conference, became counsel for the URA.[5]

The creation of the URA demonstrated Lawrence's understanding of the politics of urban redevelopment. While he did not initiate the idea of an authority, he was quick to grasp its potential. As a quasi-independent body, it enabled the government to interact on equal terms with the Allegheny Conference, the Pennsylvania Economy League, the Pittsburgh Regional Planning Association, and other private sector organizations interested in renewal of the city. The makeup of the authority, moreover, completed the interlocking directorate that became the parent of the Renaissance. Lawrence also sat on the sponsoring committee of the Allegheny Conference. Kaufmann and Perry represented the conference, and Kaufmann sat on the board of the Pittsburgh Regional Planning Authority. Van Buskirk sat on the executive committee of the Allegheny Conference and was chief spokesman for the Mellon interests. Other individuals, such as Martin, Hazlett, and Richards, represented several of the private organizations simultaneously. Finally, while it was probably not necessary to appoint a city council member to the authority—the council was unlikely to oppose the mayor on any program—the selection of William Stewart gave that body a voice in the renewal process. Lawrence, following the policy of "virtual representation" he used in selecting political candidates, seated a council member on every subsequent city authority. The council responded by supporting renewal programs with enthusiasm. Its active involvement in the redevelopment, in turn, provided an important campaign issue on which to stand for reelection.[6]

David Lawrence played several important roles in the physical redevelopment of Pittsburgh. By virtue of his positions as mayor, leader of the dominant political party, and chairman of the URA, he became the chief spokesman and cheerleader for the various projects. It was a role he relished and played with particular adroitness. Beginning in 1947, he accepted nearly every invitation to speak about the plans for the Gateway Center project and urged support for it. Community development, in his eyes, became a civic virtue. Only the "meanest spirited citizen" would offer opposition. He regularly devoted the majority of his annual state of the city messages, delivered over local radio and reprinted in the press, to the theme of urban redevelopment. In each address he outlined the plans for the coming year, commended the previous year's progress, and praised the efforts of those involved. Opposition to the redevelopment of the city, he told his listeners one year, was "morally unacceptable." He even abandoned his old disdain for planning and planners. "Nobody in this city jibes at long-haired planners or theorists or double-domes. It isn't good politics anymore and it never was good sense."[7]

Lawrence also used the public relations power of his office to scold those who resisted redevelopment in any way and to court those who could be of assistance. When land speculators threatened to force the prices of land parcels in the Gateway Center area to prohibitively high levels, thus placing the renewal project in jeopardy, he warned that taxes could be increased to thwart any potential windfall. When lack of progress in removing the wreckage from the Wabash fire appeared to be an obstacle to completing a redevelopment agreement with the Equitable Life Assurance Society, he wrote to Charles Graham and the five insurance companies involved. The letters were released to the local press to apply public as well as official pressure to the offending parties. When the numerous independent bus companies repeatedly resisted using off-street terminals to help eliminate traffic congestion, Lawrence, after several meetings with their representatives, lost his patience. Pounding on the table, he announced that citations would be issued, beginning the next day.[8]

In addition to acting as the spokesman and muscle behind the Renaissance, Lawrence courted potential outside investors, a task he greatly enjoyed. When a task force from Equitable visited Pittsburgh in early 1947 to look at the site, Lawrence and other members of the URA escorted the visitors on a tour of the area, hosted a luncheon, and took them to Mount Washington, overlooking the city, for a long-range view of the area. While he seldom took part in the actual negotiations with Equitable, the mayor repeated his tour guide and luncheon activities several times before contracts were eventually signed in February 1950.

Though not nearly as public as his efforts to champion the redevelopment of the city, Lawrence's continued cultivation of mutually beneficial relations between the public and private sectors was perhaps more important. He scrupulously avoided efforts by his political allies to turn the rebuilding process over to the machine and was quick to praise the business elements, particularly the Allegheny Conference, for their contributions. This appreciation became a common theme of Lawrence's during his remaining years in office.

Lawrence also maintained warm, although not close, relationships with a number of key people in the redevelopment process. Richard Mellon's chief lieutenants, Arthur Van Buskirk and Adolph Schmidt, worked with Lawrence as successive vice chairmen of the URA. In addition, as the Pittsburgh Renaissance gained national fame, they frequently traveled with the mayor to other cities to extol its successes. Their frequent interactions produced a lasting mutual respect, which they no doubt communicated to the "General." Mellon, in turn, indicated that he shared their views when, much to the chagrin of the Republican organization, he all but endorsed the mayor for reelection in 1953. At the groundbreaking ceremonies of Mellon Square, the one-block-square park in the center of the business district that was his gift to the city, Mellon told the crowd, "I want you to know, that Mayor Lawrence has been most cooperative. If it hadn't been for Mayor Lawrence and his associates, we might have been many years in getting this project started." The statement, according to Schmidt, was carefully planned to indicate R. K. Mellon's support for Lawrence without actually rejecting his own party's choice for mayor, Leonard Kane. Other prominent corporate executives with whom Lawrence successfully developed a close working relationship included Edgar Kaufmann, a member of the URA until his death in 1955, Leland Hazard, vice-president of Pittsburgh Plate Glass, and Gwilym Price, president of Westinghouse. In none of these instances did Lawrence develop a close personal relationship, nor was one expected. Similarly, political views remained entrenched at opposite poles. Rather, a sense of trust grew. Lawrence viewed himself as the central element in the public-private sector relationship and worked to reinforce the mutually positive attitudes. "I am very proud that the mayor can be a unifying force in this community and not a divider," he told the Press Club on the eve of his fourth campaign for mayor. "I am very proud that the mayor can muster the full energies of this powerful and productive city and set them to work in common causes, instead of wasting them in internal conflict."[9]

Lawrence's relationship with Pittsburgh's city council also played a crucial role in the redevelopment of the city. Although council members attributed their almost total compliance with the mayor to "like minds" on most issues, the fact remains that Lawrence dominated the council by his decisive influence in the selection of candidates. For thirteen years the council provided the mayor with near unanimous votes on every important issue brought before it, including bond issues for improvement of the city's infrastructure, rezoning, land condemnation, creation of a parking authority, tax increases, and, of course, the mayor's annual budgets. From the beginning of Lawrence's first term in 1946 through his last day in office in 1959, the council rejected fewer than half a dozen minor requests by the mayor.[10] Most of these passed on later readings. The view from the business community deeply involved in the Renaissance was that the municipality was run much like a well-organized corporation. The chief executive, Lawrence, made the major decisions, and his staff, including the council, carried them out. Although overly simplistic, this understanding resulted in a confidence among the business community that agreements between it and Lawrence would be put into effect. The mayor ran an efficient organization that implemented a large variety of renewal proposals, many of them controversial, with little delay or political infighting.

Finally, although all of Lawrence's roles were intertwined, his position as chairman of the URA affected the Renaissance most directly. The authority became involved in every major project undertaken during the Lawrence administration, and Lawrence conducted virtually every meeting.[11] He continued as its chairman, commuting from Harrisburg and Washington, D.C., to attend meetings, until his death in 1966. He interacted with both local and outside business interests when necessary to spur action on projects, testified before local and state legislative and legal bodies in support of redevelopment issues, and generated public support, particularly in his state of the city addresses, for URA programs. Most important, he provided symbolic leadership for the public sector. The combination of the mayor and Van Buskirk, representing the Mellon interests, as chairman and vice-chairman gave the organization instant credibility.

▽

The physical redevelopment of the city began at the Gateway Center project and spread outward. The redevelopment of the twenty-three-acre site was inherited by Lawrence when he took office in 1946. Allegheny Conference planners conceived the redevelopment along with a plan for a park at the city's apex. The mayor enthusiastically endorsed the idea, calling it "a powerful force for the preservation of [property] values in the whole triangle area."[12] His willingness to create the URA and serve as its chairman grew out of his support for the Gateway Center project.

Negotiations with the Equitable Life Assurance Society stretched over four years as a number of problems developed. The original idea of an apartment complex gave way to high-rise office structures when Equitable officials pointed out that Pittsburgh, as a headquarters city, was desperately in need of suitable office space. No new office buildings had been constructed in eighteen years, and occupancy in 1946 reached 99 percent. The URA, which took over the negotiations with Equitable, agreed and began condemnation proceedings and land purchases to accumulate the necessary properties.

The first major snag developed in March 1949 when the URA members, Robin, and several others arrived in New York City to sign preliminary agreements with Equitable. With unfortunate timing, the Pittsburgh papers announced that U.S. Steel and Mellon Bank planned to erect their own headquarters buildings, but not in the Gateway

Center area. Equitable officials expressed surprise and concern that other companies might follow the example of the city's two largest corporations and leave them with empty or partially empty buildings. They now insisted on guarantees of occupancy for a minimum of twenty years and assurances that 60 percent of the buildings would be occupied upon completion. R. K. Mellon and Van Buskirk, speaking for the authority, approached many corporations to put pressure on them to sign the leases. When two of the largest objected, Mellon told them, "The Mellon family is not going to redevelop this city . . . if companies like yours are not going to play a major role, it's just as simple as that."[13]

Meanwhile the URA was taking action on its own. Jack Robin drafted a letter of intent to the Equitable president to be signed by the presidents of the various corporations expected to lease space. It committed each corporation to lease a specified amount of office space for a specified period of time. Over Lawrence's signature, a cover letter expressed "hope that the enclosed letter will be sent to Mr. Parkinson at your earliest convenience." In addition, the authority worked to reduce rents. Equitable originally pledged a payment of $2 million to the URA in return for its services in accumulating the necessary properties. The authority agreed to reduce its fee to $1 million if Equitable would lower its rents by a similar amount. The URA also secured a major tenant when it agreed to purchase the existing Jones and Laughlin Steel office building, thereby freeing the company to move to the Gateway site. (Ultimately seven Pittsburgh-based corporations moved their headquarters to the Gateway buildings, and three others, including Mellon Bank, occupied additional space. The three buildings were completed in 1953, and six additional structures and an underground parking garage were added during the next decade.) Lawrence took such great joy in announcing the final agreement between the URA and Equitable that he canceled an appointment with President Truman in order to be at the signing ceremonies on 14 February 1950. Unable to contain his pride, he delivered a brief address liberally sprinkled with hyperbole. "Thus redevelopment is Pittsburgh's greatest achievement in a generation. . . . We are taking a national lead in community planning and community advancement. Today's work has been a giant step forward."[14]

A second major obstacle to the Gateway project had become apparent approximately two week earlier at the public hearings held in city council chambers. While most of those present testified in favor of the plan, a number who owned property in the redevelopment area offered strong objections. The protests and the subsequent court tests rested on two major points. First, according to the state redevelopment law, the City Planning Commission had to certify an area as blighted before condemnation proceedings could begin, and many of the buildings did not fit that description. Second, the land was to be taken from one group of private owners to be turned over to another. On 22 April 1950, reacting quickly to a suit brought by Duffs' Iron City College, the Court of Common Pleas ruled that personal inconvenience must yield to social and economic progress. Subsequent tests in the Pennsylvania and U.S. Supreme Courts upheld the ruling. The Gateway project, the key to the physical renewal of Pittsburgh, began almost immediately.

Other proposals, plans, and projects followed quickly. The Mellon Square park complex, the enlarging and rehabilitating of Children's Hospital in Oakland, the redevelopment of the Central North Side, and other minor projects all received attention from Lawrence during the next eight years. But three programs, the South Side industrial project, construction of a civic arena, and housing for the poor demanded most of his time.

The seven-point program offered by Lawrence in the election campaign of 1945 recognized that the city's needs were multidimensional. Environmental controls and redevelopment of the central business district were desperately needed, as were efforts to expand and diversify Pittsburgh's aging industries. Once again taking his cue from a statement of goals developed by the Allegheny Conference on Community Development, Lawrence had promised to create an industrial expansion committee. His fiscal conservatism convinced him that the city's health depended upon the strength of its industrial base, but flood and smoke control and labor problems initially diverted his attention. The weak economy, however, remained a serious concern and Lawrence raised it for discussion at the organizational meeting of the URA in November 1946. The authority, which as yet had no funds of its own and no full-time staff, recognized that it could do little and turned to its private sector ally, the Allegheny Conference. At the request of the mayor, the conference agreed on 10 February 1947 to establish an Industrial-Economic Research Council to determine ways to expand existing industries and to "determine what new diversified industries are best suited to the area." The conference supplied funds to hire an industrial economist as consultant.[15]

The rapidly improved environmental conditions, a strong postwar economy, and the efforts of the conference and the URA led to spectacular successes. During a two-year period, General Motors Corporation, Continental Can, Pittsburgh Plate Glass, Pittsburgh Coke and Chemical Company, the Koppers Company, Copperweld, and Allis-Chalmers all announced the building of new plants in the area. The city administration cut red tape where it could but generally played a minor role. The improved local environment and national economic conditions induced the growth.

The South Side expansion of Jones and Laughlin steelworks, however, required the concerted efforts of the Lawrence administration and the URA. Early in 1948, the company announced plans to install six new "giant" open hearth furnaces in an expansion expected to produce more than two thousand additional jobs. The firm indicated it had not yet determined the location of the new furnaces. Possibilities included its South Side Pittsburgh works, Aliquippa in Beaver County, and Cleveland, Ohio. The URA decided to enter into negotiations to induce Jones and Laughlin to select the Pittsburgh location, a 19.5-acre site containing sixty-one workers' houses and several small commercial establishments. Robin and Hazlett were directed to enter into negotations with the steel firm. The project became the first industrial redevelopment project of its type in the United States.

As had been true in making land available for the Gateway project, the existence of the authority gave Pittsburgh a clear advantage over the other two sites. With the approval of the city council and City Planning, the URA had the power to condemn the existing structures, negotiate with the owners, purchase the property, and sell the entire site to Jones and Laughlin. In contrast, the firm faced the harrowing prospect of negotiating with individual owners in the other two locations. In mid 1949 it announced that it had reached a "general understanding" with the authority. The URA would be responsible for land acquisition and would negotiate with the city to vacate streets, would install utilities, and would purchase any publicly owned properties. These three conditions, of course, were never in doubt, since the chairman of the URA was also the mayor and leader of the nine Democrats on the city council. Jones and Laughlin would pay all costs and a $50,000 fee to the URA for its services and would install the furnaces in the stipulated area.[16]

Lawrence personally cleared another hurdle when he met with Philip Murray, president of the CIO, whom he knew well. The problem was that the houses that had to be condemned were owned by steelworkers. After a long discussion, Murray agreed that the workers had to be made to see that the job security of the whole South Side depended on the viability of Jones and Laughlin, and he offered to help.[17]

The council hearing on 10 November 1949 was a carefully orchestrated performance designed not only to secure council approval but to convince the media and public of the merits of the program. Fred Bigger, chairman of the City Planning Commission spoke first, explaining that the "blighted" condition of the proposed site meant that Jones and Laughlin would rid the city of an existing slum. The council chairman, Thomas Kilgallen then introduced the chairman of the URA, reminding the audience that Lawrence was chairman because the other four members insisted. Lawrence explained that the city had been in danger of losing not only the Jones and Laughlin expansion but the entire industry. Then, using the identical words he used to the council about the Gateway area, he professed his empathy for the residents. "I know a lot about the problem of dislocation, because when the railroad came to the Point, they took over our home and I know something about the problem. I would like to approach it from the standpoint of Pittsburgh and saving Pittsburgh." He would repeat this argument before the council in 1952 regarding a proposed Jones and Laughlin expansion in another Pittsburgh community and in 1963 regarding property clearance for the Children's Hospital project. His guiding principle for the Renaissance was that individual rights were to be respected but must always give way to the greater common good. The city, in Lawrence's view, was not merely an entity in which private entrepreneurs and speculators operated profit-making ventures. The public-private sector coalition guaranteed that the "Private City" concept that was the driving force in nineteenth-century Philadelphia was obsolete in mid-twentieth-century Pittsburgh. After a brief presentation by Robin, the city council, as expected, approved the project by a unanimous vote.[18]

Once approvals were secured and contracts signed, Lawrence as usual turned the program over to the technical experts. He visited the area several times during the early negotations to meet with residents to assure them that they would receive fair settlements, but he generally turned to other matters. Lawrence also attended the settlement signing ceremonies held in a South Side tavern. "I'll never forget that night," Ted Hazlett recalled. "We went to a beer garden over there and had a long table with interpreters [many of the residents had difficulty with English] and all these deeds we had prepared, and signed everybody up and then we opened up the beer kegs."[19]

It is difficult to determine whether residents were adequately compensated for their property. Settlements were modest, but the structures and the land upon which they were built carried assessments well under the city average. Payments in every case exceeded assessments by more than 10 percent. Those who were represented by counsel, retained by a newly formed citizens' protective society, clearly considered the settlements fair. The URA arranged agreements with the families without once having to resort to condemnation proceedings.

Jones and Laughlin completed its multimillion-dollar project within several years and returned to the authority in 1952 with plans to expand its Hazelwood–Glen Hazel plant just across the Monongahela River from the South Side plant. In total the firm spent more than $25 million in expanding its Pittsburgh plants.[20] In addition to its economic impact the Jones and Laughlin South Side expansion was vitally important to the redevelopment process in Pittsburgh. It was the first capital expansion project undertaken by the URA, and for it the authority created a model procedure to which it returned repeatedly in the next several years.

▽

Of all the redevelopment projects, none evoked more controversy and involved Lawrence more than the one that began most innocuously. On 4 February 1949, Edgar J. Kaufmann, a devoted supporter of the arts, sent a letter to Mayor Lawrence pledging a $500,000 contribution for "the construction of an arena . . . which will be suitable for the presentation of light opera of the type produced by the Civic Light Opera Association and for other purposes." The gift was to be matched by a similar amount from the city treasury. The Kaufmann Foundation and the Allegheny Conference would "arrange and pay for preliminary surveys for the project, including studies of the practicability and cost of a removable roof." The city was to select the site for the auditorium, accept responsibility for its operation, and receive full title to the building. Several days later, Lawrence asked the city council to accept the gift, adding that "the city's contribution may be provided from bond funds, thus easing any immediate demands upon the city budget. It is my belief that the project will actually be self-liquidating . . . because of the return to the City Treasury from the ten percent levy on admissions."[21] The Allegheny Conference and the Pittsburgh Regional Planning Association offered to conduct a site selection study at no expense to the city. The council voted eight to one to accept the offer.

The selection committee originally considered fifteen sites. Its choice, by an overwhelming majority of its members, was in the East End at the terminus of North Negley Avenue, near Highland Park.[22] The site encompassed most of the estate of millionaire Robert B. King, an uncle of Richard King Mellon, and included several other private homes. The area was bordered by large middle- and upper-middle-class homes, most of which were less than forty years old. It is difficult to imagine a more improbable choice. Introduction of a public arena would have had a detrimental effect on the stable neighborhood, which could by no stretch of the imagination be called blighted. Furthermore, despite the site's proximity to trolley lines and its distance from the central business district, the absence of adequate highways would have created huge traffic problems.

Twenty-four hours after a bill to condemn the area was introduced in city council, petitions bearing more than one thousand signatures arrived. A few days later at a public hearing, three hundred East End residents, most of them in opposition, jammed council chambers. J. Vincent Burke, an attorney representing the signers of the petitions, attacked the "terrible power of eminent domain." He charged that in taking land for entertainment purposes, the city would be exceeding its power. Councilman Eddie Leonard joined the opposition, airing his favorite grievance against the Lawrence administration—the closed-door caucus. He was told that neither the mayor nor any member of council had anything to do with the selection. (Nor, curiously, did the city planning office.) "Everyone knows that the Allegheny Conference controls both political parties," Leonard retorted.[23]

However, what proved to be the most effective part of the protest came last, when seventy-four-year-old Robert B. King hobbled to the stand. Dressed in black tie and hard collar and leaning on his cane, King, whose wife had died three weeks earlier, called the proposal his second tragedy in less than a month.

> I am in favor of light opera and musical comedy but I am against the proposal by promoters who may think that this particular site which is now a refuge for birds and wild life, can be man-made by destruction into something better than God made it. This neighborhood represents my lifetime's work in a development that has given the people a pleasant and peaceful place in which to live. . . .
>
> After long thought and careful consideration, I make this suggestion which I hope you will regard as constructive: If the city will agree to let me live out my life unmolested, where I am now living, I will agree to give to the city the property . . . upon the condition that the city use the property . . . for park purposes only, which all of the people may enjoy forever and upon the condition that no arena or other building be erected to the detriment of my neighbors and neighborhood.[24]

King ended to a thunderous ovation and, according to the press, a few tears from the overflow audience. He became an instant folk hero with the press.

The mayor and council were unmoved. The site, Lawrence believed, was in the best interests of the city. The following Monday, at the usual private session, the caucus decided to accept the selection committee's recommendation agreeing that the site was clearly the best of all possible choices, and rejected the King proposal. The council approved the site on 18 July, and Lawrence signed the ordinance two days later commenting, "We are doing exactly the right thing and every public official who is worth his salt has to make decisions which some people oppose and the only standard is to determine what serves the greatest good of the greatest number. We can't have good government by pressure groups. Every test shows that this is the best available site in the city."[25]

Within two weeks the Public Works Department moved in and began to cut down trees and drill test holes. On the following day Robert King's attorney requested an injunction to stop the city until a court appeal could be filed. Judge Thomas Marshall granted the request for a two-week period beginning 3 August. In the interim several neighborhood organizations, including the East End Residents Association and the East Liberty Chamber of Commerce, joined in the opposition. Letters to the editor took both sides, but the majority supported the neighborhood position.

Two days prior to the expiration of the injunction, Lawrence surprised the city by reversing his position. In a letter to the Allegheny Conference chairman, Edward Weidlein, he announced that the Highland Park site was being dropped and that the city planning commission would be asked to recommend another site. He gave a curious set of reasons.

> Despite the opinion reached by the technicians, and accepted by us, that the Highland Park site is the best use for the purpose, so much time has been consumed in discussion and legal action that it is now physically impossible to construct the outdoor theater in time to make use of it during the summer of 1950. . . .
>
> [Therefore] we are able without sacrifice of the objectives, . . . to give renewed thought and study to the problem of the site. . . .
>
> I now propose that we initiate . . . a review and reanalysis . . . which will be understood and supported by the great

majority of our citizens. That is how all controversies must be resolved under a system of free government.[26]

Lawrence's reversal ignored his own reasoning of one month earlier and the fact that three technical groups and the architect had recommended the Highland Park site. A five-week lapse from the announcement of the project, he argued, now warranted a full reanalysis.

On the surface it appears that Lawrence was simply bowing to public pressure. That conclusion, however, is unwarranted. Though protesters were vociferous and had the sympathy of the press, they were most likely a minority. It was certainly not an issue on which future elections would be decided. Furthermore, Lawrence, in his battle to install the city's smoke control ordinances, had demonstrated that he was more than willing to take political risks on important issues. The civic arena, of course, pales in significance in comparison, yet by rejecting the chosen site he ran a far greater risk than that presented by the disgruntled citizens of the neighborhood: the Allegheny Conference, which the mayor had carefully courted, was displeased. In its response, its chairman lectured Lawrence in words almost identical to those frequently used by the mayor himself. "It must always be remembered that, if necessary, private interests must be subordinated to the public benefit. . . . The Allegheny Conference has shared the views of the experts . . . that the Highland Park site is the best one so far examined, and you and the city council have reached the same conclusion. The Executive Committee of the Conference has found no reason to change the views expressed."[27] Granted no other recourse, the conference reluctantly agreed to reexamine the issue. Lawrence's reversal had the potential for creating a serious breach of confidence between him and the conference. The reason had to be more than political expediency.

A far more logical explanation rests with the threatened court tests. Not only would a lengthy series of court cases seriously delay the project. More important was the possibility that the city's liberal interpretation of its power of condemnation might be rejected. The city had in effect decided that any project deemed to be in the public good was permissible, and the planning office followed that philosophy in exercising its power to designate an area as blighted. A more restrictive ruling by the courts would place the entire renewal program in jeopardy. It was a court case Lawrence and his advisers were most anxious to avoid. Abandoning the Highland Park site eliminated a potential legal threat to the Renaissance.

The alternative site chosen by the City Planning Commission,

Schenley Park in the Oakland district, presented no such problem because the land was wholly owned by the city. However, a court challenge on the grounds that building an arena would violate the terms by which Mary Schenley donated the land delayed construction for a full eighteen months. The city was ready to proceed by the summer of 1951 when a third alternative was considered.

The final choice grew out of a series of discussions over several years by the URA and its staff regarding the condition of Pittsburgh's Lower Hill. A high-density black and ethnic neighborhood bordering on the central business district, the Hill had long been considered the city's worst slum. With the Gateway and Jones and Laughlin South Side projects now under way, the URA turned its attention to the area above Grant Street. In January 1951 it announced its intention to act as the agency for the redevelopment of the Lower Hill. There would be no difficulty in having the area certified as blighted. A $5 million grant by the federal Housing and Home Finance Agency was expected to provide the initial funding. Additional funds were added later. For the first time in the renewal program—$100 million in private funds had already been expended or promised—the city turned to the federal government for aid.

Several months later the URA presented its program to the city council. The proposal covered more than 100 acres and would eventually affect 1551 families. It consisted of four major parts: slum clearance; construction of a "Crosstown Boulevard" highway system; development of 30 acres for new homes to be built by the Pittsburgh Housing Authority or private contractors; and clearance of an area for a sports arena, auditorium, and open-air parking lot for 2000 cars. While no mention was made of the Civic Light Opera project, it is reasonable to assume that it must have at least crossed the minds of Lawrence and Robin. They did not suggest integrating it into the Lower Hill project until March 1952, a full year later.

In carrying out the plan, the URA, while seeking public funding as a guarantee of credit to enable it to purchase the land, expected to follow the same procedure used in the two earlier programs. Cleared land would be sold to developers at a modest price. The proceeds would be used to purchase and clear additional land. Expected losses would be covered by federal and state funding programs.[28]

By early 1952, when the project was expected to get underway, a new administration, less favorable to the Lawrence regime in Pittsburgh and to the massive use of federal funds for urban renewal, had assumed office in Washington. A Republican governor, John Fine, and a Republican State Senate and House proved equally reluctant to send large grants to the Democratic administration in Pittsburgh. Thus, while planning continued, the actual purchase and demolition of properties did not begin until 1956.

The plan for an auditorium, which was incorporated into the Lower Hill project in 1953, was similarly stalled. One year earlier, the chairman of the Civic Light Opera site selection committee suggested that it might be time to consider building a multi-use auditorium in the Lower Hill as a home for the light opera, sports events, and other cultural activities. The A.W. Mellon Educational and Charitable Trust authorized $30,000 for such a study and the Heinz Foundation added another $10,000. In February 1953 Lawrence, Robin, and Martin traveled on a DC-3—supplied by the Koppers Corporation—to Palm Springs, California, to meet with a vacationing Edgar Kaufmann. Kaufmann approved the latest plans and pledged $1 million toward construction of the arena. The $500,000 increase from the earlier pledge was to cover the cost of the retractable roof. In December, Kaufmann doubled his offer.[29]

It was not until September 1955 that the entire plan was presented to and approved by the city council. The plan received unanimous support from virtually every segment of the community: local, state, and federal agencies; private sector groups such as the Chamber of Commerce, Allegheny Conference, Civic Light Opera Association, and Pittsburgh Housing Authority; and churches in the affected area, such as the African Methodist Episcopal Church.[30]

Seven months later the first properties were purchased, and demolition began in November 1956. By 1966 the area contained the arena (completed in 1961), a 396-unit apartment building (1964), the Chatham Center apartment and hotel complex (1966), and an open-air parking lot for several thousand automobiles. A vacant lot above the arena (9.2 acres) was reserved for construction of a symphony hall, a convention center, and related facilities, a project that was never initiated. The lot remains vacant today.

The Lower Hill project remains the most criticized of all those undertaken by the Lawrence administration. Almost from the start, critics labeled it urban removal rather than urban renewal. Certainly the charge that it did not contribute to desegregation of the city but merely increased the density in the black Middle and Upper Hill is accurate. Nearly 800 of the 1239 black families relocated into the already densely populated Third, Fourth, and Fifth wards; most of the others who stayed in the city gravitated to the other black neighborhoods. Almost none of the 312 white families, in contrast, settled in predominantly black neighborhoods.[31]

The problem was one of which Lawrence and the URA members were fully aware. As early as March 1953, nearly three years before the demolition began, a URA resolution pointed out that because of the lack of open housing practices in the city, relocation might have a detrimental effect. The supply of homes available to blacks, the resolution suggested, was simply not large enough to meet the newly created demand. The authority noted its support of the formation of Private Housing Incorporated (later renamed Action Housing Incorporated) to aid minority groups in resettlement. Later the URA, at the request of the housing committee of the local NAACP chapter, agreed to work with the Commission on Human Relations and the housing authority to try to solve relocation problems. The city, at the same time, attempted to increase the number of homes available to blacks by passing a Fair Housing Act in 1958. The Pittsburgh Housing Authority, with more than a decade of experience in building and operating low-rent housing units, was given the task of carrying out the actual relocation. A full-time relocation director, Ralph Harkins, negotiated individually with each home owner and attempted to find suitable replacement accommodations.

While the results were less than satisfactory, the severe criticism seems unwarranted when one examines the data. There was overwhelming evidence that the Lower Hill was a prime site for urban redevelopment. It had deteriorated beyond the point of rehabilitation. Its density of nearly ninety persons per acre far exceeded the city average, and health conditions were abominable. The incidence of tuberculosis was three times that of the rest of the city. Buildings were old and badly deteriorated. Before redevelopment 681 of the existing 901 residential structures were classified as substandard; many had been condemned as unsafe. Several of the units housed large numbers of unattached individuals, the worst being a barn that contained forty residents who paid $11.50 per week rent. A 1953 building inspector's report described the structure as "a real fire hazard" with "too many dangerous conditions to mention" and noted that after dark the halls were filled with drug dealers and buyers, prostitutes, and muggers. A series of articles by the *Pittsburgh Press* suggested that some families welcomed the opportunity to relocate, while others protested that the price offered for their property was too low. The series also revealed the mixed and somewhat colorful character of the Lower Hill. "Racket millionaires protest as bitterly about moving as families without shoes. . . . Numbers barons prowl the streets in shiny Cadillacs looking for new headquarters. . . . The 'floating crap games' are in such a state of flux that even veteran players have trouble keeping track of locations of dice tables. . . . Up on Wylie Avenue, 'Madame X,' a bejeweled gypsy, is singing the blues: 'My crystal ball is mighty cloudy these days 'cause I don't know where I'm gonna move.'" The articles noted that the housing authority, which permitted residents to remain in the structures for some time after purchasing them, "sometimes found itself managing numbers parlors or a speakeasy."[32]

Crucial problems, however, were the level of income of the residents, the availability of alternative housing, and the method of acquisition used by the federal Housing and Home Finance Agency. Nearly all permanent residents of the area were poor. Unlike the residents of the area acquired for the Jones and Laughlin project, few owned their own homes, and three fourths required low-rent housing. Approximately one-third were relocated into the Addison Terrace, Alliquippa Terrace, and Bedford Dwellings public units, but the number of units available was far short of the need. Even more crucial was the shortage of private family residences throughout Pittsburgh. In 1956, according to a survey conducted by the Allegheny Conference, only 2 percent of the existing housing stock was vacant. The proportion of homes available to black residents was even less. The settlement fees provided to home owners by the Housing and Home Finance Agency compounded the problem. Government regulations stipulated that agencies such as the URA appraise homes at fair market value plus a small bonus for inconvenience. Replacement costs were not considered. Low-income residents, receiving meager settlements, could be expected to have difficulty finding adequate housing. The shortage of private and subsidized housing and existing racial covenants made it almost impossible.

The Pittsburgh Housing Authority, nevertheless, managed to find housing rated as standard or above for 1218 of the 1299 families relocated in the city; 447 moved into public housing, while the remainder found private property for rent or sale. Approximately 80 families, mostly nonwhite, moved into substandard housing. Three years after relocation began, 67 percent of the families lived in "better housing than they had in the Lower Hill." Most, perhaps surprisingly, thought that "overcrowding was considerably relieved."[33]

Those involved with the redevelopment of the Lower Hill continue to defend the project today. Jack Robin, URA director at the beginning of the project, attempted to place it in its historical context. "At that time . . . we were talking about public housing in a subsidized form. And, Pittsburgh was one of the leading cities in doing public housing. . . . We never thought of using the power of the Authority to make below market loans for homeowners. . . . We did what the times and the government called for." Hazlett, Robin's successor, told how it felt.

> We just didn't have enough housing. . . . After you sit in your office for days with people coming in to you and crying about having to move, . . . it gets to you. The only way I could break out was to take a walk and see, actually see the conditions these people were living in. Then I would get reassured. . . . Yes, we were going to create problems in this process but what is the answer? . . . There's got to be a recognition that it takes more than all this strange sort of intellectualism that has been going on in my judgment for the last twenty years [the criticism of the project]. I still think that the people that moved out of that Hill are better housed today than they were and we also uncovered a lot of [social] problems. We stopped sweeping the dirt under the rug.[34]

At the opposite extreme, one critic (undoubtedly the most vocal), while recognizing the difficulties of housing relocation, makes a sweeping condemnation of the entire project. "Glistening in isolated splendor amid expressways and parking lots, it [the civic arena] has turned out to be something of a civic incubus. For the Negro community, it has been a highly visible symbol of old-style renewal, indifferent to the housing needs of low-income families. The atrociously planned parking lot causes long delays in exiting after a major event. . . . By any criterion, the retractable roof was a disaster. It added enormously to the expense and is hardly ever practical to open because of weather, wind or noise. The roof did not improve an acoustics problem that makes musical entertainment at the Civic Arena a painful experience for all concerned."[35]

The Lower Hill project was a mixed success, providing ammunition for both defenders and critics. The courageous undertaking—it was the largest urban renewal attempt in the nation at that date—rid the community of a long-standing slum and partially extended the central business district beyond its former narrow limits. At the same time it provided a central location for the long-sought arena and for what Lawrence hoped would become "an Acropolis—with symphony, art museum and so forth." The somewhat grandiose plans were abandoned when the Heinz family decided to rehabilitate a 1920s movie palace in the center of the city as the home for the symphony.

The charge that the redevelopers showed little concern for the plight of the residents of the Lower Hill or that housing conditions were made worse by relocation appears, in the light of the evidence, without foundation. Housing director Al Tronzo, Ted Hazlett, the URA, and many others were fully aware of the hardships caused by relocation and expended considerable effort to alleviate them. Lawrence personally petitioned Washington—unsuccessfully—several times, seeking funds to assist displaced residents, and he lent the weight of his office to support the city's Fair Housing Act. Given the available funds and a housing shortage, the authority was remarkably successful in locating equal or better housing, although, as some critics charge, the relocation process exacerbated the residential segregation problem. It also increased housing density in the Upper Hill, adding to the pressures felt by that community.

The criticisms of the arena complex, however, appear well founded. The auditorium proved unsuitable for its original purpose, and the Civic Light Opera later abandoned the area. The arena today serves as the site for professional and college sports events, circuses, and rock concerts. The Crosstown Boulevard, moreover, isolates the area from the central business district. Finally, the uncompleted section above the arena and the high-rise apartment buildings have created, in effect, a wall between the black community in the Hill District and the city center. Good intentions, as the project clearly demonstrates, often produce unexpected and undesirable results.

The Pittsburgh Renaissance, under the leadership of Lawrence, Mellon, and nearly one hundred other public-spirited citizens, was one of the nation's most remarkable urban renewal projects. Over a fifteen-year period, it encompassed more than one thousand acres in sixteen different projects. Approximately $632 million were expended, with private investments totaling almost $500 million (see Appendix A). The redevelopment, as periodicals heralded throughout the country, breathed new life into a dying city. In assessing its weaknesses and successes, Lawrence himself made the best overall evaluation when he told the Golden Age Association in 1960:

> A lot of people say we overemphasized the downtown in our program. That is not altogether true, but I have no apologies for what we did in the downtown. We had to save the core of Pittsburgh before we could do anything else with any measure of success.
>
> There is today a difference of opinion on this and related subjects. Many citizens, who only in recent years have developed an awareness of what has been taking place in Pittsburgh,

are engaging in the great American game of second guessing. One school of thought holds that there has been too much emphasis on business and industry, . . . and not enough on housing, mass transit and other human needs. . . .

Whatever the errors, . . . Pittsburgh's public and civic leadership took the only road open to it in those crucial postwar years. While most other cities returned to business-as-usual and did little, Pittsburgh moved ahead as quickly and daringly as it could with one all consuming objective in mind: To rescue the city from floods, smoke and blight and thus, to save jobs by making the community more livable for both industry and people. Where else could a start be made but in the then fluttering, economic heart of a metropolitan area of two million people—downtown?

The community's leadership had no book of rules to follow, no examples from which to learn. . . . Joint public and private action in slum clearance and redevelopment, still untested and untried, had to be played by trial and error [and] was the only available method of research—the city itself was the laboratory.[36]

1946–1959
Social Concerns and Other Matters

The business and government collaboration prevailing during the Lawrence administration produced an impressive set of physical and environmental changes in Pittsburgh and western Pennsylvania. Smoke and flood control, the nation's largest urban renewal program, industrial expansion, creation of several state and local parks, slum clearance, initial action on the development of a site for the arts and cultural activities, and an organized litter cleanup campaign all resulted from the existence of "pro-growth coalitions" present in American cities in the postwar period.[1] The movement began in Pittsburgh and clearly had its earliest and most spectacular success in the formerly "smoky city." The historic partnership, however, inevitably focused upon narrow goals and issues in which both partners had compatible interests. The concerns of the corporate community in improving the environment for commercial and industrial activities remained the prime driving force throughout the Renaissance. The business leadership reserved the right to make its own corporate decisions on investment in plants and facilities. The Lawrence administration, for its part, guided by the philosophy that a strong business environment was essential to the healthy development of the city, provided the governmental machinery to carry out the redevelopment.

Occasionally, the cooperative renewal process turned to health, social, and educational matters when individuals, such as Edgar Kaufmann, R. K. Mellon, or James Hillman, or private foundations developed an interest in such activities. But these were almost totally confined to physical and cultural improvements: parks and parklets, auditoriums for the performing arts, hospital construction, and playground and zoo improvement. The major effort at social engineering—construction of housing for the poor—became a concern of the private sector only when relocation difficulties were dramatized by the Lower Hill project. The shortage of low- and moderate-income housing prompted the Allegheny Conference on Community Development and the Pennsylvania Economy League to recommend the creation of a voluntary nonprofit agency to assist those displaced.[2] Action on the social front occurred only when other matters dictated it.

The absence of broad agreement among the private and public sector forces on important social concerns left the Lawrence administration to address them alone, and in doing so Lawrence adopted his usual pragmatic policy of dealing with immediate concerns. Long-range comprehensive programs aimed at restructuring society generated little enthusiasm or thought among his inner circle.

Lawrence's early experience in creating the statewide Little New Deal was, by his own account, one of the most significant of his entire political career. "It brought Pennsylvania into the twentieth century in terms of labor, education, health, and fair trade practices."[3] Lawrence's campaign of 1945, however, gave little indication that his city administration would carry the banner of social reform. His seven-point program was borrowed from a similar set of goals adopted by the Allegheny Conference. Specific items in the campaign platform pledged environmental and physical redevelopment, which Lawrence was convinced would benefit all social classes. In subsequent campaigns, in which he faced only token opposition from the Republicans, he confined his remarks to an enumeration of the redevelopment projects under way, asking his listeners to return him to office so "that we may finish the job." Social issues, excepting those involving alleged police corruption, were never a major part of any Lawrence campaign.

Nevertheless, they were far from unimportant to Lawrence. Repeatedly in his thirteen years as mayor, he expressed concern and supported action regarding a variety of social issues including housing, race relations, civil liberties, the rights of labor, and educational reform. At a different level, support for Israel became a special personal cause after a trip there. Such efforts added weight to the label *civic statesman,* which historians, urban experts, and journalists have attached to Lawrence.

▽

When Lawrence took the oath of office in 1946, it was generally and accurately assumed that he was a marginal friend of the black community. He had backed issues such as jobs and housing and sponsored a small number of capable black candidates such as Paul Jones, the first black on city council, and K. Leroy Irvis, a state representative. He had also pushed the Equal Rights Bill through the state legislature in 1935, but he did little to ensure its enforcement by the attorney general. His education at the hands of Robert Vann had been enlightening, but he still considered the black community as part of a larger group of unfortunate poor. Their interests, he believed, would be best served by a booming economy whether at the local, state, or national level. He courted and attempted to serve them much as he did any large bloc of votes. Patronage, economic assistance, and services were dispensed at the ward level in return for votes and campaign assistance.[4]

The issue of race relations in Pittsburgh erupted unexpectedly during the 1945 campaign when several disputes broke out in mixed white and black neighborhoods. The issues were of little lasting consequence, but they warned of more serious problems beneath the surface. Lawrence seized the opportunity to add a pledge to his famous seven points; if elected, he would create an organization designed to alleviate racial, religious, and ethnic tensions in Pittsburgh. The promise generated little interest among the press—redevelopment and an analysis of Lawrence as a boss were more interesting. The local clergy and black leaders listened, but there is no evidence that the pledge added much to Lawrence's vote total. Nor was it clear that he intended to implement it once in office. It appeared lost in the forest of strikes and redevelopment plans during the early months of his first term.

The mayor, however, did not forget. Pittsburgh's shortage of adequate housing for middle- and low-income families, discriminatory hiring practices by the city's five leading department stores, and simmering racial tensions led to a series of discussions in the summer of 1946. Political, religious, and black leaders agreed that an interdenominational, interracial council, patterned after a similar organization in Chicago, could serve a positive role in alleviating problems and reducing tensions. They further agreed that, if it was to be effective, it should be established as a regular agency of city government. On 30 November Lawrence asked the city council to establish a fifteen-member Civic Unity Council. The organization would have the power to investigate instances of racial or religious discrimination and to make recommendations for corrective measures. It would also establish "programs to promote amicable and co-operative relations between the various cultural, racial, economic, social and religious groups so that conditions which cause racial tensions may be eliminated." City council hearings brought a flood of support from interested groups. Everyone, it seemed, was in favor of racial and religious harmony. The bill passed without opposition.[5]

Lawrence's strong support gave the organization the power of the mayor's office. While it proved unable to address the root causes of racial and religious tensions—poverty and discrimination—it attacked problems as they arose and often proposed acceptable solutions. One instance was the refusal of the Pittsburgh department stores to hire blacks as sales personnel. Their employment had been confined to cleaning and warehouse work. When K. Leroy Irvis, public relations secretary of the Urban League, threatened to picket the stores, Lawrence arranged a meeting between Irvis and representatives of the five stores. The meeting failed, and Irvis called out the pickets. Angered by the store owners' reluctance to compromise and what he termed "the black eye" the city received from the picketing, the mayor intervened, applying continuous pressure to force both sides to continue negotiations and eventually arranging a meeting of Irvis, the Civic Unity Council, and Wilmer Jacoby of the Retail Merchants Association. The companies agreed to halt their discriminatory hiring. But they followed the practice, which had become common in the northern United States, of dragging their feet. A report several years later showed that each company had only a few black salespersons, most of them part-time. The Civic Unity Council concluded that legislation was needed to force an end to discriminatory practices in hiring.[6]

Lawrence agreed to support such legislation but felt that it should be enacted at the state level. A bill at the local level, his solicitor Anne Alpern informed him, would probably be ruled unconstitutional since it interfered wtih the rights of private owners. Such power, when exercised by local governments, had to be expressly granted by the state government. When a Fair Employment Practices Bill was introduced in the General Assembly in early 1949, Lawrence promised the aid of the Democratic members of the Senate Judiciary Committee in advancing it to the Senate floor. He pledged that Democratic legislators in both houses would support it, promising "by our platform and by personal conviction we are unreservedly committed to the establishment of a state Fair Employment Practices Commission (FEPC). Even though this bill is sponsored by the Republicans, we, of course, will go along." Unfortunately the overwhelming Republican majority in the committee blocked its own party's bill from reaching the Senate floor. Lawrence, now committed to a state FEPC, campaigned across the state. He also began to call for similar legislation in other states: in an address at the fortieth annual conference of the National Urban League in Grand Rapids, Michigan, he urged the states to "live the democracy for which [we are] fighting" by passing fair employment laws. "In Civil Rights, the government of this country has an immediate duty, one which will affect not only our material might but our moral right as well. No nation committed to freedom, democracy and liberty as we are, can long fight its enemies without first living what it is protecting." A subsequent attempt at passing a similar state law in 1951, however, also failed to gain the support of a majority of the Senate Judiciary Committee.[7]

When it became evident that a state law would not be forthcoming, Lawrence decided to act. Civic Unity Council members toured the country in early 1951 studying similar bills in other cities and then made recommendations to Lawrence. His legal counsel drafted a bill that Lawrence announced in August 1952. Though he suspected that it would be ruled unconstitutional, he hoped that forcible compliance would not be necessary. The mere threat of force might be enough. Lawrence conducted a brief investigation of his own, visiting Philadelphia to examine enforcement its recent fair employment law. His trip convinced him that the issue might never reach the courts. "There has been little recourse to arbitrary enforcement."[8]

The bill introduced into city council was a sweeping approach to the problem, prohibiting "discrimination in employment because of race, color, religion, ancestry, national origin or place of birth by employers, employment agencies, labor organizations and others."[9] It prohibited discrimination in promotion, tenure, firing, and salary decisions in addition to hiring. The bill established a Fair Employment Practices Commission as a division of the Civic Unity Council. At hearings held by city council, more than forty persons representing church, labor, racial, business, and other groups spoke in favor of the bill. Only one organization, the Pittsburgh Laymen's Council, spoke in opposition, claiming that the proposed commission was a Communist plot. The council voted to adopt the ordinance by nine votes to zero. George Culbertson, director of the Civic Unity Council, was named director of the FEPC.

Lawrence's gut feeling that the ordinance would not be challenged in the courts proved correct. During the next several years the commission investigated a number of cases and managed to resolve most of them amicably. The Civic Unity Council, at the same time, acting on its own and occasionally at the request of the mayor, investigated other incidents of discrimination. Lawrence extended the influence of the two organizations in 1955 when he proposed that a central agency with broader powers be created. The fifteen-member Commission on Human Relations, as it was to be known, would combine the functions of the FEPC and the Civic Unity Council but would also have authority to investigate and act on issues other than job discrimination. The bill passed in council without opposition, and the commission began operations in late 1955.

One of Lawrence's final actions as mayor of Pittsburgh was to sign into law a Fair Housing Bill. Pittsburgh became the second city in the nation to adopt such a law. An outgrowth of the difficulty in relocating blacks from the Lower Hill and other redevelopment projects, the ordinance prepared at Lawrence's request by the city solicitor applied to real estate firms, banks and other lending institutions, and owners of five or more dwelling units. It covered more than two-thirds of all such sales and rentals in the city. At city council hearings, there was overwhelming support from religious and fraternal groups, many black organizations such as the Urban League and NAACP, and a number of prominent people including the general manager of the Pittsburgh Pirates, Branch Rickey, and Mrs. Jonas Salk. Only the Pittsburgh Board of Realtors expressed strong opposition. The ordinance became effective on 1 June 1959, six months after Lawrence's inauguration as governor.

A second cause that Lawrence adopted during his tenure as mayor had none of the popular appeal of the fair employment and fair housing issues and entailed considerable risk to his political career. He became a frequent defender of the civil liberties of those accused of Communist activities or sympathies.

Pittsburgh at mid century was a hotbed of anti-Communist activity. The well-publicized battle between the leftist United Electrical Workers Union and the mainstream International Union of Electrical Workers over control of Local 601 at the East Pittsburgh Westinghouse plant raised the fear of Communist control of the labor movement in the entire western Pennsylvania area. The International Union of Electrical Workers—with support from Westinghouse, the CIO president, Philip Murray, the House Un-American Activities Committee, and Father Charles Owen Rice—eventually replaced its rival. Radical elements in the United Steel Workers and United Mine Workers similarly were purged from positions of responsibility. Fraternal associations, too, came under attack. The Serbian Progressive Club in nearby Wilmerding was placed in receivership by the courts for having radical officers. The offices of several foreign language newspapers suspected of left-wing views by the *Pittsburgh Press* were stoned and their printers harassed. The headquarters of one was eventually moved to Chicago. Several foreign language radio stations were forced off the air.[10]

Heightening the suspicion and hysteria, an organization known as Americans Battling Communism began to identify Communists or "left-wing sympathizers," whose names the Pittsburgh newspapers then published. A number who were immigrants were threatened with deportation, and many lost their jobs—one source estimated more than one hundred such firings in Pittsburgh during the era.[11]

Conditions worsened early in 1950 when Matt Cvetic revealed his identity as an undercover agent for the FBI and named some three hundred Communists or sympathizers in his lengthy testimony before the House Un-American Activities Committee in February. Judge Michael Musmanno had perhaps an even greater impact than Cvetic. Called by one authority the symbolic leader of the Italian-American community in western Pennsylvania, he had gained considerable fame as a defense lawyer in many celebrated criminal cases, including the Sacco and Vanzetti trial in 1927. He wrote of a number of books, including a highly acclaimed novel, *Black Fury,* and was the presiding judge at one of the most important trials at Nuremberg after World War II. The flamboyant judge was known for his strong anti-Communist position, which he tried to exploit in an unsuccessful attempt to win the Democratic nomination for governor of Pennsylvania in 1950. Lawrence blocked his nomination in favor of Mayor Richardson Dilworth of Philadelphia but, to avoid a costly primary battle, agreed to accept him as the candidate for lieutenant governor. Musmanno, described as "a Savonarola looking for a crusade" in 1950, now had a public forum.[12]

The publicity-seeking Musmanno launched his attack on Communism on 8 March 1950. It was, not coincidentally, less than one month after Joseph McCarthy's Wheeling, West Virginia, speech claiming the presence of "Communists in high places" had brought the Wisconsin senator instant media fame. Musmanno, supplied with information by Cvetic, refused to seat Alice Roth on the Allegheny County grand jury. "Sworn evidence has been presented which establishes to my satisfaction that Miss Alice Roth was and is a communist. I am satisfied that her surly attitude, her indecorous language, her disrespectful demeanor and her unwillingness to affirm her devotion to the United States Constitution would not make her a satisfactory grand juror. She is accordingly dismissed." His action brought newspaper articles and several thousand letters, telegrams, and phone calls of praise and congratulations. When the Pennsylvania Supreme Court overturned his decision, he responded with a blistering attack on "Fifth Columnists in our courthouses."[13]

Musmanno stepped up his attack in July by visiting the local Communist party headquarters on Grant Street. Accompanied by two detectives, he purchased a number of pieces of literature. Several days later, on the "evidence" thus obtained, he called for the imprisonment or deportation of eleven local Communists, whom he called "quasi-Quislings." Musmanno and Cvetic teamed up to raid the headquarters, confiscating a large quantity of books, pamphlets, and papers. Steve Nelson, Andrew Onda, and James Dolson, all local party leaders, were arrested and tried for sedition. Musmanno again enjoyed a rush of favorable publicity in the wake of what he called his defense of "the greatest treasure of our country. Our very liberty." The vigorous attacks against the "Communist threat" by Cvetic and Musmanno continued for the next two years. Communists, those alleged to be Communists or sympathizers or even those defending the accused, came under attack. "Our scientists are yet working on further offensive and defensive weapons. They must be protected at all costs from Communist infiltration, Communist espionage, Communist influence and Communist thievery. No sophisticated argumentation, no high-flown dialectics, no bleating about 'academic freedom' and 'witch-hunts' must allow even the shadow of a Communist to fall within the confines of the last great chance to save America and the world of decency, peace and good will to all mankind."[14]

It was in the midst of an increasingly fanatical anti-Communist crusade that Lawrence took what some observers call the most courageous steps in his political career—the defense of several people accused of Communist activities.

In early 1950, Marjorie Matson, an Allegheny County assistant district attorney, wrote a letter to the American Civil Liberties Union protesting Musmanno's refusal to seat Roth as a grand juror. "The action . . . comes as a follow-up to a wave of hysteria which has swept this community as a result of the disclosures made by Matt Cvetic." Musmanno responded with a bitter attack on Matson, but the matter appeared at an end. However, Lawrence's old enemy Charles J. Margiotti, appointed state attorney general by Republican Governor James Duff, seized the opportunity to embarrass Lawrence by ordering an investigation of Matson's background. On 5 January 1951 he sent a lengthy letter to the Allegheny County district attorney, William S. Rahauser demanding that Matson be dismissed "as it appears obvious that her Communistic associations render her unfit to hold this position." Margiotti itemized six instances of Matson's alleged pro-Communist activities.[15]

Matson responded with a categorical denial that she had ever been a member or a sympathizer of the Communist party and made a convincing point-by-point refutation of Margiotti's charges. Rahauser refused to dismiss Matson—she was given an unpaid leave of absence—but did agree to conduct his own investigation. At his request, Judge Samuel A. Weiss appointed a five-member panel of attorneys to hear the charges. Not content with this, Margiotti conducted a newspaper campaign for the next several weeks, periodically releasing pieces of "evidence" against Matson. Later, on the eve of the hearing, he announced that he would not appear before the court-appointed committee "because it would create a precedent and lower the dignity of the office of Attorney-General"; he intended to conduct his own hearing. But three weeks later, in an unrelated incident, Margiotti submitted his resignation to the recently elected Republican governor, John Fine.[16]

His resignation, however, did not alter the strong anti-Communist feelings in Pittsburgh or halt the Matson hearings, organized by Judge Weiss, which began in September 1951, one week after Andrew Onda and James Dolson were convicted of sedition. Harry Allan, an attorney and chairman of Americans Battling Communism, represented the "prosecution." In an atmosphere made sensational by detailed accounts in the media, a parade of witnesses, including Matt Cvetic, testified that Matson was known to be "sympathetic to the cause." Her legal defense of several prominent Communists and a series of letters to President Truman protesting the New York trial of eleven top Communists as "violating their civil rights in a period of hysteria" were offered as evidence against her. Several witnesses recalled seeing her involved in "corridor conferences" with defense attorney Hyman Schlesinger during the trial of Nathan Albert, the local Communist party secretary.[17]

It was in the midst of the hearing that David Lawrence, responding to a plea from Matson's husband, decided to testify on her behalf. He briefly outlined his long acquaintance with Matson, a former Democratic district committeewoman. When asked about her loyalty, the mayor responded, "I think she's thoroughly American and a mighty good Democrat. She stands up for the things we are trying to do. You can't be a Democrat and a Communist. I am an admirer of her work as a lawyer, a citizen and a Democrat. I'd give her a job, any job, in the city government." He then added a comment in defense of Hyman Schlesinger, who had been accused of Communist activities. As he left the witness stand, Matson's attorney, Thomas McBride of Philadelphia, introduced himself to Lawrence. "I never met you, Mr. Mayor; I want to shake your hand." Applause filled the courtroom.[18] Several months later the hearing board issued a ruling clearing Matson of all charges, permitting her to return to her position as assistant district attorney.

The attempts to uncover Communists or their supporters in Pittsburgh did not end with the clearing of Matson and the jailing of Steve Nelson. After a summer in Europe, "observing the inroads of Communism," Michael Musmanno returned with new zeal and renewed energy. Immediately Cvetic, Musmanno, and another anti-Communist judge, Blair Gunther, brought charges of "subversion and giving aid and comfort to the enemy" against Roy Harris, a composer-in-residence at Chatham College. Harris planned to conduct a symphony he had composed in 1943 and dedicated to the Russian people then suffering under the German invasion. The Veterans of Foreign Wars and several other groups announced that they planned to stage a protest at the performance, and Musmanno demanded that Harris destroy the work or rededicate it to the "heroic armed forces of our own United States." The mayor's help was enlisted. Lawrence, who did not know Harris, issued statements supporting him, announced that he would attend the concert, and testified on his behalf before the Americanism Committee of the Allegheny County American Legion. Musmanno and his colleagues later dropped the charges when it became clear that public support for their cause was waning.[19]

In an era when careers were ruined and families destroyed by the hint of association with Communist party members or those labeled as sympathizers, Lawrence's willingness to appear in two celebrated cases illustrates his strong belief in the civil liberties of all. While the threat to his own career turned out to be minimal, some risk did exist. The potential costs were unknown at the time. He volunteered his support because he strongly opposed the demagoguery he found in the anti-Communist effort. The incidents, moreover, were a reminder of his own trials. Individuals whom he believed to be innocent were being attacked in order to further the political aims of the accusers. Regardless of political or social views, those who, in his eyes, were wrongly accused, received his support. Several years later he served as a character witness at the tax evasion trial of a longtime political opponent, Republican Governor John Fine and testified on behalf of the Pittsburgh assistant police superintendent, Lawrence Maloney, at his embezzlement trial.

The courage Lawrence showed by his defense of accused persons in controversial causes was matched by his efforts to raise new taxes to continue Pittsburgh's redevelopment program. His effort to impose a wage tax upon the city in late 1953 demonstrated his resolve to act in what he deemed the best interests of the city regardless of the political consequences.

The question of additional revenue was a concern of the administration almost from the beginning of Lawrence's first term. A deficit existed when he took over from Scully, and redevelopment, although much of it was privately financed, placed great burdens on city government. However, from the outset, Lawrence made clear his opposition to either a sales or a wage tax. State law permitted these but stipulated a flat rate, which Lawrence dubbed a "soak the poor" tax.

For his first several years as mayor, he maintained an unwavering opposition, accepting instead state authorization for taxes on amusements and personal property. In 1949 he refused to support a wage tax for Allegheny County; in 1951 he vigorously denied charges that he intended to impose one on the city; and in 1952 he reiterated his position. He apparently felt so strongly that he was willing to postpone aspects of the redevelopment program to avoid the tax.

It is thus easy to understand why the city was shocked when, in his budget message to the council in December 1953, Lawrence hinted that he might reverse his position. The council was not surprised. The tentative 1954 budget had been discussed briefly at several Monday caucuses with the mayor's staff, and the possibility of a deficit—always abhorrent to Lawrence—was clear. New revenues would have to be found to avoid the possibility. It was actually the finance committee of the council that decided to adopt a wage tax. Lawrence received the news in a rather unusual fashion. He and Councilman Fred Weir were attending a banquet in the William Penn Hotel. "I went up to the washroom of the seventeenth floor . . . and Lawrence came in and got into the stall next to me . . . and he whispered, 'What did you guys do today?' I said 'We decided on the wage tax,' and he said, 'Okay.' That was it. Later he said, 'Whatever you decide on I'll back you to the hilt.'"[20]

Lawrence's presentation to an already committed city council took the form of an education session for the press and others in attendance. Projecting a budget deficit of nearly six million dollars resulting from salary raises and an increase in the size of the police and fire forces, the mayor analyzed four possibilities: a real estate tax increase, unacceptable because it "might encourage an exodus to the suburbs and destroy prospects for continued gains in property values"; a transfer of the city's water system to an independent authority, which would probably not raise enough to cover the shortfall; the refunding of maturing municipal bonds, which he rejected outright because "you can do that just so long before you go stone broke"; and a wage tax, to which he was still philosophically opposed but which ought to be considered along with the other alternatives because it would raise the needed funds. His rather transparent strategy appeared to be to present four choices, three of which were unacceptable, and then let the citizens talk themselves into accepting the wage tax. Accordingly, he requested that the council conduct hearings to determine the attitude of residents.[21]

For three days in early December, city council chambers were the site of heated, often angry presentations to overflow crowds. A few speakers endorsed the wage tax idea but most attacked it, and Lawrence as well. Union representatives, in particular, accused the Democrats of getting elected under false pretenses and of deserting labor.

Lawrence was silent about the matter until the middle of December, when he made his decision known. "Pressed by sheer necessity, Pittsburgh is about to levy an earned income tax which we have fought off for years. . . . We have simply run out of revenue sources and nothing else that is not destructive will serve us in our need." It was Lawrence's habit not to spend time agonizing over a decision once it had been made. The wage tax was no exception. Instead he berated his critics for their shortsightedness. "Nobody has suggested closing tuberculosis or polio hospitals or shutting down parks, and no one has urged that the city stop collecting garbage. . . . Nor has anyone demanded that city employees be shut off from a cost of living raise or that the city stop paying wages. But nobody except the mayor and council has had the elementary courage to advocate any form of taxation which would accomplish all these things and keep the city solvent. Well, that is what they elected us for and I can assure you tonight we will not shirk our jobs."[22]

The mayor waged an almost solitary fight for the next six weeks while opposition mounted. Labor unions were the most vociferous, but many others joined in the battle. Several labor leaders and dissident Democrats, stating that there was little room left for them in the party, began talking of forming a third political party in Pittsburgh. Republican Congressman James Fulton raised the specter of the "ripper bill" when he called for replacing the mayor with a city manager. Citizens wrote to Lawrence and the council threatening to "bolt" to the Republican party. A number of suburban residents objected to what they called a commuter tax. "It's taxation without representation," one outraged worker wrote. "And that's tyranny."[23]

Perhaps most offensive to Lawrence was the opposition of several prominent Democrats whom he had helped elect, in particular William McClelland, the county coroner, David Roberts, the prothonotary, and County Commissioner John Kane. Lawrence brused off the criticism of his fellow Democrats with the terse comment, "I am sorry if any of my colleagues in the Democratic Party disagree with the program which is being advanced to solve the city's financial problems. However, we have the responsibility of meeting the city's obligations and they do not."[24]

The Pittsburgh newspapers, meanwhile, editorialized against the tax almost daily. The *Pittsburgh Press,* always a strong supporter of the mayor, published six editorials in ten days in December. In early January it also ran a series of articles entitled "Where Your Tax Dollar Goes" designed to identify waste in city government. The "Letters to the Editor" columns of the three daily papers routinely carried denunciations of the mayor and council.

Lawrence remained on the attack. Campaigning as he normally would for election, he called press conferences, spoke at meetings and on radio and television, and invited union officials for private talks in his office.

On 25 January 1954, following a final desperate attempt by labor groups and a rambling discourse by a prominent Lawrence foe, Mrs. R. Templeton Smith, the council passed the measure by eight votes to one. Upon signing the bill, Lawrence again felt compelled to offer a defense. "I am under no illusion that we have acted to achieve a momentary popularity. . . . But I am sure that the council and the mayor have acted to protect the best interests of Pittsburgh and its people and that in the end such forthright action is what the citizens desire from their public officials. The politician with no sense of responsibility is the worst enemy of democratic government." His statement repeated the message he had offered again and again during the six difficult weeks: he asked citizens to join once more in a cooperative rebuilding effort "to show the whole world how an American city can find itself and build anew for a better future."[25]

Although Lawrence's action had no long-term political repercussions, he spent the next several months defending and paying a price for his decision. Early in February he sent copies of a ten-page radio address of 27 December to all 2288 Democratic committee members to help them defend the party against the continued criticism among their constituencies. One month later, in an obvious snub, Lawrence was not invited to attend the state CIO conference being held in his own city. County Commissioner Kane welcomed the delegates. The mayor was singled out for an explicit attack when the thirty union executives called for his removal as Democratic national committeeman.[26] The organization later took its most serious slap at him when it endorsed McClelland for governor over Lawrence's choice, George Leader.

Labor unions and other groups continued to attack Lawrence throughout the summer, and he was not invited to speak for weeks after he signed the bill. A six-week trip to Europe and the Middle East came as a welcome relief. By the time he returned in August, much of the furor had died down and he muted it still further with a request to the city council to reduce the wage tax from 1 to 0.5 percent for 1955. The official announcement came less than one month before the November elections and caused his opponents and the press to speculate that it was at least partially motivated by political considerations.

Not all social issues that concerned Lawrence were domestic: one to which he became committed was the creation and development of the state of Israel. He first became involved with the Zionist movement in mid 1946 when he was invited to speak at a meeting of 1200 supporters at Carnegie Music Hall. The meeting was arranged by Rabbi Irving Miller and businessman Alex Lowenthal, chairman of the Pittsburgh Zionist Emergency Council, to protest the British government's policy toward Jews in Palestine and the surviving Jews in Europe. Lawrence, a featured speaker, earned a rousing ovation when he added the "voice of the city" to a resolution of protest to be sent to the British government and to President Truman.[27]

There is nothing in Lawrence's background to indicate any earlier strong commitment toward the creation of a Jewish homeland. Rather, it appears that he was acting as a prudent politician, and he made several similar speeches during the next two years. Two factors turned his support into fervor, and the cause came as close to a crusade as any issue excepting the Democratic party and highway safety, in his entire lifetime.

First, during his early years of speaking on behalf of the creation of a Jewish state, he was greatly impressed with the dedication and zeal of the local activists. "Anyone who works as hard as you people do deserves the support of all of us. You can't help be successful. If the Irish worked as hard as you do they would have had their independence from the British a long time ago," Lawrence noted, in a rather stretched analogy.[28] Lawrence carried his Jewish-Irish analogy a step further after trips to both countries, when he frequently contrasted conditions among Irish-Americans and those he found in Israel.

Second, Lawrence visited Israel in 1951. David and Alyce were frequent travelers to Europe, usually visiting Ireland, England, and several countries on the Continent. In 1951, at the urging of Florence Reizenstein, he included a one-week stay in Israel on his itinerary. Reizenstein, an important Pittsburgh fund-raiser in the Jewish cause, had been to Israel several times since its founding. She offered to meet the Lawrences, act as tour guide, and introduce them to David Ben Gurion and other leaders. Lawrence spoke glowingly of Israel upon his return. "Everybody there seems to be working on the team, working for the country. The devotion of the people to their nation and to their aims is something out of this world." Lawrence thereupon became even more effective at raising funds for Israel. Zionist activists never had trouble selling bonds when he spoke.[29]

Lawrence continued his fund-raising efforts for Israel for the rest of his life, and he also enlisted the aid of others, including Vice-President Alben Barkley, and former President Truman. When David Ben Gurion visited the United States, he included Pittsburgh on his itinerary. He spoke at a massive Jewish fund-raising rally and, as a favor to Lawrence, attended a luncheon with local Democratic officials.

Lawrence's European trips thereafter never failed to include a stop in Israel, which he visited in 1954, 1958, and 1962. His five-week trip in 1954 was a gift from a group of Pittsburgh Jews in gratitude for his fund-raising efforts. The log of Lawrence's 1958 trip suggests that his feelings for Israel were reciprocated by Israeli officials. During a five-day period he dined with Prime Minister Ben Gurion, Mayor Gershon Agron, and Benjamin Mazar, president of Hebrew University, among others. He attended a Hadassah presentation to Ben Gurion, at which he was introduced from the podium. At a private meeting, Ben Gurion impressed Lawrence with his "wide knowledge of American Affairs." The highlight of the trip, however, was the dedication of the David L. Lawrence Forest at Malikiya, financed by funds raised by Lawrence and the Pittsburgh United Jewish Appeal. Later, he helped raise funds to establish a chain of youth centers in Israel, one of which is dedicated to him.[30]

Lawrence's work for the cause of Israel did not go unrewarded in Pittsburgh. The Jewish community consistently voted overwhelmingly Democratic. "I can only think of one or two Republican Jews," Lowenthal noted. "Leon Falk was one and I think I knew another but I can't recall his name." Jews also provided unflagging support following the passage of the unpopular city wage tax. "Our phone stopped ringing after that," a member of his staff recalled. "Except for the Jews. They kept calling. They stuck by us. Lawrence never forgot that."[31]

Lawrence's activities involving minority residents, civil liberties, the wage tax, and Israel demonstrate that he was moved by more than political concerns. He also played a decisive role in the regulation of utilities in the state, the development of educational television, and the mediation of labor-management disputes. He refused to avoid controversial issues, although they often brought at least temporary discomfort and some risk to his political career. His ability to grow while on the job, moreover, became a hallmark of his administration. He approached new problems and situations in a systematic manner and more often than not was able to arrive at a reasonable solution from among the available alternatives. When he was not initially wholly committed, as in the case of support for Israel, his political instincts carried him through until he developed his own convictions. Finally, as was illustrated by the wage tax issue, he was not reluctant to reverse his position, no matter how strongly he had been committed to a principle. When conditions dictated a new course of action, he relied upon higher principles—the greater good of the community—to set the direction. But the experience taught him a valuable lesson, which he admitted in 1957 when his opponent in the mayoralty election, Judge John Drew, taunted him about the wage tax issue. "In 1953, I had to change my mind and eat my own words. That was not pleasant, I assure you. But if I were faced with the alternative of a personal retreat from a position publicly taken or of leading the city into disaster . . . I would make the same choice again. But, I would give a friendly warning to all young men embarking on a political career to be more mindful of the uncertain future than I was in this case."[32]

1946–1959
A Bit of Tarnish: Graft and Corruption

David Lawrence's impatience with details served him well in the redevelopment process. He relied upon technical experts and expected them to accomplish the objectives that had been established by the administration in cooperation with the private sector leadership. The technical corps, in turn, appreciated the freedom to operate in an environment free of politics or bureaucratic meddling. When political decisions were required to smooth the path toward an objective, they knew the mayor would act decisively and quickly. They also knew that he would not permit the redevelopment projects to become glutted with patronage employees. Each project director and the heads of the authorities exercised full control over hiring and firing. The city ultimately benefited from the efforts of a large number of talented individuals who joined together in the exciting work of rebuilding the city.

The mayor's habit of delegating responsibility and the structure of the political organization he had created did not lead to the same fortunate results in the public service sector of the administration. Scandals and corruption involving various city services, law enforcement, and public works agencies tarnished his administration from the beginning. Although he consistently condemned such activities and was never personally implicated, he was never able to rid the administration of this unsavory element. When he became aware of wrongdoing, he was often reluctant to take corrective action. If he did so, intraparty battles would inevitably erupt that would hinder the completion of his urban renewal mission. Consequently he acted only when developing scandals demanded an immediate and certain response. Thus the city's most powerful politician proved incapable of ridding his administration of its most persistent problem.

The tradition of corruption was deeply embedded in Pittsburgh's political history. From the turn-of-the-century Flinn-Magee machine to the Lawrence administration, city government had seldom been free of scandal—kickbacks, influence peddling, protection rackets, vice operations, and jury tampering—despite occasional reform movements.[1] In the mid 1930s, the Democratic party, in need of experienced ward workers and influential neighborhood residents, welcomed new recruits who switched parties, and it asked few questions about their private activities or their associates. Lawrence, in his attempt to strengthen the organization following the abrupt resignation of McNair, vested additional power in the ward chairmen, permitting them considerable control over local patronage.

▽

The Scully administration, the first one over which Lawrence exercised considerable control, encountered only one major scandal. Several investigative reports by Ray Sprigle of the *Pittsburgh Post-Gazette* indicated that illegal gambling, numbers establishments, and prostitution operated on the streets of the city with relatively little interference from the police. There were nearly one thousand police officers in the city but more than five thousand people writing numbers. Few of the latter made much money, Sprigle wrote, because of the high cost of police protection. A policeman identified for Sprigle one of the beneficial side effects of the illegal operation. "When are you guys going to lay off the numbers racket? It's the lesser of two evils. If this numbers racket is put out of business, it will mean a lot more work for the police and the courts. And it's going to cause a lot of trouble for businessmen and citizens. . . . I'm talking about the leaders of this racket. . . . They used to be in the bootleg racket. Before that in better times they were petty thieves and at election time they would crook the ballot boxes. You let the numbers rackets go out of business and all those yeggs are going back into larceny."[2]

The long history of corrupt practices in Pittsburgh could be eliminated only by an administrator who made the effort a major priority of his term of office. Lawrence, however, had set other priorities. Even the social concerns that occupied a great deal of his time paled in significance to the task of rebuilding the city. What he considered minor corruption was simply a distasteful but unavoidable cost of running the city. "Lawrence was never puritanical about what you might call police corruption," Jack Robin explained. "He regarded that as a fact of life. What the hell can you do about it anyhow? And, if the ward leaders, and the aldermen, and the police inspectors were doing this or that in relation to gambling etc., he wasn't going to run around chasing them to uncover corruption. . . . If you're discreet and keep out of trouble, whatever you do, that's your business. . . . He never worried if anybody in the Police Department or the Democratic organization had whatever arrangements they made to anybody who could contribute to their welfare."[3] Lawrence's attitude and the priorities of the Renaissance made corruption in his administration almost inevitable. His occasional efforts at reform almost always occurred in the wake of a sensational scandal or violent crime. When public concern died down, it was "business as usual."

The first hint of corruption came a few months after his inauguration in 1946. Two small-time numbers operators, Frank Evans and Freddie Garrow, were murdered in a gangland style slaying. It was the third such incident since the beginning of the year. The other victims were also involved in numbers, and one, Gus Gianni, had recently lost a close race for First Ward alderman. All four crimes, Police Superintendent Harvey Scott concluded, were part of a numbers war for control of the East Liberty neighborhood. Lawrence responded to the news by "declaring war on the racketeers. We will not rest until the city is cleared of these rats." Under orders from the mayor, Scott led a series of raids, in which only one prominent operator, "Pittsburgh Hymie" Martin, and seventy-three small fry were caught. The police conducted several more raids in the following weeks, but their efforts continued to produce petty gamblers and numbers players, all of whom were eventually released or given small fines by the courts. The raided betting shops reopened or moved to new addresses within weeks.

The concern over vice in Pittsburgh and corruption among the police subsided during the next few months as Lawrence battled to bring a resolution to the Duquesne Light and Power Company strike. An occasional raid resulted in a few arrests, but the concerted effort to rid the city of rackets, which Lawrence had promised during the summer, never materialized. He apparently had no serious intention of disturbing the accommodation that existed between the police and the gambling establishment.

But Lawrence had reckoned without one of the few Republicans in office, the district attorney for Allegheny County, Artemas C. Leslie, who had been appointed in 1945 by a mainly Republican Court of Common Pleas to fill a vacancy. The son of a former Republican boss, Max Leslie, he created his own raiding squad of county detectives. In a deliberate attempt to embarrass the Democratic administration, he ordered a series of raids on known city establishments.

One in particular, the Enright Smoke Shop, was only one hundred yards from the East Liberty police station. County detectives seized dice tables and other gambling paraphernalia. Leslie, who faced a re-election race in the fall of 1947, ordered raids sporadically during the spring of that year, thus keeping himself and the gambling issue in the news headlines. In May 1947 he wrote to the mayor informing him of the presence of nineteen gambling establishments within the city limits and brazenly calling upon him to submit "a written report of the action taken by you and your police department." Leslie released the letter to the press.[4]

Lawrence referred the letter to Superintendent Scott, who ordered simultaneous raids on all the establishments. Only seven arrests were made. *Pittsburgh Press* police reporters noted that "more persons would have been arrested if there hadn't been a leak, either from the Police Department or the District Attorney's office." At a news conference, Lawrence bristled at the suggestion that police knew about the establishments but refused to act. "When such places come under the notice of the police, they close them up," he snapped.[5]

It was clear to Lawrence that the district attorney was in a position to embarrass the Democratic administration. Leslie would, no doubt, step up his campaign against the rackets and dishonest police as the November election neared. Lawrence would be blamed for both, and the district attorney would rely on the argument that a Republican law enforcement officer was needed to fight corruption. Leslie would have to be replaced. Earlier in the year, Lawrence had named William Rahauser, an old-line Democratic worker and former state senator, as his candidate to oppose Leslie. Rahauser, although one of Lawrence's best candidate choices, began the campaign at a disadvantage: his ties to the party marked him as a Lawrence man, and he could hardly sell himself as a crusader against "crime within the administration."

Lawrence attempted to even the score by defusing the rackets issue. He would create his own racket-busting squad. Unlike precinct police, who could operate only within their own district, his new team had authority to strike anywhere in the city. Lawrence's choice to head the squad was a short, stocky police lieutenant, Lawrence Maloney. A seven-year veteran of the force, Maloney had previously worked for the city as a janitor, fireman, and sanitary inspector. He was also Democratic committeeman in the Tenth Ward. Maloney's Marauders, as the press quickly dubbed the squad of six plainclothes officers, roamed the city raiding gambling, prostitution, and other vice establishments at will. They were often followed by newspaper photographers and reporters who recorded each raid in detail. Maloney became an instant celebrity, and the public was informed that the administration was striking back at vice.

Lawrence meanwhile conducted a vigorous campaign on behalf of Rahauser. He spoke nightly and canvassed a number of the prominent residents who had backed him in 1945 to elicit their support. Businessmen's and lawyers' groups for Rahauser were formed at his request. He ordered party officials to go all out to elect Rahauser and threatened that if they did not, they would "suffer the consequences," that is, lose patronage rights.[6]

It is difficult to determine whether Lawrence's creation of the Maloney force or his orders to the party regulars had any impact on the election itself. The Democratic party won its most impressive victory of the century, sweeping all contested offices by huge majorities. Rahauser led the ticket by an impressive number of votes in a landslide over Leslie.[7] The district attorney's office was safely under control.

The new year brought several mild attempts by Lawrence to control vice, but at the same time he bypassed a major opportunity to remove the detective corps from politics when, under pressure from the ward chairmen, he opposed a proposed state law that would have placed detectives and inspectors under civil service protection. He offered a lame explanation for his opposition: "You must have different types of people for different types of work. Suppose you want someone to speak a foreign language. You would have to set up a different type of test. We need a number of detectives who speak foreign languages." (Pittsburgh had, at this time, less than 5 percent of its population who spoke foreign languages exclusively.) Under pressure from the ward chairman, Lawrence was unwilling to support the type of reform which would grant the police force political independence.

Conditions deteriorated during 1948. An editorial in the *Pittsburgh Press* noted that "gambling joints, all-night liquor clubs and similar dives practically run wide open. . . . And the numbers racketeers are getting bolder all the time. They are so rich and powerful, so generally immune from police harassment, it seems that the small squad headed by Mr. Maloney hardly makes a dent in the industry." Several months later, Al Florig, a private detective and former police officer, sent a letter to the mayor, city council, and the press charging that organized crime was operating openly in Pittsburgh under "police and political protection." He indicated, as an example, that he had information from an anonymous witness about "high stakes gambling at the American Hunting and Fishing Club in East Liberty."[8]

Lawrence initially tried to ignore Florig's charges, attributing them to the overactive imagination of a disgruntled former employee. However, he called several high-level meetings with Rahauser, Alpern, Scott, and others. He suggested that Florig had been fired from both the city and county law enforcement departments and that no one would pay attention to him. Rahauser and Alpern countered that regardless of Florig's credibility, others would use the issue of corruption to attack the Democratic administration. It was time to attack the issue head on. The mayor eventually agreed and on 24 July announced to the press that he was asking Rahauser to convene a grand jury with broad investigative powers to examine two major issues: the extent of gambling and other illegal vices in the city; and the extent to which crime and vice were protected by the police or politicians. The district attorney was to "do everything in the power of his offices to expedite a Grand Jury inquiry which will determine the truth or falsity of certain accusations made in regard to law enforcement in the city." Lawrence added, "These accusations come from a source whose past record does not vouch for his responsibility."[9]

The grand jury of nine men and nine women convened on 7 August 1948 and remained in session until the last day of September. It heard 238 witnesses in all and documented that several dozen fled the city to avoid subpoenas to testify. Among those who did appear were Superintendent Harvey Scott, Councilman Joe McArdle, more than forty policemen, the editors of all three Pittsburgh newspapers, and several hundred individuals known to operate or frequent gambling establishments. Principal witnesses were Florig, who testified twice, Sam and Tony Grosso, who were at the start of their careers as numbers kings of western Pennsylvania, and Lawrence himself.

The grand jury had no difficulty in establishing the presence of a wide-open gambling operation in the city. Singled out as major operations were thirteen clubs, including seven in East Liberty. Others were located in the business district, on the North Side, and in Oakland. Horse rooms and gambling casinos, operated by front men who held legitimate business licenses, were identified all over the city. The real owners of these establishments had been a carefully guarded secret. The jury also uncovered numerous after-hours clubs offering gambling and illegal slot machines. A downtown hotel, the Fort Pitt, was singled out as the site of "two of the largest horse rooms in Western Pennsylvania operating for a number of years unmolested by the hotel detective or any of the hotel officials or employees," an operation linked to a multimillion-dollar betting syndicate in Yonkers, New York. Sixty-six persons were recommended for indictment, a list, as one newspaper put it, that was the "Who's Who in the gambling world." It included Sam and Tony Grosso; Tom and Vincent Prezioso (alias Christy); casino operator George Quinlan, a one-time partner in sportsman's James Rooney's slot machine company; and William "Woogie" Harris, credited with bringing the numbers operation to Pittsburgh.[10]

The grand jury questioned more than fifty people to determine whether a link existed between the rackets and the police or politicians. Florig testified that "racketeers, in order to operate, must kick in to the Democratic slush fund. If they don't, they can't operate because police would close them down within an hour." Cutting a wide swath with his accusations, he stated, "Organized crime cannot operate in the city without an okay from the mayor down through his official family to the cop on the beat." Lawrence, who appeared several days after Florig, disputed all the accusations. He called for anyone with evidence of wrongdoing by the police or anyone in the administration to present it to the authorities.[11]

The grand jury concluded that Florig had invented his "mystery informer." "No such person existed," they noted. Nor was any "evidence produced that would indicate that there was any organized protection of the gambling rackets either by the police or the politicians." However, the police department was not completely exonerated. The grand jury cited numerous sections of the city where gambling and vice operated without interference from the law. "Whether this was due to any corrupt motive . . . or to an utter lack of interest on the part of the police for the suppression of this type of crime, we have been unable to determine." The East Liberty district, headed by inspector John Dean, was singled out as the most lax in the city; the central city, the North and South sides, Hazelwood, and several other districts were criticized for the do-nothing attitude of the police; and other districts were cited and inspectors named where police were either corrupt or incompetent.[12]

The report also criticized the relationship between the police and the Democratic party, citing the case of a police inspector who also served as a ward chairman and as a constable in the district to which he was assigned. Other inspectors and police served as district committeemen in their assigned districts, and one was a member of the state legislature. Somewhat ironically in view of his later indictments, Lieutenant Maloney and his band of "marauders" were praised by the grand jury, which recommended that the squad be continued and increased in number.

Lawrence, his safety director, James Fairley, Scott, and the members of the mayor's inner cabinet deliberated only five days before arriving at a plan to implement the recommendations of the grand jury. Lawrence's statement carefully responded only to the specific charges. Two high-ranking police officers, John Dean and William Sullivan, were suspended with a request that they resign, and a third, also suspended, resigned three days later. Others singled out for criticism received only a reprimand from Superintendent Scott. Lawrence announced the continuation of the Maloney squad, to be "reinforced with such added personnel as it needs to do a thorough job." Five men were added on 15 October.[13]

In response to the criticism that many policemen had been assigned to the same beats for years and had become well acquainted with the racketeers, the mayor ordered that all inspectors and lieutenants be transferred every six months. Finally he banned police officers from holding political office in the district to which they were assigned. Lawrence's statement also noted his pleasure that the charges of protection of gambling rackets by police and politicians "proved untrue," since the grand jury had found no evidence to support them. He also praised what the grand jury called the police bureau's "excellent record in cleaning up crimes of violence."[14]

The measures Lawrence took fell far short of the needed reform of the police bureau. The relationship between the police and ward-level politics remained the heart of the problem. Unwilling to anger ward politicians, who formed the foundation of the Democratic organization, the mayor left untouched the hiring and promotion policies that vested authority at the local level.[15] Lawrence's "reform" also permitted the continued participation by law enforcement officials in political activities. His ban applied only to political office in one's own working district. Moreover, officers were still permitted to work for candidates for government or party offices in any district in the city. Indeed, the party continued to expect police officers to work on its behalf in each campaign, and ward chairmen expected a similar service from those officers they sponsored for employment. The new regulations also permitted police officers to run for election for ward-level constable or magistrate positions. In addition, these positions remained in the control of ward officials.[16]

Lawrence's halfhearted attempt at reform promised no further investigation of the police force, nor did he suggest raising salaries to make beat policemen less susceptible to bribes or protection money. Further, he steadfastly refused to fire Harvey Scott, who had served as police superintendent since 1939, in spite of strong advice to do so by several members of his executive staff.

It is tempting to perceive a direct relationship between Lawrence's failure to act on the issue of police involvement in politics and the upcoming mayoralty campaign. He certainly did not wish to risk the enmity of many of the party's best workers immediately before a possibly difficult primary battle. Eddie Leonard had already begun hinting that he might be a candidate. With hindsight, its seems the prudent move would have been decisive action to sever the police-politician connection, which was under heavy criticism from the media, prominent citizens, and Lawrence's Republican opponents. Leonard, as it turned out, never mentioned the issue. But the Republican candidate, Tice Ryan, put up nearly one hundred advertising billboards showing a huge pair of clutching hands reaching after a small child on the street and with the caption "Make our Homes and Streets Safe!—Vote Republican." Ryan emphasized the theme of police corruption and public safety in his addresses throughout the campaign.

In refusing to carry out the police-politics separation, Lawrence opted to follow a principle he had held since his early days in politics: loyalty was a paramount virtue worthy of reciprocation. The ward politicians and the police, regardless of corruption, served the party faithfully, many for nearly two decades. Lawrence feared that he would lose his political base if he abandoned them. In this regard, while he emerged as a modern municipal leader in the city's rebuilding process, he remained a nineteenth-century political boss. Neighborhood-level politics formed the basis of the system, and it had to be preserved. The district and ward politicians could not be expected to put forth a sustained effort merely to see their man elected. Rewards, in terms of patronage and some amount of power, remained unavoidable. The "booty" the party workers received was simply part of the political cost of running a municipality. Lawrence, to his credit, hoped to minimize it as much as possible.

An article in the *Pittsburgh Press* of 5 June 1949 provided evidence that the grand jury and the subsequent "Lawrence reforms" had been a classic exercise in futility. "The special Grand Jury carried a 'big stick' when it investigated the rackets eight months ago, but since then the courts and the police have been 'speaking softly' to the racketeers.

> Only one of the 65 [sic] persons indicted as a result of the probe went to jail. He got an eight months sentence but served only 2.5 months getting an 'Easter parole' on April 14.
>
> Today the numbers arrests have fallen off almost to a vanishing point. But anyone who thinks the racketeers are out of the numbers business doesn't know the facts of life. Many of

> the old numbers stores closed when the Grand Jury and Maloney's Marauders were generating the heat last year are open again. And new ones have been added to take care of the trade.

Thirty-three of those indicted either were found guilty or so pleaded but received only light fines averaging less than $300. Only one of the offending gambling clubs remained closed.

The mayor's satisfaction over the competence of the police force in dealing with crimes of violence also turned to ashes. In the year following the grand jury hearing, several unsolved murders raised questions about the ability of the department to deal with homicides, quite apart from vice and gambling. The police appeared particularly inept in the case of the rape-murder of a prominent Shadyside woman.[17] At approximately 11:15 P.M. on 25 November 1949, Jean Brusco was beaten with a beer bottle and dragged to a nearby alley, where she was raped and brutally murdered. A milkman found the body at 8:00 A.M. the next day in the back yard of an apartment house, approximately two hundard yards from her home. Parts of her torn clothing were scattered about the yard. Events that occurred in the nine-hour interim further besmirched the already tarnished reputation of the police bureau.

The initial attack on Miss Brusco occurred under a street light in full view of Mrs. Ellen Flannigan from her third-floor apartment on Howe Street. Mrs. Flannigan immediately called the East Liberty police station, located a few blocks away. The police did not appear on the scene until one hour later. When they did respond, it was to the wrong house. Following what was later described as a thorough search of the area, the police concluded that the victim had been kidnapped. A general alarm giving the description of Miss Brusco and her assailant was issued at 1:50 A.M., a full two and one-half hours after the attack. Police on the scene continued their search until 5:00 A.M. but were unable to locate a body.

Stung by press reports of police bungling and complaints from Shadyside residents, the mayor demanded an immediate report from Superintendent Scott. The report, however, left unanswered the crucial questions about the delays, errors, and failures. It also conflicted on a number of important details with a report in the *Pittsburgh Press* that was based on its own inquiries among residents of the area.

Thoroughly annoyed by the superintendent's report, Lawrence ordered an immediate police board of inquiry. To calm the public's fears, made emphatic by the flood of phone calls and letters to the mayor's office, he simultaneously promised to add 100 more policemen to the force of 1125. On his order to revise assignments so that a maximum number of men were on night duty, Scott created a night force of 402 beat patrolmen and a daytime shift of 92.

The police inquiry, conducted by Louis Rosenberg, the assistant city solicitor, revealed numerous police errors, inaccuracies in the reports submitted to the superintendent, and a general slovenly attitude. The sergeant in charge, for example, testified that he realized that he had given the investigating squad the wrong address, but he was being relieved from duty at the time. In reply to Rosenberg's questioning, he could give no reason for his failure to rectify or report his mistake other than "I don't know" and "I didn't give it a thought." The policy board of inquiry, agreeing that the case had been bungled, recommended that the seven policemen involved in the episode face a hearing on charges of neglect of duty.

Lawrence, not willing to wait for the results of the hearing, removed the velvet gloves with which he had handled the police bureau. On 13, 14, and 16 December, he called in senior officers, beginning at the top with a meeting with Scott, Fairley, the assistant superintendent, Andrew Charles, and eight inspectors. When the meeting concluded, "eleven men with red faces filed from the office." One was heard to remark, "He means business, doesn't he?" "The biggest trouble with the police department is the failure to enforce discipline—handing out cream puff penalties to subordinates who should be fired or suspended," Lawrence said afterward. He delivered the same message at the other two meetings, one with thirty-five lieutenants and one with nearly one hundred precinct sergeants and detectives. Referring to charges of political influence in the department raised several days earlier at a city council meeting by Mrs. R. Templeton Smith, Lawrence told them, "Political influence is out the window. The only measure we will recognize in the future is the ability to do the job."

Once again Lawrence's lectures had minimal effect on police behavior. Reprimands, cajoling, and threats brought only short-term results. Members of the bureau concluded that the mayor was unwilling to carry out his threats. Although seven officers were found guilty of the neglect charges and one was found guilty of incompetence, only one, a sixty-five-year-old officer, was instructed to retire while the others were fined fifty dollars each. None received suspensions or demotions.

It was almost inevitable that Ray Sprigle would follow the grand jury hearing and the inquiry into the Brusco fiasco with an investigation of his own. Sprigle, a tough-talking police reporter, often became news himself because of his Runyonesque appearance and the accuracy of his revelations. An ever present corncob pipe jutting from the corner of his mouth and a Stetson pushed to the back of his head, Sprigle was a recognized figure in Pittsburgh "gaming circles." He built his reputation on a 1926 exposé of racket conditions in various sections of the city and a series in 1931 that helped convict Mayor Kline on illegal contract charges. A third series in 1936 charged that numbers operators paid 60 percent of their gross income in bribes to police and politicians. "You'll take care of the constable of the ward in which your headquarters are. You'll sweeten a couple of deputy constables, too. You'll take care of the alderman. If your writers operate in other wards, you'll take care of the aldermen, constables and deputies there. You'll take care of the police inspectors in every district in which you operate and the lieutenants too—if they're that kind of inspectors—and too often they are. You'll take care of anywhere from one to fifty policemen in the neighborhoods where business is best and you have a crew of writers working. If there are any plainclothesmen on the numbers detail, you'll sweeten them too." At election times, "the operator has to kick in campaign funds, until both you and your roll are dizzy . . . and when you mean campaign funds you mean everyone that might be running from constable to President."[18]

Sprigle's fourth series, entitled "Inside the Rackets," began on 20 February 1950, approximately eighteen months after the grand jury investigation. His reports demonstrated that nothing had changed. "Comparing Pittsburgh's Police Bureau with those in Columbus, Milwaukee, and St. Louis results in a damning indictment of the administration and of law and order in our city. The problem is politics."[19]

Sprigle may have slightly overstated the case, as he often did, but his evidence of a police-politics liaison proved more accurate than the clean bill of health provided by the 1948 grand jury hearing. Of 10 inspectors, the level immediately below the superintendent, only 3 had worked their way up through the ranks. Two held ward chairmanships and received their positions after their districts turned in consistently high majorities for the party; 1 (Maloney) served as district committeeman; others owed their appointments directly to ward chairmen; 1 owed his to the intervention of County Chairman John Kane. Political influence was even more apparent at the detective level, where only 7 of 37 had worked their way up. Former occupations included sidewalk pitchman, prison guard, Pennsylvania Station redcap, boxer, truck driver, barber, and hotel clerk. The last of these was the brother of Inspector Frank Ferris, who was also Twenty-fifth Ward chairman. Detectives were also active in politics, serving as ward chairmen (2), district committeemen (11), constable (4), and alderman (2). A number of beat-level policemen evidently learned that promotions came to those with political ties: 47 of 705 surveyed by Sprigle also served as Democratic committeemen in their home districts.

The crusading reporter then attempted, although with much more speculative "evidence," to tie the police-politics arrangement to the rackets still rampant in the city. "Racket bosses elect and finance aldermen and constables. The ward chairmen then maintain and protect the operation of the racket bosses in their wards through control of the police department and police inspectors." Even the popular "marauder," Maloney, was accused of selecting the site of his raids by political considerations; most of the raids netted only small fry, and few convictions resulted, in spite of the publicity. For all the impressive number of arrests, most pleaded guilty and paid small fines; only half a dozen actually went to jail.

The fourteenth and last article in Sprigle's series placed responsibility for the sorry condition of the police bureau squarely on the mayor's shoulders. "For half a century, politics has always kept a dirty finger in the operation of Pittsburgh's police system," and Lawrence "brought it to a perfection it had never known before." "The absolute political master of his own party," only he could reform and rehabilitate the police system.

Encouraged by the Sprigle series, several church and women's groups and a Shadyside Citizens' Committee demanded action on the still unsolved Brusco case. They echoed the reporter in urging the mayor to take the police department out of politics. The Shadyside group also asked for the resignation of Superintendent Scott.

Pressed by the constant criticism and the growing problems within the bureau, Lawrence was forced to abandon his protection of political policemen. On 20 March 1950 the council, at the mayor's request, passed a measure that prohibited police officers from holding office or participating as campaign managers or directors in elections. Nothing, of course, prevented them from being active behind the scenes. In 1953, for example, eight policemen contributed $350 or more to support the Democratic candidates. A number of others contributed smaller amounts and still more worked on behalf of the organization candidate. A 1972 study of staffing policies revealed that many continued to benefit from political activities and friendships.[20]

While Lawrence had some success in removing politics from the police bureau, events during the next seven years show his inability to gain control over it. Two months after the Sprigle series, a state police raid on a Hill District gambling spot produced a small, brown notebook belonging to Willie "Little Brother" Jones, which contained penciled records of those bribed and the amounts they received. One week's entries ran, in part, "Anabel $45; cops $406; cops $6; cops $2; Lt. $5; No. 2 car $4; Dot $10; Lt. $25." Another entry was "'Pap' $25"; Fifth Ward chairman and magistrate "Pappy" Williams denied that it referred to him. On the same day, Superintendent Scott released results of an ongoing investigation within the department of officers receiving unauthorized sick pay. It involved at least twenty-five members, and preliminary evidence indicated that some had received as much as $800. The offenders were eventually ordered to repay all funds not due them, and several drew suspensions.[21]

The scandalous behavior within the bureau reached its peak on 22 June when Scott appeared at a grand jury hearing intoxicated. Judge Sara Soffel refused to permit him to testify, cited him for contempt of court, and ordered him to reappear the following week in "a state of sobriety." When aides reached Lawrence, who was in Ireland on vacation, he exploded. "I'm tired of these damn problems with the police," he shouted into the phone. "Suspend him. Get him out of there." Lawrence, however, could not bring himself to fire the man who had been a loyal follower. In spite of his obvious inadequacies and the opportunity he presented for a change in the police leadership, Lawrence relented and gave him a second chance: a six-week suspension and an official reprimand. It should be pointed out that Scott had strong backing from the AFL Central Labor Union, a group that Lawrence had been avidly courting since its defection to the Eddie Leonard camp in the previous mayoralty election.[22]

Scott was reinstated on 5 August, but he sealed his fate the following year when he became involved in a brawl with several patrons, the female proprietor, and a policeman in an East Liberty restaurant. Lawrence finally gave the dismissal order. "Scott saved our ass by getting drunk, then brawling in public," said Walter Giesey, the mayor's executive secretary. "We could fire him." Scott's behavior had made it impossible for his political allies, particularly the AFL, to condemn the mayor.[23]

Lawrence now had the opportunity to turn the police bureau away from political appointments, and he lost no time in acting. The following day he announced that career policeman James Slusser, who had served as patrolman, captain, and assistant superintendent, would assume the superintendency. Slusser had not been supported by either ward chairmen or other political leaders in his climb to the top, and his appointment over the heads of police officers with many more years of experience and more political influence was meant to be a sign that the police bureau would now be run differently. His selection was hailed throughout the city. Even Mrs. R. Templeton Smith and the Allegheny County League of Women Voters praised it. "It was the first time she ever said anything nice about anything that happened in the Lawrence administration," Giesey recalled.[24]

The young, energetic Slusser leaped into his new job determined to rid the department of the shadow that had hung over it for so long. He ordered stepped-up raids on rackets of any type, informing the department at a full-dress assembly that inspectors would be "held responsible for their own districts. All known rackets will be closed down." He also warned officers that discipline would be tightened immediately.[25]

The new superintendent soon learned that there were strings attached to the mayor's pledge of a free hand in operating the department. Shortly after he had been sworn in, "a total stranger walked into his office and announced that he was Slusser's new inspector." Slusser threw him out. Later in the day he received a phone call from the mayor demanding an explanation of his rudeness: the stranger had received the appointment through his ward chairman. To avoid internal conflict in the machine, "the mayor backed the ward chairman instead of his superindendent and the man was on the job the next day."[26] Without Lawrence's support, Slusser could not possibly clean up the half-century-old departmental cesspool.

The cancer of rackets and corrupt police continued to plague Lawrence into the final year of his administration and even beyond. In mid 1957 a racket war between rival groups and a series of bombings provided campaign material for the Republican mayoralty candidate, John Drew. Calling upon the mayor and the district attorney to take action to end the "surging racket war" he added, "It is the sworn duty of the mayor to enforce the law and provide the public with reasonable protection. This cannot be done with coverups, politically-dominated police districts and association with known racketeers." Drew's charges were given added weight when it was revealed that three policemen deliberately concealed the identity of racket boss Tony Grosso after he was allegedly roughed up by a rival gang in Market Square. Lawrence intervened and fired all three officers, who had sixty years of combined service, an action that prompted the Fraternal Order of Police to suggest that "the severe punishment was imposed only because this is an election year."[27]

Lawrence received a rude reminder of his inability to control the police force five years later, when his "favorite cop," racket buster

Lawrence Maloney was tried for extorting and accepting bribes amounting to hundreds of thousands of dollars from racketeers in Pittsburgh. The testimony of Clarence Cooper, a twenty-eight-year veteran of the police force, revealed the extent of the police-racket association. "I began collecting money from a number of lottery operations in 1953 for Inspector John Flavin and when Maloney was promoted from inspector to assistant superintendent [he] set up a new plan where I collected for everyone."[28]

Maloney was acquitted at a first trial, in which several convicted racketeers testified for the state, while Lawrence, Slusser, three Court of Common Pleas judges, a State Supreme Court justice, and a state senator attested to Maloney's good character. At a subsequent federal trial for income tax evasion, two kingpins in western Pennsylvania gambling operations gave evidence against him. Tony Grosso, whose empire a state crime commission valued at $12 million per year, testified that Maloney's "business" grossed on average $2500 per week. "Maloney received $1,000 per month for protection, . . . $1,000 at Christmas time and $1,000 when he went on vacation each year." Grosso also testified that he was made to pay $7000 at each election time and another $2500 for police and political officials. Meyer "Slick Man" Sigal, head of Third Ward operations since 1937, indicated the sophisticated nature of Maloney's operation. Sigal paid $1950 for a month with four Mondays and $2150 for one with five. (Monday was traditionally the largest grossing day of the week.) He added another $1000 to Maloney's Christmas fund and $5000 for his yearly vacation, and supplied whiskey by the case for parties. At one point when he was late in paying, one of his stores was raided, and four people were arrested. When he asked why he had "been hit by a four bagger," Maloney told him to search his soul to see if he had done anything wrong. Others who testified that they had made payoffs included such colorful underworld characters as Martin "The Wig" Walkow ($200 per month), Hyman Schwartz ($5200), Walter "Pavo" Crisanti ($150 per week), and Abe "Piggy" Rabinowitz.[29] (Sigal and others also testified to payoffs to other members of the police force and several magistrates.) Maloney again won acquittal by explaining that he had won his extra unearned income at the racetracks. David Craig, appointed safety director by Lawrence's successor, Joe Barr, was not convinced of Maloney's innocence. Immediately after the trial, Craig lifted his suspension, paid him his back pay, and fired him on the grounds that so much time spent at the racetrack constituted conduct unbecoming to an officer. Maloney died of bone cancer a few years later.

Lawrence's problems with the police and rackets in Pittsburgh show a pattern of indecision formed by four decades of ward politics. He had two conflicting goals. On the one hand, he believed he needed the lower echelon of the Democratic party to enable him to remain in office and complete the rebuilding job to which he had committed his administration. On the other, to rid the city of rackets and corruption required a complete overhaul of the system that had swept the Democrats into power. When a reform was eventually effected by Craig in 1967, he "cut the hell out of the patronage system and politics. He literally threw ward chairman out of the police stations and out of the department." Such a reform, Lawrence felt, would endanger the party and the city's Renaissance. It seems clear that, while Lawrence was always aware of the police-politician-racketeer relationship, he subconsciously ignored the magnitude of the corruption. He normally focused on what he termed the "majority of good policemen," dealing with offenders only when they embarrassed or hurt the administration. As late as 1957 he insisted that only a few police officers had ever been involved in corrupt activities.[30]

▽

The problems caused by the police-politician alliance had their counterparts in city service agencies: supplies, lands and buildings, and public works. Public officials, who received their jobs through political efforts or associations, often abused their positions for private financial benefit. As with the police, although it involved only a minority, corruption had existed for nearly a half-century in Pittsburgh. It also required a great deal of the mayor's time, threatened his administration, and had a lasting negative effect.

For half of its length (1949–56), the Lawrence administration remained under the shadow of what became known as the "free work scandal." The incident began with an obscure accident in Butler County, north of Pittsburgh, and mushroomed into a bitter political battle that brought disgrace and prison to some and another scandal to the Lawrence administration. While the details were often obscured by a reenactment of the Lawrence-Margiotti dispute the 1930s, an examination of the scandal demonstrates that political appointees in the Public Works Department were no less susceptible to illegal temptations than those in the police bureau.

On the morning of 26 April 1949, a truck owned by the Allegheny Asphalt and Paving Company was traveling north on Route 8 in Butler County. The truck lost a wheel, causing an accident in which a passenger, Sam Dileisi, a stonemason employed by the city, was killed. The driver, George Manko, also a city employee, sustained multiple injuries but recovered. When questioned by a *Pittsburgh Sun-Telegraph* reporter, he indicated that he and Dileisi had been heading for the summer home of the city council president, Thomas Kilgallen. They also planned to stop at the home of Howard "Buck" Gross, head of the city's skilled laborers.

The issue seemed to disappear in a few weeks, but, one year to the day after the accident, it was announced that Mrs. Dileisi was bringing a $60,000 damage suit against Kilgallen, Gross, Manko, and the Allegheny Asphalt and Paving Company. The company routinely collected more than a million dollars a year from the city in paving contracts, and its owners, Michael and Daniel Parish, were known to be close friends of David Lawrence. The attorney who announced the suit was none other than Charles Margiotti. It is not clear how Mrs. Dileisi managed to retain Margiotti, whose normal clients were high-paying criminal defendants. Margiotti's biographer suggests that Mrs. Dileisi sought him out, but Bloomfield residents who knew Mrs. Dileisi suggest that Margiotti, smelling a political scandal involving the Lawrence administration, offered his services.[31] The lawsuit rekindled the still smoldering fire of antagonism between the mayor and Margiotti.

City officials refused to comment on a case in litigation. The mayor did order Anne Alpern to look into the matter, but she ran into a stone wall when Margiotti refused to permit her to question his client. Almost simultaneously, the city controller, Edward Frey, of the Roberts-McClelland faction of the Democratic party, announced he was conducting his own investigation. Mrs. R. Templeton Smith also announced that she would conduct an "impartial" investigation unless the "governor sends state troopers to Pittsburgh to conduct a thorough investigation." With three investigations and a scheduled jury trial in the offing, the press asked for a full grand jury investigation. Lawrence, caught in a political pincer move, succumbed to the pressure and on 9 June asked the city council to investigate the accusations of "improper use of city labor and/or materials for the improvement of private properties," and other issues raised by "various anonymous and acknowledged statements appearing in the public press."[32] A hearing was set for 13 June.

At the council hearings, Mrs. Dileisi testified that Allegheny Asphalt had paved the private lane leading to the homes of Kilgallen and Gross, that her husband and others worked on the homes on city time, and that city materials were used on the Kilgallen home. Kilgallen and Gross both denied all the charges. The hearing took an unexpected turn when Robert Laun, a payroll clerk in the Department of Lands and Buildings, committed suicide. His wife later told the council that Gross had ordered him to tamper with employees' time cards, but her testimony was declared inadmissible hearsay.

On 30 June the council recommended the firing of Gross and Manko, administered an official reprimand calling Kilgallen honest but indiscreet, and criticized Frey for using bad judgment. Margiotti, Mrs. Smith, and the papers termed the council's final report a whitewash. Two days before the council made the report public, Lawrence, apparently satisfied that the matter was under control, left for Europe with his wife and son Jerry on a planned five-week vacation.

A series of totally unexpected events in the next two weeks caused the mayor's hasty return. Two days after the conclusion of the council hearings, Republican Governor Duff stunned Democrats by announcing Charles J. Margiotti as his new attorney general. The following day, prompted by strong suspicions that Margiotti would begin anew the free work investigation, the Allegheny County district attorney, William Rahauser, petitioned the courts for permission to launch a grand jury investigation. Rahauser's suspicions proved correct when Margiotti announced on 6 July that he intended to supersede the district attorney to conduct his own investigation. The following day he appointed W. Denning Stewart to direct a broad investigation of the Lawrence administration. Rahauser responded that he would not step down unless ordered to do so by the Pennsylvania Supreme Court. Lawrence returned to Pittsburgh and made a prepared statement at a hastily called news conference. As before, when he defended the police department from outside attacks, he viewed the challenge as a threat to his treasured rebuilding program. "It is my duty to see that no political attack will be permitted to tear down this city administration and the enormous program of progress which it is putting into effect. No one is going to do that without the fight of his life, and I hereby serve notice on Charles J. Margiotti and his strange bedfellow James H. Duff, that they are in such a fight—beginning now."[33]

For the next several months the particulars of free work were obscured in the details of the political battle. Brutal attacks and counterattacks by both sides questioned the integrity, honesty, and moral qualities of the opponents. The only lighter moment came when the Italian Sons and Daughters of America inadvertently invited both Lawrence and Margiotti to a Kennywood Park picnic. Lawrence was eating his dinner when a round of applause broke out at the appearance of the Italian attorney general. Lawrence, "at the sight of Margiotti, dropped his knife and fork, arose from the table and . . . in a minute was gone." The press naturally delighted in reporting any such incident and every acerbic comment of the combatants, calling the affair "one of the most poisonous vendettas ever hatched in this state of vicious political slugging." Lawrence was particularly hurt when the papers began to rehash the 1939–40 scandals.[34]

Meanwhile, Rahauser won the first round, in the Court of Common Pleas, when it was ruled that Margiotti had no right to supersede him. Margiotti, as expected, carried the case to the State Supreme Court, where, in a partisan vote of four Republican justices to two Democratic, the lower court decision was overturned. Margiotti was to have a free hand in investigating the Lawrence administration. Judge Sara M. Soffel was selected to preside over a special grand jury.

The hearings began on 16 October and dragged on for fourteen months, investigating both free work and the presence of rackets and vice in Pittsburgh and neighboring towns. An interim presentment of 14 December dealing with free work recommended the indictment of Killgallen, Gross, and Frey for cheating and defrauding the city. It also recommended indictments against the Parishes for bribery and corrupt solicitation. (The special grand jury had no indicting power of its own. It could only recommend indictments to a regular grand jury.) The report noted that a large number of city employees had worked on the Kilgallen and Gross homes, that unaccounted-for city wages amounted to more than $180,000, and that Laun's time book was unquestionably altered. It also charged that the Parishes supplied trucks, asphalt, and labor to Kilgallen "for the purpose of influencing decisions . . . in his official capacity as President of Council in any matters affecting that company [Allegheny Asphalt] . . . which might come before council."[35]

The political nature of the dispute became even more apparent early in 1950 when the twenty Democratic state senators made it clear to the incoming Republican governor, John Fine, that they would not approve any members of his cabinet until they had an opportunity to vote on the retention of Margiotti. The tactic worked perfectly, and Margiotti resigned on 14 February with the magnanimous statement to the governor: "You should not be hindered because I have been made the target of one man's political revenge. If this be the cost of public service, I willingly pay the price but not at your expense."[36] The probe in Pittsburgh would continue, but without continual prodding of the firebrand lawyer. Lawrence had won round two.

During the next several years, developments continued. Gross died before his trial could begin, and Frey was found not guilty. The

Parish brothers won a directed verdict of not guilty when a visiting judge determined that the state had not produced enough evidence to determine that they had bribed Kilgallen. Kilgallen's own trial was postponed several times, and charges were ultimately dropped in 1956. (He had left the political scene in 1951 when the party's executive committee, embarrassed by the scandal, refused to endorse him for reelection.) The special grand jury, meanwhile, recommended many more indictments, including that of Mayor Lawrence for misdemeanor in office on the grounds that the city purchased light bulbs from the Broadway Maintenance Company for $5.65 each. The bulbs cost the company 25¢ each. The presentment also charged that the E. W. Coal Company supplied inferior coal to the city. In an ill-disguised attempt to include the mayor in the charges, the jury noted that "the responsibility for the awarding, performance and payment for these city contracts must be accepted by the mayor. . . . The waste of public funds cannot be excused on the basis of reliance upon subordinates." Lawrence, back in Europe to complete the vacation he had started the previous summer, this time refused to return. "Its ridiculous," he told the press by transatlantic phone. "It's another effort by Stewart to drag me in, in every way he can."[37] The regular grand jury later refused to indict Lawrence but did act positively on the recommended indictments of seven others. Of these only one was convicted, for issuing contracts to the E. W. Coal Company when it was not the lowest bidder.

Other free work scandals surfaced during the remaining years of the Lawrence administration, but it appears that, though some wrongdoing occurred, those directly responsible for the department concerned tried to correct the situation. In three incidents that the administration itself announced in early 1951, the offending workers were all fired or suspended. When informed of the third incident, Lawrence called in Alpern and the public works director, James Devlin, for a dressing down similar to the ones he had given the police force, thundering, "I want this stopped. I want this cleaned up. I don't care who's involved. I don't care what ends you go to." A few days later the *Pittsburgh Press,* not convinced of his sincerity, delivered a ringing editorial entitled "City Hall Ought to Get Hold of Itself." Lawrence responded with a full-page, point-by-point defense of his administration. "there are about 6,000 city employees and of that number of people, you will always find a few who will abuse any privilege." The city had taken steps to correct the abuses, and he promised to "root out and, to the best of my ability, drive out of public life any proved crook or condoner of crookedness." He concluded his statement with a lecture to the press on its responsibilities. "A free society depends upon a free government and free government can rest only on the confidence of the citizens. If the people of this country are to be persuaded, in a wave of hysteria, that all government is corrupt and dishonest, and that all public officials are either fools or knaves, then and only then will we be ready for the dictatorships which the Communists and Fascists are so eager to impose."[38]

The scandals in the Lawrence administration lingered but never reached the same feverish pitch again. One persistent rumor that Lawrence found impossible to shake was that he either partially owned the Allegheny Asphalt and Paving Company or that he received kickbacks from the Parish brothers. The company managed to submit the low bid on every city paving contract from 1945 through 1953; only one other company offered competitive bids. The company became the final target of the 1951 special grand jury, which investigated for several weeks but failed to uncover any evidence of a special connection, other than friendship, between Lawrence and the Parishes. The issue was dropped before Christmas 1951 but reappeared several times during the remainder of Lawrence's administration. The prosecution attempted to raise it in the 1954 Parish trial resulting from the free work incident but was rebuffed by the presiding judge. It also became an issue during the 1957 mayoralty race, and two prominent Republicans spent nearly forty thousand dollars in the early 1960s but uncovered nothing of substance.[39] The rumor persists in Pittsburgh political circles to this day, but friends and associates of Lawrence point to the modest estate that he left when he died as evidence that he never personally benefited from his friendship with the Parishes. No evidence to the contrary has ever surfaced.

The corruption and absence of ethical standards that permeated the police bureau and to a degree the Public Works Department no doubt tarnished the illustrious career of David Lawrence as mayor of the city of Pittsburgh. As undisputed political and governmental leader of western Pennsylvania, he was both able and obligated to rid the city of its unsavory elements. His officials, at his insistence, generally acted swiftly to deal with wrongdoing in the public works and lands and buildings departments when public pressure forced such action. However, in situations where he believed corrective action threatened urban renewal or the unity of the Democratic party, he carried a light stick.

1946–1959

Politics as Usual

David Lawrence's life was filled from morning until night, seven days a week. Urban redevelopment, strike mediation, lobbying for state and national legislation, courting business and professional groups, supporting minority group interests and fighting the brushfires created by the police and other groups—all these commanded his attention. He also attended carefully to the time-consuming obligations of his office: attending fund-raising affairs and ceremonial dinners, cutting ribbons, conducting press conferences, escorting dignitaries, and appearing at social and charitable functions. He almost never said no to such requests. He participated actively in the U.S. Conference of Mayors and twice served as its president. In 1953 he received the conference's award for distinguished public service for his efforts in rebuilding Pittsburgh and his contributions to the conference itself. The only other person so honored by the organization was U.S. Secretary of State George C. Marshall. The breadth of his interests and his boundless physical energy become even more impressive when one recalls that he was plagued with an unrelenting eye ailment that limited his vision, often brought headaches, and required periodic surgery for a detached retina. He was completely immobilized for several weeks, his eyes covered with bandages, following such surgery.

Certainly his family saw little of him during his thirteen years as mayor, but the pattern of absence had been established early. His surviving children, two of whom married shortly after he assumed office, were accustomed to a household without their father. At least when he was mayor, he spent most of his time in the city and usually appeared at home at night or on weekends. His youngest child, Jerry, who was seven when Lawrence became mayor, frequently visited his father at the office, joined him on campaign tours, and accompanied him to sporting events and political rallies. The two probably spent more time together at affairs such as these than they did at home.

Left more and more alone, although the house still contained a bounty of relatives, was his wife, Alyce. The relationship between her and her husband, which never quite recovered from the loss of their sons, remained strained for the rest of their lives. Alyce continued to drink, certainly more than her slightly puritanical husband could tolerate, although she usually maintained control over what today would be called an alcohol dependency. If she drank what Lawrence considered an excessive amount when he was at home, an argument often erupted. Rather than remain in a difficult situation, Lawrence often escaped by calling his ever available friend Frank Ambrose, who would arrive within minutes to find the mayor standing in front of the house holding a small overnight bag. "Take me to the William Penn," he would instruct Ambrose. He would remain there for perhaps twenty-four hours. He thought that walking out was the best way of dealing with the problem.[1] The couple apparently did not discuss their relationship. Mrs. Lawrence accompanied her husband to Harrisburg when he became governor but refused to join him in Washington during the four years that he served on the staffs of Presidents Kennedy and Johnson.

Neither his duties as mayor, his family responsibilities, nor marital difficulties, however, kept Lawrence from engaging in his greatest love, politics. If anything, he became more active in political affairs at the local, state, and national levels than ever before. He retained his interest in the minute details of local politics, prodding, questioning, and encouraging ward chairmen and district committee members at his customary Sunday meetings at party headquarters or at local rallies.

At the county level, he nurtured an occasionally uneasy alliance between himself and a potential rival, County Commissioner John Kane. Lawrence was careful to show deference to him and to avoid any show of power. When Kane insisted on a position on the state Democratic executive committee, Lawrence readily agreed. The commissioner seldom attended any meetings, but Lawrence never suggested that he be replaced. Matters of protocol also became opportunities for Lawrence to demonstrate to Kane that he held him in high regard. For example, they never met in Lawrence's office; when a need for discussion arose, Lawrence always went to Kane's office. In 1950 when Natalie Saxe, advance agent for the Democratic gubernatorial candidate, Richardson Dilworth, arrived in Pittsburgh, Lawrence insisted that she first pay a call on John Kane.[2]

Occasionally the relationship became ludicrous, as when they had difficulty agreeing on who would speak first on the telephone. The matter was resolved when their aides suggested that the one whose secretary placed the call be the first to get on the phone. Largely because of Lawrence's careful behavior, disagreements between the two, often over the choice of a candidate, never resulted in a political break.[3]

Lawrence's interest and influence in statewide politics continued during his mayoralty although he gave up his post as state Democratic chairman. He did not require a state party position to be able to exercise power. With the removal of Senator Joseph Guffey in 1946, Lawrence's control was occasionally challenged but unrivaled until Milton Shapp appeared on the scene in 1966.

At the national level, Lawrence's exhilarating experience as Democratic national committeeman from Pennsylvania in 1944 left him with a hunger for greater involvment. He relished the intrigue and maneuvering, and his ability to deliver delegate votes and to influence the national leadership soon made him the spokesman for the urban political leaders. His influence was felt at each Democratic National Convention from 1944 through 1964.

With rare exceptions, politics in Pittsburgh after 1945 ceased to be a contest between Democrats and Republicans. The domination of the Lawrence-built party was so great that only the races for county district attorney in 1947 and 1951, influenced by the police scandals, presented any challenge at all to the Democrats. Year after year the Republican candidates for local office presented themselves for the biennial November sacrifice. The majorities of the Democratic candidates grew larger with each election until the GOP found itself in the position of its political opponents thirty years earlier—finding willing candidates became more and more difficult. Newspapers, radio, television, and even former political allies made the situation more difficult for the GOP by calling for the reelection of Democrats. At each election after 1945 (when the *Post-Gazette* endorsed Republican Robert Waddell), all three city newspapers supported Lawrence. They regularly called for the election of a Democratic council, although each occasionally endorsed a lone Republican candidate while expressing concern over "the trend toward a one-party system." The AFL Central Labor Union, which supported Eddie Leonard in 1949, joined in the rush to support Lawrence thereafter, as did numerous professional and business groups. The Democratic party outspent the

Republicans by $75,000 or more in the 1949, 1953 and 1957 mayoralty campaigns, an indication of its new strength. Lawrence thoroughly enjoyed the dilemma of his Republican opponents. "It is laughable to read that the GOP doesn't have the cash for this campaign. I have prayed for that all my life."[4]

Perhaps most difficult for the Republican party to accept was the seeming desertion of the Mellon interests, along with that of many prominent members of the Allegheny Conference on Community Development. Richard King Mellon's 1953 statement praising Lawrence produced shock waves among local Republicans. One can only speculate on the number of votes Lawrence received as a result, but he easily defeated his opponent, Leonard Kane, whose only claim to fame was that his brother J. M. Kane was Republican county treasurer. Running in the aftermath of the police and political scandals, Lawrence overwhelmed his opponent by almost 55,000 votes, winning thirty of the thirty-two wards. His Democratic running mates won every other contested race, including four judgeships on the Court of Common Pleas, giving the party a majority there for the first time in the city's history.

Four years later, at the annual dinner of the Allegheny Conference, Mellon, as if to underscore his support, insisted that Lawrence have his picture taken with him, Adolph Schmidt, and other corporate leaders. Speakers at the dinner praised Lawrence for his role in rebuilding the city. Arthur Van Buskirk, executive secretary of T. Mellon and Sons, added his voice when he announced a short time later that he endorsed Lawrence for a "fourth term in office to finish the Pittsburgh program." Prominent Republicans were becoming the mayor's most influential political allies. *Fortune* and *Time* added to the Republican party's woes when they published election-eve issues naming Lawrence as one of the nation's outstanding municipal managers.[5] Former Common Pleas Judge John Drew, who agreed to run against Lawrence after five others declined, suffered the largest defeat of all Lawrence opponents, in spite of offering his own seven-point program of reform. "Mr. Pittsburgh," as two newspapers began to label him, won by nearly 60,000 votes, again sweeping all but two wards.

As is characteristic of cities in which one party dominates, the challenges Lawrence faced came from within his own party, and it was opposition that he found almost impossible to tolerate. He branded renegades as disloyal and disruptive opportunists, and, when he could, he purged them from the party ranks.

One of the first to go was John Huston, whom Lawrence had supported for city council in 1933 following his conversion to the Democratic cause. He received the party's endorsement for register of wills in three successive elections. Huston showed that his ambition exceeded his commitment to his new party when in 1941 he tried to win the nomination for mayor over the party's endorsement of Cornelius Scully for reelection. Following a primary defeat, he rejoined the organization on the eve of the general election to claim a share of the credit for Scully's close victory. He was rewarded two years later when the executive committee endorsed him for reelection to the register's position. But Huston was not content. He openly campaigned for the committee's support for mayor in 1945, and when it turned to Lawrence, Huston went on the attack. His campaign, charging the party's choice with a variety of evils and moral indiscretions, was the most brutal Lawrence ever faced. Lawrence, nevertheless, easily won the Democratic nomination, and this time the door was closed on any attempted return by Huston. Stranded, he announced his return to the GOP in September 1945 and resumed his invective against Lawrence, this time on behalf of the Republican candidate, Waddell.

Lawrence's public stance toward Huston was an almost stoic silence, but privately he let party leaders know that he must be eliminated at the next opportunity—the 1947 election. Huston, in spite of his return to the GOP, boldly sought the Democratic endorsement for a fourth term as register of wills two years later, thus presenting Lawrence with the perfect opportunity to discipline him and set an example for other would-be independents. The executive committee unanimously rejected Huston's bid. When he refused to accept the decision, registered Democrats handed him a stunning defeat in the primary, bringing a quick end to his political career and ridding Lawrence of one of the most troublesome elements in the party.

Another minor political figure became, as Lawrence put it, too ambitious for his own good. Joe McArdle, the son of longtime City Councilman P. J. McArdle, won reelection to the city council in 1945, the year of Lawrence's first election. With a reservoir of popularity built by his father, he led the ticket that year, with five hundred more votes than the newly elected mayor. McArdle proved to be a cooperative member of the Lawrence team for the first half of his term, attending the Monday morning caucuses and regularly voting with the other members of the council for legislation requested by Lawrence. His willingness to support the Lawrence program resulted from an arrangement he negotiated with the council president, Thomas Kilgallen, whereby, in return, McArdle was allowed to name a police inspector.[6] The break between Lawrence and McArdle occurred when Lawrence fired Inspector John Dean after his indictment by the grand jury in 1948. McArdle responded swiftly with an angry statement before a startled city council, charging the mayor with "inexcusable dereliction of duty and gross incompetence in his direction of law enforcement by the city police." Lawrence refused to comment but angered the councilman further several weeks later by passing over his choice for Dean's replacement.[7]

McArdle, with no options available, responded like a spoiled child. He announced that henceforth he would join Councilman Eddie Leonard in boycotting the "mayor's private Monday sessions," and he opposed virtually every Lawrence-supported piece of legislation to come before the council in the next ten months. Lawrence, refusing to become embroiled in a public controversy, remained silent, as he had in dealing with Huston. A debate, of course, was unnecessary since the organization had a strong majority on the council. He saved his only comment until the nominating session of the executive committee in July 1949. This was one of the few times when Lawrence did not wait for a consensus to develop: he expressed his determination to have McArdle dropped from the party ticket. McArdle used the afternoon council session as a forum for his angry response, calling Lawrence "the Stalin of Pittsburgh." He was in the campaign to stay, he said.[8] It was a battle he could not win without party support. McArdle suffered a resounding defeat in the primary and campaigned for the Republican mayoralty candidate in the fall election. Two years later McArdle moved to the party his father had deserted in 1933. In return for his support for the Republican gubernatorial candidate, John Fine, he received a minor post in Pittsburgh under the auspices of the state insurance commissioner.

Lawrence demonstrated the depth of his animosity toward McArdle when, several years later, he arranged to have him fired immediately following the election of Democratic Governor George Leader. He also revealed a mild pettiness, by refusing to call the access to Pittsburgh's Mt. Washington by its proper name—McArdle Roadway, "just as when he became governor, the Harvey Taylor Bridge [named after the Republican state chairman] was the Forrester Street Bridge."[9]

Lawrence reacted swiftly against Huston and McArdle, who had proved irritating but were never political threats to him personally or to the party. He could purge both with relatively little trouble. His treatment of three other dissenters, however, indicates that, as usual, the health of the party remained his paramount objective.

In Eddie Leonard's serious challenge in the Democratic primary in 1949, for example, his labor support gave him a leverage that neither Huston nor McArdle had. It was clear that his permanent separation from the party could cause serious damage. Thus, the ever pragmatic Lawrence not only agreed to permit Leonard's return to the party but openly courted him.

Lawrence again ignored opposition within the party several years later in his relationships with David B. Roberts, the powerful Fifth Ward chairman and prothonotary, and his ally, William McClelland, the county coroner. The crude Roberts had little education, whereas McClelland was well educated and polished. But in other ways they had much in common. Neither was a party man. Both were former Republicans in the Pinchot administration, and both joined the rush to the Democratic party in the mid 1930s. Roberts demonstrated his importance to the party by consistently delivering substantial majorities from his district. In return he received numerous patronage positions, which he used to increase his control of the ward. McClelland, whom Lawrence had appointed in return for his early support of the Democratic party, nearly always sided with Roberts, usually in opposition to Lawrence. Both announced their intention to run for mayor in 1945 but dropped out when Lawrence secured the nomination. The three men disagreed occasionally over the next several years but remained cordial and mutually supportive, although the fastidious Lawrence developed a mild personal dislike for the grossly overweight, unkempt Roberts.

The break occurred over two events that took place in late 1953. The first dispute centered on the question of filling a mid-term city council vacancy. Under some pressure from the black Civic Unity Council to demonstrate his support for black candidates, Lawrence supported F. Paul Jones, a highly able attorney who had been Lawrence's protégé since the early days of the Roosevelt administration. Lawrence considered him a highly capable team player. A resident of the Fifth Ward, he had, however, spent little time in the rapidly growing black ghetto.

David Roberts and the Fifth Ward Democratic committee had another candidate in mind: Robert "Pappy" Williams, who had worked his way up through the party ranks, serving as block worker and district committeeman before replacing Roberts as Fifth Ward chairman. Almost as if to demonstrate that he could play power politics in the same league with Lawrence, Roberts called for a vote of the ward committeemen on their choice for city council—Jones or Williams. The following day, a triumphant Roberts announced the committee's 42 to 0 vote supporting Williams to the press declaring, "The committee people are the ones who work to get out the vote when party candidates run. We should be consulted when anyone from our ward is up for a job."[10]

Lawrence, who always maintained tight control over the party endorsement process, immediately rejected the prothonotary's argument. Ward committeemen, and even chairmen, were expected to work for the party in return for patronage appointments and other small perks. They had no say in leadership matters. Furthermore, Lawrence was beginning to dislike and mistrust Roberts. Rejection of Williams would demonstrate to Roberts the source of real power within the party. He might command the loyalty of the Fifth Ward, but Lawrence's power spread across the whole city. The mayor's choice, Jones, was appointed by an obedient city council to fill the vacant seat early in 1954.

Lawrence became embroiled in a second battle with Roberts and McClelland in the midst of the controversy over the council vacancy. In mid December they attacked the mayor's proposed wage tax and, as opposition to it mounted, they stepped up their campaign. Lawrence ignored them throughout the tax battle, presenting instead arguments on the necessity of the levy, which he continually characterized as "personally distasteful to me." He waited until his moment of victory, the signing of the bill, to vent his anger at what he began to call the "Roberts-McClelland faction." In a prepared statement handed out to reporters—Lawrence refused to sign the tax bill in public—he attacked the two men without naming them. "It is significant that in all the controversy over the earned income tax . . . the criticism . . . has been most vociferous from those whose offices are so minor in nature that they have never faced the responsibility of raising money—although they have been very successful throughout their lives in drawing a pay envelope from the public funds. . . . The politician with no sense of responsibility is the worst enemy of Democratic government."[11]

The three men continued a seesaw battle for the next four years. When Lawrence blocked McClelland's gubernatorial nomination bid in 1954, the coroner refused to bow out. In the primary, McClelland nearly defeated George Leader, losing statewide by only 65,000 votes. Most embarrassing to Lawrence was the coronor's upset of the Democratic organization in all but two western Pennsylvania counties, including Allegheny, and in the city of Pittsburgh. Lawrence attributed the unprecedented defeat to a backlash against the wage tax and never forgave Roberts and McClelland. They opposed almost everything Lawrence did, and the arguments grew most heated at party executive meetings, which McClelland and Roberts attended by virtue of their positions as elected row officers.[12]

The two malcontents earned Lawrence's enmity, but they apparently understood that they were on safe ground. Each carried his own constituency, which Lawrence believed was necessary to the continued success of the Democratic party. Moreover, it was always possible that, in the event of an open break, County Commissioner John Kane would join their side. Lawrence, they knew, would strike a compromise. The battle over slating Joe Dobbs to replace McClelland as coroner when the latter became county commissioner reveals the lengths Lawrence would go to avoid the intraparty fight. "Joe Dobbs," Fenrich noted, "was McClelland's right hand man. . . . the newspapers were saying we ought to have someone with a background in medicine, medical examiner . . . and Lawrence pleaded with McClelland. 'They're going to beat us. You're going to lose that damned office. Pick anybody, but get a guy with a background. We'll put Joe Dobbs somewhere else.' But they insisted. Lawrence said, 'Allright, but God damn it mark my words. I'll work for him. I'll raise money, I'll contribute everything else a hundred percent, but we're going to lose that office.' And sure enough we did."[13]

Party regulars, upset over the frequency of their opposition, urged Lawrence to dump Roberts and McClelland, but he steadfastly refused. Overestimating their strength and their potential for damage to the party, he was content to give them an occasional reminder that he remained the major source of power in the party. In 1958, for example, the party executive committee denied endorsement for renomination to two protégés of the Roberts-McClelland faction, State Representatives Daniel Verona and Matt "the Rock" Anderson, and slated attorneys K. Leroy Irvis and James F. Clark in their place. In what was acknowledged by both sides as a test of power, Irvis and Clark won easy victories, which gave Lawrence a considerable measure of satisfaction. Roberts and McClelland, however, were secure as long as Lawrence ran the organization. He would not endanger its well-being by becoming embroiled in an open struggle for power. Their dependency on the man they fought so consistently and his overestimation of their power became apparent when, one year after Lawrence's death, the executive committee refused to endorse either for reelection. Both were defeated in the subsequent election.[14]

▽

The inability of the Democratic party to dominate the state as it did western Pennsylvania, rather than diminishing Lawrence's interest in statewide politics, added spice to the challenge. Though he gave up his post as state chairman shortly after becoming national committeeman, he remained the major power on the party's policy committee, which continued to be dominated by western Pennsylvania political leaders. The eastern leaders recognized Lawrence's control.[15]

With seemingly full control of the western Pennsylvania electorate, Lawrence launched a new election strategy in an attempt to gain control of the state from the Republicans. Beginning in 1950, he consistently encouraged the nomination of candidates from the eastern part of the state. An attractive Philadelphian or other easterner at the head of the ticket, he surmised, was necessary to capture the eastern independent vote. Western Pennsylvanians could be counted upon to return a substantial Democratic majority regardless of the residence of the candidate.

Michael Musmanno, the Communist-hunting judge from Pittsburgh, nearly upset Lawrence's strategy when he announced early in 1950 that he intended to seek the Democratic nomination for governor. Labor and ethnic leaders, who traditionally supported him, flocked to his side. Pittsburgh's popular "labor priest," Charles Owen Rice, urged local and state leaders to endorse Musmanno, as did twenty-one borough, township, and ward leaders from Allegheny County. Lawrence, however, would not be pressured. Musmanno had proved several times before that he could not be counted upon to follow the wishes of the party, and, being from western Pennsylvania, he was unlikely to draw the necessary eastern votes to bring a victory. The state policy committee decided to support the recently victorious Philadelphia city treasurer, Richardson Dilworth.

Dilworth, along with Joe Clark, had upset the Philadelphia Republican regime for the first time in the century and was probably Lawrence's best choice in his entire career. A Yale-educated millionaire, Dilworth had won medals in both world wars, was an outstanding lawyer, and gained a reputation as a reformer by his unrelenting attacks against a corrupt city organization. He was once described by a Republican writer as "charming, generous, unstable, not remarkably scrupulous, brave, ambitious, fond of high living, eager to make a splash, and fundamentally innocent."[16] He was considered by supporters and many detractors to be a dedicated public servant.

In his attempt to maintain party unity and strengthen the Dilworth candidacy among Philadelphia'a large Italian-American population, Lawrence prevailed upon Musmanno to run for lieutenant governor. Dilworth expressed serious concern, but Lawrence, acting as intermediary between the two unlikely running mates, persuaded him to put aside his reservations. Musmanno, he assured Dilworth, pledged to avoid "lone wolf" campaigning and to accept his speaking assignments from the Democratic State Committee.

It was an agreement doomed to failure from its inception. Musmanno, about to launch his anti-Communist crusade in Pittsburgh, could not be held back. He outcampaigned the more restrained Dilworth, but, in the eyes of the press and many of his would-be supporters, he frequently overstepped the bounds of common decency. "The shrill, sometimes demagogic pronouncements also called attention to his own abuses and pointed up Musmanno's ambivalent stands on law and order as opposed to the right to dissent." By the end of September, Musmanno and Dilworth were conducting independent campaigns whose pronouncements often contradicted each other. Lawrence, when his attempts to corral Musmanno proved futile—the feisty candidate spoke when and where he wanted—turned his attention and energies toward the Dilworth cause. He spoke frequently all over the state on his behalf, often suggesting that what he himself had done for Pittsburgh, Dilworth would do for the state. He also gave Saxe and other members of the Dilworth staff a quick education in campaign politics.[17]

Once again, Lawrence's statewide efforts ended in failure, although the strategy appears to have been successful. The Democratic candidates carried Philadelphia and Pittsburgh, and Musmanno's name on the ticket drew large majorities in the Italian sections of both cities. Musmanno led the ticket in Allegheny County. Their success, however, was not enough to overcome the large majority that their Republican opponents piled up in the rural counties. The well-known liberal views of Dilworth, several campaign errors, and the conservative trend sweeping the country were enough to bring about a close 80,000-vote defeat. Lawrence was far from discouraged.

When the Democratic policy committee met in Harrisburg in the fall of 1953, the Philadelphia and Pittsburgh newspapers speculated that the party heads were laying strategy for Richardson Dilworth's second gubernatorial attempt. Musmanno had been effectively shunted aside by his successful run for the State Supreme Court the previous year, and former U.S. Senator Francis Myers, practicing law in Washington, D.C., had no interest in the office. Lawrence ended speculation that he himself would join the race by stating firmly that under no circumstances would he be a candidate, for he still had work to do in Pittsburgh.[18] He appeared ready to give his support to a second try by Dilworth, now Philadelphia district attorney. With no other candidates on the horizon, the time seemed ripe for a united effort to place a Democratic administration in Harrisburg. The Republican administration of Governor Fine cooperated by passing an unpopular tax package.

Events in Philadelphia and Pittsburgh, however, dramatically changed the scene and caused Lawrence to intervene at the last moment to exert his influence. In Philadelphia a dispute over the removal of patronage from municipal government threatened to create a split in the party that would certainly hinder Dilworth's chances of carrying the state in 1954. In Pittsburgh, meanwhile, Lawrence's wage tax had undoubtedly removed some of the bite of the planned Democratic attack against the Fine administration's state levy. It prompted the candidacy of William McClelland, who was immediately supported by Roberts. With the announcement by a Philadelphia ward chairmen's group that it backed McClelland, who already had considerable support in western Pennsylvania, Lawrence was faced with the unthinkable possibility that a McClelland steamroller might seize control of the policy committee. Lawrence's control was threatened, not only at the state level but in his home territory as well.

Drastic action was necessary to prevent the two factions from ripping each other apart to the advantage of the Republicans. As delegates began arriving in Harrisburg for the scheduled policy committee meeting, they learned that it had been postponed for one week. State Committee Secretary Genevieve Blatt explained to them that "the session was postponed because several members could not attend," and the wires sent to members the day before had apparently failed to reach them in time. A number of angry delegates, mostly McClelland supporters, charged that the real reason was to provide Dilworth additional time to solve his Philadelphia problems. Blatt later admitted the validity of the charges.[19]

Lawrence's trip to Philadelphia the following day gave credence to the accusations. In a last attempt at negotiating a truce, he met behind closed doors with the principals of the dispute and other leading Democrats. But his attempt was unsuccessful, and three days later Dilworth, thinking he had little chance to win, withdrew his candidacy.[20] Following the overwhelming Eisenhower victory in 1952, it appeared to him to be a Republican year.

Lawrence's worst fears had come true. The postponed policy committee meeting was due in three days with only McClelland in the race. The nomination, the newspapers speculated, might go to him by default. Several names had surfaced over the weekend, but none was considered a serious challenger. The possible alternatives included former Lieutenant Governor Thomas Kennedy, whom Lawrence had rejected in 1938 partially because of his long-standing conviction that a Catholic candidate could not win. Nothing had changed, in Lawrence's mind, to make Kennedy more acceptable to the voters in 1954. Colonel John Rice of Gettysburg, the unsuccessful candidate for governor in 1946, was also suggested, but he declined to run, though indicating that he "might accept a draft." Of all the candidates mentioned, only the name of first-term State Senator George Leader of York County generated any interest. Oftentimes characterized disparagingly as a chicken farmer—the family did own a chicken ranch—Leader's father had been a three-term state senator. The younger Leader became county Democratic chairman in 1948 and was elected to the State Senate in 1950. Two years later, at the age of thirty-five, he ran well ahead of the national presidential candidate, Adlai Stevenson, in a losing cause for the position of state treasurer. Young and charming in a boyish way, the articulate Leader might be an ideal candidate in a race that many Democrats felt was lost anyway. A solid run, even if unsuccessful, would give the energetic candidate additional valuable exposure.

Contrary to popular belief, the nomination of Leader as gubernatorial candidate on 27 February surprised neither Leader nor the party heads. It was a textbook example of behind-the-scenes political maneuvering that often characterizes American politics. Lawrence, playing coy, expressed reservations about Leader's age but agreed to give him serious consideration, not letting on that he had already made inquiries about him. "What Dave wanted to see was what I could go out and scratch up for myself. Then if I was an acceptable candidate, I would be his candidate. . . . I worked very long and hard . . . on the telephone and personally, and had some help from Andrew Bradley and others. . . . I must have had two-thirds of the votes." On the morning of the policy committee meeting, Lawrence summoned Leader to his hotel suite, and when he was satisfied that Leader had the necessary support, "he said, 'Yes, you're the person'."[21]

The meeting of the policy committee proved anticlimactic: Leader received unanimous endorsement. Lawrence demonstrated his power by preventing McClelland's name from being entered in nomination. Of course, he could not prevent him from running his own independent campaign in the primary. McClelland carried western Pennsylvania but was soundly defeated in the rest of the state. In Philadelphia County, Leader had a substantial majority that enabled him to carry the state by approximately sixty thousand votes. Attempts by Lawrence during the primary to get McClelland to withdraw from the race proved futile.

The Republicans, who countered the Leader nomination with the selection of Lieutenant Governor Leonard Wood, began the campaign with a 900,000-vote advantage in registration and a state payroll of 60,000 workers. They also had substantially more money. The Democratic State Committee had raised only $60,000 for its entire state primary campaign. Reverse sides of the same issue were espoused during the campaign, the Republicans charging that the Democrats would enact a state wage tax as soon as they took office, and Democrats attacking Governor Fine's sales tax as unjust and hinting that it might be unconstitutional. Leader made a pledge he would later regret: that he would do everything in his power to repeal the tax.

Dilworth was not the only politician who misjudged the political climate in 1954. The Eisenhower victory in 1952, as many analysts have since pointed out, was one of personality rather than party and proved to be a misleading indicator of the political sympathies of the electorate. Democrats captured eight governorships formerly held by their opponents and held all ten that they had formerly controlled. Key victories occurred in New York, Minnesota, and Pennsylvania, where Leader won a 300,000-vote victory. The Pennsylvania outcome represented a 600,000-vote turnaround since Eisenhower's victory. Leader's majority in Lawrence's home county, which had supported McClelland in the spring, was 87,000; in Pittsburgh, 58,000; in Philadelphia, 121,000. The shift from Republican to Democratic spread throughout the state as twenty-seven counties switched; the Democrats retained nine and the Republicans thirty-one. The Republican counties, however, included the eight sparsely populated ones along the state's northern border (82,000 votes), and seven in the bible belt in the center of the state (fewer than 200,000 votes). The Democrats also gained control of the State House for the first time in a decade and were only one senator short of a majority in the upper house as well. The organization had pulled off its biggest upset since the Earle victory in 1934.[22]

Lawrence could barely contain himself on the morning following the victory. He called the Democratic sweep "the greatest victory for the state of Pennsylvania since the early days of the Roosevelt years." Referring to the Little New Deal, much of which was repealed by subsequent Republican administrations, he predicted, "We will finally complete the job we began under the Earle administration." By speaking in the plural, the mayor gave a clue that the Leader administration was to be a team organization. He did not intend to send his candidate to Harrisburg without help. He persuaded James Finnigan, a Democratic power in Philadelphia, to accept the post of secretary of the Commonwealth. He also arranged to have his close political ally Joe Barr elected Democratic state chairman to play the role of unofficial whip that he himself had played so well two decades earlier. *Post-Gazette* political writer John Jones credited Lawrence with helping "to create and shape the twenty odd member 'brain trust' of professional and business experts that will strive to keep Pennsylvania at the top of America's list of favored states."[40] Leader credited Lawrence with suggesting a number of "outstanding appointments," but not all were made with only administrative expertise in mind—ethnic background and geographical representation were also taken into account.[23]

Lawrence willingly sent a number of "his people" to Harrisburg to participate in the Leader administration, but when he was offered the post of secretary of commerce, he adamantly refused again, arguing that he was needed in Pittsburgh.[24] Unspoken, of course, was the memory of his earlier unpleasant experience in the state capital. A number of reporters speculated that Lawrence might view the offer as a vindication, but he was enjoying too great a sense of fulfillment as mayor and Democratic power broker to return to the site of his earlier torment. He instead prevailed upon his long-term associate and right hand, John Robin, to take the post in his place.

Lawrence's refusal of a cabinet post, of course, did not mean that he intended to play no role in the Leader administration. As he had done so many times before, he operated from behind the scenes to influence the legislature to support the Democratic program, going to Harrisburg and lecturing the Democratic caucus when necessary.[25] Lawrence was determined that the first Democratic state administration since the Depression would succeed in enacting an impressive program, but he was careful to avoid the boss image. Democratic House and Senate leaders viewed his guidance as firm but never authoritarian, and George Leader willingly accepted his active role in the administration. "On a few occasions we had some real differences as you would expect and Dave pushed pretty hard, and I pushed back pretty hard."[26]

It was indeed the "pushing back and forth" that intrigued Lawrence. He loved the challenge of building a successful coalition, seeking compromise, and reaching an objective. To him it was the essence of politics, and he never apologized for being a politician. One could not succeed in state and local government without being a good politician. Even the weddings of his daughters became political events. When his oldest daughter, Anna Mae, married in 1946, the family attempted to keep the wedding "small" by cutting the guest list to around five hundred. The practical Lawrence approved of the moderation, but the politician in him could not bear "to make five hundred or so people mad," so he declared, "Everybody's invited." A crowd of more than one thousand attended church services. Two years later Mary Alice's wedding was arranged for 10:00 A.M. on Thanksgiving Day. Almost simultaneously John Kane's daughter Rita's wedding invitations were sent out for precisely the same hour on the same day. Local politicians would have to decide which to attend. The mayor averted a political crisis by announcing "The time of my daughter's wedding will be moved back an hour and a half in order that everyone who wishes to attend both ceremonies can be present and have plenty of time to get to the East End in time to attend Mary Alice's marriage."[27] Once again Lawrence's willingness to compromise resolved the dilemma.

▽

By the middle of his first term of office as mayor, Lawrence had gained a wide reputation for his ability to mediate seemingly intractable disputes. Labor-management relations, intraparty battles, and public-private sector differences were all influenced by his deft touch. His reputation as a power broker on the national scene, however, was just beginning to grow. He had played minor roles at several Democratic National Conventions and was a major factor in the nomination of Harry Truman for vice-president in 1944. As his stature grew with each political victory and each success in urban redevelopment, he began to assume the role of spokesman for the influential group of big-city mayors. His advice, assistance, and support were sought at each national convention by presidential and vice-presidential hopefuls.

Although no one could know it at the time, the quick action of Lawrence, Robert Hannegan, the national chairman, and a few others in stalling the renomination of Henry Wallace for vice-president in 1944 catapulted Harry Truman into the chief executive's office within ten months. It also earned Pittsburgh's mayor the lasting gratitude of the president. The two politicians corresponded frequently, exchanging congratulations on political victories and holiday and birthday wishes, and meeting occasionally to exchange views on political matters, especially as they related to Pennsylvania. Truman acknowledged a gift of Clark's Teaberry Chewing Gum, produced in

Pittsburgh, by assuring Lawrence that it would be "used in the proper way for the benefit of the country."[28] While theirs could not yet be considered a close relationship, the two men were growing quite fond of each other. Lawrence further endeared himself to Truman when he stepped in to prevent a professional embarrassment to the president's daughter Margaret as she was embarking on her concert career. Lawrence discovered that a May 1947 concert date in Pittsburgh had "no advance sale worth talking about. The thing had all the earmarks of a boomerang." Drawing on funds from the party treasury, he purchased one thousand tickets and had them distributed to public and parochial school students. He also issued instructions to party workers throughout the city to attend the concert. The standing room only crowd, although musically unsophisticated, treated the star to an evening of wild enthusiasm. "We put on a real concert and it was a howling success," Lawrence recalled proudly. "I remember how grateful he [Truman] was to me when I came in [to Washington] and he said a thing that's always stuck with me. . . . Here he was in the Office of the President, he said, 'You know Dave, she's all I got. I'll never forget you.'"[29]

Lawrence's respect for Truman grew during the president's first term in office. "It was interesting to watch the evolution as he got into office. . . . First he was timid and approaching it slowly, realizing whatever inadequacies he might have had. You could just see him picking up the threads that Roosevelt had left down. In the course of about a year or so he was in absolute command of the situation, of himself, and of the various governmental agencies."[30]

Firmly committed to Truman, Lawrence traveled to the Democratic National Convention in Philadelphia determined to fight any efforts to dump him in favor of Dwight Eisenhower, currently the favorite among many Southern Democrats, or any other challenger. Early in March 1948, he had attacked the threat of the Southern coalition to "defeat the President's bid for a nomination or to leave the party." "This country has no place for a reactionary Democratic party," he told party workers at several Jefferson-Jackson Day dinners. "This party must remain a liberal party or lose its position of leadership. The President hasn't advocated anything in his civil rights stand that Thomas Jefferson didn't stand for—and he was a Southerner. So was Andrew Jackson and he stood for the same things and he was a Southerner. Woodrow Wilson was from Virginia and he advocated the same program. . . . I don't know why the Southern political leaders are against Truman for advocating the same thing. President Truman deserves our gratitude, our loyalty, our help for his civil rights program."[31] The president, in Lawrence's view, deserved the renomination on merit. Furthermore, to nominate anyone else would violate Lawrence's long-held policy of supporting the incumbent.

The convention itself illustrated Lawrence's role as a national leader in a party that appeared to some political observers to be operating without a leader. Genevieve Blatt called it the "most depressing convention we ever entered. It seemed like we were just going through the motions." Pittsburgh's mayor, delivering the welcoming address, tried to ignite the delegates by delivering a stinging attack on the Eightieth Congress and Pennsylvania Republican boss Joseph Grundy, president of the politically powerful Pennsylvania Manufacturers' Association. Lawrence, the compromiser and frequent fence-sitter, then announced the strength of his support of Truman. "The party must continue to make clear the contrast between Republicans and Democrats as I believe President Truman has made it clear in his courageous showdown with the Republican Eightieth Congress."[32] Lawrence's address failed to produce enthusiasm among the delegates, described by the press as inattentive, but it signaled that the state he represented was prepared to deliver its seventy-four delegate votes to Truman. Working behind the scenes, he met several times with a number of city bosses, including Jacob Arvey of Chicago, Carmine Di Sapio of New York, and Frank Hague of Jersey City. One by one they all joined in support of Truman.

Lawrence, as well as countless other political observers, gave credit to Senator Alben Barkley of Kentucky for delivering the knockout blow to any potential challengers to Truman's renomination. Barkley electrified the crowd with a one-and-a-half-hour address denouncing the Republican Congress and praising the president, which was followed by a quick nomination of Truman on the first ballot. The Missouri Democrat arrived, to wild cheering, at approximately 2:30 A.M.

A more objective analysis of the proceedings, however, suggests that the party professionals had decided to accept Truman well before Barkley generated the first real enthusiasm of the week-long convention. Eisenhower had firmly stated that he was not a candidate for nomination by either party, and only his strongest supporters gave serious consideration to a draft movement. The Southern Democrats, angered over the civil rights issue, could come up with no alternative who would attract majority support, In reality, the president had no opposition although many who supported him expressed grave reservations. Even Lawrence later admitted that he was disturbed because he did not think Truman was going to win.[33]

Speculation about the vice-presidential choice began immediately after Truman's triumphant entry into the convention hall early on Thursday morning, but the question had apparently been settled days before. John Jones of the *Post-Gazette* related the events.

> It was on the Sunday night before the convention opened. I got a tip from a fella in the Bellevue Stratford. He said, "You're missing a story. . . . You go down to the Warrick Hotel and you wait there. In about a half an hour, forty-five minutes you're going to see the god damndest assembly of Democratic bosses you ever saw get off that elevator."
>
> So I took his advice, . . . and sure enough there was Bill Malone of San Francisco. There was Arvey from Illinois. There was Frank Hague from Jersey City; somebody from St. Louis, somebody from Boston and Lawrence. I asked him [Lawrence] when he got off the elevator, what he was doing there. . . . And he told me the whole story. He said, "We are going for Barkley for vice-president." I replied, "I don't know if the President is going to buy it or not." "We are sending a delegation down tomorrow to put it before him," he responded. "Some people outside our circle would like to see a fella like [Supreme Court Justice William O.] Douglas. But I don't think the President wants Douglas and I don't think Douglas wants the job because he doesn't consider Truman liberal enough."[34]

Lawrence and Arvey met with Truman the next day and convinced him that Barkley's support among Southern and border state Democrats made him the best choice. Another contender, Senator Joseph O'Mahoney of Wyoming, remained popular in the Midwest but could do little to aid the ticket in the South. Truman readily agreed and let it be known that he preferred Barkley to the other candidates. The Kentucky senator won nomination on the first ballot.

The crucial battle of the Democratic Convention of 1948, however, focused on neither the presidential nor vice-presidential nominations but upon two alternative civil rights platform issues. Lawrence was in the midst of the fight throughout the convention. He made known his position favoring a strong civil rights plank before the convention when he joined James Roosevelt, Mayor Hubert Humphrey of Minneapolis, and Jacob Arvey in urging its adoption. When asked if his position meant that he had given up on an attempt to pacify the South on the civil rights program, he snapped, "It's not a question of pacification. It's a matter of principle." Two weeks later, along with Truman and Humphrey, he made clear his willingness to support his principles when he rejected a weakened civil rights provision. He issued a simple but firm order to his state's delegates. "Be in your seats at today's session especially when the platform is presented. Many things in that platform will be important to us in Pennsylvania, such as what the platform says about civil rights, the Taft-Hartley Labor law and Palestine; The Palestine question will be particularly important in our large centers where there is a big Jewish vote. And some southerner might want to poll the delegation so you'd better be there to answer."[35] When Lawrence returned home after the convention, he informed the press that it was the most satisfying of the nine he had attended. He obviously enjoyed his position in the center of the political storm.

It was at the 1952 convention, however, that Lawrence played his most significant role. Before the convention, a group of supporters from Illinois had generated a popular boom for Adlai Stevenson, then a candidate for reelection as governor of Illinois. Stevenson consistently rebuffed their overtures, refusing to become an active candidate for two offices at the same time. As the convention opened, the front-runners appeared to be Barkley, Estes Kefauver, and Stevenson. Truman had already announced that he would not be a candidate, and Barkley followed suit on the third day. The "draft Stevenson" committee met with Lawrence before the convention, and he made it clear that he favored their candidate but felt that, unless he made known his candidacy, his chances were slim. "He would not intimate, even to Arvey, that he would accept the nomination so that we in turn could tell others," Lawrence said later. "That was a tremendous handicap with the politicians who were thinking of their futures—where they would stand with whoever was finally elected."[36] Lawrence professed his own reluctance, but nevertheless he promised to do what he could.

The amateur status of the "draft Stevenson" group became clear at a meeting to discuss the draft. Admitting that it expected perhaps a hundred votes on the first ballot, the committee appeared at a loss as to what to do next. "Our Draft Committee had assumed, when we opened headquarters on July 16, that all we had to do was to serve as a clearing-house of information for delegates and as a center for the stimulation of news about Stevenson. We soon discovered the truth of what Dewey Fleming wrote in the *Baltimore Sun* on Friday the 18th: 'Chicago is filling up with a throng of leaderless and bewildered delegates and minor local bosslets looking vainly for someone to tell them which way to go and what to do.'"[37] This meeting broke up with no resolution or plan. Lawrence was called upon for help, and he arranged a Sunday morning meeting at the Blackstone Hotel attended by James Finnegan, president of the Philadelphia city council, former U.S. Senator Francis Myers, State Senator Joe Barr, and Genevieve Blatt. Philadelphians Richardson Dilworth, Joseph Clark, and Matthew McCloskey, all Kefauver supporters, and John Kane, then backing Harriman, were not invited.

The small group of insiders decided that a symbolic act of support for Stevenson was needed to launch a movement toward him. Contrary to prior agreements with members, Lawrence called a surprise caucus of the Pennsylvania delegation for 7:00 P.M. Sunday night. The first caucus to be held, it was heavily covered by the press, radio, and television. As national committeeman, Lawrence was the first to vote in the preferential ballot. He spoke one word: "Stevenson." His vote was enough to entice other delegates to join him. Stevenson carried the straw ballot with 32 votes; Kefauver received 15.5. Pennsylvania became the first large state to announce its support of Stevenson. The Kefauver supporters were angry, and Kane was outraged. He was still fuming three days later when Richardson Dilworth visited him to attempt to convince him to switch his support from Harriman to Kefauver. "I went up to see Mr. Kane," Dilworth explained.

> He was angry and incensed. He was ashen gray. His left hand was swollen. I was afraid he was going to have a stroke. Mr. Kane started on a tirade against Dave Lawrence. I tried to calm him but the bitterness just spouted from him for an hour and a quarter. I couldn't get a word in edgewise.
>
> He went way back to 1912. He got an accumulation of resentment off his chest that apparently had been building up for years. He cited instance after instance where Dave Lawrence had crossed him. He was raging. He was bitter. He was almost apoplectic. I was frightened and concerned but I couldn't calm him down. "If it's the last thing I do," he declared, "I will prevent Dave Lawrence from being re-elected mayor of Pittsburgh next year."[38]

Lawrence, Finnegan and several other key members of the Pennsylvania delegation met again with the Illinois group immediately after the Sunday caucus. The pros were now ready to take over. Lawrence described his first reaction to the amateur group: "If you ever saw a shenanigan organization, there it was. The first thing they wanted to do was to elect me as floor leader for Stevenson. I explained why that was the last thing they should do—the opposition would tag me as a city boss and say the bosses were trying to dominate the convention."[39] Lawrence instead recommended former Senator Myers who had served as majority whip and was known and respected by northern and southern party leaders. Those present immediately supported Lawrence's suggestion.

From that moment the Lawrence-Finnegan-Myers influence was apparent. They were involved in every key decision in the draft movement and were instrumental in converting key delegates from other important states. "Lawrence was constantly in touch," Blatt related. "He was the telephone artist. He had people on the line all the time. He wasn't running around. . . . [Finnegan and Myers] checked in with him constantly."[40] At the final poll of the Pennsylvania delegation before the balloting, Lawrence delivered an impassioned plea.

> He has proven to be the best vote-getter in the Democratic Party, bar none. He has out Smithed Al Smith in Illinois. Stevenson carried Illinois by over 592,000 votes—far ahead of what the national ticket has been able to do here.
>
> It is not necessary to ask him what he would do about corruption. He has cleaned up the machine in his state. He has fought for a real fair employment practices commission. He does not need to say what should be done. He has done it.
>
> There is the most natural flow of votes to this man that I have ever observed. It reminds me of the trend to Roosevelt in the convention twenty years ago. I feel honestly that he can better unite the party than anyone else.[41]

Lawrence accurately saw the trend toward Stevenson, but several crucial questions remained. First, Truman's position following the withdrawal of Barkley was unknown. It was unclear how many Barkley delegates Truman controlled, but Lawrence, aware that neither Kefauver nor Senator Richard Russell was acceptable to the president, decided to smoke him out. After the speech nominating Stevenson, Lawrence moved for a poll of the Missouri delegation on the floor of the convention. When Truman alternate Thomas Gavin announced his support for Stevenson, all doubt about the president's choice evaporated. Barkley supporters could switch in good conscience.

A second problem, however, proved more complicated. The requirement that all seated delegates pledge support to both the nominated candidate and the platform, with its strong civil rights plank, portended a Dixiecrat walkout similar to that of 1948. Lawrence and

Franklin D. Roosevelt, Jr., sitting on the credentials committee, drafted a compromise rule, but delegates from Virginia, South Carolina, Louisiana, Mississippi, and Texas refused to go along. Lawrence then showed that his zeal for Stevenson outweighed even the civil rights issue. Speaking to the committee before national television cameras, he announced that he would vote to seat the Mississippi delegation regardless of its opposition. "This election is not won, . . . and in November, we may find ourselves in a real need for all the electoral votes we can get. . . . You must remember that Mississippi is not alone in this so-called Dixiecrat movement."[42] The committee voted to seat all five delegations, leading one Pennsylvanian to claim that Lawrence's action was that of a political sidewinder. When a floor challenge to the Virginia seating was raised by the Minnesota delegation, Lawrence again acted to prevent a regional division. Pennsylvania led the way to rejecting the challenge 650 to 518.

Three ballots were required to nominate Stevenson. Kefauver led on each of the first two, although Pennsylvania gave Stevenson 36 and 40 votes respectively. With Lawrence and Myers continuing to pressure their delegates, the opposition folded on the third ballot. Dilworth perhaps best illustrated Lawrence's hold over the delegation with his comment that, when the chips were down, he had to go along with the mayor. "I'd like a crack at [the governorship] again in 1954. How could I with Dave Lawrence against me?"[43] When Pennsylvania's turn came on the third roll call, Myers announced all 70 votes for Stevenson, giving him 542 of the 615 needed for nomination. Even Kane had capitulated. The Pennsylvania vote signaled the end of the struggle. The Stevenson draft had succeeded.

The triumph left Lawrence, "looking like the cat that swallowed the canary. Mr. Lawrence stood behind the speakers' rostrum and smacked his lips as the jubilant throng swirled through the amphitheater" during the "spontaneous" demonstration for Stevenson. "The mayor, smiling from ear to ear, stood by himself and watched the parade sweep on. He had picked a winner."[44]

Stevenson's November defeat at the hands of Eisenhower failed to dampen Lawrence's enthusiasm. He stood almost in awe of Stevenson, with his correct mixture of high social background, education, and political savvy, and predictably began to campaign for his renomination as early as the fall of 1955, one full year before the next convention. Lawrence was frequently asked to comment on his choice for the nomination, and he provided a stock answer. "Stevenson is the best equipped man in the country today to be president and he has the personality to get himself elected. There have been few, if any, men in our national history who have been so precisely trained for the presidency." Convinced that the American people would now judge Eisenhower not as a military hero, but as a "civil administrator who has demonstrated his lack of training for the job," Lawrence eagerly awaited the next campaign. "I would not expect Adlai Stevenson to lead the American Expeditionary Forces brilliantly, and I do not blame Dwight Eisenhower for failing to perform the President's job."[45]

The 1956 Democratic National Convention lacked the intrigue and excitement of the one held four years earlier. No longer plagued by Stevenson's refusal to declare himself a candidate, the party gave him its endorsement on the first ballot. When a controversy over the choice of a vice-presidential candidate—Kefauver or John F. Kennedy—threatened to erupt into a divisive battle, Lawrence joined Stevenson and Finnegan in advocating an open convention ballot. In spite of Kennedy's youthful appeal and considerable pressure from his father, Lawrence rejected his bid. His old fear of Catholic candidates, according to Genevieve Blatt and many others, pushed him into the Kefauver camp. Local Catholic politicians, including himself, had won elections, but no evidence existed to indicate that the voters were any more ready than in 1928 to support one for national office. By supporting Kefauver, Lawrence was also fulfilling his part of a deal he had made earlier in the year: Stevenson supporters would accept Kefauver as vice-presidential nominee if the expensive primary fights could be discontinued.[46]

Pennsylvania joined in the Eisenhower landslide, giving the president 600,000 more votes than the Stevenson-Kefauver ticket. For the second consecutive time, Lawrence had been instrumental in engineering the nomination of the Democratic national candidates—and by all accounts he relished his efforts at kingmaking—but unfortunately, his would-be king was not embraced by the American people. Lawrence was without question one of the major powers in the Democratic party, but he had been unable to do the thing that gave him the most joy—win the election. The one consolation was that "in America you get the chance to try it again, four years later. And we will be ready," he predicted.[47]

1959–1963
Return to Harrisburg

Lawrence's smashing sixty-thousand-vote mayoralty victory in 1957 seemed to signal the highlight of an illustrious career. John Drew, the most capable of his Republican opponents, presented only token opposition; the remainder of the Democratic ticket won with equal ease. Democrats controlled virtually every elected position in the city and Allegheny County and held the local judiciary, the governorship, and a U.S. Senate seat. The redevelopment of the city was well under way, with a number of projects nearing completion. Awards and praise from the national media and local and national organizations were bestowed on the "Renaissance mayor" almost weekly. He and Aldolph Schmidt spent a great deal of time traveling to other cities to tell the story of Pittsburgh's rebirth. The trips, which he thoroughly enjoyed, were a testament to the remarkable successes in Pittsburgh, but they reminded Lawrence of his own personal triumphs. He often commented in his talks on his modest youth, living at Pittsburgh's now completely redeveloped Point. A most poignant reminder occurred when the two men spoke at Boston's historic Faneuil Hall. Schmidt recalled that on the train back to Pittsburgh, Lawrence was quiet for a long while. "And finally he turned to me and said, 'To think, with my beginnings [that] I would live to speak in Faneuil Hall.' And tears began to come out of his eyes. It was one of the great moments of his life."[1] The sixty-eight-year-old mayor, now considered the senior statesman among urban political leaders, could conclude his career by placing the finishing touches on the redevelopment of the city he loved so much and by accepting the accolades of public officials, the media, and citizens throughout the country. His last four years as mayor, or an additional four if he so chose, would be his swan song in public life.

Those who considered Lawrence near the end of his political and governmental career, however, counted on neither his vitality nor his commitment to the Democratic party. Within six months of his victory over John Drew, he started along a new career path that would return him to the scene of his earlier legislative triumphs and political tragedy.

Following on the heels of the 1954 victory and a gradual but distinct shift in registrations away from the GOP, 1958 seemed like a Democratic year. Perhaps as a result, the scramble for the Democratic nomination for governor began earlier than usual. The contenders were: William McClelland, the Pittsburgh coroner; Mayor Richardson Dilworth of Philadelphia; James Knox, Allegheny County controller; Judge Michael Musmanno of the Pennsylvania Supreme Court; and Lieutenant Governor Roy Furman. Of these, the two with most support were Dilworth and Furman. But Dilworth did not have the backing of the Philadelphia machine, and many party leaders considered him too liberal. Furman, on the other hand, was not acceptable to Governor George Leader, who was running for the U.S. Senate. Yet none of the other candidates had enough support to be a compromise choice.

In spite of an early statement that he considered Dilworth "the most colorful and capable of those mentioned," Lawrence had followed his customary practice of waiting to see which candidate could generate enough support to carry the party. Now, anxious to forestall a primary battle, he called a meeting in Harrisburg of party leaders, including Joe Barr, the state chairman; Michael Lawler, Lackawanna County chairman; Bill Green, Philadelphia County chairman; Jim Clark; and Dilworth. The meeting proved more volatile than anyone had expected.

Lawrence, Barr, and Lawler, who could be counted upon to side with the two Philadelphia leaders, remained relatively quiet. "Green and Clark," Leader's executive secretary, David Randall, later stated, "were vehement against Dilworth and vented their vehemence on Leader." The governor, following a technique in handling Green which he had successfully used in the past, accepted the verbal abuse without protest. "Periodically during Leader's administration," Randall explained, "when he wanted to do something Green would not approve, Leader would have Green up to the mansion, tell him what was proposed, and then be smit hip and thigh by Green into the wee hours of the morning. Green would exact some price and Leader would then go off and do what he proposed. The technique worked because Green always provided a united Philadelphia delegation in the House (30 votes) and Senate (8 votes) for Leader's proposals."[2]

Green's attack lasted nearly two hours and convinced Dilworth that "if Leader would not stand up to Green, he would not stand up and fight for Dilworth as a gubernatorial candidate." Resigning his position as mayor to run with a man he considered "weak-kneed" would be too great a price to pay. Dilworth left the meeting and phoned Natalie Saxe, his executive secretary, to inform her that he couldn't run with a man who wouldn't stand up to pressure. If he couldn't win the endorsement on his own, he would not run. He would not oppose the party by running on an independent Leader-Dilworth ticket. The meeting broke up with no resolution of the dilemma.[3]

As time drew near for the policy committee meeting, it became clear that the situation had not changed. The only candidate who appeared to have a chance to win the support of a majority of the committee, Furman, was unacceptable to Leader. Delegates began to speak openly of dumping Leader to enable them to put together an acceptable slate of candidates. One other name, however, began to be mentioned as the only candidate around whom all members of the party could unite: David Lawrence. In Pittsburgh, Jack Robin, now executive vice-president of a Philadelphia urban redevelopment organization, met with Lawrence and Walter Giesey for dinner at the Carlton House Restaurant. Robin produced a list of questions. "Who can unite the Democratic Party? Bring organized labor together? Attract the independents? Get the Jewish vote? . . ." Lawrence looked at the list and responded, "That's what we have been trying to find out." "But it's you Dave. You're the one who can do it," Robin answered. The old pro was stunned. "His face actually went stark white for a moment," said Robin. If Lawrence were actually shocked by the suggestion, he quickly recovered. He emphatically set it aside, indicating that he was too old and didn't really want it. Earlier, in response to a question by Harrisburg reporters as to whether he could, under any circumstances, see himself as a candidate for governor, he insisted, "None, indeed. I am devoted to this program in Pittsburgh. A lot depends upon me. I don't say this egotistically, but I have been, on one angle of it, the key person organizing it. . . . I can't conceive of any situation where I would walk away from it."[4]

Leader meanwhile had suggested Lawrence to several associates, indicating that he would be willing to run with the mayor of either of the state's largest cities. Lawrence was also being discussed as a possible candidate with increasing frequency among Philadelphia leaders, but he continued to resist. Matthew McCloskey, a power in the party in Philadelphia, meeting with Lawrence in Washington, D.C., to sound him out, received an unequivocal answer. "I am not going to run. . . . You and I have been friends a long time. I don't want you to [support] any such policy as this; under no circumstances. I will be furious and I'll kill it right in the bud. I am not going to run."[5]

The confused situation continued right up until the policy committee meeting on 3 March at Democratic headquarters on South Third Street in Harrisburg. Lawrence spoke vigorously for Knox as compromise candidate, but the Leader, Green, and Dilworth camps continued to resist. Musmanno and McClelland meanwhile remained on the sidelines hoping lightning would strike. It was Leader, according to several sources, who first mentioned the name of Lawrence openly when he indicated that he was willing to run with any one of three men—Dilworth, Attorney General Thomas McBride, or Lawrence. The meeting dragged on for five hours. Then several of the principals, including Dilworth, Green, and Lawrence, excused themselves to go to the rest room. The atmosphere there was apparently conducive to compromise, and a deal was struck. Dilworth took himself out of the race in return for Green's agreement to support him for reelection as mayor.[6]

Dilworth's withdrawal left Lawrence as the only possible strong candidate. The man who had built his political career on seeking consensus to avoid internal disputes was caught on his own election principles. As he had done thirteen years earlier, he raised numerous objections to his candidacy: age, unfinished work in Pittsburgh, and religion. This time, however, Lawrence did not leave the meeting to phone his wife before finally permitting his name to go before the policy committee. He called Alyce immediately after receiving unanimous endorsement. The committee finished its work the following day by endorsing Judge John Morgan Davis as candidate for lieutenant governor. Davis, who resided in the eastern part of the state, was selected to provide geographic and religious balance to the ticket.[7]

The Republicans had just as much difficulty in selecting a candidate as did the Democrats. The bright and persistent three-term governor of Minnesota, Harold Stassen, announced his candidacy early in the year. Twice an unsuccessful candidate for his party's nomination for president, Stassen had moved to the Keystone State to become president of the University of Pennsylvania in 1948. In 1953 he became foreign policy adviser to President Eisenhower. A second announced candidate, William S. Livengood of Somerset County, had served four terms as secretary of internal affairs. But the Republican party ignored the experience of both Stassen and Livengood. To face the Democratic party's most experienced professional, the Republican old guard chose Arthur T. McGonigle, a self-made millionaire from Reading who had served a brief term as chairman of the party's state finance committee but had never run for elected office. His main achievement was building the rundown Bachman Bakeries into the largest pretzel manufacturing firm in the nation.

The Democratic party relaxed when McGonigle easily defeated Stassen and Livengood in the Republican primary. "Stassen was the one candidate who could have pulled Republican, independent and switch-over Democratic votes in November and beaten Lawrence."[8]

The election of the Pittsburgh mayor, in spite of the political inexperience and lack of voter recognition of his opponent, was far from a certainty. McGonigle cleverly turned jokes about his business—"the twisted candidate," and "the man with the dough"—to political advantage by flooding the state with hundreds of thousands of miniature pretzel pins. By midsummer he was no longer an unknown. More serious were the questions regarding Lawrence's candidacy. The effects of his age, his religion, and his image as a political boss on the voters were all unknown quantities.

The vigor with which Lawrence campaigned answered any doubts about his physical stamina. He began three weeks before Labor Day, campaigning in thirteen traditionally Republican counties. By November he had spoken in all sixty-seven counties on more than one occasion and had delivered a number of statewide radio and television addresses. The tactic, which he had perfected years before, of attending a rally for a few moments, making brief comments, then rushing off to another similar meeting enabled him to appear before a number of groups on any one visit to a county. In October he averaged ten appearances per day. By election day, according to one estimate, he had spoken at more than five hundred gatherings.

McGonigle made no reference to Lawrence's age or religion but struck out again and again at "political boss" Lawrence, the Pittsburgh wage tax, and the police scandal. In one address, for example, he charged that "Pittsburgh, under boss Lawrence, is wide open. Police there are in league with the underworld. The rackets there are pouring huge sums of money into the Democratic campaign." He did not need to add that the state, under Governor Lawrence, would become a haven for illegal activities.[9]

Lawrence, in refusing to respond to McGonigle's charges—he never once in the entire campaign mentioned his Republican opponent by name—followed a campaign strategy identical to the one he used in his first run for mayor in 1945. He attempted to build the broadest base possible, courting in particular the business and professional communities. Traveling in an eight-year-old car driven by his son Jerry, he spoke before chambers of commerce, managerial groups, and professional organizations all over the state. The Philadelphia Democratic organization arranged meetings with bankers, corporate leaders, and industrialists. Quite naturally, he pledged the same type of cooperation he had fostered in Pittsburgh. He promised to "call upon the ablest citizens from every walk of life and every political persuasion to participate in government service." His work as mayor of Pittsburgh, he frequently told audiences, had shown what public-spirited citizens working together could do. Though he visited every area of the state, he concentrated his efforts on the metropolitan centers of western and southeastern Pennsylvania, Harrisburg, and Erie and the hard coal region of Scranton and Wilkes Barre. His senatorial running mate, George Leader, was assigned to the bible belt, where he was strong.[10]

Just as Lawrence's first mayoralty campaign was based on a seven-point program of revitalization , he now offered a twenty-seven-point plan to "bring Pennsylvania into the twentieth century." Pennsylvania, being larger than Pittsburgh, evidently required four times the number of points. He promised something for everyone, including traffic safety and highway reforms, hospitalization and nursing care for the aged, an agricultural development program, a system of college scholarships, opposition to "right to work" laws, and a fair employment practices law. Lawrence pledged a businesslike administration and promised to set up a blue-ribbon panel to study the state's budgeting and taxation system. He no doubt pleased business interests when he promised that any taxation policy would ensure that Pennsylvania's corporations would remain competitive with those in neighboring states. He also demonstrated considerable political courage when, in the midst of the campaign, he indicated that, if elected, he intended to retain the controversial sales tax instituted by Republican Governor Fine. He later said he preferred it to a graduated or flat wage tax similar to the one he sponsored in Pittsburgh.

Throughout the campaign both sides brought in "heavy ammunition" to convince the voters. Within a two-week period in October, both President Eisenhower and Vice-President Nixon delivered addresses at the Syria Mosque in Lawrence's backyard. Former President Harry Truman repaid an old political debt to Lawrence by speaking on his behalf in New Castle, and former Governor George Earle, now a Republican, turned out to give his endorsement to his former cabinet head.

On the night of the election, Lawrence gathered with his usual band of Pittsburgh supporters to monitor the election results. As the returns began to arrive, he sensed immediately that something was wrong. The western Pennsylvania results, which arrived at party headquarters earliest, were far below anticipated results. Pittsburgh, which gave the mayor a 68,000-vote majority, performed as expected, but the county organization fell far short, giving him only a 54,000-vote majority (Pittsburgh included). The slim margin proved much too small to carry Leader, who lost in Allegheny County to Hugh Scott by 33,000 votes, and it jeopardized Lawrence's chances as well. Lawrence's anxiety eased somewhat when he received a call from William Green in Philadelphia informing him that he would carry that county by 175,000 votes. At 2:45 A.M. he was finally able to make a brief victory statement. A short time later, after phoning condolences to Leader, he rapped his ring on the table, announced, "That's it," and left for home.

Although he had carried only seventeen of the sixty-seven counties, he had squeezed out a 76,000-vote win. Lawrence's coattails, however, were far too narrow to carry either Leader or many state legislators to victory. Republican Hugh Scott outpolled Leader by 112,000 votes. State legislature results gave Lawrence a split General Assembly to work with: Republicans retained control of the Senate, 26 to 24, but lost the House, 104 to 106. Democratic voters in both of the state's largest cities, moreover, apparently "cut" Leader, who finished behind Lawrence by 45,000 and 86,000 votes in Philadelphia and Allegheny counties respectively. Leader and an aide later alleged that Lawrence and Barr had made a deal with the Republicans—that their supporters would vote for Scott—in order to protect the governorship and the power and patronage that went with it. When Lawrence telephoned immediately after his victory, he offered Leader the position of secretary of welfare. "I think he was sorry that the strategy went as far as it did," said Leader.[11]

The following day, Lawrence admitted to being mystified by the election results. "I found that I did not fare as well as expected in certain districts and industrial communities." Of Leader's loss he said, "The effort of Mr. Leader to put over a state wage and income tax apparently stuck in people's minds." He made no reference to any attempts by party regulars to "cut" or "trade" Leader. Given time to reflect on the election results, however, Lawrence returned to his old bugaboo, the Catholic issue. Appearing on "Meet the Press" in August 1959, he said that he felt his religion had affected him adversely in the upstate areas of Pennsylvania.[12]

Though a subsequent analysis of the 1958 election results indicated that Lawrence's fears were unfounded, he continued to act as if the issue were a formidable obstacle. Two independent studies demonstrated that Lawrence benefited slightly from his religion in the counties of high Catholic concentration. In low or moderately Catholic counties, the relationship between voting patterns and religion was found to be negligible.[13]

The interim between Lawrence's election and his inauguration as governor was perhaps the most sentimental period of his life. He was feted almost daily by various groups—the Press Club, the Allegheny Conference, the Chamber of Commerce, ward organizations, and the Allegheny County Civic Club, which hosted a grand farewell dinner at the Penn Sheraton Hotel ballroom. Democrats from all levels competed to pay homage to the party's "favorite son" but he was particularly moved when Republican Arthur Van Buskirk commented at the Civic Club dinner: "Of course Dave, there are those Pennsylvanians, both in your party and mine, who look on you as an old ruffian from across the mountains who has played too closely with a lot of Republicans. The same good folks think I have been too intimate with the Democrats. Fortunately, these criticisms don't bother either of us because we know in good conscience that our joint efforts in the Allegheny Conference have never been selfish but solely for the community's welfare."[14]

In expressing his pride in the city's achievements, Lawrence was careful to acknowledge the support of various sectors of the community. "There can be no question that our accomplishments—and there have been many—have been possible only because of our capacity to unite every aspect of our community life, to work in cooperation and fixed determination for wide-scale community development." Organized labor, the business community, professional and technical specialists, and Democratic politicians—particularly Commissioner John Kane and the city council—were singled out for special praise.[15]

Lawrence made it clear that he was reluctant to leave the city and served notice that he intended to continue to influence local affairs. He told the radio and television audience in his final state of the city address, "I will never lessen my interest in this community, which is the birthplace of my mother and father, the place where I was born and where I have lived all my life. In the months ahead. . . . I will never have any doubts about where my roots are and where my affections are. I will be proud to tell the world that I am still a Pittsburgher—and always will be." The city council received a quick and clear message in late November when, perhaps testing what they perceived to be a new independence, they voted six to three against an amusement tax the mayor favored. It was not revealed what Lawrence said at a private caucus the following day, but a chastened council provided the usual nine to zero vote in favor of the ordinance on a second vote. In presenting an austerity budget to the council in mid December, he let it be known that even though he would "be on assignment for the next four years," he expected his proposals to be implemented. Finally, while he praised his successor, Council President Thomas Gallagher, he let it be known that he intended to participate in the selection of the city's next full-term mayor.[16] Indeed, less than one month after he left the city, he named several acceptable candidates. Gallagher was not on the list.

▽

The heavy snowfall that covered the city of Harrisburg on 20 January 1959 caused the cancellation of the five-hour inaugural parade but failed to dim the spirits of thousands of politicians and well-wishers who jammed the hotels and bars to celebrate the installation of the state's first Roman Catholic and oldest governor. Mostly Democrats from western Pennsylvania, they had special cause for revelry. The ceremony, to be held in the State Farm Show arena, was not only the crowning of their leader of forty years but the first time in the history of Pennsylvania that a Democrat had succeeded a Democrat in the state's highest office. In spite of the snowfall, Lawrence arrived at the arena precisely on time, attired in morning clothes and a high silk hat. He was accompanied by Alyce, their three children, and several grandchildren. The oath of office was administered by a former Lawrence choice for governor, State Supreme Court Justice Charles Alvin Jones.

Lawrence's inaugural address, delivered before a cheering crowd of five thousand, indicated that his administration was to be similar to his four terms in Pittsburgh. He devoted nearly half of his speech to the problems that were to be given priority in his administration. Identifying a number of economic issues related to the national economic recession of 1958, he promised a broad effort to foster an economic and industrial renaissance. "We will have a policy of action—action not by government alone, but by industry, by finance, by labor, by community organizations so that the resources of Pennsylvania are mobilized before it is too late." The second issue, which he had raised a number of times during his campaign, was taxes. Faced with a $141 million deficit left by the Leader administration and nearly $400 million in state bond obligations, he again indicated that new taxes would be required to continue to operate the state government. He asked both parties to help. "I hope we can avoid a Democratic tax program or a Republican tax program, a governor's tax program, a House tax program, a Senate tax program. I hope we can achieve . . . a Pennsylvania tax program approved by all."[17] To achieve that goal he had appointed a bipartisan Tax Advisory Committee (the Hood-Kennedy committee) to study budgeting problems and supply tax recommendations within the month.

Lawrence and his wife divided the evening between two gala balls attended by nearly eight thousand people. The governor, who led grand marches under the crossed swords of the plume-helmeted Pennsylvania National Guard at both festivities, clearly enjoyed himself. He and Mrs. Lawrence were described as radiant as they danced the "Governor's Waltz" at each affair, and they remained at the Scottish Cathedral ballroom to dance and greet old friends and supporters until 11:30 P.M.

Mrs. Lawrence must have felt like Cinderella when she returned to the ninety-five-year-old Governor's Mansion on Front Street. The huge structure, badly in need of repair and renovation, was dark and drafty. More significantly, Alyce Lawrence was used to living in a house full of friends and relatives. In Harrisburg she would have only the household help. "It had to be one of the saddest days of my young life," her grandson David Donahoe related. "The day he was sworn as governor we all went down [to Harrisburg] and the next day we were going home. The governor's mansion that they lived in for a year was this horrible, big old house in downtown Harrisburg. It was huge. It had to be torn down, it was so bad. But I remember leaving, and how horribly sad she was, because the one thing she had in Pittsburgh, if he was away, was everyone else. Now we were all leaving. . . . It was a terribly sad occasion."[28] Alyce Lawrence endured her time in Harrisburg, becoming what one reporter called the "most inaccessible of First Ladies."[18] Four years later, when her husband took a position in Washington, she refused to accompany him and returned instead to her South Aiken Avenue home in Pittsburgh.

The new governor, although he shared his wife's dislike of Harrisburg, had no time for feelings of sadness. While his family was saying goodbye to Mrs. Lawrence before leaving for home, he was already at work. With his usual twelve- to fourteen-hour working day, he was establishing the priorities and routines for his administration. He began the day by meeting with his entire cabinet, nearly all of whom were holdovers from the Leader administration. (Pittsburghers Anne Alpern, David Kurtzman, and Park Martin were the most notable newcomers.) In a two-hour meeting open to the press, he delivered a stern message to his top aides. He would not tolerate the type of administration that had led to scandals during his predecessor's governorship. (He might have added those that brought down the Earle administration in 1938 or plagued Pittsburgh during his entire thirteen years as mayor.) "I will insist upon efficiency and honesty. We must perform the services offered by the State government better than ever before. . . . Whenever any of you has the slightest suspicion of dishonesty on the part of any employee, . . . I want you to inform me . . . immediately." No doubt recalling the damage done to the administration by Attorney General Margiotti during his first stay in Harrisburg, he made it clear that differences would not be tolerated. "If at any time you find yourself in such serious disagreement with these [the governor's] goals and procedures that you cannot give this administration your unstinted loyalty, then you should no longer be a part of the administration."[19]

Lawrence then turned to a problem that was to receive highest priority during the early months of his administration—balancing the budget. The administration and the blue-ribbon tax panel had already begun its search for new sources of revenue, he told his cabinet heads. "However, until we find a solution to our fiscal problems, I have no alternative than to insist on austerity." There was to be a hiring freeze on all but the most vital positions, expenditures were to be reduced, and no equipment or supplies were to be purchased without approval from the office of the governor. (He set an example by canceling an order for a new official car, retaining instead one with more than 100,000 miles.) Workers in every department were expected to perform the job for which they had been hired. "If there is any person in the employ of the state not willing to work and work hard, he had better leave now. We will not tolerate . . . any five percenters or ten percenters or whatever they are." Non-Pittsburghers among the group were no doubt startled at the abruptness with which the meeting came to an end when Lawrence stood up and clapped his hands. It was a signal they would have no difficulty recognizing over the next four years.[20]

Later, after the administration gained control of its fiscal problems, cabinet heads were given the same degree of freedom that Lawrence had allowed when he was mayor. Members of the administration soon found out that much of the day-to-day business of the state government would be conducted by Lawrence's able aide, Walter Giesey, another transfer from Pittsburgh. As long as a department performed to expectations, however, little interaction with the executive office was expected or required.

The governor followed his cabinet meeting with a brief press conference with journalists from across the state assigned to Harrisburg. As he had in Pittsburgh, he intended to cultivate the goodwill of the press by offering easy access to the chief executive. Unless urgent matters interfered, biweekly press conferences would be conducted. Faced with a generally friendly press, Lawrence usually enjoyed the mild give-and-take of these early-morning sessions. But he immediately established one ground rule that was never violated.

> Duke Kaminsky of the *Philadelphia Bulletin* was the most sarcastic of all the newspaper guys on capitol hill. He liked to dig, and the first day that Governor Lawrence was there and called a press conference, Duke came in and said, "Well what's boss Lawrence going to do now?" Lawrence heard him and said, "Duke, whoever told you I was boss? Who did I ever boss? Can you find me a person whom I ever bossed?" Then he said, "Now let's get things straight right now. I am not a boss, and have never been a boss, and if that term is ever used again in my presence, you'll never be at another news conference." From that point on, Duke knew who the hell was boss.[21]

Kaminsky and the others learned that first day the lesson Lawrence had taught *Pittsburgh Post-Gazette* reporter John Jones fifteen years earlier. The term *boss* was never uttered again at a press conference and seldom appeared in reports filed by the Harrisburg correspondents.

Late in the afternoon of his first day in office, Lawrence, in an attempt to build bipartisan cooperation, met with the four top leaders of each party in the legislature. He knew full well from his earlier Harrisburg experience that there was a big difference between "a 9 to 0 majority in city council and an even split in the legislature." Stressing that his door would always be open to members of the House and Senate, he heaped on the honey. "All legislators will be treated courteously and with consideration because their problems are the problems of the people and everybody must work together. I want to try to inject some of the Pittsburgh spirit [of cooperation] into the state legislature." During the next four years he spent almost as much time with Republican leaders Harvey Taylor and Albert W. Johnson as he did with the Democrats. The ability to get along with the opposition, learned decades ago in the offices of Billy Brennen, would again pay dividends. Leader's long tax battle with the legislature reaffirmed for Lawrence the wisdom of cooperation. "We have profited from the mistakes of the previous setup," he said. When his tax program appeared in jeopardy, he was asked how hard he intended to push to ensure its passage. "I'm not going to sacrifice the program by doing any pushing at all," he replied. "My job is to try to get the legislative agreement on a tax program. I'm not going to be obstinate." Lawrence's efforts brought lasting results, for his four years in office were characterized by a remarkable degree of cooperation.[22]

Aided by the youthful (thirty-four-year-old) Giesey and a highly talented administrative staff and cabinet, the administration wasted no time in attempting to carry out Lawrence's campaign program. Within six weeks of his inauguration, the governor submitted a biennial budget to the General Assembly and recommended a tax program to finance it. In addition, more than seventy bills to carry out parts of his program were introduced during his first fifty days in office. They included registration and regulation of lobbyists, prohibition of billboards along interstate highways, stringent air pollution bills, a strengthening of the Fair Employment Practices Act, and a requirement for smallpox vaccination of preschool children. He also outlined a tough new highway safety program to crack down on speeding and other traffic violations. The distribution of bills and his pronouncements on matters of priority made it clear that three concerns would dominate the Lawrence administration: fiscal responsibility, highway traffic safety, and a number of social issues, several of which had received attention during the Little New Deal of the Earle administration.

Governor Lawrence's twelve-member Tax Advisory Committee was not only bipartisan; its members included representatives from business, organized labor, and industry and governmental officials from Erie, Altoona, and Philadelphia.[23] The huge deficit from the Leader administration and mounting obligations related to the state's weak economic position made the group's task formidable. By 1 February they submitted a report recommending tax increases of $400 million within two years, including an increase in the sales tax from 3 to 3.5 percent, an extension of the tax to cover items hitherto excluded, and new levies on many consumer items, personal property, and natural gas. A cigarette tax of 1¢ per pack would fund the $120 million Korean War veteran's bonus. The committee recommended neither a wage nor an income tax, which Lawrence had pledged during his campaign not to impose. The governor submitted the plan, virtually without change, to the legislature along with a record $1.9 billion two-year budget.

To carry the tax program through the General Assembly, Lawrence reinstituted the "educational meetings" so effective during his term as secretary of the Commonwealth. Democratic senators and representatives were called in during the evening hours for a "chat" with the governor. House and Senate leaders Joe Barr, Charles Weiner of Philadelphia, and Hiram Andrews held frequent caucuses to ensure the support of reluctant party members. Lawrence's old ally Barr was particularly effective.[24]

Lawrence's best efforts on behalf of the tax package were reserved for lobbying with the Republican leadership. He met with the four men many times between 1 February and 15 April, when the bulk of the program was actually passed. Perhaps indicative of his fiscal conservatism was the strong relationship he developed with the most conservative member of the Republican group, the House minority leader, Albert W. Johnson of Smethport. Although the two differed on almost every other matter, they formed an alliance on fiscal concerns that lasted throughout Lawrence's four years in office. Johnson's support was particularly vital even though the Democrats controlled the House by a slim majority. Conservative Democrats representing rural areas frequently sided with the Republican minority on fiscal matters, and thus bipartisan support was required for passage of any tax bill.

When the 3.5 percent sales tax bill appeared permanently stalled, Lawrence agreed to remove beer, liquor, and used automobiles from the package. The revised version was pushed through the General Assembly on 15 April with all Democrats from both houses voting yes. Five ranking Republicans in the Senate joined the Democrats to give the bill a twenty-six to twenty-three majority.

The measure, however, provided only 56 percent of the $400 million needed to solve the state's financial problem. The amount was only slightly more than that needed to pay for the deficit from the previous administration. When opposition from special interest groups threatened the remainder of the package, Lawrence called in leaders of nearly 150 organizations dependent upon state funds and told them: "It is the duty of those who need state aid to get across the needs of your causes. There has never been a body here to lobby for the taxes to fulfill your needs." He indicated that nonessential items such as aid to colleges, hospitals, and libraries would all suffer if his program failed to win approval, and he warned that he would not permit further deficit funding. "My own sense of responsibility will forbid me from funding a deficit. Hard as the choice may be, it will be the . . . moral duty of the governor to assign a priority to the direct appropriations of the Commonwealth against the preferred appropriations." Later he told the Municipal Forum of New York: "I proudly lay claim to the political philosophy of the liberal, a moderate liberal, perhaps. . . . But, I am equally proud to call myself a fiscal conservative."[25]

The success of the tactic became evident when senators and representatives were besieged with letters and telegrams in support of the additional taxation. Particularly effective were the powerful Pennsylvania State Education Association, with more than sixty-five thousand members, associations of hospital doctors and nurses, and the Association of Library Trustees, with three thousand members throughout the state.

The governor battled, cajoled, and pleaded with both Republicans and Democrats during the next several months. He agreed to reduce some of the business taxes in return for an increase in the sales tax to 4 percent. He also smoothed over a defection by half of the powerful Philadelphia bloc by agreeing to name a Philadelphia representative to a Senate-House conference committee empowered to write a tax bill in final form. At other times he applied public and private pressure through the use of the media, meetings with interest groups, and the party caucus. His soft talk and barter approach occasionally gave way to anger and bullying, as when he threatened to add stiff new regulations to his lobbying bill unless special interest groups ceased applying "undue pressure" to members of the legislature. By mid August there were enough new tax levies to reduce the deficit by more than $100 million and put the government on a pay-as-you-go basis. In addition, in order to improve the business climate in the state, he reduced business's share of the state's tax burden by nearly 25 percent over the next two years.

The Lawrence administration began with an austerity program designed to reduce government expenditures and bring the financial crisis under control. The situation, however, was never considered permanent. The 1959–61 budget presented the first annual billion-dollar plan for government spending. Subsequent budgets were nearly as large. In all, the state spent a record $4 billion during Lawrence's four years in office. Nevertheless, the government continued to operate in the black, for each new program was matched by a tax program to pay for it. When the General Assembly balked at imposing new revenues, as it did over a $5 million program to repair hazardous schools, the governor vetoed the program rather than "risk an unbalanced budget."[26] By the end of his term, he had not only eliminated the deficit but turned in a $16.6 million surplus for the fiscal year 1961–62. It was the first balanced budget in seventeen years.

▽

In spite of his conservative fiscal policy, Lawrence launched the most comprehensive program of social legislation since the days of the Earle administration. Following a year-long battle with real estate interests, a Fair Housing Act, which prohibited discrimination in the sale or rental of multiple-dwelling housing units and created a Human Relations Commission for investigation and enforcement, became law in February 1961. He created a Governor's Council on Economic Development, which eventually recommended programs to attract industry to Pennsylvania and legislative measures to alleviate the economic problems of the working class. Administration-sponsored legislation established a liberal comprehensive minimum wage, improved benefits for workers injured on the job, and increased payments for unemployment compensation and for disability due to job-related illnesses. Child labor laws were strengthened to include additional industries and large commercial farms and provide protection for children of migratory farm laborers.

The Lawrence program of social legislation was aided by the narrow election victory in 1960, which produced a paper-thin margin in the House of 109–101 and a 25–25 tie in the Senate. Again working both sides of the political aisle, Lawrence pushed a program of medical care for the needy over age sixty-five and a revised dependent child care act that forced county governments to assume protective responsibility for needy children. When state legislation proved inadequate, he traveled to Washington to lobby for legislation at the federal level. In January 1960, for example, he testified before the U.S. Senate to urge enactment of a bill to provide additional funds for urban renewal and public housing. He also asked for an increase in the funds allotted for replacement housing and moving expenses for citizens displaced by urban renewal. A short time later, when he testified before a White House Commission on Aging in favor of the controversial Forand Bill designed to provide medical care for the aged, the seventy-one-year-old governor showed that his fiscal conservatism applied to the federal as well as the state government. "I am convinced also that one way of meeting the need is to build improvements into the social security system. Such new provisions can be paid for through small premium payments made through the working life of the individual."[27]

The Lawrence administration successfully supported a wide range of other programs including aid to public libraries, funds for a state park and conservation program (Project 70), reforms to the state hospital system, and approval of race track betting. On the two closest to his heart, however, the governor could report only mixed results. Ever since the death of his sons, he had expressed an interest in highway safety. Formerly a fast driver himself, he rarely got behind the wheel after the accident, although his poor eyesight was at least partly the reason. As mayor he had demanded stringent enforcement of traffic laws even during the period when the police seemed to be enforcing little else. In mid 1946, at a Governor's Conference on Highway Safety, he issued his first call for strict laws. "I would like to see the police given the power to take the reckless driver to the cell block," he said, adding that he also advocated permanent revocation of licenses for habitual offenders and drunk drivers.[28] During the next several years Lawrence attended national and state highway safety conferences and repeatedly called for tougher state laws. As a candidate for governor, he had made the need for greater highway safety a part of his campaign, advocating the use of radar to catch speeding drivers, but the issue apparently concerned few other Pennsylvanians and, except when his son Jerry was arrested for speeding, hardly drew any notice. Four months after becoming governor, he presented a massive program for highway construction and stringent new safety laws to the General Assembly. When the Republican-controlled 1959–60 legislature handed Lawrence one of his few legislative defeats by refusing to pass his bill, he issued an executive order to put the measures into effect. The far-reaching thirteen-point program contained the following measures:

1. a system of suspensions for violations of the motor code;
2. legalized use of radar to catch speeders;
3. periodic physical re-examination for drivers;
4. traffic training schools for offenders;
5. chemical testing of suspected intoxicated drivers.

"This program will make Pennsylvania foremost in the field of traffic safety. . . . It can become the national model . . . for reducing accidents, saving lives and lessening injuries."[29] To launch his program, Lawrence reaffirmed a "no-fix" ticket policy instituted by his predecessor, Governor Leader. Newspapers had a field day for the remainder of Lawrence's administration announcing the names of prominent drivers arrested for speeding or other moving violations. Serious injuries and traffic fatalities fell by 22 and 16 percent respectively during the final two years of Lawrence's term.

Lawrence's other favorite project was educational reform. Shortly after becoming governor, he appointed the twenty-one-member Governor's Committee on Education to study problems "from kindergarten through college" in Pennsylvania. The high-powered group visited hundreds of schools, conducted extensive hearings, examined thousands of school records and documents, and met with hundreds of educational leaders from all over the nation. Following nearly a year of intensive work, it presented Lawrence with one of the most comprehensive programs of educational reform ever produced:

1. a 50 percent increase in teachers' salaries by 1970; tougher teaching standards and training;
2. conversion of all state teacher colleges into liberal arts colleges; establishment of a system of community colleges in all urban districts;
3. creation of state scholarships for the top 5 percent of each year's high school graduates;
4. establishment of a $1 million college loan fund;
5. increased state subsidies to local school districts;
6. incentive payments to districts with classes for emotionally disturbed, gifted, or culturally deprived children;
7. minimum curriculum standards from kindergarten through twelfth grade;
8. consolidation of school districts with fewer than four thousand students.[30]

Nearly every one of the report's 145 proposals attracted both enthusiastic support and vehement opposition, but Lawrence accepted the report in total. In a special appearance before a joint session of the General Assembly, he called for bipartisan support, repeating a phrase made famous during his successful battle to increase the state sales tax. "There should be no Governor's program, no Republican program, no Democratic program." Instead he urged a "people's program."[31] To generate support, Lawrence embarked on a brief statewide tour, on which he was joined at one point by James B. Conant of Harvard University. As expected, the cost of the program and the plan to consolidate school districts drew the most objections. Lawrence refused to implement any of the salary or local subsidy proposals unless the legislature passed companion funding bills to pay for the increased costs. The House Republican leader, Albert W. Johnson, who had delivered crucial GOP votes supporting the sales tax increase, this time refused to help. The sales tax bill had merely enabled the government to pay bills it was already obligated to pay. Tax legislation to support the school program, on the other hand, gave state government entry into what many considered the sacred territory of local government. In Johnson's view, the two issues bore no similarity. When Lawrence indicated that he would veto any education bills unless the General Assembly voted the appropriate funds, most of the education committee's proposals died without benefit of legislative action.

The lone part that did pass, school district consolidation, rather than providing the advantages of a quality education to all, resulted in numerous court cases as community after community attempted to delay or avoid its implementation. Though a small number of mostly rural school districts did merge into larger units, most systems managed to forestall the action until the "friendly" Scranton administration produced an emasculated version of the act.

▽

Harrisburg offered David Lawrence new challenges and worlds to conquer, but it provided neither the satisfaction of his work in Pittsburgh nor the exhilaration he received from his political efforts. He and Alyce willingly abandoned the rundown Governor's Mansion in Harrisburg to live in a state-owned home in nearby Indiantown Gap. Where he lived was of little concern to him, for he left Harrisburg at nearly every opportunity, defying any signs of advancing age. He delivered nearly one thousand formal speeches during his governorship, seventy of them in major cities in the six months prior to the 1960 Democratic National Convention. During a typical three-day period he visited eight cities, toured three state mental institutions, attended several meetings of union officials, attempted to solve a political dispute in Philadelphia, gave a speech to the state AFL-CIO in Green Bay, Wisconsin, dedicated a tunnel, opened a fair in Pittsburgh, and attended a Little League banquet in Philadelphia. Lawrence's young grandson David Donahoe was a frequent companion. "I spent summers with him in Harrisburg. We went to everything. He traveled to various parts of the state and we went to fairs, to funerals and to political gatherings and tours."[32]

In addition to traveling to his many speaking engagements throughout the state and beyond, Lawrence returned to Pittsburgh nearly every weekend to catch up on the business of the Urban Redevelopment Authority (he was still its chairman), to meet on Saturday mornings with his successors in the mayor's office, and to conduct business or play pinochle with party regulars at the Benedum-Trees Building. Mrs. Lawrence occasionally accompanied him on his visits to Pittsburgh, and three trips abroad during his four years as governor gave them both respite from the Harrisburg environment.[33] Two shorter trips, however, one to Pittsburgh and the other to Los Angeles, gave Lawrence his greatest satisfaction.

On 24 September 1959, Soviet Premier Nikita Khrushchev visited Pittsburgh as part of his highly publicized ten-day tour of the United States. Lawrence, as governor of Pennsylvania, attended a luncheon at the University of Pittsburgh and accompanied him on a tour of the Mesta Machine Works in West Homestead. The two men exchanged quips during their walk through the plant, but Lawrence exhibited no humor as he spoke at a luncheon for 450 community leaders. Instead, he used the occasion to lecture the Communist party chairman on the realities of American politics. "To those who do not know us well, we may seem a divided people," he said, looking directly at Khrushchev.

> We are not a one party nation. As everyone here knows, except perhaps our guests from abroad, I do not belong to the President's political party. Next year in 1960, I will do everything I can to convince my fellow citizens that the choice of my party should be elected President rather than the candidate chosen by the party now represented in the White House.
>
> But as everyone here must know, in any grave crisis in our foreign relations we are immediately as one with the President. . . . So I would like to re-emphasize what Chairman Khrushchev has heard wherever he has gone in this country. . . . In America, politics stops at the water's edge. In his negotiations with the statesmen of the world, President Eisenhower speaks for a united country.
>
> America will confidently follow where he leads.[34]

Lawrence attempted to impress upon his guest the American heritage of freedom and democracy by calling his attention to Pennsylvania's historic sites. He wished he could show him Independence Hall, the site where the constitution, "our basic framework in self government," was drafted, or Gettysburg, "where the cause of human freedom triumphed forever in this nation over the cause of slavery and human degradation." One week later Lawrence wrote, "I don't know of anything I have ever done out of which I have ever gotten more satisfaction. I felt my responsibility very keenly, due to the fact that I was probably the highest ranking Democrat who was to have the opportunity to tell Mr. Khrushchev the position of the Democratic Party. I felt it was especially important because the very next day he was going into a meeting with the President at Camp David."[35]

Khrushchev responded to Lawrence's comments in a somewhat rambling forty-five minute address, acknowledging the unity of which the governor spoke but pointing out that "our people are [also] united. They support the Communist party, the one party, but the best party of all the parties in the world. . . . It is one party but it is better than both of yours."[36] The two then exchanged further comments and ideas, and Lawrence clearly enjoyed the repartee. It was the kind of political infighting he had learned as a child, listening to the discussions of his father and, later, Billy Brennen. Neither side gave any quarter, nor was any expected. Lawrence seemed refreshed and exhilarated by the experience. It lifted his spirits as he returned to Harrisburg to resume the battle to pull the state out of its financial morass.

The governor's second major trip from Harrisburg had a more lasting impact on the nation than his Pittsburgh exchange with Khrushchev. The 1960 Democratic National Convention was viewed as crucial by party leaders. The Republican party had held control of the White House for eight years, and another Republican victory might usher in a domination of the nation's highest office to match that of the Roosevelt-Truman span. But the popular Eisenhower would not be a candidate for another term, and the Democrats, if they could avoid their usual internal divisions and select a strong candidate around whom the various factions could unite, stood a chance of victory.

The Democratic party, balanced among a number of special interest groups, produced its normal abundance of candidates. Hubert Humphrey, the darling of the liberals, and the youthful John Kennedy, who had nearly won the vice-presidental nomination in 1956, battled each other in selected primary elections across the nation. Stuart Symington, who incorrectly saw himself as the candidate of the city bosses, remained in the wings hoping for a deadlock between the two main contenders. He would be the most readily acceptable to all the minority factions. The Senate majority leader, Lyndon Johnson of Texas, adopted the same strategy as Symington, relying on the anti-Kennedy feelings of the South and the old-line New Deal operators in the Northeast. Adlai Stevenson was again reluctant to run. Reporter Theodore White called him "uncertain, willing yet unwilling to be President."[37] The possibility of another Stevenson draft in the event of a deadlock would not disappear until the governor of Pennsylvania announced his choice on 12 July.

Lawrence, now the leader of the big-city bosses and one of the most powerful national committeemen, played his usual waiting game in the months prior to the convention, refusing to support any candidate until he was certain of his chances of victory. With a compromise candidate a distinct possibility, an uncommitted Pennsylvania delegation could play an important power-brokering role.

Though Lawrence's high regard for Stevenson was well known—one reporter called it "an almost youthful adoration"—the Kennedy supporters did everything they could to dissuade him. Early in the year a small group of Democratic leaders—including Carmine Di Sapio of New York, John Bailey of Connecticut, Jacob Arvey of Chicago, Mike Di Salle of Ohio, Pat Brown of California, and Lawrence—had conducted sporadic discussions. "We would get together to talk about the possibility of who could win. Winning was the main objective. Personalities were secondary. . . . We [had] just had two losses in the White House. . . . We decided that we could not go with another loss. Kennedy appeared to be the type that would represent the philosophy of the Northeast." Lawrence immediately raised the issue of Kennedy's religion. In the gubernatorial election, Lawrence had won by a much narrower margin than he had expected. "Having just come through that," he later observed, "I figured, well, hell, he'll lose Pennsylvania sure." The group, however, decided to support Kennedy and pressured Lawrence to accept their decision. He refused, urging them to wait for the results of the primaries.[38]

Lawrence's old political ally from Philadelphia, Matt McCloskey, had made a second attempt to pry a Kennedy commitment from the governor. At the request of Joseph Kennedy, a longtime associate, McClosky traveled to Harrisburg to ask the governor to "come out for Jack early in the game." Following a lengthy discussion, Lawrence told him what he had told the city bosses: "It's too early; all you have to do is get all the big political bosses to be for him and you'll ruin him. Let him win a few primaries so that we know that is what the people want and then we can vote for him."[39] Lawrence, as usual, was waiting for a consensus to develop before he took a stand.

When McCloskey reported back to Joe Kennedy, he was furious and decided to pay a visit to Lawrence. "I told his father the same thing," Lawrence recollected. "Of course, he didn't like it either." Lawrence's concern had local implications as well. "I was thinking—I was governor and I had the House and didn't have the Senate, and I could see losing a lot of these Dutch Democratic Counties—that I would lose the legislature. And I didn't want that to happen because I had two more years in Harrisburg and it was tough enough the way it had been the other two years. So finally—that was the thing that concerned me. And I . . . was very enamored of Stevenson, because I think of him as one of the ablest men in the world and the ablest man I ever met."[40] Kennedy left Lawrence without the desired commitment.

Lawrence deliberately maintained his poker face in his public pronouncements. In a 1959 appearance on "Meet the Press," he deftly dodged the issue by suggesting that both Stevenson and Kennedy would make excellent presidents. In response to a direct question on the impact of Kennedy's religion, he responded with classic obfuscation. "Now I don't want to dismiss that with the idea that I don't think it may enter [into the election], because at certain times it does, depending on a lot of other major circumstances. If Kennedy went into the fight with some major issue that the people were voting on—like if you voted for Kennedy you were for it, say, like the right-to-work law in the California and Ohio fights last year. [Both states elected Catholic governors by large majorities.] Then they forgot about that [the Catholic] question. At least, its submerged or subordinated to the issue."[41]

As the Democratic National Convention approached, Lawrence did his best to keep the Pennsylvania delegation uncommitted. In addresses and comments to the press, he praised nearly all the named candidates. His aide Walter Giesey, at the same time, was issuing statements to the press declaring his boss "neutral and determined to remain neutral until the Democratic National Convention."[42] A quick endorsement by Symington to a brief "Lawrence for vice-president" boom failed to win the desired return endorsement from the governor.

Lawrence's neutrality, however, was not holding his own Pennsylvania delegation. Victories by Kennedy delegates in a number of the state's primary districts and a surprising Kennedy write-in vote of 180,000 prompted a number of public endorsements by prominent officials. Senator Joseph Clark, Matthew McCloskey, and a number of other Philadelphians announced their support of him. Milton Shapp, a Philadelphia cable television millionaire, tried to start a boom for Kennedy by arranging "to have the senator come to Philadelphia to meet some of my friends" and mailing about four hundred intivations to a fund-raising luncheon to area businessmen. Philadelphia boss William Green, in an attempt to keep that part of the state in the neutral camp, responded with an angry phone call. "Shapp, what the hell's this Kennedy luncheon all about?" he demanded. "Bill, I just want some of my friends to meet the senator and maybe get some Presidential support for him." There was about a ten-second pause, and then Shapp received a prime lesson. "Shapp, I'll make a deal with you," Green shouted. "I'll stay out of the electronics business and you keep your fucking nose out of politics. When I decide who I want, I'll let you know. Now knock it off. . . . I don't want you or anyone else doing a damned thing until I tell you. Get it?" Within thirty minutes Shapp received a call from Kennedy's advance man in Pennsylvania telling him "not to do anything in a formal way. Just keep Kennedy interest going."[43]

In spite of the efforts of Green and Lawrence, however, other party leaders in the state joined the Kennedy camp. Organization Democrats in Cambria and Armstrong counties and Lawrence's ever present opponents McClelland and Roberts in Pittsburgh made public statements supporting the Massachusetts senator. On the eve of the convention, Kennedy had half of the state's eighty-one-delegate vote, according to a count by McClelland. Lawrence, as chairman of the delegation, responded to the growing Kennedy support by ruling against the unit rule for his group. If McClelland's calculations proved accurate, a vote for the unit rule would give Kennedy all of the state's delegate votes and prevent Lawrence from playing a role in the decision-making process. He refused to have his hands tied.

Lawrence arrived in Los Angeles a full day ahead of the Pennsylvania delegation. John Bailey, a Kennedy supporter, met with him at his hotel, the Biltmore, also the headquarters of the Kennedy team. Having pressed the advantages of his candidate, Bailey secured no commitment, but Lawrence did agree to meet with Kennedy the following day. At that meeting, which included McCloskey, Lawrence asked a number of questions. He was particularly interested in Kennedy's choice for national party chairman—Lawrence had carried on a running feud with the current chairman, Paul Butler—and his thoughts on a running mate. Kennedy's vice-presidential list included most of the prominent Democrats except Lyndon Baines Johnson. It was at this point that Lawrence first mentioned the Texas senator. "None of the men on the list are going to bring anything to the ticket. Why wouldn't you go for Lyndon Johnson?" Lawrence asked. When Kennedy responded, "Dave, you know that there is no way Johnson is ever going to take that," Lawrence told him of an earlier meeting in Washington between himself, Johnson, Sam Rayburn, and McCloskey. Over Rayburn's objections, Johnson had agreed that, if he did not win the first position, he would "do anything my party wants me to do." Kennedy expressed some disbelief, but Lawrence guaranteed that if "you'll ask him . . . he will take it." The meeting ended without any commitments from either side, but Lawrence had planted a seed and agreed to stay in touch with Kennedy headquarters. The Lawrence-McCloskey meeting had a strong impact on Kennedy. The following day, Joseph Alsop and Philip Graham paid a similar visit to Kennedy to discuss the merits of Johnson as a vice-presidential candidate and were astonished at his quick acceptance of the idea. "Joe and I were a bit shaken by his positiveness. His brother Bobby had told me earlier that Johnson would not be considered."[44]

Lawrence now made his last effort on behalf of the man he once called "the greatest statesman of our day." He first visited the Illinois delegation to learn the extent of support for Stevenson. Arvey and a number of the delegates made it clear that, while they felt an obligation to remain with their state's favorite son through the first ballot, their preference was now Kennedy. Lawrence's resolve for his hero was shaken. "In Illinois, those fellows there weren't for him. Hell, he hadn't his own state. . . . And so I saw the situation, then I figured well I'm just hurting myself politically to stand out against Kennedy when they want to be for him. . . . I had finally made up my mind. . . . If I lost the state legislature, then I was going to be in a terrible dilemma in the final two years of my administration."[45]

Late that Sunday night, Jerry Lawrence drove his father eight miles to the Beverly Hills Hotel to meet face-to-face with the man he had championed for nearly a decade. The two men discussed the situation for several hours. Lawrence gave Stevenson one last opportunity to declare himself openly. If he refused, the governor would support Kennedy on the first ballot and perhaps the second. Only in the event of a deadlocked convention would he return to the candidate from Illinois. Stevenson again declined to run and told Lawrence, "Do what you have to, Dave." His aide Bill Wertz asked, "Governor, are you sure that's the message you want to give Governor Lawrence?" "Adlai could have said anything but that and he would've stopped Pennsylvania from going to Kennedy," said another Stevenson aide. "Dave Lawrence was the ace in the hole and we let him go." When Stevenson repeated his statement, Lawrence told him he was joining the Kennedy camp and suggested that Stevenson place the name of John Kennedy in nomination. Stevenson responded that he could not do that "because of the people who came to California on their hard-earned money"; he just could not let his delegates down.[46] Whether Lawrence continued to hope for a Stevenson candidacy is unclear. But he would not be among the drivers of a Stevenson bandwagon, as he had been in 1952 and 1956.

Three candidates—Kennedy, Johnson and Symington—and Stevenson's stand-in, Mike Monroney, spoke to the Pennsylvania caucus the following morning. Monroney, Johnson, and Symington were greeted with polite applause. Kennedy received a standing ovation. Lawrence announced to his own delegation, in a private session following the candidates' presentations, that he would support Kennedy on the first several ballots. That was all that was needed. Other uncommitted delegates waiting for some sign from their leader now rushed to join the Kennedy effort. On the first Pennsylvania caucus vote, Kennedy received sixty-four of the eighty-one votes, bringing obvious joy to the Kennedy supporters.

The steamroller for Kennedy was momentarily halted by the wild Tuesday demonstration that followed Senator Eugene McCarthy's nomination speech for Stevenson. The half-hour celebration threatened to stampede the convention for the two-time candidate. Normally controlled groups rushed onto the convention floor to show their support. In the Pennsylvania delegation, even the always sedate Genevieve Blatt, a long-term protégé of Lawrence's, grabbed the Pennsylvania banner and joined in. The demonstration, however, proved meaningless. Pennsylvania gave Kennedy 68 votes to put him over the 650 mark, with 761 needed to nominate. When Wyoming voted unanimously for Kennedy, any remaining suspense vanished. In spite of Lawrence's persistent reservations about the candidate's religion—he had again expressed his fears following the state's Monday caucus—the forty-three-year-old Massachusetts senator became the party's nominee with a narrow surplus of 45 votes.

Thursday 15 July was another crucial day in Los Angeles. Following the first-ballot victory the previous evening, the Kennedy forces met nearly all day in the nominee's suite at the Biltmore. An adjoining suite was set up for Lawrence, Carmine Di Sapio of New York, and several other big-city bosses. In view of his significant role in the nomination and his standing among the group, Lawrence was selected as their spokesman. Convinced that Kennedy's greatest weakness was in the South, they authorized Lawrence to push for the selection of Johnson as Kennedy's running mate.

All day, party leaders filed in and out of the Kennedy suite to press their case for an acceptable candidate. Labor leaders made clear that Lyndon Johnson was not among their choices. Influential senators and representatives stopped by to make a pitch for a favored candidate. The Kennedy forces, including the candidate's brother Robert, had their own choices. Lawrence met with Kennedy several times during the day to urge the selection of Johnson. Early in the morning, to escape the crowd milling about in the "command" suite, Kennedy, McCloskey, and Lawrence met in the bathroom of suite 9333. Kennedy searched for further assurances that Johnson would be a willing candidate. "Now look Dave, I don't want to go down there and ask that guy. Are you sure now?" Lawrence and McCloskey repeated the substance of their Washington meeting with Johnson and guaranteed that he would accept. "We . . . had to authorize Kennedy to say to Johnson, if there was any question about it, that the reason he came was . . . because the two of us had assured him that this is what Johnson had said."[47] Organized labor, they added, would support the ticket, for the labor leaders had nowhere else to go.

Kennedy then visited the Johnson suite two floors below his own to sound him out without actually making an offer. When Johnson indicated that he would accept, his name immediately appeared on the list of possible candidates. The debate in the Kennedy suite continued until late afternoon, with Lawrence paying several visits. Shortly after 3 P.M. a solid offer was tendered to Johnson and he accepted.

Lawrence's influence was acknowledged: he was asked by both Kennedy and Johnson to place the name of the Texan in nomination. In a short but power-packed speech, he made the reasons for his support clear. Lyndon Johnson, the ideal candidate for vice-president, would help in the South and in borderline states and would add tremendous strength to the ticket.[48] Although he remained skeptical about the effects of Kennedy's religion until election day, the Democrats had fulfilled Lawrence's fondest wish. They remained united while putting together a winning ticket.

A happy Lawrence returned home to organize a concerted effort for the Democratic candidates. He personally campaigned extensively across the state, and the candidates of both parties made several visits to Pennsylvania. The Kennedy motorcade through the state drew crowds estimated at nearly one million. On election day, as Kennedy eked out a bare majority over Richard Nixon nationwide, he won by 116,000 votes in Pennsylvania. In addition, Kennedy carried with him enough candidates for the legislature to give the governor a narrow but workable majority in the House and a twenty-five to twenty-five tie in the Senate. Lawrence's concern over the influence of Kennedy's religion in Pennsylvania proved surprisingly accurate with one important exception. He lost the "least Catholic" counties by a greater margin than Stevenson had in 1956 and managed small gains in the "moderately Catholic" counties. In the Catholic centers, however, he had a victory of more than 255,000 votes—a turnaround in excess of 600,000 over the previous presidential election. His victories in Philadelphia and Allegheny Counties alone totaled nearly 450,000 votes.[49]

Lawrence returned from the Kennedy inauguration festivities, where he enjoyed a place of honor on the presidential stand, as he had in January 1934. Democrats were now in positions of power in Pittsburgh, in Harrisburg, and in Washington. To make matters even better, his party controlled Philadelphia, and Democratic registration in Pennsylvania now exceeded that of the Republicans. Completion of his legislative program and election of a Democrat to succeed him in the state capital would make "retirement" to the life of a senior statesman and adviser to presidents and other public officials nearly perfect.

He generally succeeded in the first goal, missing only on a tough strip mining bill and portions of his educational reform bill. The second goal appeared to be an even safer bet. His administration had created a balanced budget, suffered no scandals, and passed an impressive legislative package. He enjoyed recognition throughout the state and had been hailed for nearly six months in 1960 as a kingmaker. The election of Kennedy seemed to guarantee his influence in Washington. When the Democratic leaders met in early 1962 to select the person they hoped would be his successor, Mayor Dilworth of Philadelphia finally received the long-sought nomination. The Republicans, however, countered with their best candidate of the century, William Scranton. A Pennsylvanian of wealth and standing, from the city bearing his name, the Yale-educated Scranton was a party's dream come true. He was tall, handsome, self-assured, and knowledgeable about state issues, and he appeared to the voters sincere about his desire to serve.

Dilworth made matters worse by running what one reporter called "one of the poorest campaigns in modern Pennsylvania history."[50] A scandal in his Philadelphia administration and suburban discontent over Governor Lawrence's school reorganization bill haunted him throughout the campaign. He missed the opportunity to show off his renowned hard-hitting style in a televised Kennedy-Nixon type debate, giving the advantage to his lesser-known opponent. Scranton, on the other hand, hit the Democrats where they were most vulnerable, attacking the boss politics of Lawrence and Green and the increased taxes under two Democratic governors.

In Lawrence's view, Pennsylvania voters had turned their backs on him and his administration by handing Scranton a 486,000-vote victory. The Republican candidate won sixty-two of the sixty-seven counties. "I don't think we got a damn vote for balancing the budget. Not a vote," a dejected Lawrence commented. "All the work we put into that to get this state on its feet. I never heard anybody saying, 'I'm going to vote for these guys because they balanced the budget'."[51]

Lawrence's hopes to leave a Democratic administration in Harrisburg to complete the programs he and Leader had started were dashed, and many speculated that he would return to Pittsburgh in semi-retirement when his term was completed. They failed to take into account his never ending desire to be in the middle of the decision-making action.

Pittsburgh

Pittsburgh on a rare clear day around 1945. The two bridges in the foreground and the warehouse railroad complex at the Point were removed between 1951 and 1957. Carnegie Library, Pittsburgh

Pittsburgh after completion of the Renaissance. Associated Photographers/ Dick Brehl

Detail of the Point in 1910, Lawrence's neighborhood. Carnegie Library, Pittsburgh

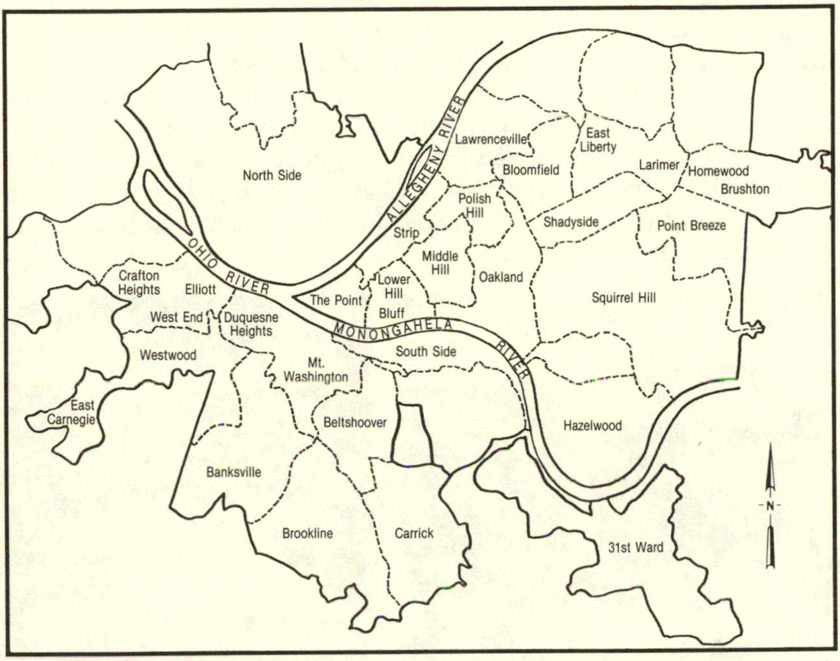

Selected neighborhoods, Pittsburgh.

Pittsburgh wards.

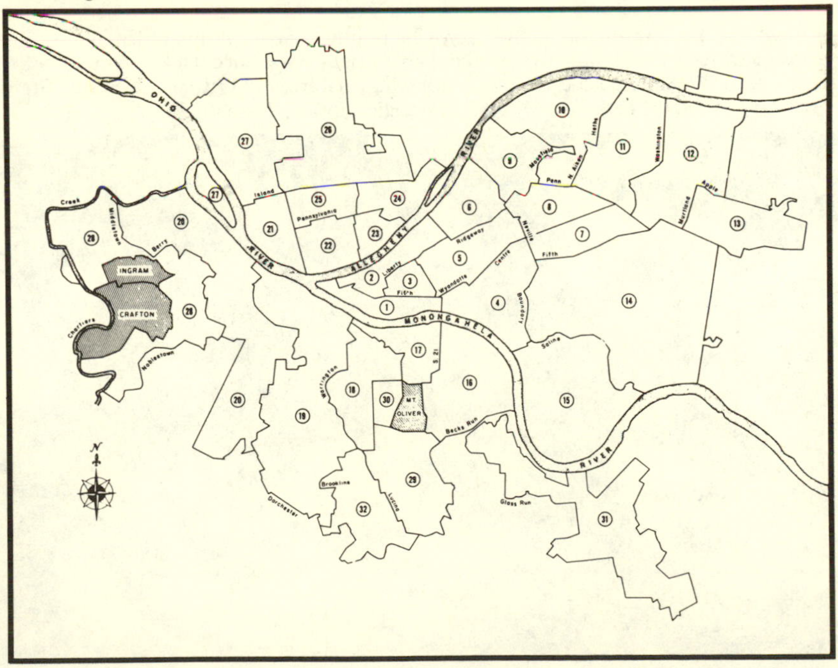

Strike

In 1946, during Lawrence's first year as mayor, the Duquesne Light workers struck the company. The city was without electricity for twenty-seven days. Lawrence and his aides worked around the clock to bring both sides to a negotiated settlement. In the minds of many, particularly the city's corporate heads, Lawrence's image as a partisan spokesman for organized labor was put to rest as a result of his efforts. Their changed perception of Lawrence played a major role in the success of the private-public partnership which spearheaded the redevelopment of the city.

(Above left) Lawrence speaks to the citizens of Pittsburgh on the status of the strike negotiations, September 9, 1946. Carnegie Library, Pittsburgh
(Above right) Lawrence catches a quick nap following the announcement of settlement of the power strike. The photo, by Morris Berman of the *Sun Telegraph,* was carried nationally by the wire services and featured on the cover of *Newsweek*. Carnegie Library, Pittsburgh

(Below) Too busy to dine out, the mayor had dinner served in his office as negotiations continued to avert a power strike. Left to right: Lawrence, Jack Robin, City Solicitor Anne X. Alpern, Federal Conciliator Charles Katz, and William Chestnut, State Secretary of Labor, February 26, 1946. Carnegie Library, Pittsburgh

A Lifetime in Government

During Lawrence's fifty-year career, he moved easily from the local to the national arena. He had many companions along the way, both political and nonpolitical, as he signed bills, pounded gavels, and even shoveled dirt.

(Below right) As Convention Chairman, Lawrence brings down the gavel to open the 1948 Democratic National Convention in Philadelphia, July 13, 1948. Carnegie Library, Pittsburgh

(Below left) Secretary of the Commonwealth and democratic state chairman, Lawrence attends the 1936 Democratic convention, June 21, 1936. Carnegie Library, Pittsburgh

The mayor signs the city's Fair Employment Practices Commission into law, December 5, 1952. Five leading supporters of the bill look on. Left to right, first row: Lawrence, Mrs. Daisy E. Lampkin, Mrs. Louis J. Reizenstein. Rear: Rev. N. H. Moor, Frederick McKee, and Boyd Wilson. Carnegie Library, Pittsburgh

(Above) Genevieve Blatt and Governor George Leader join state national committee-persons, Emma Guffey Miller and Lawrence, at the 1956 Democratic National Convention in support of Adlai Stevenson, August 16, 1956. Carnegie Library, Pittsburgh
(Below) Lawrence, a strong supporter of the Jewish state of Israel, lends his assistance in the Bonds for Israel drive. Left to right: Adolph Schoenbrun, Lawrence, Mrs. Sam Helman, Sam Felman. Carnegie Library, Pittsburgh

Lawrence and several of his closest aides receive election returns in customer's fashion at Democratic headquarters in the Benedum-Trees building. Democratic gubernatorial primary May 20, 1958. Left to right: City Councilman Fred C. Weir, Judge William S. Rahauser, County Controller James W. Knox, County Democratic Chairman B. B. McGinnis, and Mrs. Lawrence. Carnegie Library, Pittsburgh

(Below left) Lawrence and Senator Joseph Guffey during one of their friendly periods. (Below right) Mrs. Lawrence and longtime Democratic supporter Matthew H. McCloskey, at the Democratic National Convention in Philadelphia, July 15, 1948. Carnegie Library, Pittsburgh

Groundbreaking for construction of the Mellon Square Park and underground garage. The land was a gift of the Mellon family to the city. Looking on are Richard King Mellon (left) and George Main, parking authority chairman, September 29, 1953. Carnegie Library, Pittsburgh

County Commissioner John Kane, Judge Michael Musmanno, and Lawrence on the occasion of Musmanno's victory, July 13, 1950. Carnegie Library, Pittsburgh

(Above) Peter Flaherty, center, with Mayor Joseph Barr and Governor Lawrence, in the days before Flaherty was "Nobody's boy." Carnegie Library, Pittsburgh
(Below) Lawrence with Millard Tawes, governor of Maryland (left) and Lyndon B. Johnson (center). Carnegie Library, Pittsburgh

1963–1966
In Service to the Nation

Speculation regarding the next phase of David Lawrence's career naturally occurred anywhere Democrats gathered. Many felt he would return to the city of his birth, adopt a semiretired position, and watch over the finishing touches of the Pittsburgh Renaissance. He was still chairman of the URA and had maintained close relations with Mayor Joseph Barr during his absence.[1] Retirement would give him an opportunity to watch the seeds he had sown bear fruit. He could continue to have a dominant hand in local politics, where he was regarded as without peer in either prestige or power. Close supervision might shape the party so that it retained his imprint long after he retired from the scene. Those who predicted a Pittsburgh residency pointed out that Mrs. Lawrence longed to return to be near her children, grandchildren, and other relatives. She had developed osteoporosis and was frequently bedridden. Returning to Pittsburgh would give her great comfort.

There were, of course, those who speculated that Lawrence would never retire, not even part-time. It was "not in his blood." One rumor suggested that he might return to Pittsburgh to take a high-level position in the management of the Mellon Foundation. Another offered the unlikely suggestion that incoming Governor Scranton might ask Lawrence to remain in Harrisburg as an adviser on urban affairs. In November several newspapers speculated that he might be in line for a high-level position in the Kennedy administration. Among those presidential posts most frequently mentioned were postmaster general and ambassador to Israel, neither of which was open at the moment.[2] He denied that any post had been offered to him and indicated that he had no interest in moving to Washington.

Three weeks before the conclusion of his term as governor, however, Lawrence received a letter from the president asking him to come to Washington to discuss the chairmanship of a newly created President's Committee on Equal Opportunity in Housing. "We have given a great deal of attention to the qualifications the Chairman should have, and on the basis of every test you turn out to be the obvious choice. I believe the Chairman should be a man of proven administrative ability, one who possesses a national stature, an individual whose reputation for fairness will make him as acceptable in the South as in every section of the country and, if at all possible, one who has had personal experience in administering state statutes or city ordinances of a similar character. Additionally the Chairman should command respect not only from negro and other minority groups, but also from politicians and industrial leaders."[3]

Lawrence was, in fact, the obvious choice. Throughout his public career he had championed the cause of equal opportunity for decent housing for all. He had demonstrated a concern for housing assistance as early as 1949 when, as president of the U.S. Conference of Mayors, he led the fight for the Federal Housing Act. Several years later he led a delegation of mayors to petition House Speaker Sam Rayburn to use his influence to move a stalled omnibus housing bill, which, among other things, provided funds for public housing, out of committee. As mayor of Pittsburgh he instituted one of the nation's first fair housing ordinances, arguing that such legislation was more properly the responsibility of the state and federal government. As governor he pushed for a statewide act, which he signed into law in 1961. Not content with state action, he lobbied the federal government, in 1959, lecturing a U.S. Senate subcommittee on the necessity for the federal government to supply housing for low-income families.[4] In addition, Lawrence was an excellent candidate for the position because he was known among Southern politicians as a moderate on civil rights. He could be expected to move cautiously.

The position intrigued Lawrence because, as Kennedy explained, "the chairman will have great latitude in establishing his own method of operation." He would be named a special assistant to the president, a position that made him responsible only to the president. The size of the committee, the mode of operation, and the procedures for processing complaints were all to be determined by the chairman and the committee. The executive order that created the committee prohibited "discrimination because of race, color, creed, or national origin in housing and related facilities owned or operated by the Federal Government." The prohibition affected 225,000 public and community housing units already built by the federal government and all private homes to be constructed using Veterans Administration or Federal Housing Authority loans. The order further called for activities "to promote the abandonment of discriminatory practices in housing and related facilities provided with federal assistance."[5] Those who drafted the order apparently had a form of public education in mind but did not provide any specific guidelines.

Lawrence and Walter Giesey met with the president on 10 January. Following a twenty-minute conference, Lawrence agreed to accept the position provided he could bring Giesey along as his aide. It was a detail he had not mentioned to his longtime executive secretary—he assumed Giesey would comply with his wishes, and he did. Ten days after leaving the governor's post, Lawrence, his wife, his son Jerry, and Walter Giesey went to Washington for swearing-in ceremonies. The Pennsylvania politician launched a new phase of his career at age seventy-three. He later explained that his quick compliance was due to two reasons. The first was "a firm belief that when the President of the United States asks you to do something, you have no right to refuse. The second reason was my conviction that attaining equal opportunities for all our citizens is one of the most challenging and imperative domestic responsibilities we face as a nation." Walter Giesey also suggested that the position offered him an opportunity to "depressurize" from the rigors of government without the abrupt departure he faced at the conclusion of his term of office as governor.[6]

The first task facing the chairman of the new committee was to select the eight public members. Using his broad contacts among state and municipal leaders, he drew up a list of nominees, including representatives from organized labor, financial institutions, and the building industry, and an attorney.[7] Four cabinet officers and the heads of the Veterans Administration, the Housing and Home Finance Agency, and the Federal Home Loan Bank board were also members. They set up office in a handsome suite in the Executive Office Building and agreed to meet on a regular basis to hear complaints of noncompliance and to plan strategy for the public education campaign designed to bring about voluntary compliance. For Lawrence and Giesey, who threw themselves wholeheartedly into the program, the experience was from the very beginning one of both exhilaration and frustration.

Even before all the public members were approved, Lawrence launched the education phase. On 24 March he began a series of addresses and conferences that would eventually take him into more than thirty states to meet and speak with several hundred groups interested in housing and equal rights. He attended every one of the conferences. During the first several months he was virtually a one-man show. Speaking to a five-state housing conference in Springfield, Missouri, he launched his crusade not only for compliance with the executive order but also for the broader goal of eliminating discrimination in the entire housing field. He emphasized its importance by pointing out that "racial discrimination in housing is a basic cause of other types of discrimination that have received much more publicity. Breaking through the barriers in housing will release, at the most dangerous point, the mounting racial pressures in our cities resulting from artificial restrictions on local housing markets." In the next several months he delivered messages in Chicago, Cleveland, Brooklyn, Washington, D.C., and Pittsburgh. In each case the message was similar, but he presented it in language adapted to his audience. In Washington, he presented a "rational" message to an American University forum: open housing communities can work successfully and does not result in devaluation, a fact that he demonstrated with examples from Pittsburgh and the state of Pennsylvania that supporting integration need not be political suicide. Speaking before a Catholic group in Cleveland, he took a strongly moral approach, beginning by quoting liberally from a pastoral letter from the archbishop of Baltimore and concluding with the reminder that the challenge of instilling a new morality in America was not as formidable as that facing the Apostles, the early Christian missionaries, or St. Patrick in Ireland.[8]

The analogy seemed appropriate as Lawrence traveled throughout the country to drive out the demons of prejudice and racism that prevented people from living in a home of their choice. He adopted the cause thrust upon him by the president as a personal crusade. Using what he perceived to be the success of the initial conferences as a basis, he and Walter Giesey devised a strategy to reach key housing personnel. Beginning in May 1964, the committee launched an ambitious program aimed at educating the public, sponsoring a series of conferences on equal opportunity in housing designed to take its chairman and staff into dozens of metropolitan areas throughout the nation.[9] At the initial meeting in Boston, Lawrence spoke to representatives of more than seventy public and private groups involved in the housing industry, including community fair housing committees, banking interests, real estate brokers, labor unions, the Chamber of Commerce, and numerous clergy. He spared no feelings when he told them that their city had been selected because there was still a great deal of discrimination there.

Each conference was to be an exercise in self-examination and was expected to lead to a set of policy recommendations for the host city. Although Lawrence seldom participated in the small group work sessions of the conferences, it was a format with which he was most comfortable. Examine a problem, develop solutions, and then work out the details of a workable plan. Reasonable persons, when faced with a set of problems, could be expected to reach an acceptable accommodation. Although it is difficult to point to direct, tangible results of the conferences, he was convinced that they were effective vehicles to shape public policy and he attended every one over the next two years.

While Lawrence generally relied on "education" and "persuasion" to enlighten others, he demonstrated that he could still use force when necessary. He angrily berated the National Association of Real Estate Boards after it said in a policy statement that realtors had no responsibility to help blacks find better homes. "Property rights and human rights are not contradictory. Each should be respected. Since the human rights of many Americans have not been fully realized, it is the responsibility of us all, including those of the real estate business to work energetically and positively to correct those conditions." The association, which had never been particularly cautious about housing matters, could not now "assume a position of impotence or neutrality in improving housing opportunities in this nation. Nor can it defend hostility to such equality as indicated in the reaffirmation of past policies which have tended to encourage and sustain such unhealthy conditions."[10]

An exchange of accusations and denials between Lawrence and the association produced no positive results toward the goal of the housing committee but drew attention to the glaring weakness in the president's executive order. It applied only to housing purchased with Veterans Administration and Federal Housing Authority mortgages, approximately 20 percent of all housing transactions. The committee was expected to use moral suasion to bring about equal opportunity in the purchase of homes financed through conventional mortgages—about 70 percent of all housing transactions.

It was a weakness immediately identified by Ferdinand Kramer, one of Lawrence's first recruits to the committee "The order is not broad enough in that it leaves out certain agencies who have the same benefits of government guarantees on deposits as some of the agencies under the order. This leaves a loop hole so that those who do not care to abide by the President's Executive Order can finance their construction activities through [other] agencies. . . . I believe this is a serious deficiency and that the committee should consider the possibility of remedying this." Lawrence shared Kramer's misgivings, and broadening the executive order to include other housing and lending agencies became a goal of the committee almost upon its inception.[11]

Its first effort proved deceptively successful. On 26 April 1963, Lawrence announced that his group, only partially formed, had requested that the president ban the creation of new government facilities in areas where discrimination in housing existed. Kennedy, while not agreeing to a formal extension of the order, indicated that he would attempt to follow the suggested policy and authorized Lawrence to release the contents of his petition. That same day, however, three government members of the committee, Robert Weaver, head of the Federal Housing Authority, Deputy Attorney General Nicholas Katzenbach, and Joseph Murray, chairman of the Federal Home Loan Bank, cautioned that the government must move slowly and carefully in accordance with the existing order before trying to expand it.[12] The two statements signaled the beginning of a four-year conflict.

The public committee members, with Lawrence in agreement, petitioned the president in September 1963 to broaden the order to include conventional financing. This extension, when combined with the agencies already affected, would cover an estimated 90 percent of all new housing. The president's advisers indicated that, while there was no legal question involved with regard to savings and loan associations, there was some doubt about his authority to include commercial banks, and Kennedy responded that he did not believe it appropriate at that time to extend the order. Four months later the committee, hoping to renew its plea, met with President Kennedy's successor for the first time. Johnson, however, was forewarned of their interest, and Lee White, a White House aide, suggested that expansion might have an adverse effect on the proposed civil rights bill currently under discussion in the Congress.[13]

Lawrence agreed on the wisdom of the president's decision, and the issue was placed on the back burner.[14] Between January 1964 and election day, the committee made no further requests. It would be in a much better position to press the issue, Lawrence told them, when Johnson occupied the White House following his own election. In addition, pressure by the committee, particularly if it should become public, might jeopardize either the president's civil rights program or his chances for reelection. The committee agreed to lie low, although Kramer, who led the proexpansion group, offered occasional reminders to Lawrence that the issue was not forgotten.[15]

Following Johnson's overwhelming victory in November 1964, Lawrence was ready to resume the fight, but the president heeded the advice of his aides, who urged him to avoid extension. He relied instead upon the time-tested method of forming a committee, headed by Vice-President Humphrey, to look into the matter.[16]

By mid March 1965, Lawrence and his committee had grown impatient and prepared a formal petition for extension of the order to commercial banks, mutual savings banks, and savings and loan associations.[17] The petition was hand delivered to the president on 16 March. Lawrence followed the recommendation with his personal letter urging the president to respond favorably.

During the next several months a series of discussions took place among Lawrence, Humphrey, various cabinet officers, and members of the presidential staff. It immediately became clear that Weaver and the government officials were on the opposite side of the fence from Lawrence and the public members of the committee. Lawrence pressed for extension of the order but Katzenbach, Treasury Secretary Fowler, and other White House staff members continued to urge a more cautious approach. Vice-President Humphrey, Walter Giesey noted, played the role of mediator "although he was sympathetic to our side."[18] It appeared that an impasse had been reached.

Lawrence tried to bring pressure on the reluctant government officials by including cautious but pointed remarks regarding the "limitations of the 1962 Executive Order" in his addresses to various housing conferences across the nation. Whether it was the effect of his comments, the overall educational efforts of the committee, or the increased concern over civil rights permeating the nation in the mid 1960s remains unclear, but various allies began to appear. The president received a score of letters urging extension of the order from human rights committees, Urban Leagues, and the American Civil Liberties Union. The National Committee Against Discrimination in Housing, representing thirty-seven civil rights agencies, strongly protested the recommendation of the Department of Justice that the president reject expansion. The Greater Baltimore Real Estate Board, disregarding the advice of its national association, issued a statement urging an immediate and far-reaching extension. Several months later the National Association of Real Estate Boards, responding to a call from Lawrence to cease ignoring its responsibilities, adopted a resolution favoring the requested expansion. Ferdinand Kramer of Chicago and Louis Weinstein of Massachusetts raised additional concern in government circles by threatening to resign from the committee unless the issue was soon resolved.[19]

A memo by White House aide Joseph Califano to the president indicated that the efforts of the various groups were beginning to pay off. "There is tremendous pressure from civil rights leaders and the President's Committee on Equal Opportunity in Housing to do something about all other housing, preferably by extending the current Executive Order. To avoid an explosion some action must be taken soon." The memo then explored the alternatives, including a new proposal—legislation by Congress.

> The advantages of the Executive Order route are that the civil rights leaders and your Housing Committee would applaud you, and you avoid the difficulties of a tough legislative battle. The disadvantages are the opposition you would get from bankers (for using them as the instrument), the chance that you would lose in court and be accused of overextending your authority and the fact that you would be moving in the most sensitive of the civil rights areas all alone, without Congressional help.
>
> Legislation would be far less vulnerable to defeat in the courts and might not arouse too much opposition from segments who oppose excessive use of Federal (executive) power. It has the great advantage of having the Congress behind you. . . .
>
> There are serious difficulties with legislation. The most significant is in getting it passed. . . . Merely moving on this area will present a significant problem for many Congressmen—particularly the new Democrats elected in marginal districts. Nevertheless, . . . it will be essential to promise a legislative program in this area in 1966. . . .
>
> If we do nothing, both the [White House] Conference [On Civil Rights] and the [Housing] Commission will not only recommend extension of the Executive Order, they will probably attack you for delay. It is possible that two or more members of the Housing Committee might resign (the only thing that has avoided some resignations during the past few months has been the supreme skill of Governor Lawrence). Further, it is only a matter of time before some Republicans (like Javits and Kuchel) recognize the importance of this to the Negro voter and begin to ride you on it.
>
> This is a close question. Governor Lawrence favors the Ex-

> ecutive Order route. Joe Fowler, Nick Katzenbach, Lee White and I favor the legislative approach.

Califano concluded by suggesting that, if the president approved, the White House Conference on Civil Rights, chaired by Humphrey, should be induced to recommend legislative action, and the members of Governor Lawrence's housing committee should be assured that a *"legislative program in this area will be forthcoming next year* [1966]."[20]

Johnson accepted the recommendation. It was only a matter of time, Lawrence and his committee were told, until a federal open housing bill became law. Given such assurances, particularly by Vice-President Humphrey, in whom members had strong confidence, the committee abandoned its long battle to force an extension of the Kennedy executive order. However, what neither Lawrence nor the committee knew was that Johnson's memo to Califano giving the go-ahead for the legislation included a handwritten note, which read, "Favor Jan. 1967 leg.—So Cong. won't get beat." Johnson got his wish. A lengthy congressional battle over the bill, including a successful Senate filibuster in 1966, delayed passage for nearly two and one-half years. Kramer carried out his threat and resigned in January of 1967 because he felt there was nothing further to be gained by his membership. He made one last plea for an extension of the executive order and suggested that, failing that, the committee be disbanded.[21] Lawrence, who believed that it was the committee's responsibility to continue the battle, hid his own frustration by offering encouraging words to housing conferences across the country.

In private, he confided to an old Pennsylvania associate that the job "is about to drive me up a wall. In all my life I have been in jobs where I called the orders. I gave the orders and people had to get cracking; when I told them to do something they did it. Now I have got to sit here and wait . . . for any length of time for things to get going, for people to get ready to do something. When I was governor or mayor, . . . things had better get going as soon as they were underway." Washington, D.C., was becoming a tiresome place. The urban housing conferences filled only part of his time, and while he occasionally advised the president on urban affairs and political matters, time hung heavy on his hands. The issue of extending the prohibition against discrimination in housing to commercial banks and savings and loans was now in the hands of the Congress and would become part of the Civil Rights Act of 1968. Though he never said so, Lawrence, according to Walter Giesey, probably intended to resign his position following the passage of a fair housing bill. His grandson David Donahoe sensed that he was ready to leave Washington and return home.[22]

▽

Lawrence, of course, had never relinquished his contact with affairs in Pittsburgh or with Pennsylvania politics, but he found it increasingly difficult to maintain control. He retained his position as chairman of the URA and returned home to attend each executive meeting. As an admittedly unreformed sports addict, he was deeply interested in plans to build a new stadium and athletic complex. Weekends were spent in Pittsburgh meeting with Mayor Barr, presiding over political meetings at party headquarters, or playing pinochle with Frank Ambrose and a few other old cronies. "Invariably on a Friday it got so I would expect a call," Al Tronzo reported. "Sometimes it would be, 'Are you going down to the Y this evening?' Or . . . 'Meet me in front [of party headquarters]' which was a pleasant command. We would be going to the Y, just that pleasant walk."[23]

Weekend visits and periodic telephone calls and occasional reports from associates back home, however, were not enough to enable him to maintain control of either the city or the state. Events were beginning to slip from his grasp. The city council was showing its independence from the mayor, and a young politician who received his first job through Lawrence's intercession, Peter Flaherty, was starting to question the efficacy of machine politics and would eventually defeat the organization by running on an antimachine platform. The victory of a Republican district attorney, Robert W. Duggan, in Allegheny County was viewed by some as indicative of a growing weakness in the Democratic organization due to Lawrence's absence.

> I just felt real sorry for him. He just seemed to be out of the mainstream and in a place where he really didn't want to be and yet he wanted to do this assignment and do it as well as he could. And furthermore, he was down there and the Pennsylvania papers were late arriving, and he didn't have unlimited access to a phone. . . . I don't think he had quite the clout in Pennsylvania in '63 and '64 as he had previously. He still had a lot because there were still people who felt a great deal for him and still looked to him for counsel. But on the other hand they had to do the day to day work without benefit of him around and they began to feel that maybe they were the leaders instead of him. . . . There were a lot of contenders and he was trying to

keep them all happy, and he couldn't do it from that position the way he could do it up here.[24]

The first cracks appeared in the statewide organization in January 1964 when the Philadelphia Democratic organization announced, without Lawrence's agreement, that it intended to support State Supreme Court Judge Michael Musmanno for the U.S. Senate nomination. Musmanno, whom Lawrence had rebuffed in several elections, was selected by the Philadelphia committee for his ability to attract the large Italian vote, which was considered crucial if the city was to be won away from the Republican incumbent, Hugh Scott, a native son. Musmanno's former anti-Communist activities and his theatrical style on the State Supreme Court added to his attractiveness as a candidate and, ever ambitious, he appeared to be the only person anxious to take on the popular Scott. He seemed to aspire to any office that offered upward mobility. The only other logical candidate was Lawrence's former protégé Genevieve Blatt, now secretary for internal affairs. She had led the party ticket in the previous election, had an admirable record in every office she had held and, of course, was a longtime favorite of Lawrence's. But she had had a difficult campaign in 1962 and was reluctant to run against Scott. She speculated that Lawrence might oppose her candidacy because Scott was too strong and because the electorate was not ready for a woman candidate for senator. The Philadelphia organization rejected Blatt because it considered her too independent and because she had the support of Senator Joe Clark, a strong opponent of the eastern city's machine. Her admission that she neither informed Lawrence nor asked for his support when she decided to run is indicative of a changed Pennsylvania political world. She had always sought his opinion, if not approval, in the past. She vehemently opposed Musmanno in discussions with Lawrence, arguing that he had refused once to resign from the bench while running for a nonjudicial office and he would do it again, a practice she found unethical. Lawrence showed little reaction and gave no indication that he was going to back Musmanno the following day. Blatt suspected that he had already given his word to the Philadelphia delegation but was unable to tell her.[25]

Unlike previous nominating meetings, which often gave evidence that the important decisions had already been made, the 1964 caucus appeared disorganized and leaderless. Seven names received consideration for the U.S. Senate nomination, but none was close to a majority on the first ballot.[26] Lawrence, Joe Barr, and most of the western Pennsylvania delegation initially supported Blatt, while the

Philadelphia delegation gave its votes to Musmanno. The meeting at this point grew stormy, supporters of each of the candidates hurling charges at others in the room. Most vocal was Lawrence's old foe William McClelland. In what was merely another round in the never ending anti-Lawrence battle, McClelland announced his support of David Roberts. Later, when calm was restored, Lawrence, Barr, and a number of others from western Pennsylvania joined Frank Smith in support of Musmanno. He was selected by a vote of thirty-seven to sixteen over Genevieve Blatt. Milton Shapp, the Philadelphia industrialist, received three votes.[27]

Though Blatt felt the entire endorsement process had been stage-directed, the meeting demonstrated that Lawrence no longer dominated the political scene in Pennsylvania. Whether he agreed to support Musmanno before the meeting, as Blatt charged, or after the first ballot revealed his strength, the power of the Philadelphia delegation headed by Smith was apparent. Musmanno in the past had demonstrated his rebellious nature often enough to lose Lawrence's support permanently. Furthermore, it was his anti-Communist raids in Pittsburgh that had given Charles Margiotti an opportunity to strike a second blow at Lawrence while he was mayor. Musmanno had openly courted the Philadelphia delegation for nearly a year. His attempt to outmaneuver Lawrence for the endorsement was blatant and played into the hands of Frank Smith. It was the type of action Lawrence would earlier have beaten back with great relish. This time, however, he was powerless. In the interest of party harmony, he joined with the majority, becoming one of the players rather than the dominant figure in the contest.

As a good party regular, he supported the party's choice in the primary even though the woman he admired more than any other remained in the race, as she had promised. Someone had to stop the unethical Musmanno, she reasoned. Lawrence campaigned only half-heartedly that spring, explaining that his work in Washington kept him from more active participation. The primary campaign degenerated into a name-calling battle between Musmanno and Blatt's principal supporter, Joe Clark, but Blatt, as expected, kept to the high road, campaigning on her record and her considerable knowledge of national and international affairs.

On a cold, wet primary election day, the Philadelphia delegation, which had forced Musmanno on the party, lacked the power to produce the big vote needed to give him the nomination. Registered Democrats throughout the state gave another indication of the absence of their strong leader when fewer than one-half turned out to vote. Philadelphia and Pittsburgh, the organization strongholds, together gave Musmanno fewer than one hundred thousand votes over Blatt. She won nearly every county, defeating him by just over thirty-two hundred votes statewide. Musmanno, however, refused to concede. He contested the election through the Philadelphia County Elections Board, the Court of Common Pleas, the State Supreme Court—of which he was still a sitting judge—and the U.S. Supreme Court. Ironically on Columbus Day 1964, the U.S. Supreme Court refused to hear the case.

The court's rejection put an end to Musmanno's battle, validating the primary victory of Genevieve Blatt. The fight, however, had destroyed any chance Blatt had of defeating Hugh Scott. She barely had time to mount a campaign before election day. Nevertheless, she nearly pulled off a spectacular upset, losing by only 26,000 out of a total of more than 4.6 million votes cast. Her loss in both Philadelphia and Allegheny counties caused the newspapers of both regions to question what had happened to the once strong Democratic organizations. Lawrence, curiously, failed to note the absence of leadership in either area. While regretting the outcome, he laid the loss at the feet of Blatt, suggesting that her inability to carry the ethnic, particularly Italian, neighborhoods in Philadelphia and Pittsburgh led to her defeat. Election returns from South Philadelphia and the Italian wards in Pittsburgh show the accuracy of Lawrence's analysis, but he overlooked the fact that Musmanno had failed to do as well as expected in either area. In fact, Democratic voting returns from nearly all sections of the state were lower than in previous years. The organization was clearly less effective in 1964.[28]

To Lawrence the election outcome did not indicate a weakness in party leadership but was simply further evidence of the folly of primary battles, a tenet of his since 1931. In 1966 he was faced with irrefutable evidence he could no longer ignore. His absence from the day-to-day scene, the anti-organization spirit of the era, and no doubt his advancing age were having their effects. The organization he had built almost single-handedly was rapidly disintegrating.

Early in January 1966, Milton Shapp, a fifty-three-year-old millionaire electronics manufacturer from Philadelphia, met with David Lawrence in Washington, D.C. Shapp had campaigned hard for John Kennedy and made a brief attempt to win the U.S. Senate nomination in 1964. Lawrence was pleased when Shapp made a quick exit from the race after failing to win the party's endorsement, but he could not be counted among his supporters. Shapp was too brash, had too much money, and expected to move in at the top of the party. He was unwilling to pay his dues. In addition, he made no attempt to fit into the Philadelphia organization. He was not a maverick like McClelland and Roberts, who refused to support party causes but reaped the benefits of party membership. Milton Shapp was a true independent. In early 1966 he owed allegiance to no one.

Shapp boldly informed Lawrence that he intended to enter the Democratic primary election for governor of the state but that he would not seek the endorsement of the state policy committee. Lawrence could barely control himself. He argued that Shapp would only hurt the party and ensure a Republican victory.[29]

On the surface, political analysts would find it difficult to quarrel with Lawrence's conclusion. Shapp was totally unknown. A Shapp poll in Johnstown and Erie turned up only one of two hundred voters in either city who had ever heard of him. He had never run for political office before. He had absolutely no support among Democratic leaders. He was physically unimpressive—short, stoop-shouldered, with the kind of loose jowls cartoonists love to draw. He spoke slowly in a nasalized monotone—no one would ever vote for Milton Shapp because of his style of delivery. Finally, he was a Jew in a state that had never elected a Jew to a major office.

Shapp, however, had two advantages that appeared to be lacking among Pennsylvania Democrats in 1966: money and organization. As a multimillionaire committed to winning election to high office, he was willing and able to finance his own campaign. He hired two aides, Joe Napolitan and Oscar Jager, who put together an organization and a campaign unlike any ever seen in Pennsylvania. Napolitan became the advertising man, fashioning the image and making certain that no detail was overlooked. "With skillful TV and still photography and a minimum of personal appearances," he wrote to the candidate, "we can compensate for the fact that you don't look like Clark Gable. You wouldn't even if you grew a mustache. But I wish to hell you'd get rid of those maroon socks."[30] Jager, who prepared Shapp's speeches, carefully highlighted the one advantage he had over other candidates, his intelligence. It was Jager who insisted that Shapp run a strongly issue-oriented campaign to demonstrate his understanding of complex issues.

The State Democratic Committee met in Harrisburg on 15 February to select its candidates for the primary. Although Shapp had already announced his candidacy, no one appeared concerned over his challenge. The eastern members of the committee, as they had in 1964, made their wishes known, and the endorsement of Robert Casey, a young state senator in the John Kennedy mold from Scranton, seemed a certainty following an unsuccessful attempt to lure George Leader from political retirement. If he had any objections, Lawrence did not raise them. "I don't think Lawrence ever bought the business that Casey was like Kennedy. But he didn't really have anybody else he could counter with so he went along with their endorsement."[31] Lawrence's absence had left him unaware of the rising young candidates within the party. The meeting was to have been a pro forma endorsement, but Milton Shapp stole the show. His performance should have given the party leaders an indication that he would be a formidable opponent.

As a member of the committee, Shapp explained, "I was eligible to attend the meeting but waited until all the county chairmen and committee members were inside the hall." Then, "with cameras whirring, I opened the doors and made my entrance." He marched directly to the podium and read a brief prepared statement to the effect that he welcomed the support of all registered Democrats in Pennsylvania but did not seek the endorsement of the state committee. "I want to be the candidate of all Pennsylvania Democrats not just the candidate of their party's leaders," he said, looking straight into the television cameras.[32] When he left, the cameras showed the two large auditorium doors closing behind him, symbolically separating him from the party organization. Shapp was in a perfect position to brand whoever the organization endorsed as the handpicked candidate of the bosses. His theatrical performance received television coverage, not only throughout the state but on national networks as well. The campaign had been launched in grand style.

When the endorsement meeting resumed following a brief recess to "settle the audience," the party leaders proceeded as usual. Casey was endorsed on the first ballot, as were all the other candidates. Endorsement of a candidate for lieutenant governor was postponed for two weeks to give Casey an opportunity to participate in the decision. The slate no doubt had Lawrence smiling. The candidates for the five major contested offices represented all the elements he looked for in a ticket: three Protestants, two Catholics; three from the eastern part of the state, two from the west; two women; one black, two Irish-Americans, one part-Italian, and one Serbo-Croatian. (In addition, the candidate for lieutenant governor, Leonard Staisey, was almost totally blind.) Speaking later at a Democratic fund-raising dinner, Lawrence called it a UN ticket, reminiscent of the Allegheny County slate he put together in the mid 1930s.

Casey ran an efficient campaign, appearing before enthusiastic crowds throughout the state. Although polls taken several weeks before the mid May primary showed him to be well ahead of the challenger, the organization could produce neither workers nor funds to sustain his early lead.

The Shapp campaign, aside from the dramatic first day, had gotten off to a rocky start, but by mid March many of its problems had been eliminated. It focused on advertising organized by Napolitan, speeches by the candidate, and press releases written by Jager. The "man against the machine" advertising blitz, which used billboards, buses, television, radio, newspapers, and direct mail, was described as "the most intensive media campaign in the state's political history." Shapp out-traveled his Democratic opponent, delivering four or five speeches a day, each on a different issue, thus enabling Jager to prepare separate press releases and emphasizing Shapp's command of a wide range of issues.[33]

Following the pattern set by David Lawrence years before, Shapp's committee organized support groups among blacks (a major coup was the endorsement of Martin Luther King, Jr.), ethnic voters, business groups, veterans' organizations, and labor unions (starting with the United Electrical Workers at his own electronics firm, Jerrold). Shapp even hired his own poll watchers on primary election day to watch over his interests in predominantly organization districts.[34]

In retrospect, the results of the 1966 Democratic primary should have been easy to predict, but the organization appeared stunned by its second consecutive defeat. Shapp outpolled Casey by nearly 50,000 votes. Lawrence, at his customary spot behind the desk at Democratic headquarters in Pittsburgh to oversee the returns, read the figures in a low voice as the ward and county tally sheets were passed on to him. As the evening wore on he grew grimmer. When a Shapp supporter appeared to "offer friendship," he was ordered to leave. What became clear was that both the Allegheny County and Philadelphia organizations had failed to deliver the expected support. Casey carried the two Democratic strongholds by only 1344 and 8226 votes respectively. The once powerful organization had been beaten almost single-handedly by an unknown political novice. The so-called Lawrence machine had demonstrated its vulnerability.

Fortunately for the organization, the campaign had been surprisingly free of rancor, and Milton Shapp realized that he would need the party to defeat his Republican opponent. Lawrence appeared equally anxious to effect a reconciliation—Shapp, after all, was highly preferable to any Republican. Less than two weeks after Shapp's stunning victory, Lawrence told the Pennsylvania Federation of Democratic Women, "I intend to do everything I can to make certain that *all* Democratic candidates win in November. Mr. Shapp deserves a united enthusiastic Democratic party and that is what we are and what we intend to be. All of us accept the decision of the voters." Shortly thereafter, Shapp met with Lawrence at the Pittsburgh Hilton Hotel to inform him that he was now the candidate of the party. Lawrence reacted like a pro, Shapp related. "Lawrence had a stake in this thing too. He wanted to get his legislators elected in Harrisburg. He wanted Democrats elected to Congress. If he and I carried on a feud—and he was in a better position to win than I—we would both be hurt." An accord was reached. Lawrence would do what he could to bring the organization around to Milton Shapp. Shapp's own people would continue to operate independently, but they would also assist other Democrats on the ticket. Lawrence also agreed to speak on Shapp's behalf in the fall campaign whenever his Washington duties permitted. In September he issued word to organization regulars that there was "to be no cutting of Milton Shapp," in the general election.[35]

▽

Lawrence kept his word, giving a number of pro-Shapp speeches in the early fall, but the biggest address was to occur on Friday evening, 4 November at Pittsburgh's Syria Mosque. It was the traditional end-of-campaign rally formerly held at Carnegie Music Hall on the North Side. Shapp and all the candidates were to be there, and there was to be a brief pep rally in front of the stage. "On the stage we had a band and Don Brockett and Barbara [a local variety act], a big show called 'Let's Clap for Shapp.' It was fantastic."[36] Lawrence, in introducing Shapp to the party regulars, would give orders to get out the vote in the election five days later.

Lawrence, as was his custom, arrived in Pittsburgh from Washington around 2:00 P.M. He flew now rather than taking the train. He was met at the Allegheny County Airport by a party worker, who drove him directly to URA headquarters. There he presided over the monthly meeting, which lasted slightly over two hours. Business included approval of the final working drawings of a Bluff Street housing project, the opening of bids on a project for the Chartiers Valley, southwest of the city, and approval of certificates of completion for an East Liberty town house project. Reflecting his current work in Washington, Lawrence expressed particular interest in the housing projects. The meeting adjourned at 5:30 P.M., probably with a sharp rap of the chairman's ring on the large oak table.[37]

Lawrence walked the several blocks to the Stouffer's Restaurant on Wood Street to meet his grandson David Donahoe, who was arriving by bus. The dinner was punctuated by Lawrence's account of his week in Washington and questions regarding the events that filled young David's week. It was a familiar and comfortable ritual for the two. Donahoe, still in high school, was to accompany his grandfather to the rally, as he had so many times in the past. When they arrived, there was virtually no one there, a fact that in itself gave an indication of the changes that had taken place. On such an occasion in the past, the hall would have been crowded by this time. Although it eventually filled to just over half capacity, clearly the old campaigner was not pleased. When asked by a passerby, "How are we doing, governor," he snapped, "Well, I'll tell you this machine that I am supposed to be the head of isn't doing so damn good tonight." His mood continued to be somewhat sour, and when the evening's events did not begin promptly at 7:30 as scheduled, he leaned over to Frank Ambrose and barked, "Tell that Jim Knox to get this damned thing started, will you!" (Knox, whom Lawrence had brought into politics in 1938, was now county chairman and had organized the event.) Ambrose immediately informed Knox that the boss was getting impatient. Knox required no second warning, and the rally began a few minutes later.[38]

Candidates for several local offices, a state judgeship, and lieutenant governor were introduced and made brief comments. The partisan audience showed its support of each, although many—like Frank Ambrose, who was missing an Elks party—would probably have preferred to be elsewhere. But the "mayor" or the "chief," as some called him, was back in town, and out of respect for him they canceled any other engagement to be present. They owed it to him.

Jim Knox briefly introduced the man who truly needed no introduction, at least to this audience, many of whom literally owed their livelihoods to him. The seventy-seven-year-old Lawrence, now nearly blind in one eye, issued a call, as he had done so many times before, for party unity. He began in a slow, deliberate voice, as if he didn't quite believe what he was about to say. "I have been up and down this state campaigning for Milton Shapp since three days after the primary. There is less defection among the Democrats at this time than I have ever seen in twenty-five years. I've never been prouder than I am now of the Democratic party." He quickly warmed up as he turned his comments toward the Republican opponents whom he had attacked thousands of times before. "The Republicans are shaking because we have a candidate who can match them in spending money. I heard this governor we have [Scranton] say he regretted that the Democrats didn't have a candidate with experience. His experience prior to running for governor was one year in Congress. Milt Shapp has been in the forefront of governmental business for years."[39]

Those close to the Democratic scene in Pittsburgh can recall the next few moments as vividly as they remember where they were and what they were doing when they heard of the death of Roosevelt, the end of World War II, or the assassination of John F. Kennedy. Frank Ambrose was looking at his watch—it was 8:30—wondering whether the rally would end in time for him to catch the end of the Elks party. Jim Knox was looking at Lawrence's "old dyed shoes." "Just the day before he said to me, 'Jimmy, where do you buy your shoes? I've got to get a pair.'" Huck Fenrich was looking over the crowd, noting those who were absent. James Helbert, political editor of the *Pittsburgh Press,* who had momentarily looked away, was startled by a crash.[40]

Lawrence hesitated, then repeated the last two words, "for years," and stumbled backward, carrying the lectern with him. He then lurched forward, saying clearly into the microphone, "I'm fainting."

Knox, seated in the first row of the auditorium, reached Lawrence immediately. "He collapsed in my arms and we laid him down on the floor." Huck Fenrich reached him second and began to massage his chest. Karen McGuire, a nurse at Ohio Valley General Hospital, rushed to the front and applied mouth-to-mouth resuscitation. Someone put in a call to the police, and within minutes an ambulance arrived from the nearby No. 4 Station. Lawrence was carried from the auditorium at 8:40 and rushed to Presbyterian University Hospital.

Back in the auditorium, a stunned Genevieve Blatt remained on the floor, where she had knelt in prayer moments after the event. Nearby Mayor Joe Barr and other Democratic officials milled around in shock. Knox called for a silent prayer. He then adjourned the meeting and the crowd left. Milton Shapp, who was late arriving at the auditorium, met the departing crowd on the front steps. Informed of Lawrence's collapse by Jerry Lawrence, he immediately went to the hospital, where an all-night vigil by family and friends began.

Lawrence, whose heart had stopped twice before he reached the hospital, never regained consciousness. He remained in the hospital for seventeen days, never aware of the flood of messages that poured in from across the nation. Nor did he learn of Milton Shapp's defeat in the gubernatorial election. Presbyterian University Hospital issued daily bulletins, but his personal physician, Campbell Moses, removed any reason for hope on 6 November. "There is no chance of recovery," he stated at a somber press conference. "Only Mr. Lawrence's good general physique has enabled him to survive beyond expectations."[41]

Dave Lawrence died at 2:55 P.M. on 21 November 1966. "He literally slept away," his doctor said. "There was no struggle. His heart stopped." The following morning the *Post Gazette* ran a cartoon by Cy Hungerford captioned "Dave's Last Fight." It showed a boxer felled by the Grim Reaper. Above the fighter were the words "Pittsburgh's old Champion." Lawrence had told *Press* writer Kap Monahan just one month earlier, "Don't retire—Don't think of it. Keep on at your work and when your time comes, why not die in harness? I intend to do just that." He had kept his last promise.[42]

Epilogue

The attention of most Pittsburghers was fixed on David Lawrence between 21 and 25 November 1966. All three of the city's newspapers ran editorials eulogizing him and carried numerous features highlighting his lengthy career. Photographic essays accompanied each article. Television station WIIC ran a one-hour special, and several radio stations did the same. The Reverend Charles Owen Rice, an old supporter who had lately become critical, provided the best summary of Lawrence's political life in a lengthy article in the *Pittsburgh Catholic.*

> The man was a pragmatic idealist. He believed in causes and he served them. He also believed in power politics and was a frank partisan. Within his own party he had his special flock which he tended with care and some stern discipline. He was always willing to pull back himself and his own faction so that the party as a whole would benefit. He was a compromiser of ambitions. He sought to reward the faithful and he looked with a baleful eye on those who would crash the inner circle without the proper apprenticeship. Enemies within the party were the objects of his private scorn, but publicly he observed the amenities as well as the realities. It is due to him that the party in this area was not torn apart by factionalism. He co-existed with men who hated him and whom he certainly did not love.
>
> It fell to Lawrence to adapt an old style political machine into modern usage. Democrats had to be elected to positions of power, but once in, they had to serve the community. The faithful had to be fed, but they could not be allowed to gorge

themselves and in office they had to perform with acceptable efficiency. It was quite a challenge and he brought it off.[1]

In a five-column obituary, the *New York Times* made a similar assessment. "He was one of those men who worked in politics as others do in law or medicine, as a profession or craft. He served his apprenticeship in a rougher period of big city politics and he learned his lessons starting at the ward level. When the style of politics changed and the ward heeler began to give way to the sophistication of public relations, Mr. Lawrence adapted. . . . While the Pendergasts, the Curleys and the Hagues were watching their machines crumble, Mr. Lawrence was being elected governor of the third most populous state in the country."[2]

Telegrams from dignitaries throughout the nation poured into the city and were printed in the papers. Among those sending condolences were President Johnson, Vice-President Humphrey, former President Truman, Senators Robert Kennedy and Hugh Scott, nearly every state governor including William Scranton, political bosses Jacob Arvey and Carmine Di Sapio, and Philadelphia Mayor James Tate. Local dignitaries such as Mayor Barr, James Knox, Senator Joseph Clark, and labor leader I. W. Abel offered comments of praise and sorrow. The business community, including Willard Rockwell, Leslie B. Worthington, and Richard King Mellon, with whom Lawrence had worked so closely in rebuilding Pittsburgh, issued public statements. Even his old political foes David B. Roberts, William McClelland, Michael Musmanno, and Eddie Leonard had words of praise for him. The board of governors of Bonds for Israel announced that it was bestowing its highest honor, the Eleanor Roosevelt Humanities Award, posthumously on the man who had raised hundreds of thousands of dollars for the Jewish state.

Lesser known Pittsburghers, seeking to share their grief, sent letters to the editors of the city's newspapers. Their outpourings appeared daily. Flags flew at half-staff on all state, county, and city property and would do so for the next thirty days. On the day of the funeral, Friday, 25 November, state, county, and city government offices were closed.

The funeral Mass for David Leo Lawrence was one of the grandest Pittsburgh had ever seen. At about 9:30 A.M. the family and close friends gathered at the McCabe Funeral Home in Shadyside for a final private prayer. When the family had completed the ritual of a last goodbye, eight plainclothesmen from the Pittsburgh police force moved in to carry the casket to the hearse. Across the street the Sisters of Charity of Sacred Heart Parish stood in the slight drizzle that began to fall. The church bells rang every four seconds.

A cortege of twenty polished black and gray cars moved through the streets of the East End toward the center of the city. Police officers along the route saluted, and people left offices and businesses to view the procession. Some were merely curious, but most were paying their final respects. "For an old professional politician who liked to see the crowds turn out, it was a fitting tribute, and he was among old friends all the way."[3] The cortege arrived at St. Mary of Mercy Church at the Point, where David Lawrence had spent many Saturdays during his youth helping his mother tend the altar, and where he later served as usher. Nearly two thousand people jammed the church. Others gathered in the basement and the church auditorium to view the proceedings via closed circuit television. An overflow crowd waited silently in the rain outside.

Inside, John Gabriel, chief sergeant-at-arms, carrying the state mace draped in black, proceeded up the aisle of the small church. He was followed by an altar boy bearing the crucifix and by Bishop John Wright and five other bishops, in addition to many lesser clergy. They were followed by the casket bearing the body of David Lawrence. The small procession passed dozens of local politicians, the thirty-two Democratic ward chairmen, several of Lawrence's old cronies such as Huck Fenrich and Frank Ambrose, and hundreds of unknown western Pennsylvanians who arrived early enough to acquire the few seats available in the church. Farther down the aisle was a special section reserved for the four hundred dignitaries who traveled from as far away as Calcutta to be present. New York Senator Robert Kennedy, whose arrival caused a stir among onlookers, was seated just behind the Lawrence family with two of Lawrence's closest and oldest associates, Joe Barr and Jim Knox.[4]

During the Mass, Bishop Wright delivered a brief eulogy. He praised Lawrence for his "humanitarian service," singling out his efforts in Pittsburgh and Washington "as a battler for fair housing." He then told the mourners: "David Lawrence's earthly story ends where it began, here at The Point of his beloved native city. . . . Thus loyal to the end, . . . he chose to be brought back precisely to this part of Pittsburgh to take his leave of his friends and precisely this church to receive the final blessing of his church."[5]

The neighborhood of his youth, like the man being eulogized by the famous and the humble, had undergone a dramatic transformation. The once shabby environment, with its warehouses, railroad yards, and rundown homes, had been replaced by gleaming office buildings and parks. As David Lawrence had transformed himself from an uneducated son of a minor politician and laborer into one of the nation's leading urban statesmen, so too did he bring his city from "unbelievable ugliness into shining beauty."[6] It was an accomplishment of which he was most proud. He would have been pleased to return to the site of his greatest achievement. It was for him, most certainly, a fitting conclusion.

Appendices

Notes

Index

APPENDIX A
Pittsburgh Renewal Projects

These tables, reporting on Pittsburgh renewal projects, were prepared by Robert Pease.

Time Table

Project	*Certified for Redevelopment*[a]	*Approval by City Council*	*Start of Acquisition*	*Start of Demolition*
J&L, South Side	4/17/49	11/22/49	1949	1949
Gateway Center	3/29/47	1/27/50	1950	1950
J&L, Hazelwood	1/30/51	10/31/52	4/53	1953
J&L, Scotch Bottom	2/15/55	10/31/52	4/53	1953
DeSota-Thackeray	3/31/53	10/28/53	3/54	1955
Centre-Morgan	3/31/53	10/28/53	3/54	1956–57
Lower Hill	8/1/50	9/16/55	4/56	11/56
Chateau St. West	7/14/59	5/5/60	1/61	6/61
East Liberty (A-B-C)	4/26/59	7/8/60[b]	3/61	10/61
Allegheny Center	12/22/59	6/12/61	10/61	10/62
Bluff Street	6/17/52	7/13/62	12/62	1/64
Sheraden Park	2/1/63	4/15/63	None	None
Allegheny General	7/20/62	7/8/63	1/64	8/64
Stadium	10/30/61	12/16/63	8/64	7/65
Allegheny South	11/22/63	4/7/64	9/64	–
Homewood North	11/30/62	2/66	–	–

a. By City Planning Commission.

b. Amended plan for East Liberty B & C approved by Council 5/22/63; start of acquisition, 11/63 and 5/64; demolition start, 6/64.

Financial Data, 1949–65

Project	Est. Public Cost (millions)	Est. Private & Inst. Investment (millions)	Estimated Taxable Assessed Values: Before Renewal (millions)	Estimated Taxable Assessed Values: After Renewal (millions)
J&L, South Side	$ .06	$ 80.0	$ 6.87	$ 21.3
Gateway Center	.60	118.0	8.30	44.8
J&L, Hazelwood	.05	1.4	1.95	1.6
J&L, Scotch Bottom	.03	.54	.32	.06
DeSota-Thackeray	.67	13.06	.35	(Exempt)
Centre-Morgan	.60	12.20	.44	(Exempt)
Lower Hill	18.60	90.0	8.94	33.0
Chateau St. West	12.10	9.0	3.52	5.4
East Liberty (A-B-C)	42.28	45.5	29.24	41.0
Allegheny Center	24.07	65.0	9.25	31.0
Bluff Street	9.23	31.0	2.59	5.0
Sheraden Park	.06	2.7	.03	1.2
Allegheny General	.03	5.5	.57	.2
Stadium	21.49	25.0	5.04	ND[a]
Allegheny South	.06	ND	.39	ND
Homewood North	3.30	ND	3.76	ND
Totals	$133.23	$498.90	$81.56	$184.56

ND = Not determined yet.

a. Publicly owned stadium land is tax exempt, but future development of air rights will produce tax revenue.

Urban Renewal Summary, 1949–65

Project	Total Acres	Acres of Clearance	Property Acquisition: Total Parcels	Property Acquisition: No. Purchased to Date	Family Relocation: No. in Workload	Family Relocation: No. Purchased to Date	Businesses Relocated to Date[d]	Buildings Razed to Date	New Family Dwelling Units: Completed or Being Built	New Family Dwelling Units: Others Proposed
J&L, South Side	32	32	177	177	203	203	6	148	–	–
Gateway Center	23	23	111	111	25	25	150	96	311	–
J&L, Hazelwood	74	74	193	193	405	405	None	159	–	–
J&L, Scotch Bottom	13	13	73	73	120	120	3		–	–
DeSota-Thackeray	3	3	41	41	78	78	13	35	–	–
Centre-Morgan	26	26	155	155	142	142	None	117	–	–
Lower Hill[a]	95	95	989	989	1,551	1,551	413	1,324	594	540
Chateau St. West[a]	98	58	814	795	743	725	222	924	–	–
East Liberty (A-B-C)[ab]	254	118	1,017	549	887	387	245	398	296	1,450
Allegheny Center[a]	103	54	406	356	402	319	409	386	–	1,550
Bluff Street[a]	43	26	261	212	225	146	45	78	–	350
Sheraden Park	46	12[c]	Publicly owned		None	–	–	–	188	–
Allegheny General	19	9	161	127	154	50	3	38	–	–
Stadium[a]	84	84	117	39	63	–	–	–	–	–
Allegheny South	5.5	5.5	4	2	None	–	–	–	–	–
Homewood North[a]	100	ND	ND	–	ND	–	–	–	–	ND
Totals	1018.5	632.5	4,519	3,819	4,998	4,151	1,509	3,703	1,389	4,046

ND = Not determined yet.

a. Federally aided projects.

b. Originally two projects; combined in 1964.

c. Housing area; remaining 34 acres public open space.

d. Figures include rooming houses, in most cases a substantial number.

APPENDIX B

David L. Lawrence: Significant Dates

1903	Clerk-typist in law office of William J. Brennen, Allegheny County Democratic Chairman.
1918	Entered army, 18 September.
1920	Elected chairman, Allegheny County Democratic Committee.
1921	Entered insurance business with Frank J. Harris; married Alyce Golden.
1922	Job as secretary of Voter Registration Commission.
1931	Ran for county commissioner and lost.
1933	Appointed collector of internal revenue by Franklin D. Roosevelt.
1934	Named state chairman of Democratic party; appointed secretary of commonwealth under Governor George Earle (1934–39).
1940	Named Democratic national committeeman from Pennsylvania (he retained this post until his death); resigned as State Democratic Party Chairman.
1942	Death of his two sons; again named Democratic State Chairman (until 1945).
1945–59	Elected mayor of Pittsburgh.
1959–63	Elected governor of Pennsylvania.
1963–66	Served as chairman, President's Committee on Equal Opportunity in Housing.

Notes

Three major groups of interviews provided information for this study. Ninety-five interviews were conducted during the early 1970s to gather information related to the Pittsburgh Renaissance. These transcripts are on file at the Archives of Industrial Society (AIS), Hillman Library, University of Pittsburgh. Also in the early 1970s, Father Thomas Donaghy interviewed more than thirty individuals for his own work on Lawrence. The Donaghy interviews are held in the La Salle College Oral History Collection, Philadelphia. My own interviews (87) were conducted between 1980 and 1985; transcripts are available at AIS.

▷ Growing Up

1. David Brody, *The Steelworkers in America: The Non-Union Era* (Cambridge, 1960), p. 55.

2. Willard Glazier, "The Great Furnace of America," in *Peculiarities of American Cities* (Philadelphia, 1883), pp. 333–34.

3. Francis G. Couvares, *The Remaking of Pittsburgh: Class and Culture in an Industrializing City, 1877–1919* (Albany, N.Y., 1984), p. 86.

4. *Pittsburgh Leader,* 18 October 1903.

5. Victor A. Walsh, "Across the Big Wather: Irish Community Life in Pittsburgh and Allegheny City, 1850–1885" (Ph.D. diss., University of Pittsburgh, 1983), pp. 182, 184.

6. Biographical sketch of Reverend John A. O'Rourke in Diocesan Documents, II (1856–1873), n.p., in Walsh, "Across the Big Wather," p. 185.

7. The 1900 U. S. Manuscript Census for Pittsburgh and Allegheny City gives the year of Lawrence's birth as 1890 but all other sources give 1889.

8. The Hopkins Real Estate Atlas, Ward 1, Pittsburgh, Pa., 1900–1907; *Pittsburgh Leader,* advertisements, June, October 1898. See also, Robert C. Alberts, *The Shaping of the Point: Pittsburgh's Renaissance Park* (Pittsburgh, 1980), pp. 36–37.

9. *Pittsburgh Post-Gazette,* 11 January 1963.

10. Interview with Anna Mae Donahoe, 9 February 1981, p. 2. Citations refer to interviews conducted by the author unless otherwise indicated.

11. Interview with David L. Lawrence by Sally Shames, 21 January 1955, unpaginated.

12. *Pittsburgh Press,* 14 March 1946; interview with Arthur J. Rooney, 25 February

1981, pp. 1, 2. Sporting life was particularly popular in the Pittsburgh of David Lawrence's youth. See Couvares, *Remaking of Pittsburgh,* esp. chap. 5.

13. Interview with David L. Lawrence by Stefan Lorant, 14 December 1963, p. 41. The DAR, according to Lawrence, rescued the blockhouse from Powers and other would-be entrepreneurs by having her evicted and hiring a caretaker to prevent future squatters.

14. Ibid.

15. Joseph A. Vares, "David L. Lawrence" (unpublished ms., 1975), p. 11. Provided to the author by Gerald Lawrence.

16. *Pittsburgh Leader,* 8 October 1903.

17. Couvares, *Remaking of Pittsburgh,* p. 67.

18. *Saturday Evening Post,* 14 March 1959, p. 80.

19. Lawrence interview by Lorant, p. 42.

20. *Pittsburgh and Allegheny Directory,* (Pittsburgh: R. L. Polk, 1904).

21. Interview with Andrew Fenrich, 15 May 1981, p. 9; interview with James Knox, 21 April 1981, p. 18.

22. Interview with A. M. Donahoe, p. 16.

23. Lawrence interview by Lorant, p. 42.

24. Ibid., p. 43.

25. *Harpers,* August 1964, p. 47.

26. Letter from John McGrady to Joseph A. Vares cited, in Vares, "Lawrence."

27. Joseph Guffey, *Seventy Years on the Red Fire Wagon: From Tilden to Truman Through New Freedom and New Deal* (Privately printed, 1952), p. 18.

28. Samuel P. Hays, "The Politics of Reform in Municipal Government in the Progressive Era," *Pacific Northwest Quarterly* 55 (October 1964): 159ff.

29. Interview with Al Conway, 20 August 1982.

30. Hays, "Politics of Reform," p. 159.

31. Ibid.

32. Joseph Hutmacher, "Urban Liberalism and the Age of Reform," *Journal of American History* 49 (September 1962): 232, 235. "The great source of working class liberalism was experience. . . . Such people were less imbued than the middle class with the 'old American creed,' which expounded individualism, competition, and laissez faire free enterprise as the means of advance from 'rags to riches.' . . . Their felt needs, largely of the bread and butter type, were of the here and now. . . . Their outlook tended to be more practical and 'possibilistic' than that of some middle-class Progressives who allowed their reform aspirations to soar to utopian heights. . . . Their view of government was much less permeated with fears of paternalism and centralization than that of traditionally individualistic middle-class reformers many of whom abated their attachment to the laissez-faire principle with only the greatest trepidation."

33. Interview with Lawrence by Lorant, p. 46.

34. Guffey, *Seventy Years,* p. 41ff. The Guffey family, despite its financial connection with the Mellons in developing the famous Spindletop oil field in Texas, supported the Democratic party for over three generations.

35. Ibid., pp. 99, 100.

36. Minute Book of the Voter Registration Commission of the City of Pittsburgh, vol. 1, 17 February 1914, p. 175, AIS.

37. Guffey, *Seventy Years,* p. 18.

38. See, for example, Lincoln Steffens, "Pittsburgh: A City Ashamed," in *The Shame of the Cities* (New York, 1904); and Bruce Stave, *The New Deal and the Last Hurrah: Pittsburgh Machine Politics* (Pittsburgh, 1970), p. 66.

39. Minute Books of the Voter Registration Commission, 1914–1924, AIS.

40. Ibid.

41. Sally Shames, "David L. Lawrence, Mayor of Pittsburgh: Development of a Political Leader" (Ph.D. diss., University of Pittsburgh, 1958), p. 13.

▷ Friends, Family, and work

1. Interview with John P. Robin, 26 March 1983, p. 19.

2. Interview with Andrew Fenrich, 15 May 1981, p. 2; interview with Robin, p. 20; interview with Anna Mae Donahoe, 9 February 1981, p. 17.

3. *Pittsburgh Post-Gazette,* 10 April 1929.

4. Copies of federal income tax returns of David L. and Alyce G. Lawrence, 1963–65, supplied by Gerald Lawrence.

5. Interview with Arthur J. Rooney, 25 February 1981, p. 4.

6. *Pittsburgh Press,* 6 November 1936.

7. Interview with A. M. Donahoe, p. 2.

8. Minute Books of the Voter Registration Commission of the City of Pittsburgh, vol. 1, 15 October 1918, 14 June 1924, AIS.

9. Interview with Andrew Bradley by Thomas Donaghy, 1 August 1974, p. 10.

10. Interview with Frank Ambrose by Thomas Donaghy, August 1974, pp. 1, 2; interview with Walter Giesey, 23 October 1982, p. 23.

11. Interview with Gerald Lawrence, 17 August 1982, p. 4.

12. U.S. Manuscript Census for Pittsburgh and Allegheny City, 1900, 1409 Rebecca Street.

13. Interview with A. M. Donahoe, p. 7. The children's birthdates are as follows: Mary, 18 June 1922, Anna Mae, 15 September 1923, William Brennen, 12 December 1925, David Leo, 28 August 1928, Gerald, 18 March 1939. The Lawrence residences were on King Avenue, Evaline Street, Winebiddle Street, and at 355 South Aiken Avenue, all in the city's East End. They lived on South Aiken from 1937 until 1966.

14. Interview with A. M. Donahoe, p. 8; interview with Gerald Lawrence, p. 6.

15. Interview with Gerald Lawrence by Thomas Donaghy, 18 August 1974; interview with A. M. Donahoe, p. 13. The two statements are remarkably similar considering that one is referring to the 1930s and the other to the late 1940s and early 1950s.

16. Interview with Gerald Lawrence, p. 6.

17. *Pittsburgh Post-Gazette,* 30 July 1920.

18. Minute Books of the Voter Registration Commission, vol. 1, 27 November 1924.

19. *Pittsburgh Press,* 3 March 1921.

20. *Pittsburgh Press, Pittsburgh Sun-Telegraph, Pittsburgh Post-Gazette,* 5–20 October 1925; *Pittsburgh Press,* 4 November 1925.

21. *Pittsburgh Press,* 31 October 1929.

22. Ibid., 1 November 1929.

23. Minute Books of the Voter Registration Commission, vol. 1, 1920, 1925, vol. 2, 1929.

24. *Pittsburgh Press,* 1 September 1925; *Pittsburgh Post-Gazette,* 30 October 1931.

25. Interview with Genevieve Blatt, 22 June 1981; interview with David L. Lawrence by Stefan Lorant, 14 December 1963, p. 48.

26. Interview with Lawrence by Lorant, p. 48.

27. *Pittsburgh Press, Pittsburgh Post-Gazette,* 5 November 1924.

28. *Pittsburgh Post-Gazette,* 18 April 1928.

29. *Pittsburgh Press,* 5 November 1928; *Pittsburgh Post-Gazette,* 2 November 1928.

30. *Pittsburgh Post-Gazette,* 3 November 1928; Bruce Stave, *The New Deal and*

the Last Hurrah (Pittsburgh, 1970), pp. 37–39; *The Pennsylvania Manual*, "Election Statistics," no. 79, 1929, p. 480ff.

31. *New York Times*, 20 July 1931.

▷ Crumbs No More

1. Interview with Arthur J. Rooney, 25 February 1981.
2. *Pittsburgh Press*, 29–30 August, 13 August 1931.
3. Interview with James Knox, 23 April 1981.
4. *Pittsburgh Press*, *Pittsburgh Post-Gazette*, *Pittsburgh Sun-Telegraph*, July 1931.
5. Ibid., 7–15 September 1931; *Pittsburgh Press*, 30 August 1931.
6. *Pittsburgh Press*, 6 September 1931; report of the Western Pennsylvania Bar Association, typescript in the Pennsylvania Department, Carnegie Library, Pittsburgh.
7. *Pittsburgh Post-Gazette*, 15, 16 September 1931; Allegheny County Employment Records, 1930–35, located in the attic of the City-County Building, Pittsburgh.
8. *Pittsburgh Press*, 13 September 1930, 19 October 1931.
9. *Pittsburgh Post-Gazette*, 28 October 1931; *Pittsburgh Press*, 29 October 1931.
10. *Pittsburgh Sun-Telegraph*, *Pittsburgh Press*, 28 October–5 November 1931.
11. *Pittsburgh Press*, 5 October 1931; *Pittsburgh Post-Gazette*, 29 October 1931.
12. *Pittsburgh Press*, 30 October 1931.
13. Ibid., 20–25 October 1931.
14. Lawrence, quoted by Bruce Stave in *The New Deal and the Last Hurrah* (Pittsburgh, 1970), p. 31; Ray Sprigle, "Lord Guffey of Pennsylvania," *The American Mercury*, November 1936, p. 283.
15. *Pittsburgh Press*, 23 October 1931.
16. Ibid., 25 October 1931.
17. Ibid., 4 November 1931.
18. Ibid., 5 November 1931; *Pittsburgh Post-Gazette*, 5 November 1931.
19. Ibid.
20. Philip Klein, *A Social Study of Pittsburgh: Community Problems and Social Services of Allegheny County* (New York, 1938), p. 129; interview with anonymous respondent by Weber, 7 October 1966; interview with Raymond Czachowski by Greg Mahalic, 1 July 1976, Pittsburgh Oral History Project, Pennsylvania State Archives, Harrisburg.
21. Klein, *Social Study*, p. 360ff; see also Stave, *New Deal*, pp. 110–12.
22. Interview with Al Conway, 20 August 1982; *Pittsburgh-Post Gazette*, 31 March 1932.
23. Lyle Dorsett, *Franklin D. Roosevelt and the City Bosses* (New York, 1976), p. 6ff.
24. Joseph F. Guffey, "Happenings at the Democratic National Convention in Chicago, 1932," Guffey Archives, Washington and Jefferson College. Guffey's memorandum confirms Lawrence's role as an observer if not a participant in the Roosevelt camp meetings at the convention.
25. Andrew Buni, *Robert L. Vann of the Pittsburgh Courier: Politics and Black Journalism* (Pittsburgh, 1974), p. 178; *Pittsburgh Courier*, 27 August 1932.
26. Buni, *Vann*, p. 194; Ira Katznelson, *Black Men, White Cities* (London, 1973), p. 84. Vann's conversion to the Democratic party was consistent with the pattern Katznelson noted in New York, Chicago, and other Northern cities. "Black leaders were chosen by the white party elite. . . . They were not descriptively representative, in that their class composition differed strikingly from that of the represented. . . . These liai-

son or buffer leaders were given a taste of honey, the illusion of political access and some visible patronage" (p. 84).

27. *Pittsburgh Courier*, 8 October 1932.

28. List of Democratic and Republican committeepersons, 1932–34. Graciously supplied to the author by Bruce Stave.

29. Ibid., U.S. Bureau of the Census, *Census Tract Tables of Population and Families: 1930, Pittsburgh* 2, (Washington, D.C., 1932), table 1.

30. Lawrence, quoted by Samuel J. Astorino, "The Decline of the Republican Dynasty in Pennsylvania" (Ph.D. diss., University of Pittsburgh, 1962), p. 179.

31. Thomas E. Williams, "Will Pennsylvania Go Democratic This Time?" *The Nation*, 9 October 1932.

32. *Pittsburgh Press*, 29 October 1932; information card circulated to all workers of Hubbard and Company, Guffey Archives.

33. *Pittsburgh Press*, 30 September 1932.

34. Samuel J. Astorino, "The Decline of the Republican Dynasty," p. 182.

35. Lawrence to Roosevelt, 7 October 1932, Personal File, "Governor Lawrence," FDR Library.

36. *Pittsburgh-Post Gazette, Pittsburgh Press*, 20 October 1932.

37. *The Pennsylvania Manual*, "Election Statistics," no. 81, 1933, p. 422 ff.; for an analysis of Pittsburgh ethnic wards in 1930 see John Bodnar, Roger Simon, and Michael Weber, *Lives of Their Own: Blacks, Italians and Poles in Pittsburgh, 1900–1930* (Urbana, Ill., 1980), p. 207 ff.; Bruce Stave, *New Deal*, pp. 37–39.

38. *Pittsburgh Sun-Telegraph*, 9 November 1932.

39. Stave, *New Deal*, p. 56.

40. Ibid. Jones held jobs under Republican Mayor William Magee as press agent and police superintendent and was the publicity agent for Republican boss Jimmy Coyne.

41. *Pittsburgh Post-Gazette*, 5 June 1933.

42. Ibid., 7 August 1933; *Pittsburgh Press*, 28 August 1933.

43. The Republican organization reported campaign expenditures of $91,744, the bulk of which was supplied by William L. and R. B. Mellon. McArdle's campaign spending exceeded $46,000, while Mackrell spent $21,000. The Democratic organization, in contrast, reported expenditures of $17,000—Benedum, Guffey, and Lawrence were listed as $1000-plus contributors—while Henry spent less than $1700. *Pittsburgh Press*, 5 October 1933.

44. *Pittsburgh Press*, 2 September 1933.

45. Ibid., 17 August–15 September 1933.

46. *Pittsburgh Sun-Telegraph*, 22 September 1933.

47. Interview with Fred Weir, 24 June 1981, p. 13.

48. *Pittsburgh Press*, 3 September 1933.

49. *New York Times*, 5 November 1933.

50. Stave, *New Deal*, p. 76; *Pittsburgh Press*, 27 October 1933.

51. Interview with Weir, p. 17.

52. Minute Books of the Voter Registration Commission, September 1933, AIS.

53. *Pittsburgh Press*, 19 October 1933.

54. *Pittsburgh Sun-Telegraph, Pittsburgh Press*, 13 June, 14 August, 16 August, 10 October, 15 October–4 November 1933.

55. *Pittsburgh Press*, 29 October 1933.

56. Ibid.

57. Stave, *New Deal*, p. 170 ff.

58. List of Democratic and Republican committee persons.

59. Stave, *New Deal,* pp. 79–80. Stave argues that the Democratic victory was not an extension of the FDR vote and that McNair's support came from a different group of voters from those who voted for Roosevelt. McNair, for example, lost all the Republican organization-controlled wards in the central city, while FDR won two-thirds of the same wards. He further argues that McNair's following derived not from the black or ethnic blocs but from the upper-class native white population. It appears, however, that Stave underestimates the extent of ethnic participation by relying on a calculation of foreign born rather than foreign stock. In Pittsburgh by 1933, the second generation far outnumbered their parents as the dominant population group.

60. Ibid., pp. 70–80.

61. *Pittsburgh Press,* 22 September 1933.

▷ Building an Organization

1. Edward C. Banfield and James Q. Wilson, *City Politics* (Cambridge, Mass., 1963); William C. Havard, "From Bossism to Cosmopolitanism," *Annals of the American Academy of Political and Social Science* 353 (May 1964): 88; Rexford G. Tugwell, *The Braintrust* (New York, 1968), p. 371.

2. Bruce Stave, *The New Deal and the Last Hurrah: Pittsburgh Machine Politics* (Pittsburgh, 1970), p. 20; Lyle W. Dorsett, *The New Deal and the City Bosses* (Port Washington, N.Y., 1977), p. 21ff; John H. Mollenkopf, *The Contested City* (Princeton, 1983) p. 16.

3. Melvin Holli and Peter d'A Jones, eds., *Biographical Dictionary of American Mayors, 1820–1980* (Westport, Conn., 1981).

4. Fred W. Perkins, "Mr. Guffey Dispenses Political Jobs," *Pittsburgh Press,* 30 September 1934; Andrew Buni, *Robert L. Vann of the Pittsburgh Courier: Politics and Black Journalism* (Pittsburgh, 1974), pp. 198–99.

5. Lorena Hickok to Harry Hopkins, 24 July 1935, Hopkins File, FDR Library.

6. *Pittsburgh Press,* 28 October 1937; interview with Rita Wilson Kane, 27 November 1983, p. 8.

7. Interview with Al Conway, 20 August 1982, p. 8; interview with Rosemary Plesett, 14 April 1983, p. 11; Commonwealth of Pennsylvania vs. David L. Lawrence in the Court of Quarter Sessions of Dauphin County, Pa., testimony of E. A. Griffith, Sept. Session, 1939, vol. 1, pp. 500–02.

8. Pinchot to FDR, 21 December 1935, President's Personal Name File, 289, FDR Library.

9. Lorena Hickok, quoted in James N. J. Henwood, "Experiment in Relief: The Civil Works Administration in Pennsylvania, 1933–34," *Pennsylvania History* 39 (1972): 58; *Pittsburgh Press,* 2 March 1935; ward data compiled from notes supplied by Bruce Stave.

10. Donald S. Howard, *The WPA and Federal Relief Policy* (New York, 1934), p. 356. The indices of poverty included homes with no income earner, general assistance cases, and employment in emergency work. Nearly 90 percent of all WPA jobs in Pennsylvania required that the recipient be listed on the relief rolls prior to receiving an appointment.

11. David L. Lawrence to Pittsburgh Democratic Ward Chairmen, quoted in the *Pittsburgh Press,* 1 March 1935.

12. *Pittsburgh Press,* 8 March 1935; Stave, *New Deal,* p. 169; interview with John P. Robin, 26 March 1983, p. 7; Interview with Al Tronzo by Dodie Carpenter, 19 August 1974, p. 2, AIS.

13. Stave data on ward committeemen.

14. Stave, *New Deal*, p. 169; William J. Keefe and William C. Seyler, "Precinct Politicians in Pittsburgh," *Social Science* 35 (January 1960): 28; interview with Jake Williams, 30 March 1983, p. 19.

15. *Pittsburgh Post-Gazette*, 2 March, 28 December 1935.

16. Interview with Conway, p. 19–20.

17. Ibid. Conway testified that nothing detrimental happened to those who failed to contribute—It was not macing, he insisted. City workers interviewed said that they seldom saw anyone refuse to give a contribution.

18. Interview with Williams, p. 18.

19. Stave, *New Deal*, p. 235; interview with Williams, p. 18; interview with John McGrady, 3 June 1983, pp. 1–3. The committeeman from the Eighth Ward resigned after joining the police; his wife was appointed to succeed him.

20. Stave, *New Deal*, p. 112; interview with Williams, p. 20; interview with Conway, p. 11.

21. Interview with Conway, p. 14; interview with Fred Weir, 24 June 1981; interview with Al Conway by Dodie Carpenter, 19 August 1974.

22. Interview with James Knox, 28 April 1981, p. 5; telephone interview with Knox, 5 October 1984.

23. Interview with Weir, p. 4; interview with John Jones, 9 February 1981, pp. 5–6.

24. Telephone interview with Knox. The job seeker in question was Peter Flaherty, who later became mayor of Pittsburgh by running an anti-organization campaign. His campaign slogan, "He's nobody's boy," conveniently overlooked the circumstances of his first political job.

25. Telephone interview with Knox.

26. Interview with Andrew Fenrich, 15 May 1981, p. 7; interview with Jones, p. 11.

27. Interview with Frank Ambrose by Thomas Donaghy, 11 July 1984, pp. 7–8.

28. Interview with Rita Wilson Kane, p. 24.

29. Interview with Knox, p. 11.

30. Ibid.

31. Interview with Walter Giesey, 23 October 1982.

32. Interview with Conway, p. 8; interview with Williams, p. 5.

33. Interview with Jones, p. 17; interview with Genevieve Blatt, 22 June 1981, pp. 5, 16; Arthur Mann, *LaGuardia Comes to Power* (Philadelphia, 1965), p. 28.

34. Interview with Blatt, p. 7.

35. *Pittsburgh Press*, 19 September 1957.

36. Ibid; interview with Morton Coleman, 15 February 1984, untranscribed.

37. Interview with William Block, 3 March 1984, p. 9.

38. Interviews with Tronzo, untranscribed, Blatt, p. 11, Robin, p. 21.

39. Interview with Robin, p. 36.

▷ Expanding the Network

1. *Pittsburgh Sun-Telegraph*, 19 September 1933.

2. *Pittsburgh Post-Gazette*, 11 November 1933.

3. The Pittsburgh public safety director controversy was eagerly covered by all three city newspapers, January–February 1934. In addition, Bruce Stave has provided an in depth analysis of the political maneuverings of William McNair during this period. See *The New Deal and the Last Hurrah: Pittsburgh Machine Politics* (Pittsburgh, 1970), p. 87ff.

4. Walter Davenport, "Mayor's Day In," *Collier's*, 21 April 1934.

5. *Pittsburgh Press,* 29 April 1934.

6. "One Month of McNair," *Pittsburgh Press,* 5 February 1934.

7. Lawrence and McNair, quoted in Stave, *New Deal,* pp. 91, 92; interview with John Jones, 9 February 1981.

8. Interview with David L. Lawrence by Stefan Lorant, 4 December 1963.

9. Bruce Bliven, Jr., "Pennsylvania Under Earle," *The New Republic,* 18 August 1937, p. 38; Paul Beers, *Pennsylvania Politics: Yesterday and Today* (University Park, Pa., 1980), p. 119; Richard Keller, *Pennsylvania's Little New Deal* (New York, 1982), p. 125.

10. Ray Sprigle, "Lord Guffey of Pennsylvania," *American Mercury,* November 1936, p. 284.

11. *Pennsylvania Manual,* "Election Returns," no. 81, p. 246ff.

12. Interview with James Law, Democratic county chairman, Luzerne County, Wilkes Barre, 8 June 1981, p. 1; *Pittsburgh-Post Gazette,* 5, 9 June 1934. Lawrence was actually required to resign either his federal post or the state chairmanship due to an edict by Secretary of the Treasury Morganthau that treasury employees holding political party posts must quit them by September 1 or forfeit their treasury jobs.

13. Sprigle, "Lord Guffey," p. 276.

14. Interview with Law, pp. 3, 4.

15. Commonwealth of Pennsylvania vs. David L. Lawrence in the Court of Quarter Sessions of Dauphin County, Pa., Sept. Session, 1939, vol. 4, p. 1808.

16. Keller, *Little New Deal,* p. 125ff. For a detailed account of the Republican campaign see chap. 5.

17. Chester Harris, *Tiger at the Bar: The Life Story of Charles J. Margiotti* (New York, 1956); Paul Beers, *Pennsylvania Politics,* p. 145.

18. Harris, *Tiger at the Bar,* p. 323.

19. *Pittsburgh Press,* 9 June 1934.

20. Ibid.

21. *Philadelphia Independent,* 4 November 1934; Andrew Buni, *Robert L. Vann of the Pittsburgh Courier* (Pittsburgh, 1974), p. 216.

22. Harris, *Tiger at the Bar,* p. 324–25.

23. Ibid., p. 326.

24. Keller, *Little New Deal,* p. 154. Italians in Philadelphia, Keller reported, shifted from 22.6 percent Democratic in 1930 to 52.2 percent in 1934.

25. *Pittsburgh Press,* 2 October 1934.

26. *The Pennsylvania Manual,* "Election Statistics," no. 81, 1933, pp. 422–24.

27. *Pittsburgh Press,* 2 October 1934.

28. Diaries of David L. Lawrence, 1936, 1940, in possession of the author, generously supplied by the Lawrence family.

29. Harris, *Tiger at the Bar,* p. 329. Margiotti was offered the position following a 16 November victory celebration at Pittsburgh's William Penn Hotel. His acceptance was announced on 23 November.

30. *Pittsburgh Post-Gazette,* 9 December 1934.

31. Interview with Al Tronzo by Dodie Carpenter, 19 August 1974, p. 4.

32. Ibid.

▷ Exercising Power

1. Interview with John P. Robin, 26 March 1983, pp. 8–9; interview with Al Tronzo by Dodie Carpenter, 19 August 1974, pp. 2–3, AIS; *Pittsburgh Press,* 7 November 1945, p. 11.

2. "Employment in Pennsylvania," *Monthly Labor Review* 40 (December 1934): 876.

3. Richard Keller, *Pennsylvania's Little New Deal* (New York, 1982), p. 190. See also David Brody, *Steelworkers in America: The Non-Union Era* (Cambridge, Mass., 1960); John Bodnar, Roger Simon, and Michael Weber, *Lives of Their Own: Blacks, Italians and Poles in Pittsburgh, 1900–1960* (Urbana, Ill., 1982).

4. Interview with Walter Giesey by Nancy Mason, 12 December 1972, AIS.

5. Ibid.; interview with Walter Giesey by Thomas Donaghy, 19 September 1975. The wording was quoted identically in the two interviews.

6. Interview with David L. Lawrence by Stefan Lorant, 14 December 1963.

7. Interview with James Tate by Thomas Donaghy, 19 July 1973, p. 4.

8. *Pittsburgh Press*, 20 November 1934; Papers of George H. Earle, Speech and News File 67, Pennsylvania State Archives, Harrisburg.

9. *Pittsburgh Press*, 20 March 1935.

10. Ibid., 1 March 1935; Keller, *Little New Deal*, p. 167, esp. chap. 6.

11. Interview with Al Tronzo, 21 February 1984; *Pittsburgh Sun-Telegraph*, 3 May 1935.

12. *Legislative Journal: House*, vol. 18, May 1935, p. 2988 ff.; *Legislative Journal: Senate*, vol. 18, May 1935, p. 2988 ff.

13. Keller, *Little New Deal*, p. 173 ff.

14. Address by Governor Earle to the General Assembly of the State of Pennsylvania, 28 January 1935, Earle Papers, Speech and News File, 67; *Legislative Journal: House*, vol. 18, 1935, p. 221. The program was taken directly from the Democratic platform of 1934.

15. *Pittsburgh Press*, 2, 9, 28 September, 31 October 1934.

16. Ibid., 13 July 1934.

17. Ibid., 11, 12, January, 2 February 1935.

18. Ibid., 3 February 1935.

19. Ibid., 5 March 1935; *Legislative Journal: House*, vol. 19, 6 March 1935, p. 892 ff.

20. *Pittsburgh Press*, 4, 19, 20 June 1935; Senate Subcommittee Hearings, 23 October 1935, reported in the *Pittsburgh Press*, 24 October 1935. The cabinet officers were, in addition to Lawrence, Harry Kalodner, secretary of revenue, Charles J. Margiotti, attorney general, Arthur Colegrove, secretary of property and supplies; and Ralph Bashore, secretary of forests and waters. Lawrence's influence is obvious when it is noted that only he resided in the Pittsburgh area.

21. *Pittsburgh Press*, 24 October 1935.

22. *Philadelphia Inquirer*, 27 September 1936.

23. Interview with Father Woody Jones by Thomas Donaghy, 13 August 1974, p. 2.

24. *Pennsylvania Manual*, "Election Statistics," no. 83, 1937, p. 195.

25. *Evening Public Ledger* (Philadelphia), 4 November 1936.

26. *Legislative Journal: House*, vol. 21, 5 January 1937, p. 45.

27. Keller, *Little New Deal*, p. 236; *Pittsburgh Press*, 7 June 1937.

28. Keller, *Little New Deal*, pp. 270–71; *Legislative Journal: House*, vol. 21, 5 January 1937–7 June 1937; *Legislative Journal: Senate*, vol. 21, 5 January 1937–12 June 1937; Bruce Bliven, Jr., "Pennsylvania Under Earle," *The New Republic*, 18 August 1937, p. 39; *Pittsburgh Press*, 27 March 1946.

29. *Legislative Journal: House*, vol. 21, 5 January 1937–7 June 1937; *Legislative Journal: Senate*, vol. 21, 5 January 1937–12 June 1937.

30. Ibid.

31. *Pittsburgh Press*, 7 June 1937.

32. Interview with David L. Lawrence by Sally Shames, 21 January 1955, unpaginated.

33. Keller, *Little New Deal,* p. 287.

34. *Pittsburgh Press, Pittsburgh Sun-Telegraph,* 17, 27 October, 15, 21 November, 3 December 1935, 23 April, 14 May 1936.

35. Bruce Stave, *The New Deal and the Last Hurrah* (Pittsburgh, 1970), p. 135; William McNair, "The Waste of the People's Money," *Saturday Evening Post,* 27 November 1935, p. 70.

36. *Bulletin Index* (Pittsburgh), 26 December 1935.

37. Lawrence to Marvin McIntyre, 6 October 1936, Democratic National Committee, Pennsylvania File 300, FDR Library.

▷ The Empire Crumbles

1. *Pittsburgh Sun-Telegraph,* 16 January 1938.

2. It is unclear whether Lewis intended to use Pennsylvania as a springboard to the presidency as some newspapers suggested. His differences with Roosevelt involved fundamental policy issues, but neither of Lewis's major biographers believe that he seriously considered the idea. Saul Alinsky, *John L. Lewis: An Unauthorized Biography* (New York, 1949), p. 161ff; Melvyn Dubofsky and Warren Van Tine, *John L. Lewis: A Biography* (New York, 1977), pp. 314, 323–34.

3. *Pittsburgh Press,* 12 February 1938.

4. Ibid.; Commonwealth of Pennsylvania vs. David L. Lawrence in the Court of Quarter Sessions of Dauphin County, Pa., testimony of Frank Taylor, Chief Clerk, Democratic State Committee, 26 February 1940, vol. 4, p. 1787; *United Mine Workers' Journal,* 13 February 1938.

5. Guy V. Miller, "Pennsylvania's Scrambled Politics, *The Nation,* 14 May 1938, p. 555; Richard Keller, *Pennsylvania's Little New Deal* (New York, 1982), p. 296.

6. In his autobiography, *Seventy Years on the Red Fire Wagon: From Tilden to Truman Through New Freedom and New Deal* (Privately printed, 1952), p. 104, Guffey contends that he was urged to announce his candidacy, but an analysis of the statements of the fifteen top state leaders shows virtually no support for him.

7. *Pittsburgh Press,* 17 February 1938.

8. Interview with Genevieve Blatt, 22 June 1981, p. 17; Guffey, *Seventy Years,* p. 103.

9. Interview with James Law, 8 June 1981, p. 14.

10. Guffey, *Seventy Years,* p. 107. In his later reminisences Guffey denied that any such clash occurred or that he wished to become a candidate himself. All available evidence, however, suggests that the Lawrence-Guffey split came into the open at that meeting.

11. Typescript statement of dispatch by Gould Lincoln, staff correspondent for the *Harrisburg Evening Star,* 28 February 1938, Guffey archives, Washington and Jefferson College.

12. *Pittsburgh Press,* 13 April 1938, 5 December 1939.

13. Ibid.; interview with Law, p. 3; Gould Lincoln statement.

14. Transcript of Margiotti radio address, 16 February 1938, Guffey Archives.

15. *Pittsburgh Press,* 5 December 1939.

16. Ibid., 19, 21 April 1938; Keller, *Little New Deal,* p. 313.

17. Margiotti clipping file, Pennsylvania Department, Carnegie Library, Pittsburgh; *Pittsburgh Press,* 26 April 1938.

18. Chester Harris, *Tiger at the Bar: The Life Story of Charles J. Margiotti* (New York, 1956), p. 373.

19. For a complete transcript of the Earle-Margiotti exchange see the *Pittsburgh Press,* 28 April 1938.

20. Grand Jury Presentment by Carl B. Shelley, District Attorney, Dauphin County, 29 April 1938. Dauphin County Court House.

21. *Pittsburgh Press,* 26 April 1938.

22. *Pennsylvania Manual,* "Election Statistics," no. 85, 1939, pp. 147–48; Miller, "Pennsylvania's Scrambled Politics," p. 555.

23. *Pittsburgh Press,* 22 May 1938.

24. Shelley amendment to the district attorney's petition, filed before the Supreme Court of Pennsylvania, Philadelphia, 9 June 1938, in Dauphin County Grand Jury Investigation Proceedings, 1938 (no. 1) 332, p. 289, (no. 2) 332, p. 342 (no. 3) 332, p. 358.

25. Interview with David L. Lawrence in Sally Shames, "David Lawrence, Mayor of Pittsburgh: Development of a Political Leader" (Ph.D. diss., University of Pittsburgh, 1958), p. 30ff.

26. "Complete Text of Governor Earle's Speech on Graft Inquiry," *Pittsburgh Press,* 13 June 1938.

27. Interview with Carl B. Shelley in Keller, *Little New Deal,* pp. 331–32; interview with David L. Lawrence, 20 May 1958; interview with Law, p. 9; Paul Beers, *Pennsylvania Politics: Today and Yesterday* (University Park, Pa., 1980), p. 131.

28. Earle Address to the General Assembly, *Legislative Journal: Senate,* vol. 22, 25 July 1938, p. 2.

29. Named to the house commission were organization Democrats Herbert Cohen, Edgar Schope, Anthony Girard, Robert Bierly, and Joseph Ormansky, and Republicans Elwood Turner and David Perry.

30. Report of the Special Commission of the House of Representatives Investigating the Official Conduct of Civil Officers of the Commonwealth of Pennsylvania under Regulations of the HR Passed July 30, 1938, in *Legislative Journal: Extraordinary session,* vol. 23, 30 July 1938, p. 947ff.

31. *Harrisburg Patriot,* 2 September 1938; Pittsburgh, Philadelphia, and Harrisburg newspapers, 4 October–4 November 1938.

32. *Pittsburgh Press,* 8, 23 October 1938.

33. *Pennsylvania Manual,* "Votes for the U.S. Senator, Governor, General Election," no. 85, 1939, pp. 153–54.

34. Keller, *Little New Deal,* p. 365.

35. *Pittsburgh Press,* 9 November 1938.

36. Interview with Fred Weir, 24 June 1981; *Pittsburgh Press,* 9 November 1938.

37. Report of the Special Commission, p. 947; *Pittsburgh Press,* 9 November 1938; interview with Tronzo, p. 24.

38. Report of the Special Commission, p. 959.

39. Ibid., p. 960ff.

⊳ Years of Trauma

1. Dauphin County Grand Jury Investigation Proceedings (no. 2), Pennsylvania State Reports, Dauphin County Court House, 1938–39, p. 340ff.

2. *Pittsburgh Press,* 7 June 1937, 22 November 1939.

3. Dauphin County Grand Jury Investigation, p. 342.

4. Commonwealth of Pennsylvania vs. David L. Lawrence in the Court of Quarter Sessions of Dauphin County, Pa., no. 501–02, Sept. Session, 1939, opening argument of district attorney Earl V. Compton, vol. 1, p. 105ff.

5. Ibid.

6. Ibid., testimony of Arthur Colegrove, vol. 1, p. 127ff.

7. Ibid.

8. Ibid.

9. Ibid., testimony of A. Spurgeon Bowser, vol. 2, p. 688 ff, 722.

10. Ibid., p. 773.

11. Ibid.

12. Ibid., testimony of Alice E. Priddy, Bertha McCleese, and Gertrude McAnulty, vol. 4, p. 1242 ff; testimony of Alyce E. Lawrence, p. 2285 ff; testimony of Mr. and Mrs. J. Patton, vol. 4, p. 2577.

13. Ibid., testimony of David L. Lawrence, vol. 4, p. 2054 ff.

14. Ibid., charge of Judge Charles Hughes to the jury, vol. 5, p. 2330; *Pittsburgh Post-Gazette*, 8 December 1939.

15. *Valley Independent*, 9 December 1939; *Pittsburgh Post-Gazette*, 8 December 1939.

16. Interview with Judge William Rahauser, 12 June 1981, pp. 6–7.

17. Telephone interview with Anna Mae Donahoe, 10 January 1985.

18. *Pittsburgh Press*, 3 February 1940.

19. Commonwealth of Pennsylvania vs. David L. Lawrence et al. in the court of Quarter Sessions of Dauphin County, Pa., no. 201, June Session, 1939, testimony of David L. Lawrence and Frank Taylor, Chief Clerk, Democratic State Committee, 26 February 1940, vol. 4, p. 1787 ff.

20. Ibid., testimony of J. R. Copenhaver, vol. 2, p. 802 ff.

21. Ibid., testimony of C. J. Margiotti, vol. 2, p. 864 ff.

22. Ibid.

23. Ibid., testimony of Ralph Bashore; letters entered into the record by James Compton, Schuylkill County Democratic Treasurer; testimony of Frank Taylor, testimony of David L. Lawrence; letter of Mr. Dereume, Jefferson County Chairman, p. 1232 ff.

24. Ibid., testimony of David L. Lawrence, p. 1787 ff.

25. Ibid.

26. Ibid.

27. Ibid., charge to the jury by Judge Charles Hughes, vol. 3, p. 2030.

28. Interview with Andrew Fenrich, 15 May 1981, p. 7.

29. Interview with Gerald Lawrence by Thomas Donaghy, 18 September 1974, p. 13; interview with Gerald Lawrence by Weber, 23 October 1982, p. 30; interview with Walter Giesey by Thomas Donaghy, 19 September 1975, p. 31.

30. Interview with Giesey by Donaghy, p. 31.

31. Interview with Frank Ambrose, 11 July 1984, p. 10; Chester Harris, *Tiger at the Bar: The Life Story of Charles J. Margiotti* (New York, 1956), p. 452.

32. *Pittsburgh Press*, 13 April 1940; *Pittsburgh Post-Gazette*, 13, 14 April 1940.

33. *New York Times*, 4 April 1940; *Pittsburgh Press*, 25 April 1940.

34. *Philadelphia Record*, 25 April 1940.

35. *Pittsburgh Post-Gazette*, 21 June 1940.

36. Interview with Joe Barr by Thomas Donaghy, August 1974, p. 8; interview with Barr by Weber, 13 February 1981. Barr's recollections of every detail of this event were identical at the time of the two interviews.

37. Interview with Jack Clinton, 8 June 1983. Clinton, one of the rear seat passengers in the Lawrence automobile remained in the hospital several months after the accident.

38. Interview with Ambrose, p. 7. Ambrose related the identical incident to Donaghy in an interview ten years earlier. See also John Bowlby, *Loss, Sadness and Depression*, vol. 3 of *Attachment and Loss* (New York, 1980); G. Gorer, *Death, Grief*

and Mourning in Contemporary Britain (London, 1965); and Colin Murray Parkes, *Bereavement: Studies of Grief in Adult Life* (London, 1972).

39. Interview with David Donahoe, 20 June 1983, p. 6 ff.

40. Interview with Rita Wilson Kane, 27 April 1983, p. 5; interview with Genevieve Blatt, 22 June 1981, p. 7.

41. Interview with Anna Mae Donahoe, 9 February 1981, p. 7; interview with Gerald Lawrence by Weber, p. 16; *Pittsburgh Press*, 3 September 1958.

42. Interview with Gerald Lawrence by Thomas Donaghy, 8 August 1974, p. 5; interview with David Donahoe, pp. 3–4.

▷ Policies, Principles, and Procedures

1. John Kottler and Paul Lawrence, *Mayors in Action: Five Approaches to Urban Government* (New York, 1974), p. 18 ff, 29. For the best analysis of the "muddling through" mayor, see David Baybrooke and Charles E. Lindbloom, *A Strategy of Decision* (New York, 1963).

2. Interview with John P. Robin, 26 March 1983, p. 42; interview with Walter Giesey by Nancy Mason, 20 December 1972, unpaginated, AIS; interview with Rosemary Plessett, 14 April 1983, p. 13.

3. Interview with David Donahoe, 25 June 1983, p. 3.

4. Interview with Msgr. Charles Owen Rice, 17 August 1982, p. 2; *Pittsburgh Sun-Telegraph*, 6 September 1950; *Pittsburgh Press*, 9 July 1946. Lawrence characterized Churchill's views as typical of "Tories who have held subject peoples in chains."

5. Interview with Genevieve Blatt, 22 June 1981, pp. 1–3; interview with Blatt by Thomas Donaghy, 25 September 1974, p. 2; interview with Rita Wilson Kane, 23 October 1982, p. 3.

6. Interview with Robin, p. 7.

7. Interview with Blatt, p. 16; interview with Giesey, 23 October 1982, p. 18; interview with Aldo Colautti, 23 June 1983, p. 7; interview with Anna Mae Donahoe, 19 February 1981, p. 7; ms. on David L. Lawrence by Thomas Donaghy, chap. 15, p. 16.

8. Interview with Walter Giesey by Thomas Donaghy, 19 September 1975, p. 15.

9. *Pittsburgh Press*, 17 January 1945; interview with Andrew Bradley by Thomas Donaghy, 1 August 1974, p. 13.

10. Interview with Rosemary Plessett by Thomas Donaghy, 24 June 1975, p. 1; interview with Blatt by Donaghy, p. 6.

11. Speech of 4 December 1965, Lawrence Papers, Pennsylvania State Archives, Harrisburg.

12. Interview with David Lawrence by Stefan Lorant, 4 December 1963, p. 10; interview with Robin, p. 23; interview with Giesey, p. 13; interview with Colautti, p. 17.

13. Interview with Blatt, p. 11; interview with Giesey by Donaghy, p. 15.

14. Interview with Gerald Lawrence, 17 August 1982, p. 8.

15. Ibid.; interview with Dan Cercone, 14 July 1983; interview with Blatt, p. 5.

16. Information on Lawrence's ability to interact with the citizens of Pittsburgh may be found throughout the nearly 100 interviews conducted for this study. Those with Adolph Schmidt, Andrew Fenrich, Frank Ambrose, Al Conway, and Walter Giesey, all previously cited, and Henry Hillman, 31 May 1984, were particularly valuable. Michener quotation is from Paul Beers, *Pennsylvania Politics: Today and Yesterday* (University Park, Pa., 1980), p. 241.

17. Interview with Giesey by Thomas Donaghy, p. 20; interview with Andrew Fenrich, 15 May 1981, p. 4 ff.

18. Interview with Robin, p. 40.
19. Interview with Colautti, p. 6.
20. Interview with Giesey by Donaghy, p. 16; interview with Rosemary Plessett, 14 April 1983, p. 14.
21. Interview with Arthur Rooney, 25 February 1981, p. 14.
22. Interview with William Block, 3 March 1984, p. 8.
23. Interview with Gerald Lawrence, p. 16; interview with Plesset, p. 9.
24. Interview with John Jones, 19 February 1981, p. 15.

▷ The Interlude

1. Interview with James Law, 8 June 1981, p. 13; interview with Al Tronzo, 2 February 1984, p. 22; interview with Fred Weir, 24 June 1981; *Pittsburgh Post-Gazette*, 18 November 1940.
2. *Pennsylvania Manual*, "Election Statistics," no. 85, 1941 p. 149 ff. In Pennsylvania, Roosevelt recorded 2,169,000 votes to Willkie's 1,889,000. In Allegheny County his margin was slightly in excess of 100,000. During the summer of 1940 Roosevelt showed his concern over the Pennsylvania outcome by hosting several harmony meetings between Lawrence and Guffey.
3. *Pittsburgh Press*, 20 May 1942, 23 October 1941.
4. *Pennsylvania Manual*, "Election Statistics," no. 96, 1943, p. 150 ff.
5. Interview with Genevieve Blatt, 19 June 1984, p. 18.
6. Interview with David L. Lawrence by Jerry N. Hess, 30 June 1966, pp. 14, 15, HST Library; *Pittsburgh Press*, 19 June 1940.
7. Interview with Lawrence by Hess, pp. 2, 4, 10, 12.
8. Ibid., p. 6.
9. *Pittsburgh Press*, 18–21 August 1944.
10. Ibid., 21 August 1944.
11. Interview with Lawrence by Hess, p. 7; interview with Blatt, p. 1.
12. Interview with Blatt, p. 2.
13. Interview with Lawrence by Hess, p. 7; interview with Blatt, p. 2.
14. Interview with Lawrence by Hess, pp. 8, 9.
15. The Roosevelt majorities were as follows: Pennsylvania, 59,000; Philadelphia, 132,000; Allegheny County, 76,000; Pittsburgh, 55,000.
16. Interview with John P. Robin, 26 March 1983, pp. 2–4.
17. *Pittsburgh Press*, 12 October 1937.
18. *Pittsburgh Post-Gazette*, 7 November 1941.
19. Interview with Tronzo, p. 16.
20. Interview with Robin, p. 17.
21. *Pittsburgh Press*, 25 March 1945.
22. Ibid., 23 March 1945.
23. *Pittsburgh Post-Gazette*, 1 April 1945.
24. Interview with Rita Wilson Kane, 27 April 1983, p. 5.
25. Interview with Robin by Robert Pease, 20 September 1972, unpaginated, AIS; interview with Robin, p. 18.
26. Interview with Robin by Pease.
27. *Pittsburgh Post-Gazette*, 20 April 1945.
28. Ibid.
29. *Pittsburgh Press*, 10 June 1945; *Pittsburgh Post-Gazette*, 15 June 1945; script of

KDKA radio address, 15 June 1945, Lawrence clipping file, Pennsylvania Department, Carnegie Library, Pittsburgh.

30. *Pittsburgh Press,* 20 June 1945. Lawrence received 50,303 votes; Huston, 22,690.

▷ A City in Trouble

1. For a detailed account of the economic state of the city in 1900, see John Bodnar, Roger Simon, and Michael Weber, *Lives of their Own: Blacks, Italians and Poles in Pittsburgh, 1900–1960* (Urbana, 1982), p. 13 ff; David Brody, *Steelworkers in America: The Non-Union Era* (Cambridge, Mass., 1960); Paul U. Kellogg, ed., *The Pittsburgh Survey* (New York, 1910). The six-volume work edited by Kellogg presents comprehensive evidence on numerous aspects of work and life in Pittsburgh.

2. Glenn E. McLaughlin and Ralph Watkins, "The Problems of Industrial Growth in a Mature Economy," *American Economic Review* 29 (March 1939); pt. 2, p. 8 ff.

3. Robert Schauffler, *Romantic America* (New York, 1913), p. 71. The phrase "Hell with the lid taken off," first used by James Parton in the *Atlantic Monthly,* 21 January 1868, is frequently and incorrectly credited to Charles Dickens or other visiting luminaries.

4. Econometric Institute, *The Long Range Outlook for the Pittsburgh Industrial Area* (New York, 1946), p. 101. The institute's overall findings were so pessimistic that the sponsoring agencies suppressed the report.

5. Jeanne R. Lowe, "Rebuilding Cities—and Politics," *The Nation,* January 1958, p. 118.

6. "Pittsburgh's New Powers," *Fortune,* February 1947, p. 77 ff.

7. Urban Redevelopment Authority, Gateway Center Project Survey, 1947, Pennsylvania Department, Carnegie Library, Pittsburgh.

8. Minute Book, Pittsburgh City Council, vol. 80, 15 August 1946.

9. Pittsburgh Housing Authority, unpublished report, 1937, Housing Authority files; Scott Nearing, *Black America* (n.p., 1929); Bodnar et al., *Lives of Their Own,* chap. 7; Econometric Institute, *Long Range Outlook,* p. 3.

10. Philip Klein, *A Social Study of Pittsburgh: Community Problems and Social Services of Allegheny County* (New York, 1938), p. 203.

11. National Climatic Center, "Climatological Data, Pennsylvania, 1936" (Asheville, North Carolina 1937); "Our Flood in Pictures," *Pittsburgh Sun-Telegraph,* 2 April 1936. For a detailed analysis of flood control in Pittsburgh see Roland M. Smith, "The Politics of Pittsburgh Flood Control, 1908–1936," *Pennsylvania History* 42 (January 1975), and "The Politics of Pittsburgh Flood Control, 1936–1960," *Pennsylvania History* 44 (January 1977).

12. Smith, "Flood Control, 1936–1960," p. 7.

13. William Denny, address to the Pittsburgh Chamber of Commerce, 1874, printed copy in possession of the author.

14. Joel A. Tarr and Bill C. Lamperes, "Changing Fuel Use Behavior and Energy Transitions: The Pittsburgh Smoke Control Movement, 1940–1950," *Journal of Social History* 14 (Summer 1981): 562.

15. *Pittsburgh Press,* 28 January 1941.

16. Ibid., 27–31 January 1941; Econometric Institute, *Long Range Outlook,* pp. 97, 98.

17. For a detailed explanation of the development of the smoke control ordinance and its implementation, see Tarr and Lamperes, "Changing Fuel Use Behavior."

18. Theodore Hazlett, Jr., "The Changing Attitude in Pittsburgh," address to Fu-

ture Springfield Inc., Springfield, Mass., 1 June 1953, ACCD archives; Burton Hersh, *The Mellon Family: A Fortune in History* (New York, 1978), p. 359; Adolph W. Schmidt, "The Pittsburgh Story," address to the International Press Institute at the University of Pittsburgh, 19 April 1958, n.p.; Pittsburgh Chamber of Commerce, "Company Relocation Prospects," October 1945.

19. Samuel P. Hays, The Politics of Reform in Municipal Government in the Progressive Era," *Pacific Northwestern Quarterly* 55 (October 1964): 162.

20. For a detailed analysis of the public and private reform elements in Pittsburgh, see Roy Lubove, *Twentieth Century Pittsburgh: Government, Business, and Environmental Change* (New York, 1969). The 1922–23 plans of the CCCP included recommendations on playgrounds, street patterns, public transit, parks, railroads, and waterways.

21. Interview with Adolph Schmidt by Nancy Mason, 9 October 1972, p. 4.

22. Interview with David L. Lawrence by Stefan Lorant, 14 December 1963, p. 7.

▷ From Political Boss to Civic Statesman

1. *Pittsburgh Press*, 15 September, 3 November 1937. Magee was elected to the city council under both party banners in 1933.

2. Luncheon Address, American Legion Post 59, Pittsburgh, Pa., in *Pittsburgh Post-Gazette*, Lawrence clipping file, Pennsylvania Department, Carnegie Library, Pittsburgh.

3. *Pittsburgh Press*, 25 September 1945. See all Pittsburgh newspapers, 24 September–7 November 1945.

4. Waddell to the Pittsburgh Chamber of Commerce, *Pittsburgh Press*, 29 September, 17 May, 3 November 1945.

5. John Huston, letter to the "People of Pittsburgh," printed in all three Pittsburgh newspapers, 24 September 1945.

6. *Pittsburgh Press*, 14 October 1945. The invitation to Shelley was sent by Mrs. Nellie Dressler, vice-chairman of the Republican County Committee, on behalf of the Federation of Councils of Republican Women, the Republican League of Allegheny County, the Republican Luncheon Club, and the Independent Women's Group.

7. *Pittsburgh Post-Gazette*, 27 October 1945; *Pittsburgh Sun-Telegraph*, 26 October 1945; *Pittsburgh Press*, 26 October, 4 November 1945.

8. *Pittsburgh Post-Gazette*, 7 November 1945.

9. Election returns, 1941, 1945, Allegheny County Bureau of Elections, County Office Building, Pittsburgh.

10. *Pittsburgh Press*, 9 November 1945.

11. Ibid.

12. Ibid., 6 January 1946; interview with John Jones, 18 February 1981.

13. *Pittsburgh Post-Gazette*, *Pittsburgh Press*, *Pittsburgh Sun-Telegraph*, 10 January 1946.

14. Frank Hawkins, "Mediation Becomes a Major Duty of Pittsburgh Mayor," *Pittsburgh Post-Gazette*, 10 December 1947.

15. Inaugural address of David L. Lawrence, 7 January 1946, Lawrence file, ACCD.

16. Lawrence's cabinet was sworn in the following morning. It included three holdovers from the Scully administration: Dr. I. Hope Alexander, director of public health; Anne X. Alpern, city solicitor; and George A. Fairley, director of public safety. New members included: Jimmy Kirk, city treasurer; James S. Devlin, public works director; William Driscoll, director of the department of supplies (Driscoll, a former district collector of internal revenue, had been a casualty of the Lawrence-Guffey feud),

and Homer Greene, director of lands and buildings. Also sworn in was the city's first black magistrate, Robert E. Williams, Fifth Ward constable and political leader.

17. C. W. Dressler, "Mayor Lays Down Law on Garbage," *Pittsburgh Post-Gazette,* 9 January 1946.

18. *Pittsburgh Press,* 9, 10, 15, 16, 25 January 1946; *Pittsburgh Post-Gazette,* 9, 11, 13, 15, 16, 27 January, 3, 6 February, 1946.

19. Interview with Monsignor Charles Owen Rice, 17 July 1982, p. 7.

20. *Pittsburgh Press,* 11 February 1946. The number of homes affected was relatively small because a high proportion were heated with coal. This became an important part of the ammunition later used by those opposing residential smoke control.

21. *Pittsburgh Post-Gazette,* 12 February 1946.

22. Ibid.

23. *Pittsburgh Sun-Telegraph,* 12 October 1946.

24. Ibid., 13 October 1946.

25. *Pittsburgh Press, Pittsburgh Sun-Telegraph, Pittsburgh Post-Gazette,* 13 February 1946.

26. Interview with Walter Giesey, 23 October 1982, p. 10.

27. *Pittsburgh Sun-Telegraph,* 21, 22, 24 February 1946; *Pittsburgh Press,* 21–25 February 1946.

28. *Pittsburgh Post-Gazette,* 26 February 1946; *Pittsburgh Sun-Telegraph,* 14 April 1946.

29. *Pittsburgh Sun-Telegraph, Pittsburgh Press,* 26 February 1946.

30. *Pittsburgh Press,* 22 March 1946.

31. *Pittsburgh Post Gazette,* 6 August 1946.

32. *Fortune,* February 1947, pp. 69–70.

33. *Pittsburgh Sun-Telegraph,* 27 September 1946; interview with Rice, p. 8.

34. Interview with Gerald Lawrence, 17 August 1982, p. 28.

35. Lawrence Clipping File, Pennsylvania Department, Carnegie Library, Pittsburgh, 17 October 1946.

36. *Newsweek,* 9 December 1946, p. 25.

▷ Creating a Renaissance: The Environment

1. See, e.g., George Perry, "The Cities of America: Pittsburgh," *Saturday Evening Post,* 3 August 1946; "Pittsburgh's New Powers," *Fortune,* February 1947; "Cities: Pittsburgh Comes Out of the Smog," *Newsweek,* 26 September 1949; "Pittsburgh Renascent," *Architectural Forum,* November 1949; Karl Schriftsgiesser, "The Pittsburgh Story," *Atlantic Monthly,* May 1951; Herbert Kubly, "Pittsburgh: The City that Quick-changed from Unbelievable Ugliness to Shining Beauty in Less Than Half a Generation," *Holiday,* March 1959.

2. John Jones, "So You Want to Be a Mayor?" *Pittsburgh Post-Gazette,* 28 March 1947; Mayor's Appointment Book, 27 March 1947, Pennsylvania Archives, Harrisburg.

3. Interview with John P. Robin, 26 March 1983, p. 42; interview with Walter Giesey by Nancy Mason, 20 December 1972, AIS.

4. Interview with Robin, p. 31.

5. Interview with Giesey by Mason.

6. Interview with Fred Weir, 24 June 1981, p. 6.

7. Interview with Theodore Hazlett by Joel Tarr, 22 November 1971, p. 10, AIS.

8. Interview with Park Martin by Stefan Lorant, 14 June 1955, p. 31.

9. Interview with Park Martin by Joel Tarr, 17 November 1971, p. 6, AIS.

10. Burton Hersh, *The Mellon Family: A Fortune in History* (New York, 1978), pp. 173, 363. David Koskoff, *The Mellons: The Chronicle of America's Richest Family* (New York, 1978), p. 447 ff, generally agrees with Hersh's characterization of Richard K. Mellon although suggesting that he was reared by his father Richard Beatty to take over the business holdings of his family. "There was never a touch of rebellion in R. K., never a hint of the intellectual. . . . R. K. was a conventional man, luxury model."

11. Hersh, *Mellon Family*, p. 171; interview with Arthur Van Buskirk by J. Cutler Andrews, 28 October 1971, AIS.

12. Interview with Adolph Schmidt, 14 July 1984, p. 14.

13. Interview with Park Martin by Stefan Lorant, 14 June 1955, p. 20; speech files of Park Martin, Ted Hazlett, Leland Hazard, ACCD.

14. File on meeting with the secretary of the treasury, ACCD; interview with Van Buskirk by Andrews, p. 12.

15. For a detailed account of the progress of the flood control projects see Roland Smith, "Pittsburgh Flood Control, 1936–60," *Pennsylvania History* 44 (January 1977): 3 ff.

16. *Pittsburgh Press*, 4 April, 28 June 1947, 26 July 1948.

17. The system was not completed until summer 1965 when the Allegheny River Reservoir at Kinzua, 150 miles above Pittsburgh, was dedicated.

18. Other bills in the Pittsburgh Package included expansion of county planning commission jurisdiction over suburban subdivisions; transfer to the state of responsibility for maintenance of city bridges; and an amendment to the Public Utility Act permitting the county to file and appear before the Public Utilities Commission even though the county might not be the first party at interest. All but the last two became law.

19. Interview with David L. Lawrence by Stefan Lorant, 14 December 1963, p. 14. Lawrence's version of the meeting was corroborated by interviews with Walker, Martin, Hazlett, and Robin.

20. *Pittsburgh Press*, 22 February 1947.

21. The league specifically opposed the bills regarding county-wide smoke control, refuse disposal plants, suburban subdivision development, and additional taxing powers for Pittsburgh.

22. Interview with Hazlett by Tarr, p. 3; interview with Martin by Lorant, pp. 11, 12; lecture by Theodore Hazlett, Seminar on the Pittsburgh Renaissance, University of Pittsburgh, 27 November 1972, p. 7, AIS.

23. Hazlett lecture, p. 13.

24. Ralph E. Griswold, "Fron Fort Pitt to Point Park," *Landscape Architecture* 46 (July 1956): 198. For a detailed analysis of the project see Robert C. Alberts, *The Shaping of the Point: Pittsburgh's Renaissance Park* (Pittsburgh, 1980), esp. chap. 7.

25. Inaugural Address of Mayor David L. Lawrence, 7 January 1946, ACCD. Campaign advertisements appeared in the *Pittsburgh Press, Pittsburgh Post-Gazette*, 15 October–7 November 1945. See Joel A. Tarr and Bill C. Lamperes, "Changing Fuel Use Behavior and Energy Transitions: The Pittsburgh Smoke Control Movement, 1940–50," *Journal of Social History* 14 (Summer 1981), for a comprehensive analysis of the entire smoke control issue.

26. Letters to the editor, *Pittsburgh Press, Pittsburgh Sun-Telegraph*, 7–18 April 1946; ACCD statement at a public hearing of the Pittsburgh City Council, 17 April 1946, ACCD; interview with Martin by Lorant, p. 10 ff.

27. Smoke Ordinance Hearings, Pittsburgh City Council, 17, 18 April 1946, Minute Books, Pittsburgh City Council, City-County Building, Pittsburgh.

28. Ibid.

29. *Pittsburgh Press,* letters to the editor, 5–10 February 1948.

30. Tarr and Lamperes, "Changing Fuel Use Behavior," p. 575.

31. Ibid., p. 575; Sally Shames, "David L. Lawrence, Mayor of Pittsburgh," (Ph.D. diss., Pittsburgh, 1958), p. 245.

32. Interview with John P. Robin by Robert Pease, 20 September 1972. In the midst of the controversy, Martin and two others visited the president of Equitable Life to discuss the proposed CBD project. "Parkinson listened," Martin reported, "then said, 'Well, gentlemen, you'll have to answer two questions before I say anything more. What are you doing about smoke control in Pittsburgh and what are you doing about flood control?'" Interview with Martin by Lorant, p. 15.

33. Interview with Edward Leonard, 19 June 1981, p. 3.

34. Minute Book, Pittsburgh City Council, January–June 1948; *Pittsburgh Press,* 4, 7 February 1948.

35. *Pittsburgh Press, Pittsburgh Post-Gazette, Pittsburgh Sun-Telegraph,* 3–10 February 1948.

36. Interview with Al Conway 20 August 1982, p. 24; interview with Leonard, pp. 7, 8.

37. Resolution of the Central Labor Union of the American Federation of Labor, 5 May 1949, reprinted in part in the *Pittsburgh Press,* 6 May 1949; interview with Robin by Pease.

38. *Pittsburgh Press,* 22 June 1949.

39. Ibid., 1 September 1949; interview with Robin, p. 31.

40. *Pittsburgh Post-Gazette,* 2 September 1949.

41. Fuel usage for centrally and noncentrally heated dwellings calculated from U.S. Census for Pittsburgh, 1950, by Todd Shallat, in possession of Joel Tarr.

42. *Pittsburgh Post-Gazette,* 18, 20, 21 October 1949; interview with Leonard by Weber, pp. 9, 10; interview with Leonard by Donaghy, p. 8.

43. Stefan Lorant, *Pittsburgh: The Story of an American City* (Lenox, Mass., 1964), p. 402.

▷ Creating a Renaissance: Bricks and Mortar

1. Interview with John P. Robin, 26 March 1983, p. 32; *Pittsburgh Press,* 22 March 1946, 13 December 1953. A second fire one month later destroyed the Pittsburgh Plated Products Company and the Young-Wade Machine Company.

2. Interview with Park Martin by Stefan Lorant, 14 June 1955, p. 14.

3. Interview with Arthur Van Buskirk by J. Cutler Andrews, 28 October 1971, p. 4.

4. Interview with David L. Lawrence by Stefan Lorant, 14 December 1963, p. 23ff; interview with Van Buskirk by Andrews, p. 4ff. The proper title of the organization is the Redevelopment Authority of Pittsburgh. In common usage it has become known as the Urban Redevelopment Authority or simply URA. For convenience and clarity, the popular usage has been retained throughout this work.

5. Minute Book, Pittsburgh City Council, 80, no. 49, 12 November 1946, pp. 205–06; Stefan Lorant, *Pittsburgh: The Story of an American City* (Lenox, Mass., 1975), p. 424ff; minutes of incorporation meeting of the Redevelopment Authority of Pittsburgh, 18 November 1946, Urban Redevelopment Authority, John P. Robin Civic Building, Pittsburgh.

6. It was the Pittsburgh business community that funded the URA during its first year. According to Robin, the Allegheny Conference representatives purchased

$100,000 worth of URA bonds while the Duquesne Light and Power Company, several banks, and the manufacturing interests purchased others. Robin became the full-time paid director in 1948. Interview with John P. Robin by Robert Pease, 20 September 1972, p. 30.

7. *Pittsburgh Press,* 2 May 1947; state of the city addresses, 1947–54, ACCD; speech to the American Society of Planning Officials, 15 October 1951, ACCD.

8. David L. Lawrence to Charles Graham, Pittsburgh and West Virginia Railroad, F. A. Christianson, Continental Insurance Co., J. F. Crafts, Fireman's Fund, J. A. Diamond, Insurance Company of North America, C. S. Kremer, Hartford Fire Insurance Company, and Ivan Escott, Home Insurance Company, 14 May 1947, ACCD; *Pittsburgh Press,* 1 March 1948.

9. Interview with Arthur Van Buskirk by J. Cutler Andrews, 28 October 1971, p. 15; interview with Adolph Schmidt by Weber, 14 July 1984, p. II-6; interview with Schmidt by Nancy Mason, 9 October 1972, p. 15; *Pittsburgh Post-Gazette,* 29 September 1953; David L. Lawrence, speech to the Pittsburgh Press Club, 17 September 1957, p. 3, ACCD.

10. Minute Books, Pittsburgh City Countil, January 1946–January 1959.

11. The major projects included the Gateway Center redevelopment, the Jones and Laughlin Steel Corporation expansion on the South Side, the Civic Arena and Lower Hill redevelopment project, the Oakland hospital expansion, development of Allegheny Center on the North Side, and the East Liberty renewal.

12. Shelby Stewman and Joel A. Tarr, "Four Decades of Private/Public Partnerships in Pittsburgh," a report prepared for the Committee on Economic Development, July 1981, p. 19; *Pittsburgh Post-Gazette,* 4 November 1948.

13. Interview with Van Buskirk by Andrews, p. 6.

14. Minute Book, Urban Redevelopment Authority of Pittsburgh, no. 1, 5 October 1948, p. 15, 13 February 1950, p. 72; *Pittsburgh Post-Gazette,* 14 February 1950.

15. Minute Book, Urban Redevelopment Authority of Pittsburgh, no. 1, 10 February 1950, pp. 4, 5.

16. Ibid., 21 June 1949, p. 45.

17. Interview with Theodore Hazlett by Thomas Donaghy, 31 October 1974, p. 7; interview with Hazlett by Joel Tarr, 22 November 1971, p. 12.

18. Committee on Hearings, Pittsburgh City Council, 10 November 1949, p. 435ff; Sam Bass Warner, Jr., *The Private City: Philadelphia in Three Periods of Its Growth* (Philadelphia, 1968). In Philadelphia, Warner convincingly demonstrated, government operated to further the interests of private investors. What was good for the private individual, they agreed, would also be in the best interests of the larger society. The rape of Pittsburgh's best land by industrialists during the late nineteenth and early twentieth century suggests that the concept also existed in the steel city.

19. Interview with Hazlett by Tarr, p. 13.

20. It is ironic to note that less than thirty years after this massive expansion, Jones and Laughlin virtually ceased steel production in Pittsburgh.

21. Edgar J. Kaufmann to David L. Lawrence, 4 February 1949, Minute Book, Pittsburgh City Council, pp. 80–81; Lawrence to Pittsburgh City Council, 7 February 1949, Minute Book, Pittsburgh City Council, p. 78.

22. Other sites considered included Grandview Park, Frick Park, Monument Hill, the site of the Silver Lake Drive-in Theater on Washington Boulevard, Schenley Park's Flagstaff Hill, and the lower Hill immediately adjacent to the central business district. The latter two sites were ruled out "because they are presently occupied by thickly built areas presenting a re-housing problem." ACCD minutes, 11 June 1949.

23. Committee on Hearings, Pittsburgh City Council, 8 July 1949, p. 391ff.

24. Ibid.; *Pittsburgh Press,* 7–9 July 1949. King kept his word, bequeathing his land to the city upon his death a short time later. It is now an environmental park.

25. *Pittsburgh Press,* 20 July 1949.

26. David L. Lawrence to Edward Weidlein, 15 August 1949, ACCD.

27. Edward Weidlein to David L. Lawrence, 15 August 1949, ACCD.

28. *Pittsburgh Press,* 26 March 1951.

29. ACCD Executive Committee Minutes, 16 February 1953, 22 July 1955.

30. Committee on Hearings, Pittsburgh City Council, 6 July 1955, p. 418ff.

31. "Lower Hill Relocation," mimeograph, URA, n.d., supplied to the author by Al Tronzo.

32. *Pittsburgh Press,* 22 December 1956; Pittsburgh Building Inspector's Report, 17 July 1953 (copy supplied to the author by Al Tronzo); *Pittsburgh Press,* 16–21 December 1956.

33. Anonymous Chatham College study, "Lower Hill Relocation," *Pittsburgh Post-Gazette,* 6 June 1959.

34. Interview with Robin, p. 47; lecture by Theodore Hazlett, 27 November 1972, pp. 27–28, AIS.

35. Roy Lubove, *Twentieth Century Pittsburgh: Government, Business, and Environmental Change* (New York, 1969), pp. 131–32.

36. *Pittsburgh Post-Gazette,* 6 February 1960.

▷ Social Concerns and Other Matters

1. John H. Mollenkopf, *The Contested City* (Princeton, N.J., 1983), p. 16.

2. "Allegheny Council to Improve Our Neighborhood Housing: An Action Program for Meeting the Housing Problems of Allegheny County," prepared for the ACCD by the Pennsylvania Economy League, February 1957. The private sector organizations did not become involved in housing until 1957 when ACTION-Housing was formed. This organization developed a broad program which sponsored new and rehabilitated housing, the development of neighborhood citizen organizations, and research.

3. *Pittsburgh Post-Gazette,* 27 March 1946.

4. Interview with K. Leroy Irvis, 19 June 1984, p. 3ff. It was K. Leroy Irvis's leadership in the fight against discrimination against blacks by the city's five department stores which first brought him to Lawrence's attention. "He supported us," Irvis reported, "but he did not want us to picket against the department store owners. He felt that it would give the city a black eye" (p. 14).

5. Committee on Hearings, Pittsburgh City Council, 30 November 1946.

6. Interview with Irvis, p. 6.

7. *Pittsburgh Press,* 2 April 1949; *Pittsburgh Sun-Telegraph,* 6 September 1950.

8. *Pittsburgh Sun-Telegraph,* 7 August 1950.

9. Committee on Hearings, Pittsburgh City Council, Bill 1723, 19 November 1952, p. 141.

10. Steve Nelson, James R. Barrett, and Rob Ruck, *Steve Nelson: American Radical* (Pittsburgh, 1981), p. 305. For a detailed account of the anti-Communist activities in Pittsburgh see esp. chap. 10.

11. Ibid. See also Sally Stephenson, "Michael Musmanno as a Symbolic Leader" (Doctor of Arts diss., Carnegie Mellon University, 1981).

12. Stephenson, "Musmanno," p. IV-18.

13. Michael Musmanno, *Across the Street from the Courthouse* (Philadelphia, 1954), p. 44; *Pittsburgh Press,* 31 March 1950.

14. Musmanno, *Across the Street,* p. 384. "From September 1948, to July 1950,"

Musmanno wrote, "I experienced each day, as I can out of the courthouse, a sense of frustration and almost despair. Despite the increasing concerted attempt of the whole western world to push Communism back to its Asian frontiers, the Communist Party in Pittsburgh had set up its headquarters right across the street from the courthouse. Less than 100 feet from the very room in which I renewed my court sessions, the Russian agents had planted what amounted to the equivalent of an advance post of the Russian army" (p. 53).

15. Marjorie Matson to the Pittsburgh chapter of the ACLU, quoted in Musmanno, *Across the Street,* p. 323; Charles J. Margiotti to William S. Rahauser, 5 January 1951, copy provided to the author by Warren Matson. Among the charges against Matson listed in the letter to Rahauser were "the reputation among her fellow students [at the University of Pittsburgh] of having Communistic tendencies, . . . [that] she was one of the principal demonstrators against General MacArthur when he came to Pittsburgh . . . in 1932, . . . [that she] acted as counsel for Bernard Salis arrested for distributing literature without permit."

16. Marjorie Matson to Charles J. Margiotti in *Pittsburgh Press,* 5 January 1951; *Pittsburgh Press,* 18 January 1951.

17. *Pittsburgh Press, Pittsburgh Post-Gazette,* 7–15 September 1952.

18. *Pittsburgh Post-Gazette,* 7 September 1951; interview with Warren Matson, 31 March 1983. Lawrence did not forget McBride's gesture and he became state attorney general in the Lawrence administration.

19. Stephenson, "Musmanno," p. VI-3.

20. Interview with Fred Weir, 24 June 1981, pp. 6, 7. Walter Giesey related essentially the same incident. "I was almost shocked," he said of the council's independent action. Interview with Giesey, 23 October 1982, p. 22.

21. Minute Book, Pittsburgh City Council, 26 November 1953; *Pittsburgh Post-Gazette,* 1 December 1953.

22. *Pittsburgh Press,* 18 December 1953.

23. Ibid., 18, 29, 23 December 1953. Pittsburgh Mayor Richard Caliguiri was ironically attacked in the same manner and labeled "the commuter bandit" when he attempted, in 1984 and 1986, to impose a tax on all employees who worked in the city regardless of where they lived.

24. *Pittsburgh Press,* 11, 12 January 1954.

25. Minute Book, Pittsburgh City Council, 25 January 1954; Lawrence speech of 28 January 1954, Lawrence File, ACCD.

26. *Pittsburgh Press,* 19 March 1954.

27. *Pittsburgh Post-Gazette,* 9 July 1946.

28. Interview with Alex Lowenthal, 6 August 1984, p. 7.

29. *Pittsburgh Post-Gazette,* 10 August 1954; interview with Lowenthal, p. 4.

30. Handwritten log of Lawrence's European trip, 24 May–5 July 1958, in possession of his daughter, Anna Mae Donahoe; Harry S. Truman to William Green, 3 May 1961, Lawrence Name File, HST Library.

31. Interview with Lowenthal, p. 12; interview with Giesey, p. 24.

32. *Pittsburgh Press,* 17 September 1957.

▷ A Bit of Tarnish

1. Lincoln Steffens, *The Shame of the Cities* (New York, 1966), see "Pittsburg, A City Ashamed," pp. 101–33; Harold Zink, *City Bosses in the United States* (New York, 1968), pp. 246–56; James Forbes, "The Reverse Side," in *Wage Earning Pittsburgh: The Pittsburgh Survey* (New York, 1907). For a detailed analysis of the attempts at reform,

see Benjamin Hayllar, The Accommodation: The History and Rhetoric of the Rackets-Political Alliance in Pittsburgh" (Ph.D. diss., University of Pittsburgh, 1977); Samuel P. Hays, "The Politics of Reform in Municipal Government in the Progressive Era," *Pacific Northwest Quarterly* 55 (October 1964): 157–69.

2. *Pittsburgh Post-Gazette,* 14–15 February 1936.

3. Interview with John P. Robin, 26 March 1983.

4. *Pittsburgh Press,* 14 May 1947.

5. Ibid., 13, 14 May 1947.

6. *Pittsburgh Press,* 1 August 1947.

7. Pennsylvania Manual, "Election Statistics," no. 88, 1948, p. 123ff.

8. *Pittsburgh Press,* 9 March 1948.

9. David L. Lawrence to William S. Rahauser, 18 July 1948. Shown to the author by Judge Rahauser.

10. Grand Jury Final Report, June Session, 1948, Miscellaneous Docket, Allegheny County Court of Common Pleas, 30 September 1948; *Pittsburgh Press,* 30 September 1948.

11. *Pittsburgh Press,* 15, 16, 17 September 1948.

12. Grand Jury Final Report. The jury singled out Dean's district as "an example of the utter laxity of the local police for the enforcement of gambling laws. . . . His do-nothing attitude toward the racketeers in his district demonstrates his utter unfitness to serve and protect the citizens of the community."

13. *Pittsburgh Post-Gazette,* 5 October 1948.

14. Ibid.; *Pittsburgh Press,* 5 October 1948.

15. *Pittsburgh Press,* 11 October 1948. The extent of political influence in police employment was revealed by two incidents following Dean's dismissal. Councilman Joe McArdle, ignoring the overwhelming evidence against his protégé, attacked Lawrence's action as "a new low in undemocratic processes reminiscent of the totalitarian methods of ambitious dictators." Several weeks later the post vacated by Dean became the object of hot dispute among McArdle and leaders of the Third and Sixth wards. All claimed the right to select the replacement.

16. *Pittsburgh Press,* 9 November 1949, 2 January 1951; Pittsburgh City Directories, 1950–53. Of the thirty-eight aldermen and constables who earned more than $500 for their services, thirty-one were Democratic committeemen. All of the eight who earned $4000 or more in 1950 were prominent ward politicians. Of the thirty-one aldermen and constables elected immediately after the grand jury investigation, twenty-seven held city jobs, and two were employed by labor unions. All were registered Democrats and twenty-nine were actively involved in ward level politics.

17. The following account is from the *Pittsburgh Press,* 28 November, 2, 13, 14, 16 December 1949.

18. Hayllar, "The Accommodation," p. 186; *Pittsburgh Post-Gazette,* 13 February 1936. For a detailed analysis of the colorful career of Ray Sprigle see Alan Guy Sheffer, "Investigative Reporter: Ray Sprigle of Pittsburgh" (Doctor of Arts diss., Carnegie Mellon University, 1973). Sprigle won a Pulitzer Prize in 1938 for his exposé of Supreme Court Justice Hugo Black's membership in the Ku Klux Klan. The Sprigle exposé of corruption in the Pittsburgh police bureau ran from 2 February to 7 March 1950.

19. Ray Sprigle, "Politics Blamed for Lax Police System Here," *Pittsburgh Post-Gazette,* 20 February–2 March 1950, 10, 14 July 1950.

20. Minute Book, Pittsburgh City Council, letter from David L. Lawrence, 9 March 1950; *Pittsburgh Post-Gazette,* 31 December 1953; Stanley Gorski, "The Staffing Policies of the Pittsburgh Bureau of Police" (Ph.D. diss., University of Pittsburgh, 1972), pp. 179–81.

21. Hayllar, "The Accommodation," p. 213; ledger book of Willie Jones, reprinted

in the *Pittsburgh Press,* 2, 3 April 1951; interview with Walter Giesey, 23 October 1982, p. 24.

22. *Pittsburgh Press,* 22 June 1951.

23. Interview with Giesey, p. 24.

24. Ibid., p. 25.

25. *Pittsburgh Press,* 15 August 1952.

26. Gorski, "Staffing Policies," p. 177. Gorski, the son of a prominent police officer, was able to interview a number of city policemen who have been unwilling to testify to other researchers. The incident cited here comes from the testimony of an unnamed officer.

27. *Pittsburgh Post-Gazette,* 12, 26 June 1957.

28. Commonwealth ex. rel. Maloney vs. Duggan et al., *Pittsburgh Legal Journal* 116, Habeas Corpus, no. 605, July term, 1967, and no. 2592, October term 1967, p. 2.

29. United States vs. Maloney (Pittsburgh: U.S. District Court for Western Pennsylvania) Criminal Number 64–415, pp. 756–62, 298, 316. Sigal went "out of business" in 1963 after he was convicted and jailed for bribing another police official. The offense took place in 1957 while Lawrence was still mayor.

30. Gorski, "Staffing Policies," p. 186; speech of David L. Lawrence to the Pittsburgh Press Club, 17 September 1957, p. 9, ACCD.

31. Chester Harris, *Tiger at the Bar: The Life Story of Charles J. Margiotti* (New York, 1956), p. 442; interview with Dan Cercone, 11 August 1985, untranscribed; interview with Frank Ambrose, 11 July 1984, p. 7.

32. *Pittsburgh Press,* 9 June 1950; David L. Lawrence to Pittsburgh City Council, Minute Book, Pittsburgh City Council, 9 June 1950, p. 318.

33. Interview with William Rahauser, 12 June 1981, p. 11; *Pittsburgh Post-Gazette,* 11 July 1950.

34. *Pittsburgh Sun-Telegraph,* 13 July 1950; *Pittsburgh Press,* 16 July 1950.

35. Special Grand Jury Preliminary Report, *Pittsburgh Press,* 14 December 1950.

36. Charles J. Margiotti to Governor John Fine, 24 February 1951, reprinted in the *Pittsburgh Post-Gazette,* 25 February 1950.

37. *Pittsburgh Press,* 27 June 1951.

38. Ibid., 11 March, 9 April 1951.

39. Sally Shames, "David L. Lawrence, Mayor of Pittsburgh: Development of a Political Leader (Ph.D. diss., University of Pittsburgh, 1958), p. 221. Allegheny Asphalt's total bid during the eight-year period was approximately $200,000 less than that of the competitive bidder, the Harrison Construction Company. The only other company to offer a bid was the Trimble Construction Company in 1950.

▷ Politics as Usual

1. Interview with Frank Ambrose, 11 June 1984, p. 9.

2. Interview with Natalie Saxe, 19 June 1984, p. 5.

3. Interview with Walter Giesey by Weber, 23 October 1984, p. 22; interview with Giesey by Thomas Donaghy, 10 September 1975, p. 7.

4. Allegheny County Bureau of Elections, Campaign Expense Records, 1949, 1953, 1957, County Office Building, Pittsburgh; *Pittsburgh Press,* 28 September 1956.

5. *Pittsburgh Press,* 27 June 1957; *Fortune,* November 1957; *Time,* 30 October 1957.

6. Interview with John P. Robin, 26 March 1983, p. 30.

7. *Pittsburgh Post-Gazette,* 11 October 1949.

8. Ibid., 13 July 1949.

9. Interview with Giesey, p. 8.

10. *Pittsburgh Press,* 2 December 1953.

11. Ibid., 28 January 1954.

12. Interview with Andrew Fenrich by Thomas Donaghy, 8 July 1974, p. 3; interview with Fenrich by Weber, 8 May 1981, pp. 2, 3.

13. Interview with Fenrich by Weber, p. 3.

14. Telephone interview with Fenrich, then secretary of the local party, 3 June 1985. Roberts and McClelland refused to leave the meeting, Fenrich related. The committee was forced to adjourn the meeting and reconvene at a later time that day to complete their endorsements.

15. Policy committee members were not elected. The committee consisted of representatives from four groups: (1) party officials elected on a statewide basis; (2) fifteen members appointed by the state chairman, Maurice Splain, Lawrence's chosen successor; (3) members of the state executive committee; and (4) chairmen of counties that went Democratic in the previous election, mostly from Western Pennsylvania. Natalie Saxe, Richardson Dilworth's executive secretary, testified to Lawrence's uncontested leadership: "The leading figures in the Philadelphia Democratic party [in 1950] were not divided as to who was the real boss of the Pennsylvania Democratic party. None of them felt they were." Interview with Natalie Saxe by Thomas Donaghy, 17 October 1975, p. 2.

16. Paul Beers, *Pennsylvania Politics: Today and Yesterday* (University Park, Pa., 1981), p. 196.

17. Sally Stephenson, "Michael Musmanno as a Symbolic Leader" (Doctor of Arts diss., Carnegie Mellon University, 1981), p. IV-22; interview with Saxe, p. 2.

18. *Pittsburgh Press,* 12 December 1953.

19. Ibid., 19 February 1954; telephone interview with Genevieve Blatt, 6 June 1985.

20. *Philadelphia Inquirer,* 23 February 1954; interview with George Leader, 18 August 1982, p. 4.

21. Telephone interview with Genevieve Blatt, 6 June 1985; interview with Leader, p. 6; interview with Leader by Thomas Donaghy, 10 November 1975, p. 3.

22. Pennsylvania Manual, "Pennsylvania Election Returns," no. 92, 1955, p. 99 ff.

23. *Pittsburgh Post-Gazette,* 11 November 1954, 17 January 1955; interview with Leader, p. 11.

24. *Pittsburgh Post-Gazette,* 25 December 1954.

25. Interview with David Randall, 19 June 1984, p. 2.

26. Interview with Leader, p. 12. State senators Joe Barr, John Dent, and Charles Weiner all viewed Lawrence's role as supportive rather than domineering. Interview with Joe Barr, 3 February 1981; interview with John Dent by Thomas Donaghy, 23 July 1974; interview with Charles Weiner, 3 May 1983.

27. *Pittsburgh Post-Gazette,* 9 September 1948.

28. Harry S. Truman to David L. Lawrence, Lawrence Name File, 8 September 1948, HST Library.

29. Interview with David L. Lawrence, Washington, D.C., 30 June 1966, p. 23, oral interview collection of the HST Library.

30. Ibid., p. 21.

31. *Pittsburgh Press,* 2, 31 March 1948.

32. Speech of David L. Lawrence to the Democratic National Convention, 12 July 1948, ACCD.

33. Interview with Lawrence, HST Library, p. 25.

34. Interview with John Jones, 19 February 1981, p. 11.

35. *Pittsburgh Post-Gazette,* 29 June 1948; *Pittsburgh Press,* 14 July 1948.

36. Helen Fuller, "The Man to Watch at the Democratic Convention," *Harper's Magazine,* August 1964, p. 50.

37. Walter Johnson, *How We Drafted Adlai Stevenson* (New York, 1951), p. 6.

38. Fuller, "The Man to Watch," 1964, p. 51.

39. Ibid., p. 41.

40. Interview with Genevieve Blatt, 19 June 1984, p. 10.

41. *Pittsburgh Sun-Telegraph,* 24 June 1952.

42. Ibid., 27 July 1952.

43. Ibid., 25 July 1952.

44. Ibid.

45. *Pittsburgh Post-Gazette,* 27 September, 14 October, 9 November 1955.

46. Fuller, "The Man to Watch," p. 51.

47. *Pittsburgh Post-Gazette,* 8 November 1956.

▷ Return to Harrisburg

1. Interview with Adolph Schmidt, 14 July 1984, p. III-7.

2. David Randall to Michael Weber, 26 July 1984.

3. Randall and Saxe agree upon the substance of the events at the meeting but disagree upon Dilworth's assessment of Leader's strength. Randall states that Dilworth was "wrong about Leader," misreading his tactic with Green as a sign of weakness (Randall to Weber, 26 July 1984). Saxe writes that "Dilworth (and others) had previously felt other instances of Leader's malleability by Congressman Green" (Saxe to Weber, 30 July 1984).

4. Interview with Walter Giesey by Thomas Donaghy, 19 September 1975, p. 25; phone interview with John P. Robin, 18 June 1985 (both men provided nearly identical accounts of the event); *Pittsburgh Press,* 9 January 1958.

5. Interview with Matthew McCloskey by Thomas Donaghy, 2 November 1970, p. 8.

6. Interview with George Leader, 18 August 1982, p. 13; interview with Natalie Saxe, 19 June 1984, p. 7.

7. *Pittsburgh Press,* 3 March 1958.

8. Paul Beers, *Pennsylvania Politics, Today and Yesterday* (University Park, Pa., 1980), p. 252.

9. *Pittsburgh Post-Gazette,* 9, 29 September 1958; *Pittsburgh Press,* 2 November 1958.

10. *Pittsburgh Post-Gazette,* 10 October 1958; interview with David Randall, 19 June 1984, p. 4. The Pennsylvania bible belt encompasses the central section of the state running from Harrisburg to Altoona and stretching from the New York to the Maryland border.

11. Interview with Randall, p. 5; interview with Leader, p. 17.

12. Transcript, "Meet the Press," 16 August 1959, Washington, D.C., pp. 2, 3; *Pittsburgh Press,* 5 November 1958.

13. Daryl R. Fair, "The Reaction of Pennsylvania Voters to Catholic Candidates," *Pennsylvania History* 32 (July 1965): 305–15; William J. McKenna, "The Influence of Religion in the Pennsylvania Elections of 1958 and 1960," *Pennsylvania History* 29 (October 1962): 407–19. Both studies found that religion was a much more potent factor in the presidential election of 1960. Ironically, the names of the two candidates report-

edly confused many voters and so it was not clear which was the Catholic and which the Protestant.

14. *Pittsburgh Post-Gazette*, 7 January 1959.

15. Ibid.

16. Annual State of the City Address, 10 January 1959, pp. 14–15, ACCD; *Pittsburgh Press*, and *Pittsburgh Post-Gazette*, 24 November 1958–11 January 1959; Minute Book, Pittsburgh City Council, 5 December 1958.

17. Governor David L. Lawrence, Inaugural Address, 20 January 1959, David L. Lawrence Papers, Pennsylvania State Archives, Harrisburg,

18. Interview with David Donahoe, 20 June 1983, p. 8; interview with John Jones, 19 February 1981, p. 22.

19. *Pittsburgh Press*, 21 January 1959.

20. Ibid.

21. Interview with Peter Wambach, 15 June 1982, p. 1.

22. *Pittsburgh Post-Gazette*, 13 May 1959; *Pittsburgh Press*, 11 March 1959.

23. The Tax Advisory Committee included: Clifford Hood, president, U.S. Steel; David J. McDonald, president, United Steel Workers of America; George H. Love, chairman, Consolidation Coal Company; Frank Anderson, president, Miners National Bank, Wilkes Barre; Harry Boyer, president, Pennsylvania CIO; C. Richard Fryling, president, Pennsylvania Chamber of Commerce; Mayor Arthur Gardner, Erie; Thomas Kennedy, vice-president, United Mine Workers; Councilman Joseph S. Martin, Altoona; Matthew H. McCloskey, Philadelphia contractor; Joseph McDonough, president, Pennsylvania Federation of Labor; and James Symes, president, Pennsylvania Railroad.

24. Interview with Charles Weiner, 3 May 1983, p. 6.

25. *Pittsburgh Post-Gazette*, 22 April 1959; speech to the Municipal Forum of New York, 28 December 1961, Pennsylvania State Archives, Harrisburg.

26. *Pittsburgh Post-Gazette*, 5 February 1960.

27. Ibid., 22 February 1960.

28. *Pittsburgh Press*, 19, 23 August 1946.

29. News release issued by the office of the Governor of Pennsylvania, 2 February 1960, David L. Lawrence Papers, Subject File, Highway Safety, carton 35, Pennsylvania State Archives, Harrisburg.

30. Final Report of the Governor's Committee on Education, 4 April 1961, David L. Lawrence Papers, Subject File, Education, carton 9, Pennsylvania State Archives, Harrisburg.

31. *Pittsburgh Press*, 4 April 1961.

32. Ibid., 1 September 1960; interview with David Donahoe, 20 June 1983, p. 4.

33. The trips included two-week tours of Israel and South America and a full month in Japan. On the last two, the Lawrences traveled with a group of other governors and their wives.

34. *New York Times*, 25 September 1959.

35. Ibid.; David L. Lawrence to Arthur Van Buskirk, 13 October 1959, David L. Lawrence Papers, Subject File, Nikita Khrushchev, box 24, Pennsylvania State Archives, Harrisburg.

36. *Pittsburgh Press*, 25 September 1959.

37. Theodore White, *The Making of the President, 1960* (New York, 1961), p. 46.

38. Interview with Carmine Di Sapio, 21 June 1984, p. 5; interview with David L. Lawrence by Stefan Lorant, 14 December 1963, p. 59.

39. Interview with McCloskey by Donaghy, 2 November 1970, p. 3.

40. Ibid.; interview with Lawrence by Lorant, pp. 59–60.

41. Transcript, "Meet the Press," 6 August 1959, p. 3.

42. *Pittsburgh Post-Gazette,* 1 February, 24 March 1958; *Pittsburgh Press,* 4 May 1958.

43. Typescript of autobiography by Milton Shapp, p. 224. Supplied to the author by Shapp.

44. Interview with McCloskey, p. 5; Phil Graham, "Notes on the 1960 Democratic Convention," 19 July 1960, and Joseph Alsop to Lyndon Johnson, 25 March 1964, both in White House Central Files, Executive File, LBJ Library.

45. Interview with Lawrence by Lorant, p. 60.

46. Thomas B. Morgan, "Madly for Adlai," *American Heritage,* August 1984, p. 58; interview with Gerald Lawrence, 17 August 1982, p. 33.

47. Interview with McCloskey, p. 6.

48. *Pittsburgh Press,* 15 July 1960.

49. William McKenna, "Influence of Religion," p. 416; Pennsylvania Manual, "Election Returns," no. 94, 1960.

50. Beers, *Pennsylvania Politics,* p. 23.

51. *Pittsburgh Post-Gazette,* 9 January 1963.

▷ In Service to the Nation

1. Some contend that Lawrence dominated the Barr regime, but those close to the administration insist that while Barr willingly conferred with Lawrence each Saturday, he was always his own man. The available evidence confirms this.

2. *Pittsburgh Press,* 14 November 1962; Pittsburgh *Post-Gazette,* 3 January 1963.

3. John F. Kennedy to David L. Lawrence, 2 January 1963, Central Name File, Lawrence, box 1571, JFK Library.

4. Harry S. Truman to David L. Lawrence, 15 July 1949, Central Name File, "Famous Names, Lawrence," HST Library; *Pittsburgh Post-Gazette,* 13 August 1955, 27 January 1959.

5. Executive Order 11063, 20 November 1962, President's Committee on Equal Opportunity in Housing, LBJ Library.

6. David L. Lawrence, Remarks to the American University Forum on Local Government and an Open Housing Market, 14 May 1963, p. 1, President's Committee on Equal Opportunity in Housing, LBJ Library; interview with Walter Giesey, 23 October 1984, p. 13.

7. The original eight members were Jack T. Conway, Washington; Theodore A. Jones, Chicago; Charles Keller, New Orleans; Ferdinand Kramer, Chicago; Cyril Magnin, San Francisco; Roland M. Sawyer, Pittsburgh; Earl Schwulst, New York; and Lewis Weinstein, Boston.

8. *Pittsburgh Press,* 24 March 1963; Lawrence, Remarks to American University Forum, pp. 2–4; remarks of David L. Lawrence at the First Friday Club of Cleveland, 4 April 1963, pp. 2, 4, 5, President's Committee on Equal Opportunity in Housing, LBJ Library.

9. *New York Times,* 16 December 1963. The program's goals included: (1) informing the general public of the moral rightness of equal opportunity; (2) developing open housing programs in metropolitan areas; and (3) accumulating and disseminating information.

10. Ibid., 15 June 1963.

11. Ferdinand Kramer to David L. Lawrence, 7 May 1963, President's Committee on Equal Opportunity in Housing, LBJ Library; Executive Order 11063, p. 4.

12. *New York Times*, 26 April 1963.

13. Memorandum for the President from Lee C. White, 8 January 1964, Executive File, LBJ Library.

14. David L. Lawrence to Kenneth O'Donnell, 6 January 1964, White House Central File, LBJ Library.

15. "It will not be long before the election will be over," Kramer wrote, "and we will then be face to face with the question as to whether the Order should be broadened. . . . It is my feeling that we should put to the President in the strongest possible terms, that this Executive Order should be broadened and if it is not broadened, the next step, I think, should be the suggestion that the committee disband." Ferdinand Kramer to David L. Lawrence, 19 October 1964, President's Committee on Equal Opportunity in Housing, LBJ Library.

16. Memorandum from Lee White to the President, 2 December 1964; memorandum from Jack Valenti to the President, 16 November 1964, White House Central File, LBJ Library; daily diaries of Lyndon B. Johnson, Diary Cards and Appointment File, all in LBJ Library. The Diary and Appointment file indicates no meetings between Johnson and Lawrence or his committee from 5 November 1964 to 17 February 1965.

17. "Recommendation to the President by the President's Committee on Equal Opportunity in Housing," 16 March 1965, p. 2, LBJ Library.

18. Telephone interview with Walter Giesey, 5 July 1985.

19. *New York Times*, 18 February, 19 November 1965; letters received by President's Committee on Equal Opportunity in Housing, 13 April 1965–16 December 1965, LBJ Library. The president also received letters from Dale Thompson, president of Mortgage Bankers Association of America and John Glustrom, chairman of the board, Security Corporation of America, supporting extension of the order.

20. Memorandum to the President from Joe Califano, 28 October 1965, Human Rights Collection, LBJ Library. Califano's emphasis.

21. Dictated note from Lyndon B. Johnson to Joseph Califano, 30 October 1965, Executive File, LBJ Library; letter from Ferdinand Kramer to Lyndon B. Johnson, 13 January 1967, President's Committee on Equal Opportunity in Housing, LBJ Library.

22. Interview with Andrew Bradley by Thomas Donaghy, 1 August 1974, p. 13; telephone interview with Walter Giesey; interview with David Donahoe, 20 June 1983, p. 11.

23. Interview with Al Tronzo by Dodie Carpenter, 19 August 1974, p. 13.

24. Interview with Genevieve Blatt by Thomas Donaghy, 25 September 1974, p. 11.

25. Sally Stephenson, "Michael Musmanno as a Symbolic Leader" (Doctor of Arts diss., Carnegie Mellon University, 1981), p. VII-4; interview with Genevieve Blatt, 22 June 1981, pp. 11, 12. The ABA judicial code of ethics prohibits a judge from seeking office while sitting on the bench, but the code has no legal standing. In his 1950 race for lieutenant governor, Musmanno refused to resign his position as Common Pleas judge.

26. Other candidates considered were Pittsburgh prothonotary David Roberts, Philadelphia industrialist Milton S. Shapp, U.S. Representative John Dent, and state senators Leonard Staisey and Robert P. Casey.

27. *Pittsburgh Press*, 1 February 1964.

28. David L. Lawrence to John P. Robin, 21 September 1964, Lawrence Papers, Pennsylvania Archives, Harrisburg; *Pennsylvania Manual*, Election Returns, U.S. Senate, no. 96, 1964.

29. Typescript of autobiography of Milton Shapp, pp. 335, 337.

30. Richard Stolley, "Hopeless Case of Milton Shapp," *Life*, June 1966, pp. 68A–68D.

31. Interview with Blatt, p. 17.
32. Shapp typescript, p. 335.
33. Stolley, "Hopeless Case," p. 68A; Shapp typescript, p. 344.
34. Shapp typescript, pp. 352–56.
35. Interview with Milton Shapp, 20 June 1984, pp. 5, 6, 7; *Pittsburgh Press*, 21 May 1966 (emphasis mine); *Pittsburgh Press*, 6 June, 11 September 1966.
36. Interview with James Knox, 28 April 1981, p. 21.
37. Minute Book, Urban Redevelopment Authority, 4 November 1966.
38. Interview with David Donahoe, p. 11; interview with Knox, p. 21; interview with Frank Ambrose, 11 July 1984, p. 13.
39. *Pittsburgh Press*, 4 November 1966.
40. Interview with Ambrose, p. 14; with Knox, p. 21; with Andrew Fenrich, p. 16; *Pittsburgh Press*, 4 November 1966. Accounts of the events may be found in all three Pittsburgh newspapers, 4–6 November 1966.
41. *Pittsburgh Press*, 6 November 1966.
42. Ibid., 23 November 1966.

▷ Epilogue

1. *Pittsburgh Catholic*, 10 November 1966.
2. *New York Times*, 22 November 1966.
3. *Pittsburgh Press*, 25 November 1966.
4. Among those present were Governor Richard Hughes, New Jersey; Francis Coffey, Irish counsel general; Matthew McCloskey, former ambassador to Ireland; mayors James Tate (Philadelphia), Jerome Cavenaugh (Detroit), Richard Lee (New Haven), and former Philadelphia Mayor Richardson Dilworth. Representing President Johnson, who was ill, was his special assistant, Marvin Watson. Others in attendance included Stewart Udall and Orville Freeman, cabinet members; Martin McNamara, special assistant to Vice-President Humphrey; several former Pennsylvania governors; a number of congressmen; and several prominent Republicans, including Harvey Taylor, the state chairman.
5. *Pittsburgh Post-Gazette*, 26 November 1966.
6. *Holiday*, March 1959, p. 80ff.

Index